THIRD EDITION

IMAGES OF THE PAST

T. Douglas Price

University of Wisconsin, Madison

Gary M. Feinman

The Field Museum

Mayfield Publishing Company

Mountain View, California
London • Toronto

FOR ANNE BIRGITTE GEBAUER AND LINDA NICHOLAS

Library of Congress Cataloging-in-Publication Data
Price, T. Douglas (Theron Douglas)
    Images of the past / T. Douglas Price, Gary M. Feinman. — 3rd ed.
        p. cm.
    Includes bibliographical references and index.
    ISBN 1-55934-169-88
    1. Prehistoric peoples.   2. Antiquities, Prehistoric.   3. Archaeology.   4. Indians—
Antiquities.   I. Feinman, Gary M.   II. Title.
GN740.P75 2000
930.1—dc21   00-024483
                                                                        CIP

Manufactured in the United States of America
10   9   8   7   6   5   4

Mayfield Publishing Company
1280 Villa Street
Mountain View, California 94041

Sponsoring editor, Janet M. Beatty; production editor, Carla White Kirschenbaum; manuscript
editor, Margaret Moore; text and cover designer, Jeanne M. Schreiber; art editor, Rennie Evans;
photo researcher, Brian Pecko; illustrators, Joan Carol, Judith Ogus; cover photograph, ©
O. Louis Mazzatenta/National Geographic Image Collection; manufacturing manager, Randy
Hurst. The text was set in 10/12 Berkeley Oldstyle Book by Thompson Type and printed on
45# Custom LG by Banta Company.

Text and photographic credits begin on page 545, which constitutes an extension of the
copyright page.

PREFACE

Images of the Past is an introduction to prehistoric archaeology that aims to capture the excitement and visual splendor of archaeology while at the same time providing insight into current research methods, interpretations, and theories in the field.

A number of introductory books on the subject of archaeology already exist, of course. Such volumes generally take one of two directions; they offer either a comprehensive survey of world prehistory or a primer on method and theory. Surveys of world archaeology summarize what archaeologists have learned, but they often tend to be rather dry encyclopedias of information on the many places and times that people have lived in the past. That vast body of data is formidable to the beginning student. Primers on method and theory, on the other hand, are compilations of the history, techniques, concepts, and principles of archaeology: how to search for archaeological remains, how excavations are done, how to determine the age of prehistoric materials, who Louis Leakey was, and the like.

We assume that most beginning students of archaeology want to know what archaeologists have learned about the past. We believe that a combination of what has been discovered and how archaeologists learn about the past will prove to be of most value. For this reason we are taking a new tack in this book. Rather than try to cover all of archaeology, we have chosen to emphasize certain discoveries that have produced major insights into prehistory. Our focus is on more than eighty archaeological sites from a variety of times and places around the world. These sites, then, are signposts through the past. Before that journey begins, however, some background to the methods and principles of archaeology is provided in Chapter 1.

The journey itself begins with the evidence for the first humans, some 4 million years ago, and we conclude with the stirrings of written history in the Old World and the European conquest of the New World. This survey of world prehistory is organized along chronological or geographical lines in ten chapters. Chapters 2 through 6 are in chronological order, from the earliest human remains several million years ago to the beginnings of farming around 10,000 years ago. These chapters follow the expansion of the human species from its original home in Africa into Asia, Europe, and eventually Australia and the Americas. Chapter 6 covers the beginnings of agriculture in the Old and New Worlds.

Chapters 7 through 11 are concerned with the rise of large, complex societies and early states. This second half of the text has a geographic focus, with chapters on North America, Middle America, South America, Old World states, and Europe. Within each of these chapters, we have generally followed the sequence of development through time, from earlier to later. Although the earliest state societies arose in the Old World, we have arranged the chapters from the New World to the Old in order to emphasize and compare the rise of states in both areas. This arrangement of the chapters is intended to enhance comprehension of major processes such as the origins and spread of agriculture and the rise of more complex societies.

Each chapter contains an introduction and summary. The introductions provide an overview of the time period and developments that are discussed in each chapter. They also offer continuity between the sections and contain essential maps and chronological charts for the chapters. The summaries vary in content—some provide a summation, others introduce new information and concepts, others are theoretical, and yet others are more comparative. Examples of discussions included in the summaries are the behavioral correlates of cold climate adaptations, the origins of language, and the nature of cultural complexity. The introductions and summaries should be read with some care, for they provide the glue that binds the site descriptions together.

Interspersed among the site descriptions are highlighted sections that cover some of the how and why of archaeology: essential methods, debates about archaeological interpretation, or simply certain spectacular finds. In these sections, we illustrate some of the more interesting questions archaeologists ask about the past and show various new methods employed to decipher the archaeological record.

Because prehistory is a very visual subject, we have included more than 500 illustrations. It is essential to see and study the maps, plans, artifacts, and places that comprise the archaeological record. The basic framework of archaeology is the location of prehistoric materials in time and space. For this reason there is a series of coordinated maps and time lines to show readers where these sites and materials fit in terms of geography and chronology. In addition, we've included a number of color photographs in a separate section of the text to provide some impression of the captivating beauty of the past.

Throughout the text we provide a number of learning aids to help students better understand the material that is presented. Following difficult site names, we have included a pronunciation guide in parentheses. Technical terms and important concepts in archaeology are indicated in bold type; these words can be found in a glossary at the end of the book. Where appropriate, we have tried to provide some sense of the size of areas and structures from archaeological sites with reference to modern features such as city blocks, football fields, and the like. A list of general suggested readings appears at the end of each chapter, while more detailed lists of references are found at the end of the book. Specific citations were not used in the text for the sake of continuity, but references for the information can be found under the name of the individual associated with the work in the references at the back of the book. Finally, an appendix offers some English–metric measure conversions and equivalents to help make sizes more concrete.

An important note on dates in this edition: The age of archaeological materials is given in two ways in this book. Dates greater than 10,000 years ago are described in years before the present (B.P.) or in millions of years ago (m.y.a.). Dates younger than 10,000 years ago are given in calendar years before Christ, B.C. or *anno Domini* ("in the year of the Lord"), A.D. These dates for the last 10,000 years have been corrected, or calibrated, for an error in radiocarbon dating. Another term used for more recent periods of time is millennium, 1000 years. The millennia before Christ run in reverse—for example, the first millennium goes from 1 B.C. to 1000 B.C.

Finally, about the creation of this book. We began this project because we were generally dissatisfied with the texts available for introductory archaeology. We divided up the writing according to our own areas of knowledge and activity. Doug Price is interested in prehistoric foragers and the transition to agriculture; Gary Feinman is concerned with the rise of complex societies and the organization of states. Price works primarily in the Old World with stone tools and hunter-gatherers; Feinman does fieldwork largely in Mexico and China. We hope that our interest in and enthusiasm for archaeology carry over to you in this book and that you enjoy these *Images of the Past.*

WHAT'S NEW IN THIS EDITION

Because of the many helpful comments and suggestions we have received, we have been able to revise this text in accor-

dance with both new discoveries in archaeology and the interests of our readers. The pace of discovery and insight in modern archaeology is such that each year there are dramatic changes in our understanding of the past. We hope to keep *Images of the Past* as up-to-date as a book about the past can be.

Revisions to the third edition have included substantial changes in organization and additions to the volume as well as updating of the contents. A new first chapter has been added on the principles of archaeology, providing an in-depth summary of the basic methods, questions, and goals of archaeology. This chapter covers the essentials of fieldwork to provide students with a sense of how archaeologists obtain basic information. It also includes an introduction to the important questions that archaeologists seek to answer about the past along with the basic frameworks of investigation that guide their studies. The chapter is heavily illustrated with photographs of fieldwork and illustrations of principles in archaeology, creating a method and theory primer.

The remaining chapters have been revised and updated, and new illustrations and information have been added. Our intent has been to provide the latest information available on human prehistory so that students can understand the context of new discoveries as they are discussed in the mass media. Our revisions have also been aimed at the suggestions and requests of students and professors for additional information on specific times and places. For example, we have added three new sites, including another complex civilization in Africa, illustrated by the important center of Jenné-jeno in Mali, with its fabulous architecture. The first city, Çatalhöyük in Turkey, dating to more than 7000 years ago, is profiled in this edition, along with a discussion of the ongoing excavations taking place there. The site of Abu Hureyra along the Euphrates River in northern Syria is one of the earliest known settlements of the first farmers. New radiocarbon dates from this site reveal that rye may be the earliest domesticated crop anywhere, beginning almost 11,000 years ago.

Specific revisions include an updating on the latest fossil finds in "The Dawn of Humanity," in Chapter 2. The area of fossil hominid finds and the classification of our early ancestors change with each new discovery. Charts, dates, and species names have been revised in accordance with current views. Chapter 3, on *Homo erectus*, details the latest finds of skulls and tools. Chapter 4, on the rise of *Homo sapiens,* reviews recent debates on the origins of language. The section on ancient DNA has been rewritten, and illustrations of cellular DNA and the genetic map of human expansion have been added. New genetic information on the relationship between Neanderthals and modern humans in Europe has been included. The end of the Pleistocene, 10,000 years ago, marks a major turning point in human prehistory. That is also the time we switch from a dating framework of years before present (B.P.) to the use of calendar years B.C. and A.D.

With this edition, radiocarbon dates younger than 10,000 years ago have been calibrated as calendar years so that dates are more accurate and easier to comprehend.

Chapter 6, on the origins of agriculture, has been revised with the most recent dates for early agriculture around the world and new sites added. The latest evidence from sites like Abu Hureyra, Hallam Çemi, and Çatalhöyük has been added to the text. Chapter 7, on North American Indians, has been updated throughout, and new illustrations document the majesty of these native cultures. Chapters 8, 9, and 10, on civilizations around the world, have new photos and minor changes in the text. One of the new sites, Jenné-jeno, appears in Chapter 10 on Old World civilizations. Chapter 11, on prehistoric Europe, has also been revised according to the new radiocarbon calibrations, and it now includes the latest information on the Iceman and Stonehenge.

New references have been added to the bibliographies for the individual chapters and to the summary list of references as well.

ACKNOWLEDGMENTS

Any project like this one is the culmination of the efforts and contributions of a multitude of individuals and institutions. We want to thank the many individuals who have helped with this book in a number of different ways from reviewing the text, providing new data, supplying photographs, helping us locate a variety of materials, and general support. We have done our very best to contact the copyright holders of the original work included herein and to secure their permission to reprint their material; if we have overlooked anyone, we offer our sincere apologies.

This project has been long and complex and would not have been feasible without the help of these friends and colleagues: Kim Aaris-Sørensen, Melvin Aitkens, Niels Andersen, Larry Bartram, Gert Jan Bartstra, Pia Benike, John Bennet, Richard Bradley, Maggie Brandenburg, C. K. Brain, Robert Brightman, Brian Byrd, Christopher Chippendale, Tim Champion, Grahame Clark, Desmond Clark, Carmen Collazo, Meg Conkey, Nina Cummings, George Dales, Jack Davis, Hilary and Janette Deacon, John de Vos, Preben Dehlholm, Tom Dillehay, Christopher Donnan, Scott Fedick, Lisa Ferin, Kent Flannery, Melvin Fowler, George Frison, Anne Birgitte Gebauer, Henry George, Ted Gerney, Jon Gibson, Peter Christian Vemming Hansen, Spencer Harrington, Matt Hill, Ian Hodder, Brian Hoffman, Frank Hole, Vance Holliday, F. Clark Howell, Tom Jacobsen, Dick Jeffries, Greg Johnson, Ken Karstens, Larry Keeley, Mark Kenoyer, Susan Kepecs, J. E. Kidder, Jr., Richard Klein, François Lévèque, Katina Lillios, Henry de Lumley, Tom Lynch, Joyce Marcus, Alexander Marshack, Ray Matheny, Alan May, Roderick McIntosh, Susan McIntosh, Richard Meadow, James Mellaart, A. T. M. Moore, Chris O'Brien, John Parkington, Peter Vang Petersen, Theron D. Price, Naomi Pritchard, Jeffrey Quilter, John Reader, Charles Redman, Merle Greene Robertson, Gary Rollefson, Ulrick Rossing, William Ruddiman, Denise Schmandt-Besserat, Kathie Shick, Jeff Shokler, Brian Siegel, Ralph Solecki, Charles Spencer, Dragoslav Srejovic, Sharon Steadman, Jim Stoltman, J. F. Thackeray, David Hurst Thomas, Donald Thompson, Larry Todd, B. L. Turner II, Patty Jo Watson, John Weinstein, Huang Weiwen, J. Peter White, Joyce White, Edwin Wilmsen, Peter Woodman, and Tineke van Zandt.

Several individuals deserve special mention. Linda Nicholas helped greatly with many parts of the project, but especially with finalizing large parts of the text and illustrations. Jennifer Blitz spent much of a year obtaining illustrations and permissions for the first edition with extraordinary energy and care. We're also grateful to the teaching assistants that we had over the years in our introductory course in archaeology at the University of Wisconsin: Andrew Balkansky, Linda Gaertner, Brian Hoffman, Jeff Shokler, Robert Simpkins, and Tina Thurston. At Mayfield, our editor, Jan Beatty, inspired and cajoled at the appropriate times to get the job done. Jan has become a valued friend in the process. The production team—Carla White Kirschenbaum, Margaret Moore, Jeanne Schreiber, Rennie Evans, Brian Pecko, and Randy Hurst—labored long, hard, and well to put all of this together.

We'd like to thank our reviewers for the first edition, who provided help, ideas, inspiration, and motivation to revise and refine the text: J. M. Beaton, University of California, Davis; Richard Blanton, Purdue University; G. A. Clark, Arizona State University; Steven Falconer, Arizona State University; Kenneth L. Feder, Central Connecticut State University; William A. Haviland, University of Vermont; John W. Hoopes, University of Kansas; Gary W. Pahl, San Francisco State University; Donald A. Proulx, University of Massachusetts, Amherst; John W. Rick, Stanford University; Ralph M. Rowlett, University of Missouri-Columbia; Katharina J. Schreiber, University of California, Santa Barbara; William Turnbaugh, University of Rhode Island; Randall White, New York University; David J. Wilson, Southern Methodist University; and Richard W. Yerkes, Ohio State University.

For their contributions to the second edition, we'd like to thank our thorough reviewers: Douglas B. Bamforth, University of Colorado at Boulder; Kathryn Cruz-Uribe, Northern Arizona University; Richard Effland, Mesa Community College; Lynne Goldstein, Michigan State University; John J. Killeen, Louis Berger and Associates, Cultural Resource Group; Carole A. Mandryk, Harvard University; Alan McPheran, University of Pittsburgh; Lauren W. Ritterbush, University of Kansas; Ralph M. Rowlett, University of Missouri; Michael P. Smyth, University of Kentucky; Peter S. Wells, University of Minnesota; Chip Wills, University of New Mexico; Mary K. Whelan, University of Iowa; and Richard Yerkes, Ohio State University.

Our sincere thanks to the following reviewers for their help and advice in the preparation of the third edition:

Charles A. Bollong, University of Arizona; Angela E. Close, University of Washington; James Enloe, University of Iowa; Paul E. Langwalter II, Cypress College; Marilyn Masson, State University of New York, Albany; and David Pokotylo, University of British Columbia.

To all of these individuals goes our sincere appreciation. We hope that you find the result worth your efforts, and that you will continue to provide input, suggestions, and new discoveries that will improve the next edition.

CONTENTS

The Leakey family at work in Olduvai Gorge.

A Jomon site near Tokyo.

The Black Earth site at Carrier Mills, Illinois.

Pueblo Bonito in Chaco Canyon, New Mexico.

The Main Plaza at Monte Albán, looking south from the North Platform.

The Great Wall of China, north of Beijing.

Grauballe Man, a 2000-year-old body from a Danish bog.

A chac mool at Chichén Itzá.

A funerary urn at Jenné-jeno.

PRINCIPLES OF ARCHAEOLOGY

INTRODUCTION

Images of the Past is about archaeology, covering almost 5 million years and much of the planet. But it is simply not possible to describe all of human prehistory in a single volume such as this; that would be like trying to see all the attractions in Washington, D. C., in 10 minutes. Because we can visit only some of the more interesting places, we have chosen a series of important archaeological sites that have substantially increased our understanding of the past.

We hope the pathway through the past that begins in the following pages provides you with a sense of what archaeologists know about our global past and how they have come to know it. The trail that runs through this volume and ties the past to the present involves major trends in our development as a technological species—growth, diversification, and specialization. Growth is seen in the increasing number of people on the planet and in the greater complexity of human organizations, diversity in the variable roles and social relationships that exist in society and in the kinds of environments our species inhabits. Increasing specialization is witnessed in the tools and techniques used to obtain food and manufacture objects. The story of our human past, then, is the story of these changes through time as we evolved from small, local groups of people living close to nature to large nation-states involved in global trade, warfare, and politics.

Archaeology is the study of our human past, combining the themes of time and change. These themes—change in our biology and change in our behavior through time—are also the focus of this book. Archaeology is the closest thing we have to a time machine, taking us backward through the mists of the ages. The fog becomes thicker the farther back we go, and the windows of our time machine become more obscured. In Chapter 2, we go as far back as humans can go, some 4–5 million years ago, when we took our first steps in Africa. Subsequent chapters trace the achievements of our ancestors as we expanded out of Africa, developed new technologies for coping with cold climates, crafted more complex tools and imagined art, domesticated plants and animals, moved into cities, and created written languages. But first, in this chapter, we present a foundation for comprehending the human past. That foundation requires some understanding of change through time in terms of both biology and culture, along with the basic methods and principles of archaeology.

A site is found. Intensive surface collections are made in order to pick up artifacts that may help date the site. One archaeologist holds a stadia rod to measure the elevation.

FUNDAMENTALS OF ARCHAEOLOGY

Archaeologists study past human culture, from the time of our early ancestors to the historical present. The information about the past comes from artifacts and sites. **Artifacts** are the objects and materials that people in the past made and used. **Sites** are accumulations of such artifacts, representing the places where people lived or carried out certain activities. The process of discovery, analysis, and interpretation of artifacts and sites is the basic means through which archaeologists learn about the past and also the subject of the following pages in this chapter.

The Discovery of Archaeological Sites

Much of the information gathering for archaeological studies requires **fieldwork** that is intended to locate artifacts and sites. Artifacts and sites are found either on the surface or beneath the ground. **Surveys** are used to discover artifacts on the ground, and **excavations** are used to expose buried materials. These are the primary discovery techniques of field archaeology.

   The discovery of archaeological sites depends in part on what is already known about an area in terms of its landscape, environment, and history. Prior to beginning fieldwork, archaeologists check the relevant written material on the time period and place of interest. This research reveals the present state of knowledge, indicates what is not known, as well as what is, and helps establish directions for further research. Such library research is also essential to ensure that investigations similar to those planned have not already been completed.

   The next step is to visit the local historical society or other archaeological institutions such as museums or university departments where records of the area are maintained. Such institutions generally keep an archive of information on the location and contents of known archaeological and historical sites. Study of these archives indicates what types of sites are already known and perhaps their size and the general content of artifacts. This information can provide an initial list of sites in the area and their locations on maps.

Maps are one of the most important tools of fieldwork. Topographic maps (showing the shape of the land surface with contour or elevation lines) are available for most areas. In the United States, the U.S. Geological Survey compiles and distributes these maps. Such maps contain a great deal of information about longitude and latitude, elevation, slope, and the location of water, roads, towns, and other features and are a primary tool in fieldwork.

Air photographs also can provide information on the location of archaeological sites. Old foundations or prehistoric agricultural fields, overgrown with vegetation and almost hidden on the surface, may appear in air photographs. When prehistoric structures were originally abandoned, the depressions often filled with rich topsoil, which provides better growth condition for vegetation. In fields of wheat, for example, such different soil conditions might result in a distinctive pattern showing the outlines of houses or whole villages. In many parts of the world, such patterns are best observed from low-flying planes during a dry period in the early summer.

The next step in discovering the past involves fieldwork. An archaeological survey is a systematic search of the landscape for artifacts and sites. It is not always possible to make a complete survey of the entire area under investigation. Roads, forests, other vegetation, or construction often cover substantial parts of the landscape. It may be possible to thoroughly survey only a portion of the entire area, but that portion should be representative of the larger region under investigation. The larger the proportion of the research area that can be surveyed the better.

The basic type of archaeological field survey involves systematic field walking. Field crews walk up and down cultivated fields and exposed surfaces. The intervals between the walks are determined by the size of the sites that may be in the area and the nature of the ground cover.

When an artifact is found, it is put in a bag and the location of the find is recorded. The surrounding area should be searched carefully by walking back and forth at close intervals. It is important to determine whether the object is a single, isolated find or whether there are more artifacts. Surveyors also look for unusual discolorations on the surface that might indicate features like fireplaces or pits. If there is a site, it is important to establish the area covered by artifacts to determine the size of the site and to obtain an estimate of the density of artifacts.

Information must be recorded about each find. These field notes should include information on (1) the location, site number, map number, which field, position in the field; (2) what archaeological material was found, such as types and number of artifacts, fire-cracked stones, charcoal, and so on; and (3) observations about the site, which might include discolorations in the soil that could indicate cultural layers or pits, the presence of mounds, stone foundations or walls, nearby streams or other sources of water, and other pertinent environmental information.

Archaeological remains are often buried beneath the sediments that have accumulated since their deposition. Objects found on the surface often have been brought up from deeper layers through agricultural or animal activities. Such materials usually provide only a partial indication of the information that can be obtained from a buried site.

Once buried sites have been located by survey and mapped, other kinds of fieldwork can be undertaken to learn more about them. Boring into the ground with an auger or corer brings up a column of soil showing the sequence of layers and samples of sediments at the site. Small test pits, perhaps 1 × 1 meter in size, dug into the ground can provide similar information and might be necessary to determine or confirm if a buried site is present. A number of corings and/or test pits often are made, following a regular pattern over the surface of the site. Soil samples should be collected from all parts of the site and at different depths.

Physical and chemical analysis of soil samples may provide information about the origins of the deposits, the water content and fertility of the soil, the amount of organic material, and the basic chemistry of the soil. These studies may provide further information on environmental and human activities involved in the formation and burial of the site.

Phosphate analysis of the sediments from a site may reveal traces of human activities. Phosphate is found in bone, feces, urine, and other organic matters that accumulate in and around human habitation. Phosphate appears as a strong blue color in the soil sample when hydrochloric and ascorbic acid are added. Areas with higher concentrations of phosphate show up as stronger blue colors in such analyses. Phosphate testing may supplement surface surveys in areas where vegetation prevents observations of the surface or where cultural layers are deeply buried under the topsoil. Within a known habitation area, these tests may be used to determine the extent of the site and detect special areas such as house floors.

Other objects in the soil also are informative. Materials found in soil samples often include pieces of wood and plants, seeds, fragments of insects, mollusk shells, hair, or chips of bone or stone. Such items provide information on the formation of the layers, the local environment, and the nature of past human activities. For example, if small chips that result from the manufacture of arrowheads and other stone tools are present in borings and test pits, it is likely that tools were made or used in the vicinity and that other buried artifacts may be present.

Geophysical prospecting can be used to detect disturbances in the subsoil and the presence of prehistoric features. These methods include measurements of magnetic variations in the ground, the electrical conductivity (resistivity) of the soil, and the use of ground-penetrating radar.

In sum, prehistoric sites are found through a combination of archival research and fieldwork. Archival research provides information on what is already known about an area. Fieldwork often results in the discovery of the unknown. When new sites are discovered, surface survey, testing, boring, and several geophysical methods are available to determine the size and possible contents of the prehistoric deposit. However, once a site is discovered and defined from the surface, excavations are often necessary to expose what lies beneath.

A georadar unit is walked across the site. Subsurface anomalies such as walls and fireplaces may appear in the images from the instrument.

This excavation began with the removal of the plow layer by shoveling and screening the earth to expose the intact soil beneath.

Archaeological Excavation

Excavation is the technique that archaeologists use to uncover buried remains from the past. Buried materials usually are more abundant and better preserved than those found on the surface. In excavations, accurate information can be observed on the arrangement and relationships of structures, artifacts, plant and animal remains, and other materials. Thus, excavation often is essential to obtain more information about the past.

Excavations are conducted to answer specific questions that the archaeologist would like to answer. For example, who lived at the site, what did they eat, what did they do, where did they get raw materials for making tools and equipment, what kinds of relations did they have with their neighbors, how was their society organized and structured, how did they understand the world around them?

The Excavation Director   The direction of an excavation requires a variety of skills and knowledge for planning the field season, raising money to pay for the work, supervising and training a crew of volunteers or students, recording the information from the site with drawings and photographs, and measuring and mapping the location of all finds, samples, and features. The investigator must monitor progress in the field laboratory as well, where finds are washed, sorted, cataloged, and bagged for storage. Some knowledge of preservation techniques is necessary to conserve fragile objects.

Excavations require reams of drawings, recordings, and other paperwork. The director must keep an excavation log or diary, recording the course of the excavations, the work schedule, the number of people working, accounts of expenses, dimensions and positioning of excavation areas, layout of the measuring system, and all the finds. There must be recording systems for all measurements, for observations and interpretations, and for all drawings, photos, and samples.

The Field Crew   Archaeology is the science of the past, but it is also a social experience in the present. Excavation is a labor-intensive undertaking, and the field crew is the most important part of the project. This crew is a group of individuals involved in the actual digging process, unearthing the sites and artifacts. Crews are composed of a variety of individuals, young and old, ranging from professional archaeologists with advanced degrees, to undergraduate and graduate students, and sometimes just people interested in the subject.

Fieldwork can require a few days, weeks, or months, walking miles each day with your head down in survey of the ground or moving tons of earth to expose buried levels. Excavations are hard work, often in the hot sun. Frequently they are carried out in remote places, requiring patience and endurance. Archaeology is also good dirty fun, and the experience of working, and relaxing, with others who enjoy the same things can be unforgettable. The discovery process is captivating, and sharing that excitement with colleagues and comrades enhances the entire experience.

Fieldwork is, finally, an extraordinary learning experience. One realizes the difficulties involved in recovering information from the past and comes to appreciate what has been learned to this point in time. In addition, a constant stream of questions about the past and the significance of place, artifact, and context comes to mind during the process. All in all, archaeological fieldwork can be one of the most stimulating activities there is.

Selecting Sites for Excavation   The choice of which site to excavate is determined by several factors including potential danger to the archaeological remains. Sites are often chosen for excavation because they appear to be well preserved or to contain new information that will help to better understand the prehistory of a particular region. The choice of a site for excavation is often based on the results of a survey. An initial survey of an area, including coring and testing of promising sites, might indicate that one or several sites would be worth excavating. Careful surface collection and testing must be carried out at the site selected for excavation to make sure the site can provide the kinds of information that are needed and to assist in planning the excavation.

Archaeological sites are being destroyed at a rapid rate by the growth and development of modern civilization, and there is a serious and real concern about the loss of undisturbed sites for future research. Sites threatened by modern construction are often good candidates for excavation.

Historical archives may be studied over and over again, but archaeological sites are nonrenewable resources. Excavations involve moving the earth and all of its contents from a site. Every excavation means the destruction of all or part of an archaeological site. All that is left when an excavation is over are the finds themselves, the unexcavated parts of the site, and the samples, photographs, drawings, measurements, and other notes that the archaeologists made. Accurate notes and records of the layers, structures, and artifacts at a site are essential, not only for the investigator, but also to create a permanent archive of information about the site that is available to others.

It is important to know as much as possible about a site prior to full-scale excavation in order to choose the best strategy for the project. At every excavation, the archaeologist is faced with a series of decisions about how to achieve the most and best-documented information. Under ideal circumstances a site could be fully excavated and everything recorded in the finest detail. In the real world, however, constraints on time and funding and a need to leave a portion of the site for future archaeologists make it standard practice to excavate only a part of the total site.

Maps and Grids   Accurate mapping of layers and artifacts is the key to the proper recording of information at an archaeological excavation. The exact topography, or shape, of the site must be recorded in the form of an accurate contour map made using a surveyor's level and the site grid. A grid is marked out across the surface of a site prior to excavation. This grid should be used for all horizontal measurements. A site grid represents a coordinate system usually with lines running north–south and east–west at regular intervals. Intervals along the two axes of the grid are designated with a

A contour map is made by recording the measurements of elevation taken across the site and their locations on the site grid. Contour lines are then drawn by connecting points with similar elevations. An alidade sits on the drawing table.

system of letters or numbers or both. The grid lines and measurements within each grid square are measured as distances in meters and centimeters north and east of the base lines at the edge of the excavations.

The site grid might also be oriented according to local topography or archaeological features such as mounds or middens. At coastal sites, trenches are sometimes excavated perpendicular to the coastline in order to study layers and site formation in relation to the coast. In a narrow cave, the grid is often aligned to the long axis of the cave.

Location of the site and the site grid in relation to global latitude and longitude must be determined. A control point, or site datum, must be located in the neighborhood of the excavation as a point of origin for vertical measurements. A preexisting datum point like a surveyor's benchmark may be used if available. Otherwise, a permanent feature like a rock outcrop or building foundation might be marked and used as the datum point. The location and elevation of this point must be established in relation to known points like geographic features or distant benchmarks.

Vertical location in the excavation is best determined using a surveying instrument, set at a known elevation, and sighting on a vertical measuring rod. Measurements at the site should be converted to meters above sea level, or the elevation of the datum line may simply be recorded.

Test Pits   Preliminary examination of a site involves digging a series of one or more trenches or small, vertical test pits, perhaps 1 × 1 meter in size, across the site. The test squares to be excavated might also be placed in rows or a chessboard-like pattern across the site. Alternatively, their location might be chosen at random. The size and number of test pits to be excavated depends on the kind of information being sought. In some cases it is difficult to visualize the stratigraphy, or set of layers, observed in the small test pits. One or two long trenches across the site may provide a better view of the stratigraphy.

Vertical Excavations   Excavations are generally either vertical or horizontal. Vertical excavation takes the form of test pits or trenches carefully placed across a site to expose the stratigraphy and artifact contents of a site. By studying the vertical walls (the sections) of such pits or trenches, archaeologists can study stratified layers of soil sediments.

This section of an excavation trench exposes a stratigraphy of stream and lake deposits that succeeded one another as water levels changed in this area. The upper part of the deposit is recent blown sand.

A horizontal excavation. Only one-half of a feature is excavated at first. This feature, a house depression, is being excavated with trowels. The small wall in the middle is kept as a record of the feature's stratigraphy. Artifacts, bones, and other finds are mapped by layer.

The stratigraphy, or layers, of natural sediments and human deposits reveals how the site was formed and how materials accumulated. The relationships between deposits in the stratigraphic sequence indicate the chronological arrangement of the layers. The bottom layer is deposited first as the oldest layer in the sequence. The subsequent layers are progressively younger—the law of superposition. The stratigraphic sequence provides a relative chronology whereby layers and the artifacts they contain can be determined to be "younger than" or "older than" other layers and artifacts in the same sequence.

The thickness of a layer is not determined so much by the length of time that it took to accumulate, as by the natural and human activities involved in the deposition of the materials. Heaps of shells may accumulate very rapidly into high **shell middens** (large dumps of shell from mussels, oysters, or other species); the collapse of houses with earth or sod walls results in very thick layers; stone tool manufacture can produce extensive debris. On the other hand, the place where an animal was killed and butchered—a kill site—may leave almost no archaeological trace.

Evaluation of a stratigraphic sequence involves distinguishing between natural and human activities. Such environmental factors as soil erosion or flood deposits may add to the local accumulation but may also remove part of a layer. Younger features like postholes or storage pits may have been dug into older deposits. Relationships between layers must be studied carefully to determine whether younger deposits are cut into older layers and whether animal activities, downed trees, floods, or later construction have disturbed or destroyed the original stratigraphy.

Assessment of the context and relative position of layers allows an archaeologist to interpret the depositional history from the stratigraphic sequence. An actual calendar date of the layers may be derived from artifacts with a known date found in a particular layer. For example, a hubcap from a 1935 Ford would indicate that the layer could not have been formed before 1935. The ages of many types of pottery and stone tools are known and can be used to suggest an approximate date for archaeological levels. Layers and artifacts also may be dated by means of such absolute techniques as radiocarbon and other dating methods (see p. 42).

Horizontal, or Area, Excavations   Horizontal, or area, excavations are often the next step after initial vertical trenches reveal structures or features to be uncovered. Such

Soil from the excavation is sifted through a screen to recover small items.

excavations expose large areas of ground, one layer at a time. These horizontal layers are recorded and removed individually. Area excavations are intended to recover information on site arrangement and structures. Such excavations may expose actual prehistoric living floors where a group of people carried out everyday activities.

When the site stratigraphy is relatively simple—with only one or two stages of occupation and thin cultural layers—it is possible to separate the remains from each stage of occupation. In such cases it is advantageous to expose large surfaces of the same layer to get an overview of the distribution of features and artifacts at the settlement. Following removal of the topsoil, the surface is scraped with trowels or shovels, loose soil is removed, and features and artifacts are uncovered. The uncovered surface is then carefully recorded, usually in drawings and photographs. The sediments removed during the excavation are normally shaken or washed through fine screens to recover smaller items such as bone fragments and plant remains that may have been missed earlier.

A series of different kinds of samples is taken from different layers in the walls of the sections and from the occupation floor. The excavated soils are usually sifted through screens and/or washed with water to find even the smallest objects, fragments of bone, and plant remains. Soil samples are taken to help define and characterize the deposits at the site. Pollen samples are sometimes collected to assist in defining the vegetation in and around the site. At most sites, samples of charcoal and bone are taken for radiocarbon dating.

After removal of one layer of soil and artifacts, the procedure is repeated and a new surface is uncovered and recorded. One strategy for maintaining control of the stratigraphy is to leave a number of narrow sections untouched in the excavation area. The walls of these sections are cleaned and studied as the excavation goes deeper. This kind of excavation aims at recording and then removing each horizontal layer individually.

Excavations expose postholes and the foundations of two houses, one built over the other. The dark rectangles mark the location of construction posts. Two fireplace pits can be seen at the center and right of the photo.

Toward the end of the excavation the sections are excavated. The surface of the sediments beneath the occupation layer is uncovered and cleaned. Unusual colors in the soil may reveal features such as pits and postholes, which are recorded by photos and drawings. Features are dissected by excavating one-quarter or one-half of the pit or posthole at a time in order to remove the contents and determine the function of the feature. This produces a vertical section through the middle of the feature.

Sections of all features are recorded by photos, drawings, and soil description. Postholes belonging to the same structure are grouped by examining the depth of the holes and the kind of soil present. Other features are studied to determine their function and mutual relationship. Finally, the second half of the features is excavated and the excavation is over.

Analysis of Archaeological Materials

At the end of the dig, the excavated area has to be filled up and undisturbed portions of the site protected in the best possible manner. Analysis of recovered artifacts may begin concurrently with the fieldwork in a field laboratory, or records, artifacts, and samples must be shipped back to a home laboratory to be cataloged and prepared for analysis.

All the materials collected during surveys and excavations must be cleaned, classified, counted, cataloged, and analyzed. Archaeological fieldwork produces several major categories of information: (1) artifacts—portable objects altered by human activity; (2) **ecofacts**—the remains of plants, animals, sediments, and other unmodified materials that result from human activity; (3) **features**—the immovable structures, layers, pits, and posts in the ground; and (4) sites and settlements—the set of artifacts, ecofacts, and features that defines places in the landscape where activity and residence were focused.

Items are washed, dried, and put in bags with labels showing their location in the site.

After the fieldwork come more detailed analyses of the recovered materials, the writing of excavation reports, and the preparation of publications, all of which require much more work and time than the excavation itself. One estimate suggests about 5 weeks of analysis and writing for each week of excavation. Final results of the investigations are made available to the public and to professional archaeologists through articles in scientific journals and published reports.

A variety of specialists is needed to examine and interpret the wide range of materials and information that is found at archaeological sites. Lithic specialists analyze the stone tools that are often a common material on archaeological sites. Ceramic specialists study the sherds of ancient pottery. Paleoethnobotanists study the plant remains, both visible and microscopic, that are found at a site. Archaeozoologists investigate the animal bones that represent the remains of meals and manufacturing activities. Physical anthropologists and human osteologists describe and interpret the human bones and teeth that may be found. Geoarchaeologists and micromorphologists investigate the geological setting of the site and the details of the sediments encasing the archaeological remains. Archaeometrists date those remains and the chemical characterization of prehistoric materials to learn about their composition and source.

Artifacts   Each object from the excavations must be washed to remove dust and dirt. At certain sites, each object is recorded by number in a catalog. At other sites, artifacts are recorded by material and context or by the excavation area where they were found. Numbering artifacts with permanent ink ensures that each item has a label with information on the site and location of the find.

The catalog description of each artifact includes a record of the kind of artifact, the type of raw material, the color, the overall shape and measurements, techniques of manufacturing, presumed function, decoration, and provenience information. This description could be supplemented with an accurate drawing and a photograph of the artifact. An inventory of the materials from the excavation then can be made by counting and recording the number of artifacts in each category of material, such as chipped stone, ground stone, or pottery.

Following this initial recording, artifacts are classified into other categories and types. Classification is a way of creating order in a mass of archaeological materials by dividing objects into groups on the basis of shared characteristics. One example of such classification is the initial division of the remains into artifacts, ecofacts, and features, described earlier. Another example would be the division of chipped stone artifacts into axes, scrapers, knives, and arrowheads.

Three primary attributes are used to classify archaeological artifacts: (1) form—the size and basic shape of the object, (2) technology—the characteristics of raw

Recording the dimensions of flaked stone artifacts.

An obsidian core and blade.

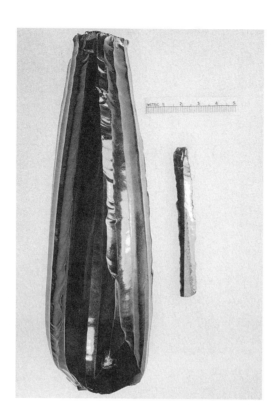

material and manufacturing technique, and (3) style—the color, texture, and decoration of the object. Most of this information is recorded in the laboratory after the artifacts have been cleaned and cataloged.

Ecofacts Ecofacts are unmodified natural items, such as animal bones and plant remains, that are usually brought to the site by its occupants and useful for the study of past human activity. They are used to reconstruct the environment of the site and the range of resources that people used. Ecofacts are classified as organic (plants and animals) or inorganic (sediments and stone). These materials are usually studied by archaeologists or specialists with training in botany, zoology, or geology.

Plant remains from an archaeological site may include pollen, seeds, leaves, pieces of wood, and the like, depending on the quality of preservation. Microscopic pollen is usually wind-deposited and may be introduced naturally to the site. Each type of plant produces a distinctively different looking pollen. Because of its long-distance distribution, pollen is likely to reflect the total environment around the site.

Changes in the types of pollen at a site through time can be used to reconstruct the vegetational history of the area and to provide a record of climatic changes. Special growing requirements and other characteristics of certain plants may reflect certain climatic conditions or specific local situations like an open versus a forested environment around a site.

Macrofossils of botanical materials are visible remains like seeds and plant parts that are more likely to be present at a site due to direct human utilization. Identification of these remains indicates what species of plants were present, whether they were wild or domestic, and in what context they were found. It is important to study the context of these remains to know how the plants were used. Plants may be collected for food, but they may also be used for production of textiles, mats, and baskets, for making poison for arrowheads, or as drugs. Types of plants and their growing condition may also provide an indicator of the nature of the local environment and climate.

Bones and teeth of domesticated sheep and pig.

Faunal analysis, or archaeozoology, is the term used to describe studies of the animal remains from archaeological sites. Animal remains are tabulated by the kinds of bones, teeth, antler, and horn that are present. Species are identified and the numbers of individuals of each species are calculated. These studies show what animals were hunted and eaten and in what proportion. The amount of meat available from each animal also might be calculated to determine their relative importance in the diet.

Faunal analysis also can provide an estimate of the ratio of adult to juvenile animals and of male to female animals. A predominance of certain age groups in a species such as deer may indicate that seasonal or selective hunting was practiced. For example, a site that contained a large proportion of 3- to 6-month-old deer would suggest the animals were killed primarily in the fall since deer are born in the spring.

The presence or absence of certain parts of the animal skeleton may indicate the way animals were butchered and whether they were dismembered on the spot or killed elsewhere and selected steaks and chops brought back to the settlement. Not all animals are necessarily hunted for food. Nonfood items such as antler, fur, bone, and hides also are important materials from hunted animals.

The most important inorganic ecofacts are the various sediments uncovered by excavation. Deposits of soils and sediments at human settlements result from both human and natural processes. These sediments and deposits are studied by geo-archaeologists. The type of sediments present might indicate the source of the material that was deposited. Examples include water-lain silts from a flood, volcanic ashes, or frost-cracked rocks from the ceiling of a cave. The study of soil chemistry is an important aspect of the analysis of soils and sediments.

Features Features must be studied largely in the field since they are fixed in the ground. Features may be structures like houses or pits, or fences or field systems defining an area used for special purposes, or constructions for certain activities like drying racks, fireplaces, and traps. They are useful for understanding the distribution and organization of human activities at a site. For example, the size, elaboration, and location of houses or burials may suggest differences in wealth and status.

Some features result from the accumulation of garbage and debris, rather than being intentionally constructed. They include shell middens, heaps of waste material

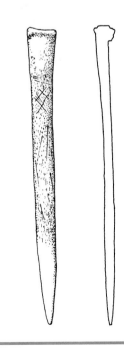

A bone point for use in a fishing spear, 7000 B.C.

A burial from the Black Earth site in Illinois, almost 6000 years old. A number of artifacts were placed in the grave with the body.

in workshops, and quarries. Studies of these features may indicate strategies for obtaining food or raw material, how the raw material was used and distributed, and whether it was scarce or abundant.

Burials and human bones are a special category of feature often found at archaeological sites. Several different kinds of burials can be found. Simple inhumations represent the laid-out burial of the whole body. Such graves usually contain an articulated skeleton with all the bones in their correct anatomical positions. Secondary burials are the result of burial of some of the skeleton, after the flesh and soft tissue have disappeared. Usually the skull and larger bones are present, often in a small pile or bundle. Cremations are burials of the ash and small carbonized bones from bodies that have been burned prior to burial. Osteologists identify and analyze such human remains. The sex of the skeleton can be determined by examining the size and shape of the pelvis and the skull and the thickness of the bones. The age of death can be estimated by the eruption sequence and wear of the teeth, the fusion (closing) of sutures between bones of the skull, and the fusion of the ends of the limb bones to the shaft.

The health status of past populations can be investigated by recording the incidence of trauma that affects the skeleton. Such diseases and injuries include bone fractures, arthritis, and periodontal diseases. Nutritional problems may be reflected in poorly developed bones and the low average height of the population. Cultural practices like cranial deformation or dental mutilation, practiced in prehistoric America, also show up in the skeletal remains.

Sites and Settlements

Settlement archaeology is the study of how and why prehistoric remains are distributed across the landscape. Investigations range from the analysis of the location of different activities within a single room to the distribution of sites in a region. Usually, three levels of locational information are investigated: (1) a single structure or occupation surface such as a cave floor, (2) a site or settlement, or (3) a series of sites within a larger region.

The spatial organization within a single structure defines areas for special activities such as grinding flour, cooking, weaving, or tool manufacturing or for certain facilities such as sleeping areas or storage. Study of such organization may indicate a division of male and female space and activities, how many people lived in a household, and the structure of the family—nuclear, extended, or polygynous, for example.

A settlement generally includes a habitation area with one or more houses and fireplaces; different activity areas for food preparation, curing of animal skins and hides, the manufacture of various artifacts, and perhaps storage equipment; and a midden or trash area. Spatial patterning within a site can provide information about the number of houses and people at the settlement and on their relationships with one another. In addition, most of the day-to-day activities of the occupants should be reflected in the various structures and activity areas found throughout the settlement. Structures at a site may be solid and substantial in the case of permanently settled communities in a village or townlike setting. Short-term or seasonal settlements, however, may leave little trace of construction.

The size of a settlement in horizontal and vertical extent depends on the number of people living there, the length of time they lived there, and the kinds of activities that took place and structures that were erected, as well as environmental factors. Sites of similar size could have been created by a few permanently settled people or through the occasional use of the same spot by a larger group of people.

Differences in the size and architectural elaboration of houses may be evidence of status differentiation, a situation in which some people have more wealth and control over goods and labor than others. The arrangement of houses at a settlement also may reflect social organization in the separation of poor and wealthy households. Concerns for privacy and protection in the form of fences, palisades, or ditches may indicate private ownership or conditions of competition or warfare. In addition, settlement studies may reveal areas of economic specialization with skilled craftspeople involved in the production of certain materials, while other items were made in individual households.

Regional settlement patterns that are recorded in archaeological surveys can provide a variety of information on the prehistoric use of the landscape. Several different

Settlement pattern in Roman Britain. Dots show the distribution of walled towns. Polygons show the regular distribution of the walled towns. Black dots are tribal centers. Large circles show the circular distribution of smaller towns around selected tribal centers. The black square is Roman London.

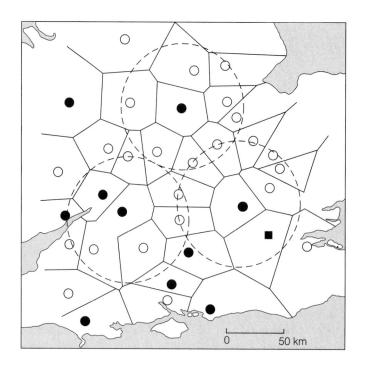

kinds of sites often are found in an area. Residential settlements of various size and duration are typical targets for investigation. Such sites can vary from camps to villages, towns, or prehistoric cities.

There are many other kinds of sites. Extraction sites are used for more specific, nonresidential purposes to obtain raw materials or resources, like quarries for stone or copper or places where animals were killed and butchered. Distinct burial areas, outside of settlements, are another kind of site. Cemeteries of inhumation graves, cremation urns, or individual burial mounds and tombs are some other types of sites that occur.

Interpretation of Archaeological Information

Archaeological information that is recovered from the ground, described and analyzed by specialists, does not directly tell us very much about the past. The analysis may tell us what kinds of objects were made, what they were made of, how they were used, and how old they are. But the questions that archaeologists seek to answer about the past concern larger concepts about the way of life of prehistoric peoples, how human societies coped with their physical and social environments, and how our predecessors viewed their world. Both the questions we ask and the ideas we use to find the answers are at the heart of interpretation in archaeology. The science of archaeology lies in bridging that distance between the information we recover and the questions we seek to answer.

The most difficult thing to predict is not the future, but the past.

Russian proverb

The kinds of questions that archaeologists ask about past societies in general terms involve technology, economy, organization, and ideology. **Technology** is the set of tools, techniques, and knowledge that allows people to convert natural resources into tools, food, clothing, shelter, and other products and equipment they need or want. Technology is the means by which people interact directly with their natural environment. It is also the aspect of past culture that is most easily observed in archaeological data. The fragments of the tools that people used in the past, made of durable materials such as stone, ceramic, and metal, are the most common archaeological

A Spanish rock painting of Neolithic hunters, ca. 8000 B.C.

remains. Changes in technology over time provide clear indicators of the development of our cultural means of adaptation.

Economy is a broad subject that concerns how people obtain foods, materials, and goods to sustain their lives. One major aspect of prehistoric economies is subsistence, which refers to the activities and materials that people use to feed themselves. Archaeologists use the term *subsistence pattern* to describe the plants and animals that prehistoric people ate, the activities required to obtain those foods, and the procurement and preparation techniques and implements used to turn those plants and animals into food. The term *hunting and gathering* describes one such pattern in which wild animals are hunted and wild plants are collected or gathered for subsistence. Agriculture is a form of subsistence that involves the herding of domesticated animals and the cultivation of domesticated plants.

Exchange is another aspect of economy. When artifacts such as stone axes, obsidian knives, metal spearpoints, or certain kinds of food have passed from person to person, archaeologists talk about "exchange." One way to study interaction within and between societies is to look at the distribution of items of exchange. Economic anthropologists distinguish three different kinds of exchange: reciprocity, redistribution, and trade. Reciprocal exchange usually takes the form of gift-giving, whereby objects of relatively equal value are given to build alliances. Redistribution involves the movement of goods to a central place from which they are portioned out to members of a society. Such a system of redistribution might be used to support an army, or priests, or the pyramid builders of ancient Egypt.

Large-scale economic transactions known as trade often involve some sort of market economy and perhaps a monetary standard. Trade takes place in our own economic system today: Objects are imported and exported for the purpose of making a profit. This level of exchange usually involves a highly complex society with professional artisans, regular supplies of raw material, extensive transportation systems, protection of markets and traders against pirates, and enough customers to make the business worthwhile.

Archaeologists often examine exchange and interaction through the study of "exotic materials." The presence of objects and materials that are not available or locally

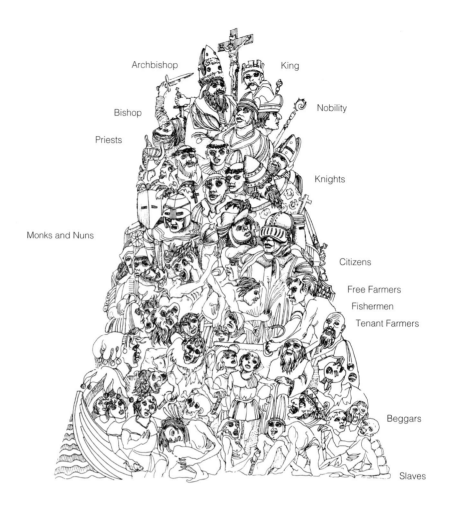

Pyramid of the social layers in a medieval European population.

Archbishop

King

Bishop

Nobility

Priests

Knights

Monks and Nuns

Citizens

Free Farmers

Fishermen

Tenant Farmers

Beggars

Slaves

produced in the study area provides immediate evidence of connections and interaction with others. Of greatest use in such investigations are artifacts or materials that come from a single location.

Organization refers to the roles and relationships in society, and concerns relations between women and men and among different segments of society, such as families, different age groups, labor units, or ethnic groups. Organization structures various aspects of society such as social interaction, economic activity, and political relationships.

Kinship and marriage systems, lineage, sodality, rank, and class are important aspects of social organization and a means of structuring social relationships. Kinship defines the relationship between individual members in society on the basis of their family relationships. Grandmother, brother, uncle, and cousin are terms that relate us to other people through kinship. Marriage systems tie unrelated individuals together through sanctioned kinship; rules for these relationships are carefully defined in society. Lineages provide a means for calculating one's relationships through lines of ancestry. Such genealogies are a way to extend relationships and determine membership in a group. Members of the same lineage often work as a corporate group.

Rank and class distinguish groups of people within society. Many societies of hunter-gatherers are described as **egalitarian,** with essentially equal relations between all members of the group. Many agricultural societies are larger and exhibit distinctive groups within the society that are defined by inherited status differences. Higher status (resulting from prestige, wealth, and/or power) characterizes elite and privileged groups in a society. Rank and class are means of defining such status groups. Rank

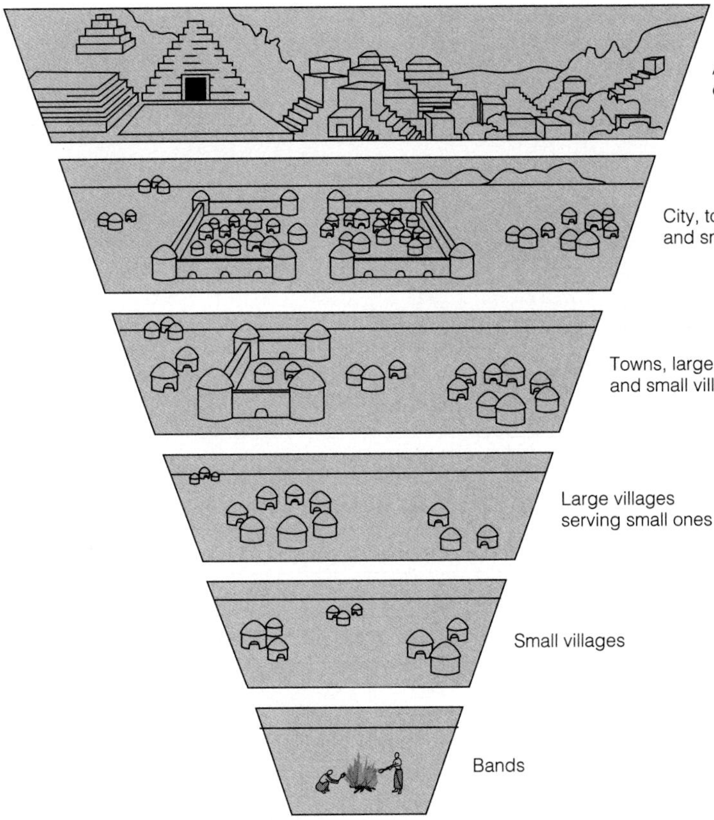

A schematic representation of the changes in social systems from bands to urban societies.

Ancient urban center

City, town, large and small villages

Towns, large villages, and small villages

Large villages serving small ones

Small villages

Bands

refers to inherited positions in societies in which everyone is ranked in terms of status relative to all other people. The firstborn of the highest ranked group is the highest position in such a society. In ranked societies, each individual has a unique place in the order of relationships. Class societies are structured by distinctions between groups, or classes, of people that define levels, or strata, in society. Class is also usually inherited but defines large groups of individuals and may determine one's job, location of residence, marriage opportunities, and financial status. The former caste system of India was an extreme example of a society structured by class.

The economic activities of prehistoric peoples also were organized in different ways. A fundamental mechanism for the organization of tasks is the division of labor. Separate groups or segments of society undertake different activities as part of the economic process. A basic example is seen in many groups of hunter-gatherers where the division of labor is by sex; males are primarily hunters and females are primarily gatherers. Both groups contribute foodstuffs to the subsistence economy of the group. Agricultural societies also see economic organization along gender lines, but the household becomes an important component of production for food and other necessary materials. Production becomes more specialized through time with entire communities involved in the production of specific items or the emergence of specialist groups of producers such as potters, metalsmiths, and bead makers. Production can assume more formal structures such as guilds or unions in larger, more complex societies.

In a general sense, political organization is a reflection of the increasing complexity that is witnessed in human society through time. As societies became larger, organizational changes resulted in closer integration and more linear decision making.

Types of societies and the appearance
of institutions.

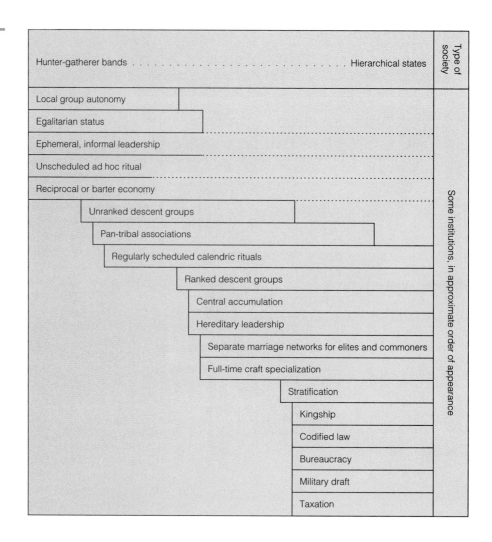

	Type of society
Hunter-gatherer bands . . . . Hierarchical states	
Local group autonomy	Some institutions, in approximate order of appearance
Egalitarian status	
Ephemeral, informal leadership	
Unscheduled ad hoc ritual	
Reciprocal or barter economy	
Unranked descent groups	
Pan-tribal associations	
Regularly scheduled calendric rituals	
Ranked descent groups	
Central accumulation	
Hereditary leadership	
Separate marriage networks for elites and commoners	
Full-time craft specialization	
Stratification	
Kingship	
Codified law	
Bureaucracy	
Military draft	
Taxation	

One of the most significant changes in organization was the shift from egalitarian to hierarchical structures that often followed the origins of agriculture. **Hierarchical** organizations have one or more levels of control above the majority of the people in the society. These higher levels are seen in elite classes or ranks that control much of the wealth, power, and decision making in society. One way to imagine such a hierarchy is to recall the nature of military organization and the chain of command from generals to lieutenants to privates. Government also operates in a hierarchical manner, from local representatives to municipal government, state government, and federal government. The sphere of control and decision making varies with the level in the hierarchy. The municipal government repairs local roads, the federal government builds an interstate system.

There are a number of ways to describe or characterize such hierarchies in human society. One of the most common terminologies uses the concepts of bands, tribes, chiefdoms, and states to distinguish different kinds of political organization in human society. Bands and tribes describe relatively small societies of hunter-gatherers or farmers in which relationships are generally egalitarian and decision making is consensual. Power and property are distributed among all the members of the population. Status is earned through achievements and is ephemeral, held only by the individual who gained it. Chiefdoms and states are larger, often territorial, societies in which relationships are unequal and organization is hierarchical. Status is hereditary and assigned or ascribed by birth order or class affiliation.

One of the more apparent (though not always present) trends in the organization of human society is an increase in complexity over time. Complexity refers to more different units in society and more integration between those units. More units are a result of social, economic, and ideological specialization. Such differentiation is reflected in the distinctions between villages, towns, and cities that began to appear with chiefdoms and states. More integration is a result of hierarchical organization and the emergence of ranked or stratified groups within society whereby power and decision making are in the hands of a few. Some of the changes in social, economic, and political organization from bands to states are summarized in the accompanying figure.

Ideology is the means by which people structure their ideas about the universe, their own place in that universe, and their relationships with one another and with other things and beings around them. Ideology is the way a people view and understand their world; that view permeates almost everything they do. Ideology is reflected in the clothes we wear, the food we eat, and the places in which we live. Ideology encompasses the norms, values, and beliefs held by a society. Ideology is reflected in **cosmology**—explanations of the origins of the universe, of life, and of society. Roman cosmology invoked the twins Romulus and Remus, mythical beings raised by a she-wolf, as the founders of Rome.

Symbols and styles are often ideological expressions. School mascots, corporate logos, flags, and certain faces incorporate and display a wide range of concepts and ideas. Ideology is often strongly expressed in ceremony and pageant surrounding important rites of passage through life: birth, adulthood, weddings, death. Ideology is often embodied in specialists who maintain ritual knowledge and direct the ceremonies and activities that keep such ideology active and pertinent. In egalitarian societies, such individuals are known as witches and **shamans**—specialists in ritual and healing, seers of the future. In hierarchical societies, such specialists are seen in powerful groups such as a priesthood.

These components of human society—technology, economy, organization, and ideology—are closely interrelated in prehistoric materials. The same artifact or object may contain aspects of each. A type of knife found exclusively in women's graves may hold information on the manufacture of tools, on the nature of women's work, on the distinction between sexes in the society, and on ideas about death. Technology, economy, organization, and ideology thus are different, but related, dimensions of past cultures and of human life and an important focus of archaeological investigations.

Rock carving of a Viking ship from Norway.

SUMMARY

THE RELEVANCE
OF ARCHAEOLOGY

Why study archaeology?

A very reasonable question concerns the relevance of archaeology. Why should we study archaeology, why is it important to know about what happened in prehistory? One basic reason to learn about archaeology is simply to participate in the contemporary fascination with the subject. Archaeology is clearly of inherent interest to the general public. Stories appear almost daily in our newspapers and on television. The World Wide Web is crowded with sites about archaeology and our human past.

But this fascination with archaeology stems from the importance of the subject. There is, of course, an exciting mystery involved in unearthing treasures from the earth, but, more than that, archaeology tells us about ourselves and how we got to be the way we are. Ultimately it is the lessons about our past that archaeology provides which convey its significance. The human condition is one that has changed and will change over time. To know our place and to have confidence about where we are going is an essential ingredient in the success of our species.

As Professor Phil Morrison of MIT has recently noted, archaeology is one of those special fields where the public appeal and interest of the subject is combined with the intellectual pursuits of science: "This is the time to extend the physical sciences and engineering into problem domains closer to the central interests of the non-scientific, to the light they increasingly throw on human nature and destiny. Archeology is surely a major example of that linkage, along with astronomy and cosmology, so close to the old existential questions of all thinking humans."

Archaeology tells about how humans, over thousands and millions of years, have survived and succeeded in the face of the difficult challenges of changing environments and competitive neighbors. We learn how past societies dealt with issues such as environmental change, overpopulation, political competition, success and failure. Maybe one of the most important lessons of archaeology is to learn that we are only building on what has been done before. Archaeology also allows us to see our place in the diversity of human societies and gain some appreciation for how we are alike and different. Perhaps as much as any discipline, archaeology tells us that we are all members of the family of humanity, traveling together on a miraculous journey through time.

SUGGESTED READINGS

Barker, P. 1993. *Techniques of archaeological excavation.* London: Routledge. *A European manual on excavation in archaeology.*

Drewett, P. 1999. *Field archaeology. An introduction.* London: Routledge. *An up-to-date manual on field archaeology and its primary methods.*

Hayden, B. 1993. *Archaeology: The science of once and future things.* San Francisco: W. H. Freeman. *A very readable and contemporary approach to the importance and practice of archaeology.*

Hester, T., H. J. Shafer, and K. L. Feder. 1997. *Field methods in archaeology.* Mountain View, CA: Mayfield. *An important guide to archaeological field methods.*

Joukowsky, M. 1980. *A complete manual of field archaeology.* Englewood Cliffs, NJ: Prentice-Hall. *Another field manual, very thorough and detailed, on methods.*

McMillon, W. 1991. *The archaeology handbook. A field manual and resource guide.* New York: John Wiley & Sons. *Handbook of archaeological field methods and information.*

Patterson, T. C. 1994. *The theory and practice of archaeology. A workbook.* Englewood Cliffs, NJ: Prentice-Hall. *An academic view of the methods and perspectives of archaeology.*

Renfrew, C., and P. Bahn. 1998. *Archaeology. Theories, methods, and practice.* London: Thames & Hudson. *A popular textbook emphasizing how archaeologists learn what they know about the past.*

Sutton, M. Q., and B. S. Arkush. 1998. *Archaeological laboratory methods.* Dubuque, IA: Kendall/Hunt. *A guide to laboratory work in archaeology involving identification, conservation, and measurement.*

Trigger, B. 1989. *A history of archaeological thought.* Cambridge: Cambridge University Press. *A major consideration of the history of archaeology and how archaeologists try to understand the past.*

2

THE FIRST HUMANS

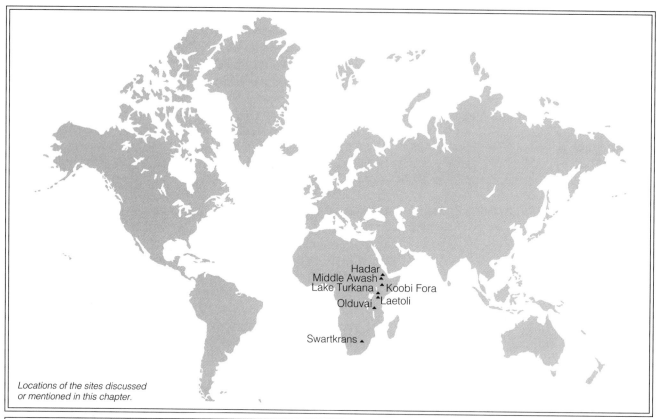

Locations of the sites discussed or mentioned in this chapter.

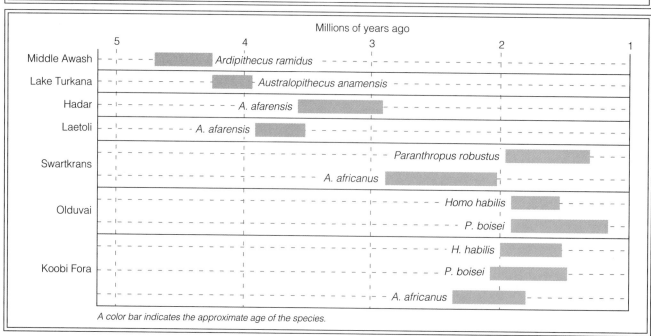

A color bar indicates the approximate age of the species.

THE DAWN
OF HUMANITY

*Our place on the planet in terms of geological
time, our relationship to other animals, and
our distinctively human characteristics*

Try to imagine the unimaginable. Sometime between 10 and 15 billion years ago, an explosion of cosmic proportions ripped time and space apart and created our universe. Hydrogen and helium hurtled through the emptiness, cast out of that original Big Bang. Clouds of these gases began to coagulate and attract other passing clouds. As these concentrations were further compacted by gravity, temperatures rose, and the energy created in the nuclear furnaces of the first stars lit up the universe.

More complex reactions in these evolving stars gave rise to heavier atoms of carbon, oxygen, magnesium, silicon, sulfur, and the other elements. Massive eruptions and disintegrations tore these early elements out of the stars and spewed them across space, creating newer and heavier stars. As they condensed, smaller conglomerations, lacking the mass or temperature to ignite, gathered around the edges of the brightly burning stars. Some of these cold outliers became hard, metallic globes; others, frigid balls of gas. The planets were born. Some gases remained on the harder planets and condensed into oceans or enveloped the surface as a primordial atmosphere. Violent electrical storms, driven by energy from the stars and massive volcanic activity rifting the surface of the forming planets, tore apart and reconstituted these elements in the early seas and atmospheres.

On the planet we call Earth, formed about 4.6 billion years ago, this alchemy of primeval forces churned out new molecules in an atmosphere of methane, ammonia, hydrogen sulfide, water, and hydrogen. Among the multitude of new chemistries created in the soup of the early earth's oceans was a remarkable combination of atoms. This was a new molecule, able to reproduce itself—to make a copy of its original. Life emerged shortly after 4 billion years ago. Like the broom of the sorcerer's apprentice in the movie *Fantasia,* once begun, the copying process filled the seas with duplicates. These reproducing molecules grew, achieved more complex forms, and became the building blocks of more elaborate organisms that developed metabolic and sexual reproductive functions. Systems for eating and internal metabolism enabled organisms to obtain energy from other life forms. Sexual reproduction allowed for a tremendous diversity in offspring, and thus a greater capacity for adapting to changing environments and conditions.

Plants appeared in the oceans and spread to the land. The atmosphere fed carbon dioxide to the plants, and they in turn replenished the air with oxygen through the process of photosynthesis. Swimming cooperatives of molecules in the oceans moved onto the land and began to use the oxygen in the air for breathing and other metabolic functions. Fish, amphibians, reptiles, insects, mammals, and birds spread across the face of the earth. And then, only a moment ago in geological time, a human creature evolved from this great chain of living beings.

GEOLOGICAL TIME

The universe is perhaps 10 billion years old. Earth is roughly 4.6 billion years old. The idea of 10 billion years, 4.6 billion years, or even 1 million years is impossible

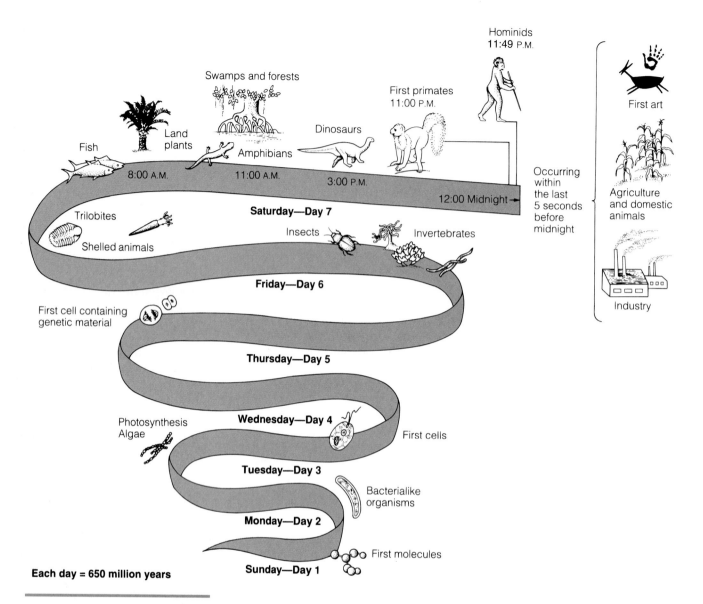

Hominids
11:49 P.M.

First primates
11:00 P.M.

Swamps and forests

Dinosaurs

First art

Land
plants

Amphibians

Fish

8:00 A.M.   11:00 A.M.   3:00 P.M.

Occurring
within
the last
5 seconds
before
midnight

Agriculture
and domestic
animals

12:00 Midnight

Saturday—Day 7

Trilobites

Shelled animals

Insects   Invertebrates

Industry

Friday—Day 6

First cell containing
genetic material

Thursday—Day 5

Photosynthesis
Algae

Wednesday—Day 4   First cells

Tuesday—Day 3

Bacterialike
organisms

Monday—Day 2

First molecules

Each day = 650 million years

Sunday—Day 1

The evolution of life on earth as a single week in time. Planet earth forms at 12:01 A.M. Sunday morning, life appears on Monday morning, fish evolve on Saturday morning, and the first bipedal homonids show up at 11:49 P.M. Saturday night.

for us to comprehend, but we need some way to appreciate this vast span of time in order to understand our past and our place in the cosmos. If we could compact the eons that have passed into meaningful units of time, the events of our evolutionary history might make more sense.

Consider a single week, from Sunday morning to Saturday night, as a substitute for our countdown to today. If one day in this 4.6-billion-year week represented over 650 million years, a single hour would be 25 million years, a minute would be 400,000 years, and the passage of a single second would take more than 6000 years. Roughly 4.6 billion years ago—the 7 days of our symbolic week—the earth formed in our solar system. The time was early Sunday morning at 12:01 A.M. By Sunday evening, a primitive atmosphere and oceans had appeared, and the first molecules began to coalesce. By Monday morning, the first traces of life emerged in the shape of bacteria that evolved and multiplied. More complex bacteria and algae, using photosynthesis, began the task of converting the poisonous, primordial atmosphere to an oxygen base on Tuesday. Not until Thursday were the first cells carrying genetic material created. Late Friday morning, the first invertebrate animals—resembling jellyfish, sponges, and worms—evolved. Before dawn on Saturday morning, the seas were teeming with shell-bearing animals, such as the trilobites. Around breakfast time on Saturday, fish and small land plants appeared. By 11:00 A.M., amphibians began to move onto the land,

Era	Period	Epoch	Millions of years ago (m.y.a.)	Important Events
CENOZOIC	Quaternary	Recent	0.01	Modern genera of animals.
		Pleistocene	2.0	Early humans and giant mammals now extinct; glaciation.
	Tertiary	Pliocene	5.5	Anthropoid radiation and culmination of mammalian speciation. Earliest apes.
		Miocene	25	
		Oligocene	38	Expansion and modernization of mammals.
		Eocene	54	
		Paleocene	65	
MESOZOIC	Cretaceous		135	Dinosaurs dominant; marsupial and placental mammals appear; first flowering plants spread rapidly.
	Jurassic		180	Dominance of dinosaurs; first mammals and birds; insects abundant, including social forms.
	Triassic		245	First dinosaurs and mammal-like reptiles, with culmination of large amphibians.
PALEOZOIC	Permian		270	Primitive reptiles replace amphibians as dominant class; glaciation.
	Carboniferous		350	Amphibians dominant in luxuriant coal forests; first reptiles and trees.
	Devonian		400	Dominance of fishes; first amphibians.
	Silurian		440	Primitive fishes; invasion of land by plants and arthropods.
	Ordovician		500	First vertebrates, the jawless fish; invertebrates dominate the seas.
	Cambrian		540	All invertebrate phyla appear and algae diversify.
PRE-CAMBRIAN			4600	A few multicellular invertebrates; earliest fossils at 3.6 b.y.a. Single-cell organisms appear.

The major divisions of geological time.

and insects appeared in a warm landscape of swamps and forests. Late that same afternoon, the first dinosaurs crawled about. Smaller, warm-blooded dinosaurs began to produce live young and nurse them. The ancestors of modern mammals appeared shortly after 9:30 P.M. Sixty-seven minutes before midnight, the common ancestor of apes and man made its home in the dense forests of Africa. The first recognizable human, walking on two legs, made an appearance at 11:49 P.M. The first art was created less than 5 seconds before midnight. Agriculture and animal domestication originated only 2 seconds before the end of the week, and the industrial revolution began just as the last bell for midnight tolled.

In order to help make this vastness of time comprehensible, geologists have divided the earth's history into a series of **eras** representing major episodes, usually distinguished by significant changes in the plant and animal kingdoms. The **Precambrian** was the first major era of geological time, extending from the origin of the earth to about 600 million years ago (m.y.a.). The succeeding **Paleozoic** era witnessed the appearance of the first vertebrate species: fish and the first amphibians. Plants spread onto the land, and reptiles began to appear. Around 225 m.y.a., the **Mesozoic** era, the Age of Dinosaurs, began following a period of extinction. The **Cenozoic,** our current era, began about 65 m.y.a. with the rise of modern mammals, birds, and flowering plants, following a major extinction of the dinosaurs. This episode of extinction is now thought to have resulted from the catastrophic impact of a meteor, causing major climatic and environmental disruption.

The Cenozoic is further divided by geologists into a series of seven **epochs,** only the last three of which are relevant to the evolution of the human species. The **Pliocene,** beginning around 5.5 m.y.a., is the geological epoch in which the first hominid, or humanlike creature, appeared. The **Pleistocene,** beginning about 2 m.y.a., was marked by a series of major climatic fluctuations. Completely modern forms of the human species appeared toward the end of this epoch. The **Recent** epoch—also called the **Holocene** (also known as the **Postglacial** or **Present Interglacial**)—began only 10,000 years ago and witnessed the origins of agriculture, the first cities, and the industrial age, includes our present time.

BIOLOGICAL EVOLUTION

The last known photograph of Charles Darwin.

Man is only one of the earth's "manifold creatures" and he cannot understand his own nature or seek wisely to guide his destiny without taking account of the whole pattern of life.

George Gaylord Simpson (1967)

Change, modification, variation—these themes describe the path of evolution from the earliest self-replicating molecules that came to life to the fully modern humans of today. The theory of natural selection, formulated by Charles Darwin and Alfred Russel Wallace in the middle of the nineteenth century, describes this process of change. Wallace and Darwin were strongly influenced by the ideas of Thomas Malthus, an English clergyman and philosopher. In his *Essay in the Principle of Population* (1798), Malthus observed that the growth rate of human population potentially exceeded the amount of food available. Malthus argued that famine, war, and disease limited the size of human populations and for that reason the number of people did not overwhelm the resources available to feed them. In essence, Malthus noted that not everyone who was born survived to reproduce.

Darwin coined the term *natural selection* to account for the increase in offspring of those individuals who did survive. He introduced the concept in his 1859 publication *On the Origin of Species by Means of Natural Selection.* During a global voyage of exploration aboard the HMS *Beagle,* Darwin had observed that most species of plants and animals showed a great deal of variation—that individuals were distinct and exhibited different characteristics. Following Malthus, Darwin pointed out that all organisms produce more offspring than can survive and that the individuals that survive do so because of certain advantageous characteristics they possess.

In other words, the surviving organisms are better adapted to the world that confronts them. For example, offspring with better hearing or eyesight can more effectively avoid predators. Nature's choice of better-adapted individuals—the "survival of the fittest," according to Darwin—leads to continual change in the species, as their more advantageous characteristics are passed genetically from one generation to the next. This basic process gave rise to the myriad creatures that occupy the world today. Evolutionary change is often described as differential reproductive success, and natural selection is the principal, though not the exclusive, mechanism responsible for it. Of course, as environmental conditions change, those physical characteristics that enhance survival and successful parenting also may vary.

Views on this process of **evolution** change over time, too. New mechanisms for evolution have been proposed, and there is discussion regarding the level at which selection operates, whether on groups or individuals. There is also debate about the pace of change—whether major evolutionary modifications occurred gradually, as Darwin emphasized, or rather abruptly and suddenly. Stephen Jay Gould and Niles Eldredge of Harvard University describe the uneven pace of evolution as "punctuated equilibrium." It now seems that some biological shifts occur gradually, as Darwin described, whereas others may occur in rapid spurts following long periods of stasis, or little change. A major theory such as evolution is modified over time, but the basic tenets of this view have withstood many tests and offer the best way to understand the emergence of life and early humans.

THE EVOLUTION OF THE
ANIMAL KINGDOM

Zoologists classify the members of the animal kingdom according to their similarities and differences. We are animals because we move and eat with a mouth, we are vertebrates because of our backbone, and we are mammals because we have warm

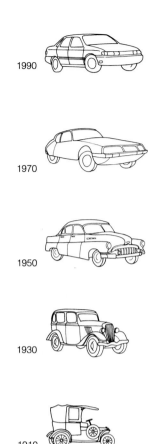

1990

1970

1950

1930

1910

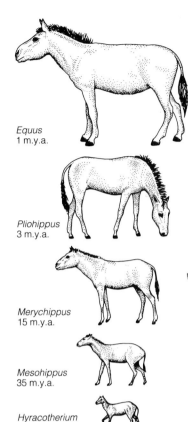

Equus
1 m.y.a.

Pliohippus
3 m.y.a.

Merychippus
15 m.y.a.

Mesohippus
35 m.y.a.

Hyracotherium
45 m.y.a.

Biological organisms and cultural artifacts evolve over time. The evolution of the automobile from A.D. 1910 to 1990. The evolution of the horse from *Hyracotherium*, 45 m.y.a., to *Equus*, 1 m.y.a.

Handwritten margin notes:

Hominoidea —
(The family that includes) includes apes + humans due to
— teeth shape
— no tail
— swinging arms

hominoids —
all present + past apes + humans

hominids —
specifically to all present + past humans

As humans, we share a common ancestor c̄ chimps + gorillas that lived sometime during last 5-10 M yrs.

blood and breast-feed our offspring. We are **primates** because we have grasping hands, flexible limbs, and a highly developed sense of vision, which we share with the other members of the primate order: lemurs, tarsiers, monkeys, and apes. We are members of the family **Hominoidea**, the taxonomic group that includes apes and humans, because of the shape of our teeth, the absence of a tail, and our swinging arms. The term **hominoids** refers to all present and past apes and humans, while **hominids** refers specifically to present and past humans. As humans, we share a common ancestor with chimpanzees and gorillas that lived sometime during the last 5–10 million years.

Present evidence suggests the following scenario for primate evolution during the Cenozoic. The first primates on earth existed about 65 m.y.a. at the beginning of the Cenozoic, when the air temperature was warm and extensive tropical forests covered much of the land surface. These early primates began as tree-dwelling insect-eaters. They had adaptive characteristics such as stereoscopic color vision, which provided depth perception and enhanced their ability to move from branch to branch and to spot insects, and a grasping ability, so they could hold on to branches and grab bugs. This heritage has provided us with an extraordinary visual ability and large centers in the brain to process the massive volume of information absorbed by the eyes. Along with the ability to hold and manipulate objects with dexterity came other changes. Arms and shoulders became more flexible for swinging in the trees, and internal organs and bones evolved toward a more vertical arrangement.

The earliest fossil Hominoidea appeared approximately 25 m.y.a. Apes are generally distinguished from monkeys and other primates by larger size, distinctive teeth, greater sociability, the absence of a tail, and a reduced sense of smell. From one of these early apes, a new group of animals, known as the **dryopithecines**, emerged during the Miocene epoch some 17–12 m.y.a. These creatures had several features, known primarily from the fossil teeth that have survived, suggesting that they were the probable ancestors of both living apes and humans. Dryopithecines were apparently

Classification of the hominids in the animal kingdom.

Kingdom: Animalia
  Phylum: Chordata
    Class: Mammalia
      Suborder: Anthropoidea
        Superfamily: Hominidae
          Family: Hominidae
            Genus: Ardipithecus
              Species: *ramidus*
            Genus: *Australopithecus*
              Species: *anamensis*
              Species: *afarensis*
              Species: *africanus*
            Genus: *Paranthropus*
              Species: *aethiopicus*
              Species: *robustus*
              Species: *boisei*
            Genus: *Homo*
              Species: *habilis*
              Species: *erectus*
              Species: *sapiens*
                Subspecies: *neanderthalensis*
                Subspecies: *sapiens*

very successful in their arboreal adaptation, ranging over much of Africa, Asia, and Europe. During this time, the earth changed dramatically. Increased geological activity in the earth's crust created new mountain ranges. Volcanoes and earthquakes were recurrent. Rainfall increased, and air temperature dropped. Widespread tropical forests began to shrink, taken over by expanding grasslands and savannas.

At some point during the later Miocene, after 10 m.y.a., an African contemporary of these primates took the path toward humanness, as seen in the evidence for more upright posture and smaller canine teeth. The fossil record from this time period is very scanty. A recent discovery in the Sumburu Hills of Kenya may represent this creature. A fragment of an upper jaw, dating to 9–8 m.y.a., has characteristics of a generalized chimpanzee-gorilla-hominid ancestor. Genetic and molecular evidence indicates that early humans were most closely related to chimpanzees and that we began to diverge from the chimpanzee lineage between 6 and 5 m.y.a. Certainly during the Pliocene, by 4.5 m.y.a., recognizably hominid members of our lineage had appeared in East Africa. The sites described in this chapter tell this story of the evolution of our earliest human ancestors.

ON BEING HUMAN

But what does it mean to be human? What makes us distinct among other species of animals? We are human because we have a skeleton designed for upright walking. We are human because we have grasping hands with opposable thumbs, capable of both strength and precision movement; but we are also human because we have *lost* the grasping, opposable toes of the other apes. We are human because we have small, flat teeth and lack the large, slashing canines of other primates. We have a distinct nose compared to apes and a face that sits beneath our brain case rather than in front of it.

We are human because we lack fur and have more sweat glands than hair follicles. We have a conspicuous penis and breasts, and we care for our young over a lengthy period of infancy and childhood. We are human because we often act according to reason rather than on instinct. We are human because we make and use tools to alter our environment and make our lives more secure and comfortable. We are human because we speak a language full of meaning and metaphor. We have a large brain relative to our body size, and enhanced intelligence as well as a complex repertoire of behaviors known as culture. **Culture** is a means of human adaptation based on experience, learning, and the use of tools. Within limits, culture enables us to modify and enhance our behavior without a corresponding change in our genetic composition. As a consequence, biological evolution and natural selection cannot explain the culturally acquired traits of the human species.

The prehistoric record of our species and its immediate ancestors is characterized by both biological evolution and cultural developments. Biological, rather than cultural, changes dominated the first several million years of our existence. The evolution of our earliest ancestors is highlighted by key changes in movement, teeth, and the size and organization of the brain. The transmission of cultural traits through learning occurs much more rapidly than Darwinian evolution. The last hundred thousand years or so of our presence on the planet are marked primarily by cultural changes rather than biological ones. The rates of these recent changes are unmatched in the entire history of life.

Upright posture, large brain size, and *tool use* are generally considered the three primary indicators of humanness among those listed above. These indicators can be seen in the bones and stones that are preserved. The major questions in human evolution, then, concern when, where, and why these distinctive characteristics appeared. What of us is preserved in the layers of geological time?

Paleoanthropology, the study of early human evolution, is an attempt to answer these and other questions, using evidence from Pliocene and Pleistocene **fossils,** the mineralized bones of extinct animals and artifacts. For this information we must turn to Africa; our oldest ancestors are known only from that continent. Some of the best evidence comes from sites at Hadar, Laetoli, Swartkrans, Olduvai, and Koobi Fora.

In each great region of the world the living mammals are closely related to the extinct species of the same region. It is, therefore, probable that Africa was formerly inhabited by extinct apes closely allied to the gorilla and chimpanzee; and as these two species are now man's nearest allies, it is somewhat more probable that our early progenitors lived on the African continent than elsewhere.

Charles Darwin (1871)

That's the thing about history, it's over before you know it.

Garrison Keillor

HADAR

A key place for finding the earliest humans

The severely eroded badlands of Pliocene and Pleistocene deposits in the Hadar region of Ethiopia.

All the evidence for the early hominids before 2 m.y.a. comes from Africa. Until 1970, there was relatively little evidence for the earliest human ancestors other than a few skulls and pieces of bone. The human characteristics of upright posture, large brain size, and tool use were thought to have evolved simultaneously as large primates moved out from the forest into the savannah. New fossil finds from Ethiopia, Kenya, and Tanzania have pushed back the age of the earliest known hominids and considerably modified our understanding of their behavior and appearance.

Shortly after 5 million years ago during the Pliocene, the first recognizably human remains began to appear in East Africa. Many of the early hominid fossils date to the Pliocene and the beginning of the Pleistocene, a time often described as the **Plio/Pleistocene.** New fossil discoveries from this time are continuously being made in East Africa, often causing our family tree to be redrawn.

One of the most productive areas of research is in a region known as the Hadar (huh-dar′), northeast of the city of Addis Ababa in Ethiopia. In this geologically active zone, the combination of

Donald Johanson (left) and coworkers at the Institute for Human Origins with the fossil remains from Hadar.

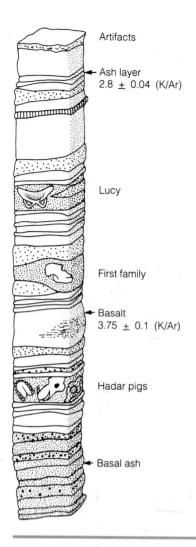

Artifacts

Ash layer
2.8 ± 0.04 (K/Ar)

Lucy

First family

Basalt
3.75 ± 0.1 (K/Ar)

Hadar pigs

Basal ash

The Pliocene stratigraphy at Hadar, showing the approximate age of the layers and where Lucy and the "first family" were found. These layers are exposed in the sides of gullies and on the surface by erosion. The fossils appear on the eroded surface.

faulting, rapid deposition, and continued erosion has exposed numerous layers from the Plio/Pleistocene that contain some of the earliest human fossils yet discovered. Donald Johanson, a paleo-anthropologist now at the Institute for Human Origins in Tempe, Arizona, and French geologist Maurice Taieb began a search for early hominid fossils in this area in 1972. One of the most complete early human skeletons ever discovered was found by this team in 1974.

Johanson spotted a small arm bone on the ground while on a survey walk. He picked it up and immediately noticed other bits of skull and bone. As he continued, more pieces were collected—fragments of vertebrae, limbs, and jaw. The next day he returned with a large crew and carefully sifted the earth at the site in order to recover all the fragments they could. The finds of Pliocene hominids usually consist of only a single tooth or at most a few bones. But after 2 weeks of searching and sifting, Johanson's team found almost 100 fragments—about 40% of a complete hominid skeleton. Unfortunately, most of the skull was missing.

For the first time, a reasonably intact early hominid was available, enough to reconstruct virtually the entire skeleton. Lucy, as this individual was dubbed by her discoverers, provides much new detail on the anatomy of torso and limbs. Lucy was probably female, small in stature—1.2 m, just under 4 ft, tall—small brained, and about 20 years old when she died. Absolute age for the skeleton is estimated as somewhat more than 2.9 m.y.a. (Absolute dating is explained later in the chapter in "Dating Methods," p. 42.)

Earlier still from Hadar, possibly dating to 3.2 m.y.a., are the skeletal parts of what has been described as "the first family"—over 200 bones from at least seven individuals, five adults and two children, found together. This is an absolutely remarkable discovery. Johanson's own description of the discoveries conveys the excitement and significance:

> Anthropology student John Kolar spotted an arm-bone fragment. From some distance away, Mike Bush, a medical student, shouted that he had found something just breaking the ground

surface. It was the very first day on survey for Mike.

"Hominid teeth?" he asked, when we ran to him. There was no doubt. . . .

Michèle Cavillon of our motion-picture crew called to me to look at some bones higher up the hill.

Two bone fragments lay side by side—one a partial femur and the other a fragmentary heel bone. Both were hominid.

Carefully, we started scouring the hillside. Two more leg bones—fibulae—showed up, but each from the same side. The same side? That could only indicate two individuals. . . .

Time was of the essence. Rainstorms during the months of our absence could wash away fragments that would be lost forever down the ravines. . . . Each day produced more remains. . . .

So we had evidence of young adults, old adults, and children—an entire assemblage of early hominids. All of them at one place. Nothing like this had ever been found! (1976, pp. 805–811)

These individuals apparently died as a group, possibly in a local flash flood, and their bodies were washed to a location where their bones were preserved until the present. The sediments in which the fossils were discovered are lakeshore and riverine deposits. There are very few remains from other species in these layers and no sign that the hominid bones had been gnawed or eaten by other animals.

The discovery of these bones from a *group* of individuals provides answers to a number of questions. The presence of so many individuals together indicates that our earliest ancestors did indeed live in groups. The individuals were relatively small (1.2–1.5 m, or 4–5 ft, tall) but strong and sturdy. The small heads had human molars and small canine teeth. However, an apelike gap exists between the incisor teeth and canines. The skeleton below the neck was almost completely human, but the arms were long and the bones of the hand were heavy, with large muscle attachments. The anatomy of the leg and pelvis indicates that they walked upright. Other information on early hominid patterns of growth, differences between children and adults and between males and females, the dexterity of the hands, and more, will emerge as the study of these extraordinary remains continues.

In 1994, fieldworkers in the Hadar region discovered the first intact skull of an *Australopithecus afarensis*. This skull confirmed the upright posture of a relative of Lucy's, dating to 3 m.y.a. More significantly, the skull was a male's and documented significant **sexual dimorphism,** or size differences, among these early hominids. Pronounced differences in body size between the sexes in primates is generally correlated with **polygynous** mating systems, in which males compete for females. Males would have been approximately 1.5 m (5 ft) tall, weighing 50 kg (110 lb); females like Lucy were 1.0–1.2 m (3.5–4.0 ft) tall and weighed closer to 35 kg (75 lb). This difference between the sexes is also found in modern chimpanzees but is greatly reduced in more recent human species.

Lucy –
Australopithecus
afarensis,
~ 3 Ma

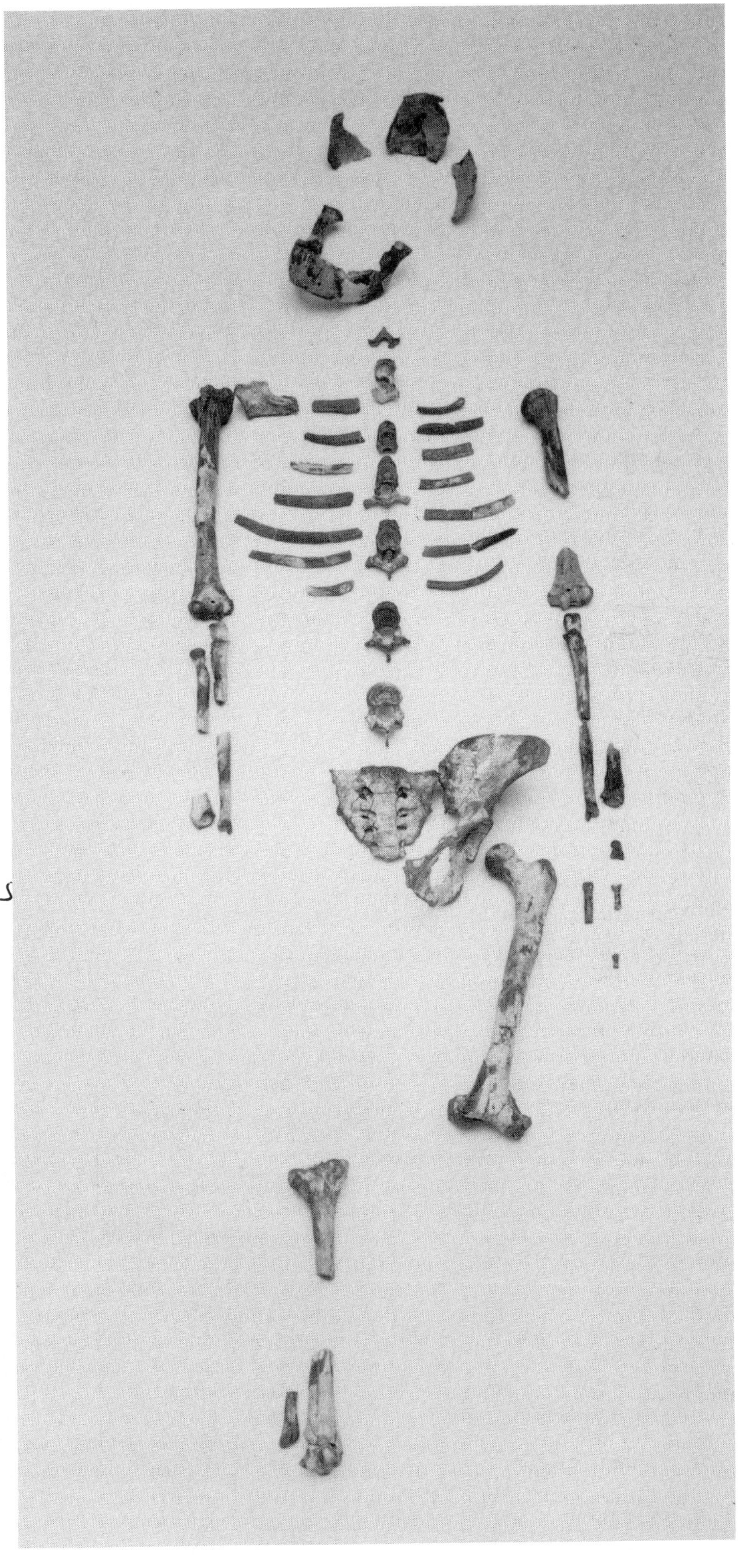

The skeleton known as Lucy from Hadar, one of the most complete of an early hominid. Almost 40% of the bones are present. A member of *Australopithecus afarensis,* Lucy was approximately 1.2 m tall and 3 million years old.

THE FAMILY TREE

The evidence and interpretation of our earliest biology

Human evolution—the changes in the skeleton and biology of our species over the last several million years—is a fascinating subject, yet one for which there is only sparse evidence. In almost every instance, the fossil remains of our earliest hominid ancestors are very fragmentary, poorly preserved, and disturbed by natural forces—time and nature have taken their toll.

Determining the genus and species of the fossil bones of early humans is very difficult. All the fragmentary pieces of the early fossil finds represent only a few hundred separate individuals. Determining the age of fossils can also be difficult, and questions remain about whether the species existed contemporaneously or sequentially. Not surprisingly, there are controversies over what to call these first hominid forms and how to identify them. As Richard Klein, of Stanford University, has noted, paleoanthropology is more like a court of law than a physics laboratory. It sometimes seems that whenever a new fragment is discovered, we have to reassess and even redraw our entire family tree. New fossils that modify current ideas are found almost every year.

Since the initial work of the Swedish botanist Carolus Linnaeus during the mid-1700s, scientists have classified newly discovered members of the plant and animal kingdoms according to a system that organizes them into species, genus, family, order, class, phylum, and kingdom, from most specific to most general—a family tree of life. Modern humans are members of the family Hominidae of the genus *Homo* and the species *sapiens*. The first members of the family Hominidae from approximately 4.5 m.y.a. have been designated *Ardipithecus ramidus*. These two ends of our family lineage are generally accepted. In between, however, disputes rage over the designation of species, the age of fossils, and the line of human ancestry. Only the most important fossil forms and some of the controversies are discussed below.

New and very important discoveries continue to come from the eroded badlands of Pliocene deposits in central Ethiopia. Since 1992, the oldest known fossils that are distinctly human have been discovered in the Middle Awash area of Ethiopia. Seventeen fossils were found by a research team directed by Tim White of the University of California,

The skulls of *Australopithecus afarensis* (left), *Homo erectus* (center), and *Homo sapiens sapiens*.

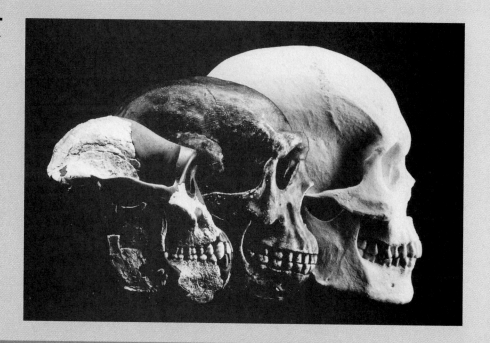

Table 2.1 Major Characteristics of the Plio/Pleistocene Hominids

	A. ramidus	A. anamensis	A. afarensis	A. africanus	P. robustus	P. boisei	H. habilis
Dates	4.5–4.3 m.y.a.	4.3–4.0 m.y.a.	4–3 m.y.a.	3–2.5 m.y.a.	2.2–1.5 m.y.a.	2.2–1 m.y.a.	2.2–1.6 m.y.a.
Sites	Middle Awash	Lake Turkana	Hadar Omo Laetoli	Taung Sterkfontein Makapansgat Lake Turkana (?) Omo (?)	Kromdraai Swartkrans	Olduvai Lake Turkana Omo	Olduvai Lake Turkana Omo Sterkfontein (?) Swartkrans (?)
Cranial capacity	Unknown (400–450 cc?)	Unknown	380–500 cc; average = 440 cc	435–530 cc; average = 450 cc	520 cc (based on one specimen)	500–530 cc; average = 515 cc	500–800 cc; average = 680 cc
Size	100 lb?	5′ 110 lb (♂) 4′3″ 70 lb (♀)	3′6″ 50 lb (♀) (♂ to 100 lb?)	Similar to A. afarensis	5′+ 150 lb	5′+ 150 lb	Limited evidence; may have been size of A. afarensis
Skull	Large pointed canines, small molar crowns, thinner enamel; foramen magnum forward	Teeth and jaw are hominid but some similarities to chimpanzee	Very prognathous, receding chin, large teeth, pointed canines with gap, arcade between ape and human, hint of crest	Less prognathous than A. afarensis; jaw more rounded; large back teeth; canines smaller than A. robustus, larger than A. afarensis; no crest	Heavy jaws, small canines and front teeth, large back teeth, definite crest	Very large jaws, very large back teeth, large crest	Flatter face, less sloping forehead, teeth similar to A. africanus, no crest
Postcranial skeleton	Arm bones with characteristics intermediate between great apes and hominids	Joints on leg bones indicate bipedal gait	Long arms, short thumb, curved fingers and toes, bipedal	—	Hands and feet more like modern humans, retention of long arms	—	Limited evidence, retention of long arms, maybe retention of primitive features of hand and foot

Source: Adapted from Feder and Park, 1997.

Berkeley, including teeth, skull, and arm bones. These fossils lie directly under a volcanic deposit dating to 4.4 m.y.a. Designated *Ardipithecus ramidus*, the species exhibits a combination of human and chimpanzeelike features. Since the initial discovery, leg bones have been found which suggest that this earliest ancestor likely walked on two legs, not four.

A. anamensis, a transitional form between *A. ramidus* and *A. afarensis*, has recently been found at Lake Turkana, Kenya, dating to 4 m.y.a. Sometime around 3.9 m.y.a., *A. anamensis* evolved into *Australopithecus afarensis*, well known from Hadar, Laetoli, and elsewhere in East Africa. (Table 2.1). *A. afarensis* exhibits more humanlike teeth and unquestionably walked upright, as seen in the footprints at Laetoli and in the fossil bones themselves.

The generally accepted picture is that sometime between 3 and 2.5 m.y.a., *A. afarensis* split into two separate lineages. One of these lineages continued as the australopithecines (a generic term for various forms of *Australopithecus*). This line included both gracile and robust

(continued)

Locations of the sites and areas listed in Table 2.1.

forms. The gracile form, with smaller teeth, skull, and body size, known as *Australopithecus africanus*, appeared shortly after 3 m.y.a. The robust forms, with big teeth and heavy jaws for chewing plant foods, are designated as genus *Paranthropus*. Several species have been identified including *aethiopithecus*, *robustus*, and *boisei*. The robust forms have been found in both East and South Africa and eventually became extinct around 1 m.y.a.

The former lineage led to *Homo habilis*, the first members of our own genus. The earliest *H. habilis* is known from around 2.5 m.y.a. and is recognized by a clear increase in brain size. (The first *H. habilis* is very close in time to the earliest known stone tools; see "The First Tools," p. 58.)

The 1986 discovery by Johanson and White of over 300 pieces of a skeleton in beds at Olduvai Gorge dating to

1.8 m.y.a. has filled in part of the picture of *Homo habilis*. For the first time, there were enough fragments of the arms and legs of an *H. habilis* creature to provide an indication of height and the proportions of the limbs. Surprisingly, this female *H. habilis* was less than 1 m (about 3 ft) tall and had very long arms, similar to Lucy and other australopithecines. Such evidence suggests that (1) *H. habilis* may still have been spending part of its life in the trees, (2) sexual dimorphism was still very pronounced, and (3) major changes in behavior and habitat of the early hominids may have taken place in the period between 2 and 1.5 m.y.a. Thus, it appears that *Homo habilis* "represents a mosaic of primitive and derived features, indicating an early hominid which walked bipedally . . . but also retained the generalized hominoid capacity to climb trees" (Susman and Stern, 1982, p. 931).

Richard Leakey, Alan Walker of Pennsylvania State University, and a few others suggest a different scenario. Louis Leakey always argued that the genus *Homo* had its roots deep in the Pliocene, and eventually he discovered several early *Homo* specimens at Olduvai and elsewhere. This view is maintained by his son Richard and others who would push the evolutionary split from a common ancestor of the *Australopithecus* and *Homo* lines much farther back in time, perhaps near the beginning of the Pliocene around 6 million years ago. They imagine that two, or more, different australopithecine groups (*P. robustus* and *A. africanus*) and one line of *Homo* (*H. habilis*) evolved at this point in time. There is very little fossil evidence between 7 and 4 m.y.a. because geological deposits dating to this period in Africa are extremely rare. Thus, the common ancestor that Leakey and others envision far back in the Pliocene remains hypothetical.

The next stage in our family tree is relatively straightforward and uncontested. *Homo erectus* evolved from *Homo habilis* about 1.8 million years ago, again in Africa (see Color Plate 1). The earliest

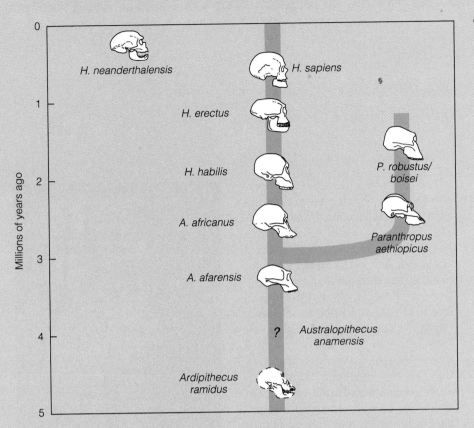

Millions of years ago

H. neanderthalensis

H. sapiens

H. erectus

H. habilis

P. robustus/ boisei

A. africanus

Paranthropus aethiopicus

A. afarensis

? *Australopithecus anamensis*

Ardipithecus ramidus

A current model of human evolution.

fossils of *H. erectus* are known from the eastern shore of Lake Turkana in northern Kenya. *H. erectus* is also the first early human form found outside of Africa, in Asia, and probably in Europe. In fact, a controversial date of 1.8 m.y.a. for an *H. erectus* fossil from the island of Java in Southeast Asia would suggest a very rapid spread of this species out of Africa (see "Trinil," Chapter 3, p. 70). *Homo erectus* walked upright and had a brain size midway between that of *Australopithecus* and fully modern humans. The time period of *H. erectus* covers more than 1.5 million years, and there were a number of changes in the species during that period. In fact, there is some controversy today about the reliability of the *H. erectus* species designation.

Sexual dimorphism was greatly reduced in *Homo erectus* and may reflect the emergence of monogamous mating systems, in which males and females each have a single mate for long periods of time. Remarkably, and probably relatedly, a major innovation in the technology of stone tools, the appearance of the handaxe and other bifacial tools occurred almost simultaneously with *Homo erectus* in Africa (see "The Acheulean Handaxe," Chapter 3, p. 92). The distribution of *Homo erectus* fossils and the archaeological evidence they produced are the subject of the next chapter.

Homo erectus gradually evolved in Africa and Asia, exhibiting slowly increasing brain size, for a million years. At some point after perhaps 200,000 years before present (B.P.), *H. erectus* fossils began to disappear and *Homo sapiens* began to appear. The timing, mechanisms, and location(s) for this evolution from *H. erectus* to *H. sapiens* are subject to debate and controversy; see Chapter 4 (see also "Modern and Ancient DNA," p. 106). Suffice it to say here that *H. erectus* is the ancestor of the first *Homo sapiens*—and ultimately of ourselves.

LAETOLI

The best evidence for the first steps toward humanness

Human
characteristics:
1. Upright posture
2. Large brain
3. Tool use

As we have noted, the three distinctive characteristics of being human are upright posture, a large brain, and tool use. The question of which came first has been dramatically answered by a discovery in East Africa. The evidence for this new posture comes not only from the fossil bones, however, but also from actual footprints preserved at the site of Laetoli (lay-toe'lee) in Tanzania, discovered by Mary Leakey in 1976. Laetoli is located about 70 km (40 mi) southeast of Olduvai Gorge. Sometime around 3.6 m.y.a., an active volcano near Laetoli covered the area with a layer of volcanic ash. Following a light rain shower, various animals moved across the damp layer of ash. A chemical reaction between rainwater and the ash quickly hardened their tracks; even the impressions of the raindrops are preserved in some areas at the site. Hares, birds, extinct elephants, pigs, buffalo, rhinos, a saber-toothed tiger, and lots of baboons left their footprints. The numerous sets of tracks do not often overlap one another, suggesting that this layer of footprints was quickly buried by more ash, ensuring its preservation. Radiopotassium dating was used to measure the age of the ash layers between 3.8 and 3.5 m.y.a. for these footprints (see "Dating Methods," p. 42).

Early hominids walked across the fresh ash as well. The 70 or so human footprints continued over a distance of more than 6 m (20 ft) and were made by three individuals. The longest track contains about 30 prints of an individual walking on two feet with a stride and balance that is clearly human. A second, smaller individual followed in the footprints of the first, and a third set of prints lies alongside the first. The footprints look human, with a well-defined arch

A view of the ash surface at Laetoli, with at least two pairs of hominid footprints and the track of an extinct form of horse running from lower left to upper right.

and an absence of the diverging toe that is characteristic of great apes. Studies of the size and depth of the prints suggest that two of the individuals were approximately 1.4 m (4 ft, 8 in) tall, and the third 1.2 m (4 ft) tall. The footpath of the second individual indicates that this early hominid stopped briefly and turned slightly to the left before continuing. Mary Leakey, the excavator of these fossil foot-

Mary Leakey recording the 3.6 m.y.a. footprints of Laetoli.

They are the most remarkable find I have made in my entire career. . . . When we first came across the hominid prints I must admit that I was skeptical, but then it became clear that it could be nothing else. They are the earliest prints of man's ancestors, and they show us that hominids three-and-three-quarters million years ago walked upright with a free-striding gait, just as we do today.

Mary Leakey (Quoted in R. Leakey, 1981)

prints, speculated about the scene:

> This motion—the pause, the glance to the left—seems so intensely human, it transcends time. Three million six hundred thousand years ago, a remote ancestor—just as you or I—experienced a moment of doubt. (Quoted in Lewin, 1988, p. 57)

The brain of these earliest hominids from the Pliocene was no larger than that of modern apes, nor had their teeth changed a great deal from those of their ape ancestors. Hominid fossil remains, particularly fragments of skulls from Laetoli and elsewhere in East Africa, demonstrate that the human brain had not yet begun its major expansion. No stone tools have been found in deposits of this age at Laetoli; such equipment was apparently not yet part of the human repertoire. What was different, however, was a shift to a new form of movement. The earliest human fossils exhibited **bipedalism**—they walked on two feet, with a stride very similar to our modern one. In fact, these earliest humans might best be portrayed with the head and face of an apelike creature atop a small, upright human body, stepping into the future. As Mary Leakey went on to say, "The outstanding evolutionary question now is: What was the selection pressure that produced bipedalism?" (quoted in Lewin, 1988, p. 57).

Dating Methods

Measuring the age of archaeological remains

Garniss Curtis, developer of the radiopotassium dating method, and his associate, Robert Drake (at left), examining the laboratory apparatus as a sample is heated to extract gases for the measurement of isotopes in a potassium-argon dating laboratory.

In the first half of this century, there was almost no way to determine the age of the remains of early humans and their artifacts. A few **relative dating** techniques were used to estimate the antiquity of bones and stones in a long sequence, but it was generally impossible to establish the absolute age of a layer or an artifact in calendar years. Relative dating methods often use stratigraphic relationships to sequence older and younger materials; lower layers of sediments in the ground, in caves, and elsewhere are, not surprisingly, older than the layers on top.

Relative dating methods also rely on the **association** of various items. For example, glass bottles have changed over the last 200 years. Bottles have become seamless, with shorter necks and narrower bodies. The known dates for certain types of bottles can be used to determine the age of other materials found with them. Similarly, the thickness of the stem and bore of clay smoking pipes from the eighteenth and nineteenth centuries followed a steady decline as the technology for manufacturing these items improved. Thus, the age of a historic trading post in Canada can be estimated by measuring the broken pieces of pipe stem found there. A photograph can be approximately dated by the known age of an automobile or other objects in the picture. The bones of extinct animals, such as elephants in France found with stone tools, were clear evidence that the artifacts were as old as the elephants, even if the exact age was uncertain.

Relative dating methods, however, are limited. It is often necessary to know the ages of archaeological materials more precisely in calendar years—**absolute dating**—in order to answer most questions about the past. Although many methods for determining absolute dates are now available, the most common techniques rely on the properties of radioactive decay in certain elements (Table 2.2). Many elements have both stable and radioactive atomic forms, known as **isotopes.** The techniques used for determining absolute dates with these elements are referred to as **isotopic**

techniques. Perhaps best known among these is radiocarbon dating, but certain other elements—potassium, uranium, or calcium, for example—can also be used for dating purposes. Radiopotassium dating, or potassium-argon dating, used to determine the age of early human ancestors and their remains, is described below. Radiocarbon dating, used to date archaeological materials and events that occurred within the last 40,000 years, is discussed in Chapter 4.

RADIOPOTASSIUM DATING

Radiopotassium dating, also known as **potassium-argon dating,** is a technique of crucial importance for determining the age of the earliest human remains. This technique can date most of the earth's history and has been used to measure the age of the oldest rocks on our planet, as well as samples of moon rocks. The first potassium-argon dates from the lava at the base of Olduvai Gorge—1.75 m.y.a.—startled the scientific community in the 1960s. These fossil remains were almost 1 million years older than previously believed. Other early hominid remains in East Africa from Laetoli, Koobi Fora, Hadar, and elsewhere have also been dated using the radiopotassium technique. Bones and artifacts are not themselves directly dated; rather, newly formed volcanic rocks or ash deposits that lie directly under or over the prehistoric materials are analyzed. These dates thus bracket the archaeological materials in time.

The technique is based on the following principles. Potassium (chemical symbol K) is found in abundance in granites, clays, and basalts in the minerals of the earth's crust. Potassium occurs in several stable forms and has one radioactive isotope, ^{40}K, with a half-life of approximately 1.3 billion years. **Half-life** is a measure of the rate of decay in radioactive materials; essentially, half of the radioactive material will disappear within the period of one half-life. Because this

Table 2.2   The Major Dating Methods Used in Archaeology

Method	Materials	Range	Principle	Limitations
Radiocarbon	Wood, charcoal, bone, carbonate	100–40,000 years	Radioactive decay	Contamination, calibration
Radiopotassium	Volcanic rocks or minerals	Unlimited but approximate	Radioactive decay	Appropriate samples are rare
Uranium series	Coral, mollusks, travertine	30,000–300,000 years	Radioactive decay	Few labs, technical problems, contamination
Geomagnetism	Undisturbed sediment or volcanic rocks	Unlimited but approximate	Alignment of particles with pole reversals	Few labs
Archaeomagnetism	Intact hearths, kilns, burned areas	2000 years	Alignment with changes in location of the earth's magnetic pole	Few labs, calibration
Thermoluminescence (TL)	Pottery, heated stones, calcite	1,000,000 years	Accumulation of TL in crystals	Environmental irradiation rate, few labs
Electron spin resonance	Heated crystalline stones, calcites, bones, shell	1,000,000 years	Accumulation of unpaired electrons in crystals	Few labs, experimental technique
Obsidian hydration	Obsidian artifacts	35,000 years	Accumulation of weathering rind on artifact	Requires local calibration
Dendrochronology	Tree rings in preserved logs and lumber	8000 years	Counting of annual growth rings	Region-specific
Fission track	Volcanic rocks, crystalline materials	100,000–1,000,000 years	Radioactive decay leaves microscopic track in crystals at known rate	Materials rare in archaeological context

potassium isotope has such a very long half-life, it is not possible to date materials that are younger than about 500,000 years old, because too little decay would have taken place to measure.

The radioactive isotope ^{40}K decays into argon (^{40}Ar), an inert gas, and calcium (^{40}Ca). The materials generally dated by the $^{40}K/^{40}Ar$ technique are limited to rocks, volcanic ashes, and other substances that contain radioactive potassium and trap the argon gas that is produced. The molten state of the rock permits the release of trapped gas in the parent rock and resets the argon reservoirs in the new rock to zero. The ^{40}Ar begins to accumulate as soon as a rock is formed. Using sophisticated counters that measure and record the amount of ^{40}Ar compared to the amount of ^{40}K remaining, researchers can determine how much ^{40}K has decayed and thus the amount of elapsed time since the rock was created.

SWARTKRANS

*South African caves with
many early human fossils*

Swartkrans (swort'kranz) is the name of one of several caves in the Transvaal region (Gautang province) of South Africa that contain both human and animal fossils from the early Pleistocene. The Transvaal is a large area in the center of South Africa underlain with limestone bedrock. This soft, permeable stone is easily dissolved by running water, which creates underground rivers, caves, and sinkholes. Streams and heavy rains from the surface wash in a variety of surface sediments, debris, bones, and other objects, which gradually accumulate in these chambers. Other agents also add materials to these deposits. African porcupines, for example, collect bones at their nests and shelters, often within the confines of caves; hyenas carry bones and other objects to their dens. Some birds, such as owls and other birds of prey, regurgitate small pellets containing the bones of the small rodents they consume. The accumulated materials eventually harden into a fresh rock known as a conglomerate, or **breccia.**

Early hominid fossils were first discovered when the breccias in these caves were commercially quarried for lime, used for making plaster and cement. Dense bone concentrations were discarded to obtain purer deposits. Eventually the antiquity and importance of these bones was recognized, and expeditions from museums and universities in South Africa and elsewhere conducted excavations to uncover more fossil materials. Collectively these excavations have uncovered the remains of more than 150 individual hominids of several species.

There are four major problems associated with studying these materials:

(1) extracting the fossils from the rock in which they are encased, (2) estimating the age of the fossils and the deposits, (3) determining the cause of death of the animals and how they got in the caves, and (4) designating the genus and species for the hominid remains.

Removal of the fossils from these deposits is very difficult. The fossil bones are embedded in breccia and in fact have become rock themselves. Excavators have used jackhammers and even dynamite to break apart the breccia to get at the mineralized bones. In recent years, large blocks of the breccia have been taken to a laboratory where acid treatments gradually dissolve the rock, thereby allowing the removal of the fossils. Because these materials are buried in the earth, geological forces have modified and distorted the stone and the fossils. The weight of deposits sometimes flattens or warps bone or crushes materials together.

The limestone deposits in these caves provide little that can be directly dated. There is no fresh volcanic ash or rock for potassium-argon dating. Most of the dates from the caves are based on the known ages of extinct animals that once existed throughout much of Africa. For example, changes over time in the size of the teeth of fossil pigs can be used to estimate the ages of the various deposits. Such dating is done by the association of hominid remains with pig teeth of known age found in the same breccia. On this basis, the early Pleistocene breccia at Swartkrans probably dates to between 1.7 and 1 m.y.a.

C. K. Brain, a paleontologist in South Africa, has been excavating at

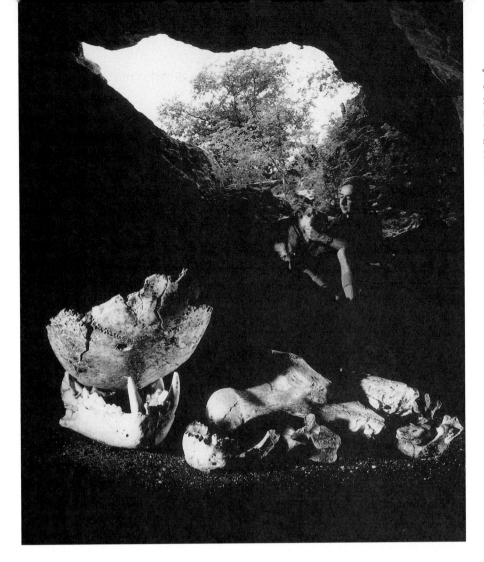

C. K. Brain and some of the fossil remains at Swartkrans cave. The canine teeth of the leopard jaw precisely fit the two indentations in the hominid skull, supporting Brain's theory that many of the early human bones are the remains of carnivore meals.

the site of Swartkrans for more than 20 years. Brain notes two major episodes of breccia accumulation, apparently of short duration on the order of 10,000 years each. Dating of the deposits is complicated by the manner in which the breccias form. There is no simple stratigraphy in which materials are piled up in regular horizontal layers; continuing water flow erodes and partially dissolves older deposits, then new episodes of accumulation fill the cavities in the old deposits. Each cave thus contains a honeycomb of deposits from various periods.

These deposits are the source for fossils of both *Paranthropus robustus* and *Homo erectus*. The partial remains of at least 80 *P. robustus* individuals have been recovered from the deposits at Swartkrans, along with fragments of bone and teeth from six individuals of *H. erectus*. These two hominid forms appear to be contemporaneous at Swartkrans, as at Olduvai. This astounding number of individuals from a single deposit raises the question of how so many came to be in one place—a question that has yet to be fully answered.

The shape and structure of the hand bones from several *P. robustus* individuals suggests that this hominid made and used some of the stone tools that are also commonly found in the cave deposits. In addition to the stone tools, there are bone artifacts with polishes that resulted from being used as digging implements, probably to obtain the roots and bulbs of plants growing in the area. Recent data from Swartkrans, from approximately 1 m.y.a., suggest that the individuals in the cave used fire, perhaps to keep preying leopards at bay. If this evidence is reliable, it records the earliest instance of the intentional use of fire. There is also some evidence for the use of fire at Koobi Fora

The skull of a *Paranthropus robustus* from Swartkrans cave.

An artist's interpretation of an australopithecine.

An artist's interpretation of the Swartkrans leopard hypothesis. A Pliocene leopard consumes a hapless australopithecine in a tree above the entrance to Swartkrans.

in East Africa perhaps 1.5 m.y.a., but this is less certain.

How the bones of so many early hominids ended up in the deposits is also not clear. This question has been the subject of lengthy debate. Raymond Dart, an anatomist in South Africa, studied the human and animal remains from the cave breccias for almost 50 years until his death in 1988. He proposed a number of theories about the life and times of *Australopithecus*. Professor Dart, the original discoverer of the australopithecines, believed that the early hominids had been extraordinary predators, hunting many animals and bringing their carcasses back to the limestone caves. Dart argued that animal bones found in the caves were the remains of meals and evidence of the prowess of *Australopithecus* as a hunter of even the largest animals. Dart's graphic depiction conveys his image of our earliest ancestors: "Man's predecessors . . . seized living quarries by violence, battered them to death, tore apart their broken bones, dismembered them limb from limb, slaking their ravenous thirst with the hot blood of victims and greedily devouring living writhing flesh" (1953, p. 209).

Dart further suggested that the high number of hominid skulls in the caves, often with the bases broken away, was evidence that early humans also hunted their neighbors. The question is one of hunter or hunted, according to Brain. Brain's detailed studies provide numerous insights about the processes of deposition in the limestone caves, and they contradict some of the arguments of Dart. Many of the cracks and breaks in the fossil remains that Dart interpreted as evidence of violent death more likely resulted from geological distortion after burial, according to Brain. Brain argues that the vast majority of larger fossils came into the cave as the remains of carnivore meals, especially of leopards. Brain points out that leopards often drag their prey into trees out of reach of other predators. The damp entrance shafts to caves such as Swartkrans would likely have been overgrown with trees, which may have been lairs for satiated leopards. Over 40% of the human fossils are immature individuals who may have been

vulnerable to leopard attacks. Brain also points to a hominid skull with two crushing indentations in the forehead, punctures that fit precisely with the huge canine teeth of a leopard.

Investigations at this important South African cave document the contemporaneity of *Paranthropus robustus* and *Homo erectus*. Swartkrans finds demonstrate that *P. robustus* almost certainly made and used stone tools, that bone tools were an important part of the equipment for these early hominids, that plants were probably important in the diet, and that fire may have been used, at least for defensive purposes.

The issue of early human diet is difficult because the remains of meals are generally not well preserved. The wild plants of East Africa probably provided a ready source of food for early hominids, but plant materials are not preserved. The relative importance of fruits, nuts, and other plant foods in the diet is not known.

Another difficult matter, and a major controversy in paleoanthropology, is the issue of scavenging versus hunting: How did early hominids obtain meat? Some scholars believe that the first humans were primarily scavengers, visiting the kills of lions and other predators, taking the morsels that remained, competing with hyenas and vultures. These scholars argue that the actual hunting of large animals was a relatively recent development in human prehistory. Others contend that early hominids were in fact hunters— stalking, killing, butchering, and eating the creatures of Plio/Pleistocene East Africa. The evidence is scanty and open to debate. Only a few facts are known: Chimpanzees and baboons occasionally hunt, kill, and consume small animals, and by the end of the Pleistocene, humans were major predators and large-game hunters, responsible in part for the extinction of certain species.

Evidence from numerous Plio/Pleistocene sites certainly suggests that humans brought various animal parts back to a common location and removed the meat and marrow with stone tools. In one instance, the large leg bone of an antelope-size creature had been broken into 10 pieces, in a fashion that modern hunters in the area today use to obtain the nutritious and tasty marrow. On this same bone, tiny scratches made by stone tools are also visible. Such **cutmarks** are sometimes found at places where large pieces of meat have been removed from the bone, suggesting that the animal was butchered for the meat. This evidence may indicate that early hominids were hunters with access to the best cuts of meat from their prey. But paleoanthropologists Richard Potts and Pat Shipman have observed that cutmarks are sometimes found over the marks left by the teeth of carnivores, suggesting the scavenging of animal carcasses. It seems clear that stone tools were used to butcher meat, but neither the presence of cutmarks indicating meat removal nor evidence of the extraction of marrow from bone demonstrates that the food was hunted, not scavenged. Recent studies of marks on bones from Olduvai Gorge suggest a sequence of large carnivore teeth, cut by stone tools, overlain by smaller carnivore tooth marks. Such a pattern suggests that the animal was killed by a large carnivore, scavenged by humans, and then eaten by smaller animals.

Comparisons of the kinds of animals represented at Olduvai Gorge and elsewhere with the prey of modern hunter-gatherers in the Kalahari Desert of South Africa support the argument that australopithecines were hunters. The range of prey types and their sizes are very similar in the two locations, suggesting that the Olduvai hominids may have been hunters, like people of the Kalahari, rather than scavengers.

The parts of animals that were brought to certain locations by early hominids also provide some clues about how the food was obtained. Scavengers can more easily obtain limb bones than most other parts of a carcass. These are the larger, harder bones of the skeleton that often remain after predators have abandoned a kill. Limb bones are also rich in marrow. Body parts from Olduvai sites and elsewhere indicate that the complete skeletons of small animals were present but that larger animals were represented primarily by limb bones. This evidence suggests that early hominids may have hunted small game but scavenged the carcasses of large game. This pattern resembles the behavior of today's chimpanzees of West Africa, which routinely hunt small animals for meat.

Still, none of these pieces of evidence is definitive. Evidence for sites where large game animals were killed is not incontrovertible until much later in the Pleistocene, after 200,000 years ago.

Ways our early ancestors obtained their food

(a)

(b)

(a) A photomicrograph of round-bottomed grooves made by hyena teeth on modern bone. (b) A photomicrograph of a V-shaped cutmark made by a stone tool on modern bone. Cutmarks on bones from Koobi Fora are a strong argument that our early ancestors were meat-eaters and hunters as well as scavengers.

OLDUVAI

A trail of biological and behavioral evolution from the early Pleistocene to the recent past

Olduvai Gorge, cutting 100 m into the Serengeti Plain and 2 million years into human evolution.

Flying low across northern Tanzania, one crosses an enormous wilderness of grassland and solitary trees, an arena filled with herds of wildebeest, giraffes, elephants, and many other animals. This is the fabled Serengeti (ser-in-get′ee) Plain—the place of safari. The level surface of the plain results from the long, gradual accumulation of geological sediments, especially volcanic materials such as ash and lava. Two million years ago, this area was a large bowl-shaped basin, ringed by a series of volcanic mountains and uplands. Active volcanoes filled the air with ash and covered the ground with molten lava, which hardened into new rock. The basin trapped rainfall, forming lakes and wetlands during the beginning of the Pleistocene. Silts and sands, carried by running water, were deposited in these lakes, which grew or disappeared over time as rainfall amounts varied with changes in climate. Along the shores of these lakes, creatures of the early Pleistocene in East Africa found food, reproduced, and died; occasionally their bones were buried and preserved in the accumulating layers of sediment.

The richness of the lakeshore environment is represented by the abundance of fossil animal bones that are found there. Antelope, giant buffalo, and wild sheep occur in large numbers, along with aquatic animals, such as the giant crocodile, hippopotamus, and various species of fish and fowl. The layers of lava, ash, and lake deposits continued to build up until the basin became relatively level, resulting in the surface of the Serengeti Plain today.

About 200,000 years ago, a particularly violent series of earthquakes and volcanic activity opened a crack in the surface. Seasonal streams cut and eroded a large gully into the layers of sediment. Gradually a canyon, some 40 km (25 mi) long and almost 100 m (325 ft) deep, wound its way from the top of the Serengeti Plain through the layer cake of deposits. This canyon is Olduvai (ol-dew-vy′) Gorge, one of the most famous prehistoric sites in the world. Each step

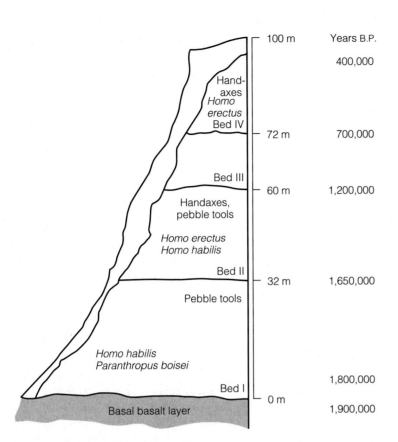

100 m
Years B.P.
400,000

Hand-
axes
*Homo
erectus*
Bed IV

72 m
700,000

Bed III

60 m
1,200,000

Handaxes,
pebble tools

Homo erectus
Homo habilis

Bed II

32 m
1,650,000

Pebble tools

Homo habilis
Paranthropus boisei

Bed I
1,800,000

0 m
1,900,000

Basal basalt layer

A schematic cross section through the 100 m of deposits at Olduvai Gorge, naming the various fossil forms and types of stone tools, with approximate ages.

Some of the more common early Pleistocene animal species at Olduvai Gorge.

Waterbuck

Okapi

Oryx

Sivatherium

Porcupine

Deinotherium

down into the gorge takes us back 6000 years in time to the layer of basalt at the very bottom, dating to 1.75 m.y.a.

Along the steep sides of this gorge, two archaeologists named Louis and Mary Leakey began an extended vigil, in quest of the remains of the earliest humans. Starting in 1931, Louis and, later, Mary Leakey made the arduous journey from Nairobi each summer to spend several weeks at the rugged exposures of Olduvai. Accompanied by their dogs, and later their several children, they searched for fossil hominids. Louis Leakey had found numerous crude stone tools in the lower layers at the gorge and was convinced that the bones of the toolmakers would also appear in this remarkable series of deposits. Not until 1959, however, some 28 years after Louis' first visit, was the persistence of the Leakeys rewarded by Mary's discovery of a very early hominid fossil, initially named *Zinjanthropus* (see Color Plate 2). At the time, the fossil was thought to be approximately 1 million years old—twice the age of the then earliest known hominid remains from Java. Zinj, as this fossil is affectionately known (or *Paranthropus boisei*, as it is scientifically termed) actually dates closer to 2 million years old.

The Leakeys' discovery brought the search for the first humans to Africa and eventually back into the Pliocene epoch. Their discovery of Zinj also brought world recognition for their efforts in the form of acclaim and funding, which supported more extensive investigations at Olduvai. With this funding, the Leakeys were able to examine a larger area of the gorge in 2 years than previously had been possible in 20 years. And this intensive work paid off in the discovery of more fossils and a whole series of archaeological sites.

Very old standardized objects of human manufacture (stone artifacts) appeared in the lower layers at Olduvai. Olduvai provided the first clear documentation that crude stone tools and the bones of very early hominids occurred at the same point in geological time. Over 70 prehistoric localities with stones or bones, or both, have been recorded in the geological layers of the gorge to date; perhaps 10 of these represent actual living areas where tools were made and used. Some of the stones are unmodified and may have been used as anvils and for other purposes. Other stones were intentionally bashed with another stone to shape and manufacture tools. These stone artifacts had strong, sharp edges, providing cutting equipment for a species lacking sharp teeth or claws.

The materials for these artifacts were often brought from the rocky hills some 10 km (6 mi) away. Raw materials were selected on the basis of specific properties. Fine-grained stone was used to make small cutting tools, while basalt and quartz were used for heavy chopping equipment. Tools described as choppers, spheroids, and discoids were created by knocking off flakes of stone from a rounded cobble or large pebble. These sharp-edged cobbles are about the size of a tennis ball and are known as **Oldowan** pebble tools, named after the gorge itself. The flakes that had been struck off these pebble tools also had sharp edges and were likely used as tools.

One of the Olduvai sites contains a large quantity of broken and fragmented bone, along with stone tools. Many of the bone fragments are clustered in an area of about 5 × 10 m (16 × 33 ft, the size of a large room), with an empty zone several feet wide surrounding this concentration. Perhaps a thorn hedge or barricade was placed in this area to protect the inhabitants in the center.

At another site in Olduvai Gorge is a group of several hundred rocks in a roughly circular arrangement, surrounded by the bones of giraffes, hippopotamuses, antelopes, and elephants. The reason for such concentrations are unknown; it is not even clear whether early hominids were responsible for killing the animals represented by the bones. However, the hominids almost certainly collected the bones. Two other sites at Olduvai are known to have been places of animal butchering. At one of the sites, known as FLK North, the bones of an elephant lie scattered on the ground along with stone artifacts. The elephant would have been much too heavy to move and was very likely butchered at the spot where it died. Most of the bones from the elephant are present,

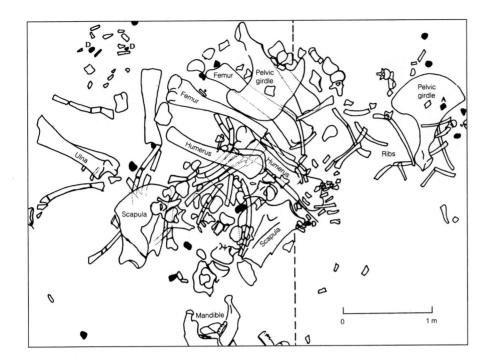

The plan of part of an excavated deposit at Olduvai, containing a concentration of elephant and other bones, with stone tools shown in solid black. This site likely represents the place where parts of these animals were butchered.

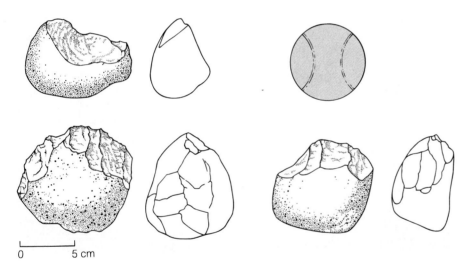

Typical Oldowan pebble tools, shown with a tennis ball for scale.

disarranged by the butchering, and surrounded by stone tools and flakes. Striations and cutmarks on the bones document the use of stone flakes to remove meat from the skeleton. (The issue of whether the hominids at Olduvai actually hunted these animals was discussed earlier; see "Hunters or Scavengers?" on p. 47).

Other evidence suggests that most of the living floors at Olduvai were occupied during the wet season. Tortoises hibernate during the dry season, making them difficult to capture, yet their remains are common at most of the sites at Olduvai. Such information suggests that our early ancestors may have been absent from the Olduvai lakeshore during the dry season, pursuing other activities and perhaps game elsewhere in the region.

Olduvai will remain one of the most important archaeological sites in the world because it contains the information that helps answer many questions— the human fossils, the early Pleistocene deposits, the association of both human bone and stone artifacts, and the fact that these materials are sometimes found where they were dropped by our early ancestors.

THE LEAKEY FAMILY

A dynasty of paleoanthropologists

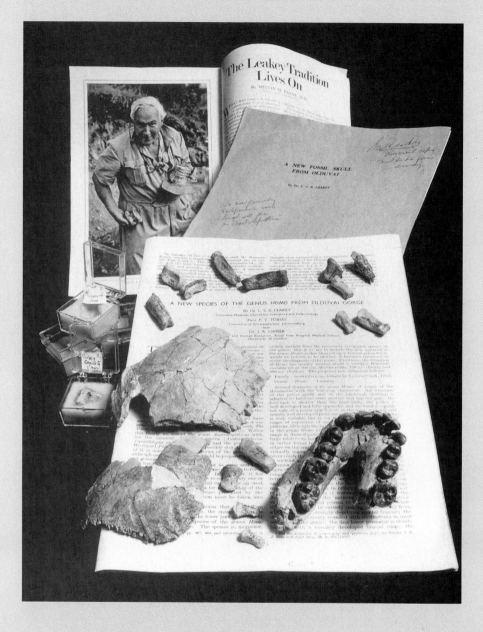

Louis Leakey and the remains of *Homo habilis* from Olduvai Gorge. This discovery demonstrated that Africa was the cradle of early human evolution and brought fame to the Leakeys.

Born to British missionary parents in Kenya in 1903, Louis Leakey became interested in prehistoric artifacts as a child. At age 16, he left for England to attend Cambridge University. A rugby injury forced a break in his studies, and he returned to East Africa on a year-long fossil-hunting expedition, engendering his interest in bones and paleontology. Leakey then returned to Cambridge, taking high honors in both archaeology and modern languages.

Leakey then received a 6-year research fellowship from Cambridge to conduct archaeological investigations in East Africa. The first expedition involved excavations at a Neolithic site, and the results were published in *Nature,* a prestigious British science journal. A second expedition centered on Gamble's Cave and provided one of the first sequences of the development of stone artifacts in East Africa. In 1931, Leakey led his third expedition to Olduvai Gorge. Here, early handaxes were found soon after his arrival, and a fragment of a human jaw was discovered nearby. Leakey argued for a great antiquity for this bone, but a British geologist, Percy Boswell, accused Leakey of incompetence in a letter to a scientific magazine. This incident left Leakey with a determination to be more exact in his statements.

Much of Leakey's research was guided by his belief that Africa was the cradle of the human race, in contrast to the generally accepted scientific view that East Asia held that distinction. One of the members of Leakey's fourth expedition was Mary Nicol, an archaeologist and illustrator, who would become his second wife in 1936. Together, Mary and Louis Leakey began their lifelong research on early humans in East Africa. The Leakeys continued their investigations at Olduvai Gorge because of its abundance of stone tools. Leakey was convinced that human fossils would also be found there, demonstrating the fact that early hominids had made the stone tools.

Leakey was appointed director of the National Museum of Kenya in Nairobi in 1945, and each summer the Leakeys would return to search for evidence of early humans in the layers of Olduvai Gorge. Finally, in 1959, after more than two decades of dogged and difficult prospecting, Mary Leakey spotted the fragments of the heavy jaw of Zinj, dating to the beginning of the Pleistocene.

The Leakeys proved that East Africa had indeed witnessed the emergence of the human species. In addition to the many important discoveries they have made, the Leakeys have pioneered the study of early stone tools and animal remains in East Africa. Louis Leakey died in London on the first of October, 1972.

After Louis' death, Mary Leakey and her children continued the search for human origins in Africa. Mary excavated at Olduvai, Laetoli, and elsewhere in East Africa, greatly enriching the record of early fossil animals and humans in this area. She compiled most of the important published descriptions of the pre-

The Leakey family at work in Olduvai Gorge.

history of Olduvai. Mary Leakey died in 1996 at the age of 83. Her son Richard became the director of the National Museum of Kenya in Nairobi and a very famous paleoanthropologist in his own right. In spite of several calamities, including the loss of both legs in an airplane crash, Richard Leakey continues as a champion of the peoples and animals of his native Kenya. His debates with other scientists over the meaning of the fossil finds are the subject of several popular books. Richard's wife, Meave, is the head of the paleontological section of the National Museum of Kenya and has been involved in the search for fossil humans in the area around Lake Turkana, continuing a family tradition.

KOOBI FORA

Important evidence for on-the-spot stone tool use and meat-eating by early hominids

Excavations at Koobi-Fora, exposing the bone and stone evidence of early hominid activities.

The majority of archaeological finds from the Plio/Pleistocene period are stone tools and isolated fragments of bone. The chances of materials of this age being preserved to the present and exposed for discovery range between slim and none. There are only a very few examples of **living floors,** actual locations where early hominids stayed for a while and left evidence of their presence. One of the best examples comes from deposits near Lake Turkana in northern Kenya. This region is known as Koobi Fora (coo'bee-for'ah), a series of rugged hills and gullies cut through geological sediments.

Some 2–1.5 m.y.a., these sediments were deposited by major rivers flowing into the lake basin. The rivers carried gravel, sand, silt, and clay that were laid down as they reached the quiet, deeper waters of the lake. Large deltas were created, providing a propitious habitat for plants, animals, and early hominids. In the rapidly accumulating deposits of this environment, bones and artifacts were buried and occasionally preserved.

More recently, as the basin has filled and lake levels have dropped, these deposits are now above water and extend to the east of the present lake for more than 30 km (20 mi). In today's arid environment, seasonal streams cut gullies through the geological layers and occasionally expose the former surfaces of the delta, along with various archaeological materials. Since the early 1970s, over 20 localities have been found where stones and/or bones from human activities have been exposed. One of these sites, designated site 50, was found eroding out at the edge of a gully some 20 km (13 mi) east of the lakeshore. The almost fresh condition of the bone resulted in a more detailed study of the location.

A major program of excavation, under the direction of the late Glynn Isaac, of Harvard University, was conducted from 1977 to 1979. Nine months of digging over that 3-year period by a crew of 6–10 people resulted in the exposure of almost 200 sq m (2000 sq ft) of deposits containing a variety of stones and bones. Radiopotassium dates on volcanic ash in the deposits indicated an age of 1.5 million years. The groups of stones and bone found on an actual living surface

Students in the Koobi Fora Archaeological Field School survey for artifacts and bones in Pleistocene deposits.

suggest that a small hominid group used this spot for several hours or days—eating, sleeping, and making tools.

Some 1.5 million years ago, this area was quite different. Site 50 was in the center of a large river floodplain, level for miles around. The river itself probably flowed directly by the site, as the deposits indicate it was a spit or sandbar along the bank at a large bend. The region was rich in animal life; the bones of many species similar to those in East Africa today were found at the site. The bones at site 50 were generally in good condition, lacking the fractures and cracks that appear as bone begins to dry and decompose. Breakage patterns indicate that many bones were intentionally fragmented by early hominids. Hammerstones and anvils were used to smash the larger bones, creating distinctive fractures and flakes. Of the more than 2000 bones recovered in the excavations, approximately 1000 could be identified as to the animal species. Various species were represented, including those from riverine environments such as hippopotamus and catfish, and a number of terrestrial species

such as giraffe, wild pig, porcupine, and gazelle.

The well-preserved condition of the bones argues that the site was buried rapidly after its abandonment. Nevertheless, the presence of fossil carnivore excrement and gnaw marks on the bones, and the absence of the soft ends of many of the bones, indicates that animals such as hyenas and other scavengers consumed some bones left behind by the hominid group, prior to the site's burial.

Studies by Nicholas Toth, of Indiana University, and Lawrence Keeley, of the University of Illinois, Chicago, have provided important clues about the use of these stone tools. Keeley used a high-powered microscope to examine the edges of stone artifacts from Koobi Fora. Experimental work demonstrated that different materials leave different kinds of traces in the form of polish on the edges of tools. At a magnification of 400×, Keeley observed microscopic polish and wear, indicating the cutting of meat, the slicing of soft plant material, and the scraping and sawing of wood, on about 10% of the flakes. Two of the flakes with evidence of meat butch-

56   CHAPTER 2   THE FIRST HUMANS

ering were found within 1 m (3 ft) of a large herbivore bone exhibiting cutmarks. Such evidence strongly supports the use of these stone artifacts as butchering tools. Evidence of woodworking suggests that wooden tools were also being made, perhaps crude digging sticks for finding roots and tubers. This indirect information is the only evidence for the use or consumption of plant materials.

One aspect of the study of such early sites involves reassembling as many of the broken pieces of stone and bone as possible. **Refitting** the pieces into their original form requires skill and patience. It's like trying to solve a three-dimensional jigsaw puzzle with no picture and many missing pieces. But the reassembled objects provide important information about the site and its activities:

1. Pieces of individual objects are generally found close to one another, indicating that disturbance of the site by natural processes following abandonment was minimal. Such a pattern suggests that this was a living surface and that objects were left close to where they were dropped.
2. The distribution of pieces of matched sets indicates that the entire area of site 50 was used by its inhabitants. This pattern strengthens the argument that the remains represent a single episode of human activity.
3. Missing pieces from objects that have been reassembled suggest that certain tools and flakes made at the site may have been transported for later use.
4. The refitted sets tell us how stones and bones were fractured originally and provide insight into the motor-coordination skills of these hominids (see "The First Tools," p. 58).

In the following passage, Isaac summarizes his impressions from the studies of Koobi Fora site 50:

> The site has provided particularly clear evidence of some things that early hominids *were* doing: they repeatedly carried stones to certain favored places and made simple sharp-edged implements from them. To those same places they seem to have carted parts of animal carcasses. Once there they presumably ate the meat and they certainly broke the bones to get at the marrow. When people ask why the hominids did not eat their meat where they obtained it, I can point out a number of potential reasons. It is possible that they simply came to eat in the shade, but it seems even more likely that they carried food to special places like site 50 for social reasons—very particularly in order to feed youngsters, or even to feed their mates and relatives. Such food-sharing behaviours certainly became a universal part of the human pattern at some stage in evolution and many archaeologists are inclined to think it might have begun by the time that site 50 formed. (1984, p. 75)

Koobi Fora has been the site of an archaeological field school for a number of years. At a field school, the methods and techniques of field archaeology are taught for course credits during the summer. Such programs are a great way to participate in the field experience and acquire basic archaeological skills. Many universities offer summer field school opportunities through the Department of Anthropology. The Koobi Fora field school in this remote part of Africa is offered by Rutgers University and directed by Dr. Jack Harris.

THE FIRST TOOLS

Simple, intentionally broken pebbles: the earliest preserved evidence for toolmaking

Simple stone tools are the earliest human artifacts that archaeologists study. It is very possible that the first humans, like chimpanzees today, used tools of wood or bone. As our closest relatives, chimpanzees provide a good model for early humans. Chimpanzees in the wild, in fact, have frequently been observed killing and eating other animals and making and using tools. In West Africa, chimpanzees often use stone or wooden objects as hammers and anvils to open nutshells. They use twigs to remove marrow from bone cavities or to extract termites from their nests. Similarly, unmodified wood, bone, and stone objects may have been used long before the appearance of deliberately modified stone tools, but these either cannot be identified or have not survived.

Intentionally modified stone tools appeared first in Africa between 3 and 2 m.y.a., probably associated with the increasing importance of meat in the human diet. Such sharp flakes and cobbles provide access to the carcasses of animals, enabling early humans to cut through thick, tough skins to remove the meaty tissue—actions simply not possible without some kind of sharp implement. Stone tools provide useful cutting edges for a species that lacks both sharp teeth and claws for slicing meat, shredding plants, or digging. As Nicholas Toth says, "Sharp-edged stones became the equivalent of canines and carnassials [meat-cutting teeth] and heavier rocks served as bone-crunching jaws" (1987, p. 121).

The oldest dated stone tools were found in the 1990s along the Gona River in central Ethiopia, dating to 2.6 m.y.a. The earliest stone tools are remarkably simple, almost unrecognizable unless found together in groups or next to other objects. Small round cobbles, the size of a large egg or tennis ball 5–8 cm (2–3 in) in diameter, weighing about 1 kg (1–2 lb), were collected from streambeds, lakeshores, and beaches.

Early stone tools were created by striking one stone against another. This process, called **percussion flaking**, results in a **flake** being removed from the parent cobble, or **core,** by a blow from another stone, called a **hammerstone**, or other hard object. Both the flake and the core then have fresh surfaces with edges sharp enough to be used for cutting. Initially the fractured cobbles themselves were thought to be the intended artifact and were called pebble tools. The flakes were thought to be by-products of the manufacturing process, a kind of waste material, often referred to as *débitage.* But it is now clear that flakes were equally important as both cutting tools and tools for making other tools, such as shaping wood, bone, or antler into new forms for new purposes. The simple action of striking one stone against another to remove a flake and create a sharp edge was a very successful invention, one that was used and refined for more than 2 million years, until the introduction of metals just 6000 years ago.

The best raw materials for stone tools during the early Pleistocene were brittle enough to break, and hard and smooth enough to provide a cutting edge. The stone also had to be fine-grained so that it would break in a predictable fashion, resulting in large flakes, rather than hundreds of shattered fragments. During this time, various rocks were used, including basalt (a hard volcanic lava), quartzite, and flint. **Flint** is one of the best and most common materials used for making stone tools.

The kinds of pebble tools found at Olduvai, Koobi Fora, and elsewhere in Africa are described as Oldowan, a tradition of toolmaking. The term Oldowan is applied to the entire group, or **assemblage,** of different stone objects found together at sites from the end of the Pliocene and the first part of the Pleistocene. These stone, or **lithic,** artifacts include both **unifacial** pebble tools, flaked on one side only, and **bifacial** pebble tools, flaked on both sides. The flakes are also occasionally further modified by additional flaking, or **retouching,** along their edges, to shape them.

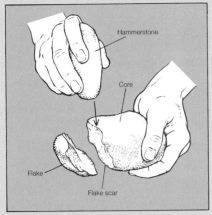

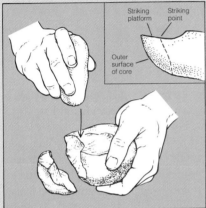

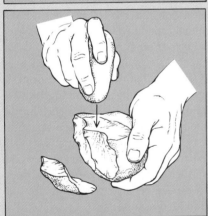

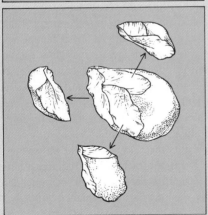

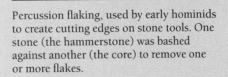

Percussion flaking, used by early hominids to create cutting edges on stone tools. One stone (the hammerstone) was bashed against another (the core) to remove one or more flakes.

We have learned other kinds of information from stone artifacts, the most durable of the remains of our ancestors. Studies by Toth have suggested that many of these flakes were made by holding the core stone in the hand and striking it with a hammerstone. Indeed, Toth argues, on the basis of the shape of the flakes, most of the flakes from Koobi Fora were produced by right-handed individuals. This handedness is not seen in the very earliest stone tools from 2.6 m.y.a. but emerged in the period between 1.9 and 1.4 m.y.a., probably correlated with the changes in the organization of the brain. The brain of modern humans is divided into two hemispheres that control different areas of thought and behavior. Handedness is a result of this lateralization of the brain. In right-handed people, the left hemisphere controls sequential abilities such as speech and more quantitative activities, and the right hemisphere regulates spatial conceptualization and more abstract behavior. These functions are reversed in left-handed people. Thus, the predominance of right-handedness in stone tool manufacture after 2 million years ago suggests that this organizational change had already taken place in the brain.

Tools provide an interface between humans and the environment, enabling us to manipulate and change our surroundings. One of the most remarkable things about stone tools is the investment they represent—a vision of the future, an anticipation of action. An object was made at one time and place, often to be used later elsewhere.

A pebble tool with one edge flaked.

Hello to all intelligent life forms everywhere . . . and to everyone else out there, the secret is to bang the rocks together, guys.
Douglas Adams, *The Hitchhiker's Guide to the Galaxy* (1980)

SUMMARY

BONES, STONES, AND HUMAN BEHAVIOR IN THE PLIO/PLEISTOCENE

*The evolution of our biology
and our activities*

As we have noted, Plio/Pleistocene evidence for early hominids consists of pieces of bones and teeth, along with small broken stones, from a few locations in East Africa and South Africa. It seems clear that the earliest hominids walked on two feet before 4 m.y.a., as seen from the early fossil evidence from Ethiopia and, slightly later, from the remarkable footprints at Laetoli. Then, sometime between 3 and 2 m.y.a., humans began to make stone tools and evolve a larger brain and were identifiable as members of the genus *Homo*. These individuals almost certainly lived in small groups, evidenced by the clusters of animal bones and stone tools at Olduvai, Koobi Fora, and elsewhere. Early hominids ate both meat and plants. How they obtained the meat is unclear, but it appears that they may have hunted small animals and scavenged the marrow-rich bones and remaining meat from the large animal kills of other predators.

Beyond these few indications, however, there is very little direct evidence for reconstructing our early pedigree and behavior. The fact that there are any reasonable explanations of our earliest evolution is testimony to the diligence and ingenuity of the scientists who study these remains. In spite of the sparseness of evidence for the biology and behavior of early hominids, there are still a number of theories about how and why we became human. This understanding comes partly from comparisons with our nearest relatives, the chimpanzees, and partly from inferences made from the evidence of the stones and bones themselves. Much of the following discussion involves such speculations about the evolution of human behavior, based on little evidence and vulnerable to considerable revision and modification.

The brain size of modern humans is roughly 1000 cubic centimeters (60 cu in) larger than that of other primates (say, a large grapefruit compared to an orange) (Table 2.3). We have a much greater ratio of brain to body size than almost any other species, emphasizing the importance of our brain for survival. Brains are costly organs, requiring about 20% of the body's energy production to operate. Brain tissue needs more than 20 times the energy of muscle tissue to function. This means that humans may need food that is denser in calories and nutrients than for most other species. Yet human infants are born with a remarkably small, underdeveloped brain, only some 25% of the adult size. While a chimpanzee's brain at birth is about 65% of fully adult size, the human brain grows and develops largely after birth, because of the narrowness of the birth canal. Having an underdeveloped brain, a human infant requires a long period of maternal care and attention. By contrast, a newborn foal, for example, can run and feed itself within a few days. In humans, the long period of infant dependency fosters a strong bond between mother and child and also permits children to know their brothers and sisters. Kinship and learning may well be enhanced as a result of such extended and intimate relationships.

Table 2.3 Average Cranial Capacity of Some Primates and Fossil Hominids

	Cubic Centimeters
Modern human	1400
Neanderthal	1450
Homo erectus	1000
Homo habilis	630
Australopithecine	450
Gorilla	600
Chimpanzee	400
Orangutan	400
Gibbon	100

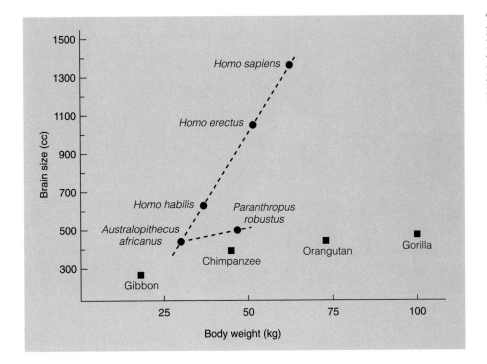

Brain size and body weight in the higher primates and hominids. Body weight is estimated for the fossil hominid forms. Notice the increase in both body weight and brain size in the line of human evolution.

A lengthy period of maternal care, however, is expensive. Small children limit the mobility and activities of the mother, including the obtaining of food. Extended care and brain development also mean longer nursing and delayed weaning. In turn, such behaviors require more food for the mother; nursing alone may increase her metabolic demands by 50% or more. The average life expectancy among the australopithecines appears to have been low, around 20 years. Such an early age of death very likely meant that children were often orphaned and had to be nurtured by the group rather than by a single parent; communal child care and feeding may well have been concomitant with the advance of our species.

Differences between humans and the apes are also represented in the secondary sex characteristics that differentiate males and females. Human female breasts are significantly larger than those of the male, a difference more pronounced than in most other species. Breast size is obviously not related to the effective feeding of offspring. The human male penis is far larger than that of other primates, including gorillas. Human females have softer skin and a higher voice and lack much of the body hair that often characterizes other primate females. The vagina in the human female points sufficiently toward the front of the body to permit face-to-face sexual intercourse.

Another biological difference lies in the absence of an estrus cycle in human females. The female members of most animal species are sexually active only for limited intervals, a period known as **estrus,** a few days each month or each year. Female apes display sexual receptivity by means of flaring or brightly colored sex organs, but ovulation is concealed in human females. Clearly there have been strong evolutionary selective forces favoring these characteristics.

Aside from biological similarities and differences with other animals and our closest relatives among the apes, are we indeed closer to the angels? We possess other attributes that distinguish us from the animals. Our large brain and intelligence enable us to make decisions and act rationally, differently than the way our basic instincts might drive us to behave. Humans have moved from purely instinctual behavior to reason and thought. We may flee a fire, but we may also turn back into that fire to save others.

Humans have technology; we make and use a wide range of tools and other devices that increase our chances for survival. Tool use by humans is often considered to be the single most distinctive characteristic of our species, even though other animals

With the stimulus of constantly available sex, protohominids had begun the most fundamental exchanges the human race would ever make. Males and females were learning to divide their labor, to exchange meat and vegetables, to share their daily catch. Constant sex had begun to tie them to one another and economic dependence was tightening the knot.

Helen Fisher (1982)

A chimpanzee using a simple tool for immediate reward. An adult chimp uses a twig to extract insects from a hole in a tree. Humans make tools in order to make other tools for later use, a unique distinction.

may use or even make simple tools. For example, the sea otter wields a rock to break open the shell of an abalone. Anthropologist Jane Goodall has observed chimpanzees using a variety of tools: thrashing about with branches for display, using clubs and missiles for defense, selecting a twig and stripping its bark to probe the nests of termites and attract them to the stick, in order to eat them. West African chimps use stone and wooden hammers to crack and open nutshells. Although tool use may not be unique to humans, using tools to make other tools does distinguish the human animal.

The evidence from Africa clearly indicates that our first step on the road to becoming human was the shift to bipedalism. It now seems clear from the evidence of *Australopithecus ramidus* that we had upright posture for perhaps 2.5 million years before either the use of stone tools or significant increases in the size of our brain. Apparently, standing upright was very important to our early survival.

Explanations for bipedalism focus on whether the feet or the hands were changing. Mary Leakey and her colleagues have suggested that we became upright in order to pursue migratory animal herds on the savanna. Bipedalism and powerful strides would be advantageous for moving long distances to follow herds for meat. And upright posture would free the hands for carrying young offspring. This hypothesis ignores the fact that australopithecine teeth seem adapted to an increasingly vegetarian diet, becoming bigger and flatter over time. Walking around on two feet could, however, be useful for collecting plant foods scattered across the landscape.

Microscopic analysis of wear patterns on fossil teeth by Alan Walker, of Pennsylvania State University, indicates that the tooth enamel among early hominids more closely resembles that of herbivores, not carnivores. Examination of the anatomy of the wrist, shoulder, pelvis, and thigh of the early australopithecines indicates a pattern of movement, or **locomotion,** different from that of both the modern apes and humans. Henry McHenry, of the University of California, Davis, notes the curvature visible in hand and foot bones, concluding that these creatures must have spent some time in the trees.

Other ideas regarding the evolution of bipedal locomotion relate to food getting, carrying, or sharing. Clifford Jolly, of New York University, has proposed that bipedalism was adaptive because it provided a means for gathering and eating young leaves, seeds, and pods of the African thornbush growing on the African savanna. Owen Lovejoy, of Case Western Reserve University, has proposed that our ancestors became two-footed because bipedalism enabled males to carry food back to a favored location to be shared with females, a concept known as male provisioning; this would have increased the birth rate and reproductive success of humans because females could support more than one dependent offspring at a time. Lovejoy wrote:

> Both an advanced material culture and the Pleistocene acceleration in brain development are sequelae to an already established hominid character system, which included intensified parenting and social relationships, monogamous pair bonding, specialized sexual-reproductive behavior, and bipedality. . . . The nuclear family and human sexual behavior may have their ultimate origin long before the dawn of the Pleistocene.
>
> The proposed model accounts for the early origin of bipedality as a locomotor behavior directly enhancing reproductive fitness, not as a behavior resulting from occasional upright feeding posture. It accounts for the origin of the home base in the same fashion as it has been acquired by numerous other mammals. It accounts for the human nuclear family, for the distinctive human sexual epigamic features, and the species' unique sexual behavior. (1981, p. 350)

We do not yet know why, in fact, certain apes became bipedal—and thus human.

In the final analysis, it is culture that distinguishes the human creature. Culture is what anthropologist Leslie White called our "extrasomatic means of survival"—the nonbiological, nongenetic behavior and sociability that have carried us through the millennia and spread us into diverse environments across the planet. Clifford Geertz, of Princeton University, has described humans as toolmaking, talking, symbolizing animals: Only they laugh; only they know when they will die; only they disdain to mate with family members; only they contrive those visions of other worlds called art. They have not just mentality but consciousness, not just needs but values, not just fears but conscience, not just a past but a history. Only they have culture (1963, p. 2).

Culture is a constellation of ideas and actions that are learned and transmitted from generation to generation. Human culture embodies the totality of behaviors and experiences that are summarized in our language and taught us by our parents and peers—a kind of group personality that provides a repertoire of actions in situations of choice. It is as impossible to have human identity without social contact as it is to have biological existence without parents. Tarzan was an ape until he met Jane. Culture enables us to eulogize our place in the universe, to create gods, to anticipate death, to travel to the stars—and to study archaeology.

SUGGESTED READINGS

Aitken, M. J. 1990. *Science-based dating in archaeology.* New York: Longman. *One of the best and more comprehensive overviews of physical dating methods used in archaeology, including radiopotassium and radiocarbon.*

Binford, L. R. 1983. *The pursuit of the past.* New York: Thames & Hudson. *A well-known archaeologist's view of the study of archaeology.*

Brain, C. K. 1981. *The hunters or the hunted? An introduction to African cave taphonomy.* Chicago: University of Chicago Press. *The classic detective story of the early human fossil remains in the caves of South Africa.*

Fisher, H. E. 1983. *The sex contract.* New York: Quill. *Another view of the origins of the species.*

Isaac, B., ed. 1989. *The archaeology of human origins: Papers by Glynn Isaac.* Cambridge: Cambridge University Press. *This volume contains the major thoughts of an important thinker on early hominids.*

Klein, R. G. 1999. *The human career: Human biological and cultural origins.* 2d ed. Chicago: University of Chicago Press. *A recent summary of the evidence and arguments concerning human evolution; detailed, accurate, and readable.*

Lewin, R. 1987. *Bones of contention.* New York: Simon & Schuster. *A popular account of fossil finds and feuds among paleoanthropologists.*

Rasmussen, D. T. 1993. *The origin and evolution of humans and humanness.* Boston: Jones & Bartlett. *A compilation of expert papers.*

OUT OF AFRICA: *HOMO ERECTUS*

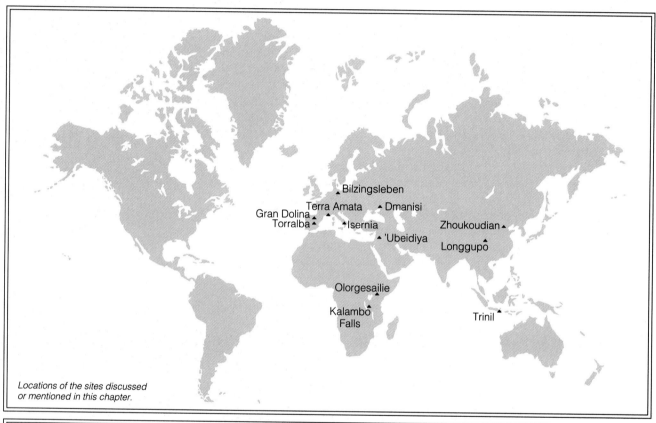

Locations of the sites discussed
or mentioned in this chapter.

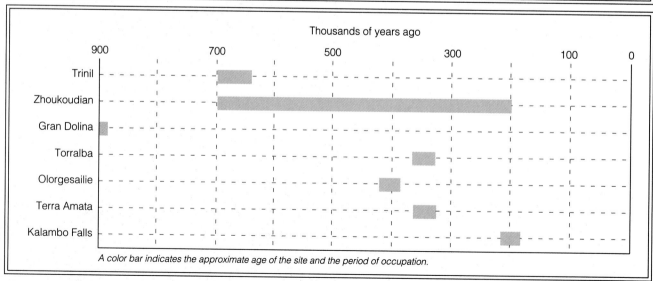

A color bar indicates the approximate age of the site and the period of occupation.

FROM HOMINID TO HUMAN

*The movement of human populations
out of Africa to other continents
after 2 million years ago*

The earliest dates for the presence of humans outside of Africa are younger than 2 million years ago, after the beginning of the Pleistocene. Our ancestors began to move into the more northern continents of Asia and Europe and to encounter new environmental conditions. The Pleistocene, also known as the Ice Age, was a time of climatic extremes in many parts of the world. Repeated, dramatic changes in temperature, sea level, and environment are hallmarks of the Pleistocene (see "Climate and Environment in the Pleistocene," p. 74). The use of hands and simple tools had been sufficient to obtain the foods available in the benign warmth of much of Africa. But expansion out of the tropics required new skills and inventions for surviving where cold weather, or the lack of food or shelter, could be fatal. It became necessary for our ancestors to modify their environment to fit their needs. The first reliable evidence for the controlled use of fire, systematic hunting, and the use of wooden spears appeared during the time of *H. erectus*. It was a time of change in stone tools, as well; the handaxe was invented as an all-purpose tool (see "The Acheulean Handaxe," p. 92).

These early migrants were almost certainly *Homo erectus,* a new species of hominid, evolved from *Homo habilis* in Africa. The timing of the spread of populations out of Africa coincides closely with the appearance of *H. erectus*. The earliest *H. erectus* fossil comes from the western shore of Lake Turkana in northern Kenya, dating to approximately 1.8 m.y.a. *H. erectus* individuals were robust, with large bones and teeth; they also had larger bodies, more or less modern in size, and significantly larger brains—around 1000 cc—than their *H. habilis* ancestors (Table 3.1). Although their brain was twice as big as a chimpanzee's, it was only about the size of a 1-year-old modern human child's. *H. erectus* skulls are characterized by a low sloping forehead, prominent brow ridges, and a protruding face. These hominids were almost fully modern in terms of movement and locomotion; they differed very little, if at all, from modern anatomy below the neck. Cranial capacity changed very little in *H. erectus*

An artist's interpretation of an adolescent and adult *Homo erectus.*

Table 3.1   Major Characteristics of *Homo erectus* Compared to Modern Humans

Trait	*Homo erectus*	*Homo sapiens sapiens*
Forehead	Absent	Vertical and rounded
Face	In front of cranium	Under cranium
Cranial capacity	1000 cc	1400 cc
Lower jaw	Larger and heavier; no chin	Smaller and lighter; distinct chin
Teeth	Larger	Smaller
Brow ridges	Heavy, extending across the eyes	Absent
Limb bones	Larger and heavier	Smaller and lighter

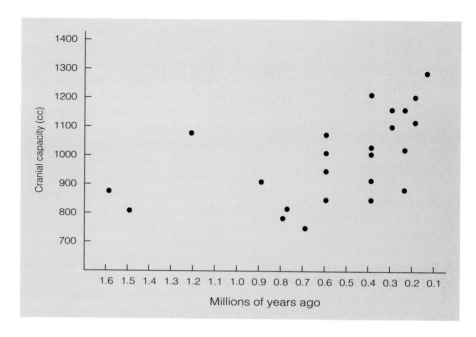

Cranial capacity versus time for *Homo erectus* skulls. Two patterns emerge: (1) There is relatively little change between 1.5 and 0.5 m.y.a. and (2) there is a dramatic increase in cranial capacity after 0.5 m.y.a., perhaps associated with the evolution of modern *Homo sapiens*.

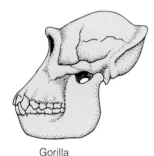

Gorilla

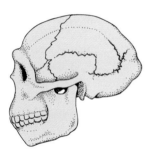

Homo erectus

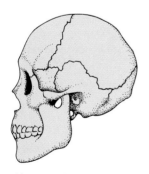

Homo sapiens sapiens

The skulls of a gorilla, *Homo erectus,* and *Homo sapiens sapiens*, shown at the same scale. The face moves under the brain case as cranial capacity expands; the teeth and jaws become smaller.

during the period 1.8–0.5 m.y.a., after which a dramatic increase occurred, perhaps in association with the rise of *Homo sapiens*.

Several sites in Asia document the presence of the first migrants. 'Ubeidiya, located in Israel a few kilometers south of the Sea of Galilee, dates to approximately 1.5 m.y.a. 'Ubeidiya contains concentrations of handaxes and other stone tools, along with animal bones, on the shore of a former lake. In this area, geological activity has tilted the layers so that the archaeological deposits are almost vertical. Even earlier, but less reliable, dates are known from central and eastern Asia. The site of Dmanisi in Georgia, containing an *H. erectus* lower jaw, has been dated by radiopotassium methods to 1.8 m.y.a. Locations of *H. erectus* finds on Java, one of the islands of Indonesia, have recently been dated using radiopotassium methods to roughly 1.7 m.y.a. (see "Trinil," p. 70). A new find from Longgupo in south-central China may go back even further. A fragment of a hominid jaw has been dated to 1.9 m.y.a. and has characteristics that may link it to a form of *Homo* even earlier than *erectus*. If these early dates prove to be accurate, *Homo erectus* would have spread very quickly across Asia after their appearance in Africa. Even at a rate of expansion of just 16 km (10 mi) per generation of 20 years, it would take only about 20,000 years to cover the distance between East Africa and Southeast Asia—around 16,000 km (10,000 mi). That brief period is indistinguishable by current chronological techniques such as radiopotassium dating. The date of the movement of human populations into Europe is another question (see "The First Europeans," p. 82).

Most of what we know about the period between 700,000 and 120,000 years ago, known as the Middle Pleistocene, comes from Europe and the Near East. Caves and rock shelters in these areas have preserved remains, attracting archaeologists interested in this period. The precise chronology for this important period in human evolution is poorly established. Because the time is too young to determine ages using radiopotassium methods and too old for radiocarbon methods, accurate dates are rare. Many archaeological sites from this period have barely survived the elements and the passage of time. Deposits have been badly disturbed; sites have suffered erosion and redeposition as the landscape has changed.

Evidence of these early humans and their activities has been discovered at the sites described in this chapter. Trinil and Zhoukoudian document the presence of *Homo erectus* in East Asia. Kalambo Falls and Olorgesailie demonstrate the continued development of the human species in Africa. Gran Dolina, Terra Amata, and other sites provide evidence for the first humans in Europe. These places take us through almost 2 million years of human prehistory, along our journey through time.

THE PALEOLITHIC PERIOD

Archaeological divisions of time

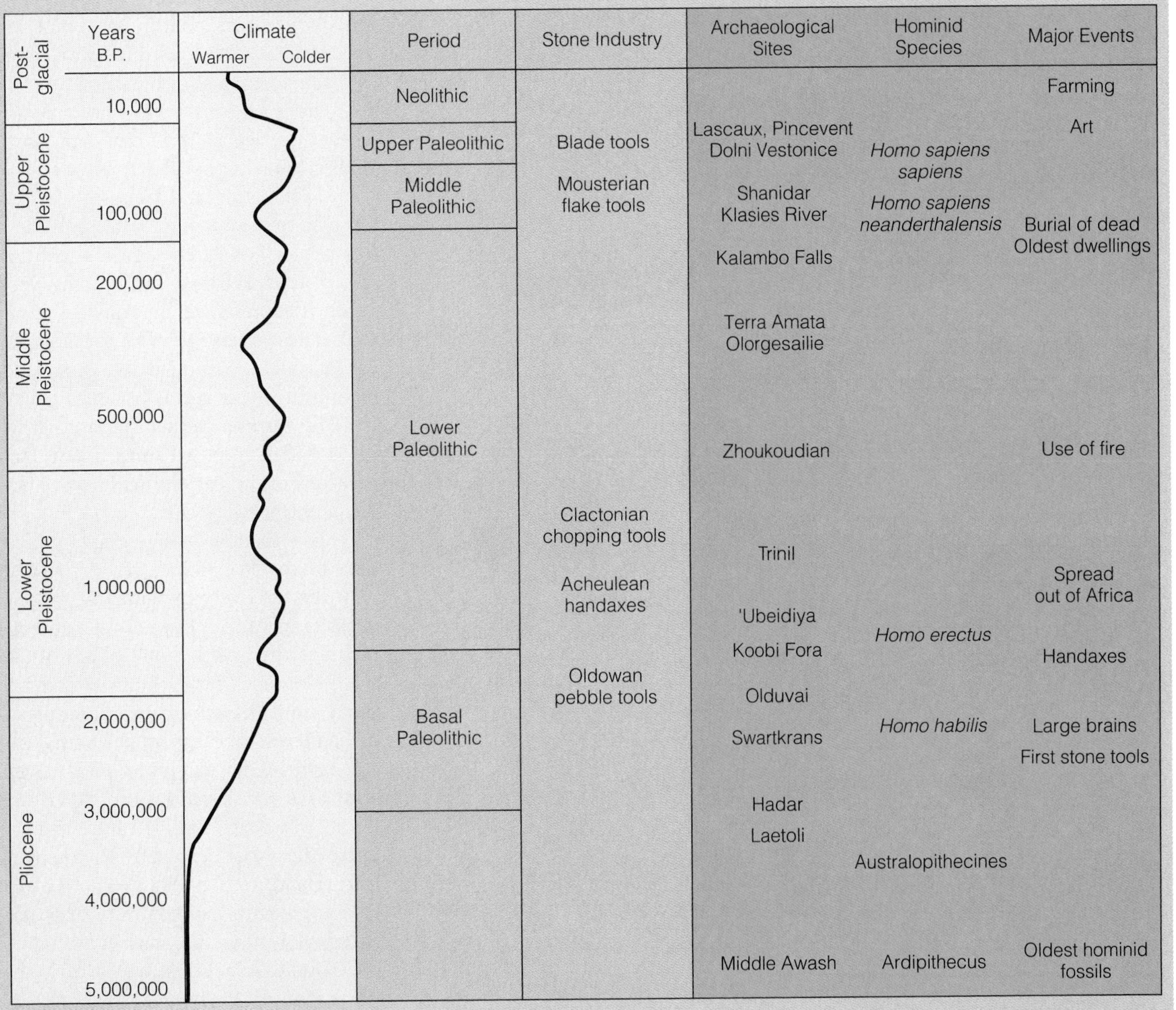

Epoch	Years B.P.	Climate (Warmer–Colder)	Period	Stone Industry	Archaeological Sites	Hominid Species	Major Events
Post-glacial	10,000		Neolithic				Farming
Upper Pleistocene			Upper Paleolithic	Blade tools	Lascaux, Pincevent Dolni Vestonice	*Homo sapiens sapiens*	Art
Upper Pleistocene	100,000		Middle Paleolithic	Mousterian flake tools	Shanidar Klasies River	*Homo sapiens neanderthalensis*	Burial of dead Oldest dwellings
	200,000				Kalambo Falls		
Middle Pleistocene					Terra Amata Olorgesailie		
Middle Pleistocene	500,000		Lower Paleolithic		Zhoukoudian		Use of fire
				Clactonian chopping tools	Trinil		Spread out of Africa
Lower Pleistocene	1,000,000			Acheulean handaxes	'Ubeidiya	*Homo erectus*	
					Koobi Fora		Handaxes
				Oldowan pebble tools	Olduvai		
	2,000,000		Basal Paleolithic		Swartkrans	*Homo habilis*	Large brains First stone tools
Pliocene	3,000,000				Hadar Laetoli	Australopithecines	
Pliocene	4,000,000						
	5,000,000				Middle Awash	Ardipithecus	Oldest hominid fossils

The Pleistocene and the Paleolithic. This chart shows the major divisions of the Pliocene and Pleistocene and years before present, along with the major divisions of the Paleolithic, important stone industries, archaeological sites, hominid forms, and significant events.

Just as geologists divide up the history of the earth into periods and epochs, archaeologists break up the prehistory of human society into more manageable and understandable units. The scheme used by archaeologists to compartmentalize prehistory focuses on changes in artifacts and material culture. Differences in the types of material used to make tools, and changes in the shapes of tools, are often the main criteria for distinguishing time periods.

The basic framework for dividing up the past was initiated in 1836, when

(continued)

Paleolithic artifacts. Top row: Lower Paleolithic handaxes. Center row: Middle Paleolithic flake core, flake tool, and Levallois point. Bottom row: Upper Paleolithic blade core, blade, and Solutrean point. There were many bone and antler tools in use in the Upper Paleolithic as well.

Christian Thomsen proposed a Three Age system for organizing the exhibits in the National Museum of Denmark, with separate rooms for stone, bronze, and iron objects. This system was quickly adopted elsewhere in Europe to designate the ages of prehistory: the Stone Age, Bronze Age, and Iron Age. These basic divisions are still used in Europe and in many other areas of the world.

The Stone Age was subsequently further divided in 1865 by English naturalist John Lubbock, who coined the terms Paleolithic and Neolithic to distinguish the Old Stone Age and the New Stone Age. The **Paleolithic** is characterized by tools of flaked flint, and the **Neolithic** is represented by polished stone tools and pottery. Further divisions of the Paleolithic were made as the age and complexity of the period became known. In 1872, the French prehistorian Gabriel de Mortillet proposed three major subdivisions of the Paleolithic: Lower, Middle, and Upper.

Since then, an even earlier subdivision of the Paleolithic was designated with the discovery of the earliest stone artifacts in Africa. The Basal Paleolithic includes the pebble and flake tools of the Oldowan industry from around 2.5 m.y.a. until the appearance and spread of handaxes. The Lower Paleolithic includes the Acheulean (ash-oo-lee′an) assemblages generally associated with *Homo erectus*. Handaxes and flake tools characterize these periods (see "The Acheulean Handaxe," p. 92). The Lower Paleolithic thus extends from approximately 1.8 m.y.a. to the beginning of the Middle Paleolithic, about 200,000 years ago.

The Middle Paleolithic is associated with Neanderthals and other forms of early *Homo sapiens* and is characterized by a predominance of flake tools in artifact assemblages. In Europe and the Near East, Middle Paleolithic assemblages are known as Mousterian. The Upper Paleolithic begins around 35,000 years ago with an emphasis on tools made on very long, thin flakes of stone, known as blades, and on tools made from a number of other materials, including bone and antler (see "The Upper Paleolithic," Chapter 4, p. 120). The finale of the Upper Paleolithic generally coincides with the end of the Pleistocene, about 10,000 years ago.

Some of the major developments in the Paleolithic include the appearance of the first stone tools around 2.6 m.y.a., the controlled use of fire around half a million years ago or perhaps even earlier, definitive evidence for the hunting of large game and the first definite structures and shelters perhaps 200,000 years ago, the intentional burial of the dead perhaps 50,000 years ago, the first art and decoration after 30,000 years ago, and the dispersal of human populations throughout the world by the end of the Pleistocene. Our human ancestors lived as hunter-gatherers for more than 99% of prehistory, successfully harvesting the wild foods of the land. Domestication—the planting of crops and the herding of animals—did not begin until the very end of the Paleolithic, around 8000 B.C.

Several important technological trends occurred during the Paleolithic, one of which was the specialization of tools. The earliest stone artifacts were general-purpose tools, extremely simple in form. Over time, there was a definite increase in the kinds of tools in use and in the total number of tools at larger sites. Efficiency in using stone also increased, as did the amount of cutting edge produced by flaking stone. For example, 0.5 kg (1 lb) of flint would produce about 8 cm (3 in) of edge on an Oldowan pebble tool, about 30 cm (12 in) around the circumference on a handaxe from the Lower Paleolithic, about 90 cm (30 in) of edges on the flake tools of the Middle Paleolithic, and in the Upper Paleolithic, the long, thin flakes would result in almost 9 m (30 ft) of cutting edge. There was also an increase in the variety of materials used to make tools during the Paleolithic. Bone, antler, ivory, and wood were commonly used by the end of the Paleolithic, although this may have been a result of better preservation at more recent sites.

The Paleolithic witnessed the achievement of humanness, a heritage that has been passed on to the inhabitants of the most recent 10,000 years of our species' past. The major developments in this recent past would not have been possible without the population expansion, innovative technology, and development of language, social relationships, and rituals that characterized the journey of our ancestors through the Paleolithic.

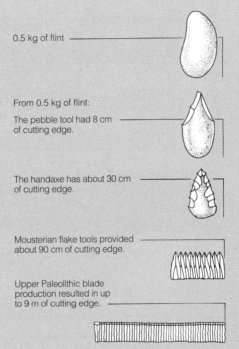

0.5 kg of flint

From 0.5 kg of flint:

The pebble tool had 8 cm of cutting edge.

The handaxe has about 30 cm of cutting edge.

Mousterian flake tools provided about 90 cm of cutting edge.

Upper Paleolithic blade production resulted in up to 9 m of cutting edge.

A major trend through the Paleolithic: increasing efficiency in the production of cutting edge. Pebble tools, handaxes, flakes, and blades were likely produced from the same original piece of flint. Blade production provides an enormous increase in the amount of cutting edge available from the same amount of material.

TRINIL

The discovery of Homo erectus *in Java*

The bank of the Solo River in Trinil where the skull of Java man was found by Eugene Dubois.

The first discovery of the fossil remains of *Homo erectus* is an unusual tale of individual intuition and conviction. The hero of this episode is Eugene Dubois, born in the Netherlands in 1858, just before the appearance of Charles Darwin's first book on natural selection. British naturalist Alfred Russel Wallace was promoting a similar theory on the evolution of species at this same time. Both Wallace and Darwin argued that the progenitors of the human species had come from a "warm, forest-clad land." Wallace had lived for almost a decade on the islands of Sumatra and Borneo. In 1869, he published a book called *Malay Archipelago,*

writing of the orangutans in this area and the potential there for human evolution: "With what interest must every naturalist look forward to the time when the caves of the tropics may be thoroughly examined, and the past history and earliest appearance of the great man-like apes be at length made known" (1869, p. 72).

Influenced by the words of Wallace, Dubois carefully studied the evidence for human evolution. Dubois wisely realized that early human remains would be found in areas with limestone caves, where the chances for preservation were greatest. He reasoned that Europe had been too cold for these early humans. He

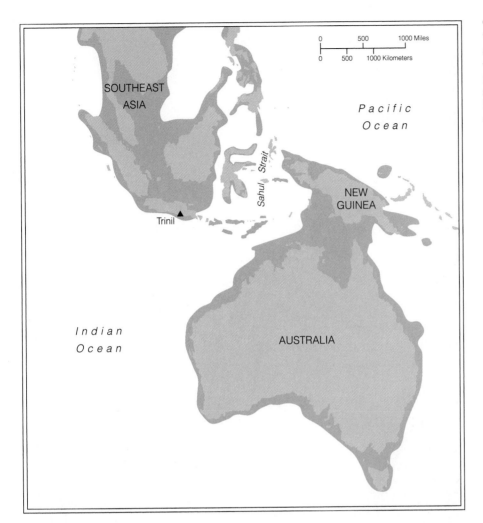

The location of Trinil. At the time that early hominids were on Java, sea level was lower and the island was part of the mainland of Southeast Asia. Darker shaded areas indicate landmasses during that time. Lighter shaded areas indicate current landmasses.

also knew that large parts of northern Europe had been scoured by erosion during the ice ages and were unlikely to have retained the earliest evidence (see "Climate and Environment in the Pleistocene," p. 74). Thus, he was convinced that he should go to the Dutch colonies in the East Indies and find human fossils—and he did.

Dubois' views were highly heretical in the context of European views of human evolution during the latter half of the nineteenth century. Early hominid remains, such as Cro-Magnon and Neanderthal, had just been discovered in Europe, and their qualifications for "humanness" were being debated. At this time the concept of a missing link—the fossil connection between apes and humans—dominated perspectives on human evolution. Many scientists did not believe apes had evolved into the human species because evidence for the connection was lacking.

Dubois had grown up in an inquiring family atmosphere. His father, a pharmacist, had taught him the scientific classification of all the plants and trees in their neighborhood. As a high school student he attended an influential lecture on evolution, and an interest in natural history and evolution dominated his subsequent intellectual life. Dubois trained as a surgeon and anatomist at the University of Amsterdam.

To pursue his interest in early hominids, he gave up his university position, joined the army as a surgeon in the Dutch East Colonial forces, and left for Sumatra with his wife and their infant in 1887. A Dutch colony and an obvious destination for the adventurer in Dubois, Sumatra was a tropical land with limestone caves and living great apes. His

Dubois and the fossil finds from Java. The skullcap of the *Homo erectus* found by Dubois in Java is shown, along with a photograph of Dubois as a young man.

duties at the small hospital in Sumatra left time to explore the countryside. He spent 2 years looking for fossil materials without success. In 1890, stricken with malaria, he was transferred to the island of Java, where the drier climate might improve his condition. There, the colonial administration provided a crew for his investigations and two officers to supervise the workers. The area was rich in fossils, and Dubois immediately began to ship specimens of extinct mammals back to the Netherlands.

One of the most productive fossil sites Dubois found was located along the eroding bank of the Solo River in north-central Java, near the village of Trinil (trin'el). Here the 15-m (50-ft) bank exposed layers of volcanic ash, river sediments, and sandstone. Hundreds of bones from such species as deer, rhinoceros, elephant, pig, tiger, hyena, and crocodile were recovered in the layers. Finally, in 1891, a tooth and then a skull were recovered that documented the presence of fossil hominids in Java. Dubois described both specimens as great manlike apes. In the next year, a human thigh bone was uncovered some 15 m (50 ft) from the skull. The femur was essentially identical to the modern form, although slightly heavier. This evidence led Dubois to designate the species *Pithecanthropus erectus*. The term *erectus*, the species name, indicates upright posture, and *Pithecanthropus*, the genus name, is from the Greek *pithecos* (ape) and *anthropos* (man). A second skull was found in the area in 1937. Today, after more than 75 specimens have been discovered throughout Africa, Asia, and Europe, these individuals from Java are included in the category *Homo erectus* to indicate their similarity to ourselves.

Dubois' discovery was of paramount importance, because it indicated that Asia, not Europe, might be the ancestral home of the human species. He returned to Europe in 1895 with the materials he had found and was met with substantial criticism and doubt. Even today, a controversy seems to arise in paleoanthropology whenever new and distinctive fossil forms are uncovered. Various authorities of Dubois' day argued that the thigh bone was too modern and could not belong with the skull. Others were unsure whether it was closer to apes or humans. Soon there were more than 15 different written opinions on the matter, espousing various ape, man, or ape-man interpretations. By the turn of the century, the controversy had driven Dubois to his home in the Netherlands, where he buried the fossils under the floor and withdrew from scientific circles for the rest of his life. Toward the end of his life, he became increasingly convinced that the remains of the Java hominids were in fact those of an ancestor to the apes, and not human after all. This end of the Dubois story is all the more poignant in light of the fact that he had been the first to discover the remains of our direct ancestor, *Homo erectus*.

At the time of its initial colonization, Java would not have been an island as it is today, but rather an extension of the peninsula of Southeast Asia, connected to the continent by land bridges during a period of lower sea level. The precise dating of Pleistocene fossil materials from Java is difficult. Just recently, a new radio-potassium date of approximately 1.7 m.y.a. was determined for the deposits in which the Trinil fossils were found. However, there are serious questions about the reliability of this date. It is now known that all of the fossils had been redeposited from their original location. Other estimates place the age of the hominid materials at around 0.75 m.y.a., but this date is speculative.

Another puzzling aspect of the Java discoveries is the absence of stone tools or other materials associated with the human fossils. No artifacts have been found in Java that can definitely be linked with *Homo erectus*. Although nineteenth-century researchers may have ignored odd-shaped pieces of stone, even more recent investigators have been unable to determine whether flakes or core tools were being made and used in the same period as the *H. erectus* fossils. Stone artifacts in the form of handaxes, choppers, and flakes were used widely in other parts of the world during this period. A number of *H. erectus* habitation sites elsewhere document both the tools and the food debris of these groups.

Microscopic examination of the scratches and wear on the teeth of the Java hominids suggests the consumption of thin, chewy plant foods. Perhaps such a diet would not require even the simplest tools. Bamboo or other materials may have been used for tools, split into pieces to create sharp edges. But the mystery of the missing artifacts on Java has not been solved; more exploration and excavation must be undertaken there to determine how these *Homo erectus* groups survived.

CLIMATE AND ENVIRONMENT IN THE PLEISTOCENE

Challenging conditions for human survival

The Pleistocene, a geological epoch and the time of *Homo erectus*, began approximately 2 million years ago in a period characterized by active volcanoes, cooling temperatures, and the appearance of several modern species of animals. Although the Pleistocene is also known as the Ice Age, there were, in fact, many glacials, or ice ages. There have been at least nine, and probably more, alternations between colder and warmer conditions, known as **glacials** and **interglacials**, during the Pleistocene.

These glacial episodes were first recognized in Europe. During the 1800s, two Swiss geologists, A. Penck and E. Brückner, identified four periods of glaciation in Europe from a series of Alpine moraines and river terraces. They named these glacial stages after local rivers—the Günz, Mindel, Riss, and Würm—from oldest to most recent. The intervening warm periods were designated Günz/Mindel, Mindel/Riss, and Riss/Würm. However, subsequent research has demonstrated that in the last million years or so, there have been a larger number of pronounced swings from warmer to colder.

It may be surprising to learn that the information for the dramatic changes in glaciation in the Northern Hemisphere comes from underwater in the Caribbean Sea, where scientists have made deep corings of marine sediments on the ocean floor. The small animal shells (foraminifera) that make up much of this sediment contain oxygen isotopes in the carbonate of the shell. **Oxygen isotope ratios** in ocean water vary with the temperature of the water, and those from deep cores of ocean sediments can thus indicate temperature change over time. The trend over the last 70 million years is clearly one of cooling temperatures. Specifically during the Pleistocene, alternations between warmer and cooler periods have been numbered sequentially and are defined as isotope stages.

It is not difficult to imagine the consequences of a sharp drop in temperature during the colder episodes of the Pleistocene. In parts of northern Canada, temperatures are cool even in summer, with lows at night around 4.5°C (40°F). The last snowfall is often in June, and the first flakes of autumn come in September. A drop in average summer temperature in this area of about −5°C (8°F) would mean that not all the winter snow would melt each year; snow would fall later in summer and earlier in autumn. Even if the snowbanks increased by only a few centimeters each summer, they would grow substantially over the course of time. For example, just 10 cm (4 in) of snow every year for 10,000 years

Oxygen isotope ratios from foraminifera in marine sediments during the Cenozoic, the last 70 million years of the earth's history. Notice the gradual decline in atmospheric temperature since the Eocene.

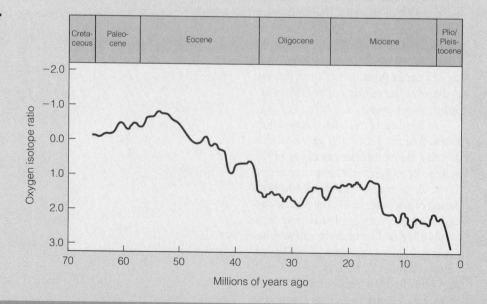

would build an enormous snowdrift over 1 km (0.6 mi) high.

Ice would form under the piles of accumulating snow. The 5 trillion snowflakes it takes to cover a football field with a foot of wet snow weigh almost 550 tons. The weight causes the mass of ice to begin to spread at the edges. In such a manner, huge sheets of ice expanded horizontally during the Pleistocene, as more and more snow and ice accumulated. It has been estimated that such ice sheets may have expanded across the landscape at a rate of as much as 100–150 m (350–500 ft) per year. In a thousand years, such a growing ice mass would cover a distance of 100 km (62 mi). In 20,000 years of accumulation, the ice would have spread 2000 km (1250 mi) from its original center.

Today, perhaps 10% of the land surface of the earth is covered by glaciers—in Antarctica, Greenland, northern Canada, Europe, and Asia, and in high mountain regions. During the last million years, sheets of continental glaciers more than 5 km (3 mi) thick grew in the Northern Hemisphere. During the colder episodes of the Pleistocene, continental ice sheets expanded from these same areas to cover perhaps 30% of the land surface.

In North America, these ice masses covered most of Canada and extended into the United States as far south as what is now St. Louis, Missouri. In northern Europe, a similar sheet moved from the Baltic Sea basin to cover Scandinavia, northern Great Britain, and parts of the Netherlands, northern Germany, Poland, and the northwestern part of the former Soviet Union. These sheets of ice acted like enormous bulldozers, grinding down the landscape as they advanced and depositing huge blankets of homogenized earth and rock as they retreated. The weight of the ice also pushed down the land surface, often to great depths. In Greenland today, for example, where the ice sheet is 2 km (1.3 mi) thick, the land surface resembles a very deep bowl, higher at the edges where the ice is thinner. The land surface

in the interior of Greenland is far below present sea level and one of the lowest spots on earth.

The mass of ice also reduced the earth's water reservoir, particularly the oceans. During the time of maximum cold when water was frozen in huge continental sheets, global sea level was reduced as much as 100–150 m (300–500 ft), completely changing the outlines of the continents and often creating connections between former islands and separate landmasses. As the massive ice sheets melted at the end of the Pleistocene, two processes operated to change the shape of the continents. At the same

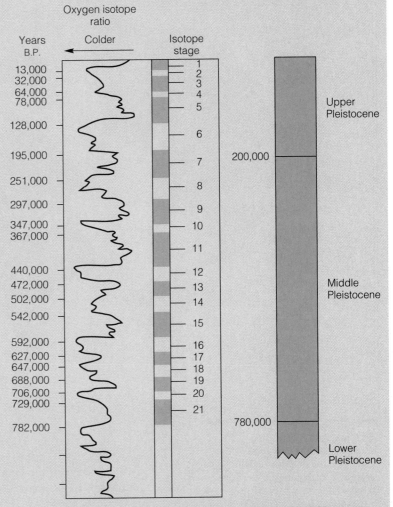

Oxygen isotope ratio

Odd-numbered stages (in color) = warmer periods, less glacial ice cover.
Even-numbered stages = colder periods, more glacial ice cover.

Pleistocene glacial chronology based on oxygen isotope ratios in foraminifera in marine sediments. Notice the many oscillations between cold and warm phases. (Data from Shackleton and Opdyke, 1973.)

(continued)

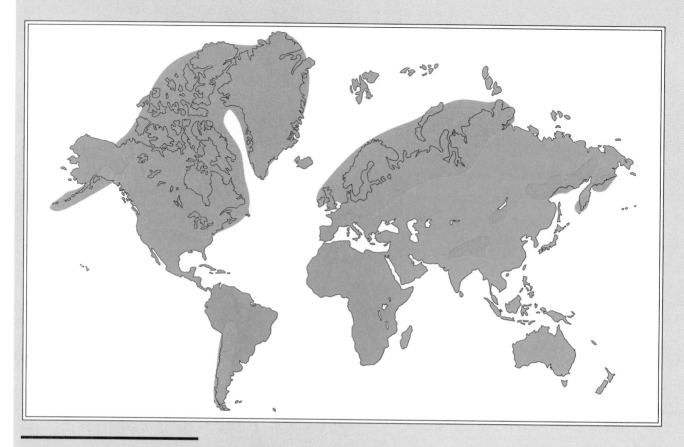

The maximum distribution of continental glaciation during the colder periods of the Pleistocene. Ice sheets are more common in the Northern Hemisphere partly because there is much more land at the higher northern latitudes.

time the melting ice refilled the seas and coastlines moved higher, the enormous weight of the ice sheets disappeared, removing a heavy burden from the land. The surface of the earth had been depressed by the weight of the ice (just as the center of Greenland is today). This surface began to come back, or rebound, as the ice disappeared. For example, the coast of Finland today is expanding at the astounding rate of several meters per century as the area rebounds from the weight of the glacial ice.

The causes of Pleistocene climatic change and continental glaciation have been debated for many years. Volcanic plumes filling the air with ash and smoke and shading the earth, or changes in the level of solar radiation, were once thought to be responsible for the onset of the Pleistocene. Recent attention has been given to the role of mountain uplift in cooling the earth's climate. Walter Ruddiman and John Kutzbach have sug-

gested that the uplift of the North American Rocky Mountains and the Himalayas of South Asia resulted in a global disruption of weather patterns and the onset of a cooler, drier climate.

Fluctuations in air and water temperature were not uncommon during the Pleistocene and are cyclical in nature. In the 1920s, Yugoslavian mathematician Milutin Milankovitch argued that the variations in the earth's orbit changed climate in a cyclical fashion. Slight variation in the precession of the earth's axis and shifts in orbit eccentricity change the distribution and intensity of sunlight reaching the planet, just as changes in our seasons are caused by movement through orbit. Milankovitch predicted cycles of 100,000, 40,000, and 20,000 years for these climatic changes, based on his calculations of the earth's orbital variation. Such a cyclical pattern seems to fit the information on climatic change found in the ocean cores. Thus, it ap-

A modern glacier.

pears that minor changes in such factors as the distance from the earth to the sun and the tilt of the earth's axis play a major role in the amount of sunlight reaching the earth, the atmospheric temperature, and ultimately the expansion and retreat of continental glaciation. This factor, now known as **Milankovitch forcing**, is considered to be the prime reason for the Holocene, the Postglacial, or the Present Interglacial. It is not at all clear that the glacial cycles of the Pleistocene have ended; we may now simply be witnessing one of the warmer intervals between fluctuations of glaciation and climatic change that occurred during the Pleistocene and repeatedly over the past several hundred million years of the earth's history.

The end of the Pleistocene is dated to 11,000 years ago (9000 B.C.) when the last ice sheets retreated. The last 11,000 years, including today, geologists call the periods of glaciation. Similarity of the present interglacial to an earlier one about 400,000 years ago suggests that the next glacial will begin in about 20,000 years.

ZHOUKOUDIAN

Bones of the dragon

The location of the excavations at Dragon Bone Hill, Zhoukoudian. The white grid painted on the back wall indicates excavation squares.

For millennia, many Chinese have believed that fossil bones have medicinal and curative powers. Called dragon's teeth, such fossils were ground into powder and sold at apothecaries throughout the country. For more than a century, paleontologists and other natural scientists have visited such shops to look for the bones of new species and to learn about potential new fossil sites. In 1899, a European doctor in Beijing found an unusual fossil tooth at one such apothecary and identified it as the upper third molar of either human or ape origin. The tooth came from a place called Dragon Bone Hill, a large limestone ridge near the town of Zhoukoudian (Joe-ko-tea-en'), 50 km (30 mi) southwest of Beijing. Before the doctor returned to Europe, he passed the tooth and the information to a Swedish geologist, John Gunnar Andersson. Andersson and his friend Davidson Black, a Canadian anatomist,

were convinced they could find an early human fossil from the place where the tooth had been found. Black persuaded the Rockefeller Foundation to sponsor excavations at the site. On the basis of two hominid teeth that were found, Black announced the discovery of *Sinanthropus pekinensis,* Chinese man of Peking, in 1927. Later the same year the first skull was found, confirming Black's bold proclamation.

For 10 years, a large workforce essentially mined the deposits in the complex of caves at Zhoukoudian, removing over half a million tons of material in the quest for fossils. Almost 2000 days, more than 6 months each year, were spent blasting out the limestone and removing rock and sedimentary deposits over a vertical distance of 55 m (180 ft), as high as a 17-story building. The large limestone chamber at the center of the Zhoukoudian caves is enormous, 140 m (450

Excavations in the lower levels at Zhoukoudian.

ft) north to south, by 40 m (125 ft) east to west, by approximately 40 m (125 ft) high—the size of a supertanker. The deposits in this chamber were almost completely removed in the course of the excavation. The crude excavation methods and untrained labor meant that stone tools and other materials were often missed and that important information about the context of the deposits was not recorded.

In his report, Black described dense layers of ash, baked sediments, and charred bone resulting from fires in the cave. These materials were thought to be evidence of the places where people lived, made tools, built fires, ate, died, and left their bones. Over 20,000 stone tools, including flakes, scrapers, and choppers (but no handaxes), were found, made from quartz, sandstone, rock crystal, and flint. These materials do not occur naturally in limestone areas and must

have been brought into the caves. The artifacts are generally very crude and irregular but do improve in quality toward the top of the deposits.

The abundant bones in the deposits come from both large and small species. Most of the large animal bones come from an extinct species of deer with enormous horns and from wild horses and giant boars, elephants, water buffaloes, hyenas, such carnivores as bears and saber-toothed tigers, and others—a total of 96 different mammalian species. The presence of these animals indicates that the climate was somewhat warmer than today. Moreover, the habitat requirements for these species suggest that the area around Zhoukoudian was a mosaic of forested hills, open plains, lakes, and rivers. The forest was likely dominated by pine, cedar, elm, hackberry, and the Chinese redbud tree. The charred seeds of hackberry fruits found in the deposits

The stratigraphy of 40 m (130 ft) of deposits at Zhoukoudian, showing the location of the *Homo erectus* skeletal remains.

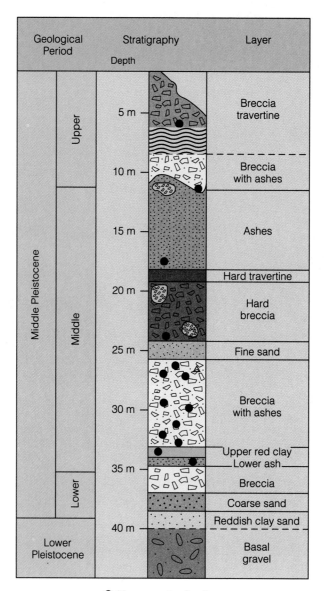

Geological Period		Stratigraphy Depth	Layer
Middle Pleistocene	Upper	5 m	Breccia travertine
		10 m	Breccia with ashes
	Middle	15 m	Ashes
		20 m	Hard travertine
			Hard breccia
		25 m	Fine sand
		30 m	Breccia with ashes
	Lower	35 m	Upper red clay / Lower ash
			Breccia
			Coarse sand
		40 m	Reddish clay sand
Lower Pleistocene			Basal gravel

● *Homo erectus fossils*

at Zhoukoudian led to the suggestion that plant foods such as these may have formed part of the diet of the human inhabitants.

By far the most important finds at Zhoukoudian were the remains of the early hominids, today designated *Homo erectus*. A total of 6 skullcaps (the face and lower portion of the crania are missing), 12 skull fragments, 15 lower jaws, 157 teeth, 7 thigh bones, 1 fragment of shin bone, 3 bones from the upper arm, 1 collarbone, and 1 wrist bone have been recovered. As in the South African caves, hominid skulls are more common than other bones of the skeleton, partly be-

cause they are more resistant to destruction and partly because they are more readily recognized. These fragments come from adult males and females and from children.

An increase in brain size over time can be seen in the materials from Zhoukoudian. Skulls from the deeper part of the deposits have a cranial capacity of about 900 cc, while those from the upper levels are closer to 1100 cc on average, within the range of variation of modern humans.

The investigations conducted by Black, and since 1949 by Chinese archaeologists, have revealed some 12 strat-

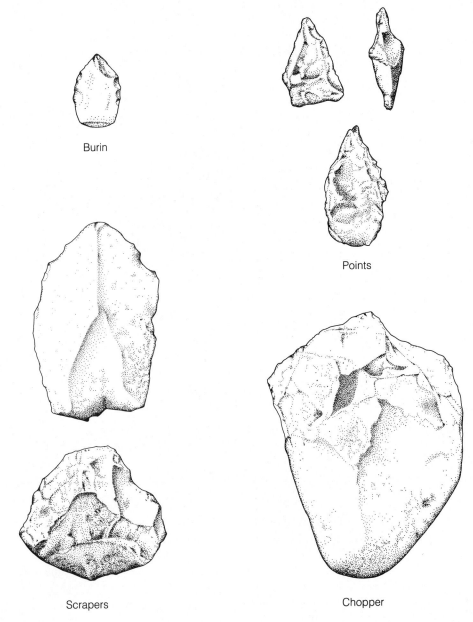

Burin

Points

Scrapers

Chopper

ified layers in the deep deposits at Zhou-koudian. The layers themselves date to at least 700,000 years ago at the bottom to roughly 200,000 years ago at the top of the sequence. The time span covered by the finds of *Homo erectus* is probably 550,000–250,000 years ago.

Unfortunately, these important fossils have disappeared. The excavations at Zhoukoudian had to be closed in 1937 with the outbreak of war between Japan and China. A decision was made to move the fossils to the United States for safe-keeping. They were packed carefully in crates and placed in the hands of a de-tachment of U.S. Marines. Somewhere between the consulate in Beijing and the port of departure from China, the fossils were lost or stolen. Today they may be destroyed, still in China, in Japan, in the United States, or at the bottom of the Pacific—no one knows. Fortunately, plaster casts were made before the fossils were lost, so that there is at least some information on their size, shape, and im-portant features. In addition, the more recent Chinese excavations since 1949 have uncovered a few more examples. Nevertheless, these priceless relics of some of our earliest ancestors would be a marvelous rediscovery.

THE FIRST EUROPEANS

An uncertain date of arrival

The size and latitudinal relationship between Europe and the United States. On the map of Europe are the locations and ages (in thousands of years) of some of the earliest archaeological sites.

Swanscombe (325)
Clacton (245)
Bilzingsleben (350)
Steinheim (250)
Verteszöllös (350)
Gran Dolina (800)
Arago (250)
Terra Amata (350)
Torralba and Ambrona (350)
Isernia (730)

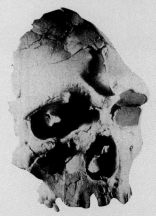

Early hominid skulls in Europe: Steinheim (top) and Arago (bottom). Dating to 300,000–200,000 years ago, these specimens likely represent an intermediate form between *Homo erectus* and fully modern *Homo sapiens*. Thus, they are now considered to represent Archaic *Homo sapiens* and the ancestors of *Homo sapiens neanderthalensis*.

As we have seen, early hominids began to expand out of Africa into Asia at the beginning of the Pleistocene, perhaps by 1.2 m.y.a. The earliest evidence for humans in Europe is less than 1 million years old. If *Homo erectus* spread into Asia, why did they not expand into Europe at the same time? The answer to this question may simply be that we don't yet have enough information, or it may relate to the geography of the European continent. New York City lies at the same latitude as Madrid and Rome. In fact, much of Europe is farther north than the U.S. border with Canada. Very cold climatic conditions would have prevailed in Europe during much of the last 1 million years, making large portions of the continent generally inhospitable to human occupation. Huge glaciers extended across the Pyrenees, Alps, Scandinavia, and Britain during the Pleistocene. A permafrost tundra covered much of the central part of the continent during the colder periods. Thus, the colder climate of Europe may have delayed human settlement until behavior and technology overcame this obstacle.

There are several archaeological sites in Europe dated before 400,000 years ago. The best candidate is from northern Spain, known as Gran Dolina, excavated since 1994. The site is around 900,000 years old. The deposits include faunal remains and 100 stone tools, largely flakes made of sandstone, limestone, quartzite, and two types of flint. No handaxes are present. There are also hundreds of bones from at least four different hominids, including a child and an adolescent. Another early site has been found in Italy, at a place known as Isernia. A few simple stone tools and animal bones were found together in deeply buried lakeshore deposits underlying a volcanic ash dating to 730,000 years ago using radiopotassium methods. Large animal species associated with the deposit are bison, rhinoceros, elephant, bear, hippo, pig, goat, and deer.

Several skeletal pieces of early humans have been found including a lower jaw from Mauer near Heidelberg in Germany, a skull from Petralona in Greece, the face of a skull from Arago in France, and a leg bone from Boxgrove in England. These European fossils date to the period after 500,000 years ago and appear slightly more modern than their *Homo erectus* neighbors in Asia. These remains are sometimes referred to as Archaic *Homo sapiens*.

A few other sites in Europe may be more than half a million years old, but reliable dates are rare. By 400,000 years ago, however, most of Europe had been occupied. Lower Paleolithic sites are found throughout the central and southern parts of the continent at places such as Bilzingsleben in Germany, Verteszöllös in Hungary, Torralba and Ambrona in Spain, and Terra Amata in France. Terra Amata is discussed in the next section of this chapter.

Bilzingsleben lies in an area of natural mineral springs; human and animal bones and small stone tools were preserved in the hardened deposits of travertine around the springs. Isotopic dates for the site indicate an age between 400,000 and 300,000 years ago, during an interglacial period. Human skull fragments were found in the deposits, along with numerous animal bones. A site very similar to Bilzingsleben exists in Hungary at Verteszöllös, roughly 50 km (30 mi) west of Budapest. Here again, the stone artifacts are curious because of their small size, probably the result of an absence of larger pieces of raw material in the area. Short cutting edges were produced on thousands of tiny pebbles, often only 2.5 cm (1 in) in diameter. Charcoal and burned animal bones document the use of fire at this site. As at Bilzingsleben, fragments of skull from early European hominids were found in the layers at Verteszöllös.

Some 150 km (100 mi) northeast of Madrid, a steep-sided valley cuts through a high plateau, creating one of the few routes between north and south in the region. During the Pleistocene, this valley almost certainly would have been an important path of migration for large animals moving between the north in summer and south in winter. Two almost identical sites, Torralba and Ambrona, are located in this valley, containing deposits of stone artifacts and the bones of extinct elephants, horses, deer, and other animals. The bones and stones accumulated here during a colder episode of the Pleistocene, probably during a glacial period, perhaps 350,000 years ago. The artifacts at the sites include objects made of stone, bone, ivory tusk, and wood. The stone artifacts belong to the early Acheulean; handaxes were made and used here, along with cleavers and a variety of other flake and core tools. Some of the stone used for making these artifacts came from tens of kilometers away.

Excavations at the site of Ambrona in central Spain, dating to 350,000 years B.P. The site documents the association of stone tools and the bones of extinct animals like the woodland elephant. Notice the linear arrangement of bones and tusks.

TERRA AMATA

Europe's oldest beach resort

The site of Terra Amata, discovered during the digging of the foundation for a new apartment building in Nice, France.

Located along the Mediterranean shore in the city of Nice, France, the site of Terra Amata was initially uncovered in 1965 during the construction of a high-rise apartment building. The place was located at the intersection of Boulevard Carnot and a side street called Terra Amata, meaning "beloved land." The director of the archaeological research center in nearby Marseilles, Henry de Lumley, was called in to look at the materials, and he immediately recognized their importance. The site was exceptional because of the antiquity of the remains; the preservation of bone, charcoal, shell, and stone artifacts; and the presence of actual living floors from the Lower Paleolithic.

De Lumley convinced the builders to stop work for 6 months in order to rescue the site. A crew of around 300 volunteers was quickly organized. Over 270 cu m (350 cu yd) of earth were moved to expose 125 sq m (1350 sq ft) of the occupation area; 35,000 prehis-

toric objects were uncovered, and the location of each was plotted on charts. Today the apartment building stands on top of what is the oldest coastal settlement in Europe. Fortunately, a portion of the underground parking area was set aside as a museum to protect and display a part of the site.

Terra Amata sits at the foot of Mont Boron, one of the dominant landmarks along the coastline of Nice. This 240-m (800-ft) high limestone ridge carries the scars of beaches formed during various high-water levels of the Mediterranean during periods of higher seas between the ice ages. The area exposed by the excavations at Terra Amata contains at least three fossil beaches and sandbars, dating to approximately 350,000 years ago. At the time of occupation, the site was located near the mouth of the Paillon River on the coast of the Mediterranean. The environment at that time was slightly cooler than today, and the water level in

A small fireplace at Terra Amata. The sand is black and red from the ash and heat of the fire. Pebbles were piled up on one side of the fire, perhaps to shield the flames from the wind.

the Mediterranean was about 25 m (80 ft) higher than at present.

Traces in the sands of this fossil beach mark a series of actual living surfaces with the remains of meals, tools, and other materials from the Lower Paleolithic. Stone tools and bones were found in one area, roughly 6 × 13 m (20 × 40 ft), the size of an average classroom. Twenty people or more might have used a place of this size. Shallow fireplaces were built in the area, with a small windscreen of pebbles and sand to protect the fire from drafts. Scorched earth and scatters of broken and burned bones mark these hearths in the sand. Artifacts and food debris concentrate around the fireplaces, decreasing in density away from the hearth.

Food remains in the form of discarded bones document a diet that included red deer (similar to the North American elk), an extinct species of elephant, rhinoceros, ibex (mountain goat), wild boar, and wild cattle. Many of the animals represented in this group were juveniles, which perhaps were easier to hunt. In addition, foods were collected from the sea; fish bones and burned shells from oysters, mussels, and lim-

pets were found in the remains at Terra Amata.

The stone artifacts here were often simple pebble tools, but a few crude hand-axes and cleavers were being used as well. The stone tools belong to the early Acheulean (see "The Acheulean Hand-axe," p. 92). Most of the artifacts were made from materials available on the beach, but some of the stone came from distances of 25 km (15 mi) or more inland. In some places, waste materials from toolmaking can be seen clustered around a small, empty area, as though an individual sat making tools as the debris accumulated around him.

Reevaluation of evidence is always important in archaeology. De Lumley originally stated that there were large huts constructed at the site, based on the presence of postholes and the distribution of artifacts. But more recent studies indicate that the evidence for a structure at Terra Amata is very weak. De Lumley also suggested that there were several repeated visits to the site, represented in the different beach layers at Terra Amata. Analysis of the location of the individual pieces of stone and bone that fit together by Paola Villa, of the University of Colorado, is

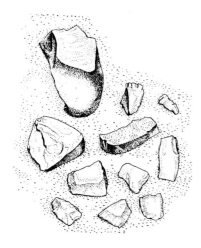

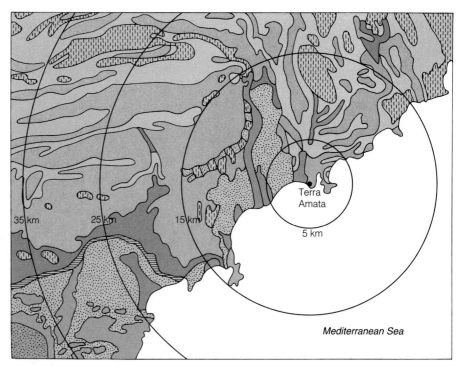

A geological map of the area around Terra Amata. The stone for the artifacts found at the site came from several different sources up to 25 km away. (The shadings and patterns represent different rock types.) Clearly these Acheulean hunter-gatherers were carrying raw materials some distance.

Refitted stone artifacts. Flakes from the same original nodule at Terra Amata have been refitted by archaeologists to study manufacturing techniques and the object of the toolmaking activity.

very informative. The distribution of these refitted pieces indicates that they were recovered from different layers over vertical distances of 30 cm (1 ft) or more. Thus, many of the levels originally distinguished at Terra Amata may not actually have been distinct initially but perhaps formed as later features at the site. The superimposed living floors that de Lumley suggested cannot be confirmed.

In spite of these cautions, Terra Amata remains one of the most important Paleolithic sites in the world. It is clear that early Europeans camped at this spot on the beach and ate a variety of food from both the land and the sea, exploiting the rich resources of the Mediterranean shoreline. Unfortunately, most of the shorelines of the Paleolithic period are today submerged beneath the sea, and we are unable to study the coastal settlements of this period.

While the Pleistocene witnessed the evolution of a number of modern mammals (e.g., elephants, horses, and cattle), many other animals that existed then are now gone. Woolly mammoths and rhinoceros, cave bears and lions and hyenas, giant deer and beavers, bison and aurochs (wild cattle) roamed over much of Europe during the colder periods of the Pleistocene. The bones of these animals from archaeological sites give some indication of the kinds of species that were present in different parts of Europe. These species were generally much larger than their modern equivalents and are now extinct.

The cave lion and cave bear are generally well known because of the large number of bones that have been found in caves. The cave bear was enormous, at least the size of a modern Alaskan grizzly, with a very large head and huge canine teeth. The cave bear ranged over much of Europe, and many of this creature's bones have been found in caves at high elevations in the Alps. Tight crevices in the caves had been polished by the passage of bears over tens of thousands of years. Thousands of skeletons of cave bears that died during hibernation have been preserved. The Drachenhöhle in Austria is estimated to have contained the remains of over 30,000 bears.

The woolly mammoth is also well known, both from the skeletal material that has been found and from a few examples of almost complete animals—soft parts, skin, and hair—found frozen in the permafrost of Siberia and Alaska. In Alaska, mammoth hairs still frozen in the ground sometimes clog the equipment of gold miners. This animal had a huge domed head, enormous curved ivory tusks, and humped shoulders. Standing approximately 3–4 m (10–13 ft) at the shoulder, its body was covered with a short, woolly undercoat and long, hairy overcoat. The mammoth inhabited arctic steppe environments and consumed a diet of tundra grasses. This species ranged from western Europe across

Notable among the mammals found in Pleistocene North America were beavers the size of a small bear, woolly mammoths, mastodons, sloths, saber-toothed tigers, bison, and horses. All of these species are now extinct.

(continued)

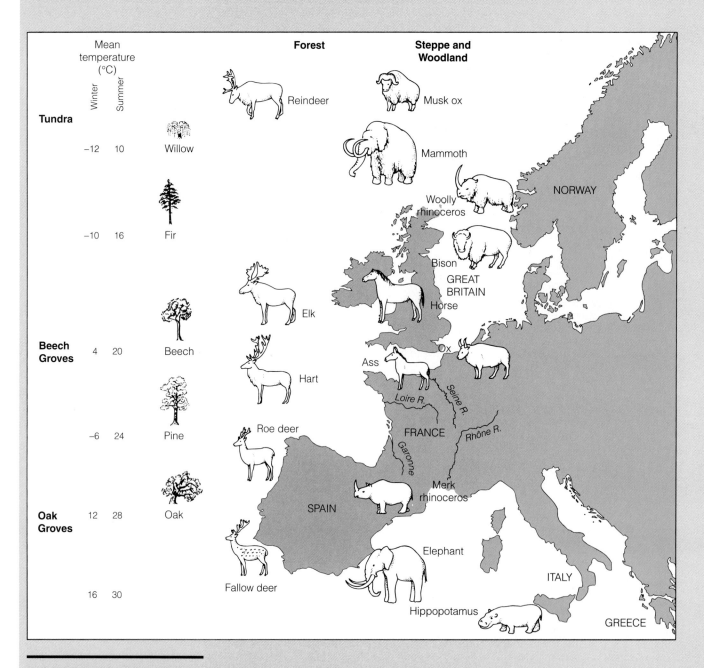

	Mean temperature (°C)			Forest	Steppe and Woodland
	Winter	Summer			
Tundra				Reindeer	Musk ox
	−12	10	Willow		Mammoth
	−10	16	Fir		Woolly rhinoceros
					Bison
				Elk	Horse
Beech Groves	4	20	Beech	Hart	Ox
	−6	24	Pine	Roe deer	Ass
Oak Groves	12	28	Oak		Merk rhinoceros
	16	30		Fallow deer	Elephant
					Hippopotamus

Some of the Pleistocene mammals of Europe, from arctic species in the north to subtropical species in the south. The plants and animals present at any one time would have depended on climatic conditions.

northern Asia and into North America during the late Pleistocene.

The giant Irish deer, from the bogs of Ireland and northern Europe, was known for the enormous antlers it carried, as much as 4 m (13 ft) across. This animal was about the size of a North American moose, but it more closely resembled an elk. Wild cattle, known as aurochs, were common game animals during the warmer periods of the Pleis-

tocene. These animals were probably adapted to grasslands and open woodlands and were particularly common in the early Postglacial.

A number of these species disappeared around the end of the Pleistocene; mammoths, cave bears, and many large species were extinct by 10,000 B.C. (see "Pleistocene Extinction," Chapter 4, p. 154). The last aurochs died in a game forest in Poland in A.D. 1627. The giant

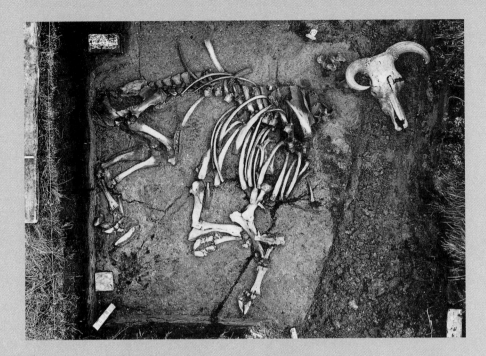

Excavation of a large bull aurochs skeleton at Prejlerup in eastern Denmark. This animal escaped from its hunters but died from its wounds.

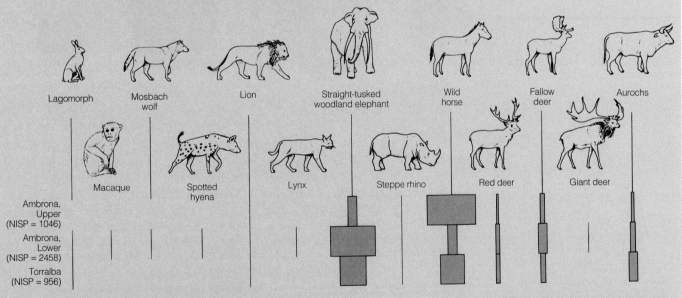

Lagomorph

Mosbach wolf

Lion

Straight-tusked woodland elephant

Wild horse

Fallow deer

Aurochs

Macaque

Spotted hyena

Lynx

Steppe rhino

Red deer

Giant deer

Ambrona, Upper (NISP = 1046)

Ambrona, Lower (NISP = 2458)

Torralba (NISP = 956)

Irish deer may have survived around the Black Sea until 3000–2000 years ago, long after it had disappeared from the European continent. The large-headed Prezwalski horse, depicted in Paleolithic cave paintings, still exists, in several European zoos. Other important Pleistocene species, such as reindeer, red deer, elk, musk ox, and brown bear, have survived to the present and continue to exist at the margins of civilization.

Species of animals represented by the bones at the Spanish Lower Paleolithic sites of Torralba and Ambrona. The width of the bar for each site and level indicates the abundance of the species. Elephants and horses are by far the most common at these sites. NISP stands for the number of identifiable bones per species.

Kalambo Falls and Olorgesailie

East Africa 200,000 years ago

Preserved nutshells and seeds from the occupation layer at Kalambo Falls, illustrating the importance of plant foods during the Paleolithic.

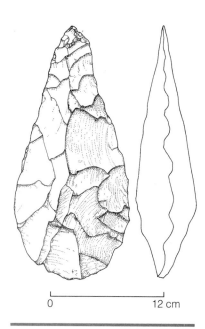

0   12 cm

Upper Acheulean handaxe from Kalambo Falls shown in front view and cross section.

The Kalambo River flows peacefully through the plateau country of East Africa, until its waters suddenly leap over the edge of the East African Rift Valley at the border of Tanzania and Zambia. There, the river falls over 250 m (800 ft) into a spectacular gorge close to the present shore of Lake Tanganyika. Deposits in the valley above the falls have provided one of the longest archaeological sequences anywhere in East Africa—or the world, for that matter. Over 200,000 years of successive human occupations are preserved in the water-lain deposits from the floods and backwaters of the river.

The site of Kalambo Falls was first discovered in 1953 by Desmond Clark, of the University of California, Berkeley, while he was examining a steeply eroded bank of the river. Preserved tree trunks and branches were present in the layers at the bottom of the bank, along with

handaxes and cleavers of the Acheulean tradition in almost fresh condition. This lowest level, designated Bed I, is over 3 m (10 ft) thick and composed of alternating layers of white sand and dark clay.

Kalambo Falls is a very unusual site for two reasons. First, evidence for the use and consumption of plants is preserved at this early site, and second, evidence for meat-eating in the form of animal bones is not represented. The acidic sediments at the Kalambo site removed all traces of bone, but the waterlogged condition of the lower layers allowed the preservation of a variety of plant materials. Bed I contains several living floors from the late Acheulean period, along with a remarkable set of plant materials, including leaves, nuts, seeds, and fruits, and some of the oldest wooden objects in the world. A club, a smoothed and pointed piece, and other wooden objects shaped by human hands were recovered

Acheulean handaxes, cleavers, and other artifacts on the ground at Olorgesailie.

Wooden artifacts, including a club (left) and a sharpened object (right) from Kalambo Falls.

from the lowest Acheulean layers. Evidence for fire is also preserved in charred logs found on the living floors.

In contrast to Kalambo Falls, the site of Olorgesailie (o-lorg-a-sigh′lee) in Kenya documents meat-eating in the Acheulean of Africa. The site was located along a sandy streambed at the edge of a former lake and contained over 400 handaxes and numerous animal bones. Much of the stone raw material for the handaxes came from nearby Mount Olorgesailie. Over a ton of lithic material was transported to the site, testimony to the importance of stone tools for these Acheulean groups.

Bone preservation was exceptionally good at Olorgesailie. Most of the animal bones come from at least 65 individuals of an extinct species of very large baboon, known as *Theropithecus*. All the skeletal elements of the baboons were represented, both large and small bones. There is strong evidence for one or more episodes of humans hunting baboons along the tree-lined stream banks at Olorgesailie. The two sites of Kalambo Falls and Olorgesailie together document the importance of both plants and animals in the diet of *Homo erectus*.

THE ACHEULEAN HANDAXE

The Swiss Army knife of the Lower Paleolithic

The evolution of the handaxe, from simple pebble tool forms through the removal of the sides and surface of the pebble. The elongated, teardrop shape is characteristic of the handaxe, giving the artifact one pointed end and one broad end.   (Used with permission from François Bordes, 1968, *The Old Stone Age.* Courtesy of McGraw-Hill Book Company.)

While pebble tools do have a cutting edge, they are extremely simple and unwieldly. These basic tools did change, evolve, and improve over time as early hominids began to remove more and more flakes from the core of raw material, reshaping it and creating longer, straighter edges for cutting. When such a core tool assumes a distinctive teardrop shape—pointed at one end, rounded at the other, retouched all over to a desired size, shape, and heft—it is known as a **handaxe,** the signature tool of *Homo erectus* and early *Homo sapiens.* The name comes originally from the French phrase *coup de poing,* an axe wielded in the hand. But the handaxe is truly an all-purpose piece of equipment that was used for cutting meat, sawing, digging, bashing, and boring large holes, among other things.

The handaxe is, in fact, a more complex tool than it first appears. The form is a shape inside a piece of stone and in the mind of the maker; a cobble must be completely modified in order for the handaxe to emerge. Moreover, the handaxe is symmetrical in outline, reflecting purpose, skill, and foresight in manufacture. Handaxes are often made from small cobbles 10–15 cm (4–6 in) long. A number of much larger examples, however, also exist, up to 30 cm (1 ft) or more in length. The oldest Acheulean handaxes are known from the site of Konso-Gardula in southern Ethiopia and date to 1.9 m.y.a., in association with early *Homo erectus.*

The 700,000-year-old site of Kilombe in Kenya contains a fascinating collection of handaxes. Here, hundreds of handaxes were discovered eroding out of the same geological layer. Remarkably, most of the handaxes are very similar in size and shape. Stone artifacts are made by a process of **reduction,** the removal of flakes from a core, and errors or mistakes cannot be erased. Nevertheless, the symmetry and relationship between length and width of the handaxes from Kilombe is striking. Small and large implements have the same length-to-width ratio, indicating the importance of the mental image the makers had of what a handaxe should look like. The handaxes from Kilombe also document the skill the makers had in producing that image in stone.

Handaxes and associated tools are referred to as **Acheulean** artifacts, after the original find location at St. Acheul in northern France. Floods of meltwater at the end of each glacial period downcut the rivers of western Europe, creating a series of terraces in the river valleys. On these terraces during the nineteenth century, near the towns of Abbeville and St. Acheul, prehistorians collected these signature tools of the Lower Paleolithic. Objects on the higher, older terraces were crude handaxes, with irregular edges and heavy flake scars on their surface. Acheulean handaxes from the lower, younger terraces were more symmetrical with straighter edges. A stone-on-stone method, or **hard hammer technique,** was used to make the more irregular tools of the early Acheulean. A **soft hammer technique** was used in making the younger, more regular handaxes. Mallets of bone, antler, or even wood can be used to remove flakes from stone. Lighter, soft hammers are easier to control, and the flakes that are removed are both thinner and wider.

Acheulean assemblages include both handaxes and a variety of other tools, heavy-duty pieces and smaller ones. **Cleavers,** handaxes with a broad, rather than pointed, leading edge, are also quite distinctive of the period. Other artifacts include a variety of flake tools such as scrapers, **burins** (stone tools used for gouging or engraving), and borers.

Fifty years ago, Harvard archaeologist Hallam Movius described the distribution of handaxes as limited to Africa, the southern two-thirds of Europe, and western Asia. More recent research, however, has expanded the known distribution of these tools; handaxes are now known from most of Africa, Asia, and Europe.

The term **Clactonian** refers to the nonhandaxe assemblages of the Lower Paleolithic. These assemblages represent an evolved Oldowan series of artifacts, including simple pebble tools and flakes. The term is taken from the site of Clacton-on-Sea in England where this distinctive set of tools, with heavy choppers, notches, and denticulates (saw-toothed), but lacking handaxes, was found during the nineteenth century. Flake tools in these assemblages are generally blocky and irregular in shape. Clactonian assemblages lack the regularly shaped core and flake artifacts of the Acheulean. Clactonian tools appear to have been made quickly for special tasks.

The distinction between handaxe and nonhandaxe assemblages is of considerable interest to prehistorians, and its significance is still not clear. Mary Leakey has found both kinds of assemblages, with and without handaxes, in the same levels of Bed II at Olduvai Gorge, suggesting that the differences in the assemblages are more likely due to the activities performed, rather than change through time. Research in England has documented the contemporaneity of both Clactonian and Acheulean assemblages, so their differences do not seem to be related to one assemblage being later than the other. Some researchers have suggested that the differences between Clactonian and Acheulean were the result of the availability of raw material, handaxes being made only where good raw material could be found nearby. Nevertheless, the presence of both kinds of assemblages at Olduvai does not support such an interpretation. The actual reason for the presence or absence of handaxes on sites of the Lower Paleolithic has not been determined.

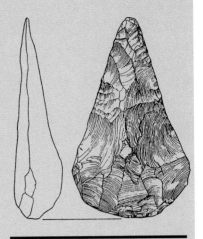

An Acheulean handaxe.

Man is a tool-using animal . . . without tools he is nothing, with tools he is all.
Thomas Carlyle (1795–1881)

SUMMARY

THE END OF THE
LOWER PALEOLITHIC

Homo erectus *in the Old World*

Homo erectus appeared shortly after the beginning of the Pleistocene, around 2 million years ago. *Homo erectus* invented the handaxe and other tools, controlled fire, spread the human lineage outside of Africa for the first time, to many parts of Asia and Europe, and appears to have thrived during this time. This is all the more remarkable because the Pleistocene was a very difficult and challenging period, with major changes in climate, environment, sea level, and the basic conditions of human life.

It is essential to understand that during this time our ancestors began to exert their influence on their environment. Clearly, the spread of early humans out of Africa was one of the most important developments in human prehistory. Following the initial appearance in southern and eastern Africa, the human species gradually increased in number and inhabited most of the more hospitable zones of the African continent. Population continued to expand, as did the geographic range of the species, and, after almost 3 million years in Africa, groups of early humans began to move north toward Asia and Europe.

The move out of the tropics demanded solutions to new problems in northern regions, especially the cold weather and a shortage of edible plants. Populations that survived easily in warm climates where roots, seeds, and nuts were often available had to find new and improved ways to stay warm and obtain enough food. An efficient cooling system for the tropics, sweat glands were of little help to furless humans in the temperate reaches of the Old World. Almost certainly, fire, shelter, and clothing—if only in the form of animal skins wrapped around the body—were used by *Homo erectus* in the course of their movement into the northern continents of Asia and Europe.

Fire must have been a major factor in the increasing success of human adaptation and the expansion into new, colder habitats. Fire is used for light, warmth, protection, and cooking. Cooking with fire provides a number of advantages in addition to making food more tender and palatable. Cooking improves the digestibility of many foods and destroys harmful toxins and microorganisms. Boiling removes juices and fats from plants and animals that are otherwise inedible. For *Homo erectus,* cooking probably made it possible to add new foods to the diet. The use of marine resources also expanded the diet of some *H. erectus* groups, as the fish and shellfish evidence from Terra Amata documents. The seas are a very rich source for food, and one that must have been exploited in the Lower Paleolithic.

Longer, colder winters in more northern latitudes also put a premium on successful predation. Meat was the primary source of sustenance during winter when roots, nuts, leaves, and other edible plants were not available. Hunting became essential to the human way of life in colder climates. Three spears found recently in Germany have been dated to 400,000 years ago. The spears, made of spruce wood, have carved points and a length of 2.0–2.5 m (6.0–7.5 ft) and appear to have been designed for throwing. In addition, a spear wound has been found in the shoulder blade of a

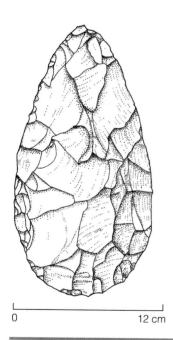

0   12 cm

Upper Acheulean handaxe from Kalambo Falls.

woolly rhino, dated to 500,000 years ago. Such evidence indicates that the early Europeans were hunting large game.

It was highly unlikely that females with infants and young children could successfully hunt regularly to provide their own food. By this point in time, a viable relationship between males and females, incorporating food-sharing as part of pair-bonding, necessarily emerged to ensure the continuance of the human lineage. Relationships between males and females and basic family structure must be related to these essential, adaptive changes. These connections—individual to individual, male to female, parents to offspring, kin to kin, group to group—are links in the chain of human society and survival.

The **sexual division of labor** exemplifies the cooperative relationship between the sexes. Roles for males, faster and larger, as hunters and for females, with young children, as gatherers of wild plant foods emerge as an efficient, synergistic pattern for the maximization of biological capabilities. Sex, and maybe love, bonded males and females for food-sharing and reproduction; maternal instincts and extended childhoods bonded mothers to children and siblings to one another. We have no information on the precise nature of prehistoric male-female relationships—whether monogamous, several females to one male, or several males to one female. But the present universality of the human family suggests a substantial length of time for this basic unit of society.

Almost certainly, some form of protofamily emerged among *Homo erectus* populations. Pair-bonding may have helped ensure the survival of offspring, as males began to recognize individual children as their own. The incest taboo, another human universal, may well have arisen at the same point in time to promote and solidify relationships beyond the group. Marriage or mating outside the family ensures alliances with other families and groups, reducing the potential for conflict. *Homo erectus,* as a creature of the Pleistocene, was a very successful member of our lineage, expanding out of Africa, taking the human species into Asia and Europe, and setting the stage for the next step in human evolution.

The sharp end of a wooden spear from Clacton, England.

SUGGESTED READINGS

Gamble, C. 1999. *The Palaeolithic societies of Europe.* Cambridge: Cambridge University Press. *A summary of the European Paleolithic, including the first inhabitants.*

Howells, W. W. 1980. *Homo erectus—who, when, and where: A survey. Yearbook of Physical Anthropology* 23:1–23. *A discussion of the anatomy and characteristics of* Homo erectus.

Klein, R. 1999. *The human career.* 2d ed. Chicago: University of Chicago Press. *Probably the most authoritative volume on the evolution of biology and culture in the Pleistocene.*

Pfeiffer, J. 1978. *The emergence of humankind.* New York: Harper & Row. *A popular and very readable account of human and cultural evolution in the Paleolithic.*

Sutliffe, A. J. 1985. *On the track of Ice Age mammals.* Cambridge: Harvard University Press. *A detailed study of the mammals of the Pleistocene.*

Tattersall, I. 1995. *The fossil trail.* Oxford: Oxford University Press. *How we know what we think we know about human evolution.*

4

THE HUNTERS

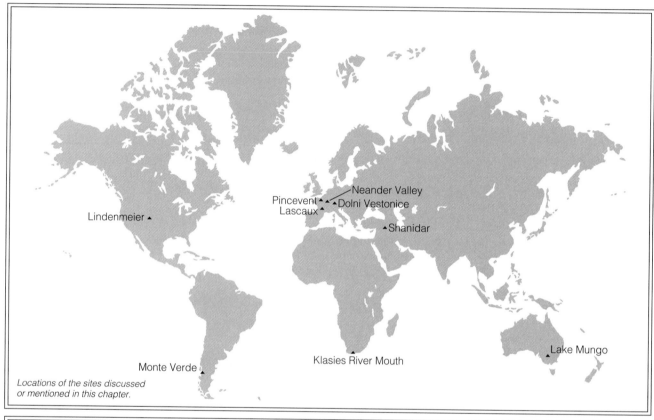

Lindenmeier ▲

Pincevent ▲ ▲ Neander Valley
Lascaux ▲ ▲ Dolni Vestonice
▲ Shanidar

Monte Verde ▲

Klasies River Mouth ▲

Lake Mungo ▲

*Locations of the sites discussed
or mentioned in this chapter.*

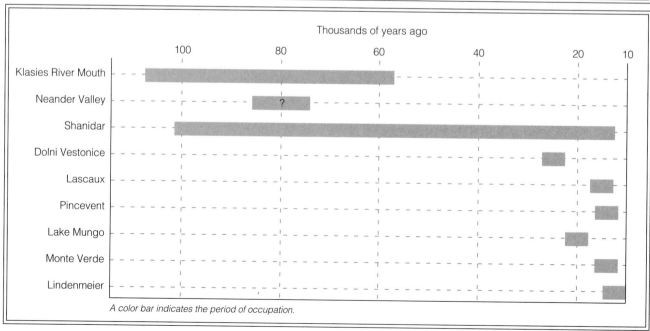

Thousands of years ago

| | 100 | 80 | 60 | 40 | 20 | 10 |

Klasies River Mouth

Neander Valley — ?

Shanidar

Dolni Vestonice

Lascaux

Pincevent

Lake Mungo

Monte Verde

Lindenmeier

A color bar indicates the period of occupation.

THE RISE OF *HOMO SAPIENS*

*Modern humans take the stage
toward the end of the Pleistocene*

Major changes in human biology and culture took place toward the end of the Pleistocene. For the first time, our human ancestors began to exhibit behaviors that were more than just practical activities, beyond the basic necessities for survival. In the Middle Paleolithic, these behaviors included burial of the dead, ritual hunting, cannibalism, and nurturing of the weak and elderly. By the end of the Pleistocene during the Upper Paleolithic, fully modern humans (*Homo sapiens sapiens*), biologically indistinguishable from ourselves, had discovered art, invented many new tools, made tailored clothing, and expanded to almost all parts of the world.

The evolution of *Homo sapiens* is one of the more intriguing questions of the later Pleistocene. As we have seen, *Homo erectus* was the first early human form found outside Africa. Around 700,000 years ago, only *H. erectus* fossils are known; by 100,000 years ago, only *H. sapiens* were present. *Erectus* became *sapiens* sometime during that period. The earlier *Homo sapiens* are usually referred to as Archaic, whereas more recent *Homo sapiens sapiens* are called fully modern humans (FMH).

The earliest fully modern humans are known from several places in South Africa, including the Klasies River Mouth Caves around 100,000 years ago. Europe and western Asia at this time were occupied by another, specialized form known as *Homo sapiens neanderthalensis*. Conventional wisdom today generally regards the Neanderthals as a rather specialized form that evolved from *Homo erectus* in the colder, more isolated areas of Europe before 200,000 years ago.

Beginning around 50,000 years ago, fully modern humans replaced Neanderthals in western Asia and then Europe. The mechanism for this replacement is the subject of vigorous debate among archaeologists and physical anthropologists. The major question is whether fully modern humans evolved only in Africa and spread from there across Asia and Europe, or whether they evolved in many places by the flow of genetic material between various human populations. These two competing explanations are known as the Out of Africa theory and the Multiregional theory. Different lines of evidence, from genetics and from the human fossils themselves, can be used to evaluate these theories. Genetic evidence relies on mutation rates in individuals with slightly different DNA to estimate how long ago a common ancestor existed. Such estimates indicate 200,000–140,000 years ago as the date for a common ancestor for *Homo sapiens sapiens* and point to Africa as the place of origin (see "Modern and Ancient DNA," p. 106).

The earliest fossil evidence also comes from Africa. A few bones from Klasies River and another site called Border Cave in South Africa indicate that anatomically modern humans were present in southern Africa before 100,000 years ago. These are the earliest known fully modern *Homo sapiens sapiens*, indicating that the time and place predicted by the genetic evidence may not be far off. From both genetic and fossil evidence, it seems very likely that fully modern humans appeared initially in Africa, sometime before 100,000 years ago.

These expanding groups of modern humans brought with them a number of remarkable innovations in human culture. Human culture, in fact, changed more

CONTENTS

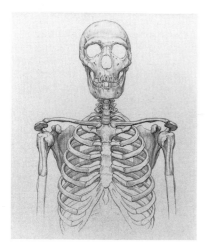

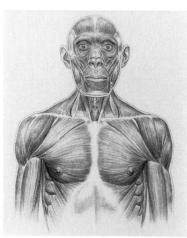

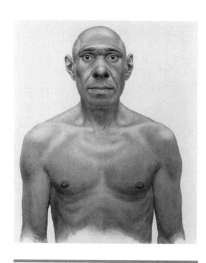

A reconstruction of the facial tissue of a Neanderthal skull. A few forensic scientists have studied the attachment of soft tissue to the bones of the face and skull and are able to reconstruct a likeness of the individual. Such skills have been applied to a Neanderthal with the result shown here. Body hair was not added to the reconstruction, with the exception of the eyebrows.

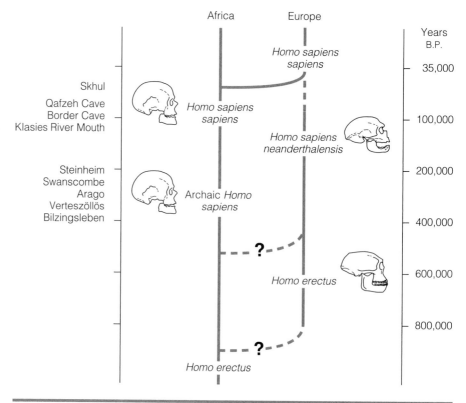

Human evolution in the Middle Pleistocene, 800,000–35,000 years ago. Current evidence suggests that *Homo erectus* expanded out of Africa into Asia sometime after 2 m.y.a. Archaic *Homo sapiens* emerged sometime after 700,000 years ago. Fully modern human forms of *Homo sapiens sapiens* began to appear sometime after 200,000 years ago, again in Africa, moving to the Near East after 100,000 years ago and replacing the Neanderthals in Europe after 40,000 years ago.

during the period shortly after 50,000 years ago than it had during the previous several million years. Richard Klein, of Stanford University, has listed some of the innovations that mark this time: great diversity and specialization in artifacts; the shaping of new materials such as bone, wood, shell, and ivory into tools; the transport or exchange of raw materials such as flint over long distances; and the first art. In Europe, this period of time is known as the Upper Paleolithic. At approximately the same time, modern-looking humans spread into Australia and New Guinea (around 40,000 years ago) and into North and South America (sometime after 15,000 years ago). Klein, and others, have suggested that these innovations represent a major change in the organization of the human brain, an advance that may be related to the emergence of complex language skills (see "The Origins of Language," p. 100).

This chapter tells the story of the Neanderthals and the appearance, expansion, and spread of *Homo sapiens* to virtually all parts of the world, as evidenced at sites such as Klasies River Mouth in South Africa, the Neander Valley in Germany, Shanidar in northern Iraq, Dolni Vestonice in the Czech Republic, and Lascaux and Pincevent in France. The evidence from Lake Mungo in Australia, and from Monte Verde in Chile and Lindenmeier in the Americas, documents the movement of humans to Australia and the New World during the last 40,000 years. (A useful distinction is made between the Old World—Africa, Asia, and Europe—and the New World of North and South America. The New World is considered new because it was discovered by Europeans at a relatively late date.)

The Pleistocene and the Paleolithic came to an end some 10,000 years ago. The glaciers retreated and warmer temperatures prevailed, and the present epoch began. The Paleolithic closed as the human species on six continents began to adapt to the warmer conditions of the Postglacial.

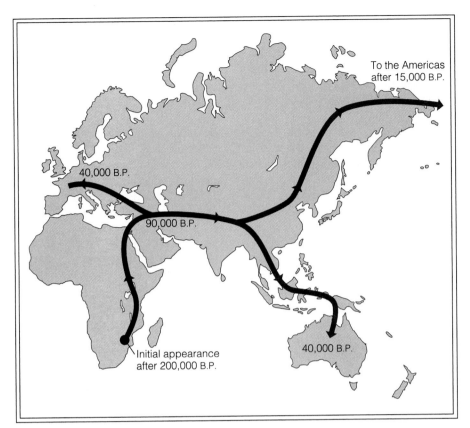

(a)

The two major competing theories about the evolution of fully modern *Homo sapiens*. (a) The Out of Africa theory involves the evolution of *H. sapiens* from *H. erectus* in Africa and the spread of that species. (b) The Multiregional theory argues that *H. sapiens* evolved from *H. erectus* in several places and that interbreeding kept them similar. Most of the archaeological evidence supports the Out of Africa theory.

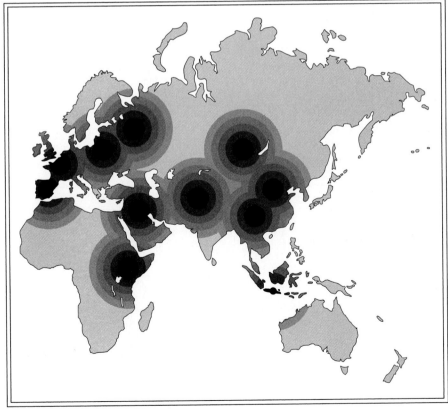

(b)

THE ORIGINS OF LANGUAGE

Why we first spoke may be more important than when

The origin of human speech and language is one of the most fascinating aspects of human adaptation and evolution, yet perhaps the most difficult to explain. Modern languages contain hundreds of thousands of words. Shakespeare's vocabulary is estimated to have been about 24,000 words; a newspaper reporter uses approximately 6000 words; the average person on the street has a speaking vocabulary of some 3000 words. We have a natural interest in when and where this ability to communicate with the spoken word originated.

Language did not appear suddenly at some point in the past without antecedents; it evolved gradually from the utterances and cries of early primates to its modern forms. On the one hand, the English language today is a huge complex of vocabulary, grammar, and structure, to which many new words are added each year. On the other hand, most animals make sounds that reflect involuntary reactions. Monkeys vocalize to express emotion but do not have voluntary control over vocalization; for one thing, they lack the vocal apparatus humans have. Chimpanzees, however, have a repertoire of 20 or more vocalizations and gestures for expressing their needs. Although these apes can manipulate symbols, they are unable to connect more than two or three concepts in a single phrase. To understand the evolution of language from gestures and cries to its complexity today, we must appreciate the path of its development.

Studies of the physical remains of early humans provide substantial information about language use by early hominids. Discovery of the hyoid bone in a Neanderthal burial from Kebara Cave in Israel showed that it was no different from our own. The **hyoid bone** holds the muscles of the tongue to the throat. The similarity between the hyoid bone in Neanderthal and in modern-looking *H. sapiens* suggests that speaking abilities would also have been similar.

An **endocast** is a copy or cast of the inside of a fossil skull, reflecting the general shape and arrangement of the brain and its various parts. Endocasts provide the only direct evidence of brain organization. The cerebrum, the upper portion of the brain, is primarily concerned with the complexities of behavior. This area is large and developed in higher primates. The size of the cerebrum, its convoluted surface, and the extent of wrinkling have increased over the course of evolution of the human species from our primate ancestors.

The organization of the cerebrum is critically important. In modern humans, the front of the brain is much larger than the back, and the sides of the brain are well developed, in contrast to chimpanzees and other apes. The two sides of our brain operate cooperatively to direct and control different aspects of our behavior and activities. This division in the organization and operation of the brain is called **lateralization.** One side of the brain controls language, while the other

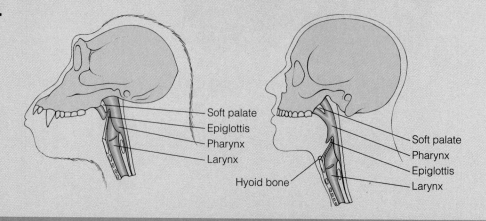

The vocal apparatus of a chimpanzee (left) compared to that of a modern human.

Soft palate
Epiglottis
Pharynx
Larynx

Soft palate
Pharynx
Epiglottis
Larynx

Hyoid bone

side regulates motor skills and perception. Lateralization is essential for language because the processing of word strings must occur in close proximity in the nerve cells of the brain. Individuals with speech problems are probably sequencing words and controlling speech from both sides of the brain.

Studies by Ralph Holloway, of Columbia University, have shown that the pattern of lateralization in fossil endocasts goes back well into the Pleistocene and probably to australopithecines as well. Dean Falk, of the State University of New York, has also been involved in the study of endocasts, pointing out that Broca's area, a brain area involved in the control of language, is larger in *Homo habilis* than in their contemporaries, the australopithecines from East Africa.

Research on human use of language has recently turned to the hypoglossal nerve, which controls the movement of the tongue. In humans this nerve is twice as thick as in chimpanzees. This thick nerve began to appear around 500,000 years ago with larger-brained members of the genus *Homo,* and it may be at this point when more sophisticated language became possible. Other fossil evidence indicates that the necessary mouth and throat anatomy was in place by at least 150,000 years ago, but it is still not clear when language emerged or whether the process was gradual or sudden.

Certainly many of the activities of our early Pleistocene ancestors would have required some form of communication. Food-sharing, social organization, and other distinctly human characteristics imply a system of verbal expression. These abilities must have evolved and expanded through time, as both brainpower permitted and need required.

One of the major unresolved issues in the development of language is the shift from a primitive language, like that of small children, to a syntactic one, with grammatical rules and structure. This development may be related in part to further changes in the human brain. Some linguists suggest that all the world's lan-

Endocasts from South African australopithecines. Notice the details of the blood vessels and other structures that have been preserved in the fossil casts.

guages evolved from a common "mother tongue," and a few would even suggest a date of 100,000 years ago for this common language. Needless to say, this is highly speculative, but it does suggest that future research may provide more information on the development of human languages. One of the more striking developments in human prehistory was the "creative explosion" that occurred about 50,000 years ago, around the beginning of the Upper Paleolithic. The changes of this period may well be related to significant advances in our language capabilities.

THE KLASIES RIVER MOUTH CAVES

One of the longest continuous sequences of human habitation in the world

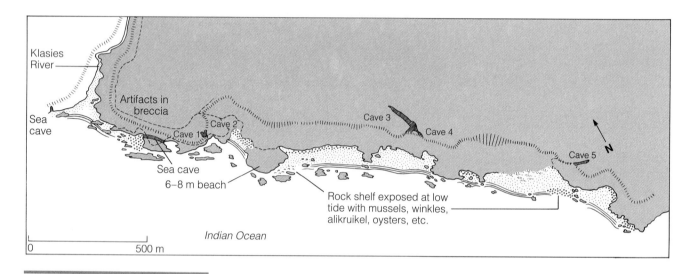

The Klasies River Mouth coastline with the location of caves, artifacts, and resources.

Caves 3 and 4 at Klasies River Mouth.

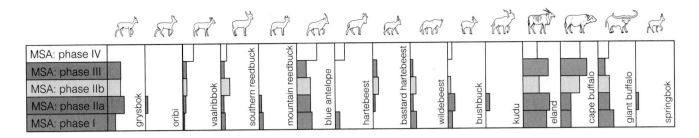

MSA: phase IV
MSA: phase III
MSA: phase IIb
MSA: phase IIa
MSA: phase I

grysbok · oribi · vaalribbok · southern reedbuck · mountain reedbuck · blue antelope · hartebeest · bastard hartebeest · wildebeest · bushbuck · kudu · eland · cape buffalo · giant buffalo · springbok

Changing utilization of species over time at Klasies River Mouth.

The sequence of layers and corresponding changes in the environment at Klasies River Mouth.

Age	Period	Deposits	Environment/Resources
10,000 B.P.	Later Stone Age	Sand with thin layers of silt and clay.	Seacoast 60 km distant. Some limpets.
	No archaeology		
70,000 B.P.	Middle Stone Age III	Shell middens and sand.	Cooler and wetter, drop in sea level. Shellfish (mussels, turbot). Open grasslands.
	Middle Stone Age IIb	Shell middens and sand.	
	Middle Stone Age IIa	Shell middens and sand; rubble and artifacts in cave.	Cooler. Increased forest and bush. Marine species: seals, birds, dolphins, whales, limpets.
120,000 B.P.	Middle Stone Age I	Shell middens and sand.	High sea level. Temperate. Mixed forest/grassland. Seals, dolphins, penguins, shellfish (limpets and mussels).

A series of caves cluster at the mouth of the Klasies (class'ease) River where it empties into the Indian Ocean in South Africa. The caves were originally cut by wave action against the high sandstone and shale cliffs in this area, at a time when sea level was higher than it is today. The caves and the sandy area in front of them were a hospitable place for human residence from 120,000 to about 60,000 years ago. Occupation was so heavy here that, in one of the caves, the accumulated debris had completely buried the opening of another, lower cave. The attractions of the site for repeated residence included the shelter of the caves; the moderate climate; the immediate availability of marine foods such as shellfish, seals, and even beached whales; the nearby fresh water; the access to large and small mammals living along the river; and good-quality stone for toolmaking.

The 60,000 years of deposits are 20 m (65 ft) deep (the height of a 6-story building) and span the entire Middle Stone Age (MSA) of southern Africa. (In Africa, the terms Early, Middle, and Late Stone Age are used to distinguish the archaeological divisions of the Paleolithic.) Although the deposits at the Klasies River are enormously deep, they accumulated at a rate of only 5–10 cm (2–4 in) every 100 years. Dating these deposits is difficult. The lower layers are beyond the range of radiocarbon dating, and other dating techniques have been employed, including oxygen isotope ratios (see "Climate and Environment in the Pleistocene," Chapter 2, p. 74). Geological cores removed from deep ocean sediments contain microscopic shells that can be measured for water temperature. It is thus possible to construct graphs of changing water temperature

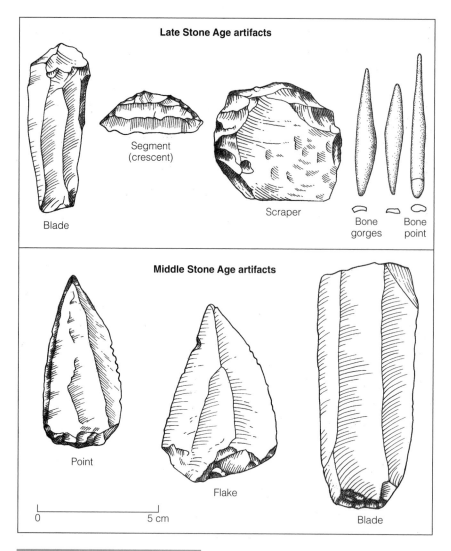

Late Stone Age artifacts

Blade

Segment (crescent)

Scraper

Bone gorges

Bone point

Middle Stone Age artifacts

Point

Flake

Blade

0   5 cm

Artifacts from the excavations at the Klasies River Mouth Caves. The Middle Stone Age assemblage is dominated by flake tools and was replaced by Late Stone Age materials in the upper levels at KRM. The Late Stone Age artifacts appear in association with fully modern humans after approximately 100,000 years B.P.

occupation layers and revealed a number of pieces of evidence of major importance for understanding Old World prehistory. Fully modern humans (*Homo sapiens sapiens*) appeared here earlier than anywhere else in the world. A handful of fossil fragments from KRM and other sites in South Africa indicate that modern-looking humans were present in this area by 100,000 years ago. The human remains from Klasies are fragmentary and show breakage, cutmarks, and burning that suggest cannibalism.

Evidence from animal bones, studied by Richard Klein, of Stanford University, documents a successful economy throughout the Middle Stone Age. A wide range of animal species is represented, and both large and small mammals were abundant. Porcupine, grysbok (a small antelope), eland (a large antelope), giant buffalo, rock hyrax (a small mammal), and the Cape fur seal were the most common. The site also records the early use of marine foods, evidenced by limpet and mollusk shells, and the bones of penguins and seals. The shells could have been collected all along the coast by wading at low tide. There are abundant carbonized organic remains in the deposits, and Deacon believes that these may represent roots and tubers that were collected and eaten by the inhabitants.

The faunal evidence from KRM can also be used to examine the hunting abilities of these Stone Age people in South Africa. Consider two possible patterns of death in a population of animals: (1) attritional, in which death is by natural causes, such as predation, disease, accident, and old age; and (2) catastrophic, in which a natural disaster, such as flood, epidemic, or mass hunting, simultaneously kills most of the members of the population. The catastrophic pattern would provide an almost complete picture of the ages and sexes of the living population, whereas an attritional pattern would be dominated by young and old animals, those more susceptible to predation and disease. Prime-age adults would be largely missing in the attritional pattern.

Comparison of the remains of two species of animals from KRM indicates that the eland, a large antelope, is repre-

extending hundreds of thousands of years into the past.

It is also possible to measure the oxygen isotope ratio in shells found in archaeological sites. The shells in stratigraphic layers from the Klasies River Mouth (KRM) Caves were measured and the results compared to the ocean sediment curve for which the age was already known. This correlation and other dating methods—including electron spin resonance, uranium disequilibrium, and amino acid dating—suggest that the age of the MSA deposits extend from 120,000 to 60,000 years ago.

Excavations over a number of years by Ronald Singer and John Wymer, of the University of Chicago, and Hilary Deacon, of the University of Stellenbosch in South Africa, have exposed the buried

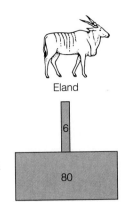
Eland

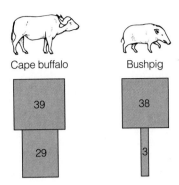
Cape buffalo

Bushpig

Nelson Bay Cave, LSA
(present interglacial
deposits)

6

39

38

Klasies River Mouth, MSA
(last interglacial
deposits)

80

29

3

sented by the catastrophic pattern, while the pattern for Cape buffalo is attritional. The eland is a relatively docile animal that can be driven into traps or falls by hunters, which probably explains the catastrophic death pattern. Cape buffalo are much more recalcitrant and dangerous. The high proportion of young in the pattern for the Cape buffalo was likely the result of selective hunting. Thus, animals that could be driven are represented by catastrophic death patterns, whereas more aggressive species were probably hunted individually with weapons. The higher number of elands at KRM, even though this species is much less common than the Cape buffalo in the environment, suggests that the MSA people were not particularly good hunters and that drives may have been more effective than stalking.

If we compare the remains of these two species from a younger site at nearby Nelson Bay Cave, dating to perhaps 10,000 years ago, the death pattern for the buffalo is the same, and eland remains are very rare. This pattern suggests that the later groups were better hunters than their counterparts at the KRM caves. The evidence is supported by the presence of bows and arrows at the time of the Nelson Bay Cave occupation.

On the other hand, Deacon believes that people of the Middle and the Late Stone Age were behaviorally similar, hunting smaller animals and both hunting and scavenging larger ones. Artifacts, hearths, bones, and shells are found in the oldest layers right next to the human skeletal remains dating to approximately 120,000 years ago. Shellfish, mostly brown mussel, were collected in quantity and shell middens accumulated. One of the shell middens is approximately 5 m (16 ft) high and is as extensive as any Late Stone Age (LSA) midden. This evidence is important because it shows regular shellfish collecting by the inhabitants and also patterned disposal of food refuse in localized heaps. This pattern suggests that people were living by the same rules for the use of space and cleanliness in both the Middle and Late Stone Age.

Deacon points out that the large mammal bones and shell middens are the most obvious food remains. Remains of plant foods appear as carbonized materials around the hearths and indicate that plant gathering was an important activity. It is this carbonized material that creates distinctive black horizons that are common features at the site. Deacon reports similar patterns of carbonized vegetation around the hearths of more recent inhabitants of South Africa. Deacon's perspective suggests that the general way of life in this area may not have changed from 100,000 years ago until the end of the Pleistocene.

MODERN AND ANCIENT DNA

Archaeology and genes

DNA (deoxyribonucleic acid) is the genetic material of all life. DNA is a long molecular chain of units called nucleotides, each composed of one of four base units (adenine, cytosine, guanine, or thymine). There are some 50,000 genes in the DNA of a human being. Genetic information is coded in a sequence of nucleotides in individual genes. Individual genes that determine the growth and characteristics of individuals are segments of DNA molecules. Molecules of DNA also have "intergenic" spaces between genes with no biological information that are important as markers for differences between individuals and between populations.

Two general kinds of studies, on either modern or ancient DNA, are being done to investigate the human past. Modern populations are studied to identify genetic differences and the time at which groups of people diverged in the past. These studies generally use DNA in blood or other cells. DNA studies of modern populations have been used to estimate the time of the first appearance of modern-looking humans and to examine the spread of Neolithic farmers into Europe, for example.

Evidence from genetic studies also provides some understanding on the point in time at which certain hominoids became hominids—when humans became a species distinct from an apelike ancestor. Biological scientists have developed a "molecular clock" that estimates the time at which different modern species separated from a common ancestor. The mechanism for this clock is change over time in the amino acids that make up DNA. Known as nucleotide substitutions, these changes are observed as mismatches in the genetic material of two species. The number of mismatches in the chromosomes of two species correlates closely with the evolutionary distance between the species.

Our closest relatives are the chimpanzee and gorilla. Comparison of amino acid sequences in humans, chimps, and gorillas indicates that the three species diverged between 5 and 4 million years ago—a date very close to that for the earliest fossil hominids. There is also intriguing modern genetic evidence regarding the evolution of *Homo sapiens sapiens*. This evidence comes from studies of **mitochondrial DNA** (mtDNA), genetic material that is assumed to mutate at a relatively rapid and constant rate. Because this type of DNA is inherited

Relative distances among various species in terms of nucleotide substitutions. The number of substitutions is shown at the bottom of the tree graph, and the estimated age of divergence between two species and their common ancestor is shown at the top.

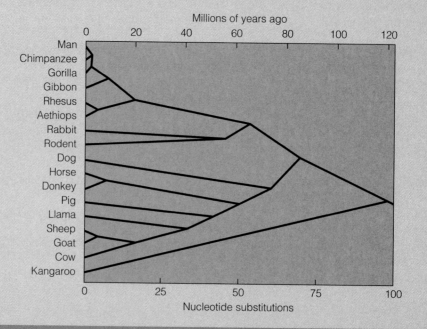

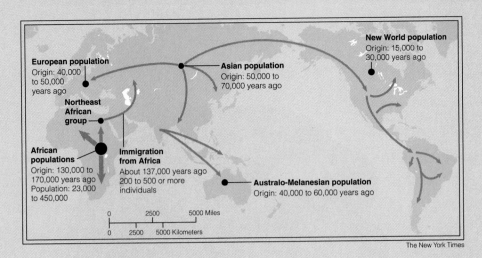

New World population
Origin: 15,000 to
30,000 years ago

European population
Origin: 40,000
to 50,000
years ago

Asian population
Origin: 50,000 to
70,000 years ago

Northeast
African
group

African
populations
Origin: 130,000 to
170,000 years ago
Population: 23,000
to 450,000

Immigration
from Africa
About 137,000 years ago
200 to 500 or more
individuals

Australo-Melanesian population
Origin: 40,000 to 60,000 years ago

0   2500   5000 Miles

0   2500   5000 Kilometers

The New York Times

Analysis of modern mitochrondrial DNA provides a map of the origin and expansion of modern humans from Africa across the continents of the Old and New World.

directly through the maternal line, it provides a continuous trail back into the past. Graphing mutations in mtDNA results in a tree with the oldest changes as the trunk and more recent mutations as the branches. The number of different mutations separating two individuals should be a function of how far back in time they shared a common maternal ancestor.

Analysis of this DNA from a number of women from around the world allows a map to be drawn of the spread of modern *Homo sapiens* after 200,000 years ago. Based on the number of accumulated mutations in the mtDNA, researchers concluded that *Homo sapiens* first appeared in southern Africa between 130,000 and 170,000 years ago. This is known as the "African Eve" hypothesis. Similar studies of the Y chromosome, present only in males, have indicated a similar date of divergence, around 200,000 years ago. These studies also suggest that modern humans moved out of Africa around 130,000 years ago, into Asia after 70,000 years ago, and into Europe after 50,000 years ago. Modern humans arrived in Australia after 60,000 years ago and came to the New World after 30,000 years ago.

The second kind of study involves **ancient DNA**, genetic material in the nucleus of cells extracted from archaeological plants and animals. Discovery of DNA preserved in prehistoric human

bone was first reported in 1989. Since that time, numerous studies have looked for and found DNA in ancient materials. Samples from human bone, for example, can provide information on sex or genealogy of an individual or on genetic relationships between populations and migration. In many cases, molecules in ancient DNA have been damaged by decay and degradation over time and are found often as short segments of the larger molecule. This breakdown of the molecule makes it more difficult, but not impossible, to reconstruct original genetic information.

Analysis of ancient DNA has been greatly improved by the development of the technique known as the polymerase chain reaction (PCR), which results in the cloning of large quantities of material for analysis even when only a very small sample is available—often the case with archaeological remains. Theoretically, even a single molecule, as well as badly degraded segments of molecules, can be analyzed with the help of the PCR technique.

Contamination is a significant problem. Since only small amounts of ancient DNA are present in samples, any contamination from living humans during excavation or laboratory analysis can mask or hide the prehistoric materials. Researchers must use great caution when removing and preparing samples for such analyses.

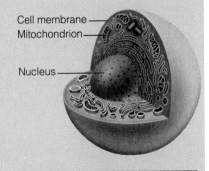

Cell membrane

Mitochondrion

Nucleus

DNA is found both in the nucleus (central ball) of cells and in floating structures known as mitochrondria.

THE VALLEY OF THE NEANDERTHALS

Close relatives with strange habits

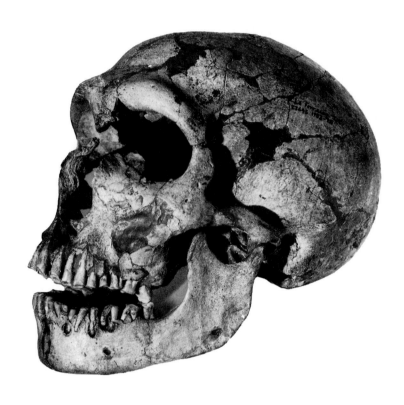

A classic Neanderthal skull from the site of La Ferrassie, France. Typical features include pronounced brow ridges above the eye orbits, a sloping forehead, and a generally robust appearance.

In 1856, 3 years before Charles Darwin published his extraordinary treatise *On the Origins of Species,* proposing natural selection as a mechanism for evolution, pieces of an unusual skeleton were unearthed in a limestone cave in the Valley of the Neander River, near Düsseldorf, Germany. Prior to this discovery, there had been no awareness of human forms earlier than *H. sapiens* and only limited awareness of a concept like human evolution. Leading authorities had described the bones from the Neander Valley as those of a deceased Prussian soldier, a victim of Noah's flood, or a congenital idiot—but definitely not an early human ancestor. Gradually, however, more examples of these individuals came to light. In 1886, at the cave of Spy (pronounced "spee") in Belgium, two similar skeletons were discovered in association with early stone tools and the bones of extinct animals, clearly proving the antiquity of humans in Europe.

In 1913, French physical anthropologist Marcellin Boule published a study of an arthritic Neanderthal skeleton from the site of La Chapelle-aux-Saints (see Color Plate 3). In this report, he described the finds from Europe as a new species, designated *Homo neanderthalensis.* Unfortunately, Boule did not acknowledge the discoveries of *Homo erectus* from Java and saw the Neanderthals as somewhere between ape and human. In Boule's own words (translated from French): "The brutish appearance of this muscular and clumsy body, and of the heavy-jawed skull, declares the predominance of a purely vegetative or bestial kind over the functions of the mind" (1913, p. 130). His work resulted in a

Table 4.1 Major Characteristics of Neanderthals Compared to Modern Humans

Trait	*Homo sapiens neanderthalensis*	*Homo sapiens sapiens*
Forehead	Sloping	Vertical
Brow ridges	Moderate	Absent
Face	Slightly forward	Below forehead; under cranium
Cranial capacity	1450 cc	1400 cc
Protrusion on back of skull	Present	Absent
Chin	Absent	Present
Appearance of skeleton	Robust	Gracile

view of Neanderthals as slow in wit, gait, and habit—an idea that continues in some quarters even today.

Gradually, however, as more *Homo erectus* and australopithecine specimens were reported and accepted into the family tree, Neanderthals have come to be recognized as closer to modern humans. Today they are classified as a member of our own genus and species but are usually distinguished at the subspecies level, as *Homo sapiens neanderthalensis*.

Neanderthals were short and stocky, averaging about 1.5 m (5 ft) in height, with bowed limbs and large joints supporting a powerful physique. Fossil skeletons of Neanderthals are recognized today by several distinctive features in the skull and teeth (Table 4.1). The cranium is relatively low, and the face is long. Prominent **brow ridges,** bony ridges above the eyes, and heavy bone structure give the skull a distinctive look. The average brain size of the Neanderthals is slightly larger than that of modern humans, probably a consequence of their generally heavier bone structure. A distinctive shelf or protrusion at the back of the Neanderthal skull is known as an **occipital bun.** The face is large, the forehead slopes sharply backward, and the nose and teeth sit farther forward than in any other hominid, giving the entire face an elongated appearance. This face is probably the result of a combination of factors, including adaptation to the cold.

The front teeth are often heavily worn, even the deciduous teeth of young children, suggesting that they were used for grasping or heavy chewing. Intrigu-

ing small scratches often occur on the front teeth, usually running diagonally. These marks are thought to be the result of "stuff-and-cut" eating habits, in which a piece of meat was grasped in the teeth and a stone knife was used to cut off a bite-size piece at the lips. Occasionally the knife must have slipped and scratched the enamel of the front teeth. Most of the scratches run from upper right to lower left, although about 10% are in the opposite direction. Such evidence confirms that right or left handedness among humans was common by this time.

The skeleton of the Neanderthals differs somewhat from that of fully modern

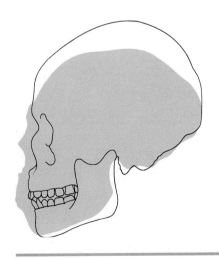

Differences between the skulls of Neanderthals and modern *Homo sapiens*. The bulging forehead, the presence of a chin, reduced brow ridges, and the absence of a large protrusion on the back of the skull, known as an occipital bun, characterize modern humans.

Typical flake tools from the European Mousterian.

forms, although they had the same posture, dexterity, and mobility. Neanderthal bones are generally described as robust; they had heavier limb bones than fully modern humans, suggesting much greater muscular strength and a more powerful grip. This strength also appears in the shoulder blades and neck, and on the back of the skull, where heavy muscle attachments are noticeable. Shoulder blade muscles would have provided the Neanderthals with strong, controlled downward movements for making stone tools or thrusting spears.

The robust appearance of the Neanderthals may be related to strength and endurance required for long-distance travel over irregular terrain or to climate. Study of the Neanderthal body indicates their shape is similar to that of the Eskimo, perhaps reflecting an adaptation to cold temperatures. Or perhaps Neanderthals had to be stronger to accomplish physically what later, fully modern humans accomplished with sophisticated tools. Neanderthal skeletons exhibit more traumatic damage, especially to the head and neck, from accident or violence than many modern populations, perhaps from close encounters with large game. The Neanderthals lived to their late thirties or mid-forties, a rather long lifespan in antiquity.

Neanderthal populations are generally associated with the manufacture of a variety of flake tools in groups of artifacts termed **Mousterian** (moose-teer′e-an) assemblages, after the site of Le Moustier in France. The Mousterian belongs to the Middle Paleolithic, approximately 120,000–40,000 years ago in Europe. Although handaxes continued to be made, large retouched flakes and **Levallois** pieces, from a technique for making thin flakes with a lot of cutting edge, are the major hallmarks of the period. Flakes are shaped into a variety of tools for more special purposes.

Neanderthal fossils and/or Mousterian assemblages are found primarily in Europe and western Asia. The Neanderthals were large-game hunters. Their prey varied across Europe; reindeer were hunted primarily in the west, and mammoths were hunted in eastern regions. Neanderthals were apparently an indigenous adaptation in Europe, well adapted to the cold conditions of the Pleistocene. However, an extremely cold period around 75,000 years ago may have pushed some Neanderthal populations southeast into the Near East and eastward into western Asia (see "The Fate of the Neanderthals," p. 118). The easternmost Mousterian sites are known from

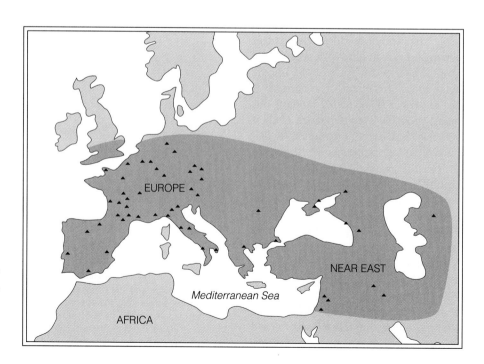

The distribution of *Homo sapiens neanderthalensis* and Mousterian sites in Europe and the Near East. *Homo sapiens sapiens* existed in most of the rest of Asia and Africa during this time.

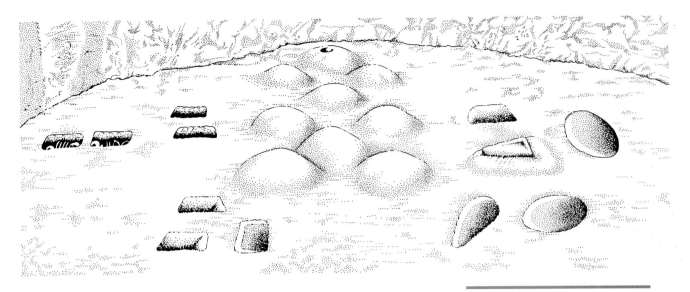

the Altai Mountains, around Lake Baikal and into western Mongolia.

Cultural innovations during this period include the first intentional burial of the dead in graves, sometimes accompanied by flowers, tools, or food. The presence of these materials in graves certainly implies concepts of death as sleep and life after death. Other more exotic practices emerge as well, difficult to understand or explain from our modern perspective. One of the most extraordinary of these is the intentional killing of cave bears, the enormous denizens of the rocky areas of Europe during the Pleistocene but now extinct. Trophy skulls and bones from these huge bears were placed in special niches and stone-lined crypts, in a fashion more elaborate than any human burial.

Finally, several examples of broken and burned human bones have been found among the remains of other animals in deposits belonging to the Middle Paleolithic period. At the cave of Krapina in Yugoslavia, the bones of at least 13 human individuals were found, along with those of various herbivores and other animals. The human bones had been burned, split to extract marrow, and treated like the bones of the animals that had provided meals for the occupants of this site. At the Grotte de l'Hortus in southwestern France, similar evidence of cannibalism was found. Heavily fragmented Neanderthal bones from at least 20 people were scattered among the numerous bones of small wild goats. Most of the human bones are skull and jaw fragments, and many of the individuals were over 50 years of age. Whether such practices were rituals of consecration of the dead, or the bones were simply individuals from enemy groups that were added to the larder, is not known. It has also been argued that the bones may have been accidentally burned and broken by later inhabitants at the site.

A reconstruction of a Neanderthal female.

Shanidar Cave

Evidence of the life and death of Neanderthals in northeastern Iraq

A common misconception has our Pleistocene ancestors as creatures of the cave, a view that has prevailed because much of the evidence from the later part of the Pleistocene comes from caves. Archaeological materials are well preserved in these places, but not necessarily because our ancestors were their constant residents. While the mouths and entrances of caves may have provided shelter for some groups, the inner recesses were almost certainly used only for special and short-term purposes.

Most of the early hominids' time was spent at open-air camps and settlements, along streams, rivers, lakes, and seas. Such places are vulnerable, however, to destruction—erosion, deep burial, underwater submergence—and many did not survive to the present. It is remarkable, in fact, that there are so many traces of the past remaining.

Caves, on the other hand, are excellent repositories for human debris. Deeply stratified deposits accumulate over millennia, incorporating all kinds of trash and food remains discarded by people living at their entrances and overhangs. The natural accumulation of sand and other sediments in caves is very slow, perhaps 1–5 cm (0.5–2.0 in) of deposits per 1000 years.

One of the most important prehistoric caves in the Near East was discovered and excavated by Ralph Solecki, of Texas A & M University. In 1951, Solecki joined an expedition to northern Iraq to help record ancient inscriptions on historic monuments dating to 800 B.C. But he was really interested in even older artifacts, particularly from the Paleolithic,

that might be found in this region. At the end of the expedition, Solecki stayed on to investigate a few caves in the area in search of an early site. One of these was the cave of Shanidar. Solecki wrote:

> My first reconnaissance of the cave left me with a very favorable impression. I spent no more than ten minutes there on the initial visit, making some rough measurements. . . . The next step was to make a test pit, or "sondage," in the earthen deposits of the cave. . . . I made some rough calculations of costs and estimated that it would take about $300 and a truck to do about a month of excavation at Shanidar Cave. I wondered about labor, since I did not see many men around the small village. But I was cheerful in the thought that at last we have found what looked like the ideal cave site. (1971, pp. 68–69)

The Zagros Mountains are a heavily folded series of sedimentary rocks that run from southwestern Iran to northeastern Iraq, dividing the high plateau of Iran from the arid stretches of Mesopotamia between the Tigris and Euphrates rivers. The northern end of the Zagros range in Iraq is rolling, rugged countryside, covered with *maqui* vegetation—scattered shrubs and dwarf oak—and tall poplars growing along the valley floors and flowing streams. In spring, the valley is colored by abundant wildflowers—red anemones and poppies, irises, grape hyacinth, and blue hollyhocks.

In this area, a number of caves and rockshelters lie at the boundary between harder and softer limestone formations. The cave of Shanidar, carved by nature into the softer limestone, is located 750 m

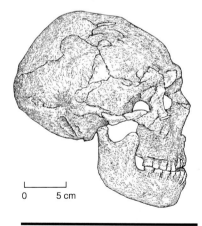

0   5 cm

A skull of *Homo sapiens neanderthalensis* from Shanidar Cave. This individual was probably killed by rocks falling from the roof of the cave.

A view of the excavations at Shanidar Cave. Excavations revealed 15 m of deposits from recent times back through deep Mousterian levels. The cave is still used today by Kurdish shepherds.

(2500 ft) above sea level, a 40-minute climb from the nearest road. The entrance to the large chamber is 8 m (25 ft) high and some 25 m (80 ft) wide. The floor of the chamber inside is about the size of four tennis courts, extending back about 110 m (350 ft). The distance from the flat earthen floor to the ceiling is roughly 14 m (35 ft), the equivalent of a three-story building. The ceiling of the cave is blackened by deep layers of soot from countless fires, interrupted by odd white spots where earthquakes have shaken off large blocks. The mouth faces south, and the morning sun reaches deep into the chamber. It is well protected from cold winter winds and has probably been occupied

off and on for the last 100,000 years or so. In recent times, Kurdish goat herders have spent the winter in a series of brush huts at the rear of Shanidar cave.

Over a series of field seasons from 1951 to 1960, Ralph and Rose Solecki explored the dry layers of Shanidar Cave. They expanded their original test trench in the center of the cave to roughly 6 m × 20 m (20 × 70 ft) and deepened it until they encountered bedrock at almost 15 m (50 ft) below the surface. It was like digging a five-level basement.

The excavations exposed four major layers of deposits in the cave, designated A–D. These materials accumulated at a rate of about 2 cm (1 in) per 100 years.

A cross-sectional view through the deposits at Shanidar Cave. The gray upper layers are recent, Neolithic, and Mesolithic deposits. The Upper Paleolithic levels (Layer C) make up the rest of the upper third of the layers, while the Mousterian makes up the bottom two-thirds of the deposits (Layer D). The triangles mark the locations of Neanderthal skeletal remains. The large chunks of rock are pieces of the roof that fell to the floor of the cave.

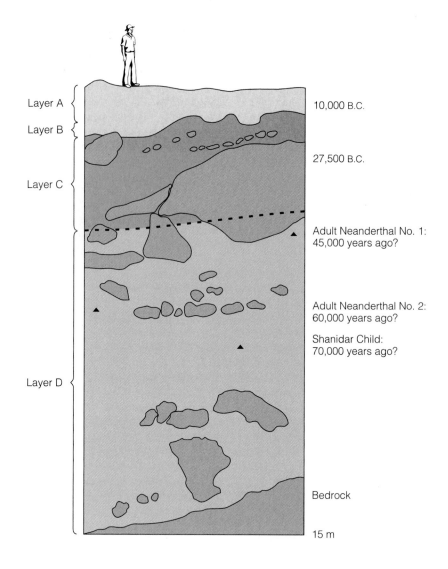

Layer A

Layer B

Layer C

Layer D

10,000 B.C.

27,500 B.C.

Adult Neanderthal No. 1:
45,000 years ago?

Adult Neanderthal No. 2:
60,000 years ago?

Shanidar Child:
70,000 years ago?

Bedrock

15 m

Layer A was the top 1.5 m (5 ft) of deposit, a black, greasy soil containing pottery, the bones of domestic animals, and grinding stones, going back from the present to the earliest farmers in the area, perhaps 7000 years ago. Layer B was made up of brown-stained sediments containing materials from the preceding period, 12,000–7000 years ago. In this layer, snail shells and the remains of a few wild animals represented the kinds of foods that were eaten. There is very little evidence of occupation in the cave during the next 17,000 years. A yellow soil with a group of massive boulders near the top, Layer C dates to 34,000–29,000 years ago. Solecki had to use dynamite to blast through the boulders and go deeper into the cave deposits. The boulders fell from the roof about 29,000

years ago, and this may be the reason the cave was not occupied for such a long period. Layer C contained stone and bone materials from the early part of the Upper Paleolithic period.

Layer D was the primary deposit in the cave, some 9 m (30 ft) of sediments dating to between 100,000 and 35,000 years ago, spanning the time of the Neanderthals and the Middle Paleolithic. Deep ash deposits in these levels testify to the large hearths that burned in the cave. The stone artifacts belong to the Mousterian and are similar in fashion to those from other sites in the Near East. The bones of wild goats, wild pigs, and tortoises are found throughout Layer D. The most important finds from this layer, however, are the skeletons of seven adults and two infants.

Several individuals in Shanidar died as a result of rocks falling from the ceiling of the cave. One of the skeletons, a 40-year-old male, had a withered humerus (upper arm bone), suggesting that his arm had been largely nonfunctional from birth. He also suffered from arthritis and was blind in one eye, probably the result of a blow to the left side of the head. This individual could not have been a successful hunter. Nevertheless, he survived with the help of the rest of the group. A second male was found somewhat lower in the layer, also crushed by falling rocks in the cave. Sometime after the rockfall, the companions of this individual returned, covered the spot with more stones, and built a large fire above his final resting place. A third male was also crushed by the collapse of the roof at another time. The ribs of this individual were scarred by a wooden spear of some kind, a wound received shortly before he died.

In another grave, four individuals were found, two females and an infant lying beneath a male. Detailed study of two of the skulls from Shanidar by Erik Trinkaus indicated that the backs of the heads were misshapen, perhaps from the use of some kind of cradling board in infancy.

The extraordinary density of pollen in the area of another burial raised the possibility that flowering plants had been placed in the grave inside the cave. Pollen from small, bright flowers that bloom in and around June—grape hyacinth, groundsel, and hollyhock—were present in abundance, along with branches from a coniferous shrub. Although the evidence is not strong, perhaps a kind of wreath was laid alongside the deceased before the grave was filled. Both compassion and aggression are thus well documented by the Neanderthal burials at Shanidar.

A skull of *Homo sapiens neanderthalensis* from Shanidar Cave. This individual was probably killed by rocks falling from the roof of the cave.

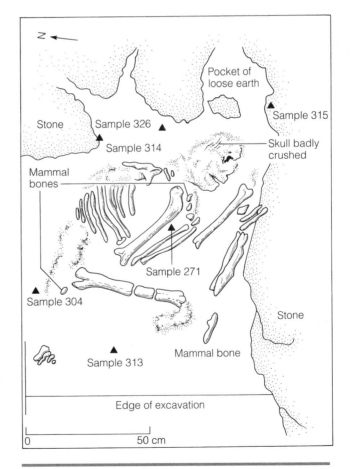

Burial IV from Shanidar, associated with large amounts of flower pollen. The drawing shows the position of the burial in the cave and the location of the pollen samples that were taken.

PALYNOLOGY

Clues to prehistoric vegetation

Although the vagaries of preservation normally remove the stems, flowers, and other bits and pieces of plants from archaeological sites, the pollen those plants produce is frequently preserved. Pollen grains are microscopic germ cells that many kinds of seed-bearing plants send into the air in order to fertilize a neighbor. Pollination by wind or insects is common in most trees, shrubs, grasses, and some flowering plants. Pollen "rain" is carried everywhere, as hay fever sufferers well know. Some types of pollen can be transported hundreds of kilometers and high up into the atmosphere. Tree pollen generally travels farther than the pollen of flowering plants.

Pollen grains are protected by a shell of material called sporopollenin, one of the most resistant substances in nature, impervious to water and soil acids. As long as sediments protect the pollen grains from oxidation, they may be preserved for thousands of years. Deposits in lakes and bogs often provide the best pollen records, but many types of sediments will preserve these grains. Pollen is also preserved in coal and has been found in rocks that are 500 million years old.

Pollen is produced in large quantities by plants and can be found in densities reaching several thousand grains per cubic centimeter of soil. Pollen grains are very specific in shape and size and can be identified as to the genus or even species of the plant that produced them. Thus, the pollen that accumulates in the sediments surrounding an archaeological site can be used to provide a picture of the area's past vegetation, climate, and environmental conditions; such study is called **palynology,** or pollen analysis.

In the field, samples of sediment for pollen analysis are taken every few centimeters from a stratigraphic column. In the laboratory, pollen grains are removed from sediment samples through a series of acidic and alkaline washes that dissolve minerals, silicates, and organic materials, leaving only the pollen grains as a residue. Microscopic examination

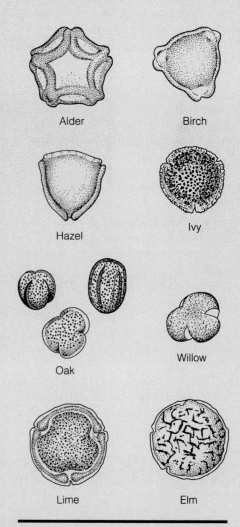

Examples of magnified pollen grains from several plant species. Identification of pollen from stratigraphic deposits provides information on changes in vegetation over time.

enables the palynologist to identify and count the grains of pollen present in the sediments. Examination of several hundred grains from each layer produces a profile of the pollen species. The palynologist then records each species in a **pollen diagram,** which summarizes both the species and the proportion of the various groups of plants found in each sample.

Species proportion

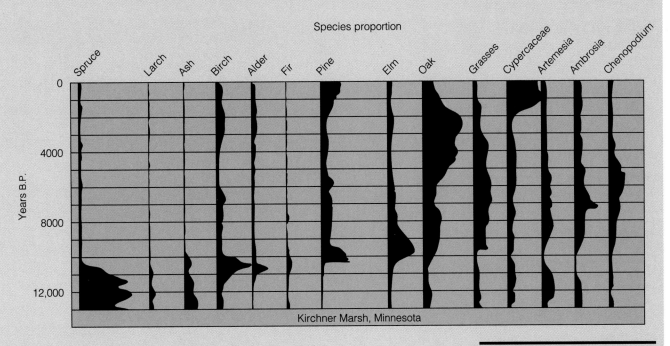

Kirchner Marsh, Minnesota

Pollen analysis can be applied to the reconstruction of local vegetation, to regional maps of plant distributions, or to the study of climatic change. For example, the ratio of tree grains (arboreal pollen, or AP) to nontree pollen (nonarboreal pollen, or NAP) might provide an indication of the density of forest and even precipitation in a given area—the more trees, the greater the precipitation. Certain marker species or changes in the pollen record may aid in the recognition of prehistoric settlements or cultivation practices. For example, the beginning of agriculture in northern Europe is often recognized by the appearance of pollen from cereals and from weeds that grow in disturbed soil, a reduction in tree pollen, and tiny pieces of charcoal from wood-burning found in the pollen samples.

A pollen chart from Kirchner Marsh, Minnesota, showing the succession of vegetation in this area following the retreat of glacial ice. The major changes include the appearance of spruce, larch, and ash, which are gradually replaced by birch and alder, then by pine, then elm, then oak. Grasses and other nontree species are indicated on the right in the chart. The black areas represent the proportion of each species at a particular point in time. The most pronounced changes are seen around 10,000 years ago at the end of the Pleistocene.

THE FATE OF THE NEANDERTHALS

A peaceful or violent end?

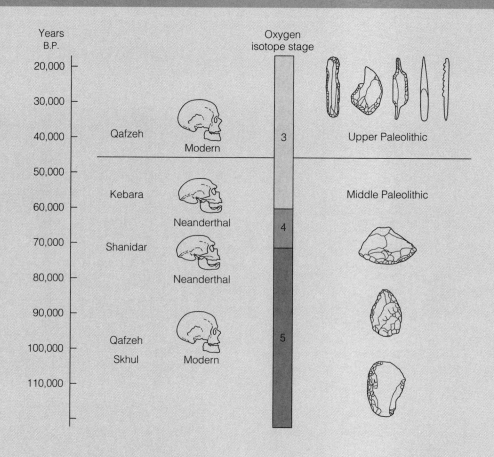

The sequence of hominids from major sites in the Near East. This important evidence indicates that fully modern humans were present in this area by 100,000 years ago, before the Neanderthals. Neanderthals were probably forced out of Europe and into western Asia during an extreme period of cold. The Neanderthals in the Near Eastern sites date between 70,000 and 40,000 years ago. Technological changes from Middle to Upper Paleolithic took place around 50,000 years ago and are not related to the human subspecies present.

Between approximately 40,000 and 30,000 B.P., Neanderthals became extinct and were replaced by fully modern humans in Europe and western Asia. The fate of the Neanderthals is open to question: Were they replaced by fully modern humans, perhaps violently, or did they interbreed and simply disappear in the mix? The evidence on this transition is quite different in the Near East and in Europe.

Current evidence from newly dated sites in the Near East suggests that the first fully modern humans appeared in this area about 100,000 years ago. At Qafzeh Cave and the site of Skhul in Israel,

A view of the caves at Mount Carmel, Israel. The site of Skhul is out of view to the left. Many of the Paleolithic sites in the Near East are found in caves that formed in limestone.

and elsewhere in the Near East, the bones of *Homo sapiens sapiens* are found in layers with Mousterian tools, dating to 90,000 years ago. At other sites such as Shanidar and Kebara, Neanderthal skeletons have been found dating to between 75,000 and 45,000 years ago. It appears that fully modern humans coexisted with Neanderthals in the Near East until around 45,000 years ago. Modern-looking humans before 45,000 years ago used Middle Paleolithic technology. The earliest evidence for Upper Paleolithic technology comes from East Africa around 46,000 years ago and includes bone tools and pendants, along with a standardized set of artifacts.

In Europe, the transition is less clear, and evidence for the first fully modern humans has them appearing much later. Neanderthals are known in Europe by approximately 200,000 years ago, yet the earliest bones of fully modern humans do not appear in this area until after 45,000 years ago. It is entirely possible that the Neanderthals found in the Near East between 75,000 and 45,000 years ago moved there from Europe during a period of intense cold.

The disappearance of Neanderthals and their replacement by fully modern humans in Europe appear to have occurred between 43,000 and 32,000 years ago, from east to west. Several pieces of evidence suggest that this was a gradual process. A Neanderthal burial was discovered in 1981 in a layer of Upper Paleolithic artifacts from St. Césaire in France, dating to 32,000 years ago. The combination of Neanderthal remains and Upper Paleolithic technology suggests that technology spread ahead of *Homo sapiens sapiens* in this area. Even earlier, at the transition between the Mousterian and Upper Paleolithic, several sites are assigned to what is called the Châtelperonnian culture, dating to around 38,000 years ago. Châtelperonnian sites contain distinctive Upper Paleolithic stone artifacts, along with typical bone tools and ornaments. Yet the human remains in these sites are from Neanderthals, again

Excavated layers at St. Césaire, France. A Neanderthal skeleton was found in the layer labeled $E_{J\emptyset}^{SUP}$.

suggesting that Upper Paleolithic technology may have spread to the Neanderthals before the arrival of fully modern humans.

The question of the fate of the Neanderthals remains. Why did they disappear? Several possibilities have been suggested in both the scientific and the popular literature. Were Neanderthals simply conquered and slain by advancing groups of technologically superior *Homo sapiens sapiens*? The Châtelperonnian evidence does not readily support such a suggestion. Did Neanderthals disappear into the gene pool of modern-looking humans, as smaller numbers of Neanderthals interbred with larger numbers of *Homo sapiens sapiens*? Ancient DNA extracted from a newly excavated Neanderthal bone in Germany suggests that there was no genetic relationship, and thus no mating, between the Neanderthals and the fully modern humans who replaced them. Thus, the end of the Neanderthals may have been more violent than romantic.

THE UPPER PALEOLITHIC

The arrival of Homo sapiens sapiens

The Upper Paleolithic is characterized by a variety of innovations that developed over the last 40,000 years of the Pleistocene. These include the arrival of anatomically modern humans in Europe; the extensive use of stone blades; the widespread manufacture of a variety of objects from bone, antler, ivory, and wood; the invention of new equipment, such as the spearthrower and the bow and arrow; the domestication of the dog; and the appearance of art and decoration.

The Upper Paleolithic also represents an important phase in the geographic expansion of the human species: There were more sites in more places than ever before. Virtually all the earth's diverse environments, from tropical rain forest to arctic tundra, were inhabited during this period. Africa, Europe, and Asia were filled with groups of hunter-gatherers, and Australia and North and South America were colonized for the first time.

The archaeological materials of this period are best known from Europe, and especially from southwestern France, an important hub of archaeological activity during the twentieth century. Here, the Upper Paleolithic replaced the Middle Paleolithic after 40,000 years ago. Excavations over the last 100 years in the deep deposits of caves and rockshelters of this area have exposed layer upon layer of remains from the last part of the Pleistocene. These excavations and studies of the contents of the layers resulted in the recognition of a sequence of Upper Paleolithic subperiods, known as the Châtelperronnian, Aurignacian, Perigordian, Solutrean, and Magdalenian. In central and eastern Europe, the Upper Paleolithic remains are designated the Gravettian, roughly equivalent to the Perigordian in the west.

The skeletal remains of *Homo sapiens sapiens* found in western Europe date to after 35,000 years ago, following the appearance of blade tools and other distinctively Upper Paleolithic artifacts. These anatomically modern individuals were originally called Cro-Magnon, after the place in France where they were first discovered. In spite of this distinctive name, they were indistinguishable from fully modern humans. Lacking the robust

A chart of the chronology, climatic changes, major cultural periods, and typical artifacts of the Upper Paleolithic. The differences between these European cultures were much greater during the Upper Paleolithic than during the Middle Paleolithic.

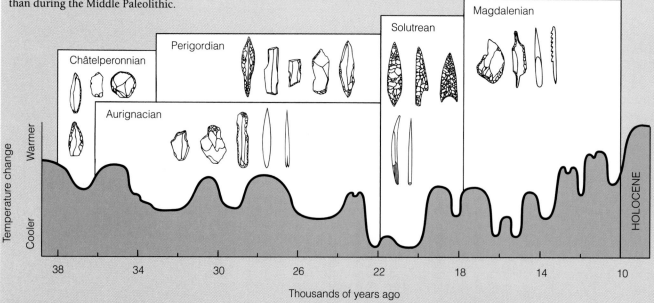

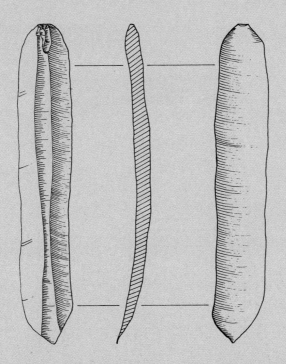

Three views of a blade: a flake with a length at least twice its width.

frame, heavy brow ridges, and protruding jaw of the Neanderthals, the *H. sapiens sapiens* face sits almost directly under a bulging forehead. A chin reinforces the smaller, weaker jaw and its smaller teeth. Cranial capacity is fully modern, and there is no reason to assume that Cro-Magnons were intellectually different from ourselves.

The material remains left by these Upper Paleolithic societies reinforce the idea that by this time our species had indeed arrived as creative creatures. Blade manufacturing techniques and blade tools characterize the Upper Paleolithic. Stone **blades** are a special form of elongated flake, with a length at least twice its width and sharp, parallel cutting edges on both sides. Blades can be mass-produced in large quantities from a single nodule of flint, removed from a core in a fashion akin to peeling a carrot. Blades also provide a form, or blank, that could be shaped (retouched) into a number of different tools. Projectile points, burins, knives, drills, and scraping tools can all be made from a basic blade form.

Another distinctive aspect of Upper Paleolithic stone tool manufacture is the appearance of special flaking techniques during the Solutrean period, to make thin, beautiful leaf-shaped points in several different sizes. Some of these points were used for spears and some perhaps for arrows, while others may have served as knives. These tools are among the finest examples of the flintknapper's skill from the entire Paleolithic. At the end of the Solutrean, however, these flaking techniques largely disappeared from the craft of stone tool manufacture, not to be used again for thousands of years.

Many new kinds of tools—made of materials such as bone, wood, ivory, and antler—also distinguish the Upper Paleolithic. Spearthrowers, bows and arrows, eyed needles, harpoons, ropes, nets, oil lamps, torches, and many other things have been found. Hafting and composite tools, incorporating several different materials, were also introduced during the Upper Paleolithic. Resin and other adhesives, for example, were used to hold stone tools in bone or antler handles.

Solutrean laurel leaf point.

(continued)

Upper Paleolithic manufacture of blades and blade tools. Blade manufacture is a kind of mass production of many elongated flakes. A pointed piece of bone or antler is struck with a hammerstone to remove the blade from the core through the indirect percussion technique.

Spearthrowers provide an extension of the arm, enabling hunters to fling their darts with greater force and accuracy. A hunter with a spearthrower can kill a large animal like a deer from a distance of 15 m (50 ft). Prior to this invention, spears may have been used primarily as thrusting weapons, requiring dangerous, close-range attacks. Spearthrowers of bone, wood, or antler usually had three components: a handle, a balance weight, and a hook to hold the end of the spear.

Spearthrowers were often elaborately decorated, with the carved figures of animals used for the weight. By the end of the Upper Paleolithic, the spearthrower was replaced by the bow and arrow as the primary hunting weapon. The bow provided an even more accurate means of delivering a long-distance, lethal blow to an animal.

Dogs were domesticated during the Upper Paleolithic, probably for the purpose of hunting. As temperatures warmed

122   CHAPTER 4   THE HUNTERS

Blades as forms, or blanks, for making other tools. Increasing specialization in the function of tools was an important trend during the Paleolithic.

at the end of the Pleistocene and the European forests moved back across the continent, woodland species of animals became more common but less visible to the hunter. A strong sense of smell, lacking in a human hunter, to locate prey was well developed in his faithful canine companion.

Fine bone needles with small eyes document the manufacture of sewn clothing and other equipment from animal skins. Several categories of carved artifacts—buttons, gaming pieces, pendants, necklaces, and the like—marked a new concern with personal appearance, an expression of self, and the aesthetic embellishment of everyday objects. This development was closely related to the appearance of decorative art. Figurines, cave paintings, engravings, and myriad decoration of other objects reflect the creative explosion that characterized Upper Paleolithic achievement. There is also compelling evidence for a celebration of the seasons and an awareness of time in the archaeological remains from the Upper Paleolithic. Finally, the suggestion of counting systems and the beginning of a calendar of sorts—or at least a recording of the phases of the moon—may have appeared at this time (see "Symbols and Notation," p. 138).

DOLNI VESTONICE

*Mammoth hunters
in eastern Europe*

An ivory carving of a mammoth from
Vogelherd, Germany (8.8 cm long).

The woolly mammoth of Pleistocene Europe was a magnificent creature. As seen in cave paintings and frozen examples from Siberia, this animal had a huge domed head atop a massive body covered with long fur. The mammoth was roughly one-and-a-half times the size of a modern African elephant and must have been formidable prey for the late Pleistocene hunters of Europe. In addition to mammoths, herds of wild reindeer, horses, woolly rhinoceros, and other species roamed the tundra of Europe. The mammoth, however, was the primary game in the east and provided the bulk of the diet for the inhabitants of this area. At one site in the Czech Republic, the remains of 800–900 mammoths have been uncovered.

The remains of the camps of these mammoth hunters were fortuitously buried under deep deposits of fine silt. This silt was originally picked up by the wind at the edges of the ice sheets, carried in the air across central Europe, and gradually deposited as blankets of sediment, known as **loess** (pronounced "luss"). Numerous prehistoric sites were slowly covered by this airborne dust; bone, ivory, and other materials have been well preserved in it. The major problem with such sites is simply finding them, because they are hidden under very deep deposits of loess.

Near the town of Dolni Vestonice (dol-nee′ves-to-neet′za), in the south-central part of the Czech Republic, the enormous bones of extinct mammoths were first uncovered in the course of removing loess for brickmaking. Although excavations were initially undertaken in

1924, the extent of the prehistoric occupation was not truly recognized until the work that began in 1947 and continues today. Large horizontal excavations have removed the deep loess deposit covering the site and exposed a large area containing dwelling structures, mammoth bones, and many intriguing artifacts dating to about 25,000 years ago.

During the late Pleistocene, the area was one of tundra and permafrost, situated north of the treeline in Europe. Little wood was available, except possibly for small stands of willow and other species in sheltered valleys. Broad expanses of grass, moss, and lichen provided food for the herds of mammoths, horses, and reindeer that were the predominant fauna of the area. The permafrost was responsible for large-scale movement of the ground surface, a phenomenon known as **solifluction.** Alternate freezing and thawing of the ground resulted in the disturbance of many of the remains at Dolni Vestonice. For this reason, it is difficult to interpret the evidence from the site.

The highest layers in the deposits, containing a campsite, are still reasonably well preserved. This camp lay on a projecting tongue of land, along a local stream that becomes a bog just at the eastern edge of the site. Part of the site sits on a ridge, providing a good view of the valley of the nearby Dyje River. The effectiveness of the mammoth hunters is dramatically portrayed in the scatters of mammoth bones marking the boundaries of the settlement. The bones of at least 100 mammoths were piled up in an area of 12 × 45 m (40 × 140 ft). Stone tools and broken bones suggest that this was a zone where animals, or parts of animals, were butchered and where skins may have been cleaned and prepared. Other piles of bones were found throughout the settlement, often sorted according to kind of bone, presumably for use as fuel and raw material for construction. Fires were lit on some of these bone piles, as evidenced by ash, perhaps as a defense against predatory animals.

Stones, earth, wooden posts, and mammoth bones were used in the construction of structures at the site. The first structure to be uncovered was a very large oval, 9×15 m (30×50 ft) in size, with five regularly spaced fireplaces inside. The size of the structure, about half

A residential structure from Dolni Vestonice showing the semisubterranean floor, with flat stones, fireplaces, and mammoth bones used for the framework. Postholes are indicated by small dark circles. The bone framework was likely covered with animal hides to complete the structure. The hut is approximately 6 m in diameter.

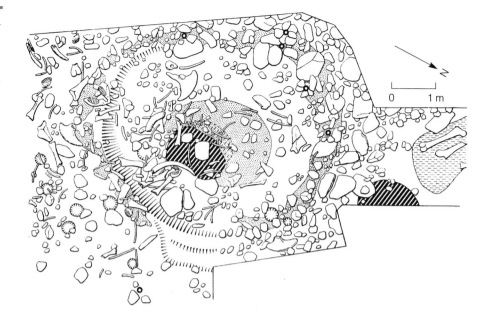

A reconstruction of a mammoth bone structure from the site of Mezerich in the former Soviet Union, which may closely resemble the structures at Dolni Vestonice.

a tennis court, and its contents suggested to the excavators that this was an open windbreak, without a ceiling, rather than a roofed structure, and that it was occupied primarily during summer. The wall posts were supported with limestone blocks and were likely covered with animal hides. At least three other roofed huts have been found in this area. These structures are partially dug into the loess; they contain one or two hearths and have numerous large mammoth bones on top of the floor. These bones are probably the remains of the framework for the roof, which would have collapsed onto the floor of the structure after the site was abandoned.

In an open area near the center of the compound was a large hearth, almost 1 m (3 ft) deep and several meters (about

10 ft) across, which may have been a common, central fire for the community. In the ashes of this fire, an ivory carving of a female figure, called the Venus of Vestonice, was found (see "Portable Art," p. 134).

Another structure, uncovered in 1951, was found some 80 m (250 ft) along the stream to the west of the main concentration. This structure was smaller, 6 m (20 ft) in diameter, and very unusual. The floor of the hut had been dug into the loess slope to level it and to provide more protection against the elements. Limestone blocks were placed against the excavated slope to buttress the wall. Posts were also supported by these blocks at the front of the hut. Hollow bird bones were found inside; they were cut at the ends and may have functioned as musical instruments. In the center of the hut was an ovenlike fireplace with a domed clay structure raised around it. The oven was made of fire-hardened earth and ground limestone. In the deep pile of ashes and waste that stood on the floor of the hut were found more than 2300 small clay figurines that must have been fired in the oven. This is the earliest example of the use of fired clay in the world, some 15,000 years before the invention of pottery. The figurines consisted of heads, feet, and other fragments of animal effigies and fired lumps of clay. Even the fingerprints of the maker were preserved in some of the pieces.

The depth and extent of deposits at Dolni Vestonice, along with the presence of both summer and winter huts, suggest that this site may have been occupied throughout the year. The remarkable artifacts and other materials found at the site confirm the impression that this is an unusual site indeed. Flint tools at the site belong to the Gravettian, the Upper Paleolithic of eastern Europe. Tools are made from narrow blades in the form of points, knives, burins, and others. There are also numerous tools made from mammoth bone and ivory: awls, needles, knives, spearpoints, lances, and digging equipment. Ornaments in the form of pendants, necklaces, headbands, and the like are made of carved bone, ivory, and shell. Some of the shells were from the Mediterranean Sea, several hundred ki-

lometers to the south, indicating either travel or trade. Other objects carved of antler or ivory, or made of baked clay, have no clear practical purpose and probably served as ritual objects in the ceremonies that took place at the site.

Perhaps the most remarkable finds may involve two representations of the same individual. Excavations in 1936 uncovered a small ivory plaque about 4 cm (1.6 in) high, with a crudely incised human face portrayed on it. The face is asymmetrical, with the left eye and the left half of the lip somewhat lower than the right. A second carved ivory head was found in 1948 in the open summer hut. This three-dimensional head also portrays an individual, and the left side of the face is somewhat distorted and asymmetrical. Finally, a burial was excavated in 1949, discovered beneath two huge shoulder blades from a mammoth. The skeleton belonged to a woman and was covered with **red ochre**, an iron mineral and pigment, and a flint point was buried near her head. A study of the facial bones of this individual showed that she suffered from partial paralysis of the left side of her face. It seems entirely possible that the two faces carved in ivory are representations of the person in the grave.

The rendering of an asymmetrical human face on a small piece of ivory (4 cm high).

The head of a woman with an asymmetrical face, carved in ivory (4.6 cm high).

The buried skeleton of an elderly female from Dolni Vestonice. The bones of the left side of the face revealed congenital nerve damage, probably resulting in an asymmetrical facial expression. The woman was buried under two mammoth shoulder blades, and the bones of an arctic fox were found next to her in the grave.

THE CAVE
OF LASCAUX

*A monument to
human creativity*

The Dordogne region of southwestern France, the center of cave art. The limestone cliffs and caves in this area were the galleries of Upper Paleolithic groups. These places have been inhabited for tens of thousands of years.

Nestled in the lovely countryside of southwestern France, the Vezere River runs past some of the most important Paleolithic sites in the world. This area, known as the Perigord, is a prehistorian's dream. The spectacular landscape contains not only hundreds of important archaeological sites, but also the kitchens and cellars of many superb French chefs. The limestone plateau is dissected by numerous streams and rivers that have carved high cliffs along the courses of the

valleys. These cliffs have many caves and rockshelters, which provided residence for generations of Paleolithic groups.

Over time, the entrances to many of these caves have collapsed and hidden the caverns completely. The cave of Lascaux (lahss′co) was discovered by chance in 1940 when a young boy noticed a hole in the ground where a pine tree had been uprooted by the wind. After dropping some rocks into the hole, he and several friends slid down the opening and into a

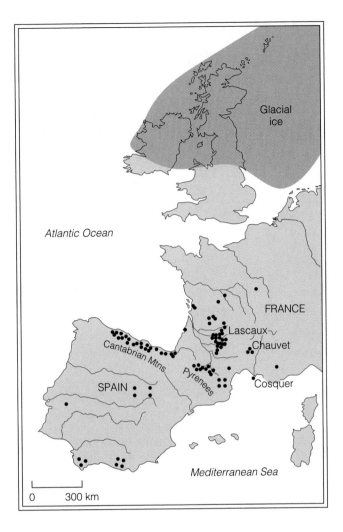

Locations of the western European painted cave sites. The painted caves are primarily in the Perigord region of southwestern France, in the Pyrenees mountains between France and Spain, and in the Cantabrian Mountains of northern Spain, as indicated by dots on the map. The map also shows the extent of continental glaciation in northern Europe during the coldest period of the Upper Paleolithic.

cave, which we now know contains the most important collection of Upper Paleolithic art in the world. Lascaux had been sealed for perhaps 15,000 years, the outside world completely unaware of the splendor it held.

After World War II, the cave was opened as an underground museum. For two decades, it was one of the major tourist attractions in France, with as many as 1000 visitors a day. Unfortunately, the flow of tourists changed the environment of the cave dramatically, raising the temperature and humidity and bringing in dust. These changes caused the growth of a fungus on the walls that began to cover and eventually flake off parts of the paintings. The cave was closed in 1963 and efforts were begun to halt the spread of the fungus, remove it, and preserve the paintings for posterity. The problem was fixed, but the cave has not been reopened to the public. Instead, the French government built a duplicate of the cave, Lascaux II, where tourists can view copies of the beautiful animal paintings that grace the walls of the original galleries.

The artwork of the Upper Paleolithic can be divided into two major categories: **mural art**—paintings and engravings on the walls of caves; and **portable art**—carvings, figurines, and other shaped or decorated pieces that can be moved from place to place. Upper Paleolithic mural art is found primarily in France and Spain, although ancient examples have also been found in South Africa and Australia. Portable art is found throughout Europe and much of the rest of the Old World. Although Upper Paleolithic mural art was also painted at cave entrances and along cliff faces and rock outcroppings, only deep inside the caves of France and Spain has it survived the erosive forces of nature.

A chart of the number and kind of hand mutilations appearing on the walls of the cave of Gargas.

3	11	1	1
9	9	1	1
3	9	1	1
1	59	1	1

Three depictions on the walls of the cave of Les Trois Frères, France, showing humans in animal skins. These individuals may be dancers, sorcerers, or hunters.

The cave interiors were not living areas; they were visited only briefly by artists and other members of society. The paintings are almost exclusively of animals; humans are only rarely represented. Human figures are depicted more commonly in engravings, both on cave walls and in portable objects. Some of the engravings of humans seem to show men wearing the skins and heads of animals. These individuals may have been dancers, participants in some ceremony, or camouflaged hunters. Single human hands are outlined on many of the cave walls. These hands may be simple signatures or graffiti, but, curiously, they are often missing several knuckles or even entire fingers. For example, at the cave of Gargas in the French Pyrenees, all but 10 of 217 hand paintings have fingers missing.

The cave paintings are rendered in outline and colored in monochrome or polychrome. Animals are most often depicted in profile. The paintings are sometimes located high on the ceiling in the darkest areas of the caves; light and some form of scaffolding must have been essential in these cases. Pieces of rope and pine torches have been found, along with simple oil lamps made of stone bowls.

Over 150 fragments of such lamps have been recovered at Lascaux. The paintings must have had a great impact, viewed in the light of a flickering torch by awed individuals deep in the earth's interior. The cave art is by and large carefully planned and skillfully executed, capturing both the movement and the power of the animals that are rendered. It is not graffiti, nor is it hastily sketched. The quality of the paintings is such that we must assume there were recognized artists in the societies of the Upper Paleolithic.

Most of the paintings at Lascaux date to around 17,000 years ago, during the Magdalenian period. The art is dated according to fragments of paints and other artifacts found in archaeological layers of known age in the cave. The paints were a blend of mineral pigments mixed with cave water, using the chewed end of a stick or pieces of hair or fur to tamp the paint onto the walls. The common colors in the paintings are black (charcoal and manganese oxide), yellow and red (iron oxides and clay), and occasionally white (clay and calcite).

Lascaux is a lengthy, narrow chamber a little longer than a football field. In spite of its rather small size, more than 600 paintings and 1500 engravings grace

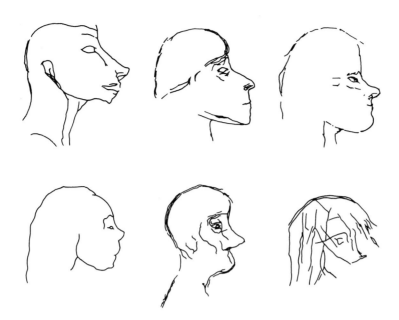

Some of the human heads engraved on the walls of the cave at La Vache.

the walls of the cave, making it the most decorated of the magnificent painted caves in Spain and France.

The opening of the cave leads into a large chamber, some 20 m (65 ft) long, filled with huge animal paintings. Four large bulls, up to 5 m (16 ft) long, stride across the ceiling. In the adjacent halls and passageways, hundreds of paintings depict bison, deer, horses, wild cattle, and other animals. Very specific characteristics, such as spring molting, are shown in some of the paintings. Animals are often depicted as pregnant or with their meaty haunches exaggerated. In several instances, feathered darts are heading toward the animals (see Color Plate 4). Certain abstract patterns also appear either in isolation or in association with animals. Rows of dots and multicolor checkerboard patterns are painted at various places in the cave.

Most of the paintings show one or a group of animals; there is little attempt at scenery or storytelling. Many of the paintings are superimposed over older ones, with little apparent regard for the previous work of other artists. Large herbivores, which provided much of the meat for Upper Paleolithic hunter-gatherers, most frequently occur in large chambers and open areas in the caves. Curiously, however, the most important game animal at this time, the reindeer, occurs only once at Lascaux. Such dangerous animals as carnivores, bears, and rhinoceros more often are found in the deep recesses of the cave and far-removed crevices.

One of the most remarkable paintings is found in a narrow, 5-m (16-ft) shaft off to the side in the cave. At the bottom of this shaft, a large woolly rhino with raised tail faces to the left, a series of dots near its hindquarters. Across a small crevice appears a striking scene of beast and man, the only human figure painted in the cave. A beautiful multicolor bison on the right is mortally wounded, its entrails spilled by a spear. The dying animal is either down on the ground or charging the human figure on the left. This figure, obviously male, is shown in merest outline, depicted with a birdlike face. On the ground nearby lies a long object with several barbs, perhaps a spearthrower, and a bird with a single long leg, possibly an important symbol. Is this painting a memorial to a hunter, a member of the bird clan or totem, killed by the bison? Does the rhino play a role in the scene? Such questions point out the difficulties involved in trying to read the minds of prehistoric people. We can speculate, but we cannot know what was intended by these paintings.

There are several schools of thought on the meaning of the cave paintings from the Upper Paleolithic. The emphasis on pregnant animals has often been interpreted to represent a concern with fertility and the bounty of nature, and an awareness of reproduction and the

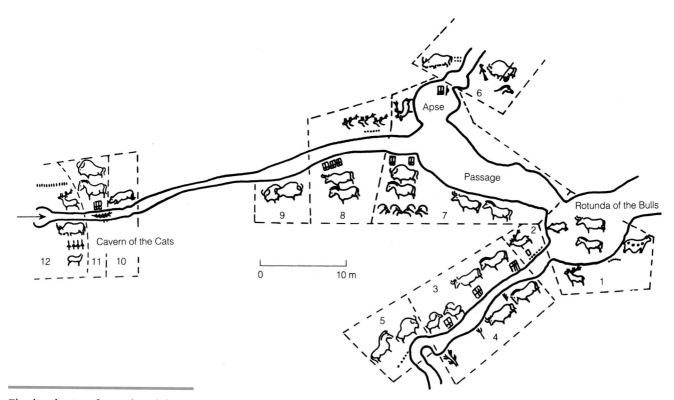

The distribution of animals and designs at Lascaux. The numbers indicate major areas of art in the cave. Large prey animals tend to be in the major galleries of the caves, while carnivores and other depictions are in less-accessible areas.

replenishment of the herds on which these people depended for food. Other scholars, pointing to the exaggerated hips and haunches of the animals and spears in flight, argue for a concern over the hunting of animals for meat. Hunting rites and ritual killings of animals before a hunt might magically help ensure success in the quest for food.

A few prehistorians suggest that the cave paintings are simply "art for art's sake," a means for artists to express themselves and to change the way their fellow humans saw the world. Still others suggest that the painted caves were primitive temples, sanctuaries for ceremony and ritual, such as the initiation of the young into society. Huge animals flickering in the light of torches and lamps deep within the bowels of the earth would provide a staggering experience for the uninitiated. Footprints preserved in the muddy floors of painted caves in France indicate that all sizes of people walked in the cave. Margaret Conkey, of the University of California, Berkeley, argues that these caves may have served as a focus of social activity for large groups of people. She suggests that the caves may have been a permanent symbol on the landscape and a place for the cere-

monies and rituals associated with the aggregation of several different groups of hunter-gatherers.

More than 200 painted caves have been discovered in France over the last 100 years. In the last decades, two major sites have been revealed. The cave of Chauvet (show'vay) was found in a tributary of the Rhône River in the south of France in 1995, containing more than 300 paintings and engravings. The site was discovered by French spelunkers who cleared a small hole at the surface and climbed down 9 m (30 ft) into a great chamber. The cave is at least five times larger than Lascaux. There are several groupings of animals, including bears and rhinos, on the walls, in addition to a number of solitary animals. Radiocarbon dates of some of the art in the cave place it at 32,000 years ago, making these the oldest known paintings in the world (see "Radiocarbon Dating," p. 142).

Another important cave, Cosquer (kos'care), was found by divers off the Mediterranean coast of France, near Marseilles, in 1992. Swimming up the opening of this cave, divers entered dry chambers containing the untouched remains of Upper Paleolithic people, footprints, lamps, torches, hearths, and the like,

Man and bison at Lascaux. This painting represents one of the very few examples of storytelling in the art of Lascaux, and it is the only painting of a human in the cave. The depiction is at the bottom of a deep, narrow shaft and has four elements: a detailed color drawing of a bison mortally wounded by a spear, a black outline of a male human with a birdlike face, a bird on a stick beneath the human figure, and a spearthrower with hook and handle lying on the ground beneath the man. The painting is subject to various interpretations, ranging from a memorial to the death of a kinsman to the depiction of an Upper Paleolithic myth.

along with many extraordinary paintings. Rising sea levels at the end of the last glaciation submerged the entrance of the cave. The opening of this cave, now almost 40 m (120 ft) below sea level, was along the shore during the Upper Paleolithic when the sea level was lower. A number of the paintings reflect the proximity of the Mediterranean shore, depicting seals and seabirds such as the great auk. Most of the art in the cave dates to around 18,500 B.P.

The magnificent art of the Upper Paleolithic represents an initial awakening of the creative spirit, an explosion of an aesthetic sense. Such a transformation may also signify major changes in the minds of Upper Paleolithic people and/or in the way they viewed the world and organized their lives and their society.

PORTABLE ART

A sense of design and beauty

Examples of Upper Paleolithic decoration of bone, antler, ivory, and wood objects. Such decoration was applied to a variety of pieces, some utilitarian and others more symbolic.

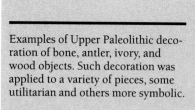

The aesthetic sense that appeared during the Upper Paleolithic with the arrival of fully modern humans is expressed in a variety of different forms. Carving, sculpting, and molding of various materials, including clay, antler, wood, ivory, and stone, is evidenced throughout this period. The decoration of artifacts and other objects occurred throughout the Upper Paleolithic beginning about 35,000 years ago. Prior to the appearance of *Homo sapiens sapiens* in Europe, there is remarkably little evidence for the non-practical modification of equipment and utensils. Only a handful of decorated objects have been found in Middle Paleolithic contexts.

Beginning in the Aurignacian some 34,000 years ago, however, bone became a common material for human use, modification, and decoration. For example, a variety of bone points date to this early period. Initially simple and plain, such points became heavily barbed and decorated by the end of the Upper Paleolithic. At the same time, carved bone and antler figurines of both humans and animals began to appear in the archaeological record.

Perhaps the most spectacular portable objects from the Upper Paleolithic are the "Venus figurines." These small sculptures appeared throughout most of Europe during a brief time around 25,000 years ago. The figures were engraved in relief on the walls of caves, carved in the round from ivory, wood, and stone such as steatite, and modeled in clay. The female characteristics of these statuettes are usually exaggerated: breasts, hips, buttocks, and thighs are very large, while the head, arms, hands, legs, and feet are shown only schematically. The pubic triangle is sometimes outlined; one figurine has a detailed vulva. Some of the figurines appear to be pregnant, while others are displayed holding a horn, perhaps a cornucopia or horn of plenty, to imply fertility, bounty, and reproduction.

Probably 80% of the prehistoric art known today comes from the last stage of the Upper Paleolithic, the Magdalenian. Objects with a short life were decorated in a cursory fashion, while more important pieces with a longer life expectancy were heavily ornamented. Spearthrowers were decorated elaborately, with carved animals serving as the counterweight and end-hook. Engraved bone was common, and such portable art was often painted as well. Body adornments, including necklaces, bracelets, and pendants, also appeared in the Magdalenian.

Portable art was more common in the larger settlements than at smaller ones. This pattern suggests a connection between art and the ritual activities that likely occurred when larger groups of people came together. Hunter-gatherers commonly aggregated in a larger group during a certain time each year to exchange raw materials and learn new information, to find mates, and to celebrate important events, such as marriage and initiation into adulthood. Rituals and ceremonies provided a common bond in both physical and psychic realms; dance, trance, and the reaffirmation of common beliefs were important aspects of such gatherings. Decorations in the form of masks, face and body painting, costumes, and the like were probably used during such ceremonial occasions (see "Contemporary Hunter-Gatherers," Chapter 5, p. 193).

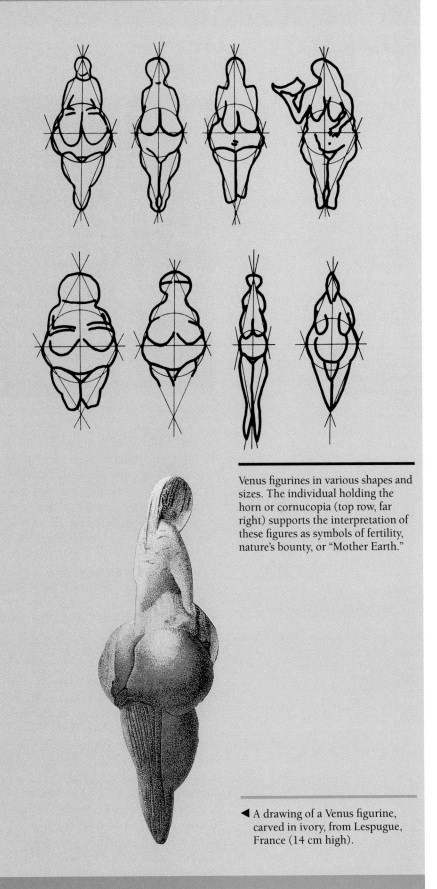

Venus figurines in various shapes and sizes. The individual holding the horn or cornucopia (top row, far right) supports the interpretation of these figures as symbols of fertility, nature's bounty, or "Mother Earth."

◀ A drawing of a Venus figurine, carved in ivory, from Lespugue, France (14 cm high).

PINCEVENT

Brief stops by reindeer hunters in the Upper Paleolithic

Two hearths at Pincevent, with the distribution of stones and bones deposited here some 12,000 years ago.

Several shallow fords on the Seine River in northern France were important crossing points for migrating reindeer herds when tundra and permafrost covered northwestern Europe at the end of the Pleistocene. The sandy banks and bars of the Seine and other rivers were the sites of the camps of Magdalenian reindeer hunters approximately 12,000 years ago. In the vicinity of Paris, the Seine may lie near the northern end of what was a major route of reindeer migration at the close of the Pleistocene, with herds moving north each spring from the south of France.

Scatters of stone, bone, antler, hearthstones, and charcoal mark these ephemeral summer encampments of reindeer hunters. A number of such sites, including one called Pincevent (ponce′von), were quickly buried and extremely well preserved. The archaeological remains are found in thin layers of clay, deposited when the river flooded annually. The river floods must have been gentle because there is little disturbance of the materials. Several artifacts were found standing upright, and two crushed bird eggs remained at the site.

At Pincevent, at least four different levels with archaeological remains have been recognized, extending over an area of 2 hectares (ha), or 5 acres, larger than a soccer field. Excavations, originally directed by A. Leroi-Gourhan and M. Brezillon, began in 1964 and continue today. The excavators intentionally exposed broad horizontal areas of the site, leaving features, artifacts, and bones in place. In this manner, entire "living floors" could be seen and the pattern of discarded materials studied to determine where people slept, cooked, made tools, and so on. The excavators also made latex rubber casts of many areas, which were then painted to reconstruct and permanently preserve the archaeological remains.

The concentrations of materials average 60–70 sq m (650–750 sq ft), about one-half of one side of a tennis court, and they probably represent single tents or structures as the residence and focus of activity of a few hunters. Each concentration contains 20,000–30,000 stone artifacts and other materials. Stone blades, a major product at these sites, had a variety of purposes. At the nearby site of

Etiolles, extremely long blades were produced, some more than 80 cm (30 in) long, from large nodules of raw material weighing 40 kg (90 lb) or more. The blades from these nodules were as long as 50 cm (20 in). The absence of wear marks on the edges of some of these blades suggests they had not been used and were being stockpiled for some later purpose.

At Pincevent, one of the most important areas excavated to date is in Layer IV. This area contains 94,000 kg (200,000 lb) of flint artifacts, the skeletal remains of at least 43 reindeer, fire-cracked rock, ochre, and several shallow pits and fireplaces. Red ochre stains are concentrated around three large fireplaces. The excavators suggest that activities were centered around three contemporary huts, each with an associated fireplace. Each hut contained a central zone for actual living space and surrounding zones of domestic activities and refuse disposal. The intensity of activity decreased with distance from the hearths. Small piles of waste materials from stone tool manufacture lie on one side of the hearths, while finished tools and red ochre are on the other side.

Near one of the hearths is a large stone that was likely the seat of a flint-worker. Most of the flint was available in the immediate area of the site. A few pieces, however, came from some distance, confirming the mobility of the hunters who stopped here. Reconstruction or refitting of the pieces removed from the flint nodules provides a good indication of how tools were made. Moreover, pieces that are missing and not found at the site provide evidence of which tools were carried elsewhere. Finally, the scattered locations of pieces that fit together indicate how the tools and waste materials were moved about at the site.

Most of the reindeer at the site were killed and butchered during summer. The distribution of bones on the living floor is similar to the flint debris. Larger bones were at the periphery, while smaller pieces and smaller fragments were found near the fireplaces. The bones from a meal were apparently tossed away from the hearth. Small fragments of antler were found near the hearths, but larger pieces

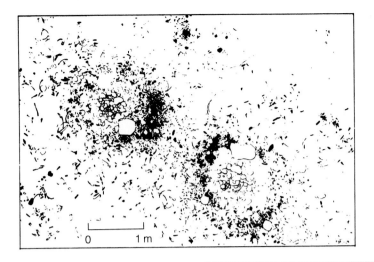

The distribution of stones and bones around two hearths at Pincevent. The large stones were used for sitting during stone tool manufacture, while the scatters of lithic debris were produced as a result.

Reconstruction of a possible tent around one of the Pincevent hearths: (a) concentration of artifacts; (b) hearth.

were discarded at the edge of the activity zone. Most antler working was apparently done at this periphery. The lack of sweeping or cleaning of the living area suggests that the occupation at Pincevent was very brief.

Lewis Binford, of Southern Methodist University, has questioned the existence of actual tents or structures at Pincevent, arguing that the distribution of materials observed in arcs of debris around the hearths could just as easily happen in the absence of tents or huts. There is no definitive evidence that the hunters built shelters on the site. Binford also argues that all the materials around the two largest hearths could have resulted from one or two individuals working and shifting position in response to wind direction. Binford based his suggestions on observations of Eskimo hunters in Alaska and the manner in which they moved away from the smoke of a fire on windy days.

SYMBOLS AND NOTATION

Evidence of seasonal awareness, numbers, and phases of the moon

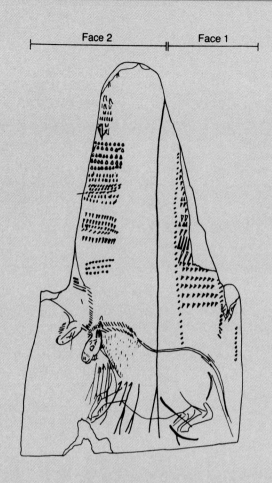

Marshack's interpretation of an engraved bone piece from the site of La Vache, France. Two horses appear at the bottom of the piece, one with a number of arrows drawn into the animal. The repeated sets of marks were made with different tools, suggesting that something was being counted or recorded.

Some of the many decorated pieces from the Upper Paleolithic contain unusual images that are not easy to understand. These designs are carved into the polished surface of bone using pointed stone tools. The motifs that often occur together suggest that specific concepts were being depicted.

One example is a bone knife from the French site of La Vache (pronounced La Vash). The design on one side of this piece has two animal heads, a doe and an ibex, wavy lines that may represent water, and three plants. The other side of the knife shows the head of a bison in autumn rut, four plant motifs that may be pine branches, a drooping stem, and three seeds or nuts. Alexander Marshack, of the Peabody Museum at Harvard University, suggests that the two sides of the knife are intended to convey images of spring and fall, a recognition of the seasons and their distinctive characteristics.

Other bone artifacts have unusual combinations of notches and patterns of dots that are more difficult to comprehend. One example of such an object comes from the cave of La Vache and dates to about 14,000 years ago. The polished fragment of long bone, about 15 cm (6 in) long, is decorated at the base with one entire horse and the head of another. About 10 pointed lines are drawn into the complete horse, perhaps symbolically representing the hunt. When the bone with the horses broke, it was reused to flake flint tools; later, elaborate sets of marks were added in a series of rows on both sides of the bone above the horses.

Marshack has undertaken a detailed, microscopic study of these objects in order to determine how the notches and dots were placed on the bone. He was able to distinguish both the type of pointed tool that made the marks and the order in which at least some of the marks were made. For example, at least four different tools were used to carve the arrows in the horse on the La Vache bone; the tally marks all occur in sets or blocks, each of which was made with a different tool in a slightly different shape. The number and pattern of the marks suggest that they were added over a period of time. On other decorated bones from the Upper Paleolithic, Marshack has observed marks in groups of 30 or 31. The number 7 also seems to regularly define groups of marks on other objects. Although such marks on bones have been considered decoration, they could signify some kind of tally, counting a series of events, or perhaps the number of hunting kills.

Possibly the most intriguing decorated bone object yet found is from the site of Abri Blanchard in France. A flat, irregular rectangle, this bone has no animal or figure engravings, but rather a se-

ries of carved and engraved notches and marks. The 80 notches cover about half the edge of the object, and the marks form a semicircular pattern of two parallel lines on the flat surface. Microscopic examination indicates that at least 24 different tools were used to make the 69 marks on the surface of this bone. Marshack believes that these marks record the phases of the moon. The shape of the marks changes with the moon's phases, over a period of about 6 months.

Marshack would argue that our Upper Paleolithic forebearers were noting the passage of time, reckoning the year according to the seasons and a lunar calendar. Marshack's discoveries are controversial, but the idea that Upper Paleolithic people were capable of counting and notation, as well as symbolic representation, does not seem far-fetched, in light of the other evidence of their creativity and accomplishments.

LAKE MUNGO, AUSTRALIA

The spread of
Homo sapiens sapiens

Although it may seem strange to find Australia in the middle of this discussion of the Upper Paleolithic, there are several important things to be learned from a consideration of the evidence from the land "down under." Australia was colonized by *Homo sapiens sapiens* around 40,000 years ago, perhaps even earlier. Rafts or boats of some kind were likely used. These first emigrants somehow crossed a body of water at least 100 km (65 mi) wide, far beyond the sight of land, to reach the island continent. There are archaeological sites at least 20,000 years old in all corners of the continent, the oldest, on the Upper Swan River, dating to around 38,000 years ago.

At this time, during one of the coldest periods of the Pleistocene, sea level was as much as 125 m (400 ft) lower than it is today. The continental shelves were exposed, and land bridges connected several areas formerly separated by the sea. Australia was connected to New Guinea and Tasmania, comprising a larger continent called Sahul. The Sahul Strait, a body of water that today is several thousand meters (more than a mile) deep, lay between Australia and Asia. At that time, Southeast Asia was a bridge of land connecting the mainland and Indonesia and Borneo. The first inhabitants crossed this deep, wide body of water to reach Australia.

Australia and Southeast Asia during the colder periods of the Pleistocene. At this time, sea level was as much as 150 m lower than it is today, and much of the continental shelf was exposed as dry land. The outlines of the continents changed considerably, and many of today's islands became part of the mainland. Australia and New Guinea joined together but were never part of Southeast Asia. One of the deepest bodies of water in the world, the Sahul Strait, would have always been sea. Thus, the early inhabitants of Australia would have crossed a large body of water to reach the continent. The Wallace Line (dashed line) marks the divide between Asian and Australian animal species.

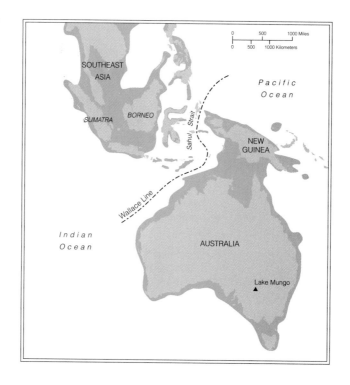

The absence of a land bridge between Australia and mainland Asia is evidenced by the fact that the animal species in the two areas are so very different. Asian placental mammals and Australian marsupial mammals have not been in contact in the last several million years. This difference was originally noted by British naturalist Alfred Russel Wallace, a contemporary of Darwin's, and the term Wallace Line is used to designate the divide between the two distinct groups of animal species.

Some of the oldest sites in Australia lie along the margins of dry lakebeds in the southeastern part of the country, an area known as Lake Mungo. Sites at Lake Mungo contain hearths and shells dating to around 32,000 years ago. This area would have contained a series of lakes with fertile shoreline in the period of initial occupation, when rainfall was higher than it is today. The sites were discovered in 1968 by a geologist who found human bones buried in a sand dune that was at least 20,000 years old. The bones appeared to have been buried at a time when the dune was active on the shore of a former lake.

Further examination of the area around the bones on the dune revealed a series of stone artifacts and several patches of charcoal, which must have been the locations of hearths. Most of the hearths contained fish and mammal bones. Bird bones, eggshell, and shell from freshwater mollusks were also found in a few fireplaces. Other sites around the fossil lakeshore have revealed concentrations of shellfish, burned areas with charcoal and fired clay lumps, probably used as cooking stones. The material culture of these early inhabitants included both bone tools and stone tools, with a large number of heavy core and pebble artifacts.

Several burials have been found, one of which, the remains of a woman 20–25 years old, is the oldest example of cremation yet known in the world. Other remains include another female and a male. Red ochre was used in some of the graves to cover a portion of the remains. All of these individuals are *Homo sapiens sapiens* and document the presence of fully modern humans in the eastern part

The elaborate art of the Australian aborigines, found throughout much of the continent. The art includes a variety of human and animal figures, and dates to the late Pleistocene.

of Eurasia, several thousand years prior to their appearance in Europe.

These early inhabitants rapidly occupied all of Australia, as indicated by the spread of radiocarbon dates across the continent. Some of the oldest rock art and wall paintings in the world are known from Australia. What is almost equally remarkable, however, is how little change took place here over thousands of years. Foraging was apparently a very successful and stable activity in prehistoric Australia. Hunter-gatherers arrived here almost 40,000 years ago, and they were still present when Captain Cook "discovered" the continent 200 years ago.

RADIOCARBON DATING

Absolute dates for the last 40,000 years

The Manhattan Project was the most secret and expensive weapons development effort of the U.S. government during World War II. Laboratories in Chicago, New York, Tennessee, New Mexico, and elsewhere employed thousands of scientists and technicians to develop the first atomic bomb. Many of the unknown details about radioactivity were revealed for the first time during this work, such as the discovery that some radioactive elements could be used to measure the age of various materials. Physicist Willard Libby, of the University of Chicago, announced the first age determinations from radioactive carbon in 1949 and received the Nobel Prize for his discovery.

The key to this procedure, known as **radiocarbon dating,** lies in the half-life of radioactive elements. As explained in Chapter 2, many elements have both stable and radioactive atomic forms, called isotopes. Some radioactive isotopes, such as potassium, have an extremely long half-life. Others have a very brief half-life; strontium-90, for example, has a half-life of 28 years. In order to determine the age of prehistoric materials, the half-life of an element must be of an appropriate period to determine the age of the material. For example, material composed of an element with a brief half-life would be gone in just a few years; none would remain in very old material for the purpose of dating.

Carbon is the most useful element for isotopic dating. Carbon is present in all living things. It has several stable isotopes, including ^{12}C and ^{13}C, and the critical radioactive isotope, ^{14}C, also known as carbon-14 or radiocarbon, with a half-life of approximately 5730 years. Because of this rather short half-life, materials older than about 40,000 years do not contain sufficient remaining radiocarbon to be dated using this method. Carbon-14 is a very rare commodity; only 6 kg (13 lb) are produced each year in the atmosphere. There are only about 60 tons on earth, so trying to find a carbon-14 atom in archaeological

The principles of radiocarbon dating.

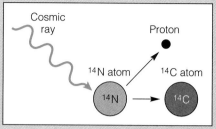

(1) Neutrons created by cosmic rays strike nitrogen-14 atoms in the atmosphere, which releases a proton and creates carbon-14.

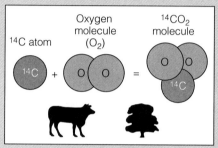

(2) Carbon-14 and oxygen enter living organisms.

(3) Carbon-14 begins to deplete.

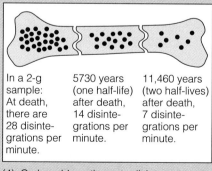

(4) Carbon-14 continues to disintegrate at an orderly, predictable rate.

materials is a bit like trying to find a specific piece of gravel in a full dump truck.

Carbon-14 is produced in the atmosphere by cosmic radiation, which was initially assumed to have been at as constant a level in the past as it is today. The radioactive carbon combines with oxygen, forming carbon dioxide, and is incorporated into plants in the same ratio as it is found in the atmosphere. Animals eat those plants or other animals. When a plant or an animal dies, the intake of carbon ceases. Thus, the amount of radiocarbon in prehistoric material is a direct function of the length of time the organism has been dead.

A variety of organic materials can be assayed by radiocarbon dating, including wood, bone, shell, charcoal, and antler. Carbon-14 often survives best at prehistoric sites in the form of charcoal, and this material has been most commonly dated using the radiocarbon method. However, wood charcoal can come from very old trees or wood and may not date the actual archaeological material accurately. If charcoal from the older rings of the tree is used for dating, the age may be off by several hundred years. For more reliable dates, plants other than trees should be used. Materials with a short life such as nutshells, corncobs, and small twigs are preferred over wood charcoal.

The actual measurement of radiocarbon is straightforward. A sample of known weight is cleaned carefully and burned to create a pure gas of carbon dioxide. The radioactive carbon isotopes in that gas are then counted. A Geiger counter is used to record radioactive emissions from the gas. Several grams of organic material are normally required to produce enough gas for counting.

New technology, however, has resulted in a reduction in the amount of material that is measured. A device called an atomic accelerator mass spectrometer (AMS) is now being used to measure the ratio of carbon isotopes in very small samples. Rather than measuring radioactivity with a Geiger counter, an AMS separates and counts individual carbon atoms by their weight, a much more accurate process. Moreover, less than 0.01 g of sample is needed, and individual pieces of charcoal or a single nutshell or cereal grain can be dated directly. **Accelerator mass spectrometry** is now being used to provide new dates from many sites and materials that could not previously be measured. The technique, which was implemented in 1980, has already produced very important results.

There are certain problems with radiocarbon dating, some involving contamination of the sample. However, as the number of actual measurements increased, it became clear to investigators that there were often regular errors in the dates. Because of these concerns, a detailed study of the method was undertaken to assess the error factor. The rings of known age from the bristlecone pine and other trees, such as the Irish oak, were compared against radiocarbon measurements of the same material. The bristlecone pine is one of the oldest living organisms on earth, reaching ages of up to 4000 years. Individual growth rings from the tree could be counted from the outer bark to the inner core, and the exact age of a ring could be measured by dendrochronology in calendar years (see "Chaco Canyon," Chapter 7, p. 292). That same ring could also be dated by radiocarbon to determine the relationship between calendar years and radiocarbon years.

This study recognized changes in the amount of radioactive carbon in the atmosphere over time and the need for a correction, or calibration, factor for radiocarbon dates to convert them to true calendar years. The assumption that radiocarbon has always been produced at a constant rate in the atmosphere was incorrect, and differences between radiocarbon years and calendar years are related to changes in the rate of cosmic ray bombardment. Radiocarbon dates that have been correctly converted to calendar years are called **calibrated dates.** The dates used for the last 10,000 years in this book are calibrated ¹⁴C dates.

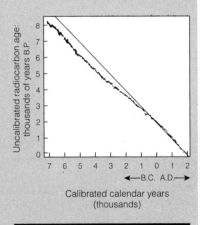

Uncalibrated radiocarbon age: thousands of years B.P.

B.C. A.D.

Calibrated calendar years (thousands)

A calibration curve for radiocarbon dates based on measurements of tree rings of known age from the Irish oak. Notice that the deviation in radiocarbon dates from calendar dates increases with time. The calibration curve provides a way to correct the deviation.

BERINGIA

The arrival of the first inhabitants in the New World

The New World and Beringia, the land bridge between northeastern Asia and Alaska, at the end of the Pleistocene, 12,000 years ago. The map shows the location of Beringia, the extent of continental glaciation, the coastline during lower sea level, and the sites mentioned in the text. These sites were occupied after the ice sheets had retreated. The dashed arrows show the possible route through a gap in the Canadian ice sheets.

The discoverers of North America walked to their new land sometime before 10,000 years ago. These individuals were neither Irish monks in leather canoes, Scandinavian Vikings in long boats, nor Italians in tiny ships, but small groups from Asia who crossed a land bridge connecting the two continents on their feet. The ancestors of the American Indians were the first inhabitants of the Western Hemisphere, a fact that was readily apparent when the Americas were "discovered" by Columbus.

Siberia and Alaska today are separated by less than 100 km (65 mi) at their closest point across the Bering Strait. The water in the strait is relatively shallow; the seafloor is roughly 50 m (160 ft) beneath the sea. During the colder intervals of the Pleistocene, when global sea levels were as much as 125 m (400 ft) below present levels, the floor of the

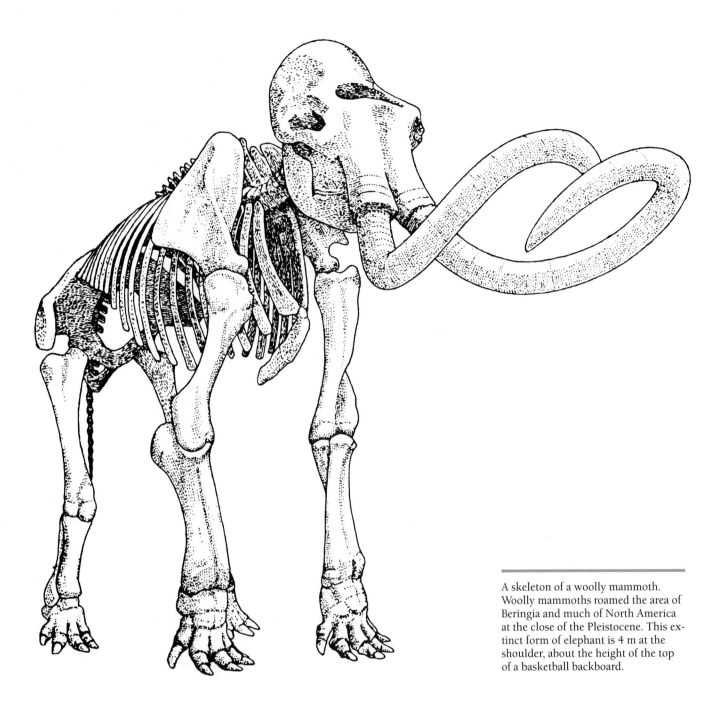

A skeleton of a woolly mammoth. Woolly mammoths roamed the area of Beringia and much of North America at the close of the Pleistocene. This extinct form of elephant is 4 m at the shoulder, about the height of the top of a basketball backboard.

Bering Strait became dry land. During periods of maximum cold and low sea level, the land area of Beringia, as it is called, would have been more than 1000 km (650 mi) wide and indistinguishable from the continents on either side. The warm Japanese Current swept the southern shore and kept most of the area free of ice. The region would have been relatively flat and treeless, a bleak and windswept plain. Scattered groups of mammoth, bison, horse, reindeer, camel, and many other species moved across this region during the cold periods of the Pleistocene. At some point in time, these herds were followed by people from northeastern Asia.

There is no doubt that the first inhabitants of this New World came from Asia; the major question is *when* they came. By 8000 B.C., human groups had occupied most of both continents, from

Paleoindian fluted projectile points. These points were attached to spears. The two points on the left are Folsom points. The two points on the right are Clovis points.

Alaska to Tierra del Fuego at the southern tip of South America.

The best place to begin considering the question of when this colonization started is at the point of entry. There were two possible barriers to the movement of terrestrial animals from northeastern Asia into central North America: (1) the Bering Strait, the body of water that separates the two continents today; and (2) an immense sheet of glacial ice that covered much of northern North America during the late Pleistocene.

Beringia was exposed as dry land for long periods during the later Pleistocene and submerged only briefly during the warmer interglacials. However, in order for people to cross, they would first have to be present in northeastern Asia. The same conditions that produced lower sea levels also meant a very harsh climate and environment in northeastern Asia, which apparently delayed human settlement in that area. Not much is known about the earliest human settlement of Siberia, but more information is gradually coming to light.

An important set of clues was found at several sites near the center of the Kamchatka Peninsula in eastern Siberia, which was part of Beringia during periods of lower sea level. The Ushki sites, excavated by Nikolai Dikov, of the Northeastern Interdisciplinary Research Institute in Siberia, contain stratified levels of living surfaces buried underneath more than 1 m (3 ft) of volcanic ash. The site of Ushki I contains a grave filled with red ochre and surrounded by several large, peanut-shaped dwellings up to 14 × 7 m in size (100 sq m, or 120 sq yards, equivalent to a large classroom). The artifacts include small, stemmed, bifacial flint projectile points similar to ones known from Alaska. The animal bones at the site reveal that the inhabitants hunted bison, reindeer, and probably mammoth, as well as catching large salmon. The lowest levels at Ushki I date to around 14,000 years ago and provide evidence that people making bifacial artifacts (a technology employed in the production of Paleoindian points) were present in this area at least 4000 years before the end of the Pleistocene.

Although the exact timing is debated, Beringia was probably dry land for long periods between 60,000 and 13,000 years ago. After 13,000 B.P., warmer climatic conditions began to melt the continental ice sheets, and the meltwater gradually returned the seas to their present levels. During the period of maximum cold and lower sea level, the continental ice sheets of northern North America stretched from the Aleutian Islands across Canada to Greenland. Alaska was cut off from the rest of North America and was more a part of Asia than the New World. A gap or corridor between the western and eastern centers of the Canadian ice sheets was probably open between 40,000 and 21,000 years ago and again shortly after 14,000 B.P. This corridor, when open, may have provided the route for the penetration of these newly arrived hunting groups into North and South America. Another possible route for the spread from Alaska into the continent lay along the western coastline of North America. That rich coastal habitat would have been ice-free and likely accessible to the hunters crossing the Bering Land Bridge. It is also possible that the strait may have been crossed at other times on the sea ice or even by boat.

Whatever the route, these emigrants must have been few in number, because they left very little evidence of their presence. Sites from this early period are quite rare, and the dates are usually debated. Only a few places, such as Monte Verde in Chile, dating to at least 13,000 years ago, provide good evidence for these early inhabitants. Monte Verde contains the remains of extinct elephants and other animals in association with stone tools.

The archaeological remains in North America from the beginning of the Holocene are generally known as **Paleoindian.** Sites from this period are recognized by the presence of a specific type of stone spearpoint, known as a **fluted point.** Paleoindian spearpoints document the presence of early Americans in North America between 11,000 and 9,000 years ago.

The best-known points from this period are called **Clovis,** after the original find spot in eastern New Mexico. Clovis people were relatively mobile groups of big-game hunters, spreading across most of North America east of the Rocky Mountains. New types of projectile points evolved following the Clovis period. Distinctive, regional types of Paleoindian points are found throughout the New World. **Folsom** points, for example, are found only in the Great Plains. A number of sites are known where animals were killed and butchered with these points, but only a few actual settlements have ever been found. The Lindenmeier site in northern Colorado is one of the rare examples of a Folsom campsite.

It appears that *Homo sapiens sapiens* came to the New World for the first time before 12,000 years ago. Groups of hunters quickly expanded across both continents and were likely involved in the extinction of a number of animal species (see "Pleistocene Extinction," p. 154). It is important to remember that the Bering Strait has probably been the point of entry for several expansions into the New World. The colonization of North and South America was not a single event, but a series of crossings. Certainly the ancestors of modern Eskimos came across the strait relatively late, perhaps 4000 years ago in boats. Thus, the timing of when the first Americans arrived is a difficult and complex issue that will continue to be investigated.

MONTE VERDE

Early hunter-gatherers
in South America

Monte Verde, 1983: a general view of the site and field laboratory. Excavation trenches can be seen running perpendicular to the creek in the lower right of the photograph. The buildings in the center of the photograph are part of the excavation headquarters.

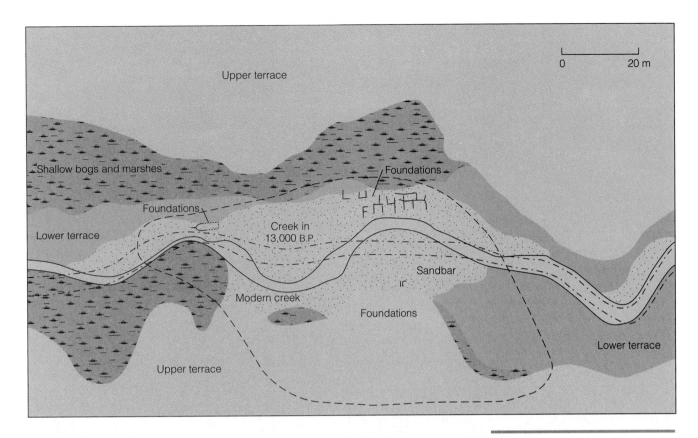

The location and plan of the Monte Verde site. The settlement lay on both sides of the creek, covering an area of approximately 7000 sq m, as indicated by the dashed line. Foundations are outlined where they have been located.

Traces of human groups in the Americas prior to 12,000 years ago are almost non-existent. There are only a few examples of archaeological sites in the New World that contain both definite evidence of an early human presence and reliable radio-carbon dates. In many instances, sites that were candidates for very early human occupation have been discounted because of contaminated carbon samples or questionable stone artifacts.

The best examples of human occupation sites before 10,000 B.C. are in South America, rather than nearer the point of entry across the Bering Strait. Monte Verde (mon′tay-ver′day) is a 13,000-year-old residential site in the cool, forested region of northern Chile. The site was discovered in 1976 by Tom Dillehay, of the University of Kentucky. While surveying in the area, he discovered bone and stone artifacts in a shallow swampy area, a peat bog, along Chinchihuapi Creek, a small, slow stream that drains this part of the rain forest of southern Chile. The site lies along the sandy banks on either side of the creek.

Excavations since the original discovery have uncovered a number of remarkable and unexpected finds for such an early site. Excellent conditions of preservation resulted in the recovery of plant remains and numerous wooden objects, along with stone flakes and broken animal bones. Wood is rare at most archaeological sites, yet it was preserved in the bog at Monte Verde. Apparently the bog developed during or shortly after the abandonment of the site and quickly enclosed all of the remaining materials in a mantle of peat. Peat provides a water-logged, oxygen-free environment where such objects can be preserved.

The timber and earthen foundations of perhaps 12 living structures were recovered in excavations. The rectangular foundations, made of logs and planks held in place with stakes of a different kind of wood, enclose rooms 3–4 m (10–13 ft) long on each side. Posts were placed along the foundation timbers and supported a framework of saplings, which may have been covered with animal skins. Small pieces of what may be

Some of the 13,000-year-old timber foundations at Monte Verde. Each rectangular enclosure measures about 2.3 × 3.3 m. Notice the dark, greasy appearance of the hut floors and the artifacts in place.

animal hide were preserved next to the timber foundation. Two large hearths and a number of shallow clay basins provided fireplaces for the inhabitants of these huts. Even a child's footprint was found preserved in the hardened clay of the basin of one of the small fireplaces.

Many of the artifacts at the site were found inside the structures. Wooden artifacts include digging sticks, tool handles, spears, and a mortar or basin, in addition to the material used for construction. Several kinds of stone tools, both flaked and ground, were found. No stone projectile points were made here, but evidence of other weapons was uncovered. Spherical stones with an encircling groove were probably bola stones, a South American throwing weapon with three leather thongs weighted at each end. The bola is thrown in a spinning fashion, and the stone weights wrap the

thongs around the prey. Other stone balls without grooves were likely used in a sling as heavy projectiles.

To the west of the living floors was a single, more substantial, rounded structure with a pointed end and a foundation of sand and gravel. The bases of wooden posts at the edge of the foundation mark the walls of the structure; a kind of yard or patio was marked off with branches near the entrance. Mastodon bones, animal skins, stone and wooden tools, salt, and the remains of several different types of plants were found in this area.

The arrangement of these structures over an area of roughly 70 × 100 m (220 × 400 ft, about the size of a soccer field) suggests a well-organized community. Dillehay estimates that the site was occupied for perhaps a year by 20–30 people. The occupants of Monte Verde apparently relied primarily on plants and large animals for their livelihood. Most of the bones came from mastodons, (a close but extinct relative of the elephant), a type of llama, amphibians, reptiles, and birds. Plant remains at the site are from species that ripen throughout the year, suggesting that this was a year-round settlement. The wetlands (marshes, bogs, and streams) of the Monte Verde area are a very rich environment, and many edible plants grow there today.

The plant remains document extensive gathering of the local vegetation. A total of 42 edible species of plants have been identified from the site. Most of the evidence is from tubers and roots that were preserved, including the wild potato. This is the oldest evidence anywhere for the potato, which was later domesticated in the Andes Mountains. The products of other plants, including seeds, berries, nuts, and fruits, were also recovered during the excavations. The number of grinding stones at the site also points to the importance of plants in the diet at Monte Verde. Herbaceous plants were found, which today are used for medicinal, rather than nutritional, purposes. A chewed cud from two kinds of seaweed and the leaf of a tree was perhaps medicinal. Exotic objects, including several of the plant species, beach-rolled pebbles, quartz, and bitumen (an adhesive tar), were also brought to the site from the Pacific coast about 25 km (15 mi) to the south.

The evidence from Monte Verde contradicts most traditional views of the peopling of the Americas. The radiocarbon date of 11,000 B.C. for this site in South America documents the fact that early Asians crossed the Bering Strait before 13,000 years ago.

The information from Monte Verde has forced a reconsideration of our interpretation of the earliest inhabitants of the New World, because it is in direct contrast to what has been observed at most sites where preservation is not nearly as good. Paleoindian sites normally contain small concentrations of stone artifacts, sometimes in association with the bones of large, extinct animals. Paleoindians are thought to have lived primarily as small, mobile groups of big-game hunters. The evidence for permanent residence at Monte Verde is in direct contrast to Paleoindian occupations elsewhere. The organic materials indicate the importance of plants, as well as animals, in the diet at that time. The existence of wood and wooden tools, more common at Monte Verde than stone artifacts, provides an intriguing look at the organic component of tools and equipment rarely seen in the archaeological record.

LINDENMEIER

Late Pleistocene hunters in Colorado

The site of Lindenmeier (at the juncture of the arrows) located between the plains and the piedmont in eastern Colorado.

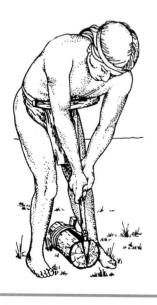

A Paleoindian flintknapper removing the flute from a Paleoindian point. A chest crutch is used to apply pressure to remove the flake from the end of the point. This flute or channel in the base of the point facilitates the hafting.

Lindenmeier, located in northern Colorado at an elevation of 2000 m (6500 ft) in the foothills of the Rocky Mountains, lies at the intersection of three major environmental zones: the eastern slope of the Rockies, the Colorado Piedmont, and the High Plains. Gullies cutting through sedimentary deposits in this area washed out and exposed the buried bones of large bison and large spearpoints. The local ranchers, who discovered these remains in 1924, wrote to the Smithsonian Institution in Washington, D.C., to inform them of the site's existence.

In 1934, Frank Roberts, of the Smithsonian, was sent to investigate the site. Roberts wanted to document the association of hunters and extinct animals in the past. Early sites in North America were almost unknown at the time. Roberts' excavations at Lindenmeier continued each year from 1934 through 1940. The field crew spent almost 600 days on the excavations, opening over 1800 sq m (almost half an acre) in the process and digging deeply into the buried archaeological deposits. This project eventually uncovered one of the largest Paleoindian sites in the New World. Roberts' careful excavations and recording procedures al-

lowed the final results of his original investigations to be published by others after his death.

Radiocarbon dates from the site place the occupation of Lindenmeier at 9000 B.C., just before the end of the Pleistocene. The climate at that time was less arid and cooler than today. The local environment at the site was more wooded, with stands of juniper and pine. Fragments of charcoal from these species were recovered from fireplaces at Lindenmeier. Ground cover would have been heavier, with thick grasses over much of the area. The area around the site can be envisioned as a lush meadow watered by an active spring, which attracted both animals and their predators. The spring, adjacent to the site, must have been the reason this spot was selected as a campsite.

More than 15,000 animal bones were recovered in the excavations. Twelve different species were represented at Lindenmeier, including wolf, coyote, fox, hare, rabbit, turtle, deer, antelope, and bison; they inhabited all three environments near the site. Antelope, wolf, and fox are native to the Rocky Mountains and the piedmont, while bison,

The 1937 excavations at Lindenmeier.

coyote, and jackrabbit are common in the High Plains. The bison was by far the most common animal represented at the site and must have provided most of the meat consumed there. This was a now extinct form of bison, a huge animal some 2 m (6.5 ft) at the shoulder. In all likelihood, the Folsom hunters cooperated to drive these animals into blind canyons and other traps where they could more easily be killed.

More than 50,000 stone artifacts have been counted from the excavated areas at Lindenmeier. Approximately 5000 of these stone pieces and 70 bones were shaped into finished tools. The bone tools included needles and simple pointed pieces. In addition, a number of bone pieces decorated with notches and engraved lines, and several bone beads, were excavated.

More than 600 projectile points were recovered, including almost 250 Folsom points. These Paleoindian spear tips are slender, bifacially worked stone points, shaped carefully on all surfaces by **pressure flaking.** To finish the point, a single long flake, or flute, is removed from the base of each side as a channel to facilitate hafting to a wooden spear shaft. This fluting flake was probably removed by pressure using a chest crutch and vise. Paleoindian points are often found with the skeletons of big game animals such as giant bison, mastodon, and mammoth. Often broken points were either resharpened or reworked into other tools, such as scrapers and knives. The repair of broken equipment was one of the characteristic activities at these campsites.

Fifteen distinct concentrations of archaeological materials were observed in the excavations at Lindenmeier. Two groups of these concentrations, designated Area I and Area II, deserve special attention. Were these two groups of artifacts and bones left by the same group on separate visits, or by two distinct groups, perhaps there at the same time? Careful measurements of the Folsom points in the two concentrations indicated two different sizes. The points in one area were slightly smaller, on average, and fashioned in a different manner. These differences suggest that two different groups of people were responsible for the two concentrations.

Further evidence for the differences between the two areas comes from the original sources for the obsidian found at the site. **Obsidian** is a type of natural glass, produced by volcanic eruptions, and highly prized for making stone tools. Sources for obsidian are limited in number and size. The obsidian in Area I came from New Mexico, while the material in Area II came from the north, near Yellowstone National Park in Wyoming. Lindenmeier thus seems to provide evidence of two or more different social groups that came together, perhaps to cooperate in bison hunting for a brief time some 11,000 years ago.

The reconstructed haft and mounting of a Paleoindian point. Note how the shaft fits neatly into the flute on the spearpoint.

PLEISTOCENE EXTINCTION

Natural versus human causes

Ovis   Bison   Camelops

Euceratherium   Odocoileus   Navahoceros   Equus

Equus asinus   Mammuthus   Stockoceros   Antilocapra

Some Pleistocene and early Holocene animals of North America.

The neck vertebra of a bison with a Paleoindian point embedded in it (at arrow).

In various places around North America—the La Brea tar pits in Los Angeles, the caves of the Grand Canyon, the bone beds of eastern Missouri—the remains of very large animals that once roamed North America have attracted a great deal of attention. Many of these animals were large carnivores and herbivores that wandered the continent over the last 2 million years. By the end of the Pleistocene, however, some 35 species of land mammals, nearly half the total number, became extinct in North America.

The giant sloth and giant beaver, the horse, camel, mammoth and mastodon, lion, cheetah, and short-faced bear, all much larger than their modern counterparts, became extinct by 10,000 years ago. The giant sloth was about the size of a giraffe and weighed up to 3 tons. Caves in the Grand Canyon have preserved many examples of softball-sized giant sloth dung. The giant beaver in the Great Lakes area weighed as much as 140 kg (300 lb). A similar, though not as complete, pattern of extinction in large mammals occurred at the close of the Pleistocene in Europe and Asia, where

mammoth, woolly rhino, cave bear, lion, and other species also became extinct.

What caused the demise of so many animals in such a relatively short period of time? Scientists, archaeologists, paleontologists, climatologists, and others have considered this question for decades. Two major scenarios have been proposed: climatic change (a natural cause) and hunting overkill (a human cause).

Each side in the debate has a set of facts and conjectures that appears to contradict that of the other. For example, those supporting overkill argue that very similar climatic changes during earlier interglacials did not result in the extinction of many species, such as the mammoth, which are adapted to a very broad range of environments. Also, the widespread appearance of Clovis hunters around 11,000 years ago coincides closely with the demise of several of the extinct species. Fluted points have been found in association with the bones of extinct mammoth, mastodon, horse, tapir, camel, and bison, suggesting that Paleoindian hunters, with easy access to

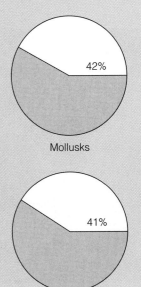

The remains of a mammoth killed and butchered by Paleoindian hunters at the Colby site in Wyoming.

Mollusks 42%

Small mammals 41%

Large mammals 50%

Percentages of extinct animals compared to the total number of species in each group.

animals virtually ignorant of human predators, quickly eliminated entire species of large animals they encountered.

Those who doubt the role of human hunters in the disappearance point out that certain extinct species are never found at kill sites. There is, in fact, no direct evidence of human predation on animals such as the giant sloth and beaver. Other nonmammalian species also suffered extinction at the end of the Pleistocene. For example, almost 45% of the bird species in Pleistocene North America disappeared by 11,000 years ago. There is little reason to suspect human intervention in the extinction of these species.

New evidence for increasing aridity at the end of the Pleistocene and its effect on animal populations argues against the role of human hunters as the sole factor in the extinctions. This climatic change caused a shift in the distribution of small species and perhaps caused the extinction of large animals. Requiring more food and more space to live, large animals, as a group, are more vulnerable to changes in their environment. They are also found in lower numbers than small animals, so the loss of a few individuals in an area could have serious consequences during mating season. Larger animals, too, have a longer generation length than smaller ones so that genetic changes move more slowly through the population. This also makes larger animals more susceptible to extinction.

Proponents of the climate change theory argue that seasonal differences in climate were not as pronounced in the Pleistocene as they are today. Late Pleistocene winters must have been warmer, and summers cooler, than they are at present. As seasonal differences increased at the close of the Pleistocene, environmental changes would have been dramatic. Such difficulties, in conjunction with effective human predation, may have been too much for those species of large animals that died out.

THE END OF THE
PALEOLITHIC

On the threshold of farming

A highly romanticized 1870 engraving of the "noble savages" of the Paleolithic.

The story of the Paleolithic is a remarkable saga—an evolutionary journey from primate to human. The major changes that occurred in human biology and culture made us essentially what we are today. We began more than 4 million years ago as chimpanzeelike primates living in open grassland environments of subtropical Africa. The climate was mild, plants grew year-round, and large predators killed and ate many animals, leaving behind bits of meat and bone marrow for hungry hominids. Sharpened edges of stone helped remove the meat, and other stones cracked the heavy bones. Biologically—lacking claws, big teeth, and speed—early humans were ill-equipped to defend themselves or their young from the predators of the plains. As social beings, however, with safety in numbers, they may have been able to drive away those ferocious carnivores.

The early hominid adaptation was a successful one that spread over most of Africa by about 2 million years ago. Brain size almost doubled during this period, and faces underwent dramatic changes. The handaxe was invented—a marvelous, multipurpose tool sculpted from a slab of stone. As hominid numbers and adaptive success increased, early humans began to move out of the African cradle into Eurasia, where a cooler, more temperate climate challenged ingenuity. The mysterious force of fire was controlled during this time for heat, light, and cooking, becoming a new ally in the continuing battle with nature. Plants were not available during the northern winters, and survival came to depend more on the hominids' abilities as hunters.

By 100,000 years ago, our ancestors had occupied much of the Old World, including the cold tundras of Pleistocene Europe and Asia. The human brain reached modern size. New tools and ideas prevailed against the harsh environment. Life became something more than eating, sleeping, and reproducing. Burial of the dead and the care of the handicapped and injured illustrate a concern for fellow hominids. A cultlike preoccupation with cave bears and some evidence for cannibalism suggest a concern with the supernatural; ritual and ceremony achieved a place in hominid activities. They probably began to dream.

The Upper Paleolithic was the culmination of many long trends—in biology and culture, in language and communication, in ritual and ideology, in social organization, in art and design, in settlement and technology—that began several million years earlier. Evolution brought humanity to our modern form, *Homo sapiens sapiens*. New continents were explored; Australia, North America, and South America were colonized. More kinds of implements were made from a wider variety of materials than ever before. Bows, boats, buttons, fishhooks, lamps, needles, nets, spearthrowers, and many other items were produced for the first time during this period. The dog was domesticated as a faithful hunting companion and occasional source of food. Caves and many artifacts were decorated with paintings, carvings, and engravings, as an awareness of art and design erupted in the human consciousness. Sites from the Upper Paleolithic were larger and more common than those from previous periods. From almost any perspective, this period of the Upper Paleolithic represents a dramatic change in human behavior, almost certainly associated with changes in the organization of the brain or in the use of language, or both. Essentially modern behavior appeared following this transformation, and the rapid change from hominid to human, from archaic to modern, from the past to the present had begun.

The end of the Paleolithic was likely the apogee of hunter-gatherer adaptations on this planet. Very successful groups of foragers lived and increased in almost all of the environments on earth. It is, in fact, this expansion in numbers that is partly responsible for the end of a hunter-gatherer way of life. Increasing populations required new and more productive sources of foods. The bounty of the land, the wild plants and animals of nature, simply were not enough to feed everyone. Experiments to increase the available amount of food were necessary. The story of the domestication of plants and animals and the beginning of the Neolithic is the subject of Chapter 6. Chapter 5 describes events after the end of the Pleistocene, leading to the beginnings of agriculture.

SUGGESTED READINGS

Bordes, F. 1968. *The Old Stone Age.* New York: McGraw-Hill. *A discussion of the tools and remains of the Old Stone Age by a noted French prehistorian.*

Fagan, B. 1987. *The great journey.* London: Thames & Hudson. *A very readable account of the arrival of the first Americans.*

Hoffecker, J. F., W. R. Powers, and T. Goebel. 1993. The colonization of Beringia and the peopling of the New World. *Science* 259:46–53. *A technical synthesis of the evidence from northern North America and Asia.*

Lieberman, P. 1991. *Uniquely human: The evolution of speech, thought, and selfless behavior.* Cambridge: Harvard University Press. *The evolution of language and other very human behaviors.*

Mellars, P. A. 1996. *The Neanderthal legacy.* Princeton, NJ: Princeton University Press. *A recent summary of the evidence for Neanderthals in Europe and their demise.*

Mulvaney, J., and J. Kamminga. 1999. *The prehistory of Australia.* Washington, DC: Smithsonian Institution Press. *The latest summary of Australian archaeology.*

Pfeiffer, J. E. 1982. *The creative explosion: An enquiry into the origins of art and religion.* New York: Harper & Row. *A popular volume on the investigation and interpretation of Upper Paleolithic art.*

Trinkaus, E., ed. 1990. *The emergence of modern humans.* London: Cambridge University Press. *A series of scientific papers on the process of becoming fully modern.*

White, R. 1986. *Dark caves, bright visions: Life in ice age Europe.* New York: American Museum of Natural History. *A wonderfully illustrated volume on the art, both cave paintings and portable objects, of the Upper Paleolithic.*

5

POSTGLACIAL FORAGERS

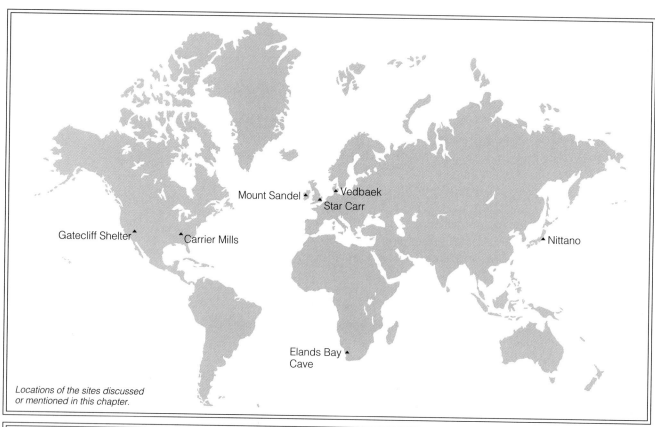

Locations of the sites discussed
or mentioned in this chapter.

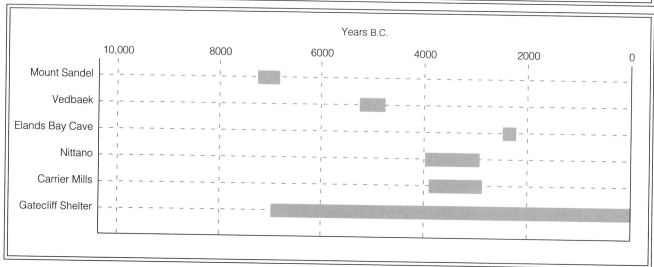

THE WORLD AFTER 8000 B.C.

New solutions to changing environments

The pace of change in human society has increased dramatically over time. For example, there were more innovations in artifacts and behavior during the Upper Paleolithic than in preceding periods. A number of major changes also took place at the end of the Pleistocene, beginning around 10,000 years ago. Large-game hunting, an adaptation that had characterized human prehistory for much of the Middle and Upper Paleolithic, began to decline as certain animal species became extinct, and environments changed in response to warming climatic conditions. Human diet became more diversified and included more plant and animal species.

This chapter examines the early part of the Postglacial period. In a few areas—the Near East, the Far East, and parts of the Americas—plant and animal domestication appeared in the early Postglacial and began to alter the long-standing, hunting-and-gathering pattern of human subsistence. (These origins of agriculture are discussed in Chapter 6.) In other places, hunter-gatherers, or foragers, continued their way of life, adapting to the changing environmental conditions of the Holocene. The term **hunter-gatherers** refers to human groups who use only the wild, natural resources of the earth, hunting animals, fishing, and collecting plants, nuts, seeds, shellfish, and other foods for their sustenance. Although different terms are used in the Old World and New World for this period—Archaic in the New World and Mesolithic in the Old World—the basic way of life was very similar.

The term **Mesolithic**, or Middle Stone Age, designates the period between the end of the Pleistocene and the beginnings of agriculture in Europe, North Africa, and parts of Asia. Only in the last 30 years has the significance of the early Postglacial period been recognized. Since the beginning of the 1800s, the Upper Paleolithic and the Neolithic have been recognized as important episodes in human prehistory. The Mesolithic, however, was regarded as a period of cultural degeneration occurring between the spectacular cave paintings of the late Paleolithic and the farming villages of the Neolithic. Today, however, the Mesolithic is recognized as a time of intensification in human activities and organization.

These hunter-gatherer societies were similar in their adaptations to other groups in Africa, eastern Asia, and North and South America, consuming a wide range of wild plant and animal species and using a highly specialized technology. An incredible range of fishing gear, including nets, weirs, hooks, and harpoons, was developed during this period. Ground stone artifacts appear as axes, celts, plant-processing equipment, and other tools. Projectile weapons were equipped with a variety of different tips made of bone, wood, antler, or stone. In those areas of Europe where bone and other organic materials have been preserved, artifacts are often decorated with fine, geometric designs. Cemeteries that are sometimes present at Mesolithic sites suggest more sedentary occupations.

Examples of Mesolithic settlements discussed in this chapter come from northwestern Europe. Mount Sandel is an Irish Mesolithic site, located at the edge of Europe, that contains very early evidence for year-round occupation by 7000 B.C. In Denmark, excavations at Vedbaek have exposed a cemetery and settlement dating to about 5000

CONTENTS

The climate, geology, and archaeological sequence in Europe and North America during the last 12,000 years.

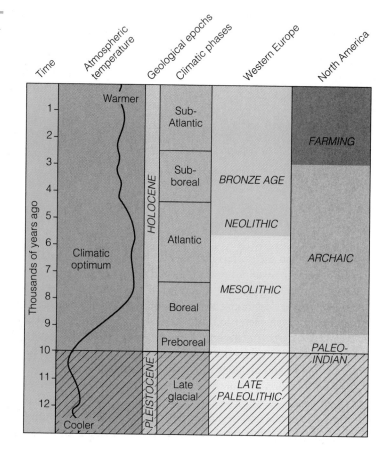

B.C. Information from these sites provides a good picture of early Postglacial hunter-gatherers.

In South and East Africa, the term Late Stone Age is used to describe the artifacts and encampments of Holocene hunter-gatherers. Although most studies concern the earlier periods of human prehistory in these areas of Africa, new information from Elands Bay Cave on the west coast of South Africa provides some indication of the way of life of these groups shortly before the introduction of herding and farming.

In Japan, the period between the beginning of the Holocene and the introduction of rice cultivation is known as the Jomon. Thousands of settlements were occupied during this time, and these food-collecting peoples created very sophisticated pottery. In fact, the earliest ceramics in the world were made in Japan approximately 12,000 years ago. Nittano, on the edge of modern Tokyo, is an example of a Jomon coastal settlement and documents the importance of fishing in this area around 5500 years ago.

In North America, the Paleoindian period of big-game hunting ended approximately 9000 years ago, about the same time many species of big game became extinct. The period between 6000 and 1000 B.C. is known as the **Archaic** and is very similar to the Mesolithic in Eurasia. Human groups began to exploit a broad spectrum of food sources. Many new sorts of subsistence pursuits seem to have begun at this time. Ground stone tools such as mortars and grinding stones have been found at some Archaic sites, indicating an increasing reliance on plant foods. Exotic materials in some regions document an increase in long-distance trade for obsidian, copper, and shell. The date for the end of the Archaic varies in different areas of North America. In some regions, such as the West Coast, the basin and range landscapes of what is now the western United States, and the subarctic and arctic reaches of Canada and Alaska, hunting and gathering persisted up to and beyond European contact. In other areas, such as the southwestern U.S. (Arizona, Colorado, New Mexico, Utah) and the major river valleys of the midwestern and southeastern U.S., a more sedentary way of life

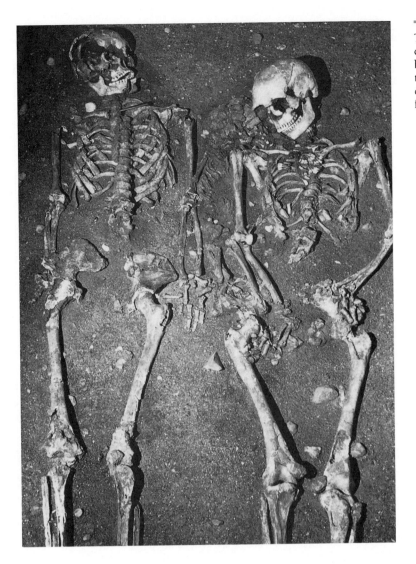

The burial of an adult male, a small child, and an adult female from Ved-baek. Notice the lethal bone point in the throat of the male and the cluster of animal teeth on the chest of the female.

involving the use of cultivated plants, or **cultigens,** began as early as 1000–500 B.C., and perhaps even earlier.

Great diversity in Archaic adaptations was also seen in eastern North America, with major emphasis on fishing, hunting, and plant and nut collecting. Archaic sites such as Carrier Mills in southern Illinois document adaptations typical of this area. Settlements were often located along lakes, rivers, and coastlines to take advantage of aquatic resources. Piles of freshwater mussel shells, the remains of prehistoric meals, are enormous; some examples up to 0.5 km (600 yd) long, 100 m (300 ft) wide, and 6–8 m (20–25 ft) high are found along major rivers in the southeastern U.S. Along the eastern seaboard, huge shell middens also accumulated, documenting the importance of marine foods in the diet of the hunter-gatherers of New England and the East Coast. In the Great Lakes region, native copper from Lake Superior was used extensively by peoples of the Old Copper culture. Copper knives, spearpoints, and various pendants and jewelry were cold-hammered from copper nuggets.

Archaic sites in the Great Plains document a major focus on bison hunting. Sites in the dry, desert West contain artifacts and organic materials that indicate an emphasis on both plant foods and hunting for subsistence. Groups in the Great Basin collected numerous seeds and nuts and hunted antelope and small game such as rabbits. Gate-cliff Shelter in Nevada contains a very deep sequence of deposits and provides a good example of such adaptations.

MOUNT SANDEL

The first human settlement in Ireland

The locations of Mount Sandel and other Mesolithic sites in Ireland.

Ireland, a remote and distinctive outpost of western Europe, is a landscape of rocky uplands and steeply cut valleys, mantled with dense vegetation that grows almost year-round in a climate tempered by the Gulf Stream. At the western edge of the continent, the island has long been isolated from Britain. This insularity has resulted in an absence of many common European mammals, such as wild cattle, elk, and roe deer. Although some late Pleistocene fauna—reindeer and giant Irish deer—may have persisted into the Holocene, there is no evidence of human exploitation of these animals. Ireland was first inhabited in the Postglacial period.

Species of economic importance included wild pig, Irish hare, Irish stoat, pine marten, beaver, otter, and brown bear. On the coast, fish, birds, shellfish, and sea mammals were incorporated into the diet.

This insular character also lent a distinctive cast to the Irish Mesolithic that became more pronounced over time. Artifacts at the earliest sites already exhibit features that are distinct from those in neighboring Scotland, only a few kilometers across the strait of the North Channel. By the end of the Mesolithic, many stone tools are uniquely Irish in design, indicating an absence of contact with the rest of Britain and the continent.

For example, there were no flint arrowheads in the later Mesolithic of Ireland, although these objects were common in England and on the continent during that period.

Investigations have fleshed out a previously vague outline of early Irish prehistory. Radiocarbon evidence for the earliest humans in Ireland comes from 7000 B.C. in the early Postglacial, at the site of Mount Sandel. This name was originally given to an Iron Age hillfort atop a 30-m (100-ft) bluff on the river, County Antrim, in Northern Ireland. The River Bann runs into the sea some 5 km (3 mi) north of the site. Today the tidal ebb and flow of the sea create an estuary below Mount Sandel, but this would not have been the case earlier in prehistory, when sea level was lower. The Bann would likely have been a series of rapids below Mount Sandel during the period of Mesolithic occupation, and the mouth of the estuary would have been a few more kilometers to the north.

Amateur archaeologists have collected Mesolithic artifacts from the fields around the hillfort for a century, documenting the presence of an earlier site. The area was excavated in advance of housing construction in the 1970s by Peter Woodman, of the University College, Cork, to determine what, if any, remains from the Mesolithic period could be salvaged. What started as a minor rescue operation quickly grew, however, into a major project, as the excavations required some 40 weeks of work over five seasons, opening an area of more than 1000 sq m (1200 sq yd).

These investigations provided the earliest evidence for human settlement in Ireland. Excavations at the site on the bluff exposed a series of large, circular structures, roughly 6 m in diameter (about 20 ft, the size of a large room), with a central fireplace and interior pits. The investigations showed that at least four huts had been rebuilt successively on the same spot. The huts were marked by peripheral rows of postholes, many more than 20 cm (8 in) deep, set at an angle in the ground. A circle of saplings or branches had been shoved into the ground and then brought together in the center

to form this structure. The ground was cleared to the subsoil in the interior of the hut, and sod may have been used to cover the outside of the structure. Estimates by Woodman suggest that 8–12 people may have inhabited this hut.

Stone artifacts in the huts included a substantial amount of waste material, along with worn or broken and discarded arrow tips and drills. Around the edges of the hut, axes and scraping tools were discarded. A number of flint blades with traces of red ochre were also found here; their use is unknown. Evidence for tool manufacture was also found to the west outside the huts. A concentration of waste and cores and an absence of finished tools characterized this area.

Fireplaces in the huts were used for cooking and heating. Their contents included stone artifacts, burned animal bones, and large quantities of hazelnut shells. The seeds of water lily and wild apple were also recovered in the excavations. Most of the identifiable bones from the site were those of wild boar; hare was also present, but rare. Bird and fish bones were common. Duck, pigeon, dove, goshawk, and grouse were taken by the Mesolithic hunters of Mount Sandel. Sea bass, eel, and especially salmon were well represented. Freshwater fish remains were not found.

The substantial nature of the residential structure, the numerous pits and rebuilding episodes, along with evidence from the diverse plant remains and animal bones, all suggest that Mount Sandel was occupied year-round. Various foods would have been available throughout much of the year, enabling the occupants to remain at the site for most or all of the seasons. Salmon were present in the streams and rivers during summer; eels ran downstream in autumn, when hazelnuts were ripe. Water lily seeds were collected in September. Most of the pig bones came from young animals killed during winter.

The evidence of year-round occupation at Mount Sandel highlights a very important aspect of this site. Mesolithic hunter-gatherers living on or near the coast were sedentary from a very early date in Ireland and elsewhere in Europe.

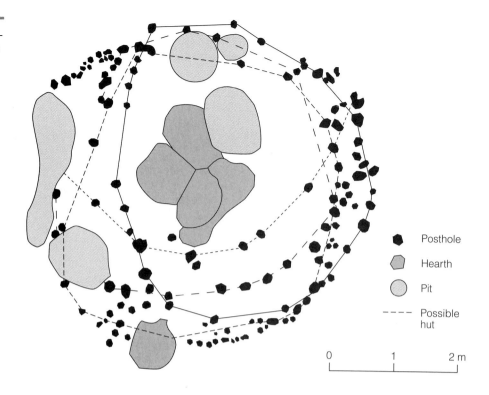

The features found at Mount Sandel—postholes, pits, and hearths. The lines show several possible huts constructed at the site.

Posthole

Hearth

Pit

- - - Possible hut

0   1   2 m

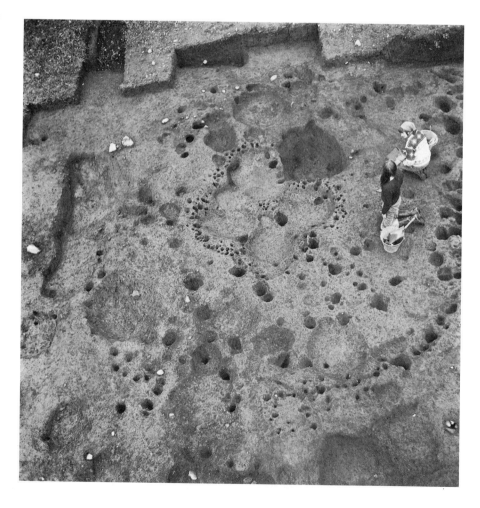

Excavations at Mount Sandel, revealing the postholes, pits, and hearths associated with a large, circular structure, 6 m in diameter.

This shift toward a less mobile way of life is one of the characteristics of the early Postglacial period.

▲ Sorting through residues from Mount Sandel to separate fragments of bone and plant remains.

▼ The seasonality of occupation at Mount Sandel. The season and relative abundance of various resources is shown by the shading. Evidence indicated that the site was probably inhabited year-round.

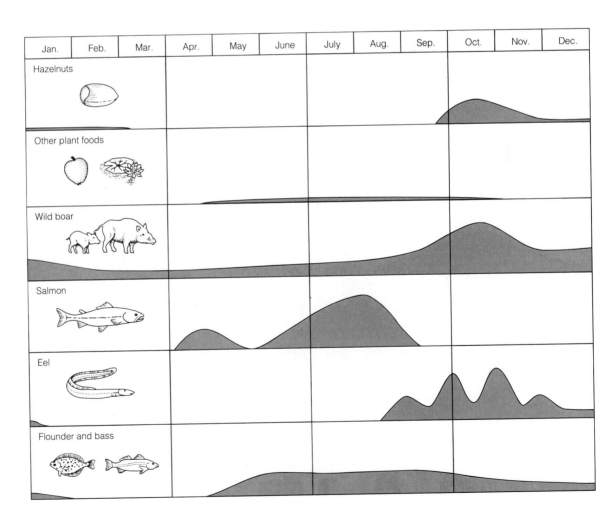

Jan.	Feb.	Mar.	Apr.	May	June	July	Aug.	Sep.	Oct.	Nov.	Dec.
Hazelnuts											
Other plant foods											
Wild boar											
Salmon											
Eel											
Flounder and bass											

THE POSTGLACIAL ENVIRONMENT OF EUROPE

The conditions of the Present Interglacial

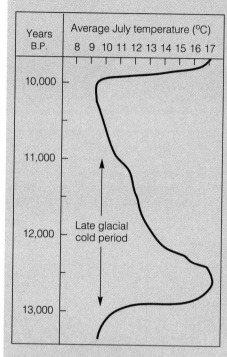

Average July temperatures for the end of the Pleistocene in northern Europe. The dramatic rise in temperature around 13,000 years ago was followed by a cooling spell until the end of the Pleistocene, 10,000 B.P.

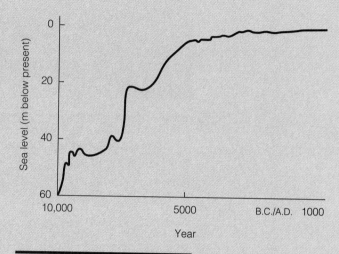

Changes in sea level over the last 12,000 years. Holocene sea levels reached modern coastlines only in the last few thousand years.

A red deer antler frontlet used as a mask or headdress, from Star Carr.

Although the basic topography of the earth has not changed significantly since the end of the Pleistocene, the environment itself has undergone dramatic modifications in vegetation, fauna, and sea level. A marked shift in climate at the end of the Pleistocene was largely responsible for such environmental changes. Dramatic deviations from modern conditions are clear. Europe was as much as 6–8°C (20°F) colder during the ice ages some 18,000 years ago, and warmer than present by 1–2°C (2–5°F) around 7000 years ago during the early Postglacial.

One of the results of the increasing temperatures at the close of the Pleistocene was the melting of continental ice sheets and a consequent rise in the level of the oceans. During the maximum cold period of the last glaciation around 18,000 years ago, the sea was as much as 125 m (400 ft) below its present level. A gradual rise in the level of the oceans began after 16,000 years ago and continued during the early Postglacial. The rate of increase was variable, but a rise of as much as 1 m (3.3 ft) per century occurred during the period of maximum warming. The rising Postglacial seas did not reach present beaches until sometime after 5000 years ago.

The higher sea levels of the Postglacial transformed the outline of the continents. Australia separated from New Guinea and Tasmania. The peninsula of Indonesia broke up into islands. The Be-

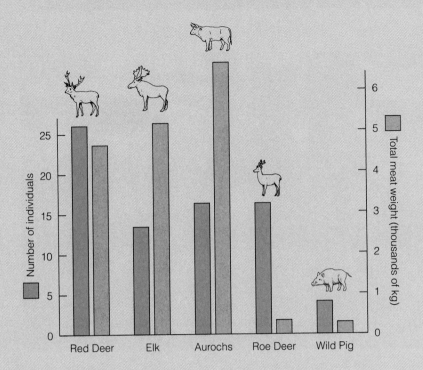

ring Land Bridge was submerged and filled by the Bering Strait. The east coast of North America moved west by more than 100 km (60 mi) in some areas. The British Isles separated from the European continent as the English Channel was flooded by rising seas.

The forest history of Europe emphasizes the complexity of vegetational development through the end of the Pleistocene and during the early Holocene. Many of the plant species that disappeared during glacial conditions in the north survived along the southern coasts of Europe. Late Pleistocene deciduous forests were restricted primarily to southwestern Europe; hazel, oak, and elm survived in western France and northern Spain. Following the close of the Pleistocene, deciduous forest spread throughout most of western Europe, with the exception of small areas of Mediterranean forest in southern Italy, southern France, northeastern Spain, and the islands of the western Mediterranean.

Along with these dramatic changes in climate and vegetation, there were pronounced changes in animal life. The large, migratory herds of reindeer, mammoth, horse, and others that roamed the tundra disappeared, either moving to the north where ice sheets previously existed or becoming extinct. In their place came the more recent species of European mammals adapted to the forest, the European elk (moose), the aurochs (wild cattle), the European red deer (elk), wild boar, and the small roe deer. These species made up the bulk of the terrestrial animal diet of Mesolithic hunters in Europe.

VEDBAEK

*Prehistoric communities
in Mesolithic Denmark*

Excavations at Vaenget Nord. The excavators removed the topsoil, leaving the Mesolithic artifacts in place to map their location and distribution.

Denmark and the rest of Scandinavia have been occupied only briefly in the scale of prehistoric time, essentially since the close of the Pleistocene and the retreat of the ice sheets from northern Europe. At that time, as temperatures rose, the tundra gave way to open woodlands of birch, pine, and eventually to a mixed forest of lime, oak, elm, and other deciduous trees. These forests were occupied initially by herbivores such as aurochs and European elk, followed soon after by wild pig, the European red deer, roe deer, and many small mammals and birds. Inhabiting the streams and lakes were large numbers and varieties of fish. The inlets and islands of the seas around southern Scandinavia would have offered a rich source of food and were the locations of human settlement during the later Mesolithic. Wild animals and plants from the land, sea, and air were the focus of their hunting-and-gathering activities. The inland forests were probably quite dense, supporting little wildlife.

By 7000 years ago, there had been a dramatic shift in human social arrangements in this area from the first small, scattered groups of inland, tundra-dwelling reindeer hunters to concentrations of more sedentary societies along the coastlines. These groups expanded their resource base, eating fish, seals, porpoises, small whales, oysters, mussels, clams, and the like. Settlements became more permanent, and the dead began to be buried in cemeteries.

An example of such a situation can be seen from an important archaeological area near the town of Vedbaek (vay-bek') near Copenhagen, Denmark. Following the retreat of the ice, the Vedbaek Valley contained a freshwater system of lakes and streams. Warming trends continued, and rising sea level filled the mouth of the valley sometime around 5500 B.C., creating a brackish inlet. The shallow waters around the shoreline and islands of the inlet were covered with stands of reeds and sea grass. Over time, the inlet filled up with deposits of reeds and leaves and other organic materials, becoming the layer of peat that it is today.

In 1975, a Mesolithic graveyard was discovered here during the construction of a new school. The cemetery is radiocarbon dated to approximately 4800 B.C. and contains the graves of at least 22 males and females of various ages. All the individuals in the burials were fully extended, with one slightly curled-up exception. Powdered red ochre was found

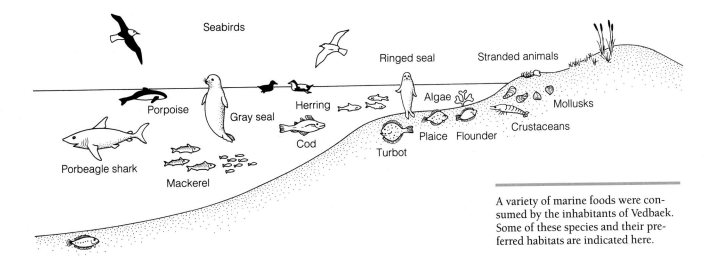

A variety of marine foods were consumed by the inhabitants of Vedbaek. Some of these species and their preferred habitats are indicated here.

in many of the graves. Racks of red deer antler were placed with elderly individuals; males were buried with flint knives; females often were interred with jewelry made of shell and animal teeth.

In one grave, a newborn infant was found buried on the wing of a swan next to his mother (see Color Plate 5). The infant was buried with a flint blade, as were all the males in the cemetery. The mother's head had been placed on a cushion of material such as an animal skin that was elaborately decorated with ornaments of snail shells and deer teeth. Similar materials were found around her waist, suggesting a skirt or costume of some kind. The cemetery also contained rather dramatic evidence for conflict among the groups occupying northern Europe at this time. The simultaneous burial of three individuals in a single grave—an adult male with a lethal bone point in his throat, an adult female, and a child—suggests both the violent death of all three and the existence of a nuclear family (see p. 161).

Since the discovery of the cemetery, Vedbaek has been the focus of intensive investigations. Over 50 archaeological sites have been located around the shore of the inlet. Some 60 species of fish, reptiles, birds, and mammals have been identified in the bone remains from these sites. These species come from every environment—the forest, streams, lakes, wetlands, the inlet, the sound, and the sea. Terrestrial animals are predominantly red deer, roe deer, and wild pig.

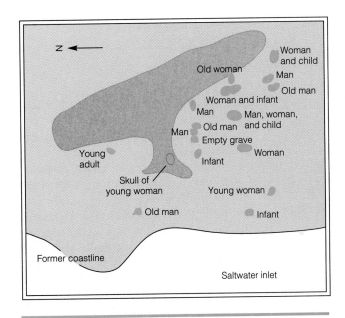

The Mesolithic cemetery at Vedbaek, near the coastline of the former inlet. The gray area is the location of the construction activities that resulted in the discovery of the burials.

Marine foods, however, provided a major portion of the diet; fish and seal bones are very common at the sites.

Mesolithic sites in northern Europe were usually located on the shore, emphasizing the importance of the sea. Distinct zones of artifact deposition can be seen at such sites. The actual living floor on dry land is characterized by the presence of hearths, pits, construction stone, and some artifacts. Stone tools and other artifacts are generally small in size, suggesting that larger refuse may have been swept up and tossed or discarded

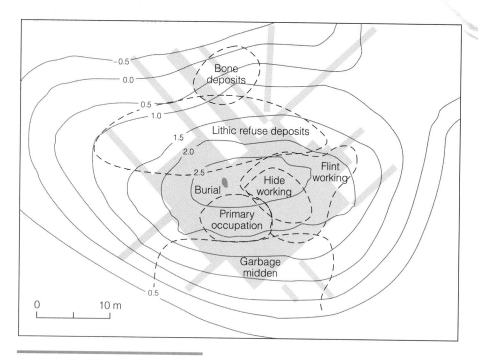

The plan of the Vedbaek site.

elsewhere. Organic materials such as bone and plant remains generally do not survive on the surface of the ground in temperate climates.

A second zone of refuse, originally discarded in the water next to the settlement, can be recognized in the layers adjacent to the occupation floor. Larger materials in this zone are well preserved, including stone, bone, antler, and sometimes wooden artifacts. Because much of the shoreline of the Vedbaek inlet was occupied during the Mesolithic, this second zone often contains a vertical stratigraphy of tools and other debris. This information has been used to construct a detailed chronology for the area. Changes in artifact types and manufacturing methods can be traced through time.

Repeated residence at the same location, however, tends to smear and obscure information about the horizontal arrangement of the prehistoric settlement, the locations of structures and associated hearths and pits. For this reason, an excavation was organized to uncover a settlement of brief occupation, where horizontal patterns of the use of living space might be examined. Several factors pointed to a site called Vaenget Nord (ving'it-nord). Today, the location of this site is marked by a grove of birch trees growing on a slight rise in the land-

scape. The rise had been a small island during the period when an inlet of the sea filled the Vedbaek Valley around 7000 years ago. The island was flooded and eventually submerged by rising sea level shortly after that date. Thus, the period when it could have been a platform for human occupation was limited in time. The age of the artifacts and radiocarbon dates reinforce these impressions. Excavations revealed that the number of artifacts per square meter was lower at this site than at the heavily used shoreline sites.

Major excavations by teams of Danish and American archaeologists began in 1980 and concluded in 1983. The excavation strategy was twofold. Narrow trenches were cut into the deep marine deposits along the former shore of the island to reveal the refuse zone. Broad horizontal units were opened on the surface of the island to expose the living floor and the distribution of artifacts, pits, fireplaces, and other items.

The surface sediments of the island are light sandy clays. The darker traces of past human activities such as digging, fire building, and the placement of posts are often retained in this light soil. On top of this natural surface of the island is a layer of cultural materials, made up of ash and charcoal, organic refuse, and the like. The thickness of this layer varied across the top of the island and was deeper along the sloping shoreline.

In two areas at the southern and eastern margins of the island, large boulders had been fractured into numerous pieces, creating a kind of pavement or landing area. In addition, there are several intact boulders on the site, concentrated in the northwest section. The excavations also exposed many very large posts. These posts are the trunks of elm or alder trees, roughly 30 cm (1 ft) in diameter, sharpened to a point and driven into the surface of the island.

The distribution of flint artifacts on the island is of major importance to understanding the activities that took place at the site. The artifacts can initially be divided into the waste products of manufacturing and repair, and the actual finished tools that were in use. The finished tools are primarily adzes, arrowheads, and burins; only a few scrapers have been recovered. Waste materials include cores for producing flakes and blades, core-shaping flakes, and a great quantity of shattered flint as a by-product of the flaking technique.

Most of the pits and hearths found in the excavation lie on the southwestern, landward side of the island. Several large fireplaces were present, often associated with concentrations of burned cooking stones and charcoal. Also in this area was a large, shallow depression that may be the location of a structure of some sort. A dense cluster of small stake holes was also observed in this area, perhaps related to the construction. Some small pits are scattered around the site. One human-size pit with a blade knife and two axes was probably a grave.

The center of the island has several distinctive features, including the large depression, numerous pits, and stake holes. Most of the projectile points came from this zone. This was likely the primary focus of the occupation. The northeast portion of the island contains evidence for hide working; most of the scrapers, truncated pieces, and unretouched blades come from this zone. Adjacent to this area is a zone of intensive stone toolmaking, rich in both *débitage* and flint tools. Most of the refitted pieces come from this area. To the south, behind these areas, is a zone of garbage dumping, containing abundant charcoal, fire-cracked stones, and only a few dispersed flakes. Along the north shore of the island is a zone of erosion, which was the beach during the time of occupation. North of the island, in what was the inlet, is the refuse zone of larger stone and organic materials discarded in the waters adjacent to the island.

Density plots of the waste material reveal areas of tool manufacture. Flint axes were made as core tools by shaping a heavy nodule of flint into an elongated implement with a sharp leading edge. These axes, averaging 1 kg (2 lb) or more in weight, were attached to long, elm handles and used to fell trees, to hollow logs, and to butcher meat. Arrowheads were made on rhomboid-shaped segments of flint blades. Analysis of the microscopic wear on the edges of the stone artifacts indicates the function of certain

An artist's interpretation of the mother and child burial at Vedbaek.

tools and blades. Some 25% of the blades showed evidence for use on such materials as plants and wood, fresh and dry hide, and meat and bone. Distribution of the blades indicates the areas of the site where these activities took place. Hide-working tools were more common in the central and northeast parts of the island.

Vaenget Nord was probably a small and specialized camp for the Mesolithic inhabitants whose more permanent homes were along the shoreline of the inlet. This small island was likely used for certain activities at specific times of the year. Plant and animal remains indicate the utilization of a variety of environments, presumably during the warmer months of the year. Hazelnut shells were also common at the site, documenting fall habitation. The island situation and the presence of bones from garfish, mackerel, and dogfish indicate the importance of the inlet and the sea to the inhabitants. Vaenget Nord was the focus of activities that involved hunting (the presence of arrowheads), the butchering of animals (butchered bones, meat polish on blades), the manufacture of tools and equipment from animal by-products such as bone (wear marks on burins) and hide (polish on scrapers and blades) and some woodworking (the presence of axes). The variety of hearths and pits, and the heaps of cooking stones, reinforce the impression of diverse activities.

BONE CHEMISTRY AND PREHISTORIC SUBSISTENCE

Information about past diet contained in human bones

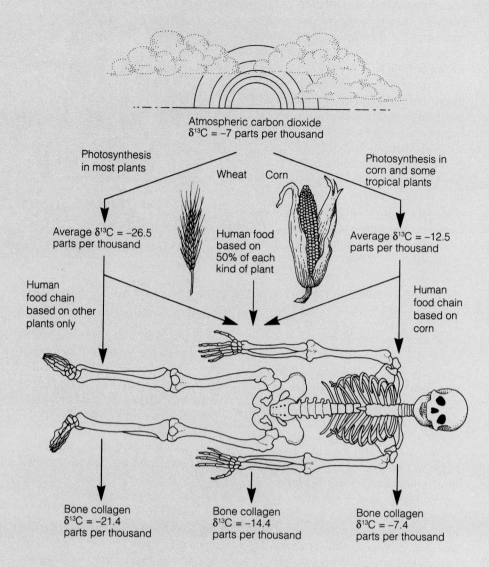

Atmospheric carbon dioxide
$\delta^{13}C = -7$ parts per thousand

Photosynthesis in most plants

Wheat   Corn

Photosynthesis in corn and some tropical plants

Average $\delta^{13}C = -26.5$ parts per thousand

Human food based on 50% of each kind of plant

Average $\delta^{13}C = -12.5$ parts per thousand

Human food chain based on other plants only

Human food chain based on corn

Bone collagen $\delta^{13}C = -21.4$ parts per thousand

Bone collagen $\delta^{13}C = -14.4$ parts per thousand

Bone collagen $\delta^{13}C = -7.4$ parts per thousand

The movement of carbon isotopes through the food chain. Differences in the types of plants consumed or the presence of marine foods in the diet will result in changes in the carbon isotope ratio ($\delta^{13}C$) in human bone. This information is used to estimate the diet of prehistoric human groups.

The nature of past human diet is one of the most important areas of prehistoric research. The quest for food directly affects many aspects of human behavior and society, including group size and social organization, residence patterns, technology, and transportation. Information on past diet has traditionally come from a number of lines of analysis: the study of preserved animal bones, plant remains, fecal matter, tooth wear and disease, and the physical characteristics of the human skeleton. New methods involving the chemical analysis of human bone provide a means of obtaining more information on paleonutrition.

Human bone is composed of organic and mineral compounds and water. Isotopic studies of the composition of bone focus on the organic portion, primarily in the form of the protein collagen. The carbon atoms in collagen occur in two major stable forms, ^{12}C and ^{13}C (carbon-12 and carbon-13). The ratio of ^{13}C to ^{12}C (expressed as $\delta^{13}C$) in bone is measured with an instrument known as a mass spectrometer and reported as a value ranging from about 0 to -30. The ratio of these two isotopes in bone reflects what is consumed in the diet.

Carbon-13 is more common in certain kinds of terrestrial plants, such as

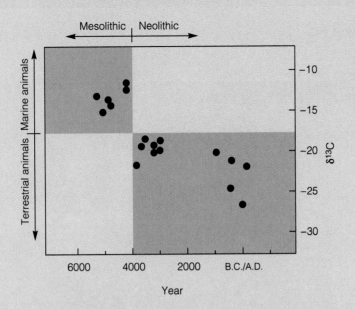

Carbon isotope measurement of human bone from Mesolithic and Neolithic Denmark. A dramatic decline in the use of marine foods came with the onset of agriculture, around 4000 B.C.

corn, and in the oceans. People who eat corn have higher ratios of carbon isotopes in their bones. Changes in this isotope ratio in prehistoric bone can indicate when corn became an important component of the diet. Such studies have been done both in Mexico, to determine when corn was first domesticated, and in North America, to record when this important staple first arrived.

Marine plants, and the marine animals that consume those plants, exhibit carbon isotope ratios ranging between -10 and $-18\ \delta^{13}C$. Values more positive than -20 indicate a predominance of marine foods in human diet, whereas more negative values are more closely related to the consumption of terrestrial plants and animals. Henrik Tauber, of the National Museum of Denmark, measured the carbon isotope ratio in the bones of skeletons from Vedbaek, along with a number of other burials from Scandinavia and Greenland. The ratios from Vedbaek range from -13.4 to $-15.3\ \delta^{13}C$ and are close to values for historical Eskimo skeletal material. Greenland Eskimos consumed marine foods extensively, perhaps as much as 70–90% of their diet, and a similar proportion of seafoods may have characterized the diet of the later Mesolithic. Saltwater fish, seals,

porpoises, whales, and mollusks contributed a major part of the diet at Vedbaek. Measurement of a dog bone from the Vedbaek area gave a reading of $-14.7\ \delta^{13}C$, within the human range, suggesting a very similar diet for the canine. Neolithic burials in Denmark show a sharp decline in carbon isotope ratios, indicative of a decrease in the importance of seafoods among the early agriculturalists.

ELANDS BAY CAVE

Late Stone Age hunter-gatherers in southern Africa

Elands Bay Cave, on the west coast of South Africa.

Much of what we know about the later prehistory of southern Africa has been discovered only in the last 30 years. During that period, John Parkington, of the University of Capetown, has been studying the artifacts and settlements of Postglacial groups in western South Africa. He says:

> We wish to know how the prehistoric populations used the area and its resources, what the relationship was between hunters and herders, what the exploitation strategies were, what precise resources were utilized and how, and what effects the resource pattern had on group size, site location, and seasonal mobility. Archaeology with an ecological viewpoint is the study of the interrelationships of technology, subsistence, and environment. (1984, p. 92)

An important question Parkington (and many archaeologists) faces is whether prehistoric hunter-gatherers moved in an annual cycle of resource use and, if so, how far. Was their movement between the coast and inland in an east-west direction, or did they move north-south within environmental zones? Or were these groups relatively sedentary and did they move only short distances when necessary?

These are difficult questions to answer. One problem is the relationship between the archaeological remains, primarily stone tools and animal bones, and the actual behavior of the prehistoric hunter-gatherers. A connection must be found between static, material objects and dynamic, human activities. Parkington has used several assumptions to make these connections. He says:

> Environments effectively comprise sets of resources, each with a specific distribution pattern. In order to extract and manipulate chosen resources, prehistoric groups needed to engage in specific activities, some of which involved the use of stone tools. Thus the accumulation of stone tools at a site reflects,

albeit in a complex way, the range of activities pursued there. Further, differences between the composition of assemblages reflect the relative importance of tool related activities at those sites. (1984, p. 96)

A review of Parkington's investigations provides some indication of the nature of archaeological research. This project focused on an area of some 22,500 sq km (8700 sq mi, about the size of the state of Vermont), between the western coast of the cape of southern Africa and interior mountain plateaus. Three major environmental zones running in north-south bands can be distinguished in the region. To the west, the Atlantic Ocean plays a major role in the climate and environment of the area. Many edible animals are available from the sea and the beach, including fish, seals, lobsters, mollusks, and seabirds. Rocky points near the mouths of rivers and estuaries are particularly good locations for obtaining shellfish and other marine species. The Strandveld is a low, sandy band, up to 30 km (20 mi) inland, between the beach and the mountains. Vegetation in this zone produces fruit, berries, and roots in season. Animal species in the area include tortoise, dassie (similar to hare), small antelope, and ostrich. Other, larger species of game such as the eland, a kind of large antelope, have disappeared since European contact. The middle Fynbos zone covers the sandstone mountains; shrubs predominate, but trees are found along rivers and at higher elevations over 1000 m (3000 ft). Plants and animals are abundant in this zone, and fish can be caught in the rivers. The Karoo is a dry lowland zone between higher elevations, drained by the Doorn River. This area is a rich pasture for winter grazing by many species of herbivores. These same species may have moved west into the Fynbos during summer when the Karoo veld (grassland) was burned brown by the sun. Human hunters may have followed the herds in a similar pattern of regular movement, known as **transhumance.**

Seasonal changes in resources are important for hunter-gatherers who depend on wild plants and animals. Most of the edible fruits and berries in the re-

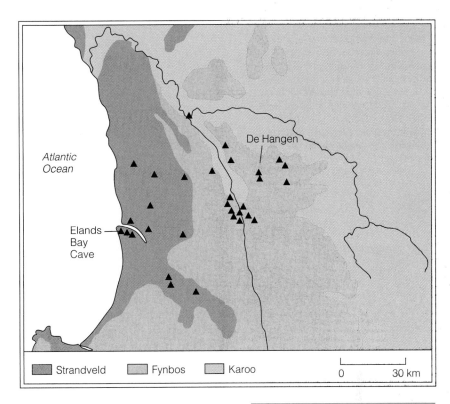

search area ripen in late spring and summer and rarely appear during winter. Diaries and other records from early European explorers in southern Africa report that the diet of the hunter-gatherers in the inland was dominated by roots the women collected daily. Roots and tubers reach maximum size in late summer and are smaller during winter.

Animal foods are generally available throughout the year, with some exceptions. Young seals are most easily captured along the coast during warmer months (August–November in the Southern Hemisphere) at breeding colonies on the beaches after their birth, or during winter when they come out of the water. Mollusks are better to eat during winter. Certain species of saltwater fish are available only seasonally on the coast. Water is also a concern in southern Africa. Precipitation is higher in the mountains. Smaller streams and freshwater springs are common in the mountains, but surface water is rare in the Strandveld and the Karoo. Several rivers run through the project area to the sea and provide some fresh water year-round.

Parkington has suggested that the archaeological remains of hunter-gatherers

Environmental zones in southern Africa, and the site locations at Elands Bay Cave and De Hangen. The triangles indicate other known sites in the research area.

Changes in the occurrence of animals by species over time at Elands Bay Cave. The layer numbers and radiocarbon dates are shown on the left side. Six species are shown: mole rat, fur seal, and four sizes of bovid (antelope). Of particular note is the increasing importance of fur seals and the trend toward smaller bovids in the upper layers.

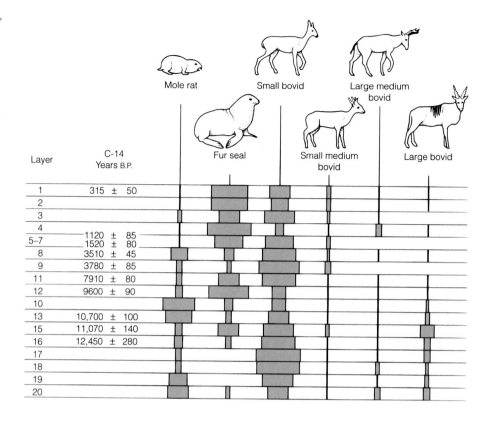

Layer	C-14 Years B.P.
1	315 ± 50
2	
3	
4	
5–7	1120 ± 85 / 1520 ± 80
8	3510 ± 45
9	3780 ± 85
11	7910 ± 80
12	9600 ± 90
10	
13	10,700 ± 100
15	11,070 ± 140
16	12,450 ± 280
17	
18	
19	
20	

found throughout this area were produced by the same or related groups of people moving seasonally in an annual cycle, from the coast to inland areas and back, to take advantage of resources when they were available. He argues that the Fynbos is best suited to summer residence, while both the Karoo and coast provide better sources of food during winter. Shellfish and marine species substitute for the absence of plant foods during the cooler months of the year.

The archaeological remains for evaluating this hypothesis come from excavations at two sites: Elands Bay on the coast and De Hangen in the inland mountains. Elands Bay Cave is located at the mouth of the Vlie River at the Atlantic Ocean. Archaeological deposits from the early Postglacial consist primarily of large accumulations of shell, known as **shell middens,** which are filled with artifacts, bones, and plant remains. All of the evidence suggests that the inhabitants at Elands Bay were on the coast for a brief time during winter, exploiting a variety of marine and terrestrial animals. The shells of mussels and limpets are the most common food remains in the shell midden. Near the cave are a series of intertidal, rocky flats, where mollusks are still very abundant today. These shells suggest that this site was occupied repeatedly in winter, because the mussels can be toxic if eaten during summer.

The shell midden also contains a variety of remains of both marine and terrestrial species. Marine fish, seals, and birds outnumber the terrestrial animals by ten to one. The presence of commercial lobster fisheries at the river mouth today confirms the abundance of these foods. Seal bones from Elands Bay Cave were similar in size and come from yearling seals. These animals tire easily during their first period at sea and wash up or haul out commonly on the beaches during late winter. Dassie bones are also present at Elands Bay Cave but not in abundance; most of the individuals are fully adult, and newborns are rare. Some of the dassies were juveniles, with newly erupting permanent teeth. In modern animals, this dental growth occurs in September and October, the end of the winter season in the Southern Hemisphere. Although grasses used for bedding, as well as seaweed and twigs, are all preserved

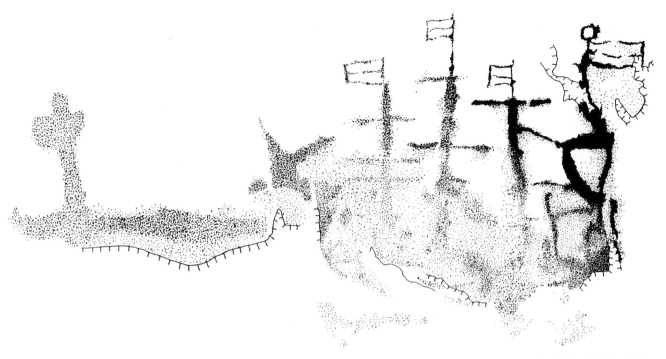

in the shell midden, there is very little evidence for the use of plant foods.

De Hangen is located in the Fynbos, some 80 km (50 mi) from the coast. Excavations at the site have also produced a variety of plant and animal remains. Long grasses were gathered during late spring and summer for bedding in the caves. Edible plant foods were very common, including seeds, fruits, tubers, and roots, more readily available in the summer months. The animal bones came primarily from tortoises, freshwater fish, dassies, and small antelopes. Most of the dassies were adult or very young when they were killed during summer. Connections with the coast are also in evidence. Several marine shells were found. Rock paintings in the mountains south of De Hangen depict sailing ships, which must have been observed from the coast.

Stone tools were made from a material available only from sources in the Strandveld. Such tools provide additional information about the pattern of residence. There are major differences in the lithic assemblages of the coast and the inland mountain area. **Adzes,** associated with woodworking, comprise more than half the tools at sites in the mountains and only about 5% of the assemblages on the coast. Adzes were probably used to make sticks for digging roots and tubers in the Fynbos area.

Pieces with one blunted edge are rare in the mountains, more common in the Strandveld. These small stone artifacts were likely used as sharp tips and barbs for arrows, and thus were found more often where hunting is the primary means of subsistence.

The archaeological remains suggest a general pattern of winter residence on the coast and summer residence in the mountains, supporting Parkington's hypothesis. This evidence also fits the pattern that might be expected given the seasonal availability of certain resources. However, the archaeological evidence does not *prove* this to be the case. Settlement could easily have been moved a few tens of meters as a few tens of kilometers. Winter sites inland, or summer sites along the coast, simply may not yet have been discovered.

Bone chemistry provides contradictory information (see "Bone Chemistry and Prehistoric Subsistence," p. 172). If the same individuals were moving seasonally from inland to coast, eating seafood for at least part of the year, a marine diet should appear in the carbon isotope content of their bones. However, analysis of human skeletal material from inland burials has failed to reveal these expected isotope ratios, suggesting that visits to the coast were not part of a regular pattern.

A cave painting of a sailing ship from one of the inland sites in the De Hangen research area, evidence of contact with the coast.

NITTANO

Coastal hunter-gatherers of Jomon Japan

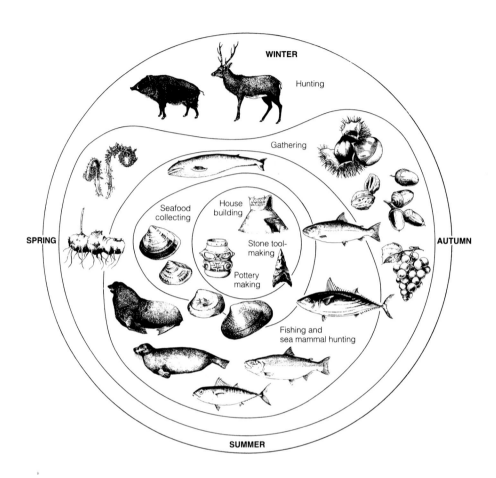

WINTER

Hunting

Gathering

SPRING

Seafood collecting

House building

Stone tool-making

Pottery making

AUTUMN

Fishing and sea mammal hunting

SUMMER

The Jomon annual cycle of hunting and gathering. The chart depicts the relative importance of different food resources and subsistence activities during the seasons of the year, with domestic activities in the center. The widths of the bands indicate the importance of the various activities.

Archaeology is a national craze in Japan where more than $1 billion a year is spent on excavations at more than 13,000 sites. In contrast, the amount spent for archaeology by the National Science Foundation in the United States is around $3 million annually.

The early Postglacial period in Japan is a long and well-documented sequence of environmental change and cultural development. Dating to 10,000–300 B.C., this period is referred to as **Jomon.** Over 35,000 Jomon sites have been discovered, concentrated in the eastern part of the country. Subsistence was based primarily on wild resources, although some cultivated plants may have been included in the diet. The importance of hunting is indicated by the abundance of arrowheads at many Jomon sites. Inland hunt-

ing focused largely on deer and boars, but bears, antelopes, monkeys, hares, martens, and other small mammals were also taken.

Marine foods and coastal settlements predominated in eastern Japan, particularly after 4000 B.C. Fishing was important at sites on the rivers, estuaries, and the ocean. Elaborate fishing gear, and even whole communities specializing in fishing, are evidenced in the archaeological record. Salmon and other freshwater fish were caught in the rivers. Bones from such deepwater species as tuna and shark were also found in the deposits. Fishing equipment included net floats of bark and pumice, net weights, fishhooks, harpoons, and dugout canoes. Over 30 species of shellfish were found in the shell middens.

Stone artifacts from Jomon Japan. Top row: a drill, a stemmed stone knife, and a scraper. The stem is for the attachment of a haft or handle. Bottom row: two projectile points and a small polished stone axe. The scale is 5 cm (2 inches) long.

Plant foods were important in the diet, and more than 180 species have been identified from Jomon settlements, including fleshy fruits such as grapes, blackberries, and elderberries, aquatic plants with edible seeds, and tubers. Nuts played a major role in subsistence; the shells of walnuts, chestnuts, acorns, and buckeyes occur at many sites. The preparation of nuts, seeds, and roots is indicated by the presence of mortars, pestles, milling stones, and other equipment. In the later Jomon, root crops such as taro, yams, and arrowroot may have been under cultivation in western Japan, along with some cereals such as buckwheat and barley. Chipped stone hoes were common at sites from this time. Rice, however, was apparently not cultivated in significant quantities until toward the end of the Jomon period.

Wood, bone, and antler were used for various tools and other objects; these items were often heavily decorated with carved designs. Jade was exchanged over long distances to be manufactured into pendants and other forms of jewelry. Pottery containers were invented very early in Japan, probably before the end

A large pottery container from the Middle Jomon period. This vessel stands 39 cm (15 inches) high.

A ditch, postholes, and hearth from a house construction at a Jomon site near Tokyo. The outer ditch is 6.4 m in diameter. The roof was probably conical in shape, constructed of timber, and thatched with reeds.

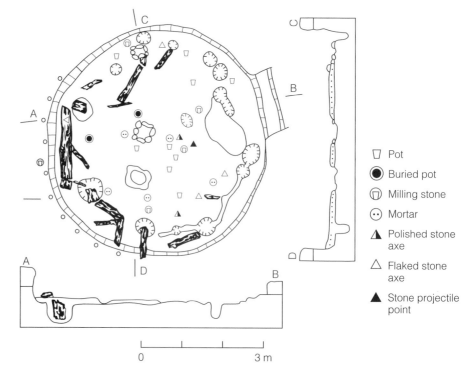

The plan and sections of a Middle Jomon circular house from central Honshu, Japan.

▽ Pot
⬤ Buried pot
⬡ Milling stone
⊙ Mortar
▲ Polished stone axe
△ Flaked stone axe
▲ Stone projectile point

0   3 m

of the Pleistocene. These fired clay vessels occur often at Jomon sites, and their forms became increasingly elaborate over time. Distinct regional varieties can be identified. The word *jomon* means **cord-marking**, referring to the kind of decoration applied to pottery before firing. Cord-wrapped sticks were pressed into the wet clay to create a design.

Jomon villages varied greatly in size and often were occupied for a long time—several hundred years or more, in some cases. Settlements along the coastline are associated with shell middens. Inland sites are found on higher, level ground. The inland settlements generally contained 4–8 pithouses, although up to 50 structures from a single site have been identified. **Pithouses** were substantial, circular or rectangular structures built of large support posts, containing elaborate, stone-lined hearths. Villages were often arranged in a horseshoe shape and may have been divided into two groups of residential units, one on either side of the horseshoe. Communal structures for various purposes were built around the periphery of the village. Burials occurred individually near houses or in the communal structures. The central open area contained few artifacts, but standing stones were occasionally erected there. In one instance, these large standing stones, 1.5 m (5 ft) high, were transported from a quarry some 120 km (80 mi) away.

The site of Nittano (ni′ta-no), near the modern city of Tokyo, is fairly typical of Jomon fishing communities along the coast. The site was excavated by Takeru Akazawa and others from the University of Tokyo. The site is marked by an extensive shell midden, at the head of a narrow, tidal inlet from the Pacific Ocean, and was occupied during the Middle Jomon period, about 4000–3000 B.C. Excavations exposed 10 layers of Jomon deposits, with a dense concentration of shells, particularly in the middle layers. Some 23 species of mollusks and 13 species of fish were identified, most of which live in the brackish waters of tidal inlets and bays. The most common mollusk in the deposits was *Corbicula japonica,* an inhabitant of freshwater streams and estuaries. Mollusks and fish were ap-

parently collected and caught in the waters of the estuary directly in front of the site. The species found in highest numbers in the shell midden came from habitats closest to the site.

Analysis of mollusk shells from Nittano indicates that the site was occupied year-round. The shells of mollusks such as oysters and limpets grow in a series of increments, represented in the shell as *daily* growth rings of calcium carbonate. Using a microscope, researchers can count and compare these rings to the known month of birth for the species, thereby determining both the age of the mollusk and the time of year it was collected. Most of the mollusks at Nittano were harvested during spring and autumn, a few during summer and almost none during winter. Evidence from several migratory fish species, which spend the summer months in estuaries and the colder months at sea, indicates that most of the fish were caught during spring, summer, and autumn.

CARRIER MILLS

*A Middle Archaic settlement
in southern Illinois*

The location of the Black Earth site, Sa-87, at Carrier Mills, Illinois. The dark areas on the ground correspond to the settlement areas at the site.

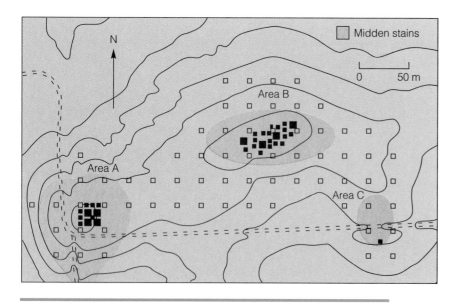

The locations of excavation units in the three areas of the Black Earth site.

The Archaeological Resources Protection Act of 1979 (Public Law 96-95; 93 Stat. 712, 16 U.S.C. 470)

This law provided for the protection of archaeological resources located on public lands and Indian lands; defined archaeological resources to be any material remains of past human life or activities that are of archaeological interest and are at least 100 years old; encouraged cooperation between groups and individuals in possession of archaeological resources from public or Indian lands with special permit and disposition rules for the protection of archaeological resources on Indian lands in light of the American Indian Religious Freedom Act; provided that information regarding the nature and location of archaeological resources may remain confidential; and established civil and criminal penalties, including forfeiture of vehicles, fines of up to $100,000, and imprisonment of up to 5 years for second violations for the unauthorized appropriation, alteration, exchange, or other handling of archaeological resources with rewards for furnishing information about such unauthorized acts. (U.S. Congress, Office of Technology Assessment, 1986)

Prior to the start of federally funded construction, the U.S. Environmental Protection Agency requires an environmental impact study to determine whether important archaeological or historical sites are in danger of destruction. Both federal agencies and private corporations must provide information on the effect their projects may have on the history and prehistory of the area. Various kinds of construction—reservoirs, highways, sewage systems, power lines, to name just a few—require such archaeological surveys and environmental impact statements. This kind of work, known as **cul-**

Excavations at the Black Earth site.

tural resource management, is an important part of the field of archaeology.

Strip mining results in the complete removal of the surface of the ground in order to excavate deep pits to extract the coal. Any buried or surface archaeological sites that are not rescued in some way prior to strip mining will simply be destroyed. In the early 1980s, the Peabody Coal Company of St. Louis, Missouri, was required to submit an environmental impact study of the Carrier Mills area in southern Illinois prior to an expansion of strip mining operations there. The area to be surveyed and tested for archaeological and historical sites covered some 57 ha (150 acres). Richard Jeffries, Brian Butler, and David Braun, of the Center for Archaeological Investigations at Southern Illinois University, Carbondale, were the directors of this 5-year project.

The survey of the Carrier Mills area discovered several large multiperiod sites, dating between 4000 and 1500 B.C. These sites were excavated carefully in order to obtain as much information as possible before the mining began. One of the three settlements, known as the Black Earth site, dates to the Middle Archaic, 4000–3000 B.C. The site sits along a low ridge, next to a series of shallow

An artist's interpretation of Middle Archaic life at the Black Earth site.

lakes and swamps to the east and west; the low, rolling Shawnee Hills lie to the south of the site. The occupants used the river, lakes, and swamps of the lowlands for aquatic resources and exploited the uplands behind the settlement for deer.

The name for the site comes from the distinct black **middens**—accumulations of trash, waste materials, and charcoal and ash from thousands of campfires—that stand out against the yellow-brown soils of the ridge. The entire scatter of artifacts at the Black Earth site covers some 53,000 sq m (13 acres). It is an enormous site, more than a city block in size. Three discrete concentrations were recognized within the larger area, designated A, B, and C. The largest, Area A, is at least 17,000 sq m (4 acres) (the size of two soccer fields), and the cultural horizon extends to 1.5 m (5 ft) below the present ground surface.

Evidence for the use of these areas and for the activities of the inhabitants comes from the prehistoric middens at the site. Deposits in the midden areas ap-

pear to be continuous, suggesting that the occupation was relatively uninterrupted. The middens contain much more sand than the surrounding natural soils, suggesting that locally available sandstone may have been brought to the site for various uses. The decomposition of this rock would explain the higher levels of sand in the midden soils. The concentration of ash, excrement, and other organic matter in the sediments changed the chemistry of the soil, resulting in more alkaline conditions, favorable for the preservation of bone and other materials.

Preserved plant and animal remains document the diet of the inhabitants. Almost 57,000 pieces of animal bone were excavated, representing some 77 species of mammals, reptiles, birds, and fish. Turtles from the nearby swamp and wetlands are among the most common remains. The bowfin, favoring swampy habitats, is the most common fish represented. White-tailed deer and turkey are the most important land animals. Rac-

B 102

Burial 102 at the Black Earth site, with a cache of artifacts near the right shoulder.

coon, opossum, elk, rabbit, beaver, and other species were also included in the game larder, but deer must have been the staple. Deer were hunted throughout the year, but more animals were killed during autumn and winter. Nonfood products, such as fur, feathers, and shells, were also important.

Hickory nutshells are very common in the middens; acorn shells also occur throughout the occupation area, along with the remains of hazelnuts and walnuts. These nuts are available in autumn and could easily be stored and used throughout the winter for food. Seeds from hackberry, wild grape, persimmon, bedstraw, and wild bean are also common. These plants ripen and are harvested during late summer and fall.

Discarded stone artifacts in the middens include a number of hafted tools: projectile points, drills, and end scrapers. Scraping tools were often made from broken arrowheads, recycled for cleaning animal hides. Ground stone tools are also common, ranging from grooved axes to grinding slabs, from counterweights for spearthrowers to hammerstones. Bone and antler tools are numerous and include awls, pins, needles, fishhooks, and other items. Almost one-third of these were made from the antler and bone of white-tailed deer. Turtle shells were used for bowls, cups, and dance rattles. Several

Extraction tasks that have been identified for the Middle Archaic component include hunting (projectile points, atlatl components, faunal remains), fishing (fishhooks, fishhook production residue, faunal remains), fowling (faunal remains), procurement of lumber (axes), nut procurement and processing (pitted stones, grinding stones, nutshell), butchering (heavy-duty scrapers, cutmarks on bone), and hide processing (scrapers, bone awls). Maintenance tasks include the manufacture of flaked stone tools (unfinished bifaces, débitage, hammerstones), ground stone tools (unfinished tools), and bone and antler tools (grooved abraders, antlers with scoring marks, production residue), and the recycling of broken tools (scrapers made from broken projectile points). One socially related task can be accounted for in the data, disposal of the dead (burials).

Richard Jeffries and Mark Lynch (1985)

Table 5.1 Grave Goods Buried with Individuals at the Black Earth Site

Function	Adult Male	Adult Female	Child
Utilitarian	Mussel shell Bone awl Worked antler Unworked deer bone Projectile point Chert core Drill Scraper Utilized flake Axe fragment	Mussel shell Bone awl Worked antler Unworked deer bone Bone needle Hafted scraper Chert biface	Mussel shell Utilized flake Ground stone
Ornamental	Shell pendant Bone pin Anculosa-shell bead Antler bead Plummet Bar gorget	Shell pendant	Shell pendant Shell bead Mussel-shell bead Circular shell disk Crinoid-stem bead
Ceremonial	Decorated bone Animal bone (not deer) Elk antler cup Red ochre Fossil Fluorspar crystal Worked shale Worked stone Hematite Water-worn pebble Banded slate Miniature grooved axe	Worked turtle shell Animal bone (bird) Red ochre	Turtle shell cup Red ochre Water-worn pebble Fluorspar crystal

recovered bone pins may have been used with clothing or in hair arrangements. These pins are decorated with incised lines in a geometric design. Beads and pendants of shell, antler, and bone also were found.

In addition to the settlement, there was a cemetery at the Black Earth site. At least 154 burials from the Middle Archaic were found. The investigators estimate that there were a total of more than 500 graves in the entire site. Infants accounted for 21% of the burials. Males slightly outnumbered females in the cemetery and had a shorter lifespan. Male life expectancy after childhood was only 32 years; for females, 38 years. Adult males averaged 1.7 m (5 ft, 6 in) in height, while females were 1.6 m (5 ft, 2 in).

Individuals were buried in shallow pits, and occasionally a cap of clay was used to seal the grave. About half the burials were found in an extended position, and the other half were curled up. Children and young adults were usually fully extended in the graves, while older adults were placed in the graves in a flexed, or curled-up, position. Four individuals were buried in unusual positions, including one man seated upright and bent over.

Grave goods provide an important sample of the tools and ornamental items of the living population (Table 5.1). Everyday objects were generally discarded when they were broken or no longer useful. Materials placed in graves, however, were likely the property of the deceased or placed with the dead as a kind of offering; these objects are intact when discovered at a burial site (see "Grave Goods," Chapter 7, p. 280).

Only about 25% of the individuals were buried with objects in their graves.

Males were buried with a wider array of goods than females or children. Males were generally buried with equipment to obtain food or other resources, while females were buried with tools to process or prepare these raw materials. Women were buried with scrapers, bone awls, and needles. Only males were buried with ornamental objects such as bone pins and decorated bones, along with projectile points, worked stone drills and axes, and small animal bones. A "medicine bundle" was placed near the head of a 43-year-old male. This cluster contained 45 objects, including eagle talons, part of a bear paw, a miniature axe, pieces of slate, red ochre, and a dog's tooth. One perforated disk of marine shell, probably from the Atlantic Ocean or the Gulf of Mexico, was found around the neck of a buried infant. Copper from the Great Lakes area was found with an adult male at Carrier Mills. A copper wedge had been placed at the top of the neck of the skeleton, perhaps as a substitute for the missing skull of this particular individual.

THE HUMAN SKELETON

A storehouse of information

Since the time of the Neanderthals, humans have buried their dead. As a result, intact human skeletons are sometimes preserved in single graves or in cemeteries. Archaeologists and physical anthropologists spend hours carefully uncovering and removing these skeletal remains from the ground. Bones and teeth are taken to the laboratory, where a surprising amount of information can be obtained from the observation and measurement of various features. Consideration of a series of burials from a single cemetery can provide information about the entire population, including demographic characteristics, life expectancy, and inheritance patterns.

The human skeleton is much more than a structural framework for supporting the body. Bone tissue contains a wide variety of information about the individual to whom it belongs. The length and thickness of bone, for example, provide an indication of an individual's size and strength. Stature can be estimated from measurements of the long bones of the arm or leg (Table 5.2). Evidence of disease or illness is also embedded in bone. It is often possible to determine age at death, the cause of death, sex, a history of disease or accident, and nutritional status from analyzing prehistoric human bone. Diet, too, may be reflected in the chemical composition of bone (see "Bone Chemistry and Prehistoric Subsistence," p. 172). The sex of a skeleton is indicated by several features. Adult males are generally taller than females, but in most cases, size alone is not a sufficient indicator of sex. Several features of the pelvis are most important for determining the sex of skeletal remains. The female pelvis is wider than that of the male and slightly different in shape.

Several indicators are used to estimate age at death, one of the most important being teeth. The age of children and adolescents is relatively simple to determine from teeth. In many mammals, the deciduous teeth of young individuals are replaced by permanent teeth, and the eruption patterns of permanent teeth are well established. For example, most 6-year-old humans are missing their two front teeth; we speak of a 12-year molar, referring to the age at which this tooth erupts.

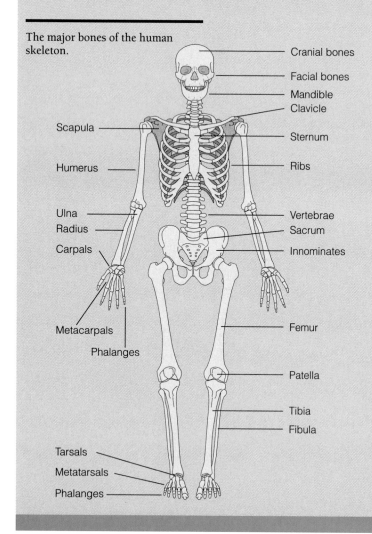

The major bones of the human skeleton.

Cranial bones
Facial bones
Mandible
Clavicle
Scapula
Sternum
Humerus
Ribs
Ulna
Radius
Vertebrae
Sacrum
Carpals
Innominates
Metacarpals
Phalanges
Femur
Patella
Tibia
Fibula
Tarsals
Metatarsals
Phalanges

Table 5.2   Estimating Stature from Femur Length

Femur Length, mm	Stature	
	cm	in
452	169	66
456	170	66
460	171	67
464	172	67
468	173	68

Source: Adapted from Jurmain, R., H. Nelson, and W. A. Turnbaugh. 1987. *Understanding physical anthropology and archaeology*, 4th ed. St. Paul, MN: West.

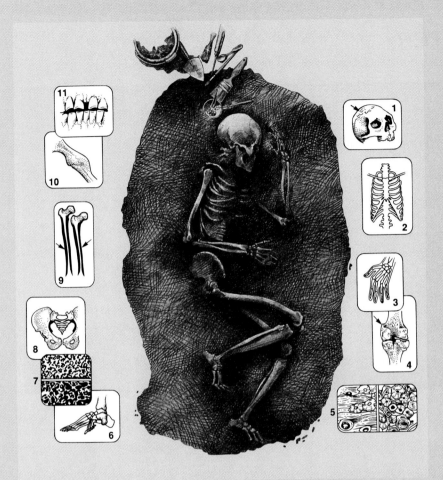

The skeleton as a storehouse of information. (1) Lesions on the skull suggest scalping at the time of death. (2) Flattened ribs and a fused breastbone result from corsets of the eighteenth century. (3) Badly twisted and eroded joints are evidence of arthritis. (4) Bone spurs appear on the knees of riders who spent too much time in the saddle. (5) Bone cells, or osteons, are denser in middle age (right) than in adolescence (left). (6) Shortened and deformed foot bones document the practice of foot binding in the China of previous centuries. (7) Osteoporosis, a loss of bone density, is more common in the elderly (bottom) than the young (top). (8) The female pelvis is wider than that of the male, for giving birth. (9) More robust femurs are evidence of a diet higher in meat; thin bones suggest a protein-deficient diet. (10) Bumps and irregularities in bone show improperly healed fractures and injuries. (11) Indentations and grooves in the teeth are found among fishermen and wool spinners, who used their teeth for cutting thread.

The size and condition of skeletal bones can also be used to estimate age at death. Body size, as indicated by the length of long bones, is one clue. However, the joint ends of long bones, called **epiphyses,** provide even more reliable information. During childhood and adolescence, as the skeleton grows and hardens, the ends of long bones are separate from the shaft to facilitate growth. However, at puberty and during adolescence, the epiphyses harden and unite with the shaft to become a single bone, terminating growth. The age of epiphysis union varies for different bones, and this information can be used to determine the age at death. By the early twenties, the development of teeth and bones is largely complete in humans. Other, less precise indicators must be used to estimate the age at death from the skeletal material of older individuals. Skeletal features used to determine the age of older adults include the pelvis and skull, and degenerative changes in bone tissue.

Stress during one's lifetime is also revealed in the skeleton. Malnourishment in childhood causes the disruption of bone growth, which shows up in the skeleton as a series of distinct features, known as Harris lines, in the ends of long bones. Tooth enamel also reflects childhood stress and malnourishment in an irregular series of lines, a condition known as dental enamel hypoplasia. Various diseases and other health problems also are reflected in bone. Arthritis is one of the most common conditions in the bones of older adults, characterized by an accumulation of bone tissue around the joints. Syphilis, tuberculosis, and other infectious diseases may result in bone loss and pitting or deformation of the skull and other bone surfaces.

GATECLIFF SHELTER

Cave deposits from the Archaic of Nevada and the desert

Removal of the sediments from the bottom layers of Gatecliff Shelter by a bucket brigade.

Gatecliff is arrowheads, baskets, charcoal, digging sticks, endscrapers, firehearths, grinding stones, horncores, insects, jasper, knives, living floors, mortars, nets, obsidian, pictographs, quartz, rattles, silt, turquoise, ungulates, vessels, whetstones, xerophytes, yarn, and zoomorphs.

David Hurst Thomas (1979)

The Great Basin of North America covers large parts of Nevada, Utah, California, Oregon, and Idaho. This region lies west of the Rocky Mountains and east of the rain shadow of the Pacific Coast ranges such as the Sierra Nevada in California. The Great Basin is, in fact, a whole series of dry, intermontane valleys and basins at relatively high elevation. The area today is essentially semiarid desert with scrub vegetation. Water is available primarily at springs that have been the focus of human settlement for thousands of years. At the end of the Pleistocene and during the early Holocene, however, many of the low areas of the Great Basin were filled with freshwater lakes, providing a fairly rich aquatic habitat.

Monitor Valley in central Nevada is a fairly typical high, intermontane basin. Here lies the site of Gatecliff, at an elevation of 2300 m (around 7500 ft). Gatecliff Shelter is an archaeological discovery that offers much more than expected. In 1970, David Hurst Thomas, of the American Museum of Natural History

in New York, was looking for a few good caves that might contain a deep stratigraphic sequence of layers for the area. Such deposits are essentially a book of information about changes in human activity and behavior. A local mining engineer told him about a place called Gatecliff, where he had seen prehistoric paintings.

Gatecliff Shelter is a large opening at the foot of a steep rocky slope. The ceiling of the shelter is heavily blackened from centuries of smoke, and the walls have been painted with small figures and other designs. A large **sondage**, or test excavation, in the cave revealed that it indeed contained a very deep, long sequence of human occupation, enduring for most of the Archaic in this area. Thomas then began a series of annual excavations at the cave that lasted seven seasons and involved over 200 people, 5000 person-days, in total. These excavations continued from the top of the ground surface at Gatecliff to a depth of more than 10 m (30 ft), one of the deepest stratigraphies in North America.

Excavations at the very bottom level of Gatecliff Shelter. Part of the stratigraphy shown here is also depicted in the drawing of the section on the right.

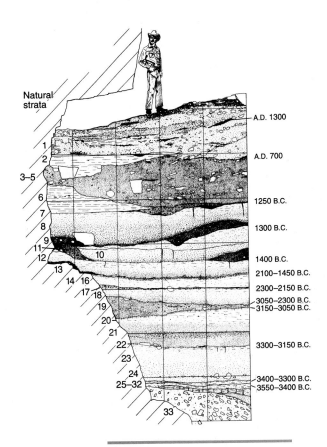

A composite drawing of the stratigraphic section at Gatecliff Shelter, with layer designations on the left and chronology on the right. Each grid unit is 1 sq m. The human figure is shown to scale.

More than 600 cu m (800 cu yd, equivalent to several large roomfuls) of earth were removed in the excavations.

The layers in the cave are very well defined; 16 individual cultural horizons can be discerned in the more than 50 layers in the cave. Sterile deposits of silt, up to 0.6 m (2 ft) thick, often buried the abandoned human occupation levels in the cave. Occasionally, alluvial materials, carried by flash floods, covered the original floor and created a new one. This process was repeated a number of times, resulting in a gradual accumulation of deep sediments in the cave.

The deposits at Gatecliff are like a book with layers as the pages. The archaeologists peel back the horizontal "pages" or layers to "read" the human activities left in the archaeological remains. Gatecliff contains an extensive record of human activities. More than 40 radiocarbon dates indicate that the lowest layers are at least 9000 years old, and the upper part of the deposit contains remains from A.D. 1400. A layer of volcanic ash toward the bottom of the deposits is known to have come from the eruption of Mt. Mazama, 6900 years ago.

The earliest evidence of human presence in the shelter dates to 5500 years ago, shortly after a piñon pine and juniper woodland began to cover the Monitor Valley, replacing the previous sagebrush steppe in the area. Most of the archaeological evidence indicates brief, episodic stays in the shelter, largely associated with male activities such as hunting and the manufacture and repair of equipment. Careful sifting of the sediments resulted in the recovery of more than 51,000 animal bones. Over 90% of the large mammal bones at the site are from bighorn mountain sheep, suggesting that this animal may have been the major focus of such high-altitude hunting

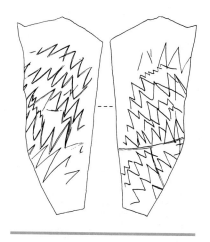

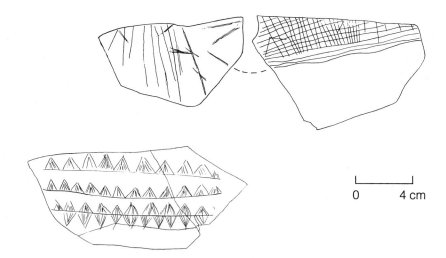

Several inscribed limestone slabs from Gatecliff Shelter.

Willow branches tied into a square knot.

camps. One of the upper layers, Horizon 2, dating to about A.D. 1300, contained the remains of at least 24 bighorn sheep that had been killed elsewhere and dragged to the shelter to be butchered. Most of the best cuts of meat—ribs, rump, shoulders, and neck—were taken from the shelter, probably to the residential community of the hunters elsewhere in the valley. The bones of rabbit and hare were numerous.

Because of the normally very dry conditions in the desert, more fragile organic remains are preserved at the site as well, including cordage and basketry. Caves are often good places for the preservation of the past. Plant remains are rather limited, however, and only a few food species were represented, particularly piñon and goosefoot (*Chenopodium*), a kind of grass with small, nutritious seeds that ripen in late summer. Piñon nuts can be harvested in autumn from the piñon pine.

The area near the back of the cave generally contained smaller objects, discarded and dropped directly after use. Larger pieces of stone, bone, and other material were tossed toward the front of the shelter, leaving the living floor in the back relatively smooth and level. More than 30 fireplaces were observed in the cultural levels, almost always built about 4 m (14 ft) from the back wall of the shelter. The deposits contained more

than 400 projectile points, many made from the locally available dark green chert. Only a few points were made from obsidian, which must have come from longer distances.

Gatecliff was apparently used only rarely as a residence for the entire local group; there is only limited evidence of female activities. Toward the end of the Archaic occupation in the shelter, however, there was a greater emphasis on grinding stones for the preparation of plant foods, along with more than 400 engraved limestone slabs. Thomas suggests that these slabs may have been left by women when they were in the area collecting seeds.

HUNTER-GATHERERS

*A lost way of life
at the margin of civilization*

About 99.8% of our human past was spent as hunter-gatherers—living in small, simple, egalitarian societies that moved around following a seasonal cycle in the quest for wild foods. Such adaptations are thought to represent the foundations of human society, from which more recent social and political arrangements have evolved. Group size and organization were highly flexible among hunter-gatherers and permitted a rapid response to seasonal changes in the food supply. For example, the Copper Eskimo of northern Canada followed a seasonal round of residential moves that focused on seal hunting in winter, fishing in summer, and caribou hunting in autumn. Some kind of an annual cycle defined the basic pattern of subsistence and settlement for many groups of hunter-gatherers.

Among these groups, leadership was ephemeral and gained through the recognition of individual abilities. Relationships between individuals were determined by kinship; status differences were negligible; everyone had access to the resources of the group. Private property was limited; labor, goods, and food were shared communally. Essential tasks for food collecting were divided according to sex; men were hunters of larger animals, while women collected plant foods and fish and trapped small animals.

Such groups survived until very recently in the more remote parts of the world. Today, the spread of farming societies and the reach of the industrialized world have basically eliminated hunter-gatherer societies. The last of these groups lived in the most marginal environments—only those areas that were of little interest or use to agricultural and industrial societies. The San, or Bushmen, of the Kalahari Desert of South Africa, the Mbuti Pygmy of the Congo rain forest in Africa, the Hadza in the tsetse-fly-ridden areas of East Africa, the Inuit, or Eskimo, of northern North America and Greenland, and the Aborigines of western Australia were among the few remaining groups of hunter-gatherers. Today, even these societies have abandoned their traditional way of life, as national governments settled them in permanent communities for purposes of education and health care. The end of the twentieth century marks the demise of the hunting-and-gathering way of life.

Our picture of hunter-gatherer lifeways is too simple, however, and reflects relatively recent changes in human society. Ten thousand years ago, hunter-gatherers occupied all the continents except Antarctica; everyone was a hunter-gatherer. Theirs was a very successful adaptation, one that had provided for the enormous expansion

Kua hunter-gatherers of the Kalahari Desert of Botswana, South Africa. Hunter-gatherers today occupy only the most marginal places on earth and have essentially disappeared.

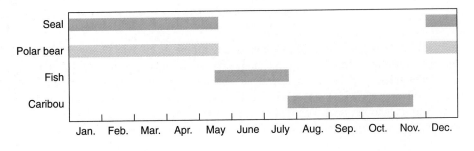

The seasonal round of the Copper Eskimo. The lighter bars indicate availability of resources; the darker bars indicate more intensive use of resources.

The estimated population and distribution of hunter-gatherers over the last 10,000 years.

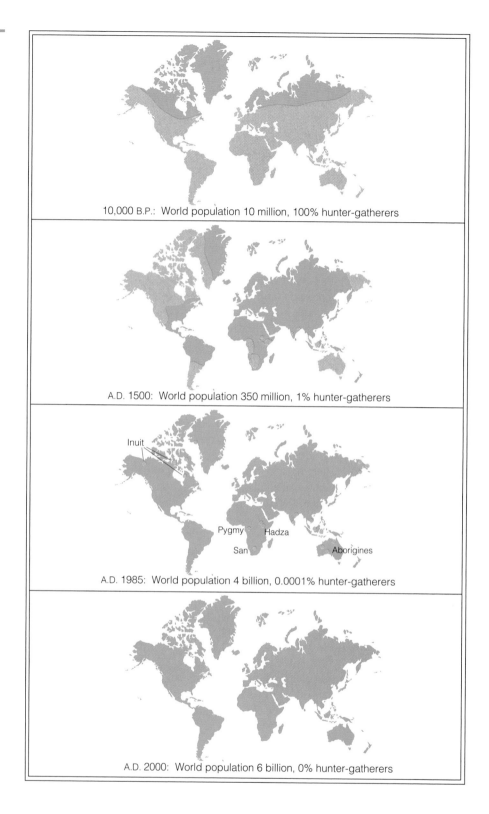

10,000 B.P.: World population 10 million, 100% hunter-gatherers

A.D. 1500: World population 350 million, 1% hunter-gatherers

A.D. 1985: World population 4 billion, 0.0001% hunter-gatherers

A.D. 2000: World population 6 billion, 0% hunter-gatherers

of the human species into a wide range of environments all over the world. Hunter-gatherer societies exhibited a diverse range of forms from large, sedentary populations with hierarchical leadership to very small, egalitarian groups moving about the landscape in search of food. In most areas, wild food was readily available to support large numbers of people. Such adaptations have been described as the "original affluent society" by anthropologist Marshall Sahlins (1968, p. 89). Leisure time was plentiful, and life must have been reasonably good. Health conditions were significantly better than among early farming populations.

By the early Postglacial, many of these foraging groups evolved quickly into larger groups, with more-sedentary occupations, more-complex technology, and more-intensive subsistence activities. Developments in technology, settlements, and subsistence practices are preserved in the archaeological record. Technology developed toward greater efficiency in transport, in tools, and in food procurement. Watercraft and paddles are found at sites in a variety of coastal and lakeside settlements. The inhabitants of Franchthi Cave in mainland Greece were sailing to the island of Melos by the end of the Pleistocene. Mesolithic coastal foragers in southern Scandinavia primarily depended on the sea for food. Settlements were generally larger, of longer duration, and more differentiated than in the preceding Paleolithic.

Sedentary occupations are known from a number of areas, including Jomon Japan, the Middle Archaic in North America, and the Mesolithic of northern Europe. Domestic dogs were used for hunting in Mesolithic Europe and in North and South America. Food procurement was both more specialized and more diversified—specialized in terms of the technology and organization of foraging activities, and diversified in terms of the numbers and kinds of species and habitats that were exploited. Plant foods became more important for subsistence, and nutshells are especially visible in the archaeological record from this period. Fishing and the exploitation of coastal and aquatic resources became very important in the quest for food. It seems clear that increasing sophistication in subsistence and settlement were important trends among Postglacial foragers.

In certain areas, the changes among hunter-gatherers at the beginning of the Postglacial led very quickly to the domestication of plants and animals and the beginnings of agriculture. These areas in western Asia, eastern Asia, western Mexico, and South America became the centers of farming adaptations, growing crops and herding animals, living in villages, and using pottery and ground stone tools. This story of the origins of agriculture is told in the next chapter.

SUGGESTED READINGS

Akazawa, T., and C. M. Aikens, eds. 1986. *Prehistoric hunter-gatherers in Japan.* Tokyo: University of Tokyo Press. *A series of articles on the archaeology of early Japan.*

Burenhult, G. 1993. *People of the Stone Age: Hunter-gatherers and early farmers.* San Francisco: HarperCollins. *A beautifully illustrated, popular book on the early Postglacial archaeology of foragers and farmers.*

Schwartz, J. H. 1995. *Skeleton keys.* Oxford: Oxford University Press. *An introduction to human skeletal morphology, development, and analysis.*

Jeffries, R. W. 1987. *The archaeology of Carrier Mills.* Carbondale: Southern Illinois University Press. *A popular account of the excavations of the Archaic site of Carrier Mills, Illinois, and of the general archaeology of this area.*

Kelly, R. L. 1995. *The foraging spectrum: Diversity in hunter-gatherer lifeways.* Washington, DC: Smithsonian Institution Press. *An archaeologist's look at hunter-gatherers.*

Lee, R. B., and R. Daly. 1999. *Cambridge encyclopedia of hunters and gatherers.* Cambridge: Cambridge University Press. *A compendium of information about hunter-gatherers around the world.*

Price, T. D., and J. A. Brown, eds. 1985. *Prehistoric hunter-gatherers.* Orlando, FL: Academic Press. *A set of papers on early Holocene foragers in a variety of places around the world.*

Zvelebil, M., ed. 1986. *Hunters in transition.* Cambridge: Cambridge University Press. *A series of papers on foragers becoming farmers during the early Holocene.*

6

THE ORIGINS OF AGRICULTURE

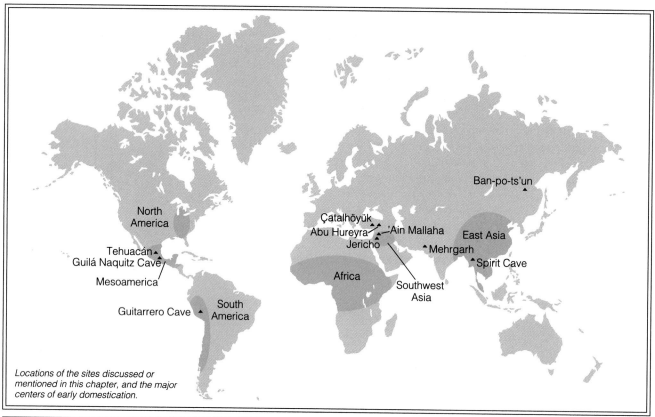

Locations of the sites discussed or mentioned in this chapter, and the major centers of early domestication.

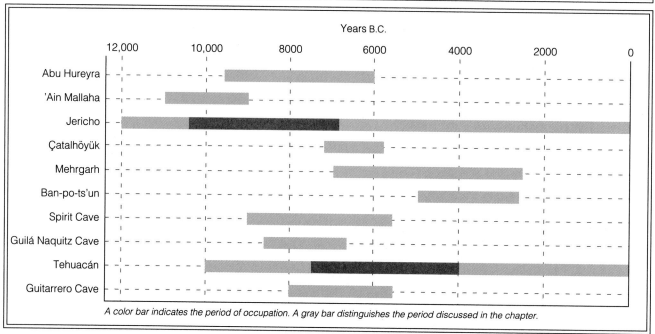

Years B.C.

	12,000	10,000	8000	6000	4000	2000	0

Abu Hureyra
'Ain Mallaha
Jericho
Çatalhöyük
Mehrgarh
Ban-po-ts'un
Spirit Cave
Guilá Naquitz Cave
Tehuacán
Guitarrero Cave

A color bar indicates the period of occupation. A gray bar distinguishes the period discussed in the chapter.

THE FIRST FARMERS

The major transition in the course of human prehistory

As we have noted, the vast majority of our history as a species was spent as hunter-gatherers. Our ancestry as food collectors, consuming the wild products of the earth, extends back more than 4 million years. Nevertheless, shortly after the end of the Pleistocene, some human groups began to produce food rather than collect it, to domesticate and control wild plants and animals. Perhaps the most remarkable transition of our entire prehistory is the almost simultaneous appearance of domesticated plants and animals in several different areas of the world between about 10,000 and 5000 years ago.

Agriculture is a way of obtaining food that involves domesticated plants and animals. But the transition to farming is much more than simple herding and cultivation. It also entails major, long-term changes in the structure and organization of the societies that adopt this new way of life, as well as a totally new relationship with the environment. While hunter-gatherers largely live off the land in an *extensive* fashion, generally exploiting a diversity of resources over a broad area, farmers *intensively* utilize a smaller portion of the landscape and create a milieu that suits their needs. With the transition to agriculture, humans began to truly master their environment.

Just because a species is exploited intensively by humans does not automatically mean it will become domesticated. Although oak trees have supplied acorns for humans for thousands of years, they have not been domesticated. **Domestication** changes the physical characteristics of the plant or animal involved. The domestication process involves both the inherent characteristics of the plant or animal species (generational length, life cycle, plasticity) and the intensity and nature of the human manipulation.

Agriculture requires several major practices for long-term success: (1) *propagation*, the selection and sowing of seeds or breeding of animals; (2) *husbandry*, the tending of plants or animals during the growth period; (3) the *harvesting* of plants when ripe or the *slaughter* of animals at appropriate times; and (4) the *storage* of seeds and *maintenance* of animals through their nonproductive periods to ensure annual reproduction. Plant propagation and husbandry involve **cultivation**—clearing fields, preparing the soil, weeding, protecting the plants from animals, and providing water.

The evidence for early domesticated plants focuses on seed crops. The best-known early domesticates are the cereals—the grasses that produce large, hard-shelled seeds, nutritious kernels of carbohydrate that can be stored for long periods. The hard cereal grains, and occasionally the stems of these plants, were often burned during preparation or cooking in the past and thereby preserved to the present.

Root crops are not well documented in the archaeological record as they lack hard parts that are more resistant to decay. Because they reproduce asexually from shoots or cuttings, it is difficult to distinguish domesticated varieties from their wild ancestors. Asexually reproducing plants may maintain exactly the same genetic structure through many generations, because a piece of the parent plant is used to start the daughter. Such plants may also exhibit great variation within a species, making

Years B.C.

Region	8000	6000	4000	2000	0
Southwest Asia	Rye, goat/sheep; wheat, cattle; barley, pigs			Camels	
South Asia		Cattle	Cotton	Chickens	
East Asia	Rice	Millet, pigs			
Africa				Millet, yams, sorghum, oil palm	
Mesoamerica	Gourds Squash		Beans	Maize	
North America				Goosefoot, sunflower, squash, marsh elder	
South America				Gourds, squash, llama, lima beans, cotton, potatoes	

The first appearance of domesticates.

domestication difficult to document. Root crops such as potatoes, yams, manioc, and taro may have been domesticated quite early. Archaeologists have started to identify them from prehistoric sites only recently.

Animals were apparently domesticated initially for meat, with the exception of the dog. Dogs were tamed from wolves very early, perhaps 14,000 years ago in the Old World, and used for hunting and as pets, or even for food. Subsequently, however, several other animal species were domesticated and herded for food and/or kept as beasts of burden. The earliest animals domesticated were pigs, goats, sheep, and cattle. The secondary products (such as milk, wool, horn, and leather) of these, and other, domesticated species also became important, as did their function as beasts of burden.

The domestication of both plants and animals may be related to the storage of food. Such cereals as wheat, barley, corn, and rice have hard outer coverings that protect the nutritious kernel for some months, permitting the seed to survive until the growing season and offering very good possibilities for storage. Meat can be stored in the form of living, tame animals that are always available for slaughter. As such, storage provides a means to regulate the availability of food and to accumulate surplus.

THE PRIMARY CENTERS OF DOMESTICATION

Questions concerning the origins of agriculture must focus on *primary* centers where individual species of plants and/or animals were first domesticated. *Secondary* areas of agricultural development received plants and animals from elsewhere, although in many of these regions, some local plants and animals also were domesticated and used along with the introduced varieties. Primary centers for domestication were in the Near East, East Asia, sub-Saharan Africa, Central America, South America, and North America. The earliest known domesticates—wheat, barley, peas, lentils, pigs, goats, sheep, and cattle—appeared in the Old World, between the eastern Mediterranean Sea and Afghanistan, shortly after 9000 B.C. Many other plants and animals—such as bread wheat, rye, figs, olives, grapes, and flax—were gradually added to this list. The origins of agriculture in the Near East are discussed in detail in this chapter because the archaeology is well known and the process of domestication may have taken place somewhat earlier than elsewhere.

Agriculture was also invented in the Far East, perhaps in two or three different areas, sometime before 6000 B.C. Millet was first cultivated and pigs were domesticated in North China in early villages dating to roughly 6000 B.C. Rice was initially cultivated in South China, possibly as early as the eighth or ninth millennium B.C., and somewhat

Harvesting and processing a cereal crop: scenes depicted on the walls of an Egyptian tomb.

later in Southeast Asia, before 4000 B.C. In all probability, root crops were under cultivation in this area, along with rice, sometime between 7000 and 3000 B.C. As a result of continuing research, we can expect the dates for all of East Asia to be pushed back somewhat earlier. Plants such as African rice, sorghum, and pearl millet were domesticated in sub-Saharan Africa after 2000 B.C. Cattle and goat herding were practiced in this area, where the new domesticates appeared.

In the New World, agriculture first developed in Mexico, in northwestern South America, and in eastern North America. In Mexico, gourds and squash were cultivated during the eighth millennium B.C.; avocados, chili peppers, beans, and possibly corn were cultivated later, before 5000 B.C. These crops provide all the essential nutrients for a healthy diet, and meat protein may not have been necessary. Domesticated animals never provided an important part of the diet in this area, although turkeys, dogs, and the stingless honeybee were domesticated.

Sites in the highlands of Peru contain evidence for the early domestication of gourds, tomatoes, beans, and potatoes by 3000 B.C. Some of these plants may have reached the mountains from an original habitat in the lowland jungles, but little is known about the prehistory of the Amazon Basin and other tropical areas of South America. Potatoes certainly were an indigenous crop; hundreds of varieties of wild and domesticated potatoes grow in this area today. In addition to plants, several animals were domesticated. The guinea pig was used for food, while the **llama** was probably domesticated and used to transport goods around the mountains of South America.

Traditional techniques for harvesting and threshing grain in the Near East have not changed for thousands of years.

The **alpaca**, a **camelid** like the llama, may have been domesticated for both meat and wool.

In addition to these major centers of domestication, the beginnings of horticulture or agriculture occurred in other areas shortly after the end of the Pleistocene. Recent evidence from New Guinea suggests that agriculture was practiced very early in this area. Radiocarbon dates from a digging stick found in what appear to be ancient agricultural fields indicate a date of around 7000 B.C. These fields were probably used for fruit and tuber crops such as yams. In eastern North America, several local plants such as marsh elder, sunflower, and goosefoot (*Chenopodium*) were domesticated by 1000 B.C., long before the introduction of corn from Mexico (see also "Agriculture in Native North America," p. 250). Clearly there was a trend toward domestication and agriculture on a global scale at the beginning of the Holocene.

EXPLANATIONS FOR THE ORIGINS OF AGRICULTURE

It is remarkable that this process of domesticating plants and animals appears to have taken place separately and independently in a number of different areas at about the same point in time. Given the long prehistory of our species, why should the transition to agriculture happen within such a brief period, a few thousand years in a span of over 4 million years of human existence? Such a dramatic shift in the trajectory of cultural evolution requires explanation.

Views on and evidence for the origins of agriculture continue to be revised and updated. We can best understand ideas about the origins of agriculture from a historical perspective, considering the early theories first. Hypothetical explanations of why domestication occurred include the oasis hypothesis, the natural habitat hypothesis, the population pressure hypothesis, the edge hypothesis, and the social hypothesis. A consideration of these ideas also reveals much about the nature of archaeology and archaeologists. Theories about the origins of agriculture have often focused on the earliest evidence from the Near East and, for that reason, may not be appropriate to all places where early domestication actually occurred.

During the first half of the twentieth century, the best information on early farming villages came from riverine areas or oases with springs in North Africa and the

The conditions of incipient desiccation . . . would provide the stimulus towards the adoption of a food-producing economy. Enforced concentration by the banks of streams and shrinking springs would entail an intensive search for means of nourishment. Animals and men would be herded together in oases that were becoming increasingly isolated by desert tracts. Such enforced juxtaposition might promote that sort of symbiosis between man and beast implied by the word domestication.

V. G. Childe (1951)

Near East—along the Nile River in Egypt or at Jericho in the Jordan Valley, for example. At this time, the end of the Pleistocene was thought to be a period of increasing warmth and dryness in the earth's climate. Researchers reasoned that because the ice ages were cold and wet, they should have ended with higher temperatures and less precipitation. Given this view of past climate, logic suggested that areas such as the Near East, a dry region to begin with, would have witnessed a period of aridity at the end of the Pleistocene when vegetation grew only around limited water sources. The **oasis hypothesis** suggested a circumstance in which plants, animals, and humans would have clustered in confined areas near water. Proponents of this idea, like the late V. Gordon Childe, argued that the only successful solution to the competition for food in these situations would be for humans to domesticate and control the animals and the plants. In this sense, domestication emerged as a symbiotic relationship for the purpose of human survival.

During the 1940s and 1950s, however, new evidence indicated that there had been no major climatic changes in the Near East at the close of the Pleistocene—no crisis during which life would concentrate at oases. The new information forced a reconsideration of the origins of agriculture. Robert Braidwood, of the University of Chicago, pointed out—in his **natural habitat hypothesis**—that the earliest domesticates therefore should appear where their wild ancestors lived. That area, the "hilly flanks" of the Fertile Cresent in the Near East, should be the focus of investigations. Braidwood and a large team of researchers excavated at the site of Jarmo in northern Iraq. The evidence from this early farming village supported his hypothesis that domestication did indeed begin in the natural habitat. Braidwood did not offer a specific reason as to why domestication occurred, other than to point out that technology and culture were ready by the end of the Pleistocene, that humans were familiar with the species that were to be domesticated. At that time, archaeologists and others considered farming to be a highly desirable and welcome invention, providing security and leisure time for prehistoric peoples. Once human societies recognized the possibilities of domestication, they would have immediately started farming.

Lewis Binford, of Southern Methodist University, challenged these ideas in the 1960s and proposed the **population pressure hypothesis.** Binford argued that farming was back-breaking, time-consuming, and labor-intensive. Citing studies of living hunter-gatherers, he pointed out that they spend only a few hours a day obtaining food; the rest of their time is for visiting, talking, gambling, and the general pleasures of life. Even in very marginal areas, such as the Kalahari Desert of South Africa, food collecting is a successful adaptation, and people rarely starve. Binford argued, therefore, that human groups would not become farmers unless they had no other choice; that the origin of agriculture was not a fortuitous discovery, but a last resort.

Binford made his point in terms of an equilibrium between people and food, a balance that could be upset by either a decline in available food or an increase in the number of people. Since climatic and environmental changes appeared to be minimal in the Near East, Binford thought it must have been increased population size that upset the balance. Population pressure was thus introduced as a causal agent for the origins of agriculture: More people required more food. The best solution to the problem was domestication, which provided a higher yield of food per acre of land. At the same time, however, agricultural intensification required more labor to extract the food.

Binford further suggested that the effects of population pressure would be felt most strongly not in the core of the natural habitat zone, where dense stands of wild wheat and large herds of wild sheep and goats were available, but at the margins, where wild foods were less abundant. This theory, incorporating ideas about population pressure and the margins of the Fertile Crescent, has become known as the **edge hypothesis.**

Binford's concern with population was elaborated upon by Mark Cohen, of the State University of New York, Plattsburgh. Cohen argued for an inherent tendency for growth in human population, a pattern responsible for the initial spread of the human

The food-producing revolution seems to have occurred as the culmination of the ever increasing cultural differentiation and specialization of human communities. Around 8000 B.C., the inhabitants of the Fertile Crescent had come to know their habitat so well that they were beginning to domesticate the plants and animals they had been hunting and gathering.

Robert Braidwood (1960)

Change in the demographic structure of a region which brings about the impingement of one group on the territory of another would also upset an established equilibrium system, and might serve to increase the population density of a region beyond the carrying capacity of the natural environment. Under these conditions, manipulation of the natural environment in order to increase its productivity would be highly advantageous.

Lewis Binford (1968)

species out of Africa, the colonization of Asia and Europe, and eventually of the New World as well. After about 10,000 B.C., according to Cohen, all the inhabitable areas of the planet were occupied, and population continued to grow. At that time there was an increase in the use of less desirable resources in many areas. Land snails, shellfish, birds, and many new plant species were added to the human diet around the end of the Pleistocene. Cohen argued that the only way for a very successful, but rapidly increasing, species to cope with declining resources was for them to begin to cultivate the land and domesticate its inhabitants, rather than simply to collect the wild produce. Domestication for Cohen was a solution to problems of overpopulation on a global scale.

Others, arguing that the transition to farming and food storage and surplus cannot be understood simply in terms of environment and population, have developed a **social hypothesis** for explaining the origins of agriculture. Barbara Bender, of the University of London, for example, has suggested that the success of food production may lie more in the ability of certain individuals to accumulate a surplus of food and to transform that surplus into more valued items, such as rare stones and metals. From this perspective, agriculture was the means by which social inequality emerged and egalitarian societies became hierarchical.

There are several other theories about why human societies adopted agriculture at the end of the Pleistocene. Geographer Carl Sauer suggested that agriculture began in the hilly tropics of Southeast Asia, where sedentary groups with knowledge of the rich plant life of the forest might have domesticated plants for poisons and fibers. Botanist David Rindos has argued that domestication was a process of interaction between humans and plants, evolving together into a more beneficial symbiotic relationship.

Some of the problems with all of these theories can be seen in a brief consideration of the evidence from the Near East. The earliest agriculture villages, places such as 'Ain Ghazal (Color Plate 6) and Jericho, were indeed located at the margins of the natural habitat. Attempts to artificially reproduce stands of wild wheat there may have resulted in domestication. However, populations were not particularly large just prior to agriculture. Several sites show signs of abandonment in the levels beneath those layers that contain the first domesticated plants. The most recent climatic evidence indicates that there was, in fact, a period of slightly cooler and moister temperatures in the Near East at the end of the Pleistocene, which may have greatly expanded the geographic range of wild wheats and barley, making them available to more human groups, and fostering the process of domestication.

Some theories may seem reasonable in one of the primary centers of domestication, but not in another. The sequence of events in two areas is of particular interest here. In the Near East, permanent settlements are known from 11,000 B.C., prior to the presence of direct evidence for domesticated plants or animals. Cultivated plants appeared about 9000 B.C.; animals were probably not herded until perhaps 8500 B.C. Pottery did not come into general use until around 7500 B.C. In Mesoamerica, however, the archaeological sequence reveals that domesticated plants first appeared around 3000 B.C., followed by pottery and permanent villages roughly 1000 years later. Domesticated animals were never important in this area. The differences in these two areas indicate that neither **sedentism**, the permanent settlement of communities, nor cultivation is totally dependent one upon the other. It is also clear that domesticated animals are not essential in all areas.

Because of the difficulties in trying to excavate phenomena like social relations and population pressure, many of the current theories are hard to evaluate. Any adequate explanation of the agricultural transformation should deal not only with how it all began, but also why it happened rather suddenly around 10,000 years ago. Population and climatic change certainly play a role in cultural evolution. But we cannot yet say precisely why plants and animals began to be domesticated shortly after the end of the Pleistocene.

The how and why of the Neolithic transition remain among the more intriguing questions in human prehistory. Simply put, there is, as yet, no single, accepted, general theory for the origins of agriculture. No common pattern of development is apparent in the various areas where domestication first took place. This chapter examines the origins of agriculture in more detail in the several primary centers where it first appeared: the Near East, the Far East, Mexico, and South America, as well as Africa and eastern North America. Because of the quantity and quality of archaeological information from the Near East, much of the discussion will focus on this area.

The Summary at the end of the chapter considers the spread of agriculture from those primary centers, like the ripples spreading from a pebble thrown in a pond, to other areas where domesticates were introduced from other places. Subsequent chapters explore the expansion of agriculture into Europe and parts of North America. We also discuss the consequences of this major change in human subsistence in terms of economy, social organization, settlement, and ideology. Human society was never again the same after the beginnings of domestication. Even societies that continued to hunt and gather after the Neolithic were dramatically, and often drastically, affected by neighboring farmers.

Wheat, one of the earliest domesticates and a major staple around the globe.

'AIN MALLAHA

*Pre-Neolithic developments
in the Near East*

Excavations at 'Ain Mallaha exposing
burials under the house floors.

Discussions about the origins of agriculture often focus on the Near East (or Southwest Asia, as it is also known) for several reasons: (1) The earliest evidence for plant domestication from anywhere in the world is found here, (2) there is a reasonable amount of information available from excavations and other studies, and (3) the Near East is often considered the "cradle of Western civilization."

The period just before agriculture, about 11,000–9000 B.C., is referred to as the Natufian. Most of the evidence for this period comes from the **Levant,** a mountainous region paralleling the eastern shore of the Mediterranean including parts of the countries of Turkey, Syria, Lebanon, and Israel. The period was characterized by an increase in the number of sites and therefore people, coinciding with a period of more rainfall and abundant vegetation. The natural habitat was rich in wild plants and animals, resources that supported permanently settled communities before any evidence of domestication.

The Natufian site of 'Ain Mallaha (ein'ma-la'ha) lies beside a natural spring on a hillside overlooking the swamps of Lake Huleh in the upper Jordan Valley of Israel (see map, p. 204). 'Ain Mallaha is one of the earliest villages anywhere in the world, dating to 11,000–9000 B.C. The entire settlement covers an open area of about 2000 sq m (a half-acre, the size of a large hockey rink), with a population estimated at 200–300 people. Excavations between 1955 and 1973 by Jean Perrot, of the French Archaeological Mission in Jerusalem, uncovered three successive layers, with the remains of permanent villages. Each layer contained a number of round houses, ranging 3–8 m (10–25 ft) in diameter. House entrances faced downhill toward the water.

The remarkable architecture consists of large substantial houses with stone foundations, standing to a height of almost 1 m (3 ft). Wooden center posts may have supported conical roofs. Stone-lined square or oval hearths and bins were found in the center of the rooms or against the walls. **Mortars** and **querns,** grinding tools and surfaces for preparing grain, were occasionally set into the floor. Although the structures were built close together, the community had a centrally located open area with round storage pits.

The ground stone artifacts include plates, bowls, mortars, and pestles, indicating a need for containers at this time. Several objects are decorated with elaborate geometric designs. Carved limestone figurines of a human body, a human face, and a tortoise were also found. The flaked stone industry is rich, with more than 50,000 pieces. The bone tools include awls, skewers, needles, and fishhooks.

The animal bones found at the site come from wild pig, three kinds of deer, wild goat, wild cattle, wild horse, and gazelle. Gazelle is the most common game animal at sites of this period. Bird, fish, tortoise, and shellfish remains were also found. The lake was clearly an important resource for these people, as indicated by the fish and shellfish remains, along with **net-sinkers,** small weights that were attached to fishing nets. The high incidence of tooth decay in the teeth of individuals buried at 'Ain Mallaha suggests that carbohydrates from cereals or other plants were consumed in quantity. Wild barley and almonds were found charred in excavations, and it is clear from the abundance of sickle blades and other plant-processing equipment that wild cereals played an important role in the diet.

Two different kinds of burials were found at 'Ain Mallaha: (1) individual interments, including child and infant burials beneath stone slabs under the house floors; and (2) collective burials in pits, either intact or as secondary reburials after soft tissue had disappeared. Most of the 89 graves were found outside the houses. Abandoned storage pits were often reused for burial purposes. Many graves contained red ochre, and limestone slabs covered several of the simple graves. Four horns from gazelle were found in one grave, and in another, an old woman was buried with a puppy. Shells from the Mediterranean and rare greenstone beads or pendants from Syria or Jordan were occasionally placed with the burials, but grave goods were generally rare.

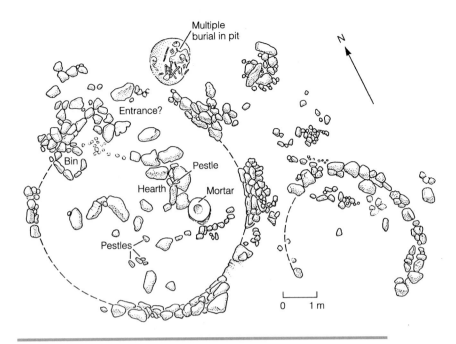

Two circular houses at 'Ain Mallaha. These structures have rock wall foundations and often contain grinding equipment, storage bins, and pits. Burials were often placed in abandoned storage pits.

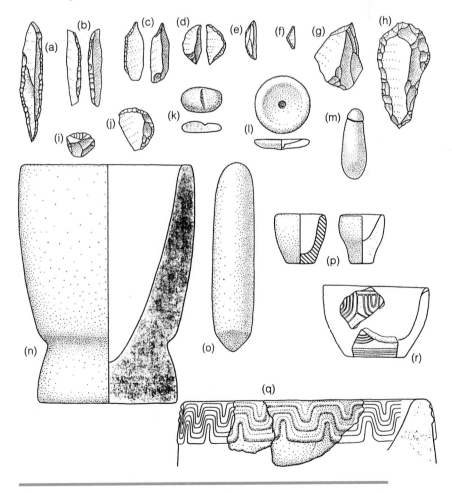

Various artifacts from 'Ain Mallaha. a–j: chipped stone tools; k–m, o: ground stone tools; n: a mortar; p–r: ground stone containers.

WHEAT, BARLEY, PIGS, GOATS, AND SHEEP

The appearance of the first farmers at the end of the Pleistocene in Southwest Asia

The Near East is a fascinating region. Perhaps too well known today for the political problems that beset it, the area is also the home of the earliest domesticated plants and animals, as well as some of the world's first civilizations. Southwest Asia is an enormous triangle of land, approximately the size of the contiguous United States. The area is bounded on the west by Turkey and the Mediterranean, on the south by Saudi Arabia and the Indian Ocean, on the north by the Black and Caspian Seas, and on the east by Afghanistan, at the edge of South Asia. The climate and environment are similar to New Mexico, Arizona, and Utah.

Southwest Asia is a series of contrasts. Some of the highest and lowest places in the world are found there, along with both rain forest and arid desert. Snow-capped mountains are visible from burning hot wastelands. Water is an important resource; arable land with fertile soil is scarce. The environment of this area can be visualized as a series of bands, driest in the south and moister to the north. Arabia is largely sand and desert; Mesopotamia, the region between the Tigris and Euphrates Rivers, is too dry for farming unless some form of irrigation is used. Many plants cannot survive in areas with less than 300 mm (1 ft) of rain each year. This 300-mm rainfall isobar stretches along an arc of mountains that ring Mesopotamia. The Zagros Mountains of western Iran, the Taurus Mountains of southern Turkey, and the highlands of the Levant along the eastern Mediterranean shore form a region where more rain falls and a variety of plants grow in abundance. This region is the natural habitat for many of the wild ancestors of the first species of plants and animals to be domesticated at the end of the Pleistocene—the wild wheats and barleys, the wild legumes, and the wild sheep, goats, pigs, and cattle that hunter-gatherers began to exploit in large numbers at the time of the first agriculture. The area is also known as the Fertile Crescent, emphasizing the variety of plants and animals that became the basic staples of many agricultural societies.

Some 20,000 years ago, a series of developments began in the Near East that set the stage for village farming. Climatic conditions during this period are not completely understood, but some general patterns are known. Around 18,000 B.C., global temperatures were some 6°C (10°F) cooler than they are today. A warming trend began about 14,000 B.C. and increased to a maximum temperature around 4000 B.C. Climate at the very beginning of the Neolithic, 11,000 years ago, was somewhat variable. Precipitation changes were not dramatic, but in an arid area, minor changes in rainfall can have a significant impact on vegetation. Rainfall was lowest during periods of maximum cooling around 18,000 B.C. As temperature and precipitation increased, the forest zone expanded in the Near East, and the number of species was greater than it is today. After about 8000 B.C., however, continuing increases in temperature likely resulted in more evaporation, so that effective precipitation began to decline and the forest cover shrank.

Within this climatic and environmental context, a gradual change from a broad-spectrum diet, focusing on the many wild species of the region, to a diet that concentrated on a few domesticated plants and animals can be seen. In the late Paleolithic, after 20,000 years ago, groups of hunter-gatherers lived in small, seasonal camps throughout the area. Although they exploited a range of resources, they focused on animals such as the gazelle. Plant foods are not common in the sites from this period.

In the period just preceding the Neolithic, there was more intense utilization of plant foods. Particularly noticeable is the range of equipment for processing plants: sickle blades and grinding stones, along with storage pits and roasting areas for preparing wild wheat. Sites were often located in areas of cultivable land, but such settlements depended on wild cereals, as evidenced in the remains of wild wheat and barley. These same locations were occupied during the Neolithic, too, probably because of the quantity or quality of arable land. Hunting continued, and more immature animals were killed, including gazelles and wild goats.

Between 8000 and 9000 B.C., changes in the size, shape, and structure of several cereals indicate that they had been domesticated. The archaeological data from Jericho and Abu Hureyra (a'boo-hoo-ray'rah), for example, mark this transition. The Neolithic, defined by the appearance of domesticated plants, began at this time. The earliest known domesticated cereal, rye, has been dated to 10,000 B.C. at the site of Abu Hureyra in Syria. In fact, eight or nine "founder" plants were domesticated during the period 9000–7000 B.C., including three cereals—emmer wheat, einkorn wheat, and barley—and four or five pulses—lentils, peas, bitter vetch, chickpea, and maybe faba beans. (Pulses are the edible seeds of leguminous plants, such as peas and beans.) Flax also was domesticated during this period and probably was used for oil and fiber; linen is made from the fibers of the flax plant. The first evidence for domestication of these founder plants comes from the same areas in which their wild ancestral stock is common. For example, genetic analysis has identified the original homeland of einkorn's wild ancestor in southeastern Turkey. The archaeological evidence can tell us when and where, but not why and how. The transition to the Neolithic is not marked by abrupt changes, but by increasing emphasis on patterns that appeared during the Natufian.

The number and size of prehistoric communities expanded greatly during the early Neolithic, as populations apparently concentrated in settlements. The first towns appeared. Major changes in human diet, and probably in the organization of society as well, began to take place. Some of the first domesticated animals may come from Hallam Çemi, a very early Neolithic site in eastern Turkey, dating to around 9000 B.C. Excavated by Michael Rosenberg, of the University of

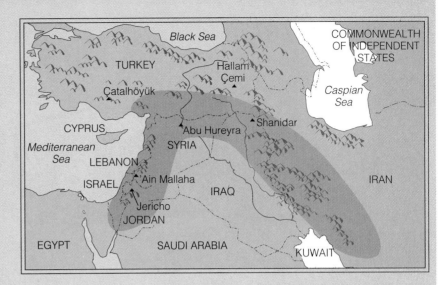

Locations of Near East sites mentioned in the chapter. The shaded area represents the Fertile Crescent.

Delaware, the site is a village of small, round houses and one larger, nondomestic building with a centrally located feasting area. The food remains at the site included wild sheep and goats, along with various nuts and wild legumes. Wild cereals were not an important part of the diet. About 10% of the animal bones came from pigs. Evidence for the domestication of these pigs is seen in the sex and age of death of the animals. Most of the bones were from young, female animals. It appears that the inhabitants were selecting suckling pigs to eat, supporting the argument that these animals were controlled, or herded. In addition, the teeth of the pigs at Hallam Çemi are smaller than those of their wild relatives.

By 7500 B.C., other domesticated animals, in the form of sheep and goats, made their first appearance in the Levant, and a number of changes in architecture occurred. Pottery was invented in the Near East around 7500 B.C. to serve as easily produced, waterproof containers. These dishes were probably used for holding liquids, for cooking a gruel made from wheat and barley (bread was a somewhat later invention), and for the storage of materials. The complete Neolithic package of domesticates, village architecture, and pottery was thus in place shortly before 7000 B.C., as the Neolithic revolution began to spread to Europe and Africa.

ABU HUREYRA

*Hunter-gatherers and early
farmers in northern Syria*

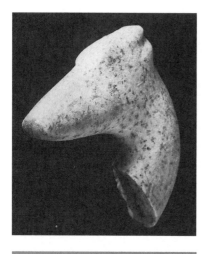

An artist's reconstruction of houses
from the Early Neolithic in the Near
East. These houses had rock wall
foundations with walls and roofs of
timber and reeds covered with mud.
In areas lacking rock, such as Abu
Hureyra, the foundations were made
of mud brick.

A miniature head of a Persian gazelle.
This exquisite piece is carved on a
granite pebble (c. 8000 B.P.). It was
broken in antiquity.

In 1974 the site of Abu Hureyra in north-ern Syria was submerged beneath the waters of a new dam on the Euphrates River. Fortunately, in 1972 and 1973, be-fore the water level in the reservoir rose and flooded the area, rescue excavations uncovered parts of this site, one of the largest early Postglacial communities in the Near East. Excavations were con-ducted by A. M. T. Moore, of Yale Uni-versity, and his colleagues.

The tell—an accumulated mound of occupation debris—covered some 11.5 ha (30 acres) with deposits from the Na-tufian and the early Neolithic, up to 8 m (25 ft) high in some places. One million cubic meters (1.3 million cubic yards) of earth were removed during the excava-tions. The primary component of the tell was the decayed mud walls of the gener-ations of houses that were built there, along with the artifacts and food remains left behind by the inhabitants. The layers contained an uninterrupted occupation of the mound from approximately 10,500 B.C. to 6000 B.C., through the Natufian and the Neolithic periods in the Near East. Abu Hureyra thus contains one of

the best available records of the changes that took place as farming and herding first began.

The mound lies at the edge of the Euphrates River, with the river flood-plain on one side and dry, level steppe on the other. The area today receives ap-proximately 200 mm (8 in) of rainfall per year; cultivation is difficult without irri-gation. During the Natufian occupation of the site, however, the climate was warmer and wetter. An open forest of oak and pistachio trees grew on the steppes nearby with dense stands of wild grasses among the trees. These grasses, probably no more than 1–2 km (about 1 mi) dis-tant, included wild wheats, rye, and var-ious pulses (lentils and legumes).

The Mesolithic occupation of the site was located on the northern side of the tell, adjacent to the Euphrates River. The settlement may have been placed here originally along the migration route of the gazelle herds. These animals were killed in great numbers during the spring migration. The Mesolithic settlement consisted of small, circular pit dwellings dug into the original ground surface.

Years B.C.	Period	Environment	Economy	Settlement	Other sites
6000 6300	Neolithic		Mixed farming cereals, legumes, sheep, goats, cattle, pigs	7 ha clustered mud-brick houses	
7500			Cereal and legume cultivation, sheep and goat husbandry	>16 ha clustered mud-brick houses	Çatalhöyük
8500		Decline in gazelle	Cereal and legume cultivation, plant gathering, gazelle hunting, domesticated sheep and goats	8 ha clustered mud-brick houses	Asikli
9000	Inter-mediate		Cereal and legume cultivation, plant gathering, gazelle hunting	Huts	Jericho, 'Ain Ghazal
9500 10,000	Natufian	Cooler and drier, retreat of forest. Dry, open steppe. Younger Dryas	Wild einkorn wheat out of habitat. Domestication of rye, plant gathering, gazelle hunting	Timber and reed huts	'Ain Mallaha, Jericho, Hallan Çemi
10,500		Open, rolling steppe and grass-land with nearby park woodland of oak and pistachio, wild cereals and legumes	Gathering wild plants, hunting gazelle	Pit dwellings	

Changes in environment, economy, and settlement types at Abu Hureyra.

These structures had a framework of wooden posts supporting the wall and roof. Almost 1 m (3 ft) of debris accumulated during this first phase of occupation, between approximately 10,500 and 9000 B.C. The population of the site is estimated to have been between 200 and 300 inhabitants at that time.

It is clear that the bulk of their food came from the wild plants, some of which were staples. The plant remains at the site indicate a year-round occupation in both the Mesolithic and the Neolithic periods. The excavators used sophisticated techniques at Abu Hureyra to recover more than 500 liters (140 gallons) of plant remains from the site. From the Natufian levels, there was evidence for wild lentils, hackberry fruit, caper berries, and nuts from the turpentine tree, related to pistachios. Most intriguing, however, were the remains of wild wheat, barley, and rye.

Around 10,000 B.C., the climate became cooler and drier and the nearby stands of wild cereals and other plants retreated more than 100 km (62.5 mi) to the higher elevations of the Fertile Crescent. Fruits and seeds of drought-sensitive plants from an oak-pistachio open woodland disappeared at Abu Hureyra. Then wild lentils and other legumes declined. Local vegetation around the site appears to have changed from moist, woodland steppe to dry, treeless steppe. At the same time, wild wheats continued to be consumed at the site in spite of the fact that their habitat in the area had been eliminated. The excavators believe that the Natufian inhabitants of Abu Hureyra practiced plant husbandry of wild cereals before changes in the glume and rachis brought about by domestication were evident. Significantly, the earliest known domesticated plant, rye, appeared at this time. Grinding stones and milling equipment also point to the importance of cereals in the diet during this period.

Experiments by Gordon Hillman, of the University of London, were designed to estimate the amount of time needed for wild cereals to change to the domesticated variety through the process of cultivating and harvesting the wild seeds and replanting them. This study indicated that the domestication of the plants could have taken place within a period of less than 300 years, perhaps no more than 25 years.

Shortly after the initial domestication of rye and the probable cultivation of wild wheats, lentils and legumes reappeared in the deposits and increased. By 8500 B.C., the range of domesticated

Two rooms of an Early Neolithic rectangular, mud-brick house. Note the filled-in doorway between the two rooms. A broken plaster storage vessel lies on the floor in the room to the left. The scale is 50 cm (almost 20 inches).

lithic periods. By the beginning of the Neolithic, however, sheep and goats had been domesticated and were being herded. After 7500 B.C., the number of gazelle bones dropped sharply and sheep and goats became much more important in the diet. During the subsequent phases of the Neolithic at Abu Hureyra, domesticated cattle and pigs were added to the larder.

Abu Hureyra grew quickly to become the largest community of its day, with 2000 to 3000 inhabitants in an area of about 11.5 ha (about 38 acres). Houses were rectangular with mud-brick walls that were plastered and white-washed. Plaster also was used to make heavy rectangular containers. Clay was used for beads and figurines, but pottery was not present in this level of the site. The importance of this community is documented by the quantity and variety of exotic materials that arrived there through trade and exchange: cowrie shells from the Mediterranean or Red Sea, turquoise from the Sinai Peninsula, and obsidian, malachite, agate, jadeite, and serpentine from the mountains of Turkey. These rare stones were made into large, thin "butterfly" beads, often found in burials.

By 6000 B.C., Abu Hureyra was abandoned. A similar pattern is seen at other Neolithic sites in the Levant at this time. It seems likely that increasingly arid conditions reduced agricultural productivity and made herding a more viable enterprise. It may be at this time that nomadic herding became the dominant mode of life, much like the pastoralists who still roam parts of the Near East with their herds of sheep and goats.

In sum, the evidence from Abu Hureyra indicates that cultivation began in the ancient Near East in a small sedentary village of gatherer-hunters around 10,000 years ago during a period of environmental change. The disappearance of the habitat for wild species coincided with the early domestication of rye and eventual cultivation of wheat, lentils, and legumes. However, the transition from wild, gathered foods and hunted animals to a dependence on domesticated varieties took 2500 years. The evidence

plants included rye, lentils and large-seeded legumes, and domesticated wheats. Clearly, plant domestication began in the Natufian period at Abu Hureyra, perhaps in response to the disappearance of the wild stands of these important foods.

Two tons of animal bone, antler, and shell also were removed during the excavations. Shells from river mussels, fish bones, and fish hooks made from bone indicate that the inhabitants obtained food from the Euphrates River as well as from the surrounding hills. Gazelle bones dominate the lower layers at Abu Hureyra and constituting 80% of all animal bones from the Mesolithic and early Neo-

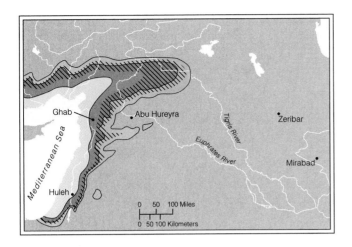

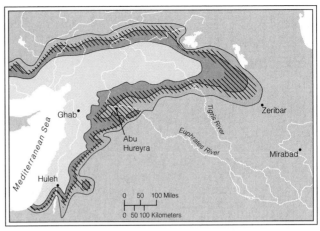

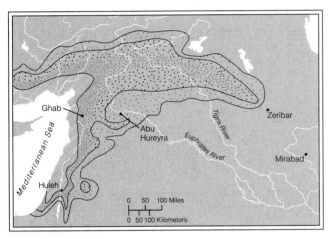

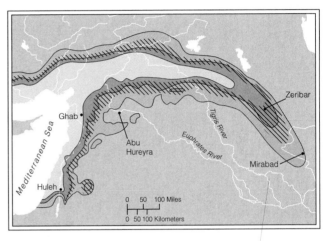

Forest and fairly dense woodland (including montane forest, au-mediterranean sclerophyllous woodland, and xeric deciduous oak-Rosaceae woodland).

Oak-terebinth-Rosaceae park-woodland (a mosaic of woodland and open areas dominated by annual grasses).

Terebinth-almond woodland steppe, involving a thin scatter of trees in what were otherwise grass-dominated steppe formations.

Areas (within the previous two zones) supporting extensive stands of wild wheats and ryes.

Steppe, dominated by wormwoods, perennial chenopods, and perennial tussock-grasses.

Mosaic of areas dominated by trees of montane forest, au-mediterranean wood-land, xeric deciduous woodland, and woodland steppe, most of them probably growing as relatively thin scatters.

The partial die-back zone, characterized by isolated pockets of trees with wild cereals and legumes (micro-refugia) that will have survived in moist hollows and at breaks in north-facing slopes, surrounded by areas littered with dead trees. The different densities of dots reflect the lower density of these scattered pockets towards the outer fringes of this zone.

The zone of total arboreal die-back, characterized by dead trees, without any of the isolated pockets of living trees of the previous zone, barring terebinths and caper bushes growing in some wadi bottoms.

suggests that not all families in the settlement were initially involved in farming and that the number increased over time. The first sheep and goat husbandry appeared around 8500 B.C., followed by cattle and pigs. The general sequence involves settlement in villages, followed by plant cultivation and subsequent animal herding. This pattern of a gradual transition from food collection to food production is typical in most parts of the world.

PALEOETHNO-BOTANY

The study of prehistoric plant remains

Table 6.1   Common Food Plants in the Early Neolithic Near East

Einkorn wheat, wild and
   domesticated forms
Emmer wheat, wild and domesticated
   forms
Rye, wild and domesticated forms
Barley, wild and domesticated forms
Chickpeas, domesticated form
Field peas, domesticated form
Lentils, wild and domesticated forms
Common vetch
Bitter vetch
Horse bean
Grape, wild and domesticated forms
Caper
Prosopis (mesquite)
Fig
Hackberry
Turpentine tree
Wild pistachio

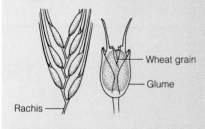

The main structural characteristics of wheat.

Preserved plants in archaeological sites are rare unless the remains have been carbonized, generally through burning or oxidation. Such burned plant materials can sometimes be obtained through a process called **flotation.** Excavated sediments are poured into a container of water, and the lighter, carbonized plant remains float to the top. In addition to the kinds of plants used, the major issues in **paleoethnobotany,** the study of the prehistoric use of plants, include the contribution of plants to the diet, medicinal uses, and domestication—the origins of agriculture.

The paleoethnobotany of the Near East is of particular interest because of the early evidence for domestication in this area (Table 6.1). Two varieties of wheat (emmer and einkorn), two-row barley, rye, oats, lentils, peas, chickpeas, and other plants were originally cultivated in the Near East. The wild forms of these species are still common today, as they were in the past. Wild emmer wheat has a restricted distribution in the southern Levant. Wild einkorn wheat is relatively widespread in the northern and eastern sections of this region. Wild barley grows throughout the Fertile Crescent. All of these wild grasses grow well in disturbed ground around human settlements. Einkorn was probably domesticated in southern Turkey, while emmer may have been first cultivated in the Jordan Valley.

Agronomist Jack Harlan, of the University of Illinois, participating in an archaeological project in southern Turkey in the 1960s, experimented to find out just how much food was available from wild wheat. Dense stands of wild einkorn wheat grow on the slopes of the mountains in this area. This wild wheat is more nutritious than the hard winter red wheats grown in the United States today. Harvesting when the wheat was ripe, Harlan collected more than 1 kg (2 lb) of cereal grain per hour with his hands and even more with a sickle. He estimated that a family of four could harvest enough grain in 3 weeks to pro-

A Dausman flotation machine in use. Water in the tank is used to separate lighter plant remains from soil and other sediments. The archaeologist uses a hose to spray some of the recovered materials.

vide food for an entire year. If this wild wheat was so abundant and nutritious, why was wheat domesticated? The answer probably lies in the fact that wild wheats do not grow everywhere in the Near East and that some communities may have transplanted the wild form into new environments.

Although artifactual evidence for the use of plants (e.g., sickles, milling stones, storage pits, and roasting areas) exists in a number of areas, domesticated varieties cannot be distinguished from wild types without actual plant parts or grain impressions in clay bricks or pottery. Paleoethnobotanist Gordon Hillman, of the University of London, studied wild einkorn and observed that simple harvesting had no major impact on the genetic structure of the wheat. Only when specifically selective harvesting and other cultivation techniques were applied could changes in the morphology of the seeds be noted. Such a pattern suggests that certain characteristics of domesticated wheat and barley, which show definite morphological differences from the wild ancestral forms, must have been intentionally selected. Results from Hillman's experimental studies suggest that the change from wild to domesticated wheat may have occurred in a brief period, perhaps 200 years or less.

According to the late Hans Helbaek, a leading paleoethnobotanist who worked on the issue of plant domestication, the most important characteristic of a domesticated species is the loss of natural seeding ability. The plant comes to depend on human intervention in order to reproduce. This change also permits humans to select the characteristics of those plants to be sown and reproduced, leading to preferred characteristics. Another major change in domesticated plants is the human removal of plants from their natural habitat and adaptation to new environmental zones. New conditions of growth would obviously select for different characteristics among the members of the plant species. Certain varieties do very well when moved to a new setting.

Wheat is an annual grass with large seed grains that concentrate carbohydrates inside a hard shell. Grain at the top of the grass stalk is connected by the **rachis,** or stem. Each seed is covered by a husk, or **glume.** The major features that distinguish wild and domesticated wheat are found in the rachis and glume. In wild wheat, each rachis of a seed cluster is brittle, to allow natural seed dispersal by a mechanism know as **shattering.** The glumes covering the seeds are tough, to protect the grain until the next growing season. These two features, however, are counterproductive to effective harvesting and consumption by humans. Because of the brittleness of the rachis, many seeds fall to the ground before and during harvesting, making collection difficult. The tough glume must be roasted so that threshing can remove it.

Domesticated wheats exhibit a reverse of these characteristics: a tough rachis and a brittle glume. These changes enable the seed to stay on the plant so

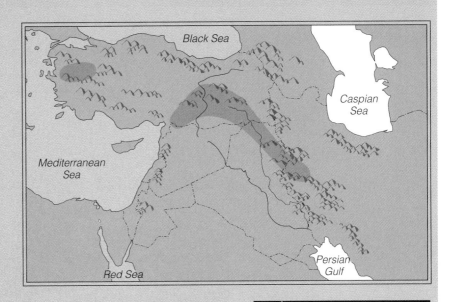

that it can be harvested in quantity and the glume can be removed by threshing without roasting. These changes also mean that the wheat is dependent upon humans for seeding and therefore, by definition, is domesticated.

One of the most exciting recent developments in paleoethnobotany has been the use of the scanning electron microscope. This instrument, with very high magnifications, has enabled researchers to identify minute scraps of charred plant remains that would otherwise be missed at archaeological sites. Electron microscopy is also being used to recognize edible plants such as roots and tubers, which were previously invisible in archaeological deposits.

The natural habitat of wild einkorn wheat (*Triticum boeoticum*) in the Near East, indicated by the shaded areas.

An assortment of seeds from the flotation of sediments at an archaeological site.

JERICHO

*One of the oldest continuously
inhabited places in the world*

The ancient tell of Jericho, at the juncture of the arrows, located near a major spring at the northern end of the Jordan Valley in the Near East. The tell is a mound of the accumulation of 10,000 years of human occupation.

*And it came to pass at the seventh time,
when the priests blew with the trumpets,
Joshua said unto the people, Shout; for
the Lord hath given you the city . . .
and the people shouted with a great
shout. . . . The wall fell down flat . . . and
they utterly destroyed all that was in the
city . . . with the edge of the sword . . .
and they burnt the city with fire, and all
that was therein.*

Joshua 6:16

The walls of Jericho fell to Joshua and the Israelites sometime around 1300 B.C. The place had been occupied, however, for thousands of years prior to their arrival. In fact, the walls of Jericho tumbled down almost twenty times in the course of its history, from either earthquake or siege. Jericho is a **tell**, a massive mound of 2.4 ha (6 acres) composed of mudbricks and trash, accumulated to a height of 22 m (70 ft) during its long period of occupation. The layers of the tell built up at a rate of roughly 26 cm (almost a foot) every century.

Jericho (or Tel es 'Sultan, as it is known in Arabic), is one of the oldest continuously inhabited places on earth. Since at least 10,000 B.C., Elisha's Foun-

tain, the spring at Jericho, has witnessed virtually continuous human settlement. The freshwater spring floods the area beneath it and supports an oasis of luxuriant vegetation in the midst of the hot and arid Jordan Valley, lying below sea level at a depth of 275 m (900 ft). The mound itself was abandoned sometime before the birth of Christ, as settlement spread to the surrounding low area.

The biblical connection has made Jericho a place of major interest and importance for archaeologists in the Near East. Today the tell resembles the surface of the moon. Craters and trenches mark the excavations of many archaeological projects that have explored these accumulated layers since 1873. Beneath bib-

Dame Kathleen Kenyon and D. Tushingham at the excavations in the lower levels of Jericho.

lical Jericho, British archaeologist Dame Kathleen Kenyon exposed a number of levels containing remains from the Bronze Age, the Neolithic, and the Mesolithic. Evidence from the early Neolithic (8500–7600 B.C.) at the bottom of the tell is of interest here. Because the mound is so deep, these lowest levels could be reached only by narrow trenches. The residential structures and artifacts exposed in Kenyon's excavations were similar to those from other Near East sites from this period. Closely packed round houses contained interior hearths and grinding equipment. Headless burials were uncovered in the houses at Jericho; skulls were found separated from the skeletons. Kenyon estimated that the early Neolithic community at Jericho had a population of about 600 people.

Gazelle bones were abundant in the lowest layers at Jericho. This important game animal probably was exploited by large drives that captured a number of animals simultaneously. Aurochs, wild boars, and foxes also were eaten. Many animals present in the surrounding hills were not hunted, including wild goats, oryx, hartebeest, and wild camels. In later periods, gazelles declined in importance, replaced by sheep and goats. The presence of equipment for processing grain

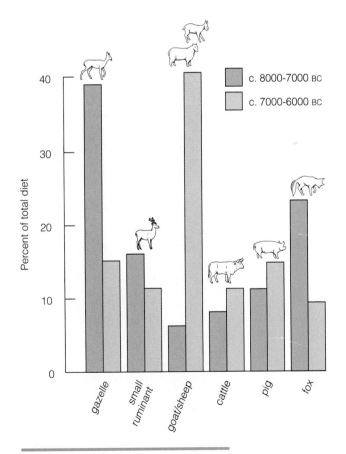

Changes in the consumption of animals between 8000 and 6000 B.C. at Jericho. Notice especially the shift from wild gazelle to domesticated sheep and goat.

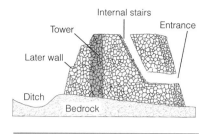

The tower, wall, and rock-cut ditch at Jericho.

The tell at Jericho. Excavations have exposed a circular stone tower, partially visible in the lower right.

(sickles and grinding stones) and storage suggests that cereals were important in the lowest levels. In the slightly higher early Neolithic layers, these cereals were domesticated and probably cultivated in the fertile soil of the Jericho oasis.

The inhabitants of early Neolithic Jericho were involved in the trading of various items over long distances. Materials such as salt, tar, and sulfur came from the area around the Dead Sea, tur-

quoise was brought from the Sinai Peninsula, cowrie shells from the Red Sea, obsidian from Turkey, and greenstone from Jordan. The reasons for such exchange probably lie in the importance of contacts with neighboring communities and in the accumulation of status items for some portion of the community.

Most remarkable of Kenyon's discoveries from this period was a large stone tower, wall, and ditch, which ap-

peared to encircle the site. These structures were built at the beginning of the eighth millennium B.C. The wall itself is 1.8 m (6 ft) thick at the base, narrowing to 1.1 m (3.5 ft) at the top, and stands 3.6 m (12 ft) high today, buried under the accumulated deposits of Jericho. The rubble-filled stone tower was also completely buried, at a height of 8.2 m (27 ft). The tower was built inside the wall and has a diameter at the base of 9 m (30 ft). An interior staircase with 22 steps leads from the bottom to the top. In front of the wall is a deep ditch, which added greatly to the height of the total structure. The ditch is some 2 m (6.5 ft) deep and 8.5 m (28 ft) wide, cut into the bedrock under the site. Such a construction project would have been a major undertaking by a small community in the eighth millennium B.C. The tower and wall were abandoned by 7300 B.C. and rapidly disappeared under the accumulating layers of the tell.

The significance of these structures has been the focus of discussion and debate. Kenyon suggested that the tell was completely encircled by the wall and ditch, with towers placed at regular intervals. However, only one tower was exposed in the excavations, and the wall was not found on the southern, lower side of the mound. Numerous unanswered questions have arisen regarding the nature of the enemy, the materials to be protected, the location of the tower *inside* the wall, the reason for its abandonment, and the size of the population. Comparable fortifications are not seen at other early Neolithic sites in the Near East, and a massive defensive structure seems out of place.

Ofer Bar-Yosef, of Harvard University, examined the evidence for fortifications at Jericho and found it lacking. Bar-Yosef interprets the wall and ditch in terms of a defense against nature, rather than against humans. In this arid region, flash floods are common, and each rainfall moves a great deal of sand and silt from higher ground to lower areas. Such erosion and deposition would have been aggravated by land clearing and the removal of trees and shrubs by the inhabitants at the site. Sediments may have ac-

cumulated on the upslope side of the tell of Jericho and at other early Neolithic sites.

To counteract this rapid accumulation of sediments at the edge of their community, the residents of Jericho, Bar-Yosef argues, built the wall and dug the ditch to hold back the sediments. The rock-cut ditch at Jericho filled with water-transported sediments shortly after it was dug. The wall was thickest in the middle portion where the sediment accumulation was heaviest. The large tower inside the wall is another matter. Bar-Yosef has noted the excellent preservation of the tower to its total height in the tell. He argues that there was likely a mud-brick structure on top of the stone tower, a building for communal storage or religious activities that made the tower a very special place in the settlement. The tower thus may represent an early shrine or temple for the community, a concept that was later transformed into the monumental ziggurats of the Mesopotamian states.

Around 7500 B.C., major changes in the architecture, artifacts, and animals occurred at Jericho. Houses became square, constructed with what have been described as "hog-backed" bricks—large, cigar-shaped mud bricks with a herringbone pattern of thumb prints on the top. Domesticated animals became important at this time; sheep and goats comprised almost half of the animal bones, along with a few wild cattle and pigs, gradually replacing the gazelle. Pigs and cattle were possibly in the process of change because their bones were slightly smaller than the wild forms, but not as small as those of the domesticated forms.

A plastered and painted skull from Jericho. The plaster remodeling of the features of human heads is found at several early Neolithic sites in the Near East and may reflect an increasing reverence for ancestors.

ARCHAEO-ZOOLOGY

The study of animal remains

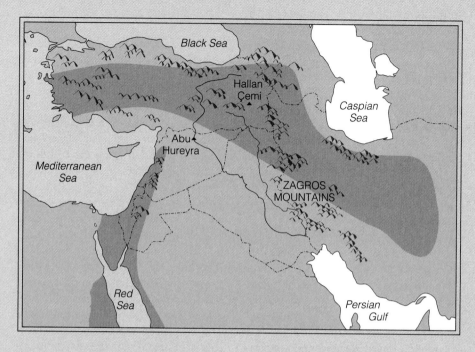

The distribution of wild goats (*Capra aegagrus*) in the Near East and Egypt, indicated by the shaded areas.

The companion of paleoethnobotany, **archaeozoology** is the study of animal remains from archaeological sites. Focusing on the hard body parts that survive—bone, teeth, antler, ivory, scales, and shell—archaeozoologists attempt to answer questions about whether animals were hunted or scavenged, how animals were butchered, how much meat contributed to the diet, and the process of domestication.

Archaeozoologists are trained to identify the genus or species of an animal from small fragments of bone, as well as the age and sex of the animals, how the bone was broken, and how many individual animals are represented in the bone assemblage. Fracture patterns in long bones may reveal intentional breakage for removing marrow. An analysis of cutmarks on bone may provide information on butchering techniques. Herded animals show certain changes in size and body parts that provide direct evidence for domestication. Domesticated species are generally smaller than their wild ancestors. The shape of the horns often changes in the domestic form, and the microscopic structure of bone undergoes modification in domestic animals. Other traits may be selected by herders to increase the yield of milk, wool, or meat. However, because such biological change takes many generations, the earliest stages of domestication may not have been recorded in the bones and horns that remain.

Brian Hesse, of the University of Alabama, Birmingham, estimated the age and sex of animals that had been killed at a prefarming site in the Zagros Mountains of western Iran. He used this information to study whether hunting or herding was practiced. The basic principle relies on the fact that herded animals are slaughtered when the herder decides; for most species, this means that the average age of death for domesticated animals is younger than for wild animals. Hunted animals are killed in chance encounters, and the proportion of adults is higher in such situations.

The ages of animals are most frequently determined by an assessment of tooth eruption and wear, along with information about changes in bone. Before 10,000 years ago, all the known sites in the Zagros Mountains show similar slaughter patterns for sheep, goats, and red deer; bone assemblages contain primarily adult animals, indicating that all were hunted in the wild. After 10,000

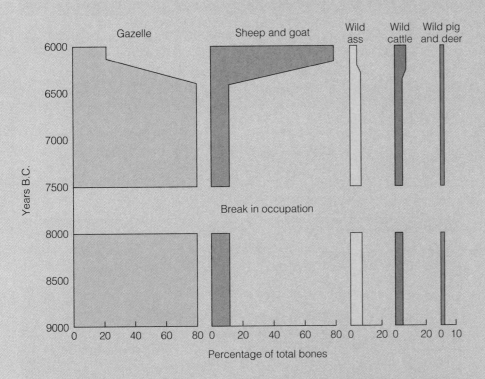

Changes in animal species at Abu Hureyra, Syria, between 9000 and 6000 B.C. The width of the bars indicates the relative abundance of the species. The most pronounced change is the decrease in gazelle and the increase in sheep and goats between 6500 and 6000 B.C. There was an absence of human occupation at this site between 8000 and 7500 B.C.

years ago, however, a number of sites contain assemblages that are dominated by the bones of younger animals. In each case, the younger groups are sheep or goats, proportionally higher than in a normal wild herd.

At the site of Abu Hureyra in Syria, a study of the bones of wild gazelles and domesticated goats and sheep has provided new information on the process of animal domestication. Around 11,000 years ago, the site was occupied by pre-farming hunter-gatherers who were hunting gazelles in large numbers. The gazelle bones and teeth include the remains of many young animals. The teeth in particular indicate that both newborns and yearlings were common in the faunal assemblage, along with adults of all ages. This pattern of newborns, yearlings, and adults, and the absence of animals of ages in between, indicates that most of the animals were killed during the same time each year, shortly after the calving period in late April and early May. These hunters were taking entire herds of gazelle as the animals migrated north during early summer. They probably used a technique that would drive an entire

herd into an enclosure or series of pit-falls, where all the animals could be killed. These hunters were so effective that the number of gazelles in the area dropped dramatically, to less than 20% of all the animals at the site, by 7500 B.C.

Goat and sheep domestication may have been a solution to the problem of decreasing numbers of gazelle. Sheep and goats were slaughtered throughout the year, in contrast to the seasonal hunting of gazelles at Abu Hureyra. Goat and sheep bones are present as about 10% of the faunal assemblages until 7500 B.C., when very rapidly they became the predominant component, at almost 80%. This period was about 1500 years after plant domestication had been initiated at the site; wheats and barley at that point provided a significant portion of the diet. It was also some 3500 years after the initial occupation of the site, documenting the sequential stages of sedentism, plant cultivation, and animal domestication typical of the Near East. Such information points to a very complex picture of animal and plant domestication in the Near East at the end of the Pleistocene.

Table 6.2   Important Animal Species in the Neolithic Near East

Gazelle
Goat, wild and domesticated forms
Sheep, wild and domesticated forms
Roe deer
Fallow deer
Cattle, wild and domesticated forms
Pig, wild and domesticated forms
Onager
Bear
Jackal
Hare
Wildcat
Fish
Bird

ÇATALHÖYÜK

The first city, central Turkey

An aerial view of Çatalhöyük.

Large communities began to appear shortly after the domestication of plants and animals in the Near East. By 8000 B.C., 'Ain Ghazal and Jericho had populations in the hundreds, sizably larger than pre-agricultural settlements. And by 7000 B.C. the first city had appeared at the site of Çatalhöyük (sha-tal'-who-yuk') in central Turkey.

The tell of Çatalhöyük is huge, 600 m (1900 ft) long, 350 m (1000 feet) wide, and almost 20 m (65 ft) high. This massive mound of houses, garbage, and burials accumulated within a period of little more than 1000 years and was abandoned around 6000 B.C. At least twice as large as early Neolithic Jericho, covering some 13 ha (32 acres), the site

was an enormous settlement with a population in the thousands, perhaps as many as 2000 families.

The original excavations at this ancient settlement were conducted by James Mellaart, of the University of London, during the 1960s. Several seasons of fieldwork at the site exposed numerous walls and floors of rooms and houses. Houses were built closely together in one, two, or three stories around small courtyards. The houses were very similar, with a rectangular floor plan of approximately 25 sq m (30 sq yd), about the size of a large living room today. The houses were divided into a living and a smaller storage area. Furniture—benches, sleeping platforms, ovens, cup-

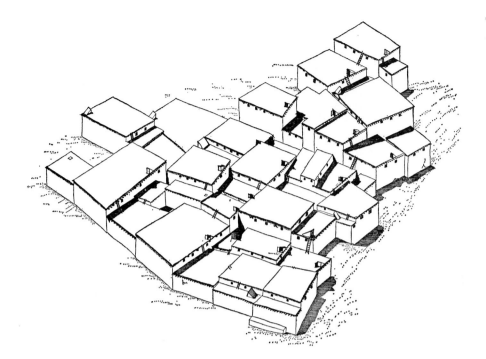

boards, and storage bins—was built into the house. The houses had no doors, and access was likely through their flat roofs.

A number of burials were found also in the houses at Çatalhöyük. These burials of men, women, and children were found under the floors and sleeping platforms. The bodies appear to have been exposed for some time prior to burial. Grave goods with the burials included jewelry such as necklaces, armlets, wristlets, and anklets of stone or shell, copper and lead beads, or weapons. A few burials contained rare objects such as stone vessels, ceremonial daggers, obsidian mirrors, polished mace heads, cosmetics, and metal beads and rings. One of the remarkable things from the early excavations at Çatalhöyük was the discovery that a large number of the structures, perhaps 20%, appeared to have been shrines. The walls of these shrines are elaborately decorated, sculpted, and painted with a variety of remarkable figures and designs including vultures, bulls, wild cats, and humans. Some of the paintings show women giving birth to bulls; others depict hunting scenes or vultures with headless humans in their talons. One of the paintings portrays an erupting volcano with a large settlement at its base.

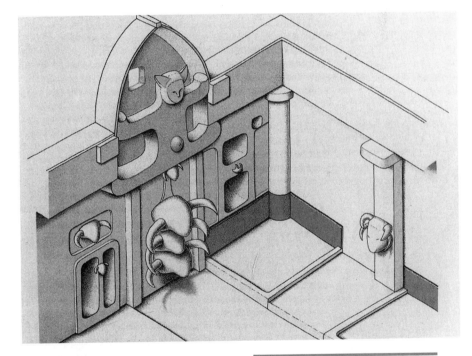

An artist's reconstruction of one of the shrine rooms at Çatalhöyük. A catlike goddess gives birth to a ram above three bull's heads.

New excavations in the 1990s have exposed more of the site and investigated in more detail the purpose and function of the various structures. These excavations, directed by Ian Hodder of Stanford University, suggest that households used their space for both domestic and ritual

A group of burials beneath a platform in one of the houses.

inhabitants depended heavily on wild flora and fauna. Important plants in the diet included domesticated wheats and barley, wild tubers and grasses, lentils, and fruits and nuts such as acorns, pistachios, crabapples, and hackberries. Cattle were an important part of subsistence at the site, but it is not yet certain if they were domesticated. Domesticated sheep and other species also were killed and eaten. There are no indications of differences in status, represented by wealth or surplus, among the houses. Çatalhöyük appears in many ways to have been a huge village of farmers rather than a complex and varied city.

Çatalhöyük was clearly a prosperous center, however, probably because of its control of the obsidian trade. Obsidian is a translucent, hard, black glass, produced by volcanoes. Molten silica sometimes flows out of a volcanic core and hardens into this stone, which was highly sought by prehistoric makers of stone tools. Obsidian, like glass and flint, fractures easily and regularly, creating very sharp edges.

In the past, obsidian was often traded or exchanged over long distances, hundreds of kilometers or more. It is available from only a few places, limited by proximity to volcanic mountains and the chance formation of a silica flow. Most sources for obsidian are known because they are rare and the material is unusual. It is also possible to fingerprint different flows of obsidian through minor differences in the chemical composition of the material, which is specific to each source, allowing pieces found elsewhere to be traced to the places where they originated. The sources of obsidian in the Near East, the Aegean area, North America, Mexico, and elsewhere have been studied using such methods. Most of the obsidian in the Near East comes from sources either in the mountains of Turkey or in northern Iran, both outside the Fertile Crescent. Information on the sources of obsidian found at early Neolithic sites provides data on both the direction and intensity of trade. Sites in the Levant generally obtained obsidian from Anatolia, while sites in the Zagros used Armenian material. The percentage of obsidian in the total flaked stone assem-

purposes and that the shrines may simply have been more elaborate households. Two or three generations of a family were often buried under the house floor. The first burials in the houses were infants and young children; later burials were older adults. This pattern suggests a family life cycle represented in the burials. Houses may have been destroyed after the family had died. The paintings and sculptures on the walls of the houses are likely associated with the burials and may have been added to commemorate the deceased. David Lewis-Williams, of the University of Witwatersrand, South Africa, has described the artwork as a symbolic membrane connecting the living to the spirit world.

Analysis of the animal bones and plant remains has provided a great deal of new information about the site. The

blage at these sites indicates that sites closest to the sources used a great deal of obsidian, while those farthest away had only a small amount available. At Jericho, for example, 700 km (400 mi) from the Turkish sources, only about 1% of the stone tools were made from obsidian.

Çatalhöyük is located almost 200 km (125 mi) from the major obsidian source in Turkey. Nevertheless, most of the chipped stone tools at the site were made of obsidian. In addition to finished tools, many unfinished obsidian artifacts were found, along with large amounts of raw material. It appears that obsidian was moved in massive quantities to Çatalhöyük. From here the obsidian was traded over a wide area of the Near East. In return the inhabitants of Çatalhöyük received copper, shell, and other exotic material. Clearly, the importance of obsidian as a desired object in trade was an essential factor in the rise of Çatalhöyük. Trade and exchange of various materials accelerated greatly during the Neolithic.

As remarkable as Çatalhöyük is, there is another site called Asikli, 100 km (62.5 mi) distant, that is even more remarkable. This mound is 1000 years older than Çatalhöyük, yet almost as large. This site contains little evidence for domesticated plants or animals. At Asikli, a population of several hundred individuals lived in a large group of mud-brick houses surrounded by a stone wall. There are at least ten levels of occupation in the mound, and the same arrangement of houses and cobbled streets is seen in each level. There is also a cluster of larger, public buildings at the site that might have been a temple complex.

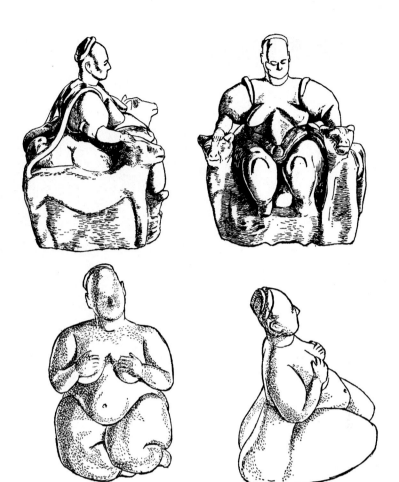

Two clay female figurines from the excavations.

Fired clay seals often were found during the excavations.

MEHRGARH

*New evidence for the early
Neolithic in South Asia*

A view of Mehrgarh, showing multi-room, rectangular structures.

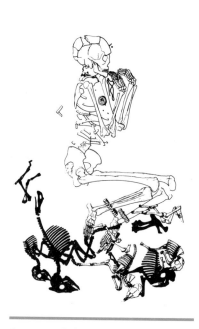

A grave with five young goats.

The Indus civilization, one of the world's early urban societies, emerged in South Asia, the subcontinent now composed of India, Pakistan, Bangladesh, and Nepal. The largest communities of this ancient civilization—the cities of Harappa, Mohenjo-daro, and others—were centered on the Indus River system in Pakistan. Until the 1970s, however, little was known about the antecedents of this ancient society. In the late 1960s, it was suggested that plant and animal domestication did not reach the subcontinent of South Asia until after 4000 B.C. The prevailing opinion was that migrants from the west, who made metals and wheel-thrown pottery, brought an agricultural way of life to South Asia just a few centuries before the rise of the Indus civilization.

More recent archaeological findings, however, have revealed an older, more indigenous picture of agricultural origins in the Indus River drainage. One key for this new perspective has come from a long-term research program, conducted by the French Archaeological Mission and the Pakistani Department of Archaeology, at the site of Mehrgarh (meh-her-gar′), located in the Kachi Plain about 200 km (120 mi) northwest of the Indus River. The site is also interesting because of its

location immediately below the Bolan Pass, which cuts through the mountains that connect the Indus River Valley with highland Baluchistan and Iran (the Near East).

In 1974, the first fieldwork at Mehrgarh by Jean-François Jarrige and his colleagues focused on a small mound. At that time, however, older pottery was collected over an area of several hundred hectares adjacent to the mound. Large-scale excavations in this area have yielded a sequence of deposits dating to the seventh millennium B.C. The earliest occupation level at Mehrgarh lacked pottery, although clay was used to make bricks for the construction of substantial, multi-room, quadrangular structures and **anthropomorphic** figurines (having human form). A count of plant impressions in the mud-bricks by Lorenzo Costantini found that barley was the most abundant cultigen in this early level. This barley had several distinctive local characteristics and may not have been completely domesticated. Other cereals grown at that time included smaller amounts of einkorn wheat, emmer wheat, and a kind of bread wheat. While the wheats appear to have been imports from the west, it remains unclear whether barley was as well.

As in the early Neolithic sites of Southwest Asia, gazelle was the most abundant of the wild animal species, which included sheep, goat, cattle, swamp deer, and a large South Asian antelope. Some goats have been identified anatomically as domesticated. In each of two burials from an early level of the occupation, five young goats were placed at the foot of an adult male, whose body was covered with red ochre. These early graves also contained a diverse combination of body ornaments made from exotic materials like seashell, turquoise, and **lapis lazuli.**

After 6000 B.C., important subsistence shifts occurred at Mehrgarh, and the first ceramic vessels were found. Richard Meadow, of Harvard University, has noted a reduction in the body size of the goats, sheep, and humped zebu cattle (*Bos indicus*) at the site, which he interprets as evidence for domestication. The relative abundance of wild species decreased, and the proportion of cattle bones increased greatly, suggesting that cattle husbandry may have begun about the same time at Mehrgarh as in sites to the west. Therefore, while sheep and goats may have been brought to Mehrgarh already tamed or domesticated, archaeological as well as recent genetic evidence suggests that local humped cattle were indigenous to South Asia.

Between 6000 and 4000 B.C., domesticated barley, well adapted to floodplain irrigation, was the predominant cultigen. Charred seeds of the plumlike jujube fruit (*Zizyphus jujuba*) and date pits (*Phoenix dactylifera*) also have been recovered. Cotton seeds were found with wheat and barley grains after 5000 B.C., the earliest date for cotton in the world.

At this time, Mehrgarh was a well-planned community composed of compartmentalized, mud-brick structures that served primarily as storage rooms. Features found in other parts of the settlement include circular fireplaces, containing burnt rocks for **stone boiling,** with bone and other debris nearby. These areas may have been used for large-scale food processing or cooking, or some other kind of communal activity.

Both specialized craft production and extensive long-distance trade, so evi-

dent at the major centers of the later Indus civilization, had clear antecedents millennia earlier at Mehrgarh. By 4000 B.C., the site spread over tens of hectares and included specialized centers where fine ceramic ware was made. For roughly the next 1500 years, Mehrgarh was an important craft center. Wheel-thrown pottery was mass-produced, and beads of lapis lazuli, turquoise, and carnelian were perforated with cylindrical drill bits made of **jasper** and rotated by a **bow-drill.** Fragments of crucibles used to melt copper also were found.

The archaeology at Mehrgarh, along with recent studies at other contemporary sites, has revised South Asian prehistory. No longer can we envision the inhabitants of the Indus River drainage as simple recipients of inventions from the west. Nor can we attribute the rise of the Indus civilization after 2600 B.C. to the diffusion of ideas from Mesopotamia. We now recognize a sequence in South Asia that documents a prepottery Neolithic phase and the indigenous domestication of humped zebu cattle, along with the development of highly specialized local craft industries.

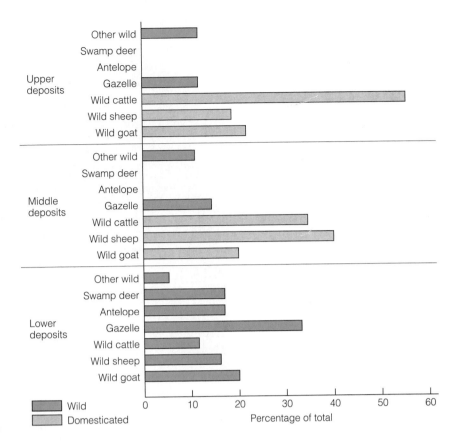

The transition from hunting to herding at Mehrgarh. In the lower deposits, all the species present are wild, including gazelle (*Gazella*), wild goat (*Capra*), wild sheep (*Ovis*), wild cattle (*Bos*), antelope (*Boselaphus*), and swamp deer (*Cervus*). After 6000 B.C. (middle deposits), the reduced size of cattle, goat, and sheep bones at Mehrgarh indicates that these animals were domesticated. After the Neolithic (upper deposits), domesticated cattle were dominant.

POTTERY

Ancient containers: a key source for archaeological interpretation

A Mexican woman making pottery vessels.

"Pottery is . . . the greatest resource of the archaeologist," wrote the famed Egyptologist W. M. Flinders Petrie (1904, pp. 15–16). Indeed, ceramics are the most common kind of artifact found at most post-Paleolithic sites. Since pottery has many purposes—cooking, storage, serving, or carrying materials—many different pieces can be used by a single household at the same time. Moreover, pottery vessels are fragile and often have to be replaced. However, fragments of pottery, or **potsherds**, are very durable and normally preserve better than many other ancient materials found in archaeological contexts.

Ceramic artifacts also are important because they can be good **temporal markers**, sensitive indicators of specific time periods. In his study of ancient Egyptian pottery, Flinders Petrie was one of the first archaeologists to recognize how decorative styles change. In addition to chronological sensitivity, pottery vessels have a series of distinctive technical, formal, and decorative attributes that can tell us many different things about the lives of the people who made, traded, and used them.

Worldwide, the increasing importance of pottery has in many cases roughly coincided with a greater reliance on domesticated foods. Fired clay containers provide clean storage for food and drink and can be used for preparing food over a fire. The earliest securely dated pottery vessels, found at Jomon sites in Japan, are 10,000–12,000 years old (see "Nittano," Chapter 5, p. 178). There may be pottery of roughly the same age from several areas of mainland China as well. Why did they occur so late in human history? Ceramic vessels do have liabilities: They are relatively heavy and often fragile. Many mobile foragers did not use ceramics, preferring lighter containers like net bags, gourds, and baskets. In the preceramic levels at Mehrgarh, for example, the inhabitants used baskets coated with water-resistant bitumen. Clearly, the development and reliance on ceramic vessels is associated with life in more settled communities. Yet some sedentary groups, such as the Native Americans of northwestern North America, did not use pottery, relying instead on a diverse array of woven baskets for storage. And pottery did not simply appear with agriculture. In both Mexico and Southwest Asia, plant domestication preceded the use of ceramics by more than 1000 years. Conversely, the world's oldest ceramic containers were made by the nonagricultural Jomon fisher-foragers of ancient Japan.

The late advent of pottery is curious because ceramic technology had been used by human societies for some time. Baked clay figurines were made at Paleolithic sites in the Soviet Union and Eastern Europe as early as 30,000–20,000 years ago. Clay figurines and mud bricks were made in the Levant 10,000 years ago, yet pottery did not appear locally until around 7000 B.C. Settled farming villagers used ground stone bowls long before they made ceramic containers. In the Americas, ceramic vessels were not made until several thousand years later, when they first appeared in lowland South America. The earliest pottery containers in Mexico and North America date to 3000–2000 B.C., before the advent of fully sedentary villages.

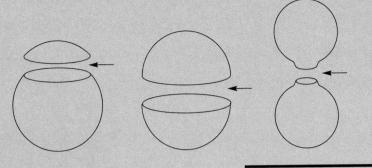

Early pottery forms in Mexico achieved by cross-sectioning gourds.

The earliest pottery from both the Old World and the New World was crafted by hand. Generally, early pottery vessels were either built up in a series of clay coils or molded using gourds. However, by roughly 4000 B.C., **wheel-thrown pottery** became an important commodity throughout the Near East and South Asia. The potter's wheel permits a single worker to make a greater number of vessels more quickly. Such pottery is also highly uniform in size, shape, and appearance. In the Americas, fired clay vessels continued to be handmade (sometimes at a high level of technological sophistication) until the European introduction of the potter's wheel in the sixteenth century A.D. Some scholars have attributed the Old World invention of the potter's wheel to the presence of wheeled vehicles, absent in the New World. Yet the pottery wheel may have preceded the use of the wheel for transport in the Old World. Furthermore, we know that some Native American groups were familiar with the concept of the wheel, because wheeled toys have been found in archaeological contexts. The absence of the potter's wheel may be related to the relative difficulty and inefficiency of transporting ceramic vessels long distances in the aboriginal Americas, where there were few domesticated beasts of burden, no wheeled vehicles, and generally less widespread sea transport than in the Old World.

BAN-PO-TS'UN

A Neolithic village in northern China

An artist's reconstruction of houses at Ban-po-ts'un. Circular structures are believed to have housed a single family; the larger, square structure is thought to have been a communal clan house.

Botanists have long recognized that many Chinese food plants were indigenous to the region. Until recently, however, archaeologists believed that the "idea" of agriculture, along with the knowledge for domesticating animals and making pottery, had diffused to the rich soil of the middle Huang Ho River Valley in northern China from elsewhere. Prior to 1960, the few known Neolithic sites with their characteristic black-and-red pottery were assigned to the Yangshao culture and presumed to date to around 3000 B.C. The general view that Near East products arrived in China about this time was supported by the presence of small amounts of foreign domesticates, such as wheat and barley, at known Yangshao sites, along with larger quantities of a locally domesticated grain (millet) and domesticated pigs.

In the last 30 years, however, information about the Chinese Neolithic has undergone a major transformation. Thousands of new Neolithic sites have recently been discovered in various areas of the country. Dozens of these sites have been excavated, and several earlier sites have been recorded. Early Neolithic sites in North China with millet and pigs have now been dated to the sixth millennium B.C., while the age for some Yangshao sites has been pushed back to 5000 B.C. Equally significant has been the discovery of Neolithic sites, such as Peng-tou-shan and Ho-mu-tu in South China, that predate 6000–5000 B.C. At these more southerly sites, the staple food plant was rice, not millet. The origin of agriculture now appears to have been an indigenous process in North and South China, since in both areas local cultigens have been

Locations of the sites mentioned in the text. The distribution of Yangshao sites is shown in gray.

found to be more abundant and earlier than exotic domesticates.

The best-known Chinese Neolithic site, Ban-po-ts'un (ban-pot'sun), is not the oldest but, rather, the first to have been excavated extensively (work was completed between 1953 and 1955). Located on a loess terrace about 9 m (30 ft) above a tributary of the Huang Ho near the city of Xian, Ban-po-ts'un covers 5–7 ha (12.5–17.5 acres). Roughly 100 houses, some circular and others square, were surrounded by a defensive and drainage ditch. Many of these structures were excavated, and the evidence indicates that the occupation at Ban-po was long and continuous. In one instance, five superimposed house floors were uncovered.

Many of the houses were semisubterranean, 3–5 m (10–16 ft) in diameter, with floors roughly a meter below the ground surface. Each house had timber beams that rested on stone bases, supporting a steeply pitched thatched roof. Floors and interior walls were plastered with clay and straw. One or two circular or pear-shaped fire pits, modeled in clay, were situated at the center of most of the dwellings. Storage pits and animal pens were interspersed among the houses at the center of the settlement.

At Ban-po, the principal crop was millet (*Setaria italica*), which was cultivated in the rich, soft-textured loess soils that surround the village. Such agricultural tools as bone hoes, polished stone adzes, axes, knives, and digging-stick weights were abundant at the site. Chestnuts, hazelnuts, and pinenuts supplemented the grain diet. The inhabitants of Ban-po-ts'un grew **hemp**, probably for use as a fiber. Silk production is suggested by a neatly sliced silkworm cocoon that was recovered. Numerous **spindle whorls,** for spinning thread, and bone needles also were found. Impressions of cloth, as well as baskets and mats, provide more evidence of weaving.

Pigs and dogs were the principal domesticated animals, although cattle, sheep, and goats also were present. Bone and quartz arrow points, bone fishhooks, and net-sinkers all were found, along with plentiful bones of several varieties of deer. Thus hunting and fishing contributed to the diet at Ban-po.

Ban-po-ts'un has yielded more than 500,000 pieces of pottery. Six pottery **kilns** were recovered beyond the ditch at the east side of the settlement, outside the residential zone. Most of the vessels were handmade into a distinctive redware. While cooking pots tend to be coarse and gritty, water vessels and food-serving bowls are made of a finer clay. Cord-marking is the most common surface decoration, although basket, textile, and fingernail impressions also are used. The black-painted geomorphic and zoomorphic Yangshao designs also are applied primarily to bowls and jars.

The inhabitants of Ban-po were buried in one of two ways. Infants and small children were placed in large redware pottery jars and interred near the houses. The cemetery for adults was located outside the enclosing ditch at the north end of the settlement, where corpses were placed in pits 2 m (6.5 ft) deep and arranged in rows. With very few exceptions, each individual was buried separately in an extended position. Ceramic vessels were included with the body in most of the graves. In a few instances, larger quantities of goods were found. The most elaborate burial was a child, who was placed in a wooden tomb that included a green jade pendant, a string of 63 bone disk beads, four ceramic vessels, and three stone pellets.

Toward the end of the occupation at Ban-po, a large rectangular structure was erected on a manmade platform (20 × 12.5 m, or 65 × 41 ft) at the center of the village. The platform was ringed by a low wall that originally may have been the foundation for a higher wall of posts.

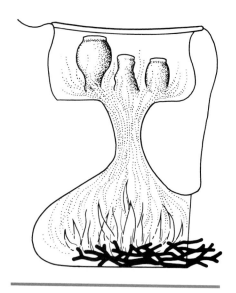

A drawing of a reconstructed section of a pottery kiln at Ban-po-ts'un.

Unlike the residential dwellings, this structure was plastered with a white limy substance that had been hardened by baking. The structure also had a hard earthen floor that appears to have been destroyed in a fire. While some archaeologists might consider this special, central structure to be a possible indicator of emergent social inequalities, Chinese archaeologists interpret the building as a communal assembly hall or clan house.

The purposefully planned layout of Ban-po-ts'un, with a large central building surrounded by a nucleated residential area inside a ditch, and exterior pottery-making and cemetery facilities, was very similar to other contemporary Yangshao villages. For example, Chiang-chai, near Ban-po, had concentric circles of oblong and rectangular houses surrounding four large structures that faced a central village plaza. Chiang-chai also was ringed by a defensive system of ditches, and the cemetery area and pottery kilns were located outside these earthworks. At all well-studied Yangshao sites, the dwelling and cemetery areas are spatially distinct.

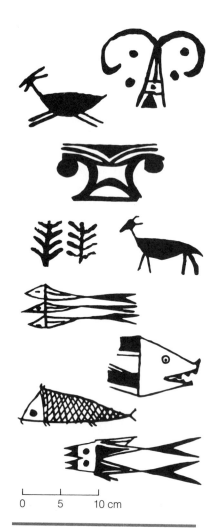

0   5   10 cm

Examples of painted designs on Ban-po-ts'un pottery.

Today, 11% of the world's arable land is planted in rice. This staple grain provides half the diet for 1.6 billion people; an additional 400 million people depend on the plant for at least 25% of their food. In fact, among the world's major grain crops, rice is the only plant that is harvested almost solely for human consumption.

Yet, despite its worldwide significance, archaeologists know relatively little about how or where rice was first domesticated. Although the plant is now cultivated in a variety of environments, it was originally indigenous to the tropics. Rice is an annual grass that shares many characteristics with wheat, barley, oats, and rye. The rice plant belongs to the genus *Oryza*. *Oryza* contains two cultivated species, the Asian *Oryza sativa* and the West African *Oryza glaberrima*, each of which includes a multitude of variants. While archaeologists know less about *O. sativa* than they do about early domesticated wheat, barley, or corn, *O. glaberrima* is even more of a mystery.

The Far East seems to have been the focus for early experimentation and cultivation of *O. sativa*. Recent archaeological research in South China suggests that rice cultivation may have occurred as early as the eighth or ninth millennium B.C. along the middle Yangtze River. By 6500 B.C., rice was an important component of the diet at sites on the flat wetlands of the Hupei Basin. Also in South China, large quantities of rice stalks, grains, and husks were preserved at the waterlogged prehistoric village of Ho-mu-tu, excavated between 1973 and 1978. The settlement contains houses raised on wooden piles above a lakeshore. Excavations revealed rice in stratigraphic levels extending back to the late sixth and early fifth millennia B.C. In one place, the rice remains were 25–50 cm (10–20 in) thick, suggesting that a threshing floor may have been preserved. Both wild and domesticated varieties have been identified at Ho-mu-tu. Remains of bottle gourds, water chestnuts, and sour jujubes were recovered, as were acorns and other nuts. The faunal assemblage includes wild deer, elephant, rhinoceros, tiger, and turtle, as well as the domesticated water buffalo, dog, and pig.

Cord-impressed pottery was found at Ho-mu-tu, and similar ceramic wares have been recovered, along with rice, at other recently excavated sites in South China. Some of these latter sites are earlier, dating to the mid-seventh millennium B.C. Rice, with both wild and domesticated characteristics, also has been recovered at excavated sites in Thailand, where it may pertain to as early as the late fourth millennium B.C. In Southeast Asia, even earlier evidence of rice domestication may lie under water, as rising sea levels have covered many Neolithic sites.

We still have fewer answers than questions about rice domestication. Yet recent research in South China indicates that the domestication of rice probably occurred there, not farther south. In the years ahead, earlier dates for rice, both wild and domesticated, will surely be found, as the archaeological record for South China is expanded and interpreted.

RICE

One of the world's most important grains

Oryza sativa, the cultivated Asian species of the rice plant.

SPIRIT CAVE

The intensive exploitation of plants in early Holocene Thailand

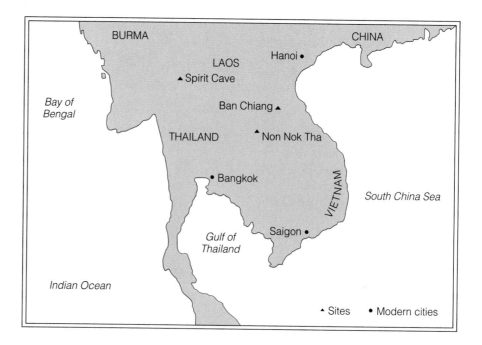

Locations of the Southeast Asian sites mentioned in the text.

In 1952, geographer Carl Sauer proposed that the cradle for the world's earliest agriculture should lie in mainland Southeast Asia, rather than in Southwest Asia, as most scholars still believe. Sauer thought that the highly diverse, tropical, and riverine environments of Southeast Asia would have provided a superb locale for the fishing and farming way of life that he surmised would constitute the earliest stage in the transition to agriculture. Like the Russian botanist Nikolai Ivanovich Vavilov before him, Sauer was aware that the wild ancestors for a wide array of modern cultigens (root, tree, and seed crops) had been traced to Southeast Asia.

For over a decade, few prehistorians gave serious consideration to Sauer's ideas because of an absence of information to evaluate them. Moreover, his proposal did not conform to the traditional views of mainland Southeast Asia as a kind of cultural recipient or backwater area that obtained most technological advances from India or China. For Thailand, traditional archaeological reconstructions suggested that the earliest domesticates came from North China after 3000 B.C.

During the 1950s, the most relevant archaeological materials for tropical Southeast Asia belonged to the Hoabinhian complex, known from a series of limestone caves and shell middens. As this complex was not well dated, the presence of cord-marked pottery with edge-ground stone axes in the upper deposits of several Hoabinhian sites was presumed to signal the introduction of agriculture from North China.

By the 1960s, however, new information revised the traditional Southeast Asian picture of a conservative Hoabinhian way of life, punctuated by a series of infusions from the north. An archaeological research program, under the general direction of Wilhelm G. Solheim II, of the University of Hawaii, produced evidence that intensive plant exploitation,

Excavation at Non Nok Tha.

pottery, and metallurgy had a much earlier history in Southeast Asia. Perhaps the most important findings came from Spirit Cave, an upland Hoabinhian site in northwestern Thailand, and Non Nok Tha, a later habitation mound in the lower northeastern part of the country.

Spirit Cave was discovered and excavated by Chester Gorman, a graduate student of Solheim's. While reconnoitering through rugged hilly terrain near the Burmese border in 1966, Gorman learned from the villagers of a nearby cave site. He found both Hoabinhian stone tools and cord-marked pottery on the surface inside the limestone chamber. Excavations revealed a stratigraphic sequence that Gorman divided into two cultural levels. The lower deposits contained standard Hoabinhian chipped stone artifacts, while polished adzes, cord-marked and burnished pottery, and polished slate knives were found in the upper soil layers. The slate knives, simi-lar to tools used to harvest rice in Java today, had not been found previously in the Hoabinhian. The most unexpected findings resulted from the careful study of plant remains and from the absolute dates generated by radiocarbon analyses of charcoal.

The first archaeologist to carefully sieve the excavated soil from a Hoabinhian site, Gorman found a great variety of seeds, shells, husks, and other plant parts. Food plants such as butternuts, almonds, cucumbers, water chestnuts, a few beans, and peppers were recovered, as were candlenuts, which may have been used for lighting. Remains of the stimulant betel nut and the bottle gourd, a probable container, also were found. Interestingly, neither of these two latter plants is now native to this area. None of the recovered plant species differs significantly from their wild prototypes, indicating that none of them was domesticated. Nonetheless, an intensive utilization

Excavation at Spirit Cave.

by Charles Higham, of the University of Otago, New Zealand, of the animal remains from Non Nok Tha, and contemporary levels at the more northerly site of Ban Chiang, indicate an increasing reliance on domesticated animals—cattle, pigs, chickens, and dogs—at these later sites as well, although hunting and fishing did continue. For Spirit Cave, Higham's identifications suggested that plant collecting and tending were supplemented by broad-based hunting, with deer, wild pigs, and arboreal animals such as monkeys the principal targets.

During the last 35 years, knowledge about the early Holocene in Southeast Asia has expanded significantly. We have learned that the broad-spectrum Hoabinhian complex extended more deeply into the past than had been previously believed, and that plant tending may have contributed importantly to the diet. By the seventh millennium B.C. (also much earlier than previously expected), new technologies, including pottery, were in evidence at Spirit Cave. However, an even more dramatic transition occurred during the next several millennia. At settled villages, like Non Nok Tha and Ban Chiang, the inhabitants lived in houses built on piles or wooden stilts, buried their dead in low mounds, and made socketed spearpoints and adzes as well as adornments of bronze, representing some of the world's earliest known bronzeworking. At these later settlements, rice agriculture and domesticated animals comprised the bulk of the diet.

While much has been learned, many questions remain. We cannot evaluate the importance of indigenous tropical domesticates, like yam and taro, because these root crops preserve so poorly in the archaeological record. The specifics of rice adoption remain a bit sketchy, although recent research places the original hearth for this key grain in South China. Consequently, while Sauer's hypothesis for indigenous Southeast Asian plant domestication may eventually hold for certain tropical roots, fruits, and tubers, concerted archaeological studies over the last decades now indicate that the region's staple grain—rice—was probably introduced into the region from South China.

(and possibly tending) of a wide variety of plants was indicated. The Spirit Cave occupation also was much older than expected. The earliest levels were at least 11,000 years old, whereas the ceramic occupation began roughly 3000–4000 years later.

Significantly, the remains of rice were absent at Spirit Cave. However, rice husks were recovered in the earliest occupational levels (4000–3000 B.C.) at the site of Non Nok Tha, where clear impressions and carbonized remnants of rice chaff were found in potsherds. Apparently the ancient potters, like their modern counterparts, mixed the plant materials into their clay as a fiber **temper**, or additive, to improve the workability of the clay and to reduce breakage. Intensive microscopic studies of rice impressions in ceramics by Douglas Yen, of the University of Hawaii, Honolulu, and others indicate that the grains were not completely domesticated and may have been hybrids, or intermediate between wild and domesticated varieties.

Rice became an increasingly important plant by the end of the several-thousand-year period between the upper levels at Spirit Cave and the lowest occupations at Non Nok Tha. Analyses

Perhaps the most surprising and significant result from archaeological research at the sites of Non Nok Tha and Ban Chiang in northeastern Thailand is the evidence for metalworking around 2000 B.C. Unlike the working of clay, bone, wood, or stone, **metallurgy** requires a greater understanding and manipulation of raw materials; metals have to be extracted from crystalline ores before they can be made into useful objects. The extraction or smelting of copper ores cannot be accomplished with the heat obtained from a typical cooking fire (600–800°C, or 1100–1500°F). Both higher temperatures and a **reducing atmosphere,** one that is oxygen-deficient, are required for the necessary chemical reaction to take place. In addition to smelting, metalworking involves other processes: mining; **annealing,** gradual heating followed by gradual cooling to reduce brittleness and enhance toughness; casting; and **alloying,** mixing two or more metals to make a new one.

More than 800 metal ornaments and weapons were uncovered at Ban Chiang, and many more were found at Non Nok Tha. Researchers used a technique called **optical emission spectrography** to determine the elemental composition of these objects. Mixing other metals (particularly tin) with copper produces alloys (such as bronze) that are harder, more enduring, and easier to cast. The characteristics of a specific metal object are affected by the proportions of different metals in the particular piece. The earliest metal object from Ban Chiang, a socketed spearpoint, contained less than 2% tin; the presence of such a small amount of tin suggests that the alloying may not, in fact, have been deliberate. However, most of the objects from both sites clearly were composed of normal tin bronze (intentionally alloyed to include about 10% tin).

Researchers have investigated the expertise of the ancient Thai metalsmiths using other procedures that reveal the grain, or microstructure, of different specimens in **photomicrographs.** The very early fourth-millennium socketed spearpoint (mostly copper), found in a grave at Ban Chiang, was cast in a two-piece mold with a core inserted during casting to create the socket. Subsequently, the point was cold-worked and annealed. Examination of the internal structure of a third-millennium bronze axe from Non Nok Tha revealed that its manufacture had required alloying, casting, cold-hammering, and annealing.

In addition to bronze tools and ornaments, iron bracelets and bangles—some of the oldest iron objects in East Asia—were discovered in later first-millennium B.C. deposits at Ban Chiang. The incorporation of iron into local metallurgy is just one indication that these early metalsmiths continually experimented and expanded their abilities to create a wider assortment of better-made tools and ornaments.

EARLY METALLURGY IN THAILAND

Bronze ornaments and weapons

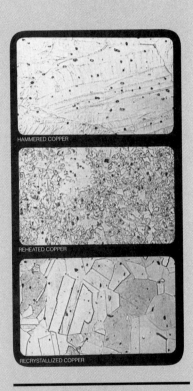

Photomicrographs of specimens of copper, showing how different ancient metalworking techniques affect the structure of the metal.

Specimens of pure copper and four copper alloys, showing marked differences when viewed through a microscope. Without magnification, the specimens display only subtle differences in hue and texture.

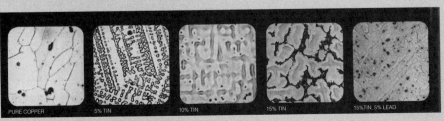

GUILÁ NAQUITZ CAVE

A preceramic seasonal campsite in Mexico

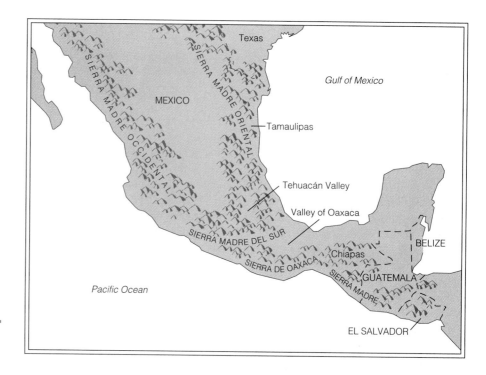

The regions of Mesoamerica mentioned in text.

We have indicated that the research problem we chose for ourselves at Guilá Naquitz was to develop a model that would not only deal with some of the underlying and more universal aspects of early domestication but also tie that process into the specific cultural pattern for the Valley of Oaxaca.

K. V. Flannery (1986)

Kent V. Flannery spent the day before Christmas of 1964 in the foothills of the eastern Valley of Oaxaca, in southern Mexico, searching for the best site to study agricultural origins in Mexico. Having just completed several seasons of fieldwork as the faunal analyst on Richard MacNeish's interdisciplinary team in arid Tehuacán 150 km (90 mi) to the north (see "Tehuacán," p. 242), Flannery wanted to see what form early agriculture might have taken in a more humid valley with greater farming potential. On that December day, Flannery found a preceramic occupation at Cueva Blanca, a site that, he says, more than any other launched his Valley of Oaxaca Human Ecology project.

On Christmas day, heartened by the previous day's finds, Flannery began to prepare a research proposal. A year later, with support from the Smithsonian Research Foundation, he returned to Oaxaca. On January 26, 1966, less than a week after beginning a reconnaissance of caves in the area, he found a rock shelter with lots of chipped stone debris and half of a projectile point on the ground surface. This small overhang named Guilá Naquitz (ge-la'nah-keets') was completely excavated. The name means "white cliff" in the native Zapotec language of Oaxaca.

At Guilá Naquitz, Flannery and his field crew carefully peeled away the layers of preceramic occupations dating to 8750–6670 B.C. Based on careful retrieval and analysis of the floral, faunal, and artifactual remains found in the cave strata, Flannery suggested that the shelter of Guilá Naquitz was occupied seasonally between August and December by small groups, or **microbands,** perhaps composed of a series of nuclear families. As in the rest of the Mexican highlands at this time, the ancient inhabitants of Oaxaca were mobile, living in several different camps during the course of their yearly activities.

Work in progress at Guilá Naquitz Cave. Many of the species of cacti and thorny bushes outside the cave have seeds or fruits that were eaten by Archaic foragers.

Maguey plant in the eastern Valley of Oaxaca. The plant also provides fibers that were used to make rope.

The archaeological contents of the cave strata indicate that the inhabitants of Guilá Naquitz consumed a diversity of plant foods, such as acorns and the roasted heart of **maguey** plants (the source of tequila and mescal today), which could have been collected in the thorn forest surrounding the site. Other plant foods, such as the seeds of the pod-bearing **mesquite** tree and hackberries, were brought back to the cave from the flatter grassland below. A small part of the diet, one that increased slightly through time, came from squash and bean plants, which may have been tended or cultivated in the disturbed terrain around the site. Use of the wild squash may have been a first step toward eventual domestication. Bruce Smith, of the Smithsonian Institution, has recently restudied squash seeds and fragments (*Cucurbita pepo*) recovered from early levels at the site. Accelerator mass spectrometry (AMS) dates taken on some of these remains indicate the presence of domesticated squash by about 8000 B.C. Neither maize cobs nor kernels were identified in ancient levels. The variety of nuts, seeds, fruits, and cactus eaten during late summer and early autumn was supplemented by a small amount of venison and rabbit meat. Although deer and rabbit bones were not abundant at Guilá Naquitz, this meat still provided much of the protein consumed in the cave.

The location of Guilá Naquitz Cave and Cueva Blanca in the Valley of Oaxaca.

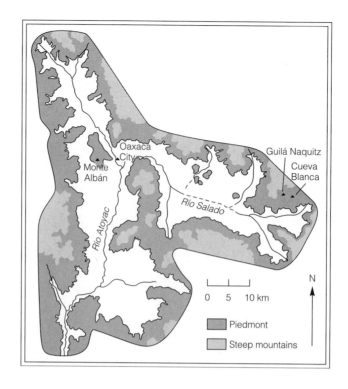

The subsistence activities of the inhabitants of Guilá Naquitz were rather conservative, changing little over the millennia of intermittent occupations. Perhaps this continuity should not be surprising. Two nutritionists, J. R. K. Robson and J. N. Elias, concluded that the diet of the cave occupants compared favorably with the contemporary diet in the United States, providing similar levels of nutrients and exceeding caloric requirements with a lower intake of food.

Whereas seasonally abundant plant foods could have been collected near the cave, stone for making tools was taken from quarries up to 50 km (30 mi) away. This better raw material was used primarily for projectile points, while more local, but less suitable, rock sources were used for more disposable tools, such as scrapers and worked flakes.

Besides recording the collection and processing of plant foods and the butchering and consumption of animals, the archaeologists at Guilá Naquitz documented the manufacture of tools, the digging of pits to store acorns, the use of fire pits to prepare food, and even the collection of leaves for bedding in the cave. Years of multidisciplinary study by Flannery and his colleagues illustrate how archaeologists can reconstruct the events of the past into a credible picture of ancient life just before the advent of agriculture in the highlands of ancient Mexico.

A fragment of knotted net from Guilá Naquitz Cave. Such nets were used as bags for transporting food to the cave.

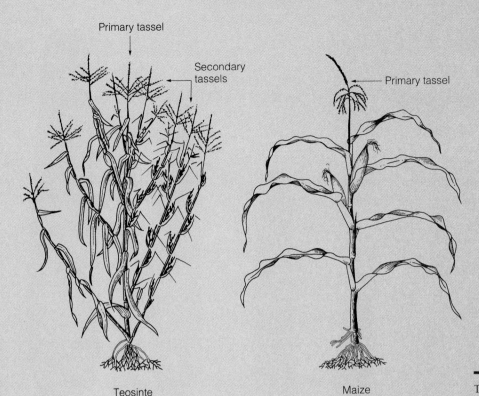

Primary tassel

Secondary tassels

Primary tassel

Teosinte

Maize

The mysterious ancestry of corn

Teosinte and maize plants.

Maize—or corn, as it is familiarly known in the United States—was unknown in Europe prior to the arrival of Columbus in the New World in 1492. By that time, the plant was cultivated by native inhabitants over much of the tropical and temperate portions of the Western Hemisphere. The great adaptability and plasticity of maize is evidenced by its position as the second or third most important food plant on earth and its current worldwide distribution. Botanical studies, however, indicate that the ancestor of modern corn (*Zea mays*) was native to southern or western Mexico.

Botanists and archaeologists have puzzled over the ancestry of maize. Domesticated varieties of such cereals as wheat, barley, and rice are structurally nearly identical to living wild species. The principal difference is that, while in the domesticated varieties the edible seeds tend to remain fastened on the plant, the wild varieties have shattering **inflorescences.** As mentioned earlier, shattering is a mechanism by which the seeds of the plant are dispersed naturally. The most recognizable feature of domesticated maize, the massive husked ear, is not present even in wild grasses most closely related to maize. In fact, the non-shattering ear of domestic corn, with its surrounding husks, inhibits seed dispersal so that without farmers to remove and plant kernels from the ear, modern maize could not reproduce for even one or two years. Because of its structure, the late George Beadle, a renowned plant geneticist, referred to domesticated maize as a "biological monstrosity."

Because of this pronounced difference between the ears of domesticated maize and related wild grasses, the debates over the origins of maize have been more contentious, and until recently have achieved less consensus, than discussions

(continued)

Increasing archaeological corncob size through time.

about the origins of most other domesticated seed plants. Although a few experts still hold the view that there was once a wild species of maize (with ears like maize) that has since become extinct (no such plant has ever been found), most participants in the debate have returned to a previously popular position that the ancestor of maize was a variety of **teosinte**, a giant wild grass so closely related to *Zea mays* that some botanists place it with corn in the same species. Teosinte still grows in the foothills and highlands of Mexico and Guatemala and, in fact, is the only large-seeded, wild, annual grass in the tropical Americas. Unlike maize, teosinte lacks a cob; instead, its seeds are contained in fruitcases. At maturity, teosinte seeds are dispersed through shattering. In other respects, the annual teosinte varieties are very similar to maize and produce fully fertile offspring when interbred with the domesticated plant.

Teosinte and maize have similar tassels, and similar DNA, amino acid, and nutritional compositions. Even examination with a scanning electron microscope cannot distinguish the pollen of annual types of teosinte from small-seeded varieties of corn (such as early domesticated maize).

In recent years, new botanical evidence has further clarified the ancestral role of the plant that the Aztecs called *teocentli* ("God's ear of corn"). Biologist John Doebley, of the University of Minnesota, and botanist Hugh Iltis, of the University of Wsconsin, Madison, compared six diverse kinds of teosinte. They found that two annual teosintes were most similar in morphology and other characteristics to maize. Later studies by Doebley determined that the specific proteins from one of these annual teosinte subspecies (*Zea mays parviglumis*) were indistinguishable from maize. The *parviglumis* teosinte was more similar to maize than any of the other teosintes. Doebley even demonstrated that a geographic cluster of the *parviglumis* subspecies growing at an elevation of 400–1200 m (1300–3900 ft) along the slopes of the central Balsas River drainage, 250 km (155 mi) west of the Tehuacán Valley, was more biochemically similar to maize than the other geographic subpopulations of this plant. In fact, recent genetic analysis by Doebley and his colleagues suggests that a small number of single-gene changes could account for the transformation of these annual teosintes into maize. The Balsas drainage, largely unknown archaeologically, may be a promising area for pursuing the domestication of maize.

To date, archaeological findings have supplemented but not resolved these debates. Archaeological deposits at Guilá Naquitz, dating to the seventh or eighth millennium B.C., contained bean and squash seeds and grains of *Zea* pollen. Yet we do not know whether the pollen came from maize or teosinte, or how the pollen was transported into the cave. Today, teosinte often grows in the same fields with beans, squash, and maize. Teosinte is a weedy pioneer that thrives in disturbed areas such as seasonally wet streambeds and abandoned campsites. Although teosinte can be neither popped nor ground into flour as easily as maize, the wild plant is occasionally eaten as a low-choice or "starvation" food in times of need. Young teosinte ears could have been eaten for their sugary taste. Seasonally, stems of the plant may have been (and are still) chewed, because the pith stores so much sugar.

According to Richard MacNeish's Tehuacán research, the earliest domesticated corn remains appear in cave deposits dating to the end of the sixth millennium B.C. These early ears were small (about the size of an index finger) and contained no more than four to eight rows of kernels. The original dating of these Tehuacán cave strata was accomplished through the conventional radiocarbon analysis of charcoal samples.

Recently, the early dates for maize have been seriously questioned, based on direct radiocarbon accelerator dating of the early maize cobs themselves. Accelerator mass spectrometry enables researchers to count individual carbon-14 atoms, rather than relying on the conventional counting of radioactive disintegrations (see "Radiocarbon Dating," Chapter 4, p. 142). As a result, they can handle much smaller samples. Recent analysis dates the early Tehuacán maize to the mid-third millennium B.C., several thousand years younger than previously thought. The new AMS dates therefore provide a new timetable for the arrival of maize in the Tehuacán Valley. Nevertheless, if maize was first domesticated to the west of Tehuacán—in the Balsas, for example—then this process may well have occurred before the new dates for early maize.

Yet the new AMS dates do not change the cultural context of maize adoption in Tehuacán. Even at 4700–4500 years ago, the highland Mesoamerican people who adopted maize were still organized in small, seasonally mobile societies. These groups added corn to their way of life without radically changing their social or economic behavior. Not surprisingly, this relatively primitive maize does not appear to have become an immediate preceramic dietary staple. Although we cannot directly determine the role of human selection in the evolution of these early ears, the Tehuacán evidence has provided a key record of increasing cob size, from the earliest tiny cobs to the much larger and more productive ears (with bigger kernels and more seed rows) grown today (see Color Plate 8). The important role of human selection in this latter process is evident.

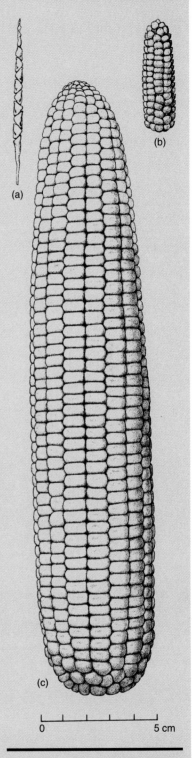

The domestication of corn: (a) teosinte, (b) early maize, and (c) modern maize, all drawn to same scale.

TEHUACÁN

The evolution of early maize

In the early 1960s, when Richard Mac-Neish began his fieldwork in the highland Tehuacán (Tay-wa-con') Valley in Puebla, Mexico, little was known about either the preceramic occupation of Mesoamerica or the beginnings of agriculture in the New World. Prior to Mac-Neish's work, **Mesoamerica,** the region—consisting of southern and central Mexico, Guatemala, Belize, El Salvador, and the western parts of Honduras and Nicaragua—that was the focus of complex, hierarchical states at the time of Spanish contact, was theorized to be a hearth of early agriculture. Yet no archaeological evidence existed to support this hypothesis.

MacNeish chose to search for the origins of maize (*Zea mays*) in the relatively small Tehuacán Valley for two reasons. First, due to the region's dryness, preservation was unusually good. Preliminary excavations unearthed fragments of basketry and plant materials in limestone cave deposits. Second, MacNeish already had recovered tiny 5000-year-old corncobs in caves in both the northeastern Mexican state of Tamaulipas and the southern state of Chiapas. He reasoned that the earliest domesticated *Zea* should be still older and would be found in a highland region like Tehuacán, located between Tamaulipas and Chiapas.

MacNeish designed his Tehuacán research to examine two critical questions: (1) What led to the domestication of maize? (2) How did these changes lay the foundation for later Mesoamerican civilization? He undertook a large survey that located more than 450 prehispanic sites over the 1500 sq km (575 sq mi) of

the valley, and excavated at a series of 12 cave and open-air deposits. Controlled stratigraphic excavations, combined with a large number of radiocarbon dates, enabled MacNeish to reconstruct an unbroken 12,000-year sequence of occupation, at that time the longest recorded in the New World. For the first time, a picture of early presedentary, preceramic society in Mesoamerica could be sketched, using both artifacts and the plant and animal remains preserved in dry caves of Tehuacán.

During the preceramic era, according to MacNeish, the few people of the Tehuacán Valley lived in microbands that dispersed periodically. Some camps accommodated only a single nuclear family, while others sheltered much larger groups. The plant and animal remains recovered from preceramic sites in Tehuacán's diverse topographic zones led to the recognition that the **seasonality** of resource availability and the **scheduling** of resource extraction were critically important in determining the annual regime. More specifically, the early inhabitants of Tehuacán scheduled their seasonal movements across the highland region, from the riverbanks to the foothills to the mountains, to coincide with the periodic availability of local plant and animal species.

For most of the preceramic era, such game as rabbits and deer supplemented plants in the diet. During the May–October rainy season, edible plants were more abundant, and a diversity of seeds, cactus fruits, and berries were exploited, in addition to the bountiful seedpods of the mesquite tree. Rabbits, rodents, liz-

Coxcatlán Cave in the Tehuacán Valley, showing its stratigraphy.

ards, and other small animals were consumed at this time of year, when the size of human groups was generally larger. Although some fruits were still available in the early part of the dry season (November and December), cactus leaves and deer apparently were the staples during the dry spells that lasted from January to April.

Although this way of life persisted for almost 6500 years, from 8000 to 1500 B.C., several important dietary changes did take place. A wild ancestor of the domesticated squash was used by 8000 years ago, probably as a container or for its protein-rich seeds. Thereafter during this 6500-year period, domesticated varieties of squash and the earliest known maize appeared in Tehuacán. The archaeological evidence suggests that these early domesticated plants did not

immediately provide a large portion of the diet, which still was based primarily on wild plants and animals. Thus, these initial experiments toward plant domestication occurred among a population that was largely mobile and remained so for thousands of years.

Somewhat enigmatically, the bone chemistry assay of human bones from the Tehuacán excavations provides a rather different picture for the period after 5000 B.C. (see "Bone Chemistry and Prehistoric Subsistence," Chapter 5, p. 172). These studies indicate a smaller amount of meat in the diet than is seen in the archaeological deposits, as well as a greater role for either early cultigens or wild *setaria* grass, the seeds of which were present but not recovered in abundance in the archaeological record. Yet the relative importance of meat inferred

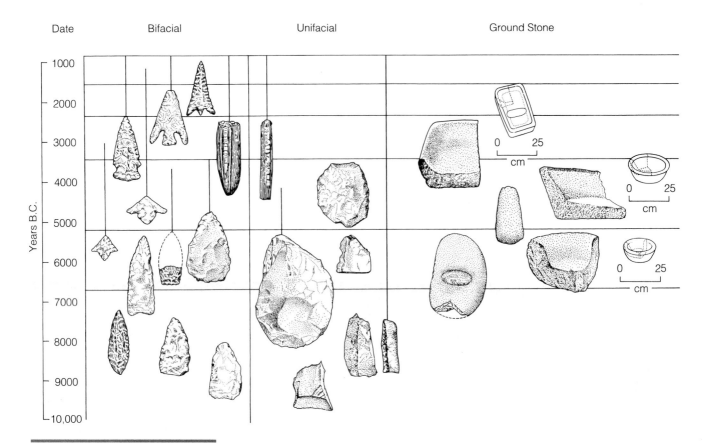

Date   Bifacial   Unifacial   Ground Stone

Changes in the flaked and ground
stone industry in Tehuacán,
10,000–1000 B.C.

from archaeological deposits is not that surprising, given that bone generally preserves better in ancient deposits than do smaller plant materials.

In addition to the gradual increase in the overall proportion of both wild and domesticated plant foods in the diet, the Tehuacán sequence reveals an increase in population and a decrease in residential mobility. Based on the size and number of sites known from the preceramic phases, the total population density for the Tehuacán Valley, though low, may have increased severalfold during this period. While the earliest sedentary villages in Tehuacán did not occur until 4000–3000 years ago, the length of site occupation increased, and the size of sites grew during the preceding millennia. A single circular pithouse, the earliest known in Mesoamerica, was found in a 5000-year-old level at an open-air site in the region. Later preceramic occupations also tend to have more storage features.

There is little question that Mac-Neish's Tehuacán research has revolu-

tionized our knowledge of early Mesoamerica, as well as our understanding of the diversity of situations in which early agriculture developed. In the Tehuacán Valley, the first experiments toward plant domestication occurred among people who remained residentially mobile for thousands of years, a sequence that is very different from what has been long known for early farming in Southwest Asia.

The wild ancestors of the major Mesoamerican cultigens—maize, beans, and squash—were all highland plants. Thus, it is not surprising that the earliest archaeological evidence for Mesoamerican agriculture has been found in highland valleys like Tehuacán and Oaxaca. The dry caves in these upland valleys are recognized for their superb archaeological preservation. Yet some of Mesoamerica's earliest sedentary villages were established in the lowlands, where the highland cultigens eventually were incorporated into a coastal subsistence economy that also included marine resources and lowland plants.

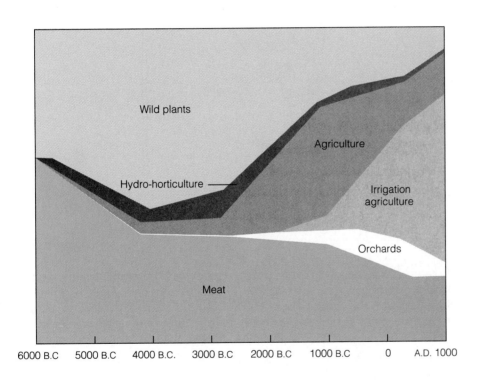

Changes in diet and farming strategies in the Tehuacán Valley, 6000 B.C.–A.D. 1000.

Wild plants

Cultivated squash and beans

Cultivated corn

Cultivated fruit and seed plants

Domesticated dog and turkey

Big and small game

6000 B.C.   5000 B.C   4000 B.C   3000 B.C   2000 B.C   1000 B.C   0   A.D. 1000

Wild plants

Agriculture

Hydro-horticulture

Irrigation agriculture

Orchards

Meat

6000 B.C   5000 B.C   4000 B.C.   3000 B.C   2000 B.C   1000 B.C   0   A.D. 1000

GUITARRERO CAVE

The origins of domestication in the high Andes

The location of Guitarrero Cave.

A century before the arrival of the Spanish in the sixteenth century A.D., the prehispanic New World's largest empire was in place along the western side of South America (see Chapter 9). This political domain stretched from the Inca capital of Cuzco, in Peru's southern highlands, down into Chile and northwestern Argentina and up through Ecuador. It encompassed high Andean mountain slopes, Pacific coastal deserts, and the western fringes of the Amazonian tropics. The Inca established a network of roads and trails to move people and goods across these diverse topographic zones.

Thousands of years before the beginnings of Inca expansion, the earliest steps toward agriculture were taken in this part of South America, where the high Andes are sandwiched by a coastal desert and a tropical rain forest. Although roads were not yet built, communication between these environments was critical to the beginnings of Andean domestication. By 10,000–8000 years ago, Amazonian plants were introduced into the Andes. After 6000 B.C., morphologically wild plants and animals from the rain forest and mountains were present at sites established along the Pacific. Yet the earliest indications for cultivation and domestication appear in the mountains.

As mentioned in the earlier discussion of Monte Verde, human groups first

Excavating the early Archaic deposits at Guitarrero Cave.

arrived in South America as mobile hunters and gatherers, using stone implements and eating a variety of foods (see "Monte Verde," Chapter 4, p. 148). They spread rapidly across the continent. Although earlier sites have been reported, archaeologists have a much more complete understanding of the last 10,000–12,000 years in the Andean highlands. One of the important sites for the early period is Guitarrero (gē-ta-rare'o) Cave, a large natural rock shelter at 2580 m (8500 ft) above sea level in the mountains of northern Peru (see Color Plate 9). First occupied more than 10,000 years ago, Guitarrero Cave served as a campsite for thousands of years, accumulating a valuable record of the beginnings of domestication in the Andes.

Thomas F. Lynch, of Cornell University, directed excavations in the cave during the late 1960s. The dry highland cave environment preserved many organic materials, and polished bone knives, fragments of gourd bowls, cordage, basketry, and textiles were recovered. The late C. Earle Smith noted that the total bulk of the inedible fibrous plants was roughly equivalent to that of the food plant remains at the site, suggesting that the Andean utilization of fibers and textiles had a very early origin. The basic twining or finger-weaving technique, used to create many of the textiles at Guitarrero Cave, is clearly an important step toward the elaborate techniques used for later prehispanic Andean fabrics.

Organic remains also revealed continuity in another important Andean cultural pattern: communication and exchange between different environmental areas. Guitarrero Cave, on the western slope of the Andes, sits in the middle of three principal environmental zones. The

Cordage recovered from Guitarrero Cave.

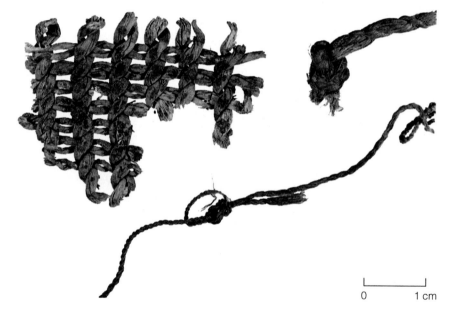

Basket fragments recovered from Guitarrero Cave.

Potato, a native South American plant.

high-altitude shelter faces the exceedingly dry, narrow Pacific coastal zone. To the east, over the Andes, are the wetter, tropical eastern slopes, or **montaña** zone, which grades down to the Amazon jungle. The presence of lima beans, a plant native to the Amazon basin, in archaeological levels dated to roughly 8000 years ago, reveals both the antiquity of pan-Andean connections, at least in an indirect, down-the-line fashion (passing from person to person, group to group over long distances), and the origins of cultivation in South America.

As with the lima bean, many wild ancestors of the major South American domesticated plants, including manioc, peanut, guava, and coca, were native to the eastern side of the Andes. Yet because of the poor archaeological preservation in the *montaña* zone, we know little about the first stages in the process of cultivation and domestication. Other root crops like the potato are indigenous to the mountain zone. Unfortunately, efforts to learn the origins of root crops are hampered because these plants reproduce asexually (see "The First Farmers," p. 197). Ten thousand years ago, Andean **tubers** and **rhizomes** (rootlike stems) were prime sources of carbohydrates for the occupants of Guitarrero Cave. Yet these plants may have been wild, collected from higher elevations.

As in highland Mesoamerica, the first steps toward cultivation and domestication in the Andean highlands resulted in few immediate changes in society. In both regions, the preceramic era was characterized for thousands of years by continued mobility and a rather resilient diet. At Guitarrero Cave, the earliest inhabitants relied for generations on a variety of tubers, rhizomes, and squash for carbohydrates, several kinds of beans for plant protein, and wild fruits, along with a variety of chili peppers, for minerals and vitamins.

Analysis of the faunal remains from Guitarrero by Elizabeth Wing, of the University of Florida, indicates that deer, camelids, rabbits, and a range of small animal and bird species were hunted. Wing observed a steady decline in the number of deer bones and an increase in camelids through time, a pattern also seen at other Andean sites from this time and particularly at sites in the higher grassland, or *puna,* region. In the Andes, the increase in camelid remains is only part of the evidence for manipulation and eventual domestication (for both meat and wool) of the larger llama and the smaller alpaca. The larger llama also served as a pack animal, carrying goods across the Andes. Another Andean species, the guinea pig, also was domesticated for meat but was not abundant at Guitarrero Cave.

Early Archaic flint scraper wrapped in deer hide and cord recovered from Guitarrero Cave.

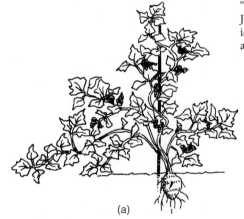

Jicama, a common native South American tuber and root plant: (a) a plant and (b) a tuberous root.

(a)

(b)

Agriculture in Native North America

Indigenous plant domestication before the spread of maize

By the time Europeans arrived in the Americas, the maize plant had spread far to the north and south. In Central and South America, the exact timing of the plant's arrival is a matter of considerable conjecture. Some scholars place maize in these regions as early as 5000 B.C. Yet, given the pathbreaking botanical and genetic work of John Doebley, an origin for the domesticated plant outside of highland Mexico seems unlikely. At the same time, if these estimates for Central and South American maize are correct, the new AMS dates for the Tehuacán maize would place the plant in those regions farther to the south before it was adopted in Tehuacán. Significantly, none of the early claims for maize outside of highland Mexico has been scrutinized as closely as the Tehuacán finds. For example, no AMS dates have been obtained directly from early maize remains found in South or Central America. At present, the best estimate is that maize arrived in South America during the last millennia B.C., where it supplemented a range of agricultural plants that were indigenously domesticated. Its arrival probably rapidly followed the plant's initial domestication in highland Mesoamerica.

The history of maize in North America is somewhat clearer. Maize reached the Southwest by 1200 B.C., and from there it apparently was carried across the Great Plains and arrived in the Eastern Woodlands by approximately A.D. 1–200. While the timing of maize's North American arrival is now better established, the role of the exotic domesticates in the beginnings of North American agriculture is still a matter of discussion. Formerly, most scholars postulated that agriculture in eastern North America began in response to the diffusion of exotic domesticated plants (specifically squash) from the south. Yet this view is beginning to be challenged in the face of mounting archaeological and genetic evidence.

In eastern North America, from Ohio to Arkansas, findings from a series of cave sites indicate that native North American seed plants were domesticated in riverine floodplain settings as early as 2500–1500 B.C. The plants include *Chenopodium* (*C. berlandieri*, also known as goosefoot or chia), marsh elder (*Iva annua* var. *macrocarpa*), and sunflower (*Helianthus annus* var. *macrocarpus*). In each case, botanical studies have shown that the domesticated varieties have larger and morphologically different seeds than the wild ancestors. As in Mesoamerica and South America, these domesticated seed plants were incorporated into the diet of mobile peoples, who also exploited a range of wild foods.

Although AMS dates on the maize found in eastern North American caves have consistently placed the arrival of this Mesoamerican plant well after the domestication of native North American seed plants, the picture is a bit fuzzier for squash (*Cucurbita pepo*). Small carbonized pieces of squash rind were recovered in flotation samples found at river valley sites in Illinois and Kentucky. These fragments yielded direct AMS dates of roughly 5000–3500 B.C. Though *C. pepo* does include some wild gourds, it is best known for its rich variety of domesticated squashes and pumpkins. Researchers also thought it was domesticated in highland Mexico around 8000–7000 B.C. The archaeological contexts that produced these early pieces of rind were outside the current range of the Texas wild gourd, another *Cucurbita* species that grows in eastern Texas. An obvious initial conclusion was that domesticated squash was introduced to eastern North America, along with the notion of agriculture, well before the cultivation of native plants.

This first scenario has been challenged by an alternative viewpoint suggesting that *C. pepo* was independently domesticated twice from different ancestral populations of wild gourds. It was domesticated in Mexico and then later in eastern North America around 2500 B.C. (around the same time the indigenous seed plants were domesticated). All

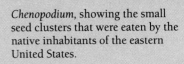
Chenopodium, showing the small seed clusters that were eaten by the native inhabitants of the eastern United States.

the early eastern North American *Cucurbita* rind samples are thin and likely came from wild gourds. Early seeds from these plants also are small, within the range of wild gourds. The earliest morphological marker, larger seed size, of *Cucurbita* domestication in eastern North America did not appear until 2500–2300 B.C. These interpretations are supported by the findings of botanist Deena Decker-Walters, of Texas A & M University, whose biochemical analyses of *C. pepo* have revealed that the species is composed of two developmental lineages, one from Mexico and the other from eastern North America. This view has re-cently been supported by the discovery of wild squash in the Ozarks of Missouri and Arkansas. This Ozark gourd occupies the same floodplain niche inhabited by two of the seed plants (goosefoot and marsh elder) that were indigenously domesticated in the East.

Based on these recent findings, the early squash rind found in eastern North America was probably from a native plant. Consequently, agriculture appears to have occurred indigenously in this North American region, well before the diffusion of the concept or any local plant from Mexico.

BREAST-FEEDING AND BIRTH SPACING

Ideas about post-Pleistocene demographic growth

Archaeological evidence indisputably shows that the beginnings of farming and sedentary life were associated temporally with an increased rate of population growth. Because the reasons for this rapid growth are difficult to understand through the archaeological record alone, archaeologists and physical anthropologists have used demographic and physiological analyses of contemporary peoples to gain insight into factors that may have prompted this transition.

Like all significant demographic shifts, the post-Pleistocene changes theoretically could have resulted from changes in migration, mortality, or fertility. Although migration may have become an important factor in certain later agricultural regions, like Neolithic Europe, it alone cannot account for the rapid growth evidenced in much of the world following food production and sedentism. Although post-Pleistocene mortality rates are difficult to evaluate, several conditions may have promoted increased mortality following agriculture and sedentism. In most instances, agricultural diets were less balanced than hunting-and-gathering diets. In several regions, tooth decay is found in adult burials only after the transition to agriculture. Animal domestication brought people and animals closer, and may have led to the genesis of contagious human diseases, apparently beginning as animal viruses or infections. Sedentary populations and higher population densities also may have increased human susceptibility to certain contagious diseases. Thus, although longer lifespans may have contributed to post-Pleistocene demographic shifts, fertility changes seem to be a more likely impetus.

Demographic studies of contemporary human groups usually, though not always, indicate that settled agriculturalists have higher fertility rates than mobile hunter-gatherers. In human populations numerous factors—including age at marriage, the length of a woman's reproductive period, birth spacing, coital frequency, and the importance of contraception—can affect the number of births each female has during her lifetime. In contemporary studies of recently settled hunter-gatherers, different sets of factors seem to contribute to the frequently noted rise in fertility with the introduction of agriculture and sedentism.

Despite these differences, shortened nursing time and earlier child weaning often do occur among recently settled foraging populations. Shorter periods of breast-feeding prompt hormonal changes that increase the chances of conception, so spacing between births often declines when women adopt a shorter nursing period. Alternatively, nursing may stimulate a woman's hormones in a manner that suppresses ovulation and menstruation, a phenomenon known as **lactational amenorrhea**. Prolonged breast-feeding is therefore frequently associated with longer spacing between births.

The Gainj of highland Papua New Guinea, a horticultural village population, have a birth-spacing pattern, without contraception, that is more similar to that of contemporary hunter-gatherers than to that of other farmers. Gainj women breast-feed their infants for an extended period, more than 3 years on average. In part, the Gainj women breast-feed because they lack adequate weaning foods (a characteristic of many hunter-gatherers as well). The Gainj agricultural staples—sweet potatoes, yams, and taro—are not easy to digest, nor are they the compact sources of nutrients required for weaning, since infants consume only small amounts of food daily.

In contrast, the Neolithic staples of Southwest Asia provided considerably better alternatives and supplements to mother's milk than are available to the agricultural Gainj. Not only were the high carbohydrate, easy-to-digest cereals (like wheat and barley) available, but milk from sheep, goats, and cattle also could be fed to infants. The increased rate of demographic growth in the post-Pleistocene Near East could have been linked to changing patterns of weaning, nursing, and hence birth spacing.

THE SPREAD OF AGRICULTURE

*The success and consequences
of food production*

Different concepts and methods are used by researchers who study the Paleolithic and those who investigate agricultural societies. Paleolithic archaeologists tend to excavate in natural stratigraphic levels, often in caves, paying careful attention to the distributions of bone and stone materials. Researchers focused on later agricultural peoples concentrate more on the stratigraphic levels revealed in the architectural remains of past structures, such as temples and houses. The latter must analyze pottery and metalwork as well as stone and bone. Because pre-Neolithic sites have fewer artifacts and are often deeply buried, systematic regional surveys, which find and map archaeological remains visible on the land surface, are rarely as practical or useful for the specialist in the Pleistocene as they are for many archaeologists who study later periods.

These differences in archaeological perceptions and practices reflect real changes in the nature of the archaeological record that began 10,000–3000 years ago in many (though not all) areas of the world. In most regions, Paleolithic sites tend to be small, thin scatters of lithic materials, reflecting generally lower populations and the tendency for occupations to involve fewer people over shorter periods of time. The low artifactual densities and the general absence of substantial structures at prefarming sites also suggest greater residential mobility.

In many regions, the presence of residential and civic architecture and cemeteries at archaeological sites is unique to prehistoric farming societies. In addition, while the artifacts of the Paleolithic—spearpoints, knives, and scrapers—tended to be largely for capturing energy (food), "facilities" or materials (stone bowls, ceramic containers) and features (pits) to store energy became much more important in later eras. Kent Flannery aptly noted that there are more storage facilities at 'Ain Mallaha alone than are known from all earlier Southwest Asian sites, indicating a sudden transition to residential stability, with its implied social and economic adjustments.

The archaeological record indicates that a more sedentary way of life, plant and animal domestication, and pottery were not adopted simultaneously, nor did these changes occur in a single or uniform sequence in all regions. For example, sedentary villages preceded any evidence for plant domestication in Southwest Asia, while the domestication of maize, beans, and squash occurred prior to the earliest Mesoamerican villages. Furthermore, although the Mesoamerican combination of beans and corn provides a complete protein source as well as adequate calories, some of the other staple grains (barley and rice) are high in carbohydrates but low in protein. In addition, the domestication of animals clearly was a much more significant part of the Neolithic transition in the Old World than in the Americas. Many of the regions of early, indigenous domestication were relatively arid (the Near East and highland Mexico). Yet this was not the case in either South China or the riverine settings of eastern North America.

Given the varied climatic, demographic, and cultural conditions of the early Holocene, the successful adoption and rapid spread of food production clearly was a

Some major African food crops (left to right): yam, finger millet, and sorghum.

widespread phenomenon. In regions where indigenous resources were not domesticated, exotic cultigens and animals often were quickly introduced and adopted. Once domesticated, wheat and barley were transmitted rapidly to the Nile Valley, many parts of Europe, and North China as a supplement to millet. In the river valleys of eastern North America, maize from Mexico was incorporated into local agricultural complexes that included different combinations of oily seed plants, such as sunflower, marsh elder, and goosefoot.

The Neolithic transition apparently was an even more complex mosaic in sub-Saharan Africa. Imported sheep and goats were introduced from Southwest Asia into diverse economies that locally domesticated more than a dozen different plant species, including finger millet (Ethiopia and northern Uganda), sorghum (Lake Chad to the Nile), African rice (middle delta of the Niger), tiny-seeded teff (Ethiopia), and yams (West Africa). While domesticated sheep and goats clearly were foreign, the origins of domesticated cattle in sub-Saharan Africa are less certain; they either were exotic or were domesticated independently in northern Africa, where they were present by the fifth millennium B.C. As in Japan, where ceramics preceded food production, pottery vessels were found at sites occupied by semisedentary fisher-foragers from the fifth and sixth millennia B.C. in the Sudan, as well as along the margins of now-dry lakebeds south of the Sahara Desert.

From a global perspective, food production emerged at a time of major cultural changes that have shaped the course of recent human history. Just as the Neolithic creates a divide in the archaeological record and among archaeologists, the beginnings of domestication are generally linked in time with more permanent or sedentary communities, changing social and political relationships, larger and denser populations, new technologies, and shifting networks of exchange and communication. Although the complexity of these relationships makes it difficult to decipher the exact causes for prehistoric changes, archaeologists have developed some ideas by studying contemporary peoples, particularly those who have recently shifted from a mobile hunting-and-gathering way of life to more sedentary and agricultural pursuits.

During the Pleistocene, human populations grew at a slow pace. If modern hunter-gatherer populations are a reliable guide, a few individuals may have separated from parent groups when resources were exhausted or when disputes became common. In larger campsites, the latter could have been a potential problem, because as the population grows, the number of interactions between individuals increases even more rapidly. By the end of the Pleistocene with the peopling of most of the continents (albeit at low densities), fissioning would have become less of an option for many groups. This pattern may partially account for observed late Pleistocene–early Holocene increases in local population densities, residential stability, greater reliance on lower-quality foods, and decreases in social group territory sizes.

Following the end of the Pleistocene, the more rapid rates of demographic growth may relate in part to changing patterns of child rearing and diet. Recently settled hunter-gatherers often witness a reduction in birth spacing. A mobile way of life limits the number of infants a family group can transport and hence care for at any one time. Intensive exercise and prolonged breast-feeding have been suggested as factors that temporarily diminish a woman's fertility. With increased sedentism, storage, and domestication, both the frequency of intensive female activity and the length of the nursing cycle may have decreased. Twentieth-century hunter-gatherers tend to breast-feed for 2–6 years because of the frequent absence or unreliability of soft weaning foods. The storable, staple cereal grains provide such an alternative "baby food" to mother's milk. In certain regions, animal milk also could be substituted.

More productive and storable food resources may have permitted larger communities and denser populations, yet a series of organizational changes often occurred at roughly the same time. For long-term maintenance and survival, larger communities would have required new mechanisms for integration, the resolution of disputes, and decision making. Kin relationships are severely tested when decisions must be made for groups of several hundred. Increased evidence for burials, ritual objects (e.g., figurines), nonresidential structures, more formal patterns of exchange, and in some cases more unequal access to goods and labor would seem to signal these very significant changes in social and political relationships. Some of these new organizational forms were hierarchical, with more permanent, formal leadership roles instituted above the remainder of the population. Such leaders or decision makers, in turn, may have fostered greater concentrations of resources and labor, leading to intensified production and even larger communities.

The transition to agriculture and sedentism occurred at the onset of a rapid succession of changes that have culminated in our modern world. The pace of these recent changes is truly remarkable when viewed from the perspective of all of human history. While neither domestication nor sedentism alone is necessary and sufficient to explain the formation of early cities and ancient states, both permanent communities and food production are critical elements of those very significant, later developments.

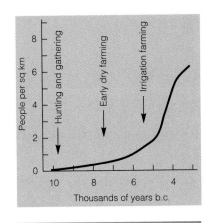

Population densities associated with different subsistence strategies.

SUGGESTED READINGS

Clutton-Brock, J. 1999. *A natural history of domesticated animals.* Cambridge: Cambridge University Press. *A detailed compendium of recent information on the domestication of animals.*

Cohen, M. 1977. *The food crisis in prehistory.* New Haven, CT: Yale University Press. *A comprehensive indictment of global population increase as the cause of the domestication of plants and animals.*

Flannery, K. V., ed. 1986. *Guilá Naquitz: Archaic foraging and early agriculture in Oaxaca, Mexico.* New York: Academic Press. *A detailed report on an important preceramic settlement in highland Oaxaca in the distinctive style of Flannery.*

Harris, D. R., and G. C. Hillman, eds. 1989. *Foraging and farming: The evolution of plant exploitation.* London: Unwin Hyman. *A volume of papers on early agriculture, presenting evidence from around the world.*

Price, T. D., and A. B. Gebauer. 1995. *Last hunters–first farmers. New perspectives on the transition to agriculture.* Santa Fe, NM: School for American Research. *A series of papers dealing specifically with the question of cause in regard to the origins and spread of agriculture.*

Smith, B. D. 1998. *The emergence of agriculture.* New York: Scientific American Library. *A well-illustrated and up-to-date summary of agricultural beginnings worldwide.*

7

NATIVE NORTH AMERICANS

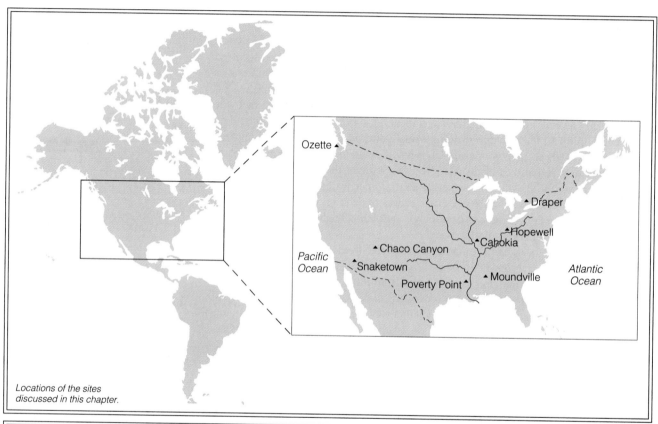

Locations of the sites discussed in this chapter.

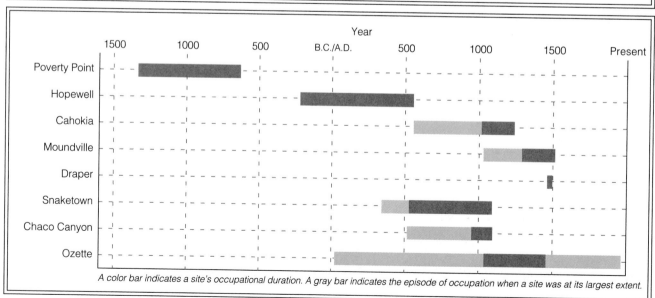

A color bar indicates a site's occupational duration. A gray bar indicates the episode of occupation when a site was at its largest extent.

THE DIVERSITY OF NATIVE AMERICAN LIFE

Hunter-gatherers, farmers, and chiefs

On the twelfth of October in 1492, when Columbus landed on a small island in the Caribbean, roughly 40 million Native Americans resided in the Western Hemisphere. These peoples spoke about 400 mutually unintelligible languages, compared to the more than 2500 languages that were spoken in the Old World. Yet the diversity of the "spoken tongues" is impressive, considering that the landmass of North and South America is less than half the size of Eurasia and Africa. One important factor influencing linguistic divergence is time, and hominids have lived for only thousands of years in the New World compared to millions of years in the Old World. At the time of European contact, the populations of the Western Hemisphere were diverse in many ways other than language. Some peoples were incorporated into the great empire of the Inca in the Peruvian Andes; others paid tribute to the rulers of Aztec Tenochtitlán in the Basin of Mexico. Yet not all Native American peoples were as socially and economically stratified as the Inca and the Aztecs. Although some Mississippian lords in eastern North America may have received tribute from surrounding populations, the sociopolitical formations in what is now the eastern United States were not as complex as those farther south. More egalitarian hunter-gatherers lived in the extreme north, on the Plains, in desert areas of the western United States and Mexico, and at the tip of South America.

The New World was first colonized by hunter-gatherers who crossed the broad Bering Land Bridge from Asia. Initially, their way of life was highly mobile. In western North America, the colonists relied in part on the hunting of large herd animals; the subsistence regime in eastern North America was generally more diversified. In much of the Americas, a long Archaic period followed the millennia (the Paleoindian period) during which several of the large herd animals that were important food sources became extinct. (See "Beringia," in Chapter 4, for a discussion of the Paleoindian period and the introduction to Chapter 5 for a discussion of the Archaic.)

During the Archaic, regional populations diversified their subsistence pursuits, each concentrating on a distinct set of local resources, hunting a wide range of animals and gathering a variety of wild plants. In the later Archaic period, cultigens were added to the diet. In midwestern North America, local seed plants were domesticated during the Archaic before the arrival of the exotic domesticates (see "Agriculture in Native North America," Chapter 6, p. 250). In certain other parts of what is now the United States, the earliest domesticated plants appear to have been imports from highland Mesoamerica. These plants—such as maize (corn), certain varieties of squash, and gourds—were domesticated initially in the south and then traded to the north in a down-the-line fashion, reaching the American Southwest. Yet in most of North America, the introduction (or local domestication) of these agricultural plants generally did not promote immediate or drastic shifts in dietary composition or residential mobility. In certain areas, such as the coastal Southeast, the increasing exploitation of riverine and marine life, in conjunction with hunting and gathering, led to increasing residential stability even before cultigens were incorporated into the diet.

Native American lifeways also were diverse at the time of the European arrival, although no populations in the continental United States lived in urban communities as dense as those in the Basin of Mexico (discussed in Chapter 8). In the desert West, mobile hunting-and-gathering lifeways persisted until historic times. Yet in parts of the Southeast, the Midwest, the Northwest Coast, California, and the Southwest, a variety of more hierarchical political formations developed during the later precontact period. These institutions were diverse, distributed mosaically, and often were short-lived in any specific locality or region. Although an increasing reliance on maize was one key factor in the development of nonegalitarian social systems in the Southeast, the Midwest, and the Southwest, such institutions were established in portions of the West Coast in the context of sedentary hunting and gathering. Other late precontact populations incorporated the plant into their diet but remained more egalitarian and more mobile.

Up to now, we have referred to **prehistory** as the time before the appearance of written records. In North America, the prehistoric era extends into the second millennium A.D. and ends with the arrival of Old World populations, who carried writing to this part of the world. The historic period begins between the sixteenth and eighteenth centuries A.D., with the specific timing varying by region, depending on the pace of European conquest and expansion. The study of the fragmentary and/or scanty historic records written by both native peoples and Europeans is called **ethnohistory.**

In this chapter, eight North American sites are discussed. In time, they span the late Archaic (Poverty Point) to the era of European contact (the Draper site and Ozette). These sites—ranging from the southern Arizona desert (Snaketown) to the floodplains of the middle Mississippi (Cahokia) to the arid lands of the Colorado Plateau (Chaco Canyon)—capture some, but certainly not all, of the tremendous variability characteristic of the later prehistory of native North America. In fact, in focusing on the above sites, as well as Hopewell (Ohio) and Moundville (Alabama), we have selected rather elaborate ancient settlements, many of which have attracted archaeological attention for decades. Many of these sites are much larger and were occupied far longer than the average prehistoric North American settlement; hence, they are relatively well known. Native Americans also lived in small communities and utilized many temporary camps, but such sites are generally less well known and therefore are not featured here.

Poverty Point (Louisiana) is one of the few late Archaic period sites north of Mexico that contains monumental earthworks. Yet Poverty Point does exemplify certain late Archaic trends in the southeastern United States: decreasing mobility, experimentation with fired clay, and the increasing role of cultivated plants in the diet. Over the next centuries, these trends became increasingly important in several areas outside the Southeast as well. For example, roughly coincident with the decline of Poverty Point in the middle of the last millennium B.C., the **Adena** complex developed in the Ohio River Valley. Adena sites tended to be associated with earthen burial mounds, larger and more elaborate assemblages of grave goods, rudimentary cultivation (of food plants as well as tobacco), and friable (soft, porous) pottery. Mobile lifeways still may have been common, yet the presence of circular houses and/or ceremonial structures, as well as the increasing abundance of pottery, suggests greater residential stability at Adena sites relative to earlier occupations in the region. In many ways, the Adena complex was directly ancestral to later Hopewell sites in southern Ohio (and surrounding states). The Hopewell site, one of the richest of these settlements, was excavated on the farm of M. C. Hopewell in the early 1890s to provide artifacts for an anthropological exhibit at the 1893 World's Columbian Exposition in Chicago.

The unequal distribution of grave goods at Hopewell sites may be evidence of social differentiation, yet it is not clear how marked those distinctions were or whether they were inherited. A similar debate concerns the nature of social organization at Poverty Point. However, by the end of the first millennium A.D., on the floodplains of the Mississippi, such inherited social distinctions appear well entrenched, at least at the Cahokia site in East St. Louis, Illinois. This ancient settlement, which contains the largest precontact pyramid built north of Mexico, includes ample indications of unequal access to wealth and power. Cahokia was one of the largest and most impressive **Mississippian** centers. Increasing reliance on corn farming at Cahokia is part of a trend found at later prehistoric sites across the eastern United States, although many Mississippian peoples retained some hunting, gathering, and fishing.

Moundville, overlooking the Black Warrior River in Alabama, was one of several important later Mississippian centers (along with Etowah in Georgia). Although these two centers are well known, in part because of their monumental mound complexes and the elaborate artifacts recovered during excavations, they were not entirely typical of corn-farming peoples of the late prehistoric period who resided in what is today the eastern United States. Archaeological findings, as well as the accounts from early European explorations into the Southeast, indicate that many indigenous peoples lived in smaller, dispersed communities and were organized in less hierarchical social formations than are evident at great centers like Moundville and Etowah.

The late prehistoric groups of the Northeast and southern Canada also appear to have been organized less hierarchically. Their villages, which were composed of multifamily **longhouses**, lacked the monumental constructions that were found at Moundville and Cahokia. The Draper site, a large Iroquoian village in southern Ontario, was almost completely excavated and thus provides a good picture of village plan and community organization in the Great Lakes region just prior to European contact.

One difference between the maize-farming peoples of the late prehistoric eastern United States and those of the West is the greater reliance on water control (irrigation) in the latter area. In the dry, changeable climate of the southwestern United States, rainfall farming would have been a risky endeavor at best. This distinction is clearly indicated in the discussion of the Hohokam of the Sonoran Desert of southern Arizona. Snaketown, an early Hohokam community between Phoenix and Tucson, was for a long time the only example of an Arizona desert village. However, spurred by the contemporary construction boom in the region, additional archaeological fieldwork at other sites has supplemented and broadened our understanding of these early villagers, documenting their evolution from local hunting-and-gathering peoples. Nevertheless, Snaketown remains a key site in the region. Early twentieth-century scholars postulated that the Hohokam migrated from Mexico; such explanations are no longer necessary to account for the transition to sedentary farming communities.

The emergence of the Hohokam tradition during the first millennium A.D. occurred with the rise of two other southwestern cultural traditions, the Mogollon and the Anasazi. While these traditions were not completely discrete, they do help characterize the great cultural variation that marked the prehistoric southwestern United States. For the most part, the indigenous peoples of the Southwest lived in small, dispersed communities; therefore, it is not surprising to find so much diversity in diet, ceramic styles, and even residential and nonresidential construction.

Periodically, the peoples of the American Southwest clustered into larger and more hierarchically organized multicommunity social networks. In general, these times of nucleation were short-lived and spatially localized. At Chaco Canyon on New Mexico's dry Colorado Plateau, the period around A.D. 900 witnessed the beginning of perhaps the most spectacular of such episodes. Although this buildup of construction and population nucleation was relatively brief, it left an impressive record.

Although the focus of this chapter is on the agricultural inhabitants of indigenous North America, we also examine the late prehistoric coastal village of Ozette in Washington. As early as 500 B.C., ranked social distinctions may have developed among certain hunter-gatherer populations in the Pacific Northwest. While Ozette dates much later, the village's destruction and burial by a mudslide resulted in unusually fine archaeological preservation. As a result, it provides a clearer picture of Northwest Coast hunter-gatherers than can be gained from earlier sites in the area.

In the chapter's Summary, we briefly discuss the changing Euro-American perspective on North American Indian sites. The archaeology of North America is extremely important because it provides a historical context for, and helps establish the rich heritage of, Native American peoples—the first inhabitants of the United States. We also raise the important issue of ethnographic analogy, and the less-than-perfect fit often found between ethnohistoric accounts and the archaeological record.

The first Americans north of Mexico have figured as little more than a few stereotyped and contradictory images in most accounts of the New World. They are generally regarded as savages with no past and no future, sparsely inhabiting a continent, and childlike both in their generosity—"selling" Manhattan Island for $24 worth of "trinkets"—and in their ferocity—scalping the victims in battle. In the West they have been seen as a jumble of opposites, as the earlier "only good Indian is a dead Indian" attitude has given way to a latter-day Hollywood "good Indian" peacemaker juxtaposed against the "bad Indian" fighter. Only most recently can a "good" Indian fight for his people's independence. Contemporary Indians are seen as a beaten people on reservations, sharing in a general "culture of poverty," a curiosity for passing tourists, while the notion persists, despite census figures to the contrary, that Indians are "vanishing" as a racial and sociocultural entity.

E. B. Leacock (1971)

POVERTY POINT

*Ancient earthworks in
southeastern North America*

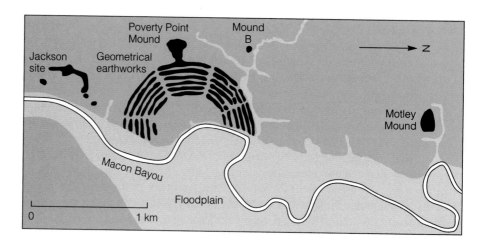

A plan of the earthworks and other
structures at Poverty Point.

The early Archaic hunter-gatherers of the southeastern United States lived in small, impermanent camps and followed a seasonal pattern of life based on a broad spectrum of plant and animal foods. The most important resources included nuts, acorns, berries, and roots, and animal species such as deer, elk, bear, fox, wolf, squirrel, raccoon, opossum, beaver, otter, freshwater mussel, fish, turkey, and migratory waterfowl. By the middle of the Archaic period, around 4000 B.C., population growth contributed to reduced residential mobility and the increasing differentiation of local cultural traditions. In coastal and riverine settings, the Archaic foragers often returned to the same location year after year in scheduled seasonal rounds to exploit localized and predictable resources. For example, deep Archaic shell middens that have been excavated along the lower Tennessee River represent the accumulated refuse of small communities that occupied these same sites repeatedly at the time of the year when shellfish were abundant.

By 1500 B.C., prior to the end of the Archaic period, several plant species were cultivated in the midwestern and southeastern United States, but foraging remained the dominant subsistence strategy. One of the first crops grown, gourds were used largely as containers. Their seeds are edible, and it appears that a reliance on this part of the plant increased over time. Other plants associated with domestication included sunflower, marsh elder, goosefoot (*Chenopodium*), and indigenous varieties of squash. New tools, including heavy ground stone implements for grinding seeds, were added to the simple portable toolkits of earlier Archaic groups. There also was an increase in food storage, and at some sites, a fairly simple and friable fiber-tempered pottery, in which fibrous plant inclusions were mixed with the

Examples of Archaic stone and bone tools: (a) stone projectile point, (b) stone pestle for grinding seeds, (c) bone fishhook, (d) bone awls, (e) bone needle, (f) stone drill.

clay, was made. Stone containers of carved **steatite** (soapstone) and sandstone are found as well. An increasing reliance on domesticated plants (as well as other riverine resources), in conjunction with the use of less portable tools, signals a change to greater residential stability.

Monumental constructions were not frequently built during the Archaic period. However, small mound complexes dating to the Middle/Late Archaic have been recorded at a few sites in the lower Mississippi Valley. These sites typically have one or two conical mounds measuring between 1 m (3 ft) and 5 m (16 ft) high. The largest and most securely dated is the Watson Brake site in northeastern Louisiana. The site's 11 mounds and connecting ridges surrounded by an elaborate earthen enclosure appear to have been constructed before 3000 B.C. The plant and animal remains recovered at the site indicate that Watson Brake was occupied seasonally. Although no evidence of domesticated plants has been recovered, the Archaic hunter-gatherers who constructed the site were already collecting the wild ancestors of several plants that were later domesticated. Excavation has revealed few clues about the purpose of the mounds and enclosure at Watson Brake.

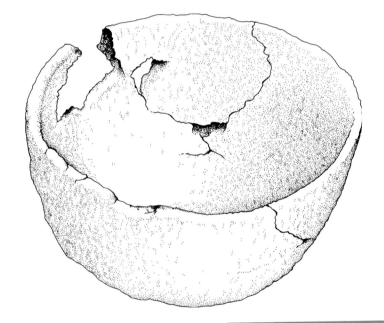

A fiber-tempered pottery bowl from the southeastern United States.

A later, much larger complex of great earthworks was constructed around 1200 B.C. at Poverty Point in northeastern Louisiana. In spite of increasing evidence of an Archaic mound-building tradition in the lower Mississippi Valley, the large-scale construction at Poverty Point continues to dwarf contemporaneous Late Archaic settlements in North America. The monumental construction at Poverty Point provides additional evidence for a

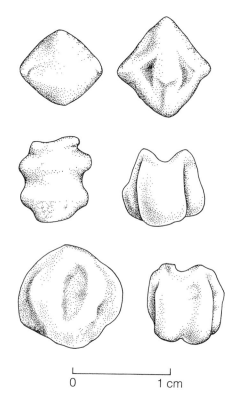

Examples of small baked clay objects found at Poverty Point and elsewhere in the lower Mississippi Valley.

0 ⊢————————————————⊣ 1 cm

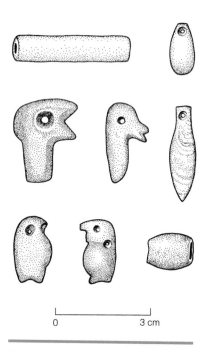

Polished stone beads, pendants, and bird effigies from Poverty Point.

0 ⊢————————————⊣ 3 cm

more sedentary residential pattern and emergence of greater social differentiation than was present elsewhere in eastern North America at this time.

Poverty Point is located on the Macon Ridge overlooking the Macon Bayou and the floodplain of the Mississippi River. A portion of the site has been eroded by recent stream action; nevertheless, what remains is impressive. The main complex at Poverty Point is a set of six concentric, earthen ridges that form a large semicircle, the outer one of which measures 1.3 km (0.8 mi) in diameter. The ridges are spaced approximately 45 m (150 ft) apart, and each one is composed of a series of separate smaller ridges, averaging 2 m (6 ft) high and 24 m (80 ft) wide. The presence of numerous **post molds** or **postholes**, soil stains indicating the past placement of wooden posts, as well as hearths and pits, indicates that the ridgetops were used as living surfaces. The level area at the center of the earthen complex is close to 1 ha (2.5 acres, larger than the size of four football fields) and contains habitation structures and associated debris.

To the west of these earthworks sits a large mound more than 20 m (66 ft)

high and 200 m (655 ft) long. A long ramp descends from the mound and faces the semicircular complex. From the mound, it is possible to view the vernal and autumnal **equinoxes** across the center of the earthworks; however, it is not clear whether this alignment was intentional. A small conical mound lies about 0.5 km (0.3 mi) north of the large mound. Another large mound, similar in form to the tall ramped mound, is 2 km (1.2 mi) away. Gully erosion down the sides of the large mounds has revealed that they were built with basketloads of clay fill.

The early population of Poverty Point is not well established, although the excavators of the site, James Ford and C. H. Webb, estimated that several hundred houses may have been occupied. Other estimates range as high as several thousand people. Smaller settlements, which lacked earthen mounds and contained fewer than 60 inhabitants, have been found up to 15 km (9 mi) away from the site. Similar settlement clusters, containing both large and small sites, also have been reported along tributary streams in other parts of the lower Mississippi Valley. Yet none of the associated earthworks is nearly as large as the impressive mounds at Poverty Point.

Most sites with artifacts similar to those found at Poverty Point occur in locations where riverine resources were available. The presence of stone adzes or hoes (some of which are well worn) originally led some researchers to suggest that cultivation may have been practiced on the floodplains. Yet ethnobotanical studies have not revealed a significant presence of cultigens. Of the indigenous eastern North American domesticates, squash is most abundant. But nuts, acorns, deer, and fish seem to have comprised equal or greater portions of the diet than cultivated plants. It appears that the stone adzes (or hoes) may have been used for clearing vegetation, or perhaps as digging tools for constructing the earthworks.

At Poverty Point, hunting, fishing, and gathering were important means of subsistence. Very little pottery, except for some nonlocal ware, has been found. However, thousands of small baked clay objects were recovered. Most of these fired concretions, sometimes referred to as Poverty Point objects, are smaller than a baseball and were made in a variety of forms, including balls, cylinders, and odd finger-squeezed shapes. These baked clay forms are thought to have served as "boiling stones" for cooking in place of rocks, which are scarce in the alluvial areas of the lower Mississippi. In this method of cooking, stones (or the clay objects) were heated and then placed in containers to boil water and cook food.

Large quantities of such ornamental objects as polished beads, pendants, and effigies were manufactured at Poverty Point, even though little stone is found on the marshy coastal plain where the site is situated. Flints and **cherts,** dull-colored rocks resembling flint, were imported from the north, and steatite from the Appalachians. Other imported stone included **galena** (lead ore), **hematite, slate,** and jasper (a high-quality flint). Poverty Point was strategically located between the sources of some of these materials and the more heavily inhabited areas to the south.

A well-developed lapidary (stone-working) industry is one of the key features that distinguishes Poverty Point and surrounding sites. At some sites, distinctive microblade drills were manufactured and used to perforate stone and bone artifacts. The distribution of stone debris and finished artifacts indicates that this craft was to some degree specialized, in the sense that different communities and specific sectors within larger sites (like Poverty Point) engaged in the manufacture of different kinds of goods. Thus, the finished items as well as the raw materials probably were exchanged over great distances.

Poverty Point and the specific cultural tradition associated with the site began to decline and change around 700 B.C., just as mound building increased dramatically in the Ohio Valley to the northeast. In these northern woodland areas, the construction of burial mounds implies an increasing preoccupation with death and mortuary ritual. Common practices included cremation and the placement of exotic objects with the dead. Ornaments made of marine shell, un-smelted native copper, jasper, slate, and

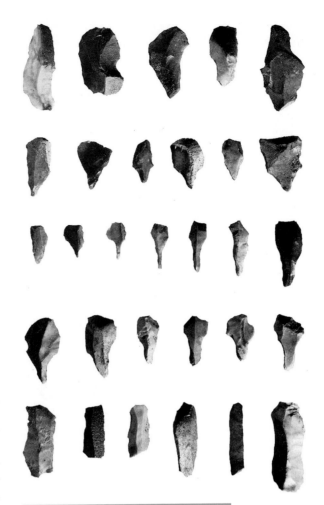

Flint tools from Poverty Point, including microblade drills (three middle rows) to perforate stone and bone artifacts.

greenstone occurred with greater frequency in these contexts. Throughout the woodlands of the eastern United States, ceramic containers became more prevalent during the last centuries B.C. The cultivation of squash and local weedy plants, which still were not staples, also became more important. These developments were foreshadowed at Poverty Point, but centuries elapsed before northeastern Louisiana again saw the scale of monumental earthen construction evident in the region at the end of the Archaic.

HOPEWELL

Prehistoric artisans and mound builders

SERPENT MOUND

Serpent Mound, situated on a prominent hilltop near Cincinnati, Ohio. The uncoiled length of the mound is approximately 400 m. The serpent's tail is slightly coiled (on the left), with its mouth clasping an oval mound (on the right).

In eastern North America, sunflower, marsh elder, and goosefoot may have been domesticated as early as 2000–1500 B.C., but it was not until the end of the Archaic that some prehistoric peoples in the region increasingly relied on the harvesting of these and other native plants. At archaeological sites dating prior to 500 B.C., the scarcity of seeds of these early domesticates suggests that these plants mainly served to buffer temporary shortages and were not yet true staples; hunting and gathering continued to provide the primary dietary resources. Nevertheless, many of these local cultigens, which produced a variety of seeds, had the advantage of being easily stored. Indigenous varieties of squash also may have been cultivated initially for their seeds rather than their flesh.

These early Archaic experiments in cultivation laid the foundation for later developments, such as Hopewell in the Midwest (200 B.C.–A.D. 600). After 500–200 B.C., native cultigens became increasingly important at many sites in eastern North America. However, food production did not completely replace hunting-and-gathering economies. Foraging remained an important part of survival; Hopewell subsistence also included a variety of wild plants and animals, including seeds, nuts, deer, turkeys, and fish. By around A.D. 100, maize was introduced into eastern North America from the west (possibly from the American Southwest, which in turn received the plant from highland Mexico, where it was originally domesticated). Yet after its appearance, maize remained a minor crop for more than 500 years in eastern North America.

About the time of the decline of Poverty Point in the lower Mississippi Valley, mound building and long-distance exchange intensified to the north in the Ohio River Valley. Elaborate earthworks—some as large as 100 m (330 ft) in diameter or more—were constructed in the shape of circles, squares, and pentagons. These earthen features appear to have been sacred enclosures rather than defensive works, perhaps serving to affirm and strengthen group cohesion and to establish the link between a local group and its social territory. One mound that seems to have been constructed midway through the last millennium B.C. was in the shape of a snake with its tail in a tight coil. This feature, called Serpent Mound, was placed along a prominent hilltop in Ohio and probably served as a sacred **effigy.** Serpent (as well as bird) imagery remained important east of the Mississippi for 2000 years.

During the last centuries B.C., the construction of burial mounds became an important part of mortuary activities throughout the midwestern United States. Early burial mounds contained up to three individuals in a log tomb. Cremations often were found in simpler graves. The unequal distribution of grave goods suggests that social distinctions were marked at death in some (though not all) societies in the eastern United States. The more elaborate graves often contained greater quantities of highly crafted and exotic grave goods that possibly served as markers of rank. These items included **gorgets,** circular ornaments that were flat or convex on one side and concave on the other, as well as axes, bracelets, beads, and rings made from copper imported from northern Michigan, carved tablets, some with abstract **zoomorphic** designs depicting birds of prey, and tubular pipes for smoking.

The Hopewell tradition first appeared in Illinois around 200 B.C. Material objects associated with this tradition quickly spread as far as upper Wisconsin, Louisiana, and New York, although the core of the phenomenon remained in the Midwest. The Hopewell tradition was not a single cultural group or society; rather, it was an exchange system for goods and information that connected distinct local populations. The complex trade network that defined this tradition has been referred to as the **Hopewell Interaction Sphere.** Goods that entered the network came from across the continent, including copper from the upper Great Lakes region and Georgia, obsidian and grizzly bear teeth from Yellowstone, chipped stone from Minnesota and North

Cremation and Burial in a Sacred Enclosure
Later Covered by a Mound of Earth

An artist's reconstruction of two stages in Hopewell burial mound construction.

Dakota, galena from Illinois and Wisconsin, shell and shark teeth from the Gulf Coast, silver nuggets from Ontario, and mica and quartz crystals from the Appalachian Mountains.

Although goods entered the Hopewell Interaction Sphere from a wide area, the focus was the Scioto River Valley in the south-central part of Ohio. Monumental mounds and extensive geometric earthworks were erected there between 100 B.C. and A.D. 600. House structures and village debris occur both within and outside the walls of these impressive earthworks. The Hopewell site in Ross County, Ohio, covered 45 ha (110 acres) and contained 38 burial mounds. Most of these mounds were small, dome-shaped structures, but one mound was 9 m (30 ft) high, 152 m (500 ft) long, and 55 m (180 ft) wide, and contained over 250 burials, as well as concentrations of grave goods. Another Hopewell burial mound complex at Mound City, Ohio, has at least 24 mounds inside a large enclosure covering 5.2 ha (13 acres). Not all the mounds at the Ohio Hopewell sites contain burials; some are effigy mounds alone.

Ohio Hopewell graves contain many objects made from unsmelted native copper, such as ear spools, gorgets, beads,

Location of Hopewell sites and other burial mound sites. Hopewell materials are found throughout the Midwest, but the focus was southern Ohio.

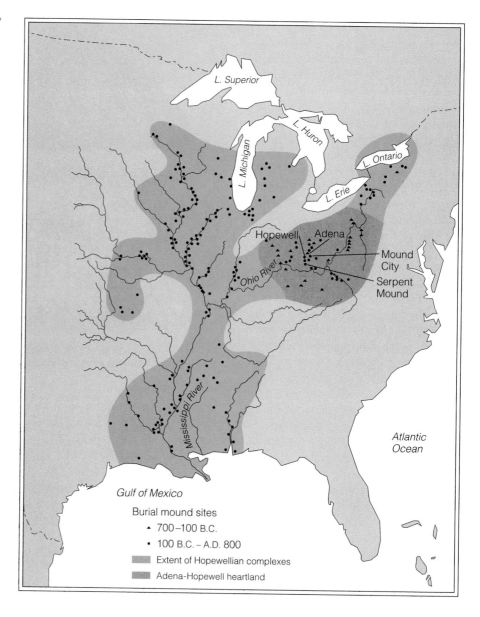

Burial mound sites
▲ 700–100 B.C.
• 100 B.C. – A.D. 800
Extent of Hopewellian complexes
Adena-Hopewell heartland

Large mica effigy of an eagle talon.

pendants, and panpipes (primitive wind instruments). Heavy sheets of copper were used to make breastplates, and large copper nuggets were fashioned into axes, adzes, celts, and awls. Sheets of mica were cut into serpents, human hands, heads, swastikas, and bird talons. Other items found in the graves include flint tools, imported conch and other shells, teeth from alligators and sharks, turtle shells, and grizzly bear canines. A certain kind of fine pottery was created to be used only as grave goods. Charms were made from galena and quartz crystals. Carved stone pipes were one of the most important trade items. These pipes feature an animal effigy (beaver, frog,

bird, bear, and even human) on top of a rectangular platform. The bowl of the pipe was positioned in the animal's back, and the smoke was drawn through a hole exiting at the end of the platform.

Several of the most elaborate Ohio Hopewell sites were excavated before 1900, prior to the use of modern equipment or contemporary standards of archaeological data recovery. Consequently, few of these contexts are well dated. The early excavators concentrated on the mounds where "museum pieces" could be recovered. As a result, Hopewell is known largely from these features and their contents. Less is known about Hopewell community patterns. While many

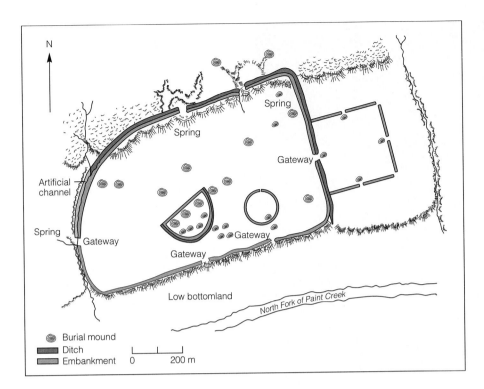

N

Spring

Spring

Gateway

Artificial channel

Spring

Gateway

Gateway

Gateway

Low bottomland

North Fork of Paint Creek

Burial mound
Ditch
Embankment   0   200 m

settlements were small and occupied seasonally, larger, more nucleated settlements in major river valleys were inhabited year-round.

Because most of the earlier excavations were in burial mounds, some archaeologists initially thought the elaborate artifacts that were recovered represented a ritual burial cult. Yet the subsequent discovery of some of these same items in domestic settings indicated that they were more likely status-specific objects that functioned in various civic-ceremonial contexts and eventually were deposited with the dead. The nature and quantities of burial goods may reflect the accomplishments and status of individuals during their lives. Only rarely were children interred with unusually large amounts of grave goods. The Hopewell groups appear to have been organized as socially differentiated societies in which people reached high status principally through their individual achievements, and less through an established structure of inherited ranks.

In general, it is very difficult to reconstruct the religion, ideological beliefs, or ceremonial activities of prehistoric peoples when written records are unavailable. Yet Robert L. Hall, of the University of Illinois, Chicago, focusing on the symbolic importance of the famous Hopewell platform pipes, provides one potentially promising example. Drawing an analogy with postcontact customs of eastern native North Americans, Hall argues that peace pipe ceremonialism served to mediate interaction over very great distances. European explorers and traders observed that violence was absolutely forbidden among the Native Americans when the pipe was being passed. Curiously, at the time of European contact, almost all smoking pipes were in the form of weapons, such as arrows. The pipes were thus thought of as ritual weapons, and during peace pipe mediations, the participants were sometimes considered to be "fighting with words."

Hall suggests that the Hopewell platform pipes also may have been ritual weapons. These earlier pipes were made in the form of the most common Hopewell weapon, the **atlatl**, or spearthrower (the bow and arrow were not in use in Ohio at this time). According to Hall's interpretation, these Hopewell effigy pipes were not simply just one of many items that were exchanged; they were part of the mechanism of exchange itself. According

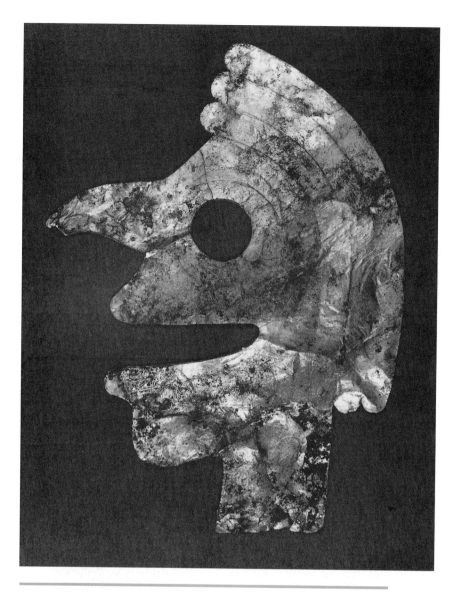

to Hall, ritual "peace pipe diplomacy" served to reduce regional differences and to promote communication and friendly contact between the disparate groups involved in the Hopewell Interaction Sphere. The Hopewell pipes were prominent items in elaborate burials, most likely because of their importance to leaders who were involved in mediation, intergroup relations, and exchange.

The Hopewell Interaction Sphere began to decline after A.D. 400. Its demise undoubtedly was related to the disruption of the trade network, but we do not know exactly what factors prompted this breakdown. One explanation is that competition in rich river bottoms between emergent slash-and-burn horticulturalists, relying increasingly on maize, led to greater competition between communities. Such frictions may have caused the closing of regional boundaries. In a few cases, dispersed settlements were replaced with small nucleated villages (enclosed by ditches or walls) located in defensive positions on blufftops. The exchange of luxury goods linked the interaction sphere. Once the complex trade network was broken, either because artisans could not obtain the resources they needed or because warfare and competition disrupted alliances, the repercussions were felt throughout the regional system.

A sheet of mica that has been fashioned into a human profile, 18 cm high.

A platform pipe in the shape of a panther. The steatite pipe is 16 cm long. Smoke was drawn through the platform below the animal's hind legs.

Most—if not all—human societies engage in the exchange of goods and information, both within their own population and with other groups. Yet the volume and the mechanisms of these transactions vary greatly. Prehistorically, many communities produced most of the items they required for subsistence and survival, only occasionally exchanging an ornament or food with neighboring peoples. Other villages and societies included many specialist producers who depended on trade for their livelihood.

Much ancient trade involved simple barter or **reciprocity,** face-to-face exchanges between known participants, such as kin or trading partners. In such small-scale exchanges, the giver assumed that a trade good or gift would be returned in the future. In the ancient Near East, pastoral herders traded mutton to sedentary farmers in exchange for grain.

Other ancient trade networks were more centralized and included "nodal" individuals (like a Polynesian chief) or central institutions (such as the Inca state) that controlled the movement, or **redistribution,** of certain goods. Items were collected from peripheral communities by a central authority, who then redistributed all or part of what was collected. In certain cases, redistribution primarily served to balance out environmental or economic differences between participating communities. Often, such systems allowed central authorities to accumulate large surpluses, as they would return only part of what was collected. Centrally stored goods could be amassed for military campaigns, construction projects, or the relief of local emergencies and natural disasters. Today, the U.S. federal income tax system acts as a very large and complex redistributive network.

Although reciprocity and redistribution were the most common mechanisms of exchange in the past, some ancient societies were involved in market transactions. For example, as we will see in Chapter 8, the market was particularly important in prehispanic Mexico. The principles of supply and demand play a larger role in marketing than they do in either redistribution or reciprocity. In contrast to redistribution, which presumes the receipt and disbursement of goods by a central figure, marketing tends to involve more individualized transactions between buyers and sellers.

Trade or exchange is best documented archaeologically by the presence of foreign or exotic goods, such as when marine shell bracelets or beads are found at inland sites many kilometers from water. However, for materials like obsidian or turquoise, determination of the source requires laboratory analysis. The point of origin of these artifacts can be identified if the specific composition of the object matches the elemental "signature" of a known source. The amount and distribution of exotic goods in archaeological contexts helps determine the means and the volume of exchange.

At the Hopewell site, one indication of a long-distance exchange network is the presence of ceremonial blades made of obsidian that probably came from the Yellowstone area of the Rocky Mountains. At Mound City, another Ohio Hopewell site, a bird effigy made with copper from an outcrop on Isle Royale in Lake Superior was found. Like the obsidian blades and the copper bird, most of the items that were traded long distances to the Hopewell sites were highly crafted and rare. In addition, many of the Hopewell goods were marked with a set of distinctive designs or motifs. Archaeologists generally assume that communities that share stylistic or ceremonial conventions are more likely to have been in contact with each other than contemporary communities that have adopted entirely different artistic conventions. Thus the relatively widespread distribution of these Hopewell motifs serves, albeit weakly, as an additional indicator for the long-distance interactions that characterized this ancient exchange sphere. Although archaeologists can often document exchange, its relative volume, and its directionality, identifying the specific mechanisms is generally more difficult.

THE ARCHAEOLOGY OF EXCHANGE

A perspective on ancient economies

Large obsidian blade from the Hopewell site.

CAHOKIA

*The largest prehistoric
community north of Mexico*

After the breakup of the Hopewell trade network in the middle of the first millennium A.D., a way of life dependent on maize agriculture developed along the lower Mississippi River bottomlands. While the spread of the Hopewell Interaction Sphere was largely ideological, the expansion of the Mississippian tradition probably involved some population movement into alluvial valleys with prime agricultural land, as well as the adoption of new symbols and subsistence systems by local populations. A key aspect of the Mississippian symbolic system was associated with warfare (another important focus was fertility). The atlatl had been the major weapon during Hopewell times. After the decline of the Hopewell phenomenon, the bow and arrow, introduced around A.D. 700–800, became the dominant weapon in eastern North America by A.D. 1000.

The lush floodplains of the Mississippi River and its tributaries were ideal for cultivating maize. Yet it was not until around A.D. 800 that maize became a major crop. Beans, another imported domesticate, and squash (local and imported varieties) also were cultivated. Yet great dietary diversity continued. Excavations at several small communities in the Mississippi Valley have revealed that maize farming was added to a diet of wild game (deer, raccoon, turkey, and seasonally available waterfowl), fish, seasonal plants (nuts, tubers, fruits, and berries), and native domesticates.

Many changes in material culture that were adopted as part of the Mississippian way of life are associated with the increasing use and storage of maize. The number and size of storage pits increased significantly at emergent Mississippian sites. In addition, flint hoes were common artifacts at Cahokia and many other Mississippian sites. Population increased rapidly in some riverine areas, reflecting the more sedentary lifeways that had been adopted, the role of storable foods in easing people through lean seasons of the year, and/or changes in labor strategies that may have given selective advantages to larger households that could clear and cultivate more land. The latter would increase the economic value of children, thereby leading to larger households and regional population increase.

Cahokia (kah-ho'kee-uh), the largest Mississippian center, was established on the east bank of the Mississippi, in Illinois, across the river from St. Louis. This area, just south of the confluence of the Illinois, Missouri, and Mississippi rivers, is known as the American Bottom. The soils are extremely fertile, and there is a great diversity of environmental zones, including swamps, ponds, forests, and wet prairie grasslands. The major rivers provided avenues for communication and transport that enabled Cahokia to become the hub of an extensive exchange system. Black chert came from the Ozarks, sheet mica possibly from North Carolina, native copper from Lake Superior, lead from northern Illinois, and marine shells from the Gulf Coast. Based on the anomalous quantity of stone scrapers found in domestic contexts, James B. Stoltman, of the University of Wisconsin, Madison, has suggested that deer hides or dried meat may have been traded south from southwestern Wisconsin.

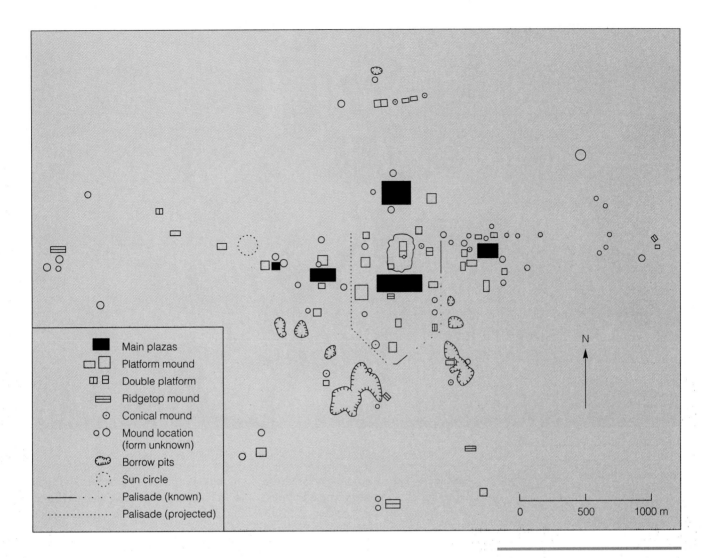

The plan of Cahokia, showing the dispersal and variety of mounds across the 13 sq km area covered by the site.

The name Cahokia was derived from an Indian group that lived in the area at the time of French colonization during the late seventeenth and early eighteenth centuries. However, the first intensive archaeological investigation of the site was not carried out until the 1920s, by Warren Moorhead under the auspices of the Illinois State Museum and the University of Illinois. This work confirmed that the mounds were humanmade, rather than just erosional remnants. Also in the 1920s, the first aerial photographs of Cahokia, probably some of the earliest shots of an archaeological site in the United States, were taken. Today, Cahokia is designated a National Historic Site, and the central part is protected, but each year the expansion of subdivisions and highways continues to destroy outlying portions of this ancient settlement. During the last decades, many of the archaeological proj-

ects at Cahokia have been salvage operations designed to recover as much information as possible prior to the destruction of a portion of the site.

Fully agricultural inhabitants first settled in the Cahokia area between A.D. 600 and 800. Small hamlets and villages consisted of small houses constructed in shallow rectangular basins. Several distinct villages were dispersed on the terrain that later was to become Cahokia. By A.D. 900, the population in the region had expanded, and a hierarchy of settlements had emerged. The larger communities or towns contained 100–150 people. These sites often included a series of flat-topped platform mounds that served as the foundations for temples, other public structures, or elite residences. Frequently, the platform mounds were arranged around rectangular open plazas. Sites often were fortified with defensive

An artist's reconstruction of Monks Mound and the central, walled part of Cahokia at its peak, around A.D. 1150.

palisades, barricades that enclosed the plazas and other nonresidential features. Houses generally were erected both inside and outside the palisades. Many of the towns were planned settlements, with rectangular single-family houses arranged in an orderly manner around the central plaza.

At its peak between A.D. 1050 and 1250, Cahokia was the largest prehistoric civic-ceremonial center north of Mexico. The site encompasses more than 100 earthen mounds in an area of 13–16 sq km (5–6 sq mi) and may have had a population as high as 30,000. The central part of Cahokia consists of a large plaza surrounded by the giant Monks Mound and 16 other earthen platforms. This entire "downtown" area covered more than 80 ha (200 acres) and was surrounded by an elaborate and massive wall. The wall served defensive purposes, as it included screened entrances and bastions. Yet it also may have been used to limit access to the central portion of the site. The people residing within the palisaded area undoubtedly were the highest-ranked individuals in the com-

munity. People of lesser status had their own houses, public buildings, and burial mound areas outside this central portion of the site.

Monks Mound, the largest prehistoric structure in the United States, consisted of four platforms, with a large public structure and some related smaller structures and walls located on the summit (see "Monumental Architecture," p. 274). The other mounds at the site occur in a variety of shapes. Conical mounds were probably used as burial mounds. Linear "ridgetop marker" mounds situated at the edges of Cahokia may have served to delineate the limits of the site. The most common mounds are large square platforms, several of which had two levels, such as Mound 42, a rectangular platform mound with a smaller mound on one corner. Excavations have revealed the presence of wood and postholes on top of several platforms, which are assumed to have served as sites for ceremonial structures. Also within the site area are features called **woodhenges,** demarcated by large upright timbers that once had been arranged in a circle.

By sighting along certain marker posts, one can observe the annual sequence of the **solstices** and the equinoxes; woodhenge features may have served as solar observatories.

Excavations by Melvin Fowler, of the University of Wisconsin, Milwaukee, at Cahokia's Mound 72 have uncovered a series of burials from the 100-year period prior to A.D. 1050. In all, there were six burial episodes, involving at least 261 individuals (118 of which are thought to have been retainer sacrifices), and each episode resulted in the expansion of the mound as prior burials were covered over. During one of the first episodes, a **cache** of offerings, including pottery vessels, projectile points, and shell beads, was placed in a pit. In a subsequent episode, a pit containing more than 50 young women and a platform with four young men, who had been beheaded and behanded, were added. The closeness in age of the women argues against their having died from disease or some common disaster. Along with the four men, they appear to have been sacrificial victims who were dispatched to accompany powerful chiefs after death. One burial contained a possible chief who was laid out on a litter composed of thousands of drilled shell beads and surrounded by offerings. Near this figure were six individuals with elaborate grave goods, including rolled sheet copper, mica slabs, polished stones, and caches of arrowheads. The complexity of the Mound 72 burial sequence, the sacrifices, and the grave goods document elaborate burial ceremonialism and marked social differentiation at Cahokia.

Cahokia was a great center, dominating the floodplain for miles around, that contained a disproportionate amount of elaborate public architecture compared to the settlements in its surrounding hinterland. The craftsmanship and diversity of the goods present in burial and domestic contexts at Cahokia were unmatched at the smaller settlements. In addition, there is every reason to believe that Cahokia was well planned and that its construction required the control of a reasonably large, organized labor force. Cahokia appears to have been at the pinnacle of a hierarchically orga-

nized and complex social system that was centered on the rich American Bottom for several centuries.

After A.D. 1250, Cahokia continued to be occupied, but many of the site's mounds fell into disuse. Population at the site and throughout the American Bottom was greatly diminished as people moved into surrounding uplands. The decline of Cahokia and some nearby settlements may have been related to the growing importance of other large Mississippian centers, such as Moundville in Alabama, that redirected channels of exchange, alliance, and communication. At the same time, the great buildup at Cahokia could have precipitated degradation of the local environment.

Whatever led to the transition, the period after A.D. 1250 was dominated by a series of important Mississippian centers that were dispersed across the southeastern United States. Archaeological findings suggest that each of these sites was smaller and less monumental than Cahokia had been. The archaeological record on this point dovetails with early documentary accounts from the period of first white contact. The earliest European travelers in the southeastern United States encountered a number of chiefs, temple mounds, and hierarchically organized societies, but none of the reported centers matched the size or monumentality of Cahokia.

The skeleton of a man lying on a burial platform made of thousands of drilled shell beads. The burial is from Mound 72.

A Cahokia pottery vessel, with sophisticated spiral scroll design, 23 cm high.

MONUMENTAL ARCHITECTURE

Monks Mound at Cahokia

Monumental construction is characteristic of complex societies. Some of the most famous structures of the ancient world are the Egyptian pyramids and the massive architecture and pyramids along the Street of the Dead in Teotihuacan, Mexico. Although large-scale constructions were erected by most ancient civilizations, the specific activities associated with these massive edifices vary from structure to structure and region to region. Some large-scale architecture served primarily to commemorate the dead, while other structures served as platforms for temples or high-status residences. In certain cases, massive architectural features (elaborate tombs or gigantic palaces) were built to confirm and glorify the power of a specific ruling individual or family, but in other places great public structures or plazas were built to hold more corporate political and ritual functions in which a larger segment of society participated. Of course, many monumental buildings served multiple functions. The study of ancient architecture allows archaeologists to identify the political and ceremonial activities carried out by peoples in the past. In some cases, the examination of ancient buildings has enabled archaeologists to estimate the size of the labor force that was required to construct them.

The largest prehistoric structure in North America (north of Mexico) is Monks Mound at Cahokia. This immense earthen mound, located at the center of Cahokia, was 30 m high (or 98 ft, as tall as a 10-story building) and larger than a city block (316 m long × 241 m wide, or 1036 × 790 ft). Covering 6.5 ha (16 acres), it contained over 600,000 cu m (21,000,000 cu ft) of earth, or the equivalent of six modern oil tankers. Monks Mound was erected in as many as 14 stages, beginning early in the tenth century A.D. The last level, the summit on which large public buildings were built, dates to the middle of the twelfth century.

In 1809, a land claim of 160 ha (400 acres), including Monks Mound, was assigned to Nicholas Jarrot, who donated this area to a group of Trappist monks. The monks, who established a monastery, gardened on the first terrace of the largest mound and built their settlement on a small mound nearby. They abandoned the site only 4 years later because of disease and hardship, but it is from this brief occupation that the largest mound at the site is now known as Monks Mound. In 1831, Amos Hill moved onto the property and built his house on the summit of Monks Mound. The area was under private ownership until 1923, when it was turned into a state park.

The form of Monks Mound is unique; it consists of four terraces or platforms. The lowest, or first, terrace extends across the south end of the structure and stands approximately 11 m (36 ft) above the surrounding ground surface. A projection that appears to have been a ramp leading to the ground is situated near the center of the southern end of the terrace. The southwest corner of this terrace is slightly higher than the rest. Excavations have shown that large public buildings were erected in this area; it likely was an important focal point for the Cahokia community around A.D. 1100. These public buildings were later covered over by another platform mound that also had a public structure on top of it. This platform mound was rebuilt several times. Later, a ridge was constructed connecting this platform with the main mass of Monks Mound to the northeast. Around A.D. 1700, Native Americans returned to the site and buried several individuals in this part of the mound.

The second terrace, extending from the first terrace back toward the northwest corner of the mound, actually consists of two flat-topped platforms at an elevation of 19 m (62 ft). These platforms were built sometime after A.D. 1250. The

An aerial view of Monks Mound at Cahokia, looking northwest. The base is approximately 300 m north to south, more than 210 m east to west, and 30 m above the surrounding fields at the highest point.

third and fourth terraces, situated in the northeast part of the structure, form the highest points of the mound.

The uniqueness and size of Monks Mound attest to its function as a symbol of civic-ceremonial power. Yet to many archaeologists, Monks Mound is more than a sacred place where annual ceremonies probably took place. The identification of ramps and stairways on the mound suggests that access to the apex of the mound, which stood far above the surrounding floodplain, was restricted, possibly limited to a small segment of Cahokia's population. Its monumentality provides an indication of the large numbers of people needed for its construction. Finally, Monks Mound, still visible today for miles around, also was the focal point of a powerful polity, a place where Cahokia's rulers surely must have displayed their political influence for many to witness.

MOUNDVILLE

A late Mississippian center in Alabama

Major changes in subsistence, material culture, and settlement patterns took place in the southeastern United States after A.D. 700. As with groups living on the Mississippi River bottomlands, corn became more important in the diet. Shell-tempered pottery appeared—a technological breakthrough that made possible the construction of larger, more durable ceramic vessels. Although most settlements in the Southeast remained small, a few larger communities with several small pyramidal earthen mounds arranged around an open plaza were established. While none of these sites yet approached the size and complexity of Cahokia, the presence of residences on the tops of some of the mounds, which were continuously rebuilt, enlarged, and inhabited for generations, suggests that a more stable or institutionalized form of elite status (perhaps inherited leadership positions) had developed in portions of the Southeast.

Although the shift to maize did not occur simultaneously throughout the area, large quantities of maize were grown in much of the Southeast by A.D. 1200. Wild plants and animals continued to be important sources of food, but maize agriculture (supplemented by beans and squash) was the economic foundation of these complex societies. The social and political hierarchies of this period were manifested in public architecture, as civic-ceremonial centers proliferated across the region. The largest of these centers was Moundville, a Mississippian community located on a bluff overlooking the Black Warrior River in west-central Alabama.

Most Mississippian settlements were linked by political, economic, and social ties into larger regional polities (political organizations) that varied greatly in size and complexity. Some were small and simple, each consisting of a single center and its immediate hinterland. Others were much larger, consisting of major centers, minor centers, and villages. The larger polities, which may have had several levels of chiefs, did not emerge until after A.D. 1200. Many of the groups actually consisted of semiautonomous polities linked together by alliances. Such formations, or confederations, were constantly subject to fragmentation and realignment, especially as distance from the paramount center increased.

Relationships between communities also were maintained through exchange. Such materials as copper, marine shell, mica, galena, fluorite, and bauxite were moved over great distances in both raw and finished form. At Moundville, non-local materials were abundant, including marine shell from the Florida Gulf Coast, copper from the Great Lakes, pottery from many areas of the Southeast, galena from Missouri, and finished ceremonial objects from Tennessee and the Spiro site in Oklahoma. Most of the artifacts made from these exotic materials tend to be associated with rich burials at Moundville, suggesting they were traded through elite channels. Other more domestic items, such as salt and chipped stone, probably were traded through reciprocal transactions at the household level.

One of the more striking features at Moundville and other large Mississippian centers is the presence of an art style

PLATE 1: Three early hominid skulls and other remains found by Richard Leakey and his coworkers in East Africa: *Homo habilis* (left), *Homo erectus* (center), and *Australopithecus robustus* (right). The discovery of these species in the same geological deposits suggests their contemporaneity.

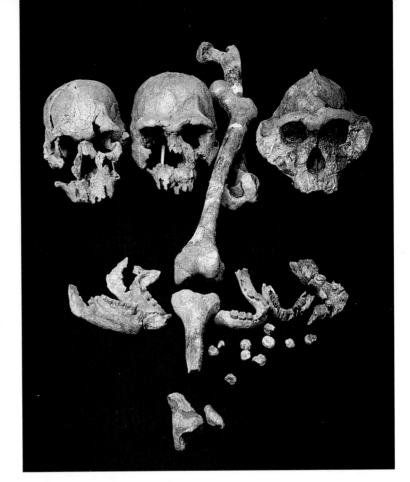

PLATE 2: The skull of Zinj, a robust australopithecine, discovered at Olduvai Gorge in Tanzania by Mary Leakey in 1959. The background shows the walls of the gorge.

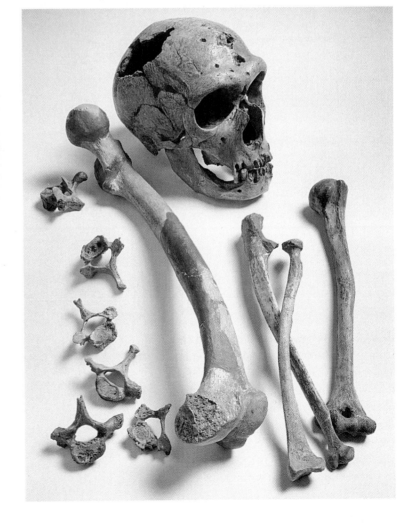

PLATE 3: A Neanderthal skeleton from La-Chappelle-aux-Saints, France, discovered early in this century. The femur and vertebrae are deformed by arthritis. These remains led Marcellin Boule to describe the Neanderthal as brutish and slow in wit, gait, and habit.

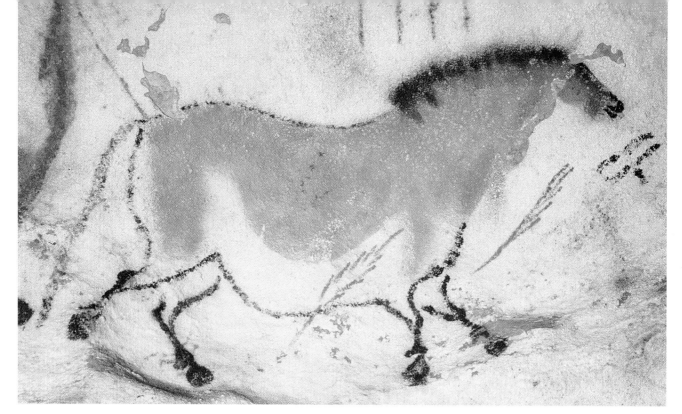

PLATE 4: The Upper Paleolithic cave of Lascaux in France, containing many paintings of a variety of animals. This running horse appears with two feathered darts or plants.

PLATE 5: The grave of a mother and child from a Mesolithic site at Vedbaek, Denmark. The mother's head rests on a bundle of teeth that would have decorated a hide blanket or piece of clothing. The newborn infant next to the mother was buried with a stone knife, as were all the males in the cemetery. The infant was buried on the wing of a swan. (An artist's reconstruction of this grave appears in Chapter 5 on page 171.)

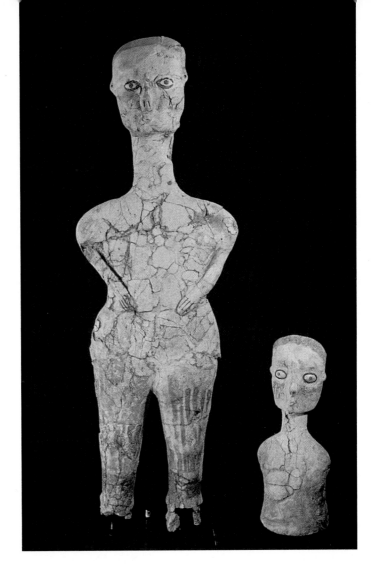

PLATE 6: A painted statue and bust of plaster from the early Neolithic site of 'Ain Ghazal in Jordan after reconstruction. The eyes are cowrie shells set in bitumen. The taller statue is 90 cm high.

PLATE 7: An aerial view of the mound of Cätalhöyuk. Paths on top of the mound lead to excavation areas and the headquarters to the left.

PLATE 8: The great diversity of modern maize, one indication of the tremendous adaptability and genetic plasticity of the plant. These varieties come from many regions of Mexico, and they prosper under different environmental and topographic conditions.

PLATE 9: A view of the Andes from Guitarrero Cave, a large natural rockshelter situated 2.5 km above sea level in the mountains of northern Peru. The site was first used by Native Americans more than 10,000 years ago, and contains a valuable record of the beginnings of domestication in the South American highlands.

PLATE 10: Chetro Ketl, one of the great houses that was built on the floor of Chaco Canyon (New Mexico). For the most part, the large pueblo of Chetro Ketl was constructed during the late tenth and early eleventh centuries A.D. The outer rooms, which faced the courtyard, were used primarily for residential activities, while the inner rooms were used for storage.

PLATE 11: Mound 1 at San José Mogote in Oaxaca, Mexico. This natural rise was artificially enhanced, raising the top of the mound further above the rest of the site. Around 600 B.C., Mound 1 became the focus for public building at San José Mogote. The *danzante*, a carved stone figure, found at San José Mogote was situated amidst a ceremonial building complex atop this mound.

PLATE 12: Part of the hill-top site of Monte Albán, Oaxaca, Mexico. The ruins of prehispanic structures are still visible at the summit, and residential terraces can be seen on the upper slopes. Monte Albán was the largest and most architecturally elaborate center in the Valley of Oaxaca for more than 1000 years.

PLATE 13: A view of the Pyramid of the Moon and the north end of the Street of the Dead from the top of the Pyramid of the Sun at Teotihuacan. These monumental pyramids are among the largest structures ever built in the ancient Americas.

PLATE 14: The Palace at Palenque, a Maya site at the foot of the Chiapas highlands in southern Mexico. The multiroom palace sits at the core of Palenque's complex of civic-ceremonial structures. The most distinguishing feature of the palace is a four-story tower, which provides a superb view of the city and the surrounding countryside.

PLATE 15: A view of the large ball court at Chichén Itzá. The Mesoamerican ballgame has a long history; however, the specific form and size of the courts varied across time and space.

PLATE 16: Recent excavations at Tenochtitlán's Templo Mayor. Today, this Aztec site lies at the center of downtown Mexico City. After the Spanish conquest, Mexico City rapidly grew up over the ancient Aztec center, and materials from the upper level of the Templo Mayor were used in the construction of Mexico City's main cathedral.

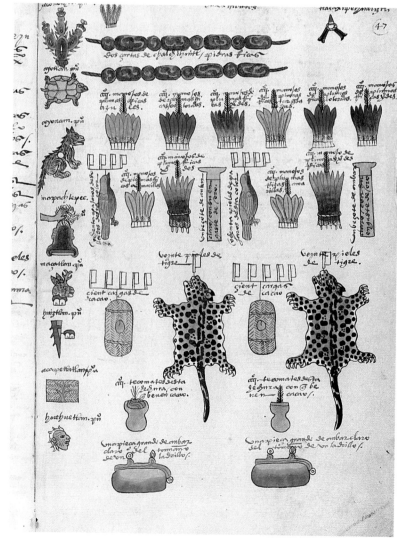

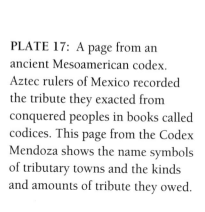

PLATE 17: A page from an ancient Mesoamerican codex. Aztec rulers of Mexico recorded the tribute they exacted from conquered peoples in books called codices. This page from the Codex Mendoza shows the name symbols of tributary towns and the kinds and amounts of tribute they owed.

PLATE 18: An elaborate sacrificial knife used by the Aztecs. The blade is made of chalcedony, a type of chert. The handle is made of wood inlaid with a mosaic of turquoise and shell.

PLATE 19: A cloth mantle of the Paracas style. Images on ritual weavings played a key role in the visual communication of prehispanic Peruvian society, particularly at the south coastal sites associated with this style. The "ecstatic shaman" shown in this weaving was a common image depicted on Paracas textiles.

PLATE 20: The north face of the fortress of Sacsahuaman at Inca Cuzco, Peru. This edifice was constructed of huge, stone blocks fitted together with great masonry skill. Some of these blocks weigh more than 100 metric tons. The fortress is perched atop a high hill that has a commanding view of Cuzco below.

PLATE 21: The superbly preserved Inca administrative center of Machu Picchu, high in the Peruvian Andes. Discovered early in the twentieth century by Hiram Bingham, the Machu Picchu ruins are a conglomerate of courtyards and stone stairways, as well as residential structures and public buildings.

PLATE 22: The Royal Standard of Ur, recovered by Sir Leonard Woolley from a complex of royal graves at Ur, an ancient city in southern Mesopotamia (Iraq). One side of the box portrays domestic activities, food production, and feasting (top). The reverse side depicts war-related images, including chariots, soldiers, and fallen enemies (bottom). In a society where most people could not read, the Royal Standard may have served to communicate socially approved modes of behavior.

PLATE 23: The ruins of ancient Mohenjo-daro, a well-preserved center in the Indus Valley of modern Pakistan. Much of the site was built on a massive mud-brick platform, which raised the settlement over the wet alluvial plain below. The balloon above the site is used by archaeologists to view and photograph the ruins from the air.

PLATE 24: An enormous pyramid complex at Giza, near modern Cairo, built during Old Kingdom Egypt (2686–2181 B.C.). The pyramids were constructed over a long period of time by a succession of pharaohs, each of whom had his own funerary monument.

PLATE 25: The Great Enclosure and other stone ruins at Great Zimbabwe. The Great Enclosure is the largest known prehistoric structure in sub-Saharan Africa. Inside the Great Enclosure were smaller stone structures, which are thought to have housed the site's ruling families.

PLATE 26: The body of the Iceman as he was first found in the Italian Alps. This Neolithic man was discovered by hikers during a warm summer when the ice that had covered him for 5000 years melted and exposed the corpse. He was first thought to be an unfortunate skier until the age of the find was realized.

PLATE 27: The funeral mask of "Agamemnon" from the excavations in the shaft graves at
Mycenae, Greece. Although this individual was determined not to be Agamemnon, he certainly
was an important Mycenaean ruler.

PLATE 28: An early Celtic bronze mirror, with engraved back, from the Iron Age in England, 36 cm in diameter. The elaborate scrolling design on the mirror is typical of Celtic art.

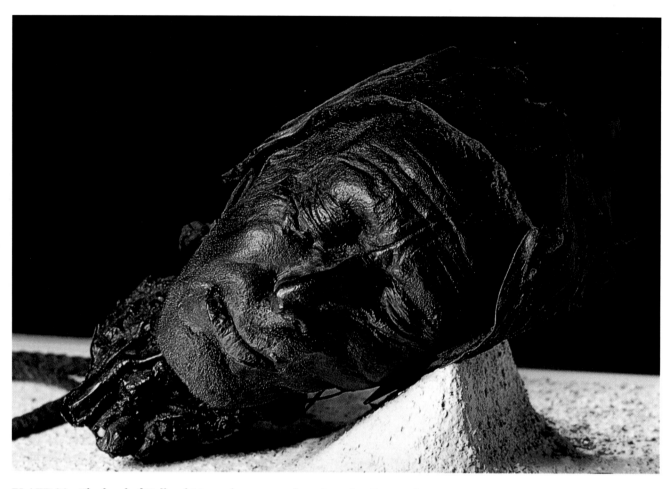

PLATE 29: The head of Tollund Man, a bog person from Iron Age Denmark.
The corpse was preserved in bog deposits for almost 2000 years.

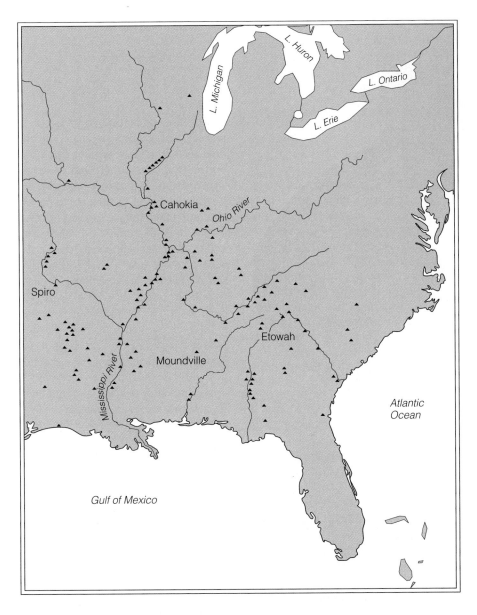

known as the **Southern Cult,** also called the Southeastern Ceremonial Complex. It was not really a cult but a network of interaction, exchange, and shared information that crossed regional and local boundaries. So-called cult items have been found from Mississippi to Minnesota, and from Oklahoma to the Atlantic Coast, although they are most abundant at certain sites in the Southeast. Such motifs as human hands with an eye in the palm, sunbursts, weeping eyes, and human skull-and-bones characterize this style. They appear on polished black shell-tempered pottery, are embossed on pendants made from Lake Superior copper, and are incised on imported Gulf conch shells. The most famous Mississippian cult objects are the so-called effigy jars that are decorated with human faces, some with signs of face painting or tattoos. Others represent sacrificial victims, with eyes closed and mouths sewn shut. Often the effigies are shown weeping, possibly denoting a connection between tears, rain, and water in Mississippian cosmology. Some of the common Southern Cult motifs—wind, fire, sun, and human sacrifice—seem to share certain thematic elements with Mesoamerica, although the basis for this similarity has not been established. The greatest concentrations of these Southern Cult objects occur in temple mounds at some

A black pottery vessel with bird effigy found at Moundville, 16 cm high.

A stone disk from Moundville, with the eye-in-palm motif (diameter about 31.5 cm).

of the major late Mississippian sites, suggesting that these goods had sacred importance.

Because of its large size (second only to Cahokia), Moundville has long attracted public attention. In 1840, Thomas Maxwell, a local planter and merchant, excavated in one mound, noted the stylistic similarities with Mesoamerica, and concluded that the site was an outpost of the Aztec empire. Several small-scale investigations of the site were made by the Smithsonian Institution during the latter part of the century, but the first large-scale excavations were not carried out until 1905–1906 by Clarence B. Moore. Excavating both platform mounds and village areas, Moore uncovered over 800 burials, many accompanied by pottery vessels and other artifacts of shell, copper, and stone. The second major episode of excavation was carried out by the Alabama Museum of Natural History. From 1929 through 1941, 4.5 ha (11 acres) of the site surface was opened, and the excavations yielded over 2000 burials, 75 structures, and many other finds. More recent work has concentrated on understanding the chronolog-

ical sequence at the site. In all, excavations at Moundville have yielded more than 3000 burials and over 1 million artifacts.

Moundville was occupied initially around A.D. 1050. At first the site contained only one mound and was one of several small ceremonial centers in the drainage of the Black Warrior River. The burials from this period indicate some signs of marked, possibly inherited, social differentiation, though not to the extent found for later occupations.

Moundville flourished after A.D. 1300, when Cahokia was already in decline. The site grew to over 150 ha (370 acres). Twenty large platform mounds were built, associated with a 30-ha (75-acre) plaza. The mounds were large flat-topped earthen structures constructed to elevate temples or the dwellings of important individuals above the surrounding landscape. The mounds were built in stages, probably as part of community rituals. The two major mounds, the largest of which was 18 m (60 ft) high and covered more than 0.5 ha (1.25 acres) at its base, were located within the plaza at the center of the site along the north-south axis. The 18 earthworks surrounding the plaza are arranged into pairs of one large and one small mound. The small mounds usually include burials, while the larger earthen structures do not. Based on parallels with later Native American groups in the Southeast, each mound pair may represent the mortuary temple and elite residence of a particular kin group or clan.

In the northeast corner of the site, the dwellings were larger and more complex than in other parts of Moundville. Broken artifacts that correspond to items found in the higher-status burials also are found in this probable elite residential area. **Charnel houses,** houses in which bones of the dead are placed, and a sweat house are located along the margins of the plaza. Commoner residential areas were placed at greater distances from the eastern, southern, and western sides of the plaza. At its height, Moundville is estimated to have been occupied by 3000 people.

Several craftworking areas have been identified away from the residential zones at Moundville. One contained a large quantity of finished shell beads, unworked shell, and beadworking tools, while another yielded hundreds of large bone awls and the stones used to sharpen them. The bone awls may have been used for processing hides. Large fire hearths, caches of shell (for temper), clay, and other items indicative of pottery production were found in a third area of craftworking.

Social differentiation was clearly expressed in mortuary goods from this later episode of occupation. The high-status segment of the society, which totaled approximately 5% of the population, was always buried in or near mounds. These individuals were always accompanied by rare and distinctive artifacts, including copper axes and gorgets, stone disks, Southern Cult items, and many shell beads. Each mound also contained lower-status individuals, who were accompanied only by a few ceramic vessels. The less elaborate burials could have been retainers who were positioned to accompany those of higher status. The largest proportion of Moundville's inhabitants were interred away from the civic-ceremonial part of the site. These graves generally included no more than a few ceramic vessels. The inclusion of people of both sexes and all ages in each class of burials suggests that access to goods (at least at death) was determined partially through birthright.

While social status at Moundville appears to have been inherited, warfare may have provided one mechanism for certain individuals to enhance their status. Evidence of warfare is present in the archaeological record at Moundville, as well as elsewhere in the Southeast. Many communities, both large and small, were surrounded by fortification walls and ditches. In addition, skeletal studies have revealed numerous indications of scalping, the taking of trophy heads, and the burial of headless bodies. Warfare is also prominent in the **iconography** of the Southern Cult. One grave at Moundville contained 11 decapitated skeletons. This grave also included ceremonial flints and shell objects engraved with elaborately dressed individuals holding decapitated heads.

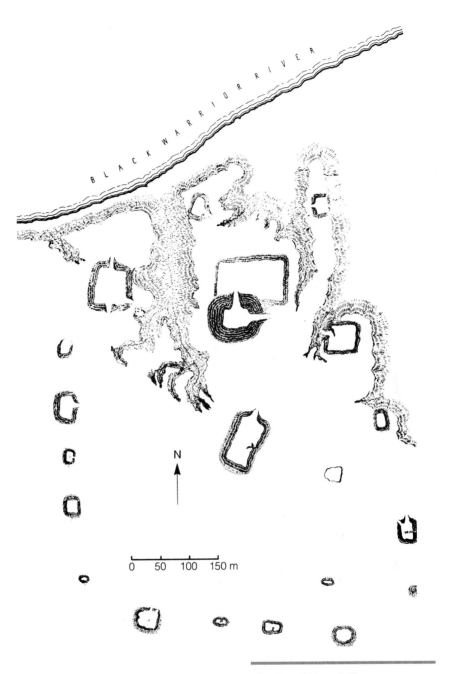

The plan of Moundville.

Mississippian culture persisted in parts of the Southeast until the sixteenth century. In the 1540s, Spanish ***conquistador*** (conqueror) Hernando de Soto encountered Creek Indian chiefs who still lived in fortified towns with temple mounds and plazas. With the European expeditions came smallpox and other Old World diseases for which the Indians had no immunity. These communicable diseases quickly decimated the Native American population, putting an end to many facets of a way of life that had endured for centuries.

Grave Goods

Indicators of social differences

Grave goods, the items buried with individuals at death, are an important source of information about the social organization of prehistoric groups. With other aspects of mortuary ritual, such as location of the burials and the "elaborateness" of tombs, grave goods inform archaeologists about the relative social position of the interred individuals. A person's status during life is generally reflected at death: elaborate burials and grave goods for people of high status, but few or no trappings for low-status individuals. Complex societies with marked social differentiation usually have a greater degree of mortuary variation than less hierarchical societies. The distribution of grave goods relative to age and sex also may indicate whether an individual had **achieved status,** earned through personal accomplishments, or **ascribed status,** inherited at birth. Some archaeologists have argued that graves of infants or children with an unusually rich array of grave goods are indicative of ascribed status, since these individuals would not have been able to achieve high status on their own.

In the Mississippian societies of the southeastern United States, social differentiation was expressed in mortuary ritual. Commoners were interred in simple graves, usually grouped in communal cemeteries or scattered near dwellings. Typical grave goods included simple shell ornaments, ceramic vessels, and domestic tools. In contrast, high-ranking people were buried in or near public buildings, often on mounds, and accompanied by elaborate grave goods.

The more than 3000 burials excavated at Moundville can be divided into several groups (Table 7.1). Seven individuals had very high status; they were probably chiefs. All male, they were buried in large mounds and were accompanied by lavish grave goods, such as copper axes, copper-covered shell beads, and pearl beads. Sacrificial victims accompanied these burials (group A in the

table). A second group of elaborate burials (group B) included both children and male adults; these graves also were placed in or near the mounds. This group was interred with copper earspools, stone disks, bear-tooth pendants, oblong copper gorgets, and artifacts decorated with symbols associated with the Southern Cult. A third group of high-status interments (groups C and D) included individuals of both sexes and all ages, buried in cemeteries near the mounds, accompanied by shell beads, oblong copper gorgets, and galena clubs. Since rare and exotic items were buried with individuals of both sexes and all ages, it appears that status at Moundville must have been ascribed rather than achieved.

Less elaborate burials at Moundville also were divisible into several groups (E–H), including a large number, mostly children and infants, that lacked any grave goods at all. Less ornate grave goods were distributed very differently than the goods associated with high-status burials. In the lower-status graves, the distribution of goods corresponded more closely with variation in age and sex. Graves of older adults generally contained pottery vessels, bone awls, flint projectile points, and stone pipes. Such other items as unworked deer bones, bird claws, and turtle bones were found exclusively with adults, while children and infants were sometimes accompanied by toy vessels and clay toys. Stone ceremonial celts (axe heads) were found only with adult males, while effigy vessels were associated with adults of both sexes. The different grave goods indicate that status for commoners was determined according to sex and age. While high or low status in general was a result of birth, ranking within each group seems to have depended partly on individual achievement or role.

Similar burial patterns are found at other contemporaneous sites in the vicinity of Moundville. But there is one major difference: The most elaborate

Table 7.1 The Complexity of Mortuary Ritual at Moundville

Broad Groupings	Burial Group	Number of Individuals	Characteristic Grave Goods	Burial Context	Age	Infant Child % Adults	Sex
Highest-status graves	A	7	Copper axes	Central mound	I C A		? Male
	B	110	Copper ear spools, bear teeth, stone disks, red or white paint, shell beads, oblong copper gorgets, galena	Mounds and cemeteries near mounds	I C A		Male and female
Other high-status graves	C	211	Effigy vessels, shell gorgets, animal bone, freshwater shells	Cemeteries near mounds	I C A		Male and female
	D	50	Discoidals, bone awls, projectile points	Cemeteries near mounds	I C A		Male and female
Lower-status graves	E	125	Bowls and/or jars	Cemeteries near mounds and in village areas	I C A		No data
	F	146	Water bottles	Cemeteries near mounds and in village areas	I C A		Male and female
	G	70	Sherds	Village areas	I C A		Male
	H	1256	No grave goods	Retainers in mounds Isolated skulls with public buildings Cemeteries near mounds and in village areas	I C A		Male and female

Source: Adapted from Peebles and Kus, 1977.

burials in the mounds of the minor ceremonial centers (those sites with only a single platform mound) did not contain copper axes—the badge of office—that accompanied the highest-ranking burials at Moundville. The highest-ranking individuals in the social system apparently resided at the region's largest and most important ceremonial center.

THE DRAPER SITE

A late prehistoric Iroquoian village in southern Ontario

Iroquois Indian basket used for washing hominy (kernels of corn).

When early European explorers and fur traders arrived in the northeastern United States and southeastern Canada, the native peoples they encountered differed in several important ways from the aboriginal populations farther south. Maize agriculture was prevalent among most of the people east of the Mississippi River, yet the native peoples of the Northeast differed from those of the Southeast in village structure and social organization. Generally, the Northeast groups were organized less hierarchically than the societies of the Southeast. In the northeastern Iroquoian communities, leaders were chosen largely for their skills in settling disputes and organizing military expeditions and for their ceremonial knowledge. Leadership roles were based more on achievement than ascription; the latter pattern was more common among the southeastern groups. Also, northern villages were composed of clusters of longhouses, often surrounded by palisades and lacking the platform mounds found at sites in the Midwest and Southeast, such as Cahokia and Moundville.

The historic Iroquoian tribal groups of the Northeast were the descendants of small, mobile bands of Archaic foragers. We have little evidence of their settlement patterns; however, a small circle of post molds at one Archaic site in Vermont suggests that they built temporary shelters framed with poles and possibly covered with bark or skins. Hunting, fishing, and collecting wild plants were the primary subsistence activities.

By the middle of the first millennium A.D., people in southern Ontario were living in semipermanent settlements during spring, summer, and early fall. These sites, usually positioned near good fishing locations, consisted of unfortified clusters of round or oblong houses. Although limited amounts of squash may have been cultivated, hunt-ing, fishing, and collecting continued to be the main subsistence activities.

After A.D. 700, major changes in settlement pattern, subsistence, and social organization occurred in the Great Lakes region. Villages were repositioned from major rivers and lakes to hilltop locations that were naturally defendable, and many settlements were surrounded by palisades. Most villages remained small (around 0.6 ha, or 1.5 acres) and were composed of small, multifamily, bark longhouses. These villages were occupied primarily in winter. By A.D. 1100, maize agriculture became a more significant part of the subsistence regime. This important dietary shift coincided with the evolution of heartier maize varieties that were better adapted to the colder, northern latitudes (where the growing season was relatively short). But even toward the end of the prehistoric era in the Northeast, maize farming did not completely supplant the hunting, fishing, and gathering of wild foods. Fishing remained an especially key part of the diet for many populations.

After A.D. 1300, the stockaded villages were occupied on a more permanent basis. Several archaeological indicators, including an increase in the complexity of village fortifications and a growing number of traumatic injuries found on skeletal remains, point to the intensification of warfare. The historically known patterns of Iroquoian internecine warfare and blood revenge may have been established by this time. Longhouse size expanded and village size increased. Some villages were as large as 6 ha (15 acres) and included 2000 people, although the average community was closer to 2.5 ha (6.25 acres) in size. In several areas, settlement pattern studies suggest that these larger villages apparently were formed through the nucleation of several smaller communities. In these larger villages, the alignment of houses was usually much more formal than in the earlier, smaller settlements.

Excavations over the last 25 years at the Draper site have provided a wealth of information on village organization in the late prehistoric period. Located 35 km (22 mi) northeast of Toronto, the site has a long research history; however, most of the settlement was excavated as part of a salvage operation initiated prior to the construction of a new Toronto airport. An unusually large village for late prehistoric Ontario, the site is particularly important because almost the entire settlement was excavated. The high cost of modern archaeological excavation makes it very rare for more than a small portion of most sites to be examined carefully. Yet in a few cases—Draper being one—the opportunity to excavate a large segment of the original village provides an usually detailed picture of community plan, changes in settlement size over time, and house-to-house variation.

The Draper site is one of more than 15 Iroquoian villages in the Duffin drainage, located in the white pine–hardwood forest region of southern Ontario. The settlement was inhabited between A.D. 1450 and 1500. This relatively short occupation is not unusual for southern Ontario, where most villages were resituated every 25–50 years, usually to new locations only 3–5 km (2–3 mi) away. Many factors have been proposed to account for these frequent relocations, including infestation of the wood-and-thatch longhouses by insects, soil exhaustion or weed competition (which would have prompted the clearing of forest for new agricultural fields), depletion of wood (for construction and firewood) and game, and community realignments due to disputes and other social stresses.

The Draper site was composed of three spatially discrete areas of occupation: the main palisaded village, a small group of seven houses located 50 m (160 ft) south of the main village, and a lone structure (Structure 42) located on a small knoll 80 m (260 ft) to the southwest. At different times in its occupation, the main village was surrounded by three or four palisade rows (each composed of wooden posts or beams). William Finlay-

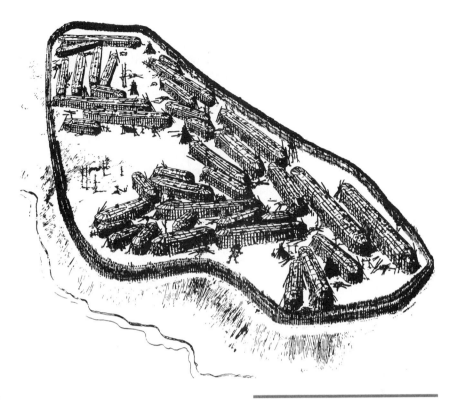

An artist's interpretation of the palisade and longhouses at the Draper site.

son, who supervised the principal excavations in 1975 and 1978, believes the settlement seems to have been planned with defensive considerations in mind.

The site began as a 1.2-ha (3-acre) village of seven to nine longhouses (accommodating roughly 400 people). All the houses were built well back from the palisades. These first houses were arranged in two clusters, with the houses in each cluster laid out according to similar compass orientations. Each set of houses may have represented a distinct social unit, perhaps a lineage or clan segment.

All the longhouses had a relatively similar set of internal features, including sweat baths, cooking hearths, pits (some of which were burials), storage cubicles, and benches (2–2.5 m, or 6.5–8 ft, wide), which were placed along the house walls. Each nuclear family within the longhouse is thought to have had its own cooking and sleeping area. The sweat baths were less abundant and were probably used in a more communal fashion. According to ethnohistoric accounts of the Huron, the Iroquoian tribal group considered to be the descendants of the people at the Draper site, sweat baths usually were taken by groups of men to prevent disease. Prior to the bath, the stones were heated very hot in a large fire, then removed and put in a pile in the center of the lodge. Sticks were arranged at waist height around the pile then bent at the top, leaving enough space between the sticks and the rocks for naked men sitting with their knees raised in front of their stomach. When the men were in position, the whole bath was covered with large pieces of bark and skins to prevent air from escaping. While in the bath, the men would often sing. These sweat-bath rituals are thought to have had an important integrative function for a group of people who resided in very close quarters.

In the first Draper village, one of the longhouses had several characteristics suggesting a special function. This large structure had one of the highest densities of wall posts and sweat baths. It also had the greatest average distance between hearths, indicating that each family group had more space than other longhouse occupants. In addition, a special hearth was placed at one end of this somewhat unusual residential structure. Finlayson suggests that this large longhouse may have been occupied by a community or kin-group leader or village chief. Such special structures may have been used for council meetings, community feasts, and ceremonies.

The Draper village underwent five expansions, eventually reaching a maximum population of 1800–2000 people. Prior to abandonment, the village was 3.4 ha (8.5 acres) in size. During each expansion episode, between three and nine houses were built. The houses often were added in clusters, with the houses having similar orientations. The additions may represent new kin segments that moved into the site. Over time, an increasing amount of space was devoted to nonhouse use; with each expansion the houses, or clusters of houses, were positioned to create new plazas. The plazas may have served as places for village ceremonies and social activities. Such integrative events may have increased in importance as the community grew. Two of the houses that were added during these expansions are thought by Finlayson to have been leaders' houses.

Two rectangular structures that abutted the palisade also were added. These buildings have been interpreted as houses set aside for visitors. According to ethnohistoric accounts, visitors were assigned to special cabins so that they could be closely monitored; they were not allowed to wander through the community.

The longhouses in the Draper site were 14.5–75.1 m (48–247 ft) long and 6.7–7.9 m (22–26 ft) wide. The narrow range of widths was probably determined by the mechanical limitations of the construction procedures and the available material (wood). In contrast, the length variation was probably related primarily to household or kin-group size.

The seven houses in the south field were smaller than those in the main village. They had a low density of pits and sweat baths, suggesting a shorter occupation. The presence of only a partial palisade, possibly used as a windbreak, suggests less concern for defense. Perhaps the occupants of this southern area moved inside the larger palisaded village when sieges occurred. Structure 42, also outside the main village, appears to have been a special-purpose structure, although its specific function remains little understood. Fragments of human bone were found on the surface prior to its excavation, but further study has not yet revealed additional signs of a burial area.

The late precontact Iroquoian villages in the Great Lakes region were not organized as hierarchically as the larger, contemporaneous Mississippian polities in the Southeast. In the latter, labor was amassed to construct large pyramid mounds at central settlements. These focal settlements differed in size and function from the many smaller villages that also comprised the settlement system. In contrast, the differences between the Draper site and surrounding settlements were not substantial. Although Draper was somewhat larger than its neighbors, the construction remains and material items at the site were basically similar to those found at surrounding communities.

Because of the tremendous changes that occurred in Native American lifeways as a result of direct European contact (and sometimes before, as the spread

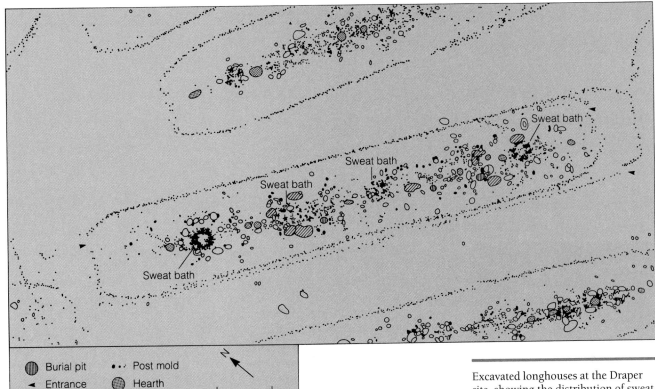

Legend:
- Burial pit
- Entrance
- Large pit
- Post mold
- Hearth
- Pit feature

N

0   5 m

Excavated longhouses at the Draper site, showing the distribution of sweat baths, hearths, burial pits, and other pit features. The longhouses are clearly outlined by post molds. Other post molds are also present inside the houses.

of disease and trade goods often preceded actual face-to-face relations), the early European historical accounts present a sketchy and sometimes inaccurate picture of the late precontact period. This potential disparity between archaeological and historical records is especially troublesome in areas where major settlements, such as the large Hohokam villages of the Arizona desert, were apparently abandoned sometime prior to European contact (see "Snaketown," p. 286). In such cases, the native peoples that the Europeans first encountered were not necessarily the direct descendants of earlier native populations, whose communities have been found by archaeologists. In other areas, the direct sequence between the historic and prehistoric peoples is somewhat clearer, such as for the Iroquoian groups of the Northeast. In these cases, historical information can more readily be used to test and support interpretations derived from archaeological data. Nevertheless, the careful researcher must be prepared to recognize diversity and changes in the archaeological and historical records.

For example, in the Great Lakes region, indirect contacts spread trade goods and disease vectors to most areas before direct meetings between native peoples and Europeans took place. In fact, some scholars have argued that the large-scale Iroquoian alliances and confederacies, which at times joined up to 25 villages and are well documented in the early historical accounts, may have been formed in response to contact-period processes. Such large linkages appear not to have been in place prehistorically. New trade demands and land pressures may have prompted the formation of new political structures. Warfare and trade certainly were important prehistorically in the Great Lakes region, but after European contact, they took on new forms. Scholars, such as those studying the Iroquoian peoples, who can use and compare archaeological and historical sources as partially independent records, stand the best chance of unraveling the multifaceted and often destructive processes that surrounded European arrival in the Americas and the effects of these processes on the native peoples.

SNAKETOWN

*A desert village in the
American Southwest*

Mano resting on a well-used metate.

Despite its often arid and unforgiving landscape, the American Southwest has a rich archaeological past. The region was first populated around 9000 B.C. by hunter-gatherers who hunted big-game species, such as mammoth and giant bison. These early inhabitants had highly mobile food-collecting strategies and manufactured sophisticated tools for hunting and butchering game and for processing hides, wood, and bone. Their remains occur primarily as small, ephemeral kill and butchering sites characterized by animal bones and flaked stone implements. By 5500 B.C., big-game hunting had declined in importance, and emphasis shifted to smaller animals and a variety of local plant resources. In southeastern Arizona and southwestern New Mexico, these wild foods included yucca, cactus leaves and fruits, and sunflower seeds.

By 1000 B.C., maize was introduced into the area from Mexico. Along with other early southwestern cultigens (beans, squash, and bottle gourds), maize has a long history of cultivation in Mexico prior to its appearance in the Southwest. Eventually, maize became the most important cultivated crop in the Southwest. However, for at least 1000 years following its introduction, most peoples of the Southwest relied surprisingly little on maize or any other exotic domesticate, and many groups retained a primarily hunting-and-gathering subsistence regime.

The earliest villages in the Southwest appeared in southern Arizona during the Late Archaic period (middle of the last millennium B.C.). This more sedentary existence was marked by the appearance of circular foundation pits,

storage facilities, crude plainware pottery jars and bowls, jewelry made from marine shells, and maize farming. By the end of the Late Archaic, agricultural villages dotted the landscape throughout the American Southwest, coexisting in some areas with groups who continued more traditional foraging practices and nomadic lifeways. In the colder, more northerly parts of the Southwest, farming was relatively risky. Perhaps that is part of the reason many early villages were positioned defensively and generally included storage facilities. In the hot Sonoran Desert of southern Arizona, crop production was more secure (as long as sufficient water was available), villages were situated more in the open, and no specialized storerooms were constructed. The presence of basketry containers, along with **metates**, grinding stones, and **manos**, companion handstones, for grinding corn or seeds, is indicative of a more settled existence in this area.

The early villages of the Southwest shared certain general characteristics. The earliest permanent dwellings were pithouses, structures in which the lower parts of the walls were actually the earthen sides of a shallow pit. The top part of the walls consisted of a framework of poles, interlaced with small twigs and then completely covered with mud on the exterior, a construction technique known as **wattle and daub.** Settlements often contained only two or three pithouses. In contrast, larger villages usually had one or more community, or special-function, structures in addition to pithouses.

Although the earliest ceramics in the Southwest were plainwares (without decoration), distinct regional variations soon developed. During the early centuries of the first millennium A.D., the three major cultural traditions of the prehistoric Southwest began to emerge: **Hohokam** (ho-ho-kham′) in the deserts of southern Arizona; **Anasazi** (ah-na-sah′zee) on the high plateaus of the Four Corners region (northern Arizona and New Mexico, southwestern Colorado, and southeastern Utah); and **Mogollon** (muh-gē-yown′) along the Mogollon Rim (in east-central Arizona) and in the mountains of southeastern Arizona and southwestern New Mexico. Each tradition eventually developed its own pattern of settlement and land use, architecture, community organization, and craft specialization. The discussion here of Snaketown (Hohokam) and the next section on Chaco Canyon (Anasazi) highlight the diversity of Native American life in the prehistoric Southwest.

The Hohokam lived in the lower Sonoran Desert region of southern Arizona and adjacent Chihuahua and Sonora in northern Mexico. The area is basin-and-range country, composed of numerous more or less parallel mountain ranges rising 300–1070 m (1000–3500 ft) above the intervening basins. The desert area of southern Arizona receives less rain than the high plateaus of the Anasazi and is intensely hot in the summer. The land supports a rich natural flora of shrubs and cacti (saguaro, barrel, cholla, prickly pear); mesquite and other trees and shrubs grow in the washes. Yet because of the somewhat unpredictable rainfall, irrigation is necessary in many areas for reliable maize farming.

After A.D. 1, a large Hohokam community called Snaketown was settled in the Phoenix Basin, a broad, low alluvial region where southern Arizona's two major rivers, the Salt and the Gila, come together. Snaketown is situated on an upper river terrace about 1 km (0.6 mi) from the Gila River at an elevation of 360 m (1175 ft). According to the late Emil Haury, who excavated at Snaketown in 1934–1935 and again in 1964–1965, good agricultural land, a river that could be tapped for irrigation, and a high water table were important features determining Snaketown's location.

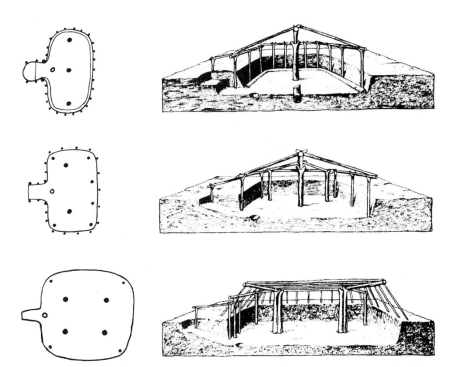

Three examples of pithouse dwellings (with postulated roof constructions) from Snaketown, from early (bottom) to late (top).

The largest of the early Hohokam pithouse villages, Snaketown may have had as many as 100 residents soon after its foundation. The early habitation levels included only residential pithouses; no public buildings were constructed. However, David R. Wilcox, of the Museum of Northern Arizona, has suggested that even early in its occupational history the site may have had a central plaza area. Maize was a dietary staple, although such wild plant foods as mesquite, saguaro, and cholla also were important.

By A.D. 600, the number of known Hohokam villages increased markedly, and the Phoenix Basin became the most densely populated area in southern Arizona. Many villages, including Snaketown, grew. At some sites, **ball courts** and platform mounds were erected (see "The Mesoamerican Ballgame," Chapter 8, p. 333). One of the most impressive of these oval Hohokam ball courts was constructed at Snaketown. Rubber balls, also found at Snaketown, suggest that certain aspects of the Hohokam ballgame may have been similar to the game played in Mexico. Hohokam platform mounds, usually low and rectangular, were made of earth and **adobe** and topped with caliche (calcium carbonate)

Snaketown during excavations in 1965.

or adobe plaster. Ceremonial structures may have been positioned on the tops of these mounds. Both platform mounds and ball courts were generally erected at larger Hohokam sites, such as Snaketown. These sites may have served as political-ritual centers for the populations of smaller surrounding settlements that lacked such nondomestic structures.

The Hohokam cultural tradition, marked by its red-on-buff pottery, reached its greatest spatial extent after A.D. 900, spreading across much of central and southern Arizona. At about this time, Snaketown covered an area over 1 sq km (about 0.4 sq mi, the size of the Indianapolis race track) and may have had a population of 500–1000 people.

The plan of the village became more complex as well. At the site's core was a central plaza surrounded by an inner habitation zone. A series of mounds and two ball courts circled this area, with an outer habitation zone beyond. In all, 60 trash-filled mounds were constructed at the site, and as many as 125 pithouses may have been occupied at any one time.

At Snaketown, craftspeople specialized in the production of ceramics and developed elaborate shell- and stone-working industries. Goods from all over the Southwest and northern Mexico were traded to the site. Some items, like the rubber for the balls, may have come from even farther south. The shell was imported from the Gulf of California and

The large oval ball court at Snaketown.

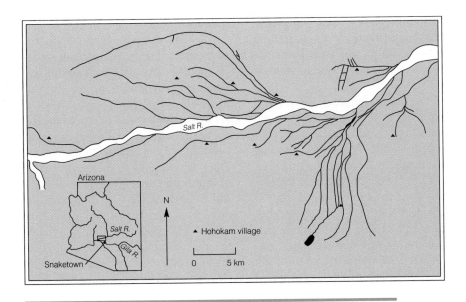

The network of Hohokam irrigation canals along the lower Salt River in the Phoenix Basin of central Arizona. Today, Phoenix covers the area where these canals were situated; only a few of the ancient canals are still visible on the surface.

A shell with an etching of a horned toad (diameter 10.2 cm).

After A.D. 1150, the spatial extent of the Hohokam and their ceramic ware decreased. Snaketown was largely abandoned, and the surrounding Gila Basin was partially depopulated. Hohokam settlement then concentrated in the lower Salt River Valley, where several villages grew very large, and the irrigation network reached environmental limitations on expansion. Pithouse villages were largely replaced by rectangular adobe enclosures built aboveground, possibly for defensive purposes. Platform mounds continued to be constructed, while ball courts declined. In some instances, residential compounds, possibly associated with higher-status households, were placed on the mounds. Multistory structures were built at some sites. Although an explanation for these changes is not well established, they do indicate that a political reorganization occurred.

When the first Spanish explorers entered the Phoenix Basin, the Hohokam were gone. The irrigation systems were abandoned, and the large villages, with their associated mounds and ball courts, lay in ruins. The Pima and Papago Indians, who consider the area to be their historic homeland, were the desert's only inhabitants and resided in small, scattered villages. Hohokam is their name for the people responsible for the ruins; the word can be translated as "those who have gone."

While archaeologists have postulated many reasons for the Hohokam demise—climatic change, invasion, flooding, environmental degradation, political collapse—no single factor seems sufficient to explain this abandonment. Yet the Hohokam left a lasting imprint on the desert landscape. Their ability to master the desert is testimony to the sophistication of Hohokam engineering skills. This fact was not lost on the early European settlers, who reexcavated and used some of the long-abandoned Hohokam canals. Several canals still in use today in Phoenix follow the route and grade of the ancient waterways.

was cut into bracelets, rings, pendants, beads, and ornaments decorated with designs etched with acid. Stone was fashioned into beads, earplugs, ornaments, carved paint palettes, axes with deep grooves for hafting, and vessels with animals in relief. Lizards were a common motif.

Other large Hohokam villages also were present in the region, especially in the Salt River Valley to the north. Although the residents of Snaketown dug several canals, it was along the lower Salt River of the Phoenix Basin that the Hohokam constructed the largest prehistoric irrigation system north of Mexico. At its largest extent, this irrigation network consisted of 14 main canals, ranging from several kilometers up to 20 km (12.5 mi) in length, that drew water from the river, and hundreds of smaller canals that carried water to the fields. Canal irrigation required a large labor investment, first to dig the canals and then to maintain and repair them.

Over the last three decades, archaeologists have paid increasing attention to the analysis of village or site plans. These studies, which require the excavation of broad horizontal areas to expose sets of associated dwellings and features, are a means of examining settlement patterns at the scale of the community. The size and spacing of houses, as well as other archaeological features—storage facilities, cemetery areas, ritual structures, for instance—can provide researchers with information on ancient household size, the nature and arrangement of social units above the level of the household, and the association of households with storage and other social and economic activities.

In the American Southwest, a long history of archaeological community pattern analysis extends back to the broad horizontal excavations conducted at pithouse villages along the Mogollon Rim by the late Paul Martin, of the Field Museum in Chicago. In a classic study, James Hill, of the University of California, Los Angeles, used architectural and artifactual indicators to identify differences in room function at Broken K Pueblo, a late prehistoric Mogollon settlement in eastern Arizona.

More recently, David Wilcox and his colleagues have made a detailed study of ancient community structure at Snaketown. Wilcox began by identifying houses that were occupied contemporaneously. He then mapped the location and orientation of each set of houses that were inhabited during the same phase. Wilcox noted when the doorways of contemporaneous structures opened onto a shared courtyard. He found that house clusters from the early occupations at Snaketown usually consisted of only two associated structures. Later residential clusters at the site had as many as six houses around a plaza. Based on his analysis, Wilcox suggests that the people residing in each cluster of houses formed an extended family group and possibly shared certain domestic activities.

Most of the Snaketown houses have similar internal features, such as small hearths near the entrance. Other domestic activities were conducted in the shared outdoor space. Outside work areas included several types of hearths, as well as postholes that seem to mark the former position of windbreaks or brush kitchens. The inside hearths were too small to hold pieces of wood large enough to produce adequate coals for cooking, which may have been done outside on a cooperative basis.

Houses within each cluster were arranged at right angles to each other, defining rectangular courtyard areas. In general, clusters that contained the most houses also had the biggest courtyard areas. Over time, the location and orientation of the houses within a courtyard area showed considerable continuity, suggesting that residential placement was not random. Most larger household clusters included one structure that was square, as opposed to the usual oblong or rectangular shape. The square structures may have been used for special or ritual activities.

After A.D. 900, the largest clusters of houses at Snaketown were situated at the core of the site near major platforms and a central plaza. These larger house clusters contained more total floor area than the house clusters at the edge of the site. The emergence of these large clusters, possibly signifying increased differentiation between family groups, occurred in conjunction with a greater emphasis on civic-ceremonial construction. Some scholars suggest these are indicators for increasing sociopolitical complexity.

STUDYING COMMUNITY PLAN AT SNAKETOWN

Household clusters at Snaketown

One objective of community studies is the examination of cohort groups at the residential level. Such units are important components (building blocks) within the social, settlement, and subsistence systems, and are for that reason a significant focus of archaeological research.

G. Rice (1987)

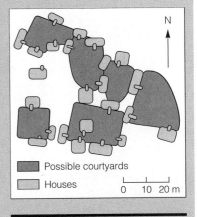

Possible courtyards

Houses

0   10   20 m

N

The distribution of pithouses and courtyards in one area of Snaketown, around A.D. 900–1100.

CHACO CANYON

A prehistoric regional center in the American Southwest

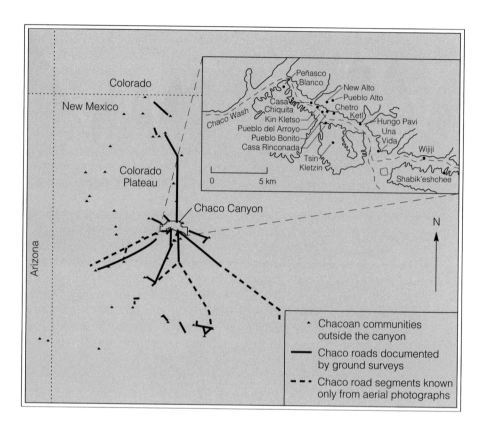

A map of Chaco Canyon, showing the principal towns and roads and the early village of Shabik'eshchee.

A black-on-white Anasazi pottery vessel.

The Four Corners region of the Southwest—the junction of Arizona, New Mexico, Colorado, and Utah—is dominated by an extensive highland (elevation above 1500 m, 5000 ft) called the Colorado Plateau. The plateau is drained by the Colorado River and its tributaries, which have cut a complex topography of mesas, buttes, valleys, and canyons into the landscape. Located in a remote part of northwestern Mexico, Chaco Canyon is one of the largest of these erosion features.

Chaco (chah'ko) Canyon, 15 km (9 mi) long, has a sandy bottom and little permanent water. The bleak environment lacks trees and experiences dramatic temperature extremes. Rainfall, characterized by infrequent summer cloudbursts that cause washes to fill temporarily with water, is marginal for farming. Today the area is seldom used for agriculture, but once it was a center of prehistoric settlement and long-distance exchange. The Native Americans depended on rainfall for **floodwater farming,** in which they channeled seasonal runoff to agricultural fields, to supplement the water supply.

Several of the most spectacular ruins anywhere in the Southwest are located in Chaco Canyon. Although brief reports of these ruins extend back to the mid-seventeenth century when military forays from Spanish outposts entered the area, the first substantial accounts were not published until 1850. At that time, James Simpson, an officer in the Army Topographical Engineers, was sent to the canyon area to investigate claims that the Navajo were harassing isolated farms and ranchos (settlements consisting of only a few houses). Simpson was overwhelmed by the massive walls, which still stood three to four stories high and formed complexes of contiguous rooms. He described and measured many of the prehistoric structures, and many other curious visitors soon followed. In 1906, Chaco Canyon was made a national monument to protect the ruins from destruction by treasure hunters and vandals.

The continuity of past and present Native American groups in the Southwest is most evident between the prehistoric Anasazi, a Navajo word meaning "ancient enemies," and the contemporary Pueblo Indians. Many Pueblo peoples consider the Anasazi area of the Colorado Plateau to be their traditional homeland. Anasazi is now the term used for one of the major prehistoric southwestern cultural traditions that developed out of the hunting-and-gathering adaptation around 2000 years ago. Prior to that time, temporary campsites and kill sites were present on the Chaco Plateau, but not in the canyon itself. The first sedentary Anasazi sites occur around A.D. 100, located on mesas away from the bottomlands of the canyon, possibly for reasons of defense. Most of these sites contained 5–10 shallow pithouses. Over the next several centuries, the diet at most Anasazi sites showed an increasing reliance on domesticated corn, beans, and squash. Yet the collecting of pine or piñon nuts and the hunting of cottontail and jackrabbits, deer, antelope, and Rocky Mountain bighorn sheep remained important.

By the middle of the first millennium A.D., villages, which may have been inhabited year-round, were located on the floor of Chaco Canyon. Once the canyon was occupied, its population grew, and though small sites remained common, some larger communities, with 50–100 pithouses, were established. **Kivas,** semisubterranean ceremonial rooms, were constructed at some sites, and the distinctive black-on-white Anasazi pottery first appeared.

Shabik'eschee (shuh-bik'eh-she), an early village in the Chaco region, has been excavated. Occupied between A.D. 550 and 750, the settlement had as many as 68 pit dwellings, a large kiva, numerous outdoor storage pits, and two large refuse heaps. Because roughly half of the excavated structures were intentionally dismantled to provide construction materials for later buildings, it seems unlikely that the entire village was inhabited simultaneously.

At Shabik'eshchee, the sides of the pithouses were lined with stone slabs and coated with mud plaster. The roofs were supported by four posts topped with crossbeams. The upper walls of the houses were formed by leaning poles and sticks against the crossbeams to the ground surface outside the excavated pit. The walls were coated with a mixture of mud, twigs, and bark. One entered the house through a small antechamber. Inside the main chamber of the house was a centrally located hearth. The kiva was larger than the pithouses, and unlike the pithouses, the interior kiva walls were encircled by a low bench.

Sometime after A.D. 700, aboveground rectangular rooms of adobe or roughly layered masonry were constructed in the Anasazi area. At first these structures may have been used for storage, while pithouses continued to serve as dwellings. In later communities, pithouses were used largely as kivas, while most dwellings were of adobe bricks and placed aboveground. The Anasazi were the first in the Southwest to build compact villages of contiguous rectangular rooms, with different areas for habitation, storage, and ceremonial activities. For the most part, these later communities were situated at lower elevations, closer to the bottomlands, perhaps reflecting an increasing reliance on agricultural resources.

After A.D. 900, there was a considerable shift in settlement as population congregated in larger, apartmentlike **pueblos,** stonemasonry complexes of adjoining rooms. Clusters of adjacent rooms served as the residences for separate families or lineages. Chaco Canyon supported at least nine large towns, or "great houses," of several hundred rooms each (see Color Plate 10), plus hundreds of smaller villages of 10–20 rooms each. The towns were large, multistory complexes, standing as high as four stories at the back wall, and averaging 288 rooms, some of which were large with

The many questions that remain unanswered about the Chacoan regional system signify both the accomplishments and the challenges of Southwestern archaeologists interested in the problem of sociopolitical development. After nearly a century of survey and excavation throughout Chaco Canyon and the San Juan Basin, investigators have accumulated sufficient settlement pattern, burial, architectural, and artifactual data to conclude that the Chacoan regional system was hierarchically organized. This conclusion has prompted three major questions that will probably guide the next several decades of Chacoan research: How did this complex system develop? What kinds of relationships existed among its different components . . . ? Why did the system collapse? These questions are challenging because they require that Chacoan archaeologists derive testable hypotheses from the various proposed explanatory models and that they then collect and analyze the data necessary for systematically evaluating these hypotheses

J. Neitzel (1989)

Pueblo Bonito. The circular features are kivas. Interior rooms were used for storage, and outer rooms facing the courtyards served as living quarters.

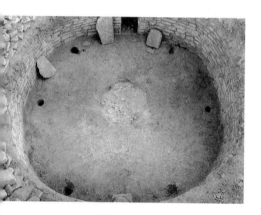

Kiva with fireplace in center.

high ceilings. The towns appear to have been built according to a preconceived plan, and there was a high degree of quality and uniformity in masonry styles. Each town also had at least one "great kiva." Placed in interior courtyards, these large kivas had a central ceremonial role in community activities. Many smaller kivas were located elsewhere in the towns and most likely served as ceremonial chambers for the various kin or family units that comprised the site population. These larger sites served as local centers for resource redistribution, long-distance trade, and ceremonial activities.

The largest and most impressive town, Pueblo Bonito, is 160 × 100 m (525 × 325 ft, or the size of two soccer fields). It is a huge, D-shaped complex composed of over 800 rooms arranged in several stories. At its height, Pueblo Bonito's population may have been as large as 1000 people, although archaeologists disagree on the number of rooms that were residential in character and the proportion of the rooms that were occupied contemporaneously. Situated at the base of a 30-m (100-ft) mesa on the north side of the canyon, the pueblo is protected by the steep cliffs of the canyon.

The occupation of Pueblo Bonito has been precisely dated using **dendrochronology**, the study of the annual growth rings of trees as a dating technique to build chronologies. This highly precise technique, pioneered by A. E. Douglass more than 60 years ago, is based on the recognition that certain trees produced distinctive ring sequences in response to shifts in temperature and precipitation. Based on the work of Douglass and his successors, a continuous tree-ring chronology for the Colorado Plateau has been projected back more than a thousand years. Tree-ring dates obtained from preserved wooden beams at Chaco Canyon place the earliest building at Pueblo Bonito at A.D. 919; town construction apparently was finished by A.D. 1115.

At Pueblo Bonito, the masonry consisted of layers of stone covering an interior core of rock and adobe rubble. The room walls were faced with adobe plaster. The rooms surrounded central courtyards. The outer rooms, which had doors and windows facing onto the courtyard, served as living quarters, and interior rooms were used for storage. The most elevated rooms were at the back of the

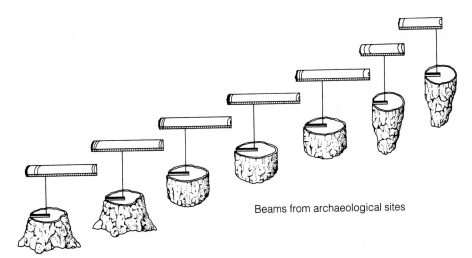

Beams from archaeological sites

Tree stumps from a living tree

Dendrochronology. The matching of tree rings from a modern tree with a known cutting date to those of progressively older tree samples results in a long sequence of distinctive tree-ring patterns that can be used to date beams from archaeological sites.

complex along its outer rim. These back rooms included one great kiva and several smaller ones. This great kiva, the largest in the community, measured 20 m (65 ft) in diameter and was encircled by a wide masonry bench.

From A.D. 1020 to 1130, the Chacoan system peaked in population and spatial size. Much of the population of the northern Southwest participated in the regional trading network centered at Chaco Canyon. Throughout this network, which covered over 53,000 sq km (20,500 sq mi), there were at least 125 planned towns with distinctive Chacoan architecture. Settlements were linked by a complex of roads radiating from the canyon, built in straight lines, not contoured to the topography, with ramps and stairways ascending the cliffs. Some were lined with masonry curbs, and some were up to 9 m (30 ft) wide, leading to sites up to 190 km (120 mi) away.

Chacoan towns evidently had the capability of mobilizing large labor parties for construction. Timber was cut from forests up to 80 km (50 mi) away. Imported turquoise was worked in Chaco Canyon; some scholars have suggested it functioned as a medium of exchange. Such exotic goods as **jet**, turquoise, shell bracelets, iron pyrite mosaics, conch shell trumpets, ornamental copper bells, and macaw feathers are found more frequently at the large central town sites than at smaller villages.

The Chaco regional system was disrupted in the mid-1100s. The popula-

tion declined, although complete abandonment of the canyon did not occur for almost 200 years. The demographic collapse in the canyon coincided with population increases in other parts of the Colorado Plateau, including surrounding upland regions. In many areas, Anasazi villages shifted to well-protected, defensive locations, such as the sheltered cliffs at Mesa Verde in southwestern Colorado. Defense was a likely motive in the resettlement of some Anasazi villages, and this pattern may reflect an era of political instability that followed the collapse of the Chacoan centers.

By roughly A.D. 1300, the Anasazi region went through another major restructuring, and many Pueblo sites were again abandoned. When Europeans arrived in the Southwest, only a small number of large nucleated settlements remained. Whether these episodes of dispersal and reorganization (first at Chaco and later in other parts of the Anasazi region) were triggered by climatic change, environmental degradation, shifting trade connections, changing political alliances, or a series of other factors remains a matter of conjecture and discussion. While the causes of these abandonments are still debated, the construction and maintenance of Pueblo Bonito, a structure that was the largest apartment building erected in the United States prior to the nineteenth century, in a dry desolate canyon, remains a powerful testament to the ingenuity of the Native Americans who lived there.

A cross section of ponderosa pine with a 108-year lifespan.

OZETTE

A prehistoric Northwest Coast whaling village

Ozette Village, located on the outer coast of the Olympic Peninsula. Cabins of the archaeologists are in the right foreground, with the excavated site just to their left.

The Pacific Coast of Oregon, Washington, and British Columbia is an environmentally rich area where land and sea hold a wealth of natural resources. The sea and the rivers contain mollusks and many species of fish, including salmon, halibut, cod, and herring. Sea mammals—such as seal, sea lion, otter, porpoise, and whale—thrive in the offshore waters. Waterfowl can be found along the shore, and farther inland there are deer, elk, bear, and other smaller animals. The area has a heavy forest cover of fir, spruce, cedar, and some deciduous trees. Although vegetable foods are less plentiful, many species of berries abound.

The earliest known inhabitants of the Pacific Northwest were mobile hunter-gatherers who moved into the area before 8000 B.C. At first, coastal foods did not comprise a major portion of the diet, but by 2000–3000 B.C., the accumulation of large shell middens at several sites indicates an increasing use of the readily available marine shellfish. Over the last 2000 years, subsistence patterns have continued to emphasize the exploitation of fish, shellfish, and sea mammals, supplemented by land mammals and birds. Such plant foods as berries, roots, and bulbs were not staples, but they were available during lean times of the year.

In later prehistory, the peoples of the Pacific Northwest were specialized hunter-gatherers who lived in permanent villages and developed large food surpluses by exploiting a variety of fish species. Although subsistence was based on wild resources, many of these societies had specialists in hunting, fishing, curing, and toolmaking. Large, permanent settlements of several hundred people appeared by A.D. 1000, despite the absence of agriculture. The abundance of giant cedar trees provided plentiful material for building houses and making dugout canoes. The natural wealth of the environment and the range of available foods allowed for the production of surplus goods and ornate material items, such as decorative wood carvings, including **totem poles,** carved boxes, canoes, and masks, as well as cedar bark baskets and textiles. Canoes made long-distance travel possible, facilitating the gathering of seasonal resources, the hunting of sea mammals, and the maintenance of far-reaching social networks.

Archaeological evidence indicates that social ranking appeared on the Northwest Coast by 500 B.C. At the time of European contact, all individuals in some Pacific Coast societies were ranked into a series of relatively higher and lower statuses, according to both heredity and wealth. There were chiefs and slaves and, in between, craftsmen, hunters, and fishermen. Most respected of all were the whale hunters. Whaling could be undertaken only by men from wealthy families; it was a hereditary right. Only chiefs possessed the necessary wealth to build whaling canoes, to outfit them, and to assemble the crew. Hunting whales in these large, oceangoing canoes was very dangerous. Bringing home one whale brought enormous prestige to a family, in addition to vast amounts of food.

One well-known Pacific Northwest settlement, Ozette, is located on the coast of Washington's Olympic Peninsula at Cape Alava, the westernmost point of the contiguous 48 states. Because the cape juts out into the Pacific Ocean, Ozette is close to the migration routes of a variety of whales, including gray, humpback, and sperm whale. The shoreline is a crescent-shaped beach protected by points of land, an offshore reef, and small islands. Abundant sea resources and a rich forest behind the beach made the cape an attractive location for prehistoric Native American groups. People settled in the area over 2000 years ago, and eventually Ozette grew into a major whaling village. Ozette is unique in that it was one of a few major whaling villages south of Alaska. Two other sites south of Ozette on the coast are located near quiet bays. Their long, straight beaches are washed by a rolling surf, making canoe travel much more difficult than at Ozette. In addition, sea mammals pass too far offshore to be worth hunting. As a consequence, these two sites show less reliance on ocean resources. Rather, the inhabitants focused on the bay and land resources, such as deer, elk, harbor seals, and salmon, in addition to oysters, mussels, and clams.

The village of Ozette stretched for almost a mile along the coast and had a maximum population of roughly 800 people. It is thought to have been a major settlement of the Makah Indians, a group that still resides on the Olympic Peninsula today. Although the population of Ozette declined after Europeans began to settle in the area during the mid-nineteenth century, it continued to be occupied until the late 1920s. Today, there are few surface remnants of the village left. Richard Daugherty, of Washington State University, began excavations at the site in the late 1960s when told of native accounts of mudslides that were believed to have periodically buried parts of the site. However, the actual discovery of the buried village area occurred accidentally after a violent winter storm in 1970. The harsh waves of the storm eroded sections of a bank and exposed a number of timbers, baskets, boxes, paddles, and other wooden artifacts, which were discovered by hikers. That spring, Daugherty began excavation of the buried houses.

Part of Ozette has been preserved by a massive mudslide that buried five houses around A.D. 1400–1500. Because the heavy layer of clay sealed these houses and kept out oxygen, perishable artifacts of wood and fiber, which normally do not preserve well in the wet environment of the Northwest Coast, could be recovered. Since the village was occupied at the time of the mudslide, the excavated material represents the entire range of wooden artifacts that were used

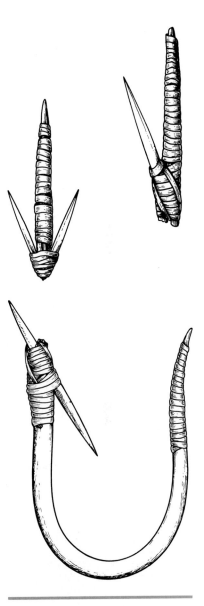

Examples of fishhooks made from bone and wrapped with bark.

A carved wooden bowl from Ozette.

A basket woven of cedar bark.

by a Northwest Coast household. In addition to the wooden planks and posts of the houses, the excavators recovered baskets, mats, hats, **tumplines** (carrying straps), halibut hook shanks, arrow shafts, harpoons, finely carved wooden clubs and combs, box fragments, bowls, wood wedges, and a variety of fishhooks and barbed fish points (used on the end of a spear to stab fish in the water). In total, over 42,000 artifacts were recovered.

As a result of the region's abundant rainfall and high groundwater, Ozette is water-saturated, like many other sites on the Northwest Coast. This condition has made normal excavation procedures difficult. When trowels and shovels were used, as they are on most excavations, they sliced through and gouged the fragile wood and fiber. To deal with this problem, a method called **wet-site excavation** was developed. With this technique, water is pumped through garden hoses and sprayed onto the deposits to remove the dirt and expose the archaeological materials. Excavators use high water pressure to remove the heavy clay deposits and lower pressure to remove dirt from more fragile artifacts. This procedure works well because the water pressure can be adjusted continually to expose an artifact without dislocating or destroying it. By using a very fine spray, excavators can carefully reveal and remove even the remains of basketry and other fibers.

The excavated houses at Ozette were very large, some 20 m (60 ft) long and 10 m (33 ft) wide, about the size of a tennis court. They were constructed of cedar planks, some up to 0.5 m (1.5 ft) wide, supported by upright wooden posts, and held in place with twisted cedar twigs. Roof boards were overlapped to keep out the rain. Raised platforms ringed the inside walls and were used for sleeping and storage. Most of the recovered artifacts were found in association with these platforms. The existence of several hearths in each house suggests that these large structures were occupied by more than one nuclear family. In one house, the highest-ranking family apparently lived in the left-rear quarter; ceremonial gear and whaling harpoons were found there. In this area, a woven cedar bark hat, traditionally worn by individuals of high status in later times, also was recovered. In another house, wood chips associated with woodworking activities were found.

Excavations at Ozette have provided ample evidence for the extensive hunting of sea mammals. Whale bones were found in the earliest levels, indicating that the prestige and practice of whaling dates back at least 2000 years. Many whale bones also were found in later levels; some of the bone was used in house foundations, to shore up walls, or to divert water and mud from sliding down the hillside onto the backs of the structures. At low tide, a cleared strip through the offshore rocks is still visible. Centuries ago, canoes could have taken this route to the open waters to encounter the migrating whales. Artifacts associated with whaling—parts of canoes, canoe paddles, and whaling harpoons—were plentiful at the site. The people of Ozette

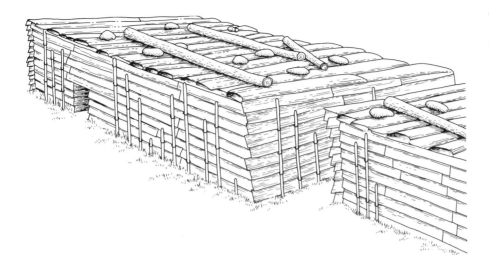

An artist's interpretation of a house at Ozette.

also hunted other sea mammals, including fur seal, porpoise, dolphin, and sea lion, which constituted the majority of mammal bones at the site. Elk and deer bones were present, but in small amounts. Although salmon bones were few at Ozette, halibut, ling cod, and shellfish were well represented.

The importance of maritime resources is also evident 3 km (2 mi) south on the beach at Wedding Rock, where at least 44 **petroglyphs,** drawings carved on rocks, have been found on beach boulders. Whale motifs are especially prevalent, including one of a pregnant whale. Although a rich ceremonialism on the Northwest Coast was associated with the hunting of sea mammals, especially whales, there is no definitive evidence that the petroglyphs were used as part of such ceremonies. One possible function of the carvings may have been to gain supernatural power over the inhabitants of the sea. Whale hunters may have made the petroglyphs to ensure good luck on whaling trips or to commemorate other important events. No method of dating the petroglyphs is yet available. However, the Wedding Rock art may have been made at the same time that the excavated houses at Ozette were inhabited, because several of the carved motifs are also present on artifacts recovered from the site.

Petroglyphs of whales and human faces at Wedding Rock near Ozette.

CHIEFS

Hereditary leadership among native North Americans

Nineteenth-century potlatch mask.

The first Europeans on the North American continent encountered a wide variety of social and political organizations among Native Americans. Some groups were organized as bands or tribes, with little formal variation in the status or rank of individuals. People filled different roles according to their talents and achievements. At the other end of the spectrum were a number of groups in which positions of authority were inherited at birth. At the top of this hierarchy of social rank were chiefs, who held political authority over individuals in the society. Native American chiefs engaged in a wide range of activities, including intersocietal politics, ceremonial leadership, and declarations of war. Yet none of these chiefly societies was as hierarchically organized or socially stratified as the largest polities to the south.

In the Americas before European contact, chiefs usually were associated with agricultural societies. Although food surpluses can be produced by most, if not all, economies, it often is easier to produce a storable surplus with agriculture. Domesticated plants are generally easier to store than wild resources, and they tend to produce a greater return per unit of land. Chiefs can extract or control food surpluses; they also can encourage their kinsmen to work to produce beyond their immediate needs. In the southeastern United States, such large sites as Cahokia and Moundville were located in very fertile areas. The large mortuary mounds and burials accompanied by elaborate grave goods indicate the presence of powerful chiefs at these sites.

Chiefs also were present in some societies that did not practice agriculture. Most societies on the Northwest Coast were based on hunting and gathering. Their economies focused on a rich and diverse base of marine resources, which permitted the accumulation of surplus. These societies also had complex social organizations and hierarchies of social rank. Only people from the highest-ranking families could become chiefs.

Chiefs did not necessarily return all the produce they collected. This surplus provided the capital to obtain exotic goods through trade. Much chiefly exchange involved the acquisition of high-status items that were either traded to establish new allies or loaned to attract followers. Often a chief's power could be measured by the number of allies and dependents he could mobilize for specific tasks.

Although the position of chief was largely acquired along hereditary lines, personal achievements also were important. Among Northwest Coast Native American groups, only high-ranking individuals could attain the position of chief. But one's role as chief had to be validated continually; failure to do so resulted in a loss of status. One way chiefs validated their position was by publicly displaying their wealth and distributing their accumulated property. At the time of European contact in the Northwest, an elaborate ceremonialism had developed, based on the **potlatch,** a large feast that included the display and dispersal of accumulated wealth to assembled guests. The mere possession of wealth did not confer prestige. But by distributing the wealth, the chief created social debts and obligations that could be called in and used to bolster his position at a later date. A potlatch gave the host far greater prestige than selling or trading, yet in economic terms the result was relatively similar: the redistribution of goods. Politically, the quest for prestige gave momentum to the whole system; the more a chief gave away, the greater his status.

To date, most archaeological interpretations have emphasized the functional or managerial advantages, especially the mitigation of food crises, associated with the emergence of chiefs. Yet such arguments are incomplete; in many cases the likelihood of major crop failures requiring chiefly intervention was low. The construction of complete explanations requires that archaeologists extend consideration beyond the benefits of chiefly societies to the political strategies of emergent leaders and the factors that allowed those strategies to work.

THE CLASH OF
WORLDS

*Changing perspectives on native
North Americans*

When European settlers and slaves from Africa first penetrated the lands of the New World north of Mexico in the sixteenth, seventeenth, and eighteenth centuries, they observed huge earthen mounds at sites in the east that were no longer inhabited, as well as well-planned mud-brick ruins in the west. Blinded by the **ethnocentrism** of the era, many of the early explorers failed to recognize any of the obvious historical connections between the land's indigenous peoples and the impressive architectural features. Frequently, the Euro-American traders and adventurers speculated that the great earthworks and pueblos were remnants of earlier constructions built by Romans, Vikings, Celts, or people from imaginary lands, like Atlantis. Few early explorers were willing to accept the possibility that the ruins were part of the heritage of Native American peoples, whose lands and resources they coveted. Sadly, such migrationist views are still all-too-frequently advanced (and may even attract occasional popular attention today), although they remain entirely without solid empirical support. (Some authors have gone so far as to postulate extraterrestrial contacts!)

Fortunately, there were exceptions, like Thomas Jefferson, who held a serious interest in the origins of the native North Americans. In the 1780s (before being elected President), Jefferson carefully excavated a burial mound on his property in order to address a series of questions that were posed in a French government questionnaire that was sent to him as governor of Virginia. Some of the queries concerned the aboriginal population of the state. Jefferson's reasoned, stratigraphic analysis showed that the excavated mound represented several discrete interment episodes, with each burial group covered and separated by a layer of stones and earth. The absence of wounds on the bodies and the presence of children suggested to Jefferson that the burials were not related to warfare or militarism, as others had surmised. He correctly concluded that the mound was constructed by the ancestors of the Native Americans who were encountered by early European colonists of Virginia.

In the nineteenth century, a principal focus of early North American anthropology was the Native American, in the past as well as in the present. Information was collected from archaeological evidence, early historical accounts, and contemporary observations. Continuities in language, ritual, and material culture were emphasized in an effort to confirm the historical relationships between living indigenous peoples, past documentary records that described the aboriginal inhabitants of North America, and artifact inventories. Although many of the associations between present and past were reasoned and justified (laying the foundation for twentieth-century archaeology and anthropology), the absence of an adequate time scale (no absolute dating techniques were yet invented) contributed to the occasional overreliance on contemporary or historical records to interpret the archaeological past. Archaeology depends on inspirations, clues, analogies, and models from more recent times to help flesh out the past. Yet archaeologists studying the prehistory of North America, as well as other areas, should be prepared to recognize changes that occurred during prehistory and immediately thereafter. Prehistoric peoples may have had a way of life and organizational formations that were markedly different from those recorded in written texts.

Many studies have documented that the contact period, the sixteenth through eighteenth centuries, was a time of great change for most, if not all, native North American groups. In many areas, such as the Southeast, Native Americans not only were savaged in combat with the Euro-American invaders (such as the nine shiploads of *conquistadores,* led by Hernando de Soto, who landed on the coast of Florida in 1539), but also were vanquished by infectious, epidemic diseases (influenza, smallpox, measles, and whooping cough) introduced to the New World. Because the aboriginal peoples had no immunity to these diseases, their effect often was calamitous, decimating the native populations. In many regions, the impact of disease may have been further intensified by social and economic dislocations occurring at the same time. Regardless of the specific causes, many Native American populations had been severely ravaged and disrupted in demographic size, subsistence, and sociopolitical organization when they first were encountered by more permanent settlers (and eventually anthropologists) during the seventeenth, eighteenth, and nineteenth centuries. As a consequence, anthropologists and archaeologists must be careful about relying too specifically on direct analogies between ethnohistoric, as well as early ethnographic, accounts and the deeper past that we see through archaeology. Nevertheless, many aspects of tradition, belief, and religion do show significant continuities between precontact and postcontact times.

The history of European colonial expansion following the late 15th century is riddled with a multitude of curious and seemingly inexplicable encounters between native cultures and Europeans, which demand the conjoining of historical and anthropological methods.

J. L. Hantman (1990)

When the Europeans first arrived in North America, few, if any, sites as large as Cahokia in the Midwest or the pueblos of Chaco Canyon in the Southwest appear to have been inhabited, or were described. Yet this fact should not lead us to doubt the Native American heritage of these sites, nor force us to inhibit our interpretation of the past by assuming that the archaeological settlements were organized in exactly the same way as the ethnographically observed inhabitants of the respective regions.

Such variation should not be surprising, because, as noted at the start of the chapter, diversity in both space and time seems to have been a key feature of the Native American way of life. In part, spatial variation may have been related to the great environmental differences that characterize the North American continent. At times, cultural changes may have been responses to documented episodes of climatic transitions. Yet such environmental factors alone cannot explain the range of prehistoric variability. Perhaps the smaller and less stratified social systems that occupied North America were generally more flexible and organizationally (and demographically) fluid than the more complex, hierarchical polities that developed in much of Middle and South America (see Chapters 8 and 9), as well as in a good portion of the Old World (see Chapter 10). Such flexibility and fluidity also may help account for the great cultural diversity of the prehistoric North American peoples.

Most people are interested in their past, their forebears, their roots. Where did they come from? How did they make their living? What were their ways of life? Our interest is generated by an almost innate understanding that our past has influenced and shaped the present. While some people show no concern with the past, others believe that the past is no different than the present, or that the only thing one needs to know about the past is written in holy scriptures. Still others may be afraid of the political or cultural realities that one may find by studying the past. Obviously, we as archaeologists agree with the English poet G. K. Chesterton, who wrote: "The disadvantage of men not knowing the past is that they do not know the present. History is a hill or a high point of vantage, from which alone men see the town in which they live or the age in which they are living" (1933, p. 105).

As people tend to be most interested in their own ancestral roots, it is not surprising that Euro-American archaeology got off to an earlier start in Europe than did systematic archaeological research in North America. This circumstance may help account for the popularity of migrationist views in the history of the latter. European countries also enacted antiquity legislation, protecting archaeological resources from destruction, decades prior to the passing of such laws by North American governments. And even today, most European nations devote more resources per capita to studying local prehistory than North American countries do. At the same time, as

Euro-American archaeologists investigate the prehistory of North America, they must remember that they are helping establish the history of living peoples—Native Americans—who care just as much (if not more) about their ancestral heritage.

Although there are gaps in this knowledge, anthropological archaeology has established that Native Americans inhabited the vast tracts of North America for close to 12,000 years. It is clear that they adjusted and adapted to highly variable environmental conditions through a broad array of social and cultural traditions and strategies. These lifeways changed over time, generally gradually, but sometimes more rapidly. Archaeologists should be sensitive to these realities, as well as to the past and present diversity of Native American peoples. We should also remember that archaeological data have a significant role to play in liberating Native American history from an exclusive reliance on documentary sources, which are primarily products of Euro-American culture.

SUGGESTED READINGS

Coe, M., D. Snow, and E. Benson. 1986. *Atlas of ancient America.* New York: Facts on File. *An elaborately illustrated volume covering all of the Americas, with excellent maps.*

Cordell, L. S. 1997. *Archaeology of the Southwest.* 2d ed. San Diego: Academic Press. *The best current synthesis of archaeology in the American Southwest.*

Crown, P. L., and W. J. Judge, eds. 1991. *Chaco and Hohokam: Prehistoric regional systems in the American Southwest.* Santa Fe, NM: School of American Research. *A scholarly compendium of papers that compare and contrast regional variation in southwestern prehistory.*

Fagan, B. 1996. *Ancient North America.* 2d ed. London: Thames & Hudson. *An amply illustrated synthesis of North American archaeology.*

Feder, K. L. 2000. *Frauds, myths, and mysteries: Science and pseudoscience in archaeology.* 3rd ed. Mountain View, CA: Mayfield. *An entertaining and informative exploration of fascinating frauds and genuine mysteries that relate to the human past.*

Fiedel, S. J. 1992. *Prehistory of the Americas.* 2d ed. Cambridge: Cambridge University Press. *A general overview for the ancient Americas.*

Jennings, J., ed. 1983. *Ancient North Americans.* New York: Freeman. *A collection of articles summarizing North American prehistory, each one written by an expert in the region.*

8

ANCIENT MESOAMERICA

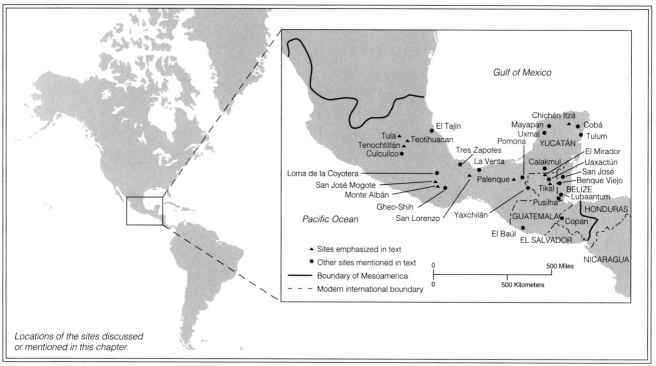

Gulf of Mexico

Chichén Itzá
Mayapan • Cobá
Uxmal • Tulum
Pomona YUCATÁN
El Tajín
Tula ▲ Teotihuacan El Mirador
Tenochtitlán ▲ Tres Zapotes Uaxactún
Culcuilco • La Venta Calakmul San José
Loma de la Coyotera Palenque ▲ Benque Viejo
San José Mogote Tikal BELIZE
Monte Albán Lubaantum
Gheo-Shih Pusilha HONDURAS
San Lorenzo Yaxchilán GUATEMALA Copán
Pacific Ocean El Baúl
EL SALVADOR

NICARAGUA

▲ Sites emphasized in text
● Other sites mentioned in text
── Boundary of Mesoamerica
--- Modern international boundary

0   500 Miles
0   500 Kilometers

Locations of the sites discussed or mentioned in this chapter.

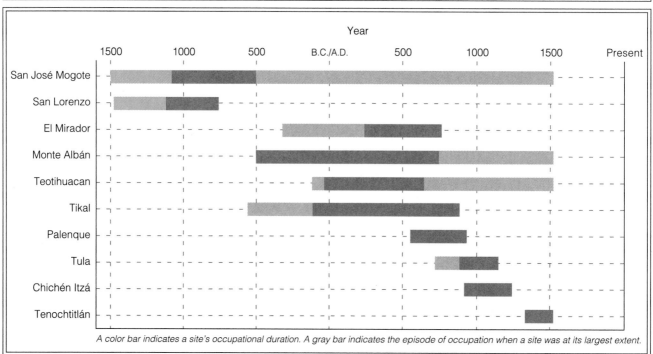

Year

| 1500 | 1000 | 500 | B.C./A.D. | 500 | 1000 | 1500 | Present |

San José Mogote
San Lorenzo
El Mirador
Monte Albán
Teotihuacan
Tikal
Palenque
Tula
Chichén Itzá
Tenochtitlán

A color bar indicates a site's occupational duration. A gray bar indicates the episode of occupation when a site was at its largest extent.

EARLY STATE DEVELOPMENT IN MESOAMERICA

The Aztecs, the Maya, and their neighbors

Archaeologists and other social scientists define a **state** as an internally specialized and hierarchically organized political formation that administers large and complex polities. States are associated with populations that are socially and economically stratified. In these societies, wealth, social status, and political power generally are inherited, whereas in unstratified societies such advantages are most often achieved through personal skills and experience. While some archaeologists have suggested that Cahokia, in the midwestern United States, was at the center of a short-lived state organization (see Chapter 7), most researchers argue that state formation in the New World did not occur north of Mexico before European contact.

Indigenous or pristine states, institutions that developed relatively free of significant external contact or outside influence, arose in Mesoamerica, South America, Southwest Asia, and China. The rise of these early polities, and several cases of secondary and tertiary state development, are presented in this chapter, as well as in Chapters 9 and 10. In this chapter (Mesoamerica) and Chapter 9 (South America), we take a more historical approach in surveying the complex processes surrounding the rise of civilizations in two areas of the New World. Although comparisons are made throughout, we adopt a more deliberately comparative perspective in Chapter 10, where we discuss early civilizations from several parts of the Old World. Chapter 10 concludes with a discussion of some of the theories that have been advanced to explain state origins.

The first indigenous states were established in the Near East during the fourth millennium B.C. For that reason, some of you may wish to review Chapter 10 before reading Chapters 8 and 9. Because so many of the theories about state origins were constructed with the Near Eastern cases in mind, we thought it would be helpful to consider these different explanations in Chapter 10 in conjunction with the Old World examples. We also wanted to discuss these theoretical positions after we had considered the variability of early states. For that reason, we begin our discussion with Mesoamerica, drawing comparisons between the highland polities (such as Teotihuacan) and those of the Maya lowlands. We then move to Andean South America in Chapter 9, where we consider some of the similarities and differences between the prehispanic Andean and Mesoamerican worlds. In Chapter 10, we offer a more global, synthetic perspective.

When Hernán Cortés and his Spanish *conquistadores* landed on the eastern coast of Mexico in A.D. 1519, they encountered a remarkably diverse landscape of cultures and environments. The terrain is a complex vertical mosaic of snow-capped volcanic peaks and arid highland valleys, lush tropical forests, "scrubby" plains, swampy lowlands and estuaries, and beautiful sand beaches. The climate ranges from the arctic cold of high mountain summits to sweltering heat at sea level, and climatic and topographic variability results in a rich mosaic of animal and plant life. Before the 1519 arrival of the Spanish, Mesoamerica—which includes central and southern Mexico, the Yucatán peninsula, and the northern parts of Central America—was also a world

CONTENTS

305

of enormous linguistic and ethnic differences. The prehispanic inhabitants spoke many languages, employed a wide range of farming and water-control strategies, and inhabited towns and cities of diverse form and function.

Yet the peoples of Mesoamerica also shared a great deal, including a reliance on similar staple foods, widespread trade, and related religious systems. This shared ceremonial realm included a calendar, stepped pyramids, ritual sacrifice of blood, writing systems, and specific styles of dress. The dietary "trinity" of corn, beans, and squash (supplemented by avocado and chili peppers) provided a remarkably nutritious diet. Maize (corn) provides most of the essential amino acids for building protein; lysine, a missing ingredient, is present in beans. An enzyme in squash contributes to the digestion of the protein in beans. Maize extracts nitrogen from the earth in which it grows; beans release nitrogen back to the soil. Corn and squash are rich in carbohydrates and calories. Beans and the avocado provide fat. The chili pepper, a regular condiment in Mesoamerican meals, is high in vitamins and aids in the digestion of high-cellulose foods.

As discussed in Chapter 6, corn, beans, and squash were domesticated by 5000–7000 years ago in the highlands of Mexico, where the wild ancestors of these plants still grow side by side. These domesticated plants spread throughout Mesoamerica by 2000 B.C. At about this same time, perhaps a few centuries earlier, people began to make simple pottery in the shape of squashes and gourds. Yet it was not for centuries (roughly 1800–1500 B.C.) that we find the first permanent farming villages in this region. This pattern differs from what we saw in parts of North America (see Chapter 7), where some residential stability was present prior to reliance on domesticated plants. The sequence of development in highland Mesoamerica appears to be the domestication of plants, followed by the invention of ceramics, and then the emergence of village society. Once the indigenous peoples of Mesoamerica had adopted a sedentary farming lifeway, the advent of the region's earliest cities and states followed after roughly 1000 years. The Spanish conquest 2000 years later effectively terminated the indigenous rule of native Mesoamerican civilizations.

Information about those civilizations and their predecessors comes from a number of sources, including Spanish accounts, prehispanic texts, archaeology, and **ethnography,** the study of culture from firsthand observation. The Spanish conquerors and priests kept diaries and descriptions of their impressions of this New World, which often incorporated the remembrances of indigenous confidants as well. These ethnohistoric sources provide an invaluable record of ancient Mesoamerican customs, beliefs, and individual histories at the time of European contact. However, they also provide an incomplete and often ethnocentric picture of the prehispanic past.

Scholars also derive information from the texts of the prehispanic peoples themselves. These records include both short accounts, written more than a millennium ago on stones, murals, and pottery, and a few later (and generally longer) books, or **codices.** The surviving codices, written on bark paper or animal skins, date principally to the end of the prehispanic era. The religious zeal of the Spanish resulted in the destruction of much that was native, including the burning of many books, the razing of temples and palaces, and the destruction of the priesthood. Decipherment of the surviving written accounts, particularly those of the ancient Maya, has greatly enhanced our understanding of rituals, militarism, and rule in prehispanic Mesoamerican civilizations. The native texts are limited in scope and geographic coverage, however, and they reflect a bias toward the events in the lives of the literate elite and rulers.

Ethnographic studies of contemporary peoples in modern Mesoamerica provide information about the organization of agricultural systems and the survival of certain prehispanic customs. Nevertheless, the Spanish presence in Latin America effectively eliminated much of what was native through law, education, and religious doctrine.

Despite these historical and modern sources of information, archaeological research is essential for a basic understanding of the emergence of Mesoamerican cities and civilizations. More than a century of investigations in Mesoamerica has begun to yield significant findings. Major tomb and temple excavations have been conducted in lowland regions of Mesoamerica, where ancient Maya ruins sat virtually undisturbed from the time of their abandonment around A.D. 900, until their rediscovery in the nineteenth century. More recent studies have analyzed villages and the hinterland of ancient cities, temples, and tombs in order to understand the organization and operation of everyday life. In Mexico's Central and Southern Highlands, where archaeological preservation is generally good and ancient ruins are often visible on the present land surface, long-term, multistage archaeological excavation and settlement pattern survey programs have been implemented.

In Mesoamerica, the beginnings of sedentary village life mark the start of the Formative, or Preclassic, period. Studies at San José Mogote document this early stage of village living in highland Mesoamerica. The rapid transformation from simple village society to the construction of impressive ceremonial centers occurred precociously on Mexico's Gulf Coast. San Lorenzo is the earliest of these lowland centers and is roughly contemporaneous with Poverty Point in northeastern Louisiana (see Chapter 7). Recently investigated, El Mirador is unusually large and spectacular for the Maya lowlands, considering its early date.

Late in the Formative period, major urban centers were established in the highlands; hilltop Monte Albán in the Valley of Oaxaca and giant Teotihuacan in central Mexico illustrate this episode of development. Following the onset of the Classic period in A.D. 200–300, Monte Albán and Teotihuacan grew significantly. The latter became one of the largest cities of the world at the time, even larger than Rome. Impressive centers, including Tikal and Palenque, also were built in the Maya lowlands during the Classic era. While the Classic Maya developed Mesoamerica's most sophisticated writing system, none of their centers equaled the population size of Teotihuacan.

Between A.D. 700 and 900, the Mesoamerican world underwent a sequence of upheavals and transitions that included the decline and depopulation of most extant centers. The succeeding Postclassic period was characterized by somewhat greater political fragmentation and fewer architecturally massive centers. Yet places like Tula, on Mesoamerica's northern frontier, and Chichén Itzá, in the northern Yucatán, did rise to power for several centuries. The greatest exception to this Postclassic pattern was Tenochtitlán, which during the last years before Spanish conquest became the largest city in the history of prehispanic Mesoamerica. Although the rulers of the latter center established a tributary domain that stretched as far as highland Guatemala, they were defeated by Cortés in less than 2 years.

Unlike most states in the Old World, Mesoamerican civilizations arose and flourished without beasts of burden, wheeled transportation, or metal tools. Yet during the 30 centuries that elapsed between the establishment of village farming communities and the Spanish conquest, this prehispanic world was the scene of highly developed statecraft, major urban centers, magnificent craftsmanship, spectacular architecture, and large swamp and lakeshore reclamation projects. Mesoamerica thus provides a physically diverse and scientifically important natural laboratory for joining historical and archaeological methods, in order to unravel and interpret societal continuity and change.

SAN JOSÉ MOGOTE

*A 3500-year-old community
in Mexico's southern highlands*

Carved stone (*danzante*) from San José
Mogote.

The preceramic era in ancient Meso-america was long, and the pace of change was relatively slow (see "Guilá Naquitz Cave" and "Tehuacán," Chapter 6, pp. 236 and 242). However, this period was marked by the origin and increasing reliance on agriculture, as well as by steady but gradual increases in settlement size and occupational stability. The contrast with the subsequent episode of rapid change is pronounced. By the latter half of the third millennium B.C., the inhabitants of both coastal and highland settlements were making and using pottery. Within a few centuries, permanent villages were established across much of the Mesoamerican landscape.

San José Mogote (san'ho-zay'mo-go'tay), one of the more thoroughly studied of these early settlements, was positioned on a low spur of land abutting the flat valley bottom in the Valley of Oaxaca (wah-ha'kah). This spot has been inhabited almost continuously to the present, and even today there is a small farming community at the site. First occupied before 1400 B.C., San José Mogote appears to be the oldest pottery-using village in the area.

A fairly complete archaeological record exists for the occupation of the site between 1500 and 1150 B.C. During this period, San José Mogote grew to become the largest—more than 2 ha (5 acres)—and most important of the more than 25 villages distributed across the Valley of Oaxaca. At this time, San José Mogote was the only settlement containing several public buildings. Most of the early villages were situated on or near the valley bottom, the prime agricultural land. The inhabitants depended on maize, avocados, and other cultigens for subsistence, supplemented by wild plants from the piedmont and mountains; deer, cottontail rabbits, and other game were hunted.

Small household units were equipped with braziers, earth ovens, and/or cooking hearths, as well as manos (grinding stones) and metates (ground stone basins) and blackened ceramic jars, for preparing and cooking food. Outside each household area were bell-shaped pits built for food storage and later used for trash disposal. Burials and other activity areas were located near the wattle-and-daub dwellings. In total, each house and its surrounding features encompassed about 300 sq m (3200 sq ft), an area about the size of a tennis court.

Clay figurines of humans and animals appear in association with rituals and burials in the first sedentary villages. Obsidian, a nonlocal stone from volcanic sources elsewhere in Mesoamerica, was found in varying quantities in each excavated residence. This evidence suggests that both trade and ritual were carried on at the level of the family during this period and that households were generally free of hierarchical control.

Household autonomy began to diminish after 1150 B.C. While most of the villages in Oaxaca remained small, San José Mogote continued to grow. Monumental architecture at the site was enhanced and enlarged. In the valley, certain craft activities were enacted only at San José Mogote. In one part of the town, magnetite (an iron ore) was polished into mirrors that were traded as far as the Gulf Coast, over 250 km (150 mi) away. At the same time, exotic equipment for ceremonial activities—such items as turtle shell drums, conch shell trumpets, and the bony tail spines of stingrays (used to draw blood in human autosacrificial rites)—were more abundant at San José Mogote than elsewhere. Obsidian also was more common here. Symbolic designs on pottery associated with the widespread connections of the Olmec

Horizon are prevalent in Oaxaca between 1150 and 800 B.C., particularly at this most important town (see "The Olmec Horizon," p. 316).

After 700 B.C., differences between communities in the valley were even more pronounced. Major public buildings, incorporating adobe bricks and huge blocks of stone, were erected atop groups of earthen mounds. The valley's largest architectural complex prior to 500 B.C. was built on a natural rise (Mound 1) that was artificially enhanced so that it rose 15 m (50 ft) above the rest of San José Mogote (see Color Plate 11). As part of this complex, a flat stone was laid on the ground as a kind of threshold in such a way that anyone passing through a corridor between ceremonially important structures would step on it. The body of an awkwardly sprawled naked individual with closed eyes, mouth open, and an open chest wound was carved on this slab. A similar theme, likely representing slain or sacrificed captives, appears slightly later with the carved stone *danzante* ("dancer") figures at the site of Monte Albán (see p. 322).

Slightly later in time at San José Mogote, the public buildings of Mound 1 were replaced by elite residential compounds, accessible only by the same stone stairway that had previously led to the public buildings. The importance of these residences also is suggested by the large storage areas associated with one of the compounds. A woman with three jade ornaments was buried in the same compound; the largest tomb at this time was situated in the central patio. Unlike the later palaces at Monte Albán, these elite compounds could have been built by the members of an extended family, without large labor gangs. Kent Flannery and Joyce Marcus, of the University of Michigan, who worked for two decades at San José Mogote, have concluded that the community's highest-ranking family, however, did have sufficient power to direct the construction of a huge public building by corvée (unpaid) labor, and eventually even to preempt that platform as a site for personal residence.

Following the establishment of the city of Monte Albán (in 500 B.C.) on a hilltop, less than 10 km (6 mi) to the

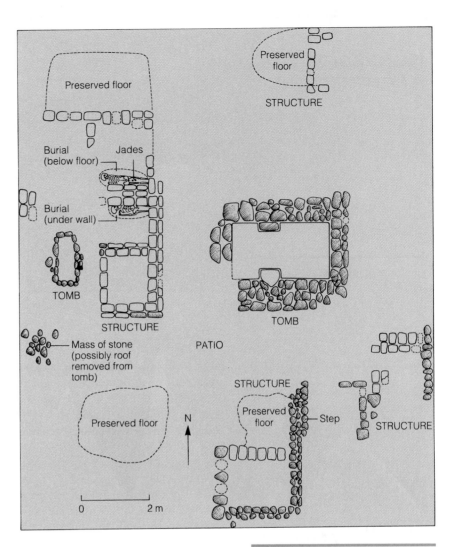

An elite residential complex with tombs on Mound I.

south, San José Mogote became one of several second-tier communities that were part of the expanding political entity that was to become the Zapotec (Valley of Oaxaca) state. San José Mogote never regained the regional and interregional importance that it had before 500 B.C. Yet for the roughly 1000 years prior, beginning with the transition from mobile hunting and gathering to a sedentary way of life, San José Mogote was the central community in the Valley of Oaxaca. In Mesoamerica, cultural change was rapid following the shift to village life. At San José Mogote, a small farming hamlet expanded into a town with ceremonial and production functions encompassing more than 1000 people. These changes, which preceded the rise of Mesoamerica's first urban civilization, are captured in the site's archaeological record.

NONRESIDENTIAL ARCHITECTURE

Clues to changes in the use of space and the nature of ritual

Cut stone architecture at San José Mogote.

Anyone who has visited the archaeological sites of Mesoamerica remembers the massive pyramids, like the Pyramid of the Sun and the Pyramid of the Moon at Teotihuacan, Temple I at Tikal, or the Castillo at Chichén Itzá. Nonresidential constructions, whether monumental, like the major Mesoamerican temple pyramids, or small, like Structure 6 at San José Mogote, can reveal significant information about the societies that built and used them. The size and complexity of construction can tell us about available labor and the power to organize and direct such projects. From the form or shape of public buildings, we can learn about the different kinds of communal activities that took place above the family level. Today such activities might include funerals, weddings, dances, sports events, parades, and political rallies. In prehispanic Mesoamerica, such activities included the ritual game played in formal ball courts (see "The Mesoamerican Ballgame," p. 333), the burial of elite individuals in ornate tombs, and various ritual sacrifices enacted in and around the temples. The use of nonresidential space also tells something about accessibility to ritual activities. For example, an open plaza, or "danceground," would have very different participants than the enclosed ritual space in the temples atop pyramid mounds.

Changing patterns in the use of public space have been documented in a series of excavations in the Valley of Oaxaca by Kent Flannery and Joyce Marcus. The earliest known communal area was identified at the center of Gheo-Shih, a preceramic temporary campsite. Excavations revealed an arrangement of boulders in two parallel rows, each roughly 20 m (65 ft) long. The 7-m (23-ft) wide space between the rows was swept clean and contained almost no artifacts, while outside the rock lines, artifacts were abundant. The space is thought to have been used for community rituals, perhaps a kind of danceground that was similar to those used by the Native Americans of Nevada during the seventeenth and eighteenth centuries A.D.

A similar cleared feature also was found in the early levels of occupation at San José Mogote, the oldest sedentary village in the Valley of Oaxaca. A new kind of construction appeared soon after the abandonment of this feature. A series of one-room structures, roughly 4 × 5 m in size (13 × 16 ft), were constructed of pine posts, walled with cane and clay, and plastered with lime. The first was built around 1350 B.C. and was continuously repaired and rebuilt on the same spot for centuries. These structures included a pit, filled with powdered lime, and a low bench along the interior wall.

The lime may have been combined with narcotics, like tobacco, and ritually smoked. Spanish chroniclers noted that the use of tobacco was prevalent among the Zapotec at the time of European contact. Although the specific rituals that took place in these early structures are unknown, only a limited number of the village's inhabitants could have participated in them. Compared to the dance-grounds, access to the sacred world may have been somewhat more restricted at this time. Furthermore, the continual upkeep and construction suggests that increasing care and energy were devoted to public buildings and group ritual.

Other elaborate public structures also were erected at San José Mogote and elsewhere in the Valley of Oaxaca during the Formative period. These buildings often were placed on flat-topped platforms of stone and adobe brick. By 600 B.C., this architecture was frequently faced with huge slabs of cut stone. Through time, the construction efforts in the Valley of Oaxaca reflected increased energy input and more restricted access to ceremonial activities. These two trends, along with the increasing diversity of Oaxacan public buildings, continued and intensified after 500 B.C. at the hilltop center of Monte Albán and elsewhere.

This sequence of nonresidential building in the Valley of Oaxaca reflects changes in a society that began as a small, mobile population. At that time, the entire population of an open-air camp could participate in ceremonies, dances, or other rituals. With sedentism, larger populations, and the development of greater social, political, and economic differences within the Zapotec population, ceremonial activities became somewhat more exclusive and restrictive. The most elaborate architectural constructions are found at larger sites, like San José Mogote and later Monte Albán. At these sites, access to these important civic-ceremonial buildings (and the activities and rituals within) was limited to a small, favored segment of the overall population.

The cleared area between the two rows of boulders, possibly used for communal rituals or dances, at Gheo-Shih.

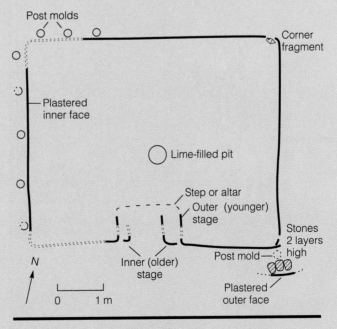

Structure 6, an early public building at San José Mogote.

SAN LORENZO

*The roots of Mesoamerican
civilization on the coastal
plain of southern Veracruz*

In 1860, a workman in southern Veracruz was clearing the dense tropical forest for a sugar plantation, when he noticed a huge, round object on the ground. He reported it to his foreman, who dispatched a crew to unearth it. What they had believed to be a large iron pot was actually the top of a colossal human head, carved of volcanic stone,

standing 1.5 m (5 ft) tall. More than 50 years later, the place of discovery was recognized as the archaeological site of Tres Zapotes (tray′zah-po′tays).

In the decades following this discovery, many other artifacts and artificial mounds were noted along the Gulf coastal plain in the states of Veracruz and Tabasco in Mexico. Yet archaeologists could not determine the age of these finds. The unique style of the monumental carved stone heads did not match the known archaeological traditions of the Maya, the Aztecs, or even pre-Aztec Teotihuacan. Few archaeologists suspected that these magnificent coastal materials were much earlier than those of the later, better-known traditions.

The age of the great basalt heads was not determined until the 1930s, when Matthew Stirling and his associates, of the Smithsonian Institution, began a 20-year project of mapping and excavation at the sites of San Lorenzo, La Venta, and Tres Zapotes. These sites were located in dense, often swampy, tropical vegetation on broad river plains along the Gulf Coast. Stirling's discoveries of carved basalt, extensive earthen mound groups, and caches of jade captured broad public and archaeological attention. Of great importance was the recovery of actual dates (around 31 B.C.) in the Mesoamerican calendar on carved stones at Tres Zapotes. These dates were older than any identified for the Maya and confirmed the antiquity of these materials, which are referred to as **Olmec** (see "The Olmec Horizon," p. 316).

Stirling's pioneering work prompted more extensive studies at both La Venta and San Lorenzo. In the late 1950s, researchers from the University of Cali-

The plan of La Venta.

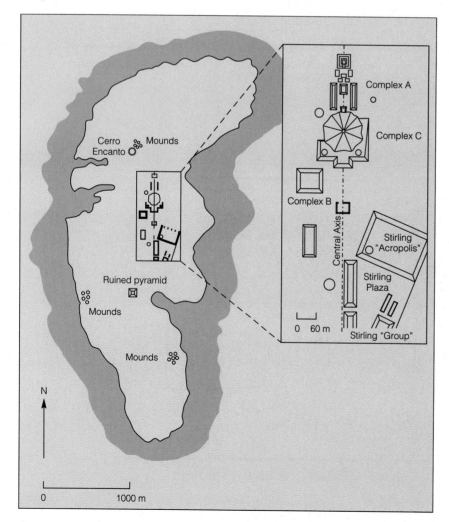

A colossal human head from San Lorenzo.

fornia, Berkeley, used the radiocarbon method to date the principal Olmec occupation at La Venta to between 900 and 400 B.C. During that period, a series of clay and earthen pyramids were constructed on a low island in the middle of a swamp near the Tonalá River. The linear complex of structures, oriented 8° west of true north, covered an area more than 1.6 km (1 mi) long. One of the structures was more than 30 m (100 ft) high. North of that high mound, a series of smaller platforms, plazas, and mounds were arranged symmetrically. Several platforms were built over mosaic pavements, each made of hundreds of blocks of greenstone. One mosaic depicts the symbolic mask or face of a jaguar. Offerings of greenstone, jade, and magnetite objects also were found in the excavations. The

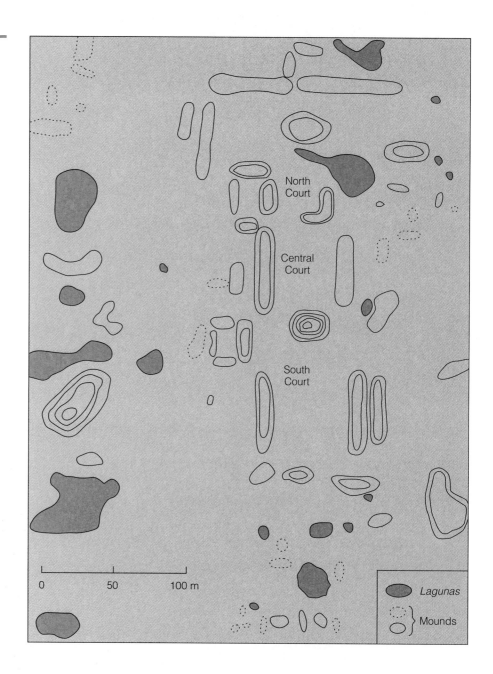

The central part of San Lorenzo, including the locations of mounds and *lagunas*.

North Court

Central Court

South Court

0   50   100 m

Lagunas

Mounds

most spectacular of these, located under the center line of the architectural complex, included 16 greenstone human figures and 6 jade celts. These polished green objects (30 cm, or 12 in, tall) had been placed upright in a ceremonial arrangement.

At its peak, La Venta was a very impressive center. The pyramids were built of clays of different colors, and the platforms were painted in various hues. Sculpted monuments, including four massive stone heads, were carved from volcanic basalt brought from about 100 km

(60 mi) away. The work at La Venta made clear the antiquity of this early Gulf Coast occupation, as well as the labor, calendrical, and craft skills that may have been controlled by the Olmec rulers. These rulers were probably the individuals portrayed in the massive stone heads.

A more recent project, conducted by Michael D. Coe, of Yale University, and Richard A. Diehl, of the University of Alabama, has provided significant information about the beginnings of the Olmec. At San Lorenzo, the Yale project mapped hundreds of monuments, mounds, and other features visible on the surface. These included 20 *lagunas,* humanmade depressions that may have begun as borrow pits where dirt was removed for the construction of earthen mounds; later they were lined with waterproof bentonite (shalelike) blocks. The *lagunas* may have been used for ritual bathing. Part of the site was located on top of an artificially enhanced natural rise that stands 50 m (164 ft) above the surrounding countryside. Excavations revealed that San Lorenzo had a long and complex occupational history, reaching its peak between 1150 and 900 B.C., somewhat earlier than the major construction phase at La Venta.

Significantly, the peak occupation at San Lorenzo was preceded by earlier village habitation. The first inhabitants settled only a small part of San Lorenzo, perhaps as early as 1500 B.C. By 1250 B.C. ceramic designs clearly related to the Olmec occupation were in use, and the villagers began to raise the natural mesa on which their houses were located. Deposits from 1250–1150 B.C. included basalt chips and lumps, discarded during monument carving, as well as Olmec black-and-white pottery.

The Yale project established antecedents for the major occupation at San Lorenzo. This latter period was characterized by a major building episode that included massive mound and plaza construction, the carving of at least eight basalt heads and other monuments, and the layout of a drainage system to take water from the artificial *lagunas.* Also during this time, San Lorenzo developed ties with other areas throughout Mesoamerica. These connections are evident in the foreign goods found both at San Lorenzo and at sites in the highlands of Mexico, as well as in the widespread presence of the shared motifs of the Olmec Horizon. These designs probably had sacred or ritual importance throughout much of ancient Mesoamerica. For unknown reasons, building activities at San Lorenzo ceased after 900 B.C. The site was replaced, probably by La Venta, as the principal center of the Olmec.

Michael Coe refers to the Olmec as Mesoamerica's first civilization. Other archaeologists, such as William Sanders, of Pennsylvania State University, and Kent Flannery, suggest that San Lorenzo and La Venta were chiefly centers associated with social inequality and permanent leaders, but not with urbanism or state government. Clearly, the Olmec centers were occupied by elites as well as lower-status people. The former wore greenstone earplugs, hung iron-ore mirrors as **pectorals** (large chest ornaments), sat on sculpted thrones of basalt, and probably planned the ceremonial architectural precincts at the major centers. The lower-status people must have farmed and helped transport the construction materials of earth and basalt.

Most of our information about the ancient Olmec comes from the ceremonial centers of a few key sites and the artifacts and sculptures associated with those high-status areas. Although in recent years archaeologists have started to collect more information about the size and layout of Olmec polities and conduct select excavations of villages and simple residences, it will be difficult to paint a more complete picture of this ancient social system until further research has been completed and fully published.

Hereditary rulership sanctified by divine descent is common to chiefdoms [societies with chiefs]. The colossal stone heads for which Early Formative Olmec culture is famous are probably portraits of the rulers of major Olmec centers. Many other of the stone monuments demonstrate in their iconography the divine descent and supernatural power of the rulers. A kinship tie between rulers at San Lorenzo and La Venta seems to be symbolized on one San Lorenzo altar, a relationship which would also imply hereditary rulership.

David C. Grove (1981)

THE OLMEC HORIZON

Exchange and interaction in Formative Mesoamerica

A jade celt, the Kunz Axe, with unmistakable features of both a jaguar and a human child (actual size is 30 cm tall).

On the Gulf Coast, the period dating between 1150 and 700 B.C. is distinguished by specific styles of monuments and art, including the massive basalt heads, large flat-topped mounds, rectangular carved stone altars, an abundance of greenstone, slant-eyed clay figurines, the half-jaguar/half-human or **were-jaguar** figure, black-and-white pottery, and the repeated use of certain stylized designs on ceramic vessels. While some of these elements, such as the huge stone heads, are known only from the Gulf Coast heartland, other traits, like the paw-wing and crossed-bands motifs on pottery, are found both locally in the Gulf Coast and at early sedentary settlements across Mesoamerica. These widespread Olmec stylistic motifs have become recognized as elements of what archaeologists refer to as a **horizon,** a broadly distributed array of archaeological traits that appears to have spread rapidly and may have been associated with a shared symbolic or ritual system.

The Olmec Horizon is not evenly distributed across Mesoamerica. Kent Flannery has noted that several Olmec designs are more common in the Valley of Oaxaca than along the Gulf Coast. Archaeologists have puzzled over the meaning of the Olmec Horizon. Some have suggested that it reflects Olmec conquests in the highlands or even an early empire, but this explanation seems doubtful, given the scale of the heartland Olmec sites and the wide distribution of the stylistic elements. The Gulf Coast Olmec were not powerful or populous enough to stake out and rule such far-reaching localities. Even the later and much larger Aztec state (with a large core population and a strong military) had great difficulty maintaining its broad tribute domain (the area from which it demanded tribute from local populations).

Other archaeologists have proposed Olmec colonization of those areas where elements associated with the horizon have been found. But this also seems unlikely; most of the participating regions had distinctive local traditions that existed be-

A stylized were-jaguar on a ceramic vessel.

A carved stone altar from San Lorenzo.

fore, and continued after, the adoption of horizon motifs. For example, in the highlands, local ceramic traditions generally were retained, incorporating the Olmec motifs into local ceramic complexes.

Perhaps the most reasonable interpretation of the Olmec Horizon is that it represents an important symbolic component in a network of interaction that linked sites on the Gulf Coast with those elsewhere in Mesoamerica. Highland resources like obsidian, jade, and magnetite were found at the Gulf heartland centers, while mollusk and turtle shell, stingray spines, shark teeth, and Gulf Coast pottery were recovered in highland sites. In general, these exotic goods are found in ritual or high-status contexts, as are the items carrying the Olmec symbols. The exotic goods and shared pottery designs may have served to enhance or affirm the social positions of certain individuals in both the Gulf Coast and the highlands. These social systems were characterized by increasing societal differentiation and the development of more formal leadership roles during this early village era.

Clearly, the shared Olmec Horizon elements had a strong ritual aspect, with certain motifs serving as symbolic representations, or icons, for specific mythic creatures, deities, or kin-group totems, like the were-jaguar. The sharing of rare materials and the ritual symbols also may have helped solidify communication and marriage alliances between groups of high-status individuals. The relative elaboration and abundance of the Olmec symbols in the heartland may signal the greater importance—and hence the expanded involvement in ritual, rule, and exchange—of the leaders at San Lorenzo compared to those at the smaller centers in other regions of Mesoamerica.

EL MIRADOR

*New perspectives on the
beginnings of ancient
Maya civilization*

The Maya civilization flourished in the tropical forests of the Petén lowlands of northern Guatemala between A.D. 250 and 900. Speculations about its beginnings have focused outside the region, partly because of the notion that the tropical forest was not suitable for large-scale agriculture. Some archaeologists saw the origin of the Maya as a direct extension of the Gulf Coast Olmec tradition, fostered by a belief that the Olmec were the "mother culture" of Mesoamerica, giving rise, like a pulsating beacon, to all later civilizations in the area. However, new interpretations of the Olmec Horizon have questioned this beacon model and have envisioned a network arrangement, in which certain concepts, knowledge, and symbols were shared by an emergent elite at a number of centers across Mesoamerica. With the recent discovery of early preceramic and ceramic sites in the tropical forest of Guatemala and Belize, the origins of the Maya can now be traced locally. Outside influences or introductions from elsewhere in Mesoamerica, or even farther afield, are not essential to explain the rise of this important civilization.

Recent investigations at El Mirador (el-mere-a-dor′, "the lookout") in the dense Petén forest of Guatemala have yielded new insights into the beginnings of Maya civilization. Surrounded by dense vegetation, more than 60 km (37 m) from the nearest modern road or town, El Mirador is almost inaccessible today. Although there have been sporadic reports of these massive colossal ruins for more than 60 years, the first scientific visit took place in 1967, when Ian Graham, of Harvard University, made a preliminary map. Investigation of such a remote site is difficult. Research teams in the 1980s, including a project directed by Ray Matheny, of Brigham Young University, had to transport food, mail, and supplies to the site by weekly mule trains; a landing strip had to be cleared to fly in equipment and personnel.

A helicoptor bringing supplies to El Mirador, which is inaccessible by road.

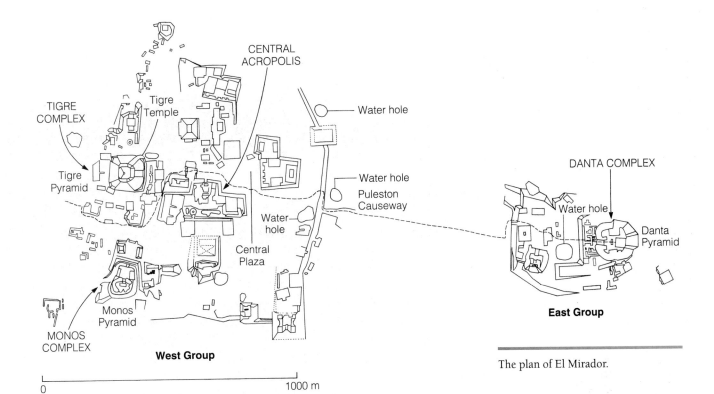

TIGRE COMPLEX

CENTRAL ACROPOLIS

Tigre Temple

Tigre Pyramid

Water hole

Water hole
Puleston Causeway

Water hole

Central Plaza

Monos Pyramid

MONOS COMPLEX

West Group

0   1000 m

DANTA COMPLEX

Water hole

Danta Pyramid

East Group

The plan of El Mirador.

Nevertheless, the preliminary findings are extraordinary. Ceramic and architectural clues, as well as a few radiocarbon assays, date most of the occupation that has been found thus far to between 300 B.C. and A.D. 250, prior to the Maya Classic period. Thus, at a time when most Maya settlements are thought to have been small, containing only a few nonresidential structures, El Mirador was huge and architecturally astounding. The site includes several hundred structures, some of which were as large as any built during the Maya Classic period. El Mirador is particularly important because there apparently was little building activity at the site during the later Classic period. Thus, unlike Tikal and most other Maya sites, the site's Preclassic structures remain relatively undisturbed by later construction.

El Mirador lies on a limestone plain dotted with broad, flat, clay-lined depressions, or *bajos,* which are filled with water for several months during the year. The site is not arranged according to a grid plan and appears to have been built in accordance with local topography. The structures at the site are distributed over 16 sq km (6 sq mi), with large, open spaces between buildings. The architectural core covers at least 2 sq km (0.8 sq mi) and is composed of a series of complexes: groups of plazas, platforms, buildings, causeways (raised roads), and other constructions. This core of the site is divided into two major building groups almost 2 km (1.2 mi) apart. The West Group is defined by a stone wall and ditch to the south and east and by steep escarpments to the north and west. Access to this area was controlled by a series of gates in the walls. These barriers may symbolically delimit the West Group as the sacred core of the site.

Three features dominate the West Group: the Central Acropolis and two enormous pyramids that comprise the Tigre and Monos complexes. The Tigre Complex, with an enormous pyramid 55 m (180 ft) high, apparently was constructed primarily during the last centuries B.C. This complex forms what Mayanists refer to as an **E Group,** an arrangement of buildings designed to mark the position of the rising sun during important solar events, such as equinoxes and solstices. Structure 34, a small temple included within the Tigre Complex, had large **stucco** sculptures on

Archaeologists uncovering a stucco mask on the Tigre Temple.

its **facade.** The sculpted stucco masks, which incorporate both human and jaguar features, are very similar in style and context to those at other sites in the Maya lowlands. The messages transmitted through these symbols may convey divine sanction for the right to rule.

Although the huge Monos Complex is still not fully explored, the Central Acropolis has been mapped and appears to be the nucleus of the site. Measuring 330 m (1080 ft) long by roughly 100 m (325 ft) wide (the area of 12 football fields), this structure supports a number of buildings, including several possible "palaces" or high-status residences.

A causeway leads from the east gate of the West Group to the East Group, 2 km (1.2 mi) away. This group is known largely for the Danta Complex, a massive series of sculpted terraces and platforms, built on a natural elevation that was leveled and modified to accommodate the monumental construction. From the top of the highest building in the Danta Com-

plex, one can see above the forest canopy for 40 km (25 mi) in all directions.

El Mirador could not have existed in a vacuum. Food and labor for construction almost certainly had to come to the site from the surrounding countryside. The movement of people and materials followed a series of six long causeways built like the spokes of a wheel from the site's hub. These impressive causeways would have been especially useful during the summer rainy season, when the *bajos* and low ground turn to heavy and sticky mud, becoming impassable.

Much of El Mirador is still unexplored, hidden under thick tropical vegetation. Some questions remain about the actual size of the site and how much of it was built prior to A.D. 250, the start of the Maya Classic period. Yet there seems little question that El Mirador and other early Maya sites have revolutionized archaeological views of both the Preclassic in the Petén lowlands and the origins of Maya civilization.

From the carved heads and thrones of the Olmec to the circular calendar stone of the Aztecs, stone was a primary medium of prehispanic Mesoamerican art. At almost every major site, archaeologists have recovered sculpted stone monuments. Such stones were used as architectural elements, for the facades of earthen or rubble-filled structures, or as free-standing monuments, such as the thrones and giant heads of the Olmec or the upright stone shafts, or **stelae**, from later periods. Such stelae often glorified the ancestries and accomplishments of specific rulers or elites.

Free-standing stelae are particularly important because they contain examples of the earliest Mesoamerican writing. The first carved stones with **hieroglyphs**, found in the Valley of Oaxaca and at the Gulf Coast site of La Venta, date to between 600 and 400 B.C. The inscription from Oaxaca contains two **glyphs**, or conventionalized symbols, that indicate "1 Earthquake." This inscription represents a date in the Mesoamerican calendar (see "Writing and Calendars," p. 346). It is the first documented use of that sacred system. These glyphs were carved between the feet of an individual who was a probable captive or sacrificial victim. In Mesoamerica, individuals often were named by their birth date, and Joyce Marcus has suggested that 1 Earthquake may be the name of the prisoner depicted. The La Venta stone, the so-called "Ambassador Monument," includes three glyphs, a central figure, and an isolated footprint. Later in prehispanic Mesoamerica, the footprint was a conventional symbol for travel or journey.

Writing, calendrics, and the use of stelae were developed to their greatest extent by the Maya of the Petén lowlands between A.D. 250 and 900. The earliest Maya stelae with written inscriptions, however, do not appear in the Petén lowlands but in the Maya highlands and at sites along the Pacific Coast. Some of these monuments include calendar dates in the Long Count, a cycle with a fixed

CARVED STONE

A medium for important prehispanic Mesoamerican messages.

Stela 1 from Monte Albán in the Valley of Oaxaca.

zero date that can record large blocks of time (see "Writing and Calendars," p. 346). The earliest Long Count dates fall in the last century B.C. and the first century A.D., years before the first Petén stela, which was erected during the third century A.D. (see "Tikal's Monument Record," p. 340).

These carved stones must have carried great importance for prehispanic Mesoamericans. Significant labor was devoted to both their construction and, at times, their destruction. At Olmec and later Maya sites, there is evidence for the intentional mutilation and defacement of these stone monuments, possibly to diminish the importance of the individuals who were represented (perhaps after their death), just as statues may be toppled in a revolution today. Yet despite the destruction, the carved stones are durable and provide an important record for archaeologists. Unfortunately, the many later Mesoamerican documents on bark paper and deer skin did not fare as well.

Inscriptions on the Ambassador Monument from La Venta.

MONTE ALBÁN

A hilltop city in the Valley of Oaxaca

The Valley of Oaxaca is divided into three major arms by the Atoyac River and its tributary, the Salado. The northern arm was the primary focus of early settlement between 1500 and 500 B.C., particularly around San José Mogote. Although several large villages were established in the valley's southern and eastern arms after 700 B.C., San José Mogote continued as the region's largest and architecturally most impressive locality. Around 500 B.C., the pattern of settlement shifted, following the establishment of the hilltop center of Monte Albán at the hub of the valley's three arms.

The monumental hilltop ruins of Monte Albán (moan'tay-al-bahn') have attracted explorers, antiquarians, and archaeologists for well over a century. Systematic excavations were begun at the site in 1931. These studies were carried out over 18 field seasons by Mexican archaeologist Alfonso Caso and his colleagues, Ignacio Bernal and Jorge Acosta. Their research involved the opening of more than 170 tombs, a series of stratigraphic excavations, and the clearing and reconstruction of many buildings. Much of their work focused on the Main Plaza at Monte Albán, an impressive concentration of architecture erected on the artificially flattened summit of the hill.

In 1971, Richard Blanton, of Purdue University, initiated a survey to map the ruins of Monte Albán and to define changes over time in the size and organization of the site. From its foundation, Monte Albán was unique in the Valley of Oaxaca. While earlier settlements were on or next to the valley bottom, Monte Albán was situated above and at some

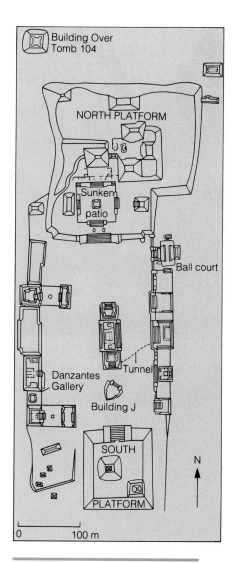

The Main Plaza at Monte Albán.

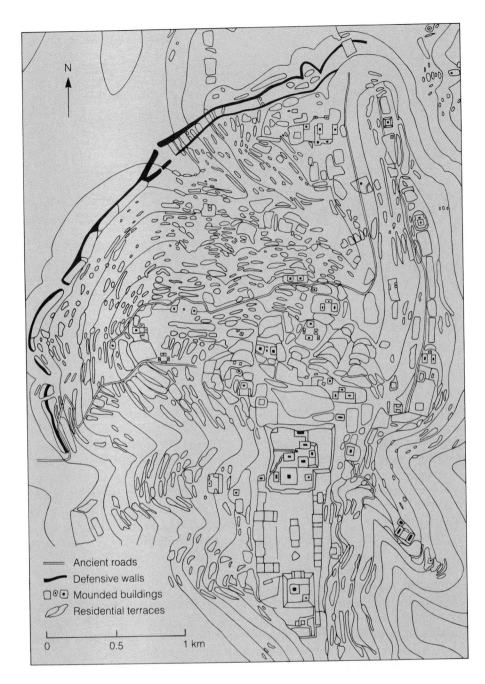

A general map of the structures and residential terraces in the core area of Monte Albán.

distance from good farmland (see Color Plate 12). Blanton's survey indicates that the city also grew very rapidly to a size of more than 1 sq km (0.4 sq mi). During the last centuries B.C., it had an estimated population of 15,000 people and, after its foundation, quickly surpassed San José Mogote in size and architectural elaboration. Soon after the establishment of Monte Albán, major building activities ceased at San José Mogote for several centuries.

During the phase known as Monte Albán I, 500–200 B.C., more than 300 stone monuments were carved and displayed in one of Monte Albán's first public buildings. Although the figures on these stones have been named the *danzantes* ("dancers"), most of them are similar to an earlier monument with a military theme at San José Mogote. Naked and sprawled in grotesque, rubbery positions, with closed eyes and blood

Danzantes on an early public building at Monte Albán.

One of the conquest slabs erected on Building J at Monte Albán.

running from one or more wounds, the *danzantes* probably represent captives or prisoners of war. Although the specific meaning of these carved stones remains uncertain, their date corresponds in time to the consolidation of power at Monte Albán and the political unification of the Valley of Oaxaca.

Many other changes took place in the Valley of Oaxaca with the rapid growth of Monte Albán. Monumental construction increased. Greater concern with the dead (and with their ties to the living) was reflected in the construction of elaborate subterranean tombs. Domestic architecture evolved from simple wattle-and-daub structures to more permanent adobe constructions. Greater regional similarities in pottery styles also were noted. New ceramic forms, including the tortilla griddle, or *comal,* and the incense burner, or *incensario,* suggest changes in both cooking technology and ritual activities at this time. The rapid growth in the number and size of settlements in the Valley of Oaxaca is further indication that this was a period of dynamic transition.

During the second phase of Monte Albán (Monte Albán II), 200 B.C.–A.D. 200, the site expanded its political, economic, and military influence beyond the Valley of Oaxaca. At the same time, a 3-km (2-mi) defensive wall was erected at the site. An unusual building with an arrowhead-shaped groundplan (Building J) was erected in the Main Plaza. Set into the walls of this structure were more than 40 carved stone panels. Each panel included a set of glyphs with a place name, or **emblem glyph,** probably identifying a location, along with an upside-down human head, which likely signified military defeat. Caso identified these slabs as the documentation of Monte Albán's conquests, and Joyce Marcus has suggested identifications for several distant localities represented on the stone slabs.

In one of these identified localities, the Cuicatlán Cañada, 80 km (50 mi) northeast of Monte Albán, Charles Spencer, of the American Museum of Natural History, and Elsa Redmond, of Columbia University, have found strong indications of Monte Albán conquest during Monte Albán II. A local community, the site of Loma de la Coyotera, was sacked and burned, with the skulls of 61 of its inhabitants mounted on a rack. This skull rack, what the Aztecs called a *tzompantli,* was found to be contemporaneous with Monte Albán II. *Tzompantli* erection was generally associated with military conquest during Aztec times and prob-

Building J on the Main Plaza of Monte Albán.

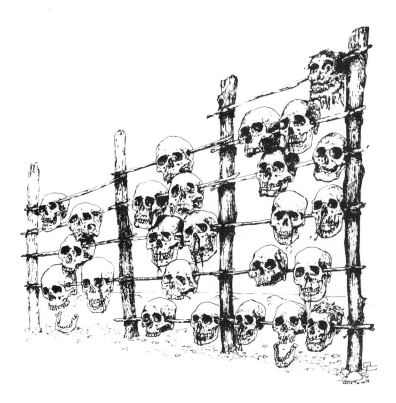

An artist's reconstruction of the skull rack (*tzompantli*) at Loma de la Coyotera.

ably served similar functions in earlier phases as well. Spencer and Redmond also found a major transition in the settlement pattern of the Cuicatlán Cañada, including the construction of a fortress that was placed to control traffic through the Cañada and between the valleys of Oaxaca and Tehuacán.

Monte Albán's dominance over the Valley of Oaxaca continued during the third phase of its history (Monte Albán III), A.D. 200–700. However, during this phase, its influence outside the valley diminished, perhaps because of the growing importance of Teotihuacan, the great urban center in the Valley of Mexico (see "Teotihuacan," p. 328). In the Cuicatlán Cañada, for example, the Monte Albán connection waned during this period, while settlement patterns and ceramic findings point to the increasing influence of Teotihuacan.

Late in Monte Albán III, Monte Albán itself reached its greatest physical size, with a population of 25,000–30,000 people. Sometime around A.D. 700, major construction at Monte Albán ceased, and the city began to decline in size and importance. Although a remnant population occupied the hilltop for much of the rest of the prehispanic era, the city never again achieved its former glory. Toward the end of the prehispanic period, a powerful ruler was buried in a tomb originally built during Monte Albán III at Monte Albán. This subsurface feature (Tomb 7) contains ancient Mesoamerica's greatest treasure, a tomb stuffed with gold, carved jaguar bones, shell, turquoise, jet, crystal, and numerous other exotic items.

Monte Albán was quite different in plan, size, and function from the contemporaneous Mesoamerican centers of Teotihuacan or Tikal or the later Aztec city of Tenochtitlán. Monte Albán's hilltop location is not typical of Mesoamerican sites as a whole. With its monumental Main Plaza, dwarfing the architecture found at contemporary sites on the valley floor, Monte Albán's politico-religious functions always surpassed its regional commercial role. In general, archaeological indicators for craft activities are surprisingly few at the hilltop city, and no central market area has yet been identi-

fied. The site was not laid out according to a grid plan. Few major roads were constructed, and access to the Main Plaza was restricted to several narrow entryways. The bulk of the population lived on the more than 2000 residential terraces carved out of the hillside beneath the Main Plaza and on adjacent hills. Held in place by stone retaining walls, each terrace contained no more than a few households.

By 200 B.C., Monte Albán was the capital of a Zapotec state whose limits stretched beyond the Valley of Oaxaca. While archaeologists have yet to unravel all the factors responsible for either the foundation of this hilltop center or the rise of the Zapotec state, these changes seem in part tied to the increasing role of militarism in Oaxaca. The *danzantes,* the conquest slabs, Monte Albán's hilltop location, and its defensive wall all point to the importance that warfare may have had. Yet the emergence of Monte Albán also coincided with marked regional population growth, as well as changes in the local systems of exchange and production, and these factors also may have had key roles in these important societal transitions.

Traditionally, archaeologists have depended on excavation as the primary means for obtaining information. Paradoxically, however, when archaeologists excavate sites, they also destroy the buried deposits of material. Unlike physics or chemistry, in which experiments can be repeated numerous times under the same conditions, archaeologists can dig a particular area only once. Excavations, therefore, proceed slowly and carefully, to record as much detailed information as possible. Because of limited time and money, we are lucky to investigate more than a small part of any one site or more than a few sites in a given area.

Sociologists would be uncomfortable describing a modern city from only a few interviews and often supplement detailed accounts with broad urban surveys or censuses. For similar reasons, geologists and geographers often combine very specific information gathered from soil probes or individual field studies with the larger-scale perspective provided by satellite imagery. Over the last 50 years, archaeologists have developed a technique, called a *systematic settlement pattern survey,* for studying areas larger than one or a few sites.

Archaeologists have for a long time used surface survey procedures to locate sites based on the presence of artifactual or architectural debris on the ground. They frequently use unsystematic surveys, or reconnaissances, to find sites to excavate. Over the last several decades, archaeologists have refined regional archaeological survey procedures. In systematic surveys, large blocks of land are thoroughly and carefully walked over to locate surface evidence of past occupations. These occupations, which are dated by the artifactual scatters associated with them, are placed on aerial photographs or topographic maps. The entire distribution of sites known for each particular period represents that era's settlement pattern.

The first systematic settlement pattern survey was carried out in the Virú Valley on the north coast of Peru soon after World War II by Gordon Willey, of Harvard University. Willey designed this study to determine the geographic and chronological position of sites, to outline the developmental history of settlement, and to reconstruct cultural institutions as far as they were reflected in the settlement data. To achieve these ends, Willey and his colleagues walked over the valley, mapping a total of 315 archaeological sites. These sites were dated and classified according to estimated function, determined primarily by site size, location, and the kind of architecture visible on the surface. Pieces of pottery on the ground surface were used to date the sites. Through this extensive surface survey, Willey obtained a regional overview of changing patterns of settlement that he could supplement with detailed excavations at a few sites.

Since Willey's pioneering study, systematic settlement pattern surveys have been undertaken in many areas, including the highlands of Oaxaca and central Mexico, the rivers and foothills of Southwest Asia, the mountain valleys of the Andes, and the deserts and plateaus of the southwestern United States. Surveys are most successful where artifacts are readily visible on the ground. Such conditions are found frequently in semiarid climates, where vegetation is limited and soil formation is slow.

Archaeological surveys provide a variety of information about the past. The number and sizes of sites enable the archaeologist to estimate ancient population size and changes in demography over time. Archaeologists also can examine the distribution of sites on the landscape in relation to different kinds of soil, topographic features, and resources.

Like household interviews and censuses, soil probes and satellite images, excavations and surveys provide complementary insights. Excavations yield detailed, specific, more precise observations at a small scale. Surveys provide broader, less fine-grained information at a larger scale. When used alone, each method can provide misleading results because of small sample size (excavation) and the reliance on surface materials no longer in their primary context (survey). The most complete descriptions are achieved when both are used.

SETTLEMENT PATTERN SURVEYS

Examining ancient demography and the distribution of sites on regional landscapes

TEOTIHUACAN

One of the world's largest cities in A.D. *500*

The Basin of Mexico, showing the prehispanic lakes, volcanoes, and major early centers.

Today Mexico City, with over 16 million inhabitants, covers most of a huge geological basin in the central highlands of Mexico. Before the enormous growth of Mexico City, the Basin of Mexico contained the largest expanse of flat, agricultural land in all of highland Mesoamerica. The basin lies at an elevation of 2100 m (7000 ft) and is ringed by a series of dormant, snow-capped volcanoes forming a palisade around its perimeter. The outlet for the basin was dammed by a number of volcanic eruptions several million years ago, forming a series of lakes. The floor of the basin originally held five shallow lakes, brackish in the north and fresher to the south. These lakes, of particular importance for the Aztec civilization, were drained by the Spanish during the Colonial period, when Mexico was ruled by the Spanish crown (A.D. 1521–1821), and only small remnants of them remain.

The Basin of Mexico was the center of at least two major prehispanic civilizations. Systematic archaeological surveys of more than half the floor of the basin, made during the past 40 years, have shown that the first sedentary villages were concentrated in the southern half. This area receives more rainfall than the northern portion of the basin and is better for farming. Prior to 500 B.C., occupation was established at a site called Cuicuilco (kwee-kwil′co) in the southwestern part of the basin. Relatively little is known archaeologically about this site. It was buried by at least two prehispanic lava flows and then covered by the urban sprawl of modern Mexico City. Only the tops of a few small pyramids rise above the mantle of volcanic stone. Yet the scale of Cuicuilco's distinctive structures and the large area of its occupation suggest that the site was the basin's first major town.

The volcanic eruptions may have helped end Cuicuilco's preeminence and may have contributed to a shift in the balance of power in the basin. By the end of the second century B.C., the site of Teotihuacan (tay-o-tee-wa'kahn) had been established in the northeastern corner of the basin, about 20 km (12 mi) from the lakeshore. Situated in low hills adjacent to a series of natural springs, Teotihuacan grew rapidly, becoming one of the region's two primary centers, along with Cuicuilco. Based on his urban survey of Teotihuacan, René Millon, of the University of Rochester, estimates that the site may have reached 6–8 sq km (2.5–3.0 sq mi) in area, with a population of at least 20,000 by this time. The population of the basin became increasingly nucleated during this period, particularly around the major centers. At the same time, areas of little habitation formed between the population clusters, suggesting the emergence of buffer zones between hostile groups.

By the first century A.D., Teotihuacan had become the primary settlement in the Basin of Mexico. While the urban center sprawled to almost 20 sq km (7.5 sq mi), encompassing roughly 90,000 people, other centers in the basin declined in size and importance. In fact, the next largest communities had populations of less than 5,000 people and comparatively little nonresidential construction. This tremendous nucleation of population and power continued over subsequent centuries, signaling the dramatic political and economic reorganization that took place during the hegemony (predominance) of Teotihuacan.

Several hypotheses have been advanced to account for the rapid growth and development of this great city. We will probably never know just how closely the growth of Teotihuacan was related to the natural disaster that buried a portion of the contemporary center of Cuicuilco in the last centuries B.C. Alternatively, William Sanders, of Pennsylvania State University, has emphasized

the importance of Teotihuacan's location, positioned to tap springs for a series of irrigation canals. For decades, Sanders and other archaeologists have been influenced by the writings of Karl Wittfogel, who emphasized the managerial costs of water control and the possible role such management had in stimulating political change. While canals were built to harness the water from these springs, the specific timing of this construction has not been verified. Sanders and others have suggested that canal construction and agricultural intensification would have been required to feed the burgeoning population of this ancient city and the basin as a whole.

Noting the abundance of obsidian at Teotihuacan, Michael Spence, of the University of Western Ontario, has suggested that the manufacture of obsidian artifacts may have played a role in the growth of the city, something like the relationship between the automobile and Detroit. In the ancient Mesoamerican world, obsidian provided the sharpest cutting edge available. It was used economically for knives and other tools, ritually to extract blood in autosacrifice (the drawing of blood from the fleshy parts of one's own body), ornamentally as part of masks and necklaces, and militarily for weapons. Raw obsidian nodules can be taken from the San Juan River, which cuts directly through the site of Teotihuacan, as well as from a large source of gray obsidian only 16 km (10 mi) away. Teotihuacan also is close to a source of green obsidian at Pachuca, roughly 50 km (30 mi) to the northeast. Pachuca obsidian, present in great quantity at Teotihuacan, was valued for both workability and the symbolic importance of its color. While Spence has emphasized the role of obsidian production and export in Teotihuacan's rise, John Clark, of Brigham Young University, has suggested that most of the surface obsidian debris could reflect production for local use. Regardless of its eventual destination, there is little doubt that the quantity of obsidian at Teotithuacan far exceeds what is typical in Mesoamerican sites.

Millon has stressed the importance of ideological, as well as economic, factors

It has mainly been the humanists who have studied the informational aspects of complex societies—art, religion, ritual, writing systems, and so on. The "ecologists" have largely contented themselves with studying exchanges of matter and energy—the "techno-environmental" factors. . . . To read what the "ecologists" write, one would often think that civilized peoples only ate, excreted, and reproduced; to read what the humanists write, one would think civilizations were above all three, and devoted all their energy to the arts. . . . I will argue that humanists must cease thinking that ecology "dehumanizes" history, and ecologists must cease to regard art, religion, and ideology as mere "epiphenomena" without causal significance.

Kent V. Flannery (1972a)

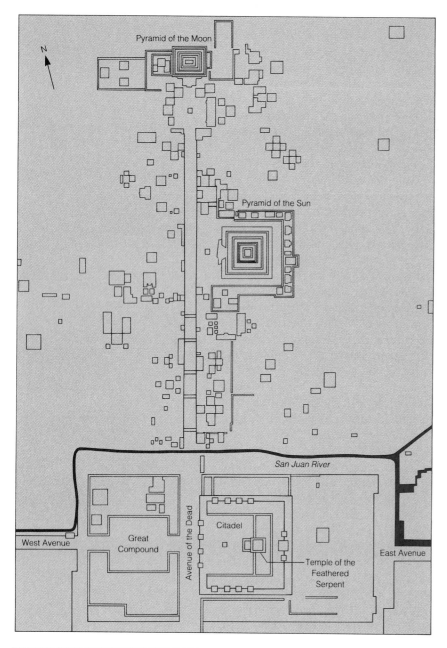

The central core of Teotihuacan.

nue and West Avenue. Together these avenues divided the city into quadrants. At their intersection were the distinctive Ciudadela ("citadel") and the Great Compound, which formed a massive architectural unit. The Great Compound is thought by some scholars to have been the city's central marketplace. The Ciudadela was a huge political and religious precinct, enclosing a sunken courtyard and the imposing Temple of the Feathered Serpent. The Ciudadela, together with all the buildings along the Avenue of the Dead, was constructed with cut-stone facing known as **talud-tablero.** This style, composed of framed panels (*tableros*) and sloping basal elements (*taluds*), is recognized as a symbol of Teotihuacan temples. Its presence on the entire 2 km (1.25 mi) of structures from the Ciudadela to the Pyramid of the Moon would seem to denote the sacred aspect of the central city (Color Plate 13).

Sabruro Sugiyama, of Japan's Aichi Prefectural University, and Rubén Cabrera, of Mexico's National Institute of Anthropology and History, have recently excavated burial chambers under the Pyramid of the Moon and the Temple of the Feathered Serpent in the Ciudadela that contain the remains of royal retainers and sacrificial victims. However, no royal tombs have been uncovered. The elaborate offerings found with the burials, such as imitation human teeth carved from shell, are quite different from artifacts found in residential areas.

The largest of the city's more than 5000 known structures, the Pyramid of the Sun and the Pyramid of the Moon dominate the surrounding landscape. The monumental Pyramid of the Sun was the largest structure ever built during a single construction episode in the ancient Americas. The structure stands 64 m (212 ft) high and measures roughly 213 m (700 ft) on a side. It contains 1 million cu m of fill (35,000,000 cu ft, equivalent to the volume of 10 modern oil tankers), which was carried to the pyramid in basketloads. The cut-stone exteriors of these massive structures (as well as most other platforms at the site) are believed to have been faced with a thick, white plaster and painted red to enhance their visibility.

in the developmental history of Teotihuacan. It was a sacred city with more temples than any other prehispanic Mesoamerican site, before or after. At its maximum size, between the fifth and seventh centuries A.D., Teotihuacan covered an enormous area of 22 sq km (8.5 sq mi), with an estimated population of at least 125,000 people. The city was planned and laid out along a rectilinear network of roads and paths. The major north-south axis, the Avenue of the Dead, intersected with lesser East Ave-

The Pyramid of the Sun at Teotihuacan.

Hidden below the Pyramid of the Sun lies a cave. It runs 100 m (330 ft) from its mouth near the base of the pyramid stairway to a spot close to the center of the pyramid. The people of Teotihuacan must have used the cave because ritual items were found within it, and in certain spots the walls of the cave were reroofed. Caves were sacred in Mesoamerican religion, associated with the creation of the sun and the moon. Archaeologist Linda Manzanilla, of the National Autonomous University of Mexico (UNAM), has noted that the cave under the Pyramid of the Sun was just one of many at the site, and she has suggested that these tunnels and caverns were the source of virtually all the volcanic stone used to build Teotihuacan.

The residential pattern for the earliest years of Teotihuacan is not well known. However, a series of distinctive multi-household residential units dating to the third century A.D. can be recognized. Some 2200 of these well-planned, single-story apartment compounds were eventually built. During the site's later history,

these compounds were the principal kind of residential structure. The interiors of the compounds were divided into different apartments, each with rooms, patios, and passageways. The exteriors were surrounded by tall, windowless stone walls of cement and plaster. The compounds varied significantly in size. Millon estimates that the average structure housed about 60 people, while the larger ones held 100 or more.

From size, architectural differences, and the kinds of artifacts and wastes found at the compounds, it is clear that the occupants of these units varied in socioeconomic position. The groups that lived in the compounds were enduring. Many of the structures were rebuilt several times over several centuries, with little change in plan. The specific relationships that linked households in a compound remain unknown. Spence's preliminary study of the skeletal materials led him to speculate that the males within one compound had fairly close biological ties, whereas the females did not. Such a pattern suggests a lineage or

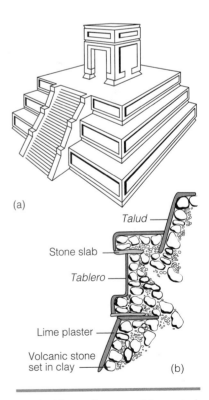

Talud-tablero architecture: (a) a typical structure; (b) a cross section showing the elements of construction.

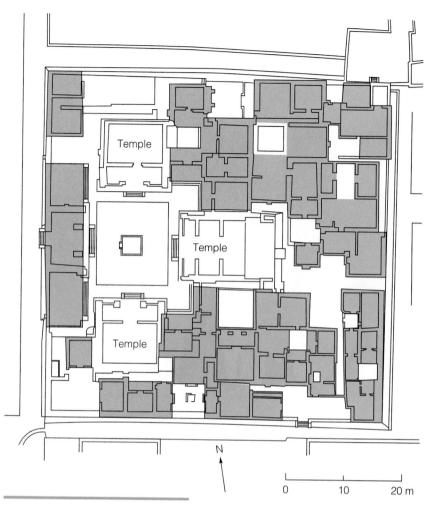

The plan of an apartment compound at Teotihuacan. The areas in color are roofed; the uncolored areas are open plazas or temples.

extended-family residence pattern that was **patrilocal**, in which females moved in with the family of the groom after marriage. Spence also has suggested that individuals within apartment compounds may have shared certain economic skills, such as working obsidian. Each compound had at least one temple or shrine, suggesting joint participation in ritual by the residents.

Certain neighborhoods at Teotihuacan were associated with foreign residents. The compound occupied by people from Oaxaca included a tomb with an inscribed stela bearing a glyph and number in the distinctive Oaxacan style. One ceramic urn came directly from the Valley of Oaxaca; other pottery vessels were made from local basin clays in the Oaxacan style. At least some of the foreign residents are assumed to have been merchants or traders.

In another neighborhood of Teotihua-

can, the houses were built of adobe following the style of the Mesoamerican Gulf Coast. Teotihuacan was involved in trade relationships that extended as far as the Gulf Coast of Mexico, the Maya lowlands, the Guatemalan highlands, and the deserts of northern Mexico. On Monte Albán's Main Plaza, carved stone monuments depict an important, yet apparently peaceful, meeting between an emissary wearing a costume from Teotihuacan and a Zapotec lord. Figures bearing symbols associated with central Mexico also are portrayed on stelae from Maya Tikal. Yet despite these long-distance exchange and diplomatic contacts, there is little evidence that Teotihuacan directly controlled much territory outside the Basin of Mexico.

Little is known about the decline of Teotihuacan in the seventh through tenth centuries A.D. The site was not abandoned, but its size decreased by more than half during this period. Militarism is a prominent theme in art during A.D. 650–750, although perimeter defensive walls were never constructed. Part of the city was burned in the seventh and eighth centuries; the fires appear to have started intermittently. The core of the city—the buildings along the Avenue of the Dead—was burned, as were temples, pyramids, and public buildings throughout the site. Millon has suggested that the conflagration was deliberate and ritually inspired, similar to the earlier desecration of the Olmec stone sculptures. In ancient Mesoamerica, the symbolic destruction of selected monuments or sacred structures was repeatedly associated with decline and the loss of power.

After A.D. 750, the enormous pyramids, the avenues and markets, and the memory of the Classic civilization were in decline. Centuries later, the Aztecs referred to the mounds of stone and broken walls as "the place of the gods." Today, Teotihuacan is one of the most important tourist attractions in Mexico. The magnificent Avenue of the Dead has been reopened and leads past the Pyramid of the Sun to the plaza and Pyramid of the Moon. The pyramids have been restored, and every year thousands climb them in awe and admiration for the achievements of the ancient Mexicans.

The late art historian Paul Kirchhoff drew up a list of cultural traits that generally defined the prehispanic societies of Mesoamerica and distinguished them from other large cultural regions in the New World, such as the Andean area in South America. Among the traits he used to define the boundaries of prehispanic Mesoamerica was the game played with a solid rubber ball. First reported in sixteenth-century Spanish accounts, the ballgame, called **tlachtli** by the Aztecs, was a team game played by somewhat different rules from place to place. Ceramic evidence suggests that some form of the ballgame was played in Mesoamerica as early as 1000 B.C., soon after the transition to village life. Ballplayers are depicted in clay figurines from central and western Mexico, as well as sites along the Gulf Coast. The pottery figures are shown wearing such playing gear as knee guards.

Archaeological evidence also suggests that the ballgame was played in different ways during its history. For example, the Spanish chroniclers witnessed a game played on a court where stone rings were used as goals. Most ball courts from before A.D. 700 do not have such rings of stone. Small shallow pits enclosed by four earthen retaining walls, known from San Lorenzo, may have served as early playing fields in the Olmec period. The earliest I-shaped ball courts with stone walls were not built until several centuries later. This more traditional form, often with sloping playing surfaces, has been found throughout Mesoamerica. (To compare the oval ball court of the U.S. Southwest, see "Snaketown," Chapter 7, p. 286.) The absence of a ball court at Teotihuacan is a mystery, since ballplaying is depicted on polychrome murals in the one of the compounds. Ballplayer figurines also have been found at the site.

The Mesoamerican ballgame was not just for the sake of sport. Spanish chroniclers describe the sixteenth-century version as very rough, played with a ball weighing up to 11 kg (5 lb). In one version, the ball had to be kept in motion and could not be hit with hands or feet. Hips, knees, and elbows were used, and injuries were frequent. In prehispanic times, the game was associated with fertility, death, militarism, and sacrifice. At the site of El Tajín in Veracruz, a stone relief panel in the ball court graphically shows one player stretched over a sacrificial stone, while another is poised with a stone knife ready to be plunged into the chest of the victim. Sixteenth-century accounts also detail the sacrifice of defeated team members. Interestingly, the ball courts at the Maya site of Chichén Itzá and at the Aztec capital of Tenochtitlán were directly adjacent to the *tzompantli*, the skull rack where the heads of war captives were placed.

THE MESOAMERICAN BALLGAME

A ritual game with symbolic and political importance

The ball court at Monte Albán.

A stone relief panel from the ball court at El Tajín.

Tikal

A Maya city in the rain forest of Guatemala

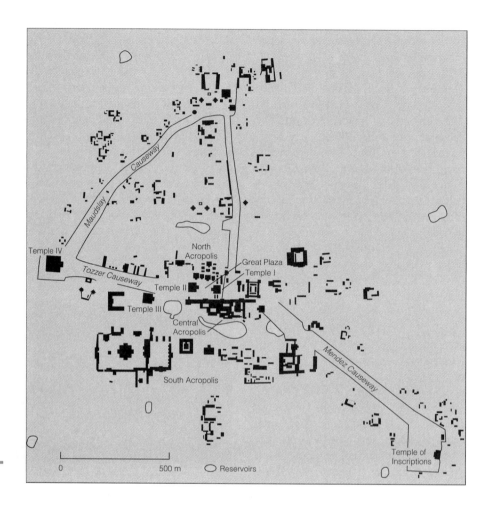

A map of Tikal.

Of all the New World states, it is perhaps the Maya that afford us the greatest opportunity for understanding the evolution, operation, and demise of a complex society. No other New World state offers us such a variety of complementary data sets, including eye-witness reports preserved as ethnohistorical documents, hieroglyphic texts that span some 600 years, regional settlement pattern data, linguistic reconstructions, subsistence data, and architectural evolution. The challenge remains for us to integrate all these lines of evidence, to highlight the differences and similarities among them, and to understand the Maya better by learning more about other Mesoamerican states.

J. Marcus (1983b)

The first adventurers and antiquarians who discovered the overgrown ruins of Maya sites in the rain forests of the Petén assumed them to be the remains of ancient cities with large populations. Yet by the early 1900s, opinion shifted to the belief that the ancient Maya resided in vacant ceremonial centers, inhabited only by small groups of priests. These individuals were purported to direct rural, peasant populations through periodic rituals at the centers. This shift in perspective, from urban to ceremonial, was the result of the concentration of archaeological investigations at the cere-

monial cores of these sites, and of preconceived notions that tropical forests could not support urban centers. Researchers failed to recognize residential architecture, and they often neglected to look for houses outside the ceremonial cores of the sites. Moreover, since today the Maya practice slash-and-burn cultivation, it was assumed that the ancient Maya used the same technique. **Slash and burn** (also called swidden farming) is a simple strategy that involves a cyclical process of field clearing, cultivation, and abandonment. Such extensive agriculture was not thought capable of sup-

A view of Tikal.

porting large urban enclaves or high population densities.

During the last three to four decades, however, new information has revived an interpretation similar to the original one. Fifteen years of investigations at the site of Tikal (tee-cahl′) by researchers at the University Museum of the University of Pennsylvania included survey and mapping, excavation in selected areas, and the recording of carved stone monuments. The Tikal survey recorded thousands of small mounds in the thick forest vegetation. More common near the center of the site, the mounds decreased in number toward the periphery. A few of the mounds were excavated and found to be residential structures. At Tikal, the quantity of these residential structures demonstrated that the site had held a sizable population. Subsequent mapping of other Maya centers has indicated that the lowland population during the Maya Classic period, A.D. 250–900, was much larger than anyone suspected, considerably larger than it is today.

Once researchers recognized the population density of the ancient Maya, new questions were raised concerning

The Temple of the Great Jaguar (Temple I).

agricultural subsistence, craft production, and sociopolitical organization. It is now clear that the ancient farmers of the lowlands used several different strategies, such as terracing and ridged fields, for more intensive agricultural production (see "Raised and Drained Fields," p. 338). Classic Maya communities apparently also had specific occupational groups, like craftsmen, in addition to the groups of peasants and ruler-priests envisioned in the ceremonial center model.

The core of Tikal is situated on a series of low ridges standing roughly 50 m (165 ft) above two swampy areas (*bajos*). Most of the great structures presently visible, clustered on the rises, date to the later part of the Classic, the period of most pronounced construction activity at Tikal and in the Maya lowlands in general. Yet excavations have revealed that many earlier buildings, some contempo-

raneous with the major Formative period occupation at El Mirador, were encased within the later structures.

For most of Tikal's history, the core of the city was the Great Plaza, although it did not dominate Tikal to the extent that the Main Plaza did at Monte Albán. In Tikal, this central open area, laid out prior to 100 B.C., stretches for roughly a hectare (2.5 acres) and was replastered four times. At the eastern end of the plaza, the Temple of the Great Jaguar (Temple I) rises to 45 m (150 ft), with its crowning roof comb peeking out above the tropical canopy of mahogany, cedar, and chicle (gum) trees. A large seated lord was originally painted in an array of colors on the face of the hollow comb. Temple I itself has three high narrow rooms with carved wooden beams spanning its door frames. The innermost of these beams, or **lintels,** portrays a Maya lord towered over by a jaguar, which may serve as his protector. Temple I was dedicated in the Late Classic period to Lord Ah Cacau, whose sumptuous grave was found beneath its base and whose portrait is found on the lintels and roof comb. Directly across the plaza from Temple I lies the slightly shorter Temple II, probably dedicated to Ah Cacau's wife.

The north side of the plaza is framed by the North Acropolis, a huge, 100 × 80 m (325 × 260 ft) platform that was continually expanded between 200 B.C. and A.D. 550. The University of Pennsylvania team, led by William Coe, intensively excavated this structure, discovering a rich succession of elaborate, elite tombs. Based on their findings, the North Acropolis appears to have been a burial place for a long sequence of Tikal's rulers.

South of the Great Plaza sits Tikal's greatest palace complex, the Central Acropolis. In total, this complex spreads over more than 1.6 ha (4 acres) and contains a maze of 42 multistory buildings with multiple rooms interspersed with internal courtyards. The elaboration of the room decorations, which included thronelike seats with armrests, implies that Tikal's lords and their retainers lived and conducted their activities here.

Other monumental buildings and important plazas are linked to the Great Plaza by broad, raised causeways called *sacbes,* or rain forest paths. The Tozzer Causeway (named for a renowned Mayanist) runs west from Temple II to one of the two tallest structures in the pre-Columbian world, Temple IV. Temple IV, some 70 m (230 ft) tall, was built in the middle of the eighth century A.D. to commemorate one of Tikal's last known rulers, Ah Cacau's son and successor, Yax Kin.

The final pyramid temple at the site, Temple III, was built as a funerary monument to Chitam, the last well-known Tikal ruler. Temple III is significantly taller than either Temple I or Temple II, attesting to the labor power that Chitam or his immediate successor could still amass. In the summit shrine, the wooden lintel framing the doorway covers 1.3 sq m (14 sq ft) and depicts a central figure carved in **bas-relief** (low relief). This corpulent person, believed to be Chitam, is

The Central Acropolis at Tikal.

flanked by two attendants. The central figure is dressed in lordly finery, including jaguar skins; he wears a jaguar headdress plumed with feathers from the **quetzal,** a native bird, and sports adornments made of jade and shell. There is little question that Chitam's reign marked the final "glory days" of prehispanic Tikal. After Chitam, little construction was carried out, and few stelae were erected. A century or two later, this giant city was abandoned by humans and eventually reverted to forest.

RAISED AND DRAINED FIELDS

Intensive agriculture in the Maya lowlands

I'm not particularly interested in ancient objects. This seemingly heretical statement for an archaeologist usually takes aback friends who believe that the best way to entertain me is to show me the local museum. On more than one occasion, I have had to explain that beautiful Classic Maya vases or finely carved jade pendants hold less interest to me—and to many of my colleagues—than the scientific investigation of ideas about why and how ancient cultures like the Maya developed.

J. A. Sabloff (1990)

Forty years ago, most Mayanists believed that the ancient Maya relied entirely on the slash-and-burn farming practices used in Yucatán today. For example, in 1956, Sylvanus Morley and George Brainerd summarized the prevailing viewpoint as follows:

> Modern Maya agricultural practices are the same as they were three thousand years ago or more—a simple process of felling the forest, burning the dried trees and bush, planting, and changing the locations of the cornfields every few years. (1956, p. 128)

Yet during the last decades, with the completion of archaeological settlement surveys, a large number of sites have been mapped. Often these sites were found to have contained a greater residential population than expected, raising questions about Maya subsistence and population. Most notably, given the long fallow cycles required by slash-and-burn farming, how did the large Classic Maya populations sustain themselves?

The late Dennis Puleston, who surveyed outlying portions of Tikal, provided an alternative hypothesis. Noting the high spatial association between the ruins of Tikal house mounds and the distribution of ramón trees (local trees bearing fruits), Puleston suggested that the fruit of the ramón, eaten today as a dietary supplement, may have been a food staple in the past. Although Puleston may have overestimated the ancient dietary significance of ramón, more recent findings have supported his view that the ramón and other fruit trees were tended by the prehispanic Maya and probably contributed to their diet.

In 1969, Puleston, collaborating with geographer Alfred Siemens, discovered raised-field complexes during an aerial reconnaissance in the vicinity of a series of Maya sites along the Candelaria River in the state of Campeche. Subsequent aerial photographs, on-the-ground checks, and archaeological excavations confirmed that the observed patterns of raised fields and interdigitated canals were constructed prior to the Spanish conquest. Since the initial work of Siemens and Puleston, these agricultural features, which are similar in function to the prehispanic central Mexican *chinampas*, also have been noted in other parts of the Maya lowlands (see "Tenochtitlán," p. 354).

Along the Hondo River in Belize, Puleston's excavations suggested that the prehispanic raised features were built up by piling floodplain sediments above the natural terrain. In other areas, canals were constructed to drain water from swampy and waterlogged zones. In both cases, cultivated fields were established above the high water table, or floodplain, during the rainy season. Yet, if necessary, these raised or drained fields could receive water supplements from the intervening canals in the dry season. In addition, the periodic cleaning of the canals further raised and naturally fertilized the fields. Although these features could be laborious to construct, the returns also were significant, allowing for a much more continuous output than that afforded by slash and burn. The canals within the raised-field systems also could have promoted fish cultivation and facilitated transport and communication. The Maya glyph signifying abundance was the water lily, a key natural floral component of the artificially constructed aquatic raised-field/canal environment.

Pollen samples from the silt of the ancient Hondo River canals have identified maize and cotton as crops grown in the raised-field complexes. Thus subsistence foods as well as nonfood plants were grown. Significantly, radiocarbon dates from the Hondo River fields place the initial construction of this artificial landscape in the first millennium B.C., prior to significant population expansion in the Maya lowlands.

In the last decade, side-looking airborne radar (SLAR) has been used to locate huge areas of suspected raised-field complexes in a large portion of the Maya region. Yet most of these proposed field

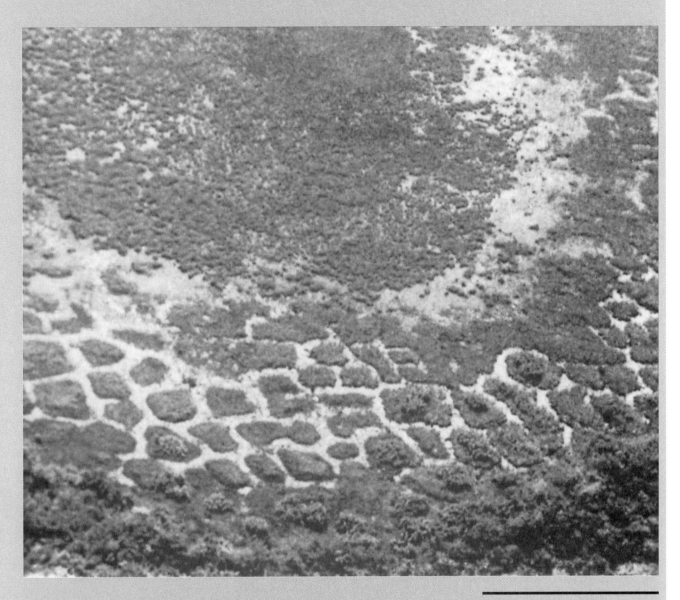

A raised-field complex in Pulltrouser Swamp, Belize.

systems have not been checked on the ground. Several other linear patterns observed by SLAR reflect no more than natural soil formations. Thus the geographic extent of ancient Maya raised-field complexes remains unknown.

In several areas, the ancient Maya supplemented extensive slash-and-burn farming with the construction of artificial terrace systems. Evidence for these agricultural features, which converted otherwise unfarmable slopes into a patch-work of level plots, has been found in both western Belize and in the vicinity of the Bec River. While doubts persist about the dating and distribution of Classic Maya agricultural systems, there is no longer any question that the Maya used a great diversity of subsistence strategies, including a series of intensive-farming techniques.

TIKAL'S MONUMENT RECORD

The rulers of Tikal

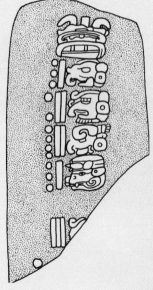

Stela 29, with a richly dressed noble on one side of the monument and glyphs arranged in a single column on the other.

Just as the ancient Maya economy was more complex than expected, recent studies in Maya archaeology and **epigraphy**, the study of inscriptions, have demonstrated that Classic Maya society was not egalitarian but, instead, was hierarchically organized. The commemoration of the births, accessions, conquests, and deaths of important rulers was a major theme of their carved stone monuments.

One of the most important monuments at Tikal, known as Stela 29, exhibits the earliest known and well-provenienced inscriptions in the Maya lowlands with a Long Count date of A.D. 292 (see "Writing and Calendars," p. 346). For archaeologists, Stela 29 is a rough marker for the beginning of the Maya Classic period, an era during which the Long Count was used on numerous Maya inscriptions. The end of the Classic period (A.D. 900) roughly coincides with the cessation of Long Count inscriptions. Stela 29 also includes the earliest emblem glyph (place name), a distinctive sign that identifies either a specific Maya center or the ruling lineage associated with that location.

In the Early Classic period, the importance of Tikal and its ruling lineage is indicated by the numerous dated monuments at the site. While other Maya centers in the immediate vicinity of Tikal also asserted their importance and autonomy by erecting fourth-century A.D. monuments, Tikal and its neighbor Uaxactún (wah-shak-toon') raised almost half of these early stelae. Stela 5 at Uaxactún, dating to A.D. 358, includes Tikal's emblem glyph, an indicator that the former site by that time may have been under Tikal's jurisdiction. Soon thereafter, several other Petén sites ceased erecting stelae, another signal that Tikal may have expanded its sovereignty early in the Classic period.

Precocious political development at Tikal and Uaxactún may have been related to the close ties that these centers developed with foreign elite. A stela erected in A.D. 377 at Uaxactún portrays a figure in non-Maya attire. Less than 2 years later, Tikal Stela 4 records the accession of a new ruler, Curl Nose, who is posed facing front rather than in profile, as was typical of earlier Maya rulers. In pose and costume, Curl Nose resembles Teotihuacan nobles, and the excavation of the tomb thought to have been his included objects suggesting a Teotihuacan connection.

This foreign link continued, although perhaps somewhat diminished, during the reign of Curl Nose's heir, Stormy Sky. The latter figure is portrayed on Tikal Stela 31, which commemorates the twentieth year of his rule. On the stela, Stormy Sky appears in Maya regalia, flanked by two subordinate figures wearing outfits more indicative of the highlands. Their shields are adorned with the face of the central Mexican rain deity prominent at Teotihuacan. During and immediately after the reign of Stormy Sky, Tikal's influence spread even farther in the lowlands, possibly stretching to distant Yaxchilán (yah-chee-lahn'), a Maya center on the Usumacinta River. Tikal's broad foreign ties and political importance may have stemmed from the site's location on land that lies between two major drainage systems, which linked the Gulf of Mexico with the Caribbean Sea, interconnecting the Maya lowlands.

Early in the sixth century A.D., a stela at Yaxchilán displayed the site's own emblem glyph, which may imply that a greater degree of autonomy from Tikal had been secured. Tikal's declining influence was signaled by a construction slowdown and a long break, from A.D. 534 to 692, in the carving of dated stelae. During the first 59 years of this period, called the hiatus, monument erection practically ceased at many sites in the southern Maya lowlands. Just prior to the hiatus, a Tikal ruler, Double Bird, was apparently defeated in battle by Caracol. During the hiatus, even the tombs of the Tikal elite contained meager offerings compared to the exotic and sumptuous items found earlier. Recent epigraphic breakthroughs stemming from the decipherment of glyphic texts from across the Maya lowlands support archaeological indications that the power of Tikal's lords may have waned during this period. At the same time, another Maya center to the north, Calakmul, ascended to much greater influence.

But by A.D. 700, political fortunes appear to have shifted again. Late in the seventh century, the most massive construction episode was begun at Tikal under the ruler Ah Cacau, who deliberately harkened back to powerful Stormy Sky. Clemency Coggins, of the Peabody Museum at Harvard University, has proposed that Ah Cacau's accession was timed to occur exactly 256 years after the inauguration of Stormy Sky. Under Ah Cacau and his immediate successors, Tikal's central Twin Pyramid groups and the most massive **acropoli**, mazelike complexes of palaces and courtyards, were built, and the site grew to more than 120 sq km (45 sq mi). At its maximum size, bounded by the swampy *bajos* to the east and west and defensive earthworks to the north and south, the site is thought to have been occupied by 50,000–80,000 people.

The later Classic period was characterized by a series of politically competitive centers, including Tikal in the central Petén, Calakmul in the north, Palenque in the southwest, Yaxchilán along the Usumacinta, and Copán in the southeast. The specific fortunes of these centers, their interconnecting networks of alliance, and the overall degree of political consolidation in the Maya lowlands appear to have vacillated over time. Yet during this era, stylistic and iconographic conventions were shared across the southern Maya lowlands. A standardized lunar calendar was employed throughout the region for almost a century (A.D. 672–751). Monuments from various centers indicate that communications between the sites were fostered by elite intermarriage, as well as by military alliances. Archaeological findings suggest that exchange also was an important means of regional integration.

Whether the Late Classic period ruling lineage at Tikal ever developed

Stela 31, showing Stormy Sky flanked by two subordinate figures.

the far-flung influence that Curl Nose and Stormy Sky apparently had earlier achieved remains a matter of scholarly debate. Although recent epigraphic findings indicate that the later lords of Tikal did extend their political influence over other Maya centers, those same texts seem to tell of increasing political fragmentation after A.D. 750. By the end of the eighth century A.D., construction at Tikal, and at many other major Maya centers, began to wane. A large percentage of Tikal's excavated house mounds were occupied during the major episode of building, yet most of the habitation after A.D. 830 was restricted to the site core, and the total site population may have been only 10% of what it was a century before. In A.D. 889, the latest monument was erected at Tikal, and the last known Long Count date anywhere was carved in A.D. 909. Tikal's fate was only part of the significant demographic decline and political breakdown, the so-called Maya collapse, that characterized almost the entire central and southern lowlands during the ninth and tenth centuries.

PALENQUE

*A Classic center at the edge
of the Maya lowlands*

The Maya and other native groups in the New World divided their physical realms into four quarters; each quarter was associated with specific colors, living things, and supernatural forces. Original Maya maps consistently place east at the top, suggesting that east was viewed as the dominant direction.

In A.D. 731, a stela was erected at the site of Copán, a large center in the southeastern part of the Maya lowlands. This monument lists the place names of four major Maya centers, each associated with one of the four cardinal directions. Preceding this list is a clause that Joyce Marcus interprets as "four on high," or "divided into four quarters." It appears that the Maya associated each section of their world with an important place or center. Not surprisingly, the monument carvers at Copán associated their site with the

foremost direction, east. Tikal was associated with the west, while Marcus has suggested that the emblem glyph associated with the south belonged to a site called Calakmul. Palenque (pa-len'kay), a center at the western edge of the lowlands, was linked with the direction north. Although these directions did not correspond closely to the actual geography, the cosmological model, dividing the Maya world between a series of centers, did reflect the political fluidity of the Late Classic Maya realm. This is not to say that the lowland Maya world contained four autonomous centers in A.D. 731. Rather, some authority at Copán perceived these four centers to be of the greatest importance.

Palenque is situated on a series of rolling hills approximately 50 km (30 mi) from the Usumacinta River, in the

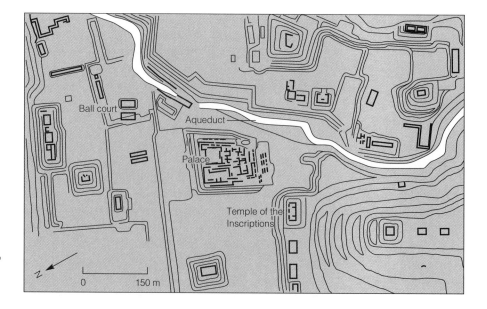

The plan of the central part of Palenque.

An artist's interpretation of the Temple of the Inscriptions, showing the staircase leading to Lord Pacal's tomb below.

state of Chiapas, Mexico. The site was occupied early in the Classic period but remained relatively small until the seventh century A.D., when a major building boom was started following the hiatus. The new structures at the site were built by a powerful lord who, inscriptions indicate, came to power in A.D. 615 and may have been named Pacal ("shield"). During Pacal's rule, Palenque also grew in size and expanded its authority over the neighboring region, and the site's emblem glyph appeared. The major structures at the site today were begun after Pacal's accession.

Lord Pacal was buried in an elaborate tomb beneath the pyramid that supports the Temple of the Inscriptions. The tomb was discovered by Alberto Ruz Lhuiller (in 1949–1958). Several years later, after clearing a staircase that led deep under the pyramid, Ruz found a large stuccoed crypt. The huge stone coffin, or **sarcophagus**, was topped with a superbly carved lid depicting the dead ruler falling into the underworld. Beneath the lid were the remains of Pacal, wearing beads and a mosaic mask of jade, surrounded by other treasures.

Epigraphic studies of the stone lid of the sarcophagus and other inscriptions at Palenque have led to the reconstruction of the long dynastic history of the site. Pacal was succeeded directly by his son Chan-Bahlum, who in a relatively short reign continued the massive construction at the core of the site. Following Chan-Bahlum's death early in the eighth century A.D., his brother Kan-Xul replaced him. During his rule, Palenque's realm reached its greatest extent. Kan-Xul also expanded Palenque's so-called Palace structure by erecting an unusual four-story tower in veneration of his father (see Color Plate 14). During winter solstices, the sun seems to set directly behind the Temple of the Inscriptions when viewed from the top of the Palace tower.

Inscriptions on the lid of Lord Pacal's coffin.

After the death of Kan-Xul, the site and its inscriptions began to wane. A series of three rulers with brief and possibly broken reigns followed. Two of Lord Pacal's later successors apparently were women. The last recorded accession date of a ruler in Pacal's lineage was A.D. 764. The last Long Count date known from Palenque (corresponding to A.D. 799) occurs on an inscribed pottery vessel and records the accession of a ruler with a central Mexican style name (non-Maya), 6 Cimi, suggesting that the site may have been taken over or influenced by foreigners late in the eighth century A.D.

Palenque was one of the earliest Maya centers to experience collapse. Monumental construction and the textual record waned during the latter half of the eighth century and ceased early in the ninth century. Pomona, a small former dependency of Palenque, displayed its own emblem glyph in A.D. 771, suggesting that it had achieved independence. Palenque was also one of the first sites to show an increasing tie to Gulf Coast or central Mexican elements. In parts of the Classic Maya world, this external bond often was associated with the cessation of monumental building and the erection of stelae. On a stela that was raised at the site of Seibal in A.D. 889, Palenque and Copán were no longer considered among the four primary centers of the Maya region. By then the realm of the Classic Maya had shrunk to little more than its former core around Tikal.

Although Palenque at its height was clearly part of the Classic Maya cultural realm, the site's distinctive layout and architecture reflected its location at the western periphery of the lowlands. Compared to the imposing appearance and vertical thrust of the architecture at Tikal and other Classic Maya centers, Palenque's major structures were broader and more dispersed, giving the site's civic-ceremonial center a more horizontal flow. Palenque also lacked a corpus of free-standing sculptured monuments (stelae and altars). Instead, hieroglyphic inscriptions generally were written on stone panels or plaster and incorporated directly into buildings.

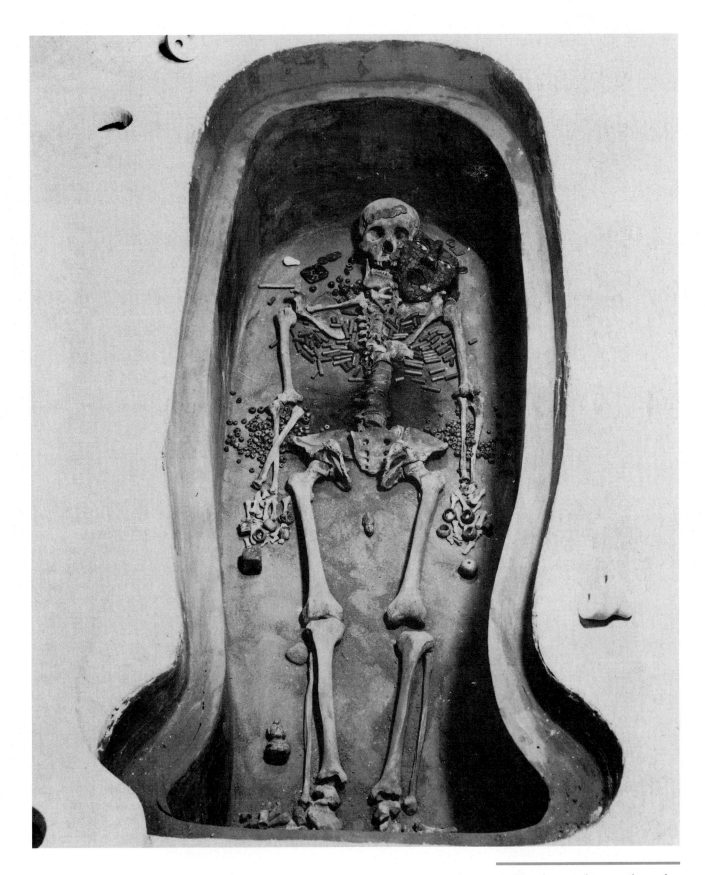

Lord Pacal's sarcophagus in the tomb.

WRITING AND CALENDARS

The Maya numerical system and Calendar Round

The earliest Mesoamerican writing appeared more than 2500 years ago, prior to the rise of the state or the existence of urban centers. Four different prehispanic Mesoamerican writing systems are known: the Maya, Zapotec, Mixtec, and Aztec. Each appears to include a mixture of **pictographic, ideographic,** and **phonetic** elements. The Mixtec and Aztec are known from late prehispanic texts written on prepared bark paper or deer skin; the older Zapotec system is preserved on inscriptions carved in stone. The Maya writing system has been preserved in late prehispanic folding books, as well as in a large body of texts on stone, pottery, and wall paintings from the Classic period (A.D. 250–900). The Maya writing system is the best known of the four, and

major breakthroughs in decipherment have come during the last two decades.

At first, the Classic Maya inscriptions were thought to relate exclusively to astronomy and calendrics, because these subjects comprised the first portions of the texts to be deciphered. Today, epigraphers recognize that the principal theme of Maya inscriptions is a political or dynastic one. As discussed earlier (see "Tikal's Monument Record," p. 340), scholars can now chart the military claims and political alliances of specific Maya rulers, and compare these textual data with the archaeological and architectural record. Carved stones have been deciphered, which commemorate significant events—birth, autosacrifice, accession to rule, marriage, military victory, death—in the lives of the Maya lords and their kin. Often the text helps frame a stylized scene of the commemorated event. The blocky hieroglyphs are presented in double columns intended to be read from left to right and top to bottom. As with ancient Egyptian monuments, the messages are generally brief and composed largely of nouns and verbs.

Prehispanic texts are closely linked to the pre-Columbian calendar. Classic Maya inscriptions are distinguished by their frequent use of the **Long Count** calendar, a system capable of tracking extended cycles of time. Although the Maya did not invent the Long Count, they refined and used it to the greatest degree. The smallest Long Count unit is the day, or *kin*. The second Long Count unit, composed of 20 *kins,* is called the *uinal.* The third unit, the *tun,* consists of 18 *uinals* or 360 *kins.* Above this third cycle are the *katun* and the *baktun,* consisting of 20 and 400 *tuns,* respectively. In accord with all prehispanic Mesoamerican numeration systems, the Long Count had a vigesimal structure, one based on multiples of 20. The only adjustment necessary to approximate the solar year was a change in the third unit, or *tun,* from 20 to 18 *uinals.*

The Long Count system enables scholars to date precisely many of the

An example of Maya hieroglyphs.

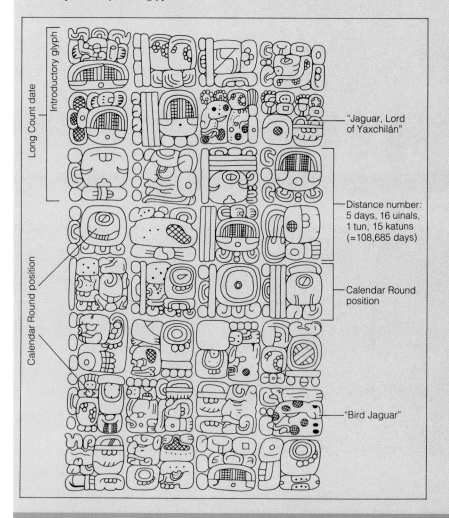

Introductory glyph

Long Count date

Calendar Round position

"Jaguar, Lord of Yaxchilán"

Distance number: 5 days, 16 uinals, 1 tun, 15 katuns (=108,685 days)

Calendar Round position

"Bird Jaguar"

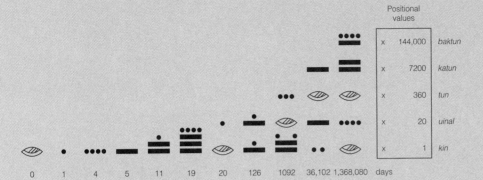

Positional values		
x	144,000	*baktun*
x	7200	*katun*
x	360	*tun*
x	20	*uinal*
x	1	*kin*

0   1   4   5   11   19   20   126   1092   36,102 1,368,080   days

The Maya numbering system and Long Count units. The base-20 system used only three symbols, the stylized shell for 0, a dot for 1, and a bar for 5. The numbers were arranged vertically (rather than horizontally, as in our Arabic numeration), with the lowest values at the bottom.

Classic Maya inscriptions. Long Count dates were calculated by the Classic Maya and their Mesoamerican forebears, who established the system by adding the total amount of elapsed time to a base date from which they began their calendar. Until this starting point was calculated, Long Count dates could not be equated with our calendric system. Some scholarly disagreement still exists, yet most researchers place the base date for the Long Count near the end of the fourth millennium B.C. (with 3114 B.C. the most widely accepted date).

In addition to the Long Count, the Maya and other Mesoamerican peoples used the Calendar Round. The main element of this calendar was the Sacred Almanac, or 260-day count. Primarily religious and divinatory in function, the almanac can be visualized as having been composed of two integrated "cogged wheels," or cycles of numbers; one cycle of numbers ran from 1 to 13, while the other cycle consisted of 20 named days. In general, these named days were similar across Mesoamerica; however, some differences did occur from group to group. The combination of a number and a day name formed a unit that would not recur until 260 days had elapsed, at which point the cycle began again. The numbers were usually expressed in typical Mesoamerican bar-and-dot fashion, with a dot equivalent to 1 and a bar equivalent to 5.

A second element of the Calendar Round was the 365-day Vague Year. This year was divided into 18 "months" of 20

days each. An extra period of 5 days was added at the end of the year. While the Classic Maya were aware that the tropical year actually was 365.25 days, they did not use a leap-year correction. The permutation of the Sacred Almanac and the Vague Year produced an 18,980-day Calendar Round that cycled back to its original start every 52 solar years.

The Maya believed that significant moments in time had their links with divinities and astrologically based auguries, and these associations were known and recorded. The Maya viewed time in a cyclical fashion. Points in time and the events assigned to them were not thought to be unique; the past, present, and future often could be woven together in prophecy and divination. Given the intricacy of Classic Maya writing and calendrics and their importance in the politico-religious sphere, it appears that this special knowledge was generally held by only a relatively small segment of the population.

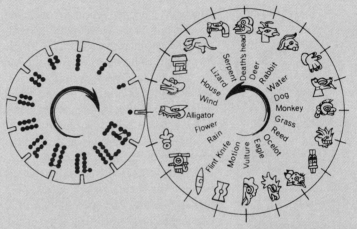

The 260-day Sacred Almanac for the Aztecs. The 20 named days intermesh with the numbers 1–13.

TULA

*Capital city of the
Toltec empire*

One of the Atlantean columns at Tula.

When the fifteenth-century Aztec ruler Itzcoatl purged the state archives, burning older documentary records, he greatly limited our ability to reconstruct the late prehispanic history of central Mexico. Fortunately, some lists of rulers, called king lists, and other fragmentary accounts of the previous periods survived. In conjunction with archaeological discoveries, these records enable us to begin to understand events in the central highlands between the decline of Teotihuacan, beginning around A.D. 700–800, and the establishment of the Aztec city of Tenochtitlán in A.D. 1325.

Sixteenth-century Spanish clerics and men of letters, curious about prehispanic civilization, inquired about the native history of Mexico. Repeatedly, their Aztec informants attributed the origins of their society to a semilegendary race known as the Toltecs. According to these part-historical, part-mythical accounts, the Toltecs were great warriors, but also peace-loving people. These mythic histories also describe the Toltecs as innovators, builders, and craftsmen, who cultivated giant ears of corn and colored cotton that did not have to be dyed. Their capital was supposedly an architectural masterpiece known as Tollan. The Aztecs traced their right to rule directly to their Toltec ancestry.

Like many such accounts, the origin myths of the Aztecs blended historical reality with fiction and distortion. Some of the stories did contain elements of truth, which enabled Mexican ethnohistorian Wigberto Jiménez Moreno to persuasively suggest that the Toltec capital was an actual place near the modern town of

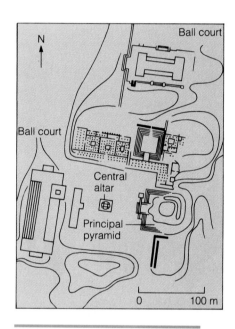

The plan of Tula.

Tula de Allende, in the state of Hidalgo. Over the last decades, several archaeological projects at Tula have substantiated Jiménez Moreno's identification.

Tula (too'la) is situated at the northern fringe of Mesoamerica, about 65 km (40 mi) northwest of modern Mexico City. The site had little significant occupation when Teotihuacan was partially burned and abandoned. The collapse of that great city, nearly coincident with the demise of monumental building at Monte Albán, marked a major transition in the highlands of Mexico. Following the fall of Teotihuacan, no single dominant community emerged in the central highlands to control the Basin of Mexico. Tula rose rapidly in this politically fragmented landscape.

Soon after A.D. 800, a substantial occupation was present at the site. Even at its height, Tula was considerably smaller than Teotihuacan or the later Aztec city of Tenochtitlán. Tula also lacks any evidence of urban planning outside its civic-ceremonial core. It reached its maximum size and its greatest influence between A.D. 950 and 1150: 13–16 sq km (5–6 sq mi) and about 40,000–60,000 people. The major structures at the site, including two large ball courts, were built during this period. Although the monumental architecture at Tula was far less grandiose than at Teotihuacan, a series of squat but substantial temple pyramids were erected. The most impressive and well-known remains at Tula are the sculpted **Atlantean columns,** which stand 4.6 m (15 ft) high. The military theme depicted by these giant basalt figures is also evident in a series of carved stone relief panels showing jaguars, eagles eating hearts, and coyotes, all creatures perhaps associated with specific warrior groups in the city.

Trade, the procurement of raw materials, and craft production were very important economic activities at Tula, as they were at Teotihuacan and Tenochtitlán. Containers of travertine, a white sedimentary stone, were made at the site, and sixteenth-century accounts describe many other fine, high-status goods produced by the Toltec craftspeople. As at Teotihuacan, areas of heavy obsidian use and/or production have been recorded at Tula. Most of the obsidian was derived from the same source that furnished workshops at Teotihuacan. Tula borders on arid regions to the north, where little can be grown except maguey. This plant is an important source of fiber, needles, sap, and other products. In ancient Mesoamerica, maguey fibers were raw material for cloth, clothing, nets, and bags. The abundance of spindle whorls at Tula indicates that the spinning of these fibers into twine also was an important economic activity. The presence of pottery and marine shells from the Pacific Coast further documents the extent of exchange with peoples in northern and western Mexico.

Both historical and archaeological sources agree that Tula had lost much of its influence before A.D. 1200. Excavations at Tula by Mexican archaeologist Jorge Acosta revealed evidence of burning and disruption at all the major structures; however, the specific date of this destruction was not determined. A recent project by Richard Diehl found that Tula was at least partially abandoned by A.D. 1200, although the extent of the collapse is unknown. Diehl's study also recorded a sizable Aztec occupation at Tula. Acosta found extensive evidence for late prehispanic looting in earlier monumental structures and even in the residential compounds. Colonial era texts of the Spanish friar Bernardino de Sahagún allude to this looting, citing the removal of Toltec artifacts from the ground.

Various written accounts provide a more intriguing depiction of Tula's end, yet their accuracy is unconfirmed. Although the accounts themselves are somewhat contradictory, the story ties the fall of Tula to a conflict between cosmic forces. The Mesoamerican cosmos was frequently symbolized as a duality. Quetzalcoatl, the representative of day, light, traditional religion, and good, was opposed to Tezcatlipoca, the embodiment of night, darkness, chicanery, and evil. In these accounts, Quetzalcoatl ("the feathered serpent"), or a ruler associated with him, is tricked, disgraced, and forced to leave the city, an event resulting in Tula's downfall.

Archaeological and historical sources both indicate that following the collapse, the Basin of Mexico and its northern fringes once again fragmented into a series of small polities, each controlling only its immediate vicinity. It was during this era of political decentralization that the Aztecs began their ascent to power.

Two obsidian blades and an exhausted core from Tula.

CHICHÉN ITZÁ

*The most magnificent late
Maya center in Yucatán*

Puuc-style architecture at
Chichén Itzá.

The collapse of major centers in the central and southern Maya lowlands during the ninth and tenth centuries A.D. coincided with an episode of development and population increase in the drier northern fringe of the Yucatán peninsula. Several clusters of larger centers were established in the northern lowlands, each marked by its own distinct architectural style.

The most widespread of these, the Puuc style, is identifiable by a mosaic of limestone masonry covering a rubble core. The earliest construction at the site of Chichén Itzá (chee-chen'eet-zah') is charcterized by this style. Chichén Itzá,

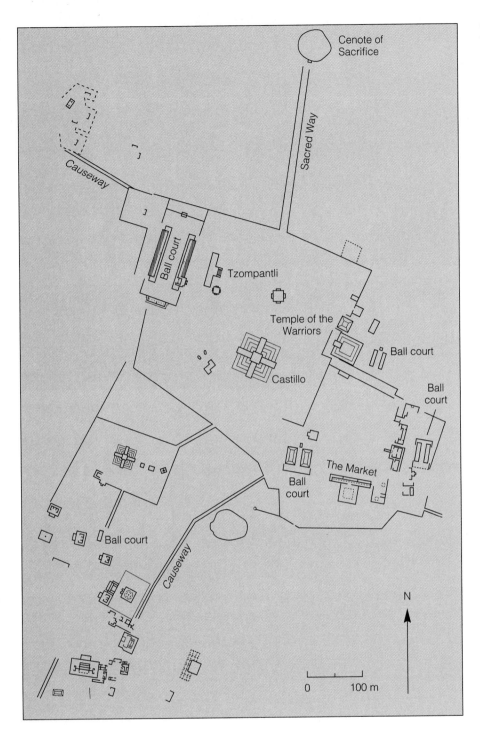

Cenote of
Sacrifice

Sacred Way

Causeway

Ball court

Tzompantli

Temple of the
Warriors

Ball court

Castillo

Ball
court

Ball court

The Market

Ball
court

Ball court

Causeway

N

0   100 m

one of the easternmost of the Puuc sites, was strategically situated toward the center of the Yucatán peninsula, near two large natural sinkhole wells, or **cenotes.** The limestone bedrock of northern Yucatán is very porous, and rainfall soaks immediately into the ground. There are no rivers and very little surface water in this area. The cenotes in the limestone landscape are a very important source of drinking water.

The flowering of the Puuc centers is associated with ceramic and architectural elements from the non-Maya areas of Mexico, perhaps the Gulf Coast. The archaeological indications of these exotic

A carved skull rack (*tzompantli*) at Chichén Itzá.

A mural from the Temple of the Warriors, showing warriors arriving in canoes.

connections fit well with later written accounts suggesting the role of "Mexicanized" Maya traders in the rise of the northern Yucatán centers during the Late Classic period. Their influence was related to a shift in long-distance trade routes and involved an expansion of circum-Yucatán sea transport at the expense of the old Petén River route across the Petén lowlands.

Late in the tenth century A.D., a second, more opulent construction boom led to the rebuilding of the center of Chichén Itzá in an architectural style more similar to that found at Toltec Tula. During this later construction phase, Chichén Itzá grew to its maximum size, more than 5 sq km (2 sq mi). The new architecture included colonnades, extensive I-shaped ball courts (Color Plate 15)

The sacred Cenote of Sacrifice at Chichén Itzá.

(the largest in Mesoamerica), relief carvings of prowling jaguars, carved warrior figures, carved *tzompantlis* (skull racks), and fascinating, sculpted *chac mools*. A **chac mool** is an altar in the form of a reclining figure with head and knees raised. The hands surround a bowl-shaped impression at the navel, where sacrifices or offerings were placed.

Some archaeologists have suggested an actual central Mexican Toltec presence at Chichén Itzá on the basis of ancient legends that tell of the god Quetzalcoatl from Tula arriving in Yucatán in A.D. 987. This interpretation is supported by murals in a temple at Chichén Itzá depicting warriors (assumed to be Toltecs) arriving in canoes and doing battle with the local populace. Yet the same textual sources that tell of foreign invaders in Postclassic Yucatán note that they spoke a Maya language, suggesting that they were not actually central Mexican Toltecs. The nature of the relationship between the two centers remains uncertain and under debate.

The later construction at Chichén Itzá reflects a strong Maya influence, with veneer masonry, mosaic facades, and the use of vaults, and they are generally more finely made and larger than similar buildings at Tula. The focus of

the new construction was a huge 12-ha (30-acre) plaza area. For almost two centuries, Chichén Itzá was the primary locus of truly monumental construction in northern Yucatán. The scale of building at the site, including 15 large plaza groups and numerous ball courts, is not found elsewhere. Yet excavations indicate that construction slowed by the middle of the thirteenth century, conforming with documentary accounts implying that Chichén Itzá's rule was broken by A.D. 1221.

During Chichén Itzá's ascendancy, and even after its demise, the cenotes remained important sites of sacred offerings. A *sacbe* (stone causeway) ran directly from the site's main plaza to one of the cenotes. Offerings of all kinds from across the Maya region, including Classic period items that may have been looted, were cast into this sacred natural well, appropriately named the Cenote of Sacrifice. According to Bishop Diego de Landa, a Spanish cleric who chronicled life in sixteenth-century Yucatán, men were thrown alive into the well as a sacrifice to the gods during times of drought. Indeed, the dredging of the sacred cenote turned up human bone as well as prehispanic copper, gold, and jade.

A *chac mool* at Chichén Itzá.

TENOCHTITLÁN

The capital city of the Aztecs:
the Venice of the New World

The Aztec civilization, the best known of any indigenous Native American state society, has aroused scholarly interest since the discovery and conquest of Mexico by the Spanish in the early sixteenth century. Although written accounts of Aztec society are rich and full of descriptive detail, the archaeological record is somewhat impoverished, in part because the Aztec capital of Tenochtitlán (ten-noch-teet-lan') is buried under the bustling metropolis of Mexico City.

In February 1978, electrical workers were digging trenches for cables in Mexico City when they found a large stone sculpture. Located 2 m (6.5 ft) below the surface, this sculpture depicted the Aztec female lunar deity Coyolxauhqui, who according to myth was slain and dismembered by her very important brother Huitzilopochtli, the war god. This discovery revived national interest in the Great Temple of the Aztecs, the Templo Mayor: a twin temple dedicated to Huitzilopochtli and Tlaloc, the rain deity. The accidental discovery initiated a long-term research project that has added greatly to our information about this city and the temple that was the physical and psychic heart of the Aztec world (see Color Plate 16).

The Aztecs, who referred to themselves as Mexica, had humble origins. The Mexica were **Chichimecs** from the northern desert who did not arrive in the Basin of Mexico until the middle of the thirteenth century A.D. Although the specific cause of this population movement is not known, it appears to have coincided with an episode of drought in the north, whic may have made that already dry area particularly unsuitable for agriculture. Alternatively, the Mexica and other northern groups may have been attracted to the economic and military opportunities afforded by the rise of Tula on Mesoamerica's northern frontier.

When the Mexica arrived, more than 50 small, autonomous **petty states** were present in the Basin of Mexico. At first, the Mexica had little choice but to settle on lands controlled by others. The established basin populations viewed the Mexica as barbarian heathens, yet they also recognized their military prowess, important during a period characterized by military conflicts and competition.

The Mexica's migrations did not end after their arrival in the basin. Feared and despised by more powerful and urban groups, they were repeatedly driven away. They took asylum on lands owned by Culhuacan, a relatively powerful petty state with ancestral ties to the ruling families at Tula. According to legend, the Mexica served the Culhua well as mercenaries. Eventually, they asked for the hand of the daughter of the ruler of Culhuacan to strengthen their bloodlines through marriage. Unfortunately one of their gods, Huitzilopochtli, spoke to the Mexica priests and asked them to sacrifice the girl. The Culhua ruler, invited to a ceremony to dedicate his daughter as a goddess, instead found a Mexica priest dressed in the flayed skin of his offspring. His wrath again forced the Mexica to retreat.

At the start of their journey, the Mexica had been told by the same god that

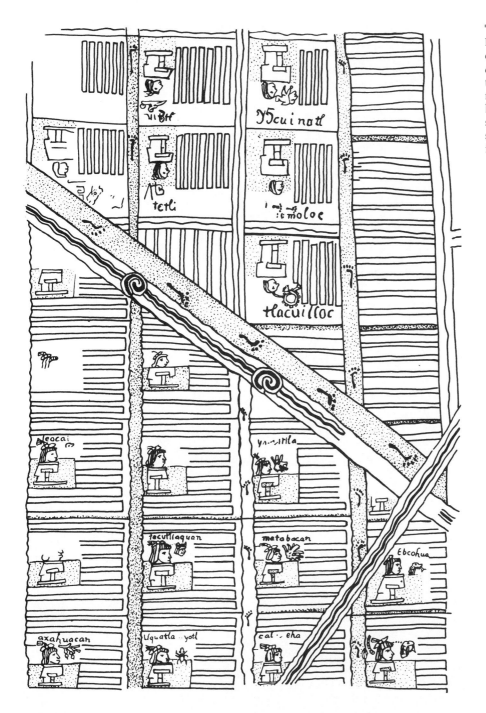

Part of an early sixteenth-century map of *chinampas* in Tenochtitlán. The *chinampas* are separated by water, and the houses of the owners, whose names are given in Spanish and Aztec hieroglyphs, are situated on squares of solid ground. Major canals are represented by wavy lines, and footprints indicate streets.

they would find an eagle perched atop a cactus plant to mark the end of their wanderings. Fleeing into the swamps of Lake Texcoco, one of the principal lakes of the basin, they found the eagle and cactus (a scene now immortalized on the flag of Mexico) on a nearby small, marshy island. The Mexica settled here and erected a temple for Huitzilopochtli. They named the settlement Tenochtitlán ("place of the fruit of the prickly pear cactus").

When Tenochtitlán was founded in A.D. 1325, the island lacked most construction materials (such as wood and stone), suffered periodic flooding, and was abundant only in insects. But the location offered several advantages. Water fowl and fish were plentiful, and the freshwater lakeshore was amenable to intensive *chinampa* agriculture. These farm plots, created by draining standing water and raising the surface of the swamp

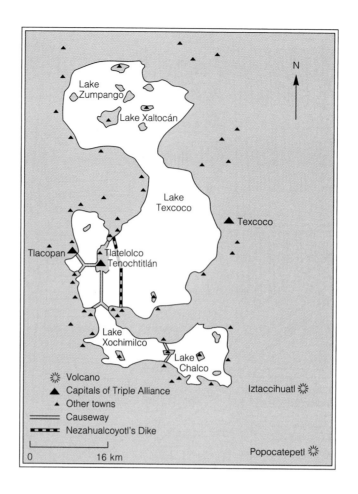

The Basin of Mexico during Aztec times.

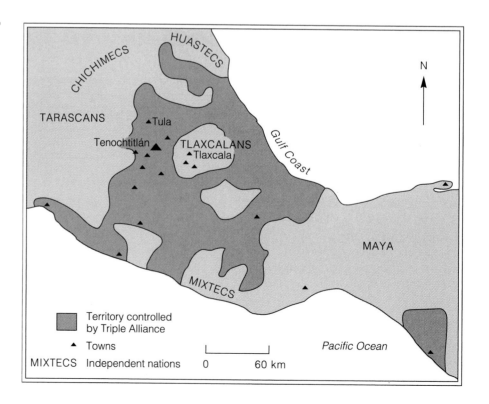

The domain controlled by the Triple Alliance.

The plan of the ceremonial core of Tenochtitlán. The shrines to Tlaloc and Huitzilpochtli sit atop the Templo Mayor.

1 Shrines of Tlaloc and Huitzilopochtli
2 Temple of Quetzalcoatl
3 Skull rack
4 Ball court

0   200 m

with soil and vegetation mats, became a major source of food production for the Aztecs. The little island was also in a prime location for controlling transportation in the basin. In ancient Mesoamerica, transport was exclusively by foot or canoe; there were neither beasts of burden nor wheeled vehicles (although toys with wheels were made). Water transport saved time and energy, especially when heavy loads were involved. Canoes plied the waters of the lake as the most efficient means of moving goods and materials between communities.

In the less than two centuries between its founding and the Spanish conquest, Tenochtitlán developed from a small island town to the largest and most powerful city in all of Mesoamerica. During its first century of existence (A.D. 1325–1428), the settlement was subordinate to more important basin centers. During this phase, the Aztec constructed *chinampas,* encouraged immigration to Tenochtitlán, and continued to gain renown for their mercenary skills. Their rulers strategically intermarried and al-

lied themselves with more established elite in the region.

By 1428, Tenochtitlán was powerful enough to join with the petty states of Texcoco and Tlacopan, forming a Triple Alliance that soon vaulted the Aztec capital to a supreme political position in the Basin of Mexico. In the years before the Spanish conquest, Tenochtitlán consolidated this political dominion while its armies defeated and demanded tribute from foreign polities across western Mesoamerica and as far away as Guatemala.

In 1473, Tenochtitlán defeated its neighbor city of Tlatelolco and incorporated the latter, including its giant marketplace, into the metropolis. The dual city was linked to the mainland by three large manmade causeways that ran from the lakeshore to the central ceremonial district of the capital. When the Spanish arrived, Tenochtitlán was a city of roughly 150,000–200,000 people. The Spanish leader Hernán Cortés was greatly impressed by the size and grandeur of Tenochtitlán, calling the Aztec city "another Venice."

Reconstruction of the Templo Mayor, superimposed over the excavated area. The main Spanish cathedral (still in place) was located next to the prehispanic temple.

Numerous craftspeople (including featherworkers, lapidaries, and reed-mat makers) were encouraged to settle in the city, adding to its importance as a commercial center. Finished goods from Tenochtitlán may have undermined local craft production in some of the communities in outlying parts of the basin. Tenochtitlán also obtained large quantities of exotic resources and finished goods as tribute payments from defeated polities. In general, nearby polities gave foodstuffs, wood, woven mats, and other heavier, more utilitarian items; more distant states sent rarer, more valuable goods. Captive states were typically instructed to send local materials. Other exotic goods were brought back to the city by the *pochteca,* a hereditary guild of long-distance traders. The *pochteca* also returned to Tenochtitlán with valuable military or political information.

The Aztec tribute demands were heavy, and noncompliance was dealt with harshly (see Color Plate 17). It is not surprising that Cortés' small band of adventurers received invaluable military and logistic support from Indian groups that despised the Aztecs. Obviously Cortés and his few hundred men would not have defeated the Aztec armies as quickly and easily without this native assistance. Once victorious, the Spanish razed the ceremonial core of Tenochtitlán, replacing the temples and shrines with churches, government buildings, and palatial residences. Mexico City rapidly grew up over the ancient Aztec center. The upper level of the Templo Mayor was dismantled, and the materials were used to build Mexico City's Main Cathedral.

During the Colonial era, Spanish power in Mesoamerica was strengthened by occupation of the same place as the prior Aztec civic and sacred authority. Eventually, in response to several destructive floods, the once productive lakes were largely drained by the Spanish. The Colonial authorities could not adequately manipulate the complex networks of dikes and canals that had been built and used by the Aztecs. The dry lake bottom now serves as the soft foundation for Mexico's earthquake-prone capital.

Early Colonial period maps and accounts indicate that the basic residential unit at Tenochtitlán was smaller than the apartment compounds at Teotithuacan. Most household compounds at Tenochtitlán were occupied by nuclear or joint families, each with its own direct access to the streets and canals of the city. Individual compounds were more easily differentiated, permitting public displays of status and wealth. In Aztec society, advances in social position could be achieved through military or economic successes.

AZTEC MARKETS

Cacao, currency, and "profit" in ancient Mexico

Aztec market scenes from the Codex Florentino. Top left: a produce market with neatly arranged wares; top right: King Ahuitzotl receiving shells, jaguar skins, plumage, jade, and cacao from the coast; bottom left: members of a slave family wearing bars across their necks as a sign of bondage; bottom right: a merchant from the coast bartering for cloth, gold ornaments, copper, obsidian tools, and maguey fiber rope from the highlands.

In today's market economies, people try to minimize costs and maximize returns in order to make a profit. Anthropologists distinguish this type of market endeavor from reciprocal and redistributive exchange networks (see "The Archaeology of Exchange," Chapter 7, p. 269). Reciprocity refers to face-to-face exchanges between known participants, such as relatives or trading partners, in which the specific return is not predefined (gift giving, for example). Redistribution is the accumulation and later dispersal of goods from a central place or by a central person (the income tax system, for example).

Aztec **marketing**, with its network of marketplaces, various currencies, and numerous participants, clearly fits within the conventional definition of a market system. The *conquistador* Bernal Díaz del Castillo wrote, in awe of the size and variety of goods offered at the main Tlatelolco marketplace in Tenochtitlán:

> After having examined and considered all that we had seen we turned to look at the great market place and the crowds of people that were in it, some buying and others selling, so that the murmur and hum of their voices and words that they used could be heard more than a league off. Some of the soldiers among us who had been in many parts of the world, in Constantinople, and all over Italy, and in Rome, said that so large a market place and so full of people, and so well regulated and arranged, they had never beheld before. (1956, pp. 218–219)

This market alone served 20,000–25,000 people on a normal day, and twice as many every fifth day when it was the focus of a cycle of changing regional markets. Many exchanges in the market were made by bartering. Others were facilitated by accepted currencies. **Cacao** beans, used to make a favorite drink of the nobility, were the most common form of money, but large cotton cloaks, quills filled with gold dust, stone and shell beads, and copper beads and axes also were employed. Cacao beans, which in fact did grow on trees, were accepted in payment for either goods or labor. Their importance was such that the dishonest buyers and sellers tried to counterfeit cacao by filling the bark or skin of the beans with earth. These fake cacao beans were then adeptly sealed and mixed into piles with true beans, where they could be passed off as genuine. The existence of counterfeit beans and the presence of market judges to catch and punish dishonest merchants both emphasize the importance of profit as a motive in this precapitalist society.

HUMAN SACRIFICE AND CANNIBALISM

Divergent interpretations of ancient rites

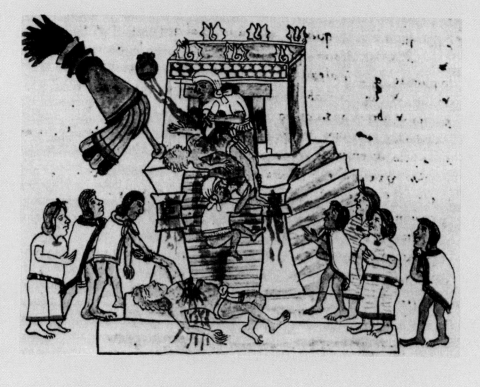

A depiction of an Aztec ritual heart sacrifice from a sixteenth-century codex.

No issue concerning ancient Mexico has attracted more attention and biting scholarly debate than human sacrifice and **cannibalism.** The Aztecs have frequently been portrayed in the popular press as violent, insatiable cannibals, practicing bloodthirsty and ghoulish acts. Ritual sacrifices have been documented archaeologically in early Mesopotamia, as well as in dynastic Egypt and ancient China. Human sacrifice has a very long history in prehispanic Mesoamerica, perhaps even back to the preceramic era in the Tehuacán Valley. Human sacrifice is depicted graphically in several Classic Maya inscriptions and is strongly suggested by the Oaxacan *danzante* stones. Ancient Mesoamerican societies also gave great ritual importance to blood. Both autosacrifice and the ritual offerings of blood are present in the archaeological and epigraphic evidence (see Color Plate 18).

Why, then, are the Aztecs so closely linked to the practice of human sacrifice? Most likely it is because the custom was featured so prominently in Spanish descriptions of central Mexico. While the Aztecs believed human sacrifice was a deeply religious practice, necessary for preserving the continuity of the universe, the Spanish Catholics saw it as the devil's work. Furthermore, the Europeans believed it to be their duty to abolish this behavior through conquest, conversion, and whatever means possible. The elimination of these customs, which horrified the Spaniards, therefore became a rationale for achieving their envisioned destiny to rule New Spain. (It should be noted that, at the time, the Spanish themselves were not above ghoulish behavior; in Spain, people were burned at the stake, while in Mexico, many Indians were mistreated and massacred.)

Anthropologist William Arens, of the State University of New York, Stony Brook, argues that the Spanish were so interested in defaming the native inhabitants and justifying their conquests that their sixteenth-century accounts cannot be trusted. Arens questions whether cannibalism even existed among the Aztecs. Although the evidence for cannibalism is not as overwhelming as it is for large-scale sacrifice, independent accounts describe the consumption of sacrificed prisoners, particularly by warriors and members of the elite.

An alternative to Arens' explanation has been advanced by Michael Harner, of the New School for Social Research, who argues that the absence of domesticated animals and the large number of people in late prehispanic central Mexico necessitated massive Aztec sacrifices to alleviate a dietary shortage of meat protein and fat through cannibalism. Harner's ecological interpretation, which lists cannibalism as the reason for massive sacrifices, has met with little nutritional, economic, or historical support. Harner argues that some 250,000 people were sacrificed each year in central Mexico, whereas most scholars place the annual figure in the tens of thousands. Harner ignores the religious context of Mesoamerican sacrifice and symbolic blood offerings, which often occurred without cannibalism. Many of the Aztec sacrificial events, which elaborated and embellished these prior customs, were dedicatory, carried out as thanksgiving rituals, and involved no cannibalism.

The diet of the people of prehispanic Mexico probably was not deficient in either protein or fat. In combination, the dietary staples of maize and beans provide a complete protein source. Such staples were sent in tribute to Tenochtitlán from surrounding polities and distributed through the market system. In one sixteenth-century account, 32 different types of wild fowl, many of which were very fatty, were described as edible; several of these were noted as abundant. Fish and other lake flora and fauna, including high-protein algae that was made into a cheeselike delicacy, also were available, as were domesticated dog and turkey. Some agricultural fields, like the *chinampas,* produced two or three crops annually.

If, as Harner implies, cannibalism provided the Aztecs with a major source of food, why were most sacrifices held immediately following the major harvest when food was abundant? In addition, why was human flesh restricted to the warriors and elite, groups likely to have the most to eat anyway? During Cortés' long siege of Tenochtitlán, the inhabitants were starving, eating almost anything, even adobe and leather. Yet human bodies lay all around, untouched.

Aztec human sacrifice is more convincingly interpreted in its historical and symbolic context. The Aztec traditions are connected with earlier Mesoamerican customs of bloodletting, dedicatory offerings, and the sacrifice of war captives in ritual events. The embellishment of the practice of human sacrifice by the Aztecs would seem associated with their distinctly militaristic background. According to Aztec ideology, they were the people chosen to nourish the deities through human sacrifice, as a hedge against uncertainty and to maintain order in the universe. As sacrificial victims were frequently (though not exclusively) prisoners or slaves, these beliefs may have motivated and fanaticized the Aztec military. The Aztecs conducted several kinds of sacrificial rituals—to bring rain, to commemorate temples, and as a kind of thanksgiving. Large sacrificial events also must have conveyed a powerful message about the strength and sanctity of Tenochtitlán to individuals both inside and outside the city.

THE END OF PREHISPANIC CIVILIZATIONS IN MEXICO

The legacy of Mesoamerica's past

People first set foot in Mesoamerica approximately 10,000–15,000 years ago. From their arrival until A.D. 1519, when the Spanish arrived, Mesoamerican societies developed and diversified independently of contacts with nonnative peoples. Over that period, a Mesoamerican world evolved, composed of diverse groups and polities connected through trade, warfare, intermarriage, and other long-distance contacts and communication. These peoples shared a common cultural background that was distinctively Mesoamerican. As we have discussed in this chapter, sedentary villages emerged across Mesoamerica during the second millennium B.C., while cities and conquest states were first established in various regions after 500 B.C.

The study of ancient Mesoamerica, therefore, enables archaeologists to examine agricultural origins, the emergence of villages and institutionalized social inequality, and the rise and fall of early civilizations. It also permits the investigation of a large macroregion that, unlike portions of the Old World, was never politically controlled by a single empire. Even the powerful Aztec armies were unable to defeat and consolidate the nearby peoples of Tlaxcala or the west Mexican Tarascans. Although long-term change in Mesoamerica did not follow the same course as in Mesopotamia and China (Chapter 10), Europe (Chapter 11), or even South America (Chapter 9), there are many features of these sequences of change and transition that can be compared.

The prehistory of Mesoamerica is documented by a variety of sources of information, including both indigenous and sixteenth-century Spanish texts and archaeological studies. With recent breakthroughs in the decipherment of Classic Maya writing systems, scholars studying these lowland societies can now view the past from an indigenous perspective that is not available for other regions of the preconquest Americas. Alternatively, the Mesoamerican highlands are well suited to archaeological surveys. In the valleys of Tehuacán, Mexico, and Oaxaca, as well as in several other highland Mesoamerican zones, the regional perspective from such surveys supplements the more specific findings from careful excavations at individual sites. We have learned that the size and number of prehispanic settlements did not increase at a uniform rate during the prehispanic era and that the pattern of population change was somewhat different in each region.

The art and architectural ruins of ancient Mesoamerican societies have captured attention for centuries. Now, as we collect more information about their makers, archaeologists have become fascinated with economies, statecraft, religious systems, and other aspects of their lifeways. The diversity of ancient Mesoamerican cities is truly astounding in size and function. Thus Mesoamerica has become a fruitful domain for the study of early urbanism and the processes associated with the rise of ancient cities. Some Mesoamerican cities, like Teotithuacan, were compact and laid out on a grid plan. Others were dispersed and positioned according to local topography, as in the Maya region during the Classic period. In Classic Maya cities and at Monte Albán, for example, the major thoroughfares were not planned to be strictly perpendicular to one another. Residential architecture also was far from uniform at major Mesoamerican cities. Craft manufacturing was central to ancient Teotihuacan, yet it played a smaller role in most other cities. Although exchange was an integrative mechanism that linked most Mesoamerican cities with their hinterlands, marketing may have had an especially crucial role at Tenochtitlán.

Even though exchange and economic production helped integrate the landscape, the volume and magnitude of trade was limited by prehispanic transport. One can only marvel at the mechanisms that allowed for the organization of tens (and even hundreds) of thousands of people. The longevity of cities like Teotihuacan and rain forest Tikal exemplify the effectiveness of the kin, ceremonial, and stately ties that integrated Mesoamerican polities. In prehispanic Mesoamerica, such features as the calendar, the ballgame, certain symbols, sacrificial (blood) rituals, public architectural conventions, and astronomical knowledge were all part of key informational systems that were shared and communicated primarily by the elite, and seemingly central to the maintenance of both their position and societal continuity.

Yet the specific ways in which these symbols were used and the nature of Mesoamerican rulership were by no means uniform across time and space. Classic Maya rule emphasized specific lords, individuals like Palenque's Pacal and Stormy Sky of Tikal, who were depicted on stelae in ornate costumes and were eventually buried in elaborate tombs accompanied by rich offerings. In contrast, we currently do not know the names of any of the rulers of ancient Teotihuacan, nor have massive burial displays been unearthed. Rule at Teotihuacan seems to have been less focused on specific individuals. Architectural emphasis was placed on large public spaces, such as inside the Ciudadela and the plaza in front of the Pyramid of the Moon. For the most part, mural art depicted ritual feasts and offerings, rather than glorifying the dynastic histories of specific kings. While Teotihuacan undoubtedly had a ruling class, the strategies of rule and the mechanisms of societal integration were different from those of the Classic Maya.

The autonomy of ancient Mesoamerican societies ended in the sixteenth century with the arrival of the Spaniards, but the ancestry and culture of the indigenous peoples has in large part survived, helping meld the contemporary lifeways of Mexico and Central America. The foods, craftsmanship, music, religion, and languages of these areas owe much to their prehispanic heritage. The demise of Aztec society, as well as that of their allies and enemies, has remarkable parallels to similar events farther south. In the northwestern quadrant of South America, the sixteenth-century Spanish clashed with a powerful indigenous Andean society, the Inca. Inca administration also had come to dominate a large cultural area, even bigger than that dominated by the Aztecs. But they, too, were conquered by the arriving *conquistadores*. In the next chapter, we examine these Andean societies and the series of processes and events that culminated in the empire of the Inca.

Most [artistic] scenes [at Teotihuacan] show human beings so loaded with clothing and insignia that faces and other body parts are barely visible. Emphasis is on acts rather than actors; on offices rather than office-holders. This, together with the multiplicity of identical scenes, suggests an ethos in which individuals were interchangeable and replaceable. . . . Supreme [Teotihuacan] political authority may not always have been strongly concentrated in a single person or lineage.

G. L. Cowgill (1997)

SUGGESTED READINGS

Blanton, R. E., S. A. Kowalewski, G. M. Feinman, and L. M. Finsten. 1993. *Ancient Mesoamerica: A comparison of change in three regions.* 2d ed. Cambridge: Cambridge University Press. *An analysis of long-term change in three Mesoamerican regions.*

Flannery, K. V., ed. 1976. *The early Mesoamerican village.* New York: Academic Press. *A humorous, yet highly instructive, volume on ancient Mesoamerica that illustrates how archaeology should proceed at various scales of analysis to interpret the past.*

Flannery, K. V., and J. Marcus, eds. 1983. *The cloud people: Divergent evolution of the Zapotec and Mixtec civilizations.* New York: Academic Press. *The synthetic overview for prehispanic Oaxaca.*

Marcus, J., and K. V. Flannery. 1996. *Zapotec civilization: How urban society evolved in Mexico's Oaxaca Valley.* London: Thames & Hudson. *A synthetic overview of prehispanic Oaxaca, focusing on the rise of early urban societies in that region.*

Sharer, R. J. 1994. *The ancient Maya.* 5th ed. Stanford, CA: Stanford University Press. *A classic text on the Maya.*

SOUTH AMERICA: THE INCA AND THEIR PREDECESSORS

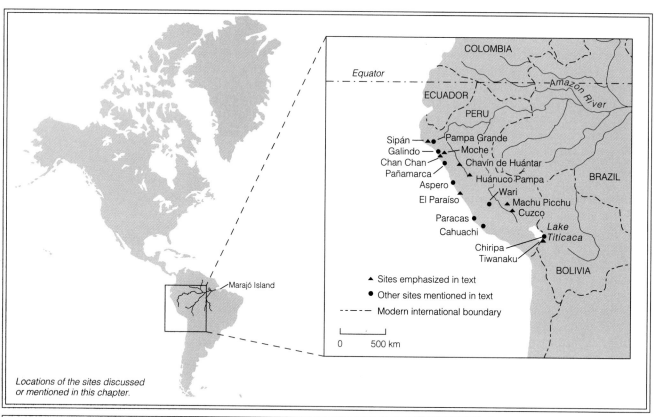

Locations of the sites discussed or mentioned in this chapter.

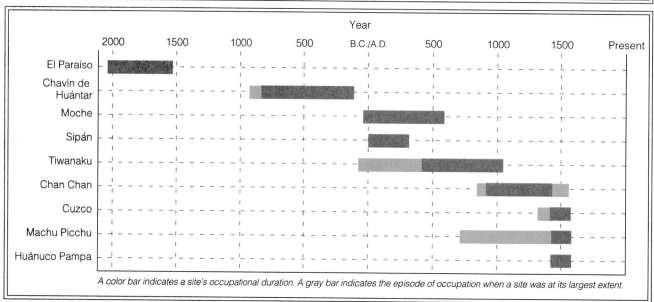

A color bar indicates a site's occupational duration. A gray bar indicates the episode of occupation when a site was at its largest extent.

PREHISPANIC SOUTH AMERICA

Early coastal villages and large mountain states

When Christopher Columbus left Spain on the voyage that brought him to America, the largest empire in the world was Tawantinsuyu, the Inca empire. Much greater in size than any fifteenth- or twentieth-century European state, Tawantinsuyu ("land of four quarters") stretched over 984,000 sq km (380,000 sq mi), about the size of Washington, Oregon, Idaho, and Montana combined. The Inca controlled the most extensive political domain that has ever existed in the Southern Hemisphere. Cuzco, the capital of the realm, governed some 80 provinces that sprawled from Colombia in the north across the Andean highlands of Argentina, Bolivia, Peru, and Ecuador to Chile in the south.

From the Pacific Ocean, the Andes rise so abruptly that a mere sliver of flat coastal land separates the high mountains from the water. This coastal strip is one of the world's driest deserts. In the high Andes, where peaks rise to more than 6100 m (20,000 feet) above sea level (the highest peaks in North or South America), humans occupied the relatively flat basins and valleys, as well as the high grassland plateaus (*punas*). The eastern side of the mountains, called the *montaña,* is wet and heavily vegetated. Farther east lies the enormous drainage basin of the Amazon, composed of tropical forests and savannas. Feathers and many tropical plants were brought from the forest into the Andean and coastal zones.

Our main focus in this chapter is Andean South America. The people of the Amazon rain forests and savannas had a unique and important prehistory as well. Yet because of the impenetrability of the lush environment, archaeologists and ethnohistorians still know much less about the latter area than about the more accessible coastal and mountain zones.

In 1948 and 1949, Betty Meggers and Clifford Evans, of the Smithsonian Institution, began preliminary investigations on Marajó Island at the mouth of the Amazon River. On this large island, 39,000 sq m (15,000 sq mi), huge earthworks were found, which Meggers and Evans interpreted as the remnants of a complex society that had moved to the island from the Andes, only to meet a rapid demise. At the time, this interpretation was well reasoned because the large scale of the earthworks was unexpected, given their absence in small, egalitarian, contemporary Amazonian Indian villages. Recent archaeological work on Marajó Island by Anna Roosevelt, of the Field Museum of Natural History, and her colleagues has revised our perspective on Marajoara origins. Their research illustrates numerous continuities between modern Amazonian people and the earlier Marajoara occupation and documents a more than 1000-year habitation sequence (400 B.C.–A.D. 1300) on the island. For example, Roosevelt found large, globular burial urns that were painted to represent crouching humans, decorated with multicolored, geometric patterns similar to the abstract drug visions illustrated by contemporary Amazonians. Marajoara art also has antecedents in earlier lowland styles, and the painting method is Amazonian (not Andean) in character. The physical affiliation of Marajoara skeletons is closer to Amazonian than to Andean people.

At the same time, reanalysis of written accounts of sixteenth-century Spanish penetration into the Amazon has led researchers to argue that many of the late prehistoric populations of this region may have been more hierarchically organized and densely distributed than Amazonian populations today. Differences, such as the cessation of inherited positions of leadership, between pre-Columbian inhabitants and contemporary groups may owe much to the diseases brought by the Europeans.

Western South America contained the continent's first agricultural settlements (e.g., Guitarrero Cave), as well as its earliest sedentary communities. We examine the prehispanic peoples of this area, beginning with the early site of El Paraíso, a sedentary coastal community dating prior to 2000 B.C., and concluding with the late prehispanic Inca sites of Cuzco, Machu Picchu, and Huánuco Pampa.

The prehistory of this part of South America is, in a general way, similar to that of Mesoamerica. In both areas, the earliest experiments with food production preceded the transition to sedentary village life. In South America the first villages date to 3500 B.C., much earlier than in Mesoamerica. In both regions, however, these first sedentary communities were situated on the coast. Soon thereafter, greater social differences and the first positions of leadership become evident in the archaeological record. In Mesoamerica, these changes occurred along with the development of an interregional style, the Olmec Horizon, represented in exotic and highly crafted items found in both the highlands and the lowlands. Between 900 and 200 B.C., a similar phenomenon, the Chavín style, was shared from the edges of the Amazon to the Pacific Coast. This style is named for the carvings found on a temple in the uplands of central Peru at Chavín de Huántar. In Peru, however, the spread of the Chavín style appears to postdate the construction of truly monumental public architecture and the emergence of social differences at coastal sites that were contemporary with earlier El Paraíso.

In South America, the last centuries B.C. were marked by the rise of major centers that became the core of states administering regional populations. We discuss Moche, on the north coast, and refer to the fantastic line drawings constructed by the Nazca in the south. We also discuss the coastal site of Sipán, where spectacular Moche-era tombs were excavated. Later, Tiwanaku, a giant economic and religious center near the southern end of Lake Titicaca in Bolivia, began to incorporate larger areas outside its local region.

As with the Aztecs in the highlands of central Mexico, the end of the prehispanic era in South America was characterized by a powerful people, the Inca, whose rulers exacted tribute from a wide domain. Yet this much larger South American empire had clearer imperial predecessors, such as the Tiwanaku polity and the Chimú kingdom. After A.D. 1000, the latter, which was centered on the north coast at Chan Chan, consolidated a large, primarily coastal domain. This political sphere was eventually engulfed by the expansive Inca, who conquered the Chimú between A.D. 1462 and 1470. We examine the nature and organization of this New World empire by looking at Cuzco, the Inca capital, the famous high mountain settlement of Machu Picchu, and the provincial administrative center of Huánuco Pampa.

While parallels can be drawn between the long prehispanic sequences in Mexico and Peru, there also were important differences. Most of the major Peruvian centers were shorter-lived than Mesoamerican sites like San José Mogote, Monte Albán, and Teotihuacan, which were inhabited almost continuously for a millennium or more. The Andean world also seems to have lacked a core region like the Basin of Mexico, which dominated the larger landscape for much of the prehispanic era. In South America, the balance of power seems to have shifted repeatedly between the Pacific Coast and the rugged uplands. Likewise, at times, the core of the Andean world was positioned in the south (as at Inca Cuzco), while at other times the Andean world's most powerful centers lay in the north at Moche and Chan Chan.

Animal domestication was more important in South America, where a variety of camelids, in addition to guinea pigs, were tamed. Since only the turkey, the dog, and the honeybee were domesticated in Mesoamerica, long-distance land transport was conducted entirely by human bearers. In South America, the llama (a camelid), used also for wool and meat, served as a pack animal for loads up to 45 kg (100 lb), making land transportation considerably less costly than it was in Mesoamerica. Llamas, like the more efficient Old World beasts of burden, subsist on grasses and other foods that humans cannot digest.

The Inca built and maintained an extensive, often paved road system (with suspension cables, stone bridges, and a system of relay runners) that crossed almost the entire empire and was unmatched in Mesoamerica. Alternatively, water crafts, including giant trading canoes, were more developed in Middle America.

In Mesoamerica, a writing system developed more than 2000 years ago. Subsequently, it diversified, with several systems, particularly that of the Maya, becoming more complex (with relatively long texts). In contrast, no archaeological evidence for prehispanic Andean writing has been found to date. The Inca did possess an ingenious numerical apparatus, the *quipu* ("knot"), which was composed of a main horizontal cord from which a series of smaller strings hung. The *quipu* was used to record numbers, by tying knots at various intervals on these strings. The knots farthest from the main cord represent the smallest numbers. Although the *quipu* makes an excellent system for recording numbers, it would have been somewhat more cumbersome to use in calculations. Nevertheless, even without a system of writing, the Inca were able to establish a larger and better integrated political system than ever existed in prehispanic Mesoamerica.

Although the written words left by the Maya and other Mesoamerican peoples are absent in the Andes, archaeologists working along the arid coast of Peru have the advantage of a quality of preservation unknown almost anywhere else. Standing adobe architecture frequently sits almost unscathed by the elements for centuries, even millennia. The recovery of large woven textiles is not unusual. Preservation can be so good that even fingernail clippings and human hair were found by Joyce Marcus using careful excavation procedures at coastal Cerro Azul, a site that postdates A.D. 1100. Marcus also found a series of mummified burials at Cerro Azul. While males generally were buried with fishing nets or slings (for hunting), females were interred with an array of different weaving implements (including camelid bone tools, bobbins made of thorn, needles, and balls of various colored yarns).

South America provides a second fascinating area for studying the emergence of an indigenous civilization. Only through archaeology can we hope to discover the remarkable similarities—as well as the all-important differences—that characterized these long cultural processes in various regions of the globe.

EL PARAÍSO

*An early sedentary village
on the coast of Peru*

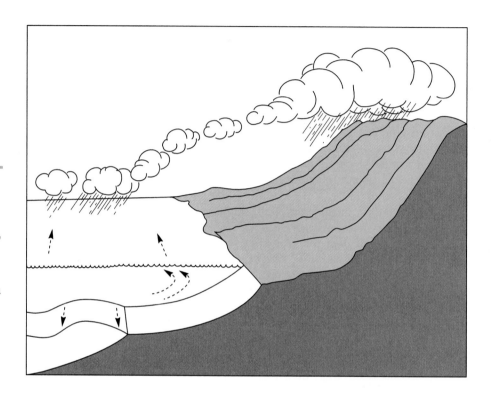

A drawing of ocean currents and coastal weather patterns. Moisture-bearing clouds moving from the Pacific Ocean are warmed by the landmass, but temperature inversions keep precipitation from falling until the higher altitudes of the Andes are reached (about 2500 m), leaving the coast dry but cool. The waters off Peru are swept northward by the coastal current. The deeper undercurrent flows southward; upwelling waters from the lower depths bring up rich nutrients that support abundant marine life.

The waters off the west coast of Peru are one of the world's richest fishing areas. A complex mixing of ocean currents provides an extraordinary source of marine foods. The shore of these abundant waters, however, is one of the world's driest deserts. The same cold waters that foster rich plankton and fish life also inhibit rainfall on the coast. This coastal zone, stretching from the shoreline to the foothills of the Andes, only rarely receives measurable quantities of precipitation. Short-lived torrential downpours occur only once or twice a decade. Streams carrying the snowmelt and rainfall from the Andes provide most of the surface water, cross-cutting the bleak coastal desert in an east-west direction. These rivers and streams are in essence isolated verdant pockets along the arid coastline.

The desert coast of central Peru was first settled after 7000 B.C. by mobile groups who exploited a wide range of environmental zones. The Pacific Ocean was a source of fish and shellfish, while deer, small mammals, and birds were hunted and wild plants collected in the coastal river valleys. The dry foothills of the western Andes become oases of scattered communities of fog vegetation, or **lomas,** between June and October (winter in the Southern Hemisphere). Here the early inhabitants ate deer and the edible seeds of grasses or sagelike plants. Grinding stones used in preparing these plant foods have been found in these areas.

After 5000 B.C., certain coastal populations relied increasingly on marine and plant products, including cultivated squash and tubers that had been introduced to the desert coast from the highlands. Settlements clustered closer to the ocean than they had previously, and Peru's first permanent, year-round villages were established shortly after 4000 B.C.,

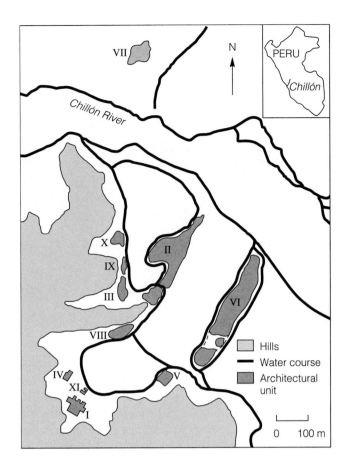

more than 1000 years before the first Peruvian evidence for pottery. These early villagers wove nets of cotton; net fragments, cotton twine, cordage pieces, and various remnants of cotton plants have been recovered from dry midden deposits at the early oceanside sites.

Around 2000 B.C., several larger settlements were established. El Paraíso (el′par-a-ease′o), the most extensive of these preceramic settlements, was located about 2 km (1.2 mi) from the coast along a permanent stream, next to a wide area of irrigable land. El Paraíso contains eight or nine large stone structures that, in total, cover over 58 ha (140 acres). The structures range in size from three to four rooms to massive complexes 300 m (980 ft) long × 100 m (325 ft) wide. The site represents one of the New World's earliest examples of monumental construction and nucleated population.

Although El Paraíso has been known to archaeologists for decades, it was not excavated until 1965 by Frederic Engel. The first excavations indicated an early preceramic date and revealed that one of the stone structures (Unit I) consisted of a series of rectangular rooms, courts, and passageways delineated by walls of 1.5–2.5 m (5–8 ft) in height. The walls were built of large stone blocks cemented together with clay and faced with a mud plaster painted with black, red, ochre, and white. The compound was filled in with rock rubble and then rebuilt several times during the occupation of the site. Recent excavations by Jeffrey Quilter, of Dumbarton Oaks Research Library and Collection, and his colleagues have confirmed that two other compounds also were preceramic. Radiocarbon dates from the three compounds indicate a short, possibly 300-year contemporaneous occupation that ended by 1500 B.C.

Despite these findings, many questions remain. How were these masonry compounds used? Although some of the rooms in Unit I contain possible offerings and may have been used for ceremonies, the diversity of artifacts (grinding stones, a wooden sling, stone and wooden tools) from the compound suggests it was not simply a religious

The north face of Unit I at El Paraíso.

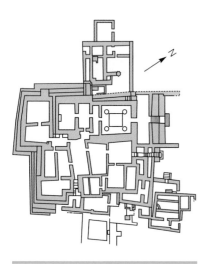

The plan of Unit I, a partially restored architectural complex at El Paraíso.

structure. Quilter found domesticated cotton, wool, and needles in one room in Unit II, suggesting that this area may have been used for making textiles. Large quantities of bird excrement, or **guano,** a bird offering, and colorful bird feathers also were found in the same room, likely evidence for the ancient practice of weaving colored feathers into high-status cloths. Other cotton was woven into nets and lines used in fishing. Although there is little consensus about the kind of sociopolitical organization at El Paraíso, large quantities of labor clearly were required to quarry and shape the stone blocks used to build the compounds. Additional coordination, planning, and muscle power were needed to repeatedly rebuild the structures.

Yet the biggest mystery concerns the diet of the residents of El Paraíso and the other preceramic inhabitants of coastal Peru. In 1975, Michael Moseley, of the University of Florida, proposed that the foundations of later Andean civilization were established during the preceramic era at such places as El Paraíso. He believed the inhabitants depended largely on marine foods. Although no one disputes the important role of foods from the sea (shellfish, marine mammals, and fish), various plants, including the starchy tropical tubers (jicama and achira), cultivated common beans and lima beans, and

domesticated chili peppers, gourds, and squash have all been recovered at El Paraíso, along with the remains of birds and small quantities of land mammals. More than 90% of the faunal remains identified by Quilter and his team belonged to bony fish and mollusks. However, the site's location, adjacent to an unusually large patch of arable land near the mouth of the Chillón River and 2 km (1.2 mi) from the Pacific, also indicates a terrestrial component important to the preceramic economy (cotton production) and diet. This inference is supported by the analysis of ten human **coprolites** (fossilized feces) from El Paraíso, which revealed that both squash and a variety of wild plant foods (including grasses, seeds, and tree fruits) comprised a significant portion of the diet.

Many questions remain regarding the early inhabitants of El Paraíso. Yet there is no doubt that the archaeological work at this site and others along the dry Pacific Coast has revolutionized our knowledge of ancient South America and its early sedentary beginnings, thousands of years ago.

In 1975, Michael Moseley proposed that complex societies with monumental architecture emerged during the preceramic period on the Pacific Coast of South America. Subsistence activities at these sites appear to have focused on marine resources. Moseley intended to refute the widely accepted belief that only agricultural economies can support the foundations of civilization. He bolstered his argument, which he called the Maritime Hypothesis, by noting the abundance of shellfish middens and fishing nets at many coastal settlements, particularly at several sites that were closer to the coast and somewhat earlier than El Paraíso.

Although there is little doubt that marine foods were an essential component in the diet of the prehispanic coastal dwellers, several studies have suggested that both wild and agricultural plants also were a significant part of ancient Peruvian subsistence. Root and seed crops have been recovered in relatively small quantities in midden deposits at El Paraíso, as well as at other preceramic coastal sites. However, the quantity of plant remains, compared to the abundance of shell, may not provide an accurate reflection of the relative importance of these foods in the ancient diet. Plant remains generally do not preserve in the archaeological record nearly as well as harder materials, such as mollusk shells. Poor preservation is a particular problem for detecting the root crops that were important in ancient Peru, because they lack the harder parts that make seed crops somewhat easier to find. The problems of preservation were aggravated in many early coastal excavations where fine screening and other meticulous recovery techniques were not used.

Several critics of the Maritime Hypothesis have noted that a subsistence regime largely dependent on the abundant marine resources of the Peruvian Pacific would have left the coastal inhabitants at the mercy of the warm countercurrents that periodically disrupt the bounty of the ocean environment. Five to ten times each century, a countercurrent, referred to as **El Niño** ("the Christ Child"), moves in from the north soon after Christmas, altering the normal patterns of water temperature, flow, and salinity, and diminishing the availability of nutrients. El Niños generally last 2–12 months and severely disturb marine life. Bountiful schools of fish and flocks of seabirds either migrate or die. Because of the irregularity of these maritime disruptions and the difficulty of storing large quantities of marine products in a warm climate, it seems likely that plant foods provided a significant portion of the ancient diet. In fact, this suggestion has been supported by Jeffrey Quilter's recovery at El Paraíso of a diversity of wild and domesticated plant foods, through both coprolite analysis and the sifting of excavated trash deposits through ¼-inch hardware cloth and 1⁄16-inch mesh. As Quilter has noted: "It was not simply the adoption of domesticated plants or the importance of seafood that led to complex societies in Peru but the roles of a variety of subsistence and other resources within the context of social interactions" (Quilter and Stocker, 1983, p. 554).

A fragment of cotton net used for fishing.

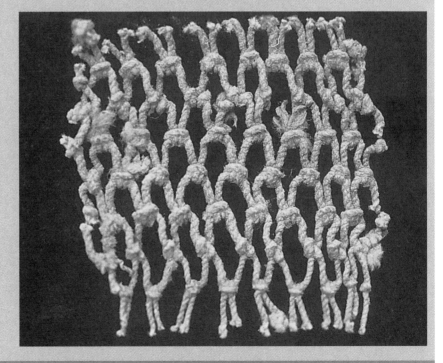

CHAVÍN DE HUÁNTAR

An early Andean center

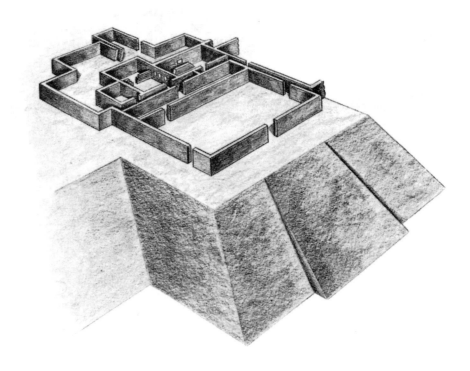

An artist's reconstruction of architecture at Aspero.

The Peruvian coast, homeland for such late prehispanic polities as the Nazca, Moche, and Chimú, also gave rise (prior to 2000 B.C.) to the first complex political systems in western South America. Centralized polities, focused on large sites that contained monumental architecture, including ceremonial mounds and plazas, developed in a number of valleys along the north and central coasts.

Excavations at the coastal site of Aspero by Robert A. Feldman, of the Field Museum of Natural History in Chicago, have revealed interconnected rooms of various sizes that were divided by stone walls. The outer rooms were usually the largest and had the widest doorways. The inner rooms, which contained cached artifacts and wall niches, were small. These central rooms, the walls of which were elaborately decorated, could be entered only by winding through the more open

larger rooms and then stepping through narrow entryways. Thus access to the inner cores of these nonresidential structures may have been restricted to a small segment of the population.

As with many ancient Native American ceremonial structures, these multi-roomed compounds were repeatedly refloored and rebuilt. In some instances, old rooms were filled with **shicra,** meshed bags containing rocks, prior to reconstruction. At about the same time, early villages in the highlands contained more-modest nonresidential structures, usually one-room, free-standing buildings. The highland structures included ceremonial hearths, wall niches, and colored plaster, features also found in the coastal compounds. Some communication and exchange of foods, shells, and colored stones occurred between the upland and coastal environments, although for more than a millennium the coast contained the larger, more socially differentiated polities.

After 1000 B.C., the balance of power began to shift upward as larger centers developed in the Andean highlands. Perhaps the best known of these sites is Chavín de Huántar (cha-veen′day-whan′tar), situated at the confluence of two rivers, more than 3000 m (10,000 ft) above sea level in what is today a typical Peruvian valley. The site is surrounded by steep slopes, including the snow-capped Cordillera Blanca, whose highest peaks rise above 5500 m (18,000 ft).

In the early years of the Colonial era, Spanish chroniclers noted the grandeur of the ruins and the beautiful decoration visible in the finely cut stones at Chavín de Huántar. Yet the historical placement of the ruins and their importance to Andean prehistory were established just over 50 years ago, through the works of the late Peruvian archaeologist Julio Tello. Tello correctly recognized the important artistic similarities between the stone carvings at Chavín de Huántar and the decorative items of pottery, stone, and metal found at other sites in the highlands and on the coast. These similar motifs define a stylistic pattern that has become known as the Chavín Horizon. Typically, Chavín carvings interweave figures that combine the natural features of people, snakes, jaguars, **caymans** (alligators), and birds, with intricate geometric and curvilinear designs.

Radiocarbon dates from Chavín de Huántar by Richard L. Burger, of Yale University, place the major occupation of the site between 850 and 200 B.C. It appears that construction of the civic-ceremonial architecture began early in the occupation but did not reach its largest (more than 40 ha, or 100 acres) and most monumental extent until after 390 B.C. By 200 B.C., the central core of the site included a complex of rectangular, stone masonry platforms covering an area greater than 4000 sq m (about 1 acre). Although the height of this construction is difficult to assess because the main structures were on a slope, the largest platform, the Castillo, or New Temple, rises about 13 m (45 ft) above the surrounding terrace.

The Castillo platform was not solid masonry but was composed of three superimposed levels of small, interlocking galleries and rooms, which were covered by flat slabs and separated by adobe and stone walls. The interior walls were sometimes painted, and the inside rooms were ventilated by a complex network of shafts. The platform exterior was faced with dressed granite, and at one time these outer walls were adorned with sculpted human and animal heads.

The so-called Old Temple at Chavín was U-shaped and consisted of a main building with two wings that enclosed three sides of a rectangular plaza. Deep inside the Old Temple stands a carved prismlike shaft of white granite. This 4-m (13-ft) high pillar, named the Great Image or the Lanzón, was pointed at both ends and was fastened to both the floor and the ceiling of the interior gallery in which it stood. Each side of the Great Image was carved in bas-relief,

Finely carved stone from Chavín de Huántar.

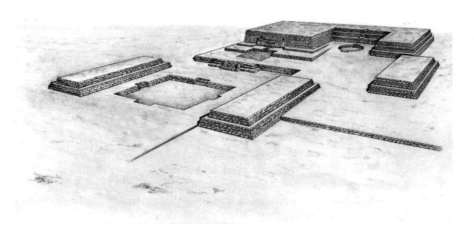

An artist's reconstruction of the Temple of Chavín. The Old Temple is in the upper right; the New Temple and its sunken plaza complex are at left and center. The sunken plaza measures approximately 500 × 500 m.

depicting a standing human figure with feline teeth and nostrils. The anthropomorphic figure was wearing earplugs, a necklace, and a belt that contained serpent-jaguar faces. The latter images also adorned the upper portion of the monolith, as a kind of headpiece perched on the serpent hair of the main figure. The Great Image was just one of a number of large stelae found at the site.

By 400–200 B.C., several thousand people lived at Chavín de Huántar, with residential areas surrounding the ceremonial complex. In size and scale of construction, the site far surpassed any other occupation in the narrow Mosna Valley, where it was located. During this period, Chavín de Huántar also became much more interconnected with large settlements in other highlands, as well as on the coast. Although some archaeologists have proposed that the sharing of the Chavín style reflects some kind of broad, centralized religious or economic control, this now seems highly improbable. Rather, this wide distribution of certain ideological and stylistic conventions may mark an intensified level of exchange, communication, and militaristic competition between highland and coastal settlements. In certain ways, the Chavín Horizon is similar to the Olmec phenomenon in Mesoamerica, although in contrast to the latter, sociopolitical differences were present in certain South American polities for centuries prior to the spread of the Chavín style.

The Lanzón in the Old Temple of Chavín.

THE TEXTILES OF PARACAS

Clues to visual communication in ancient South America

A close-up view of a Paracas mantle with the embroidered image of an elite figure and the Ecstatic Shaman (lower right).

In ancient Peru, textiles were an important means of visual communication (see Color Plate 19). This use of woven cloth to convey ritual images is perhaps best exemplified on the south coast of Peru by the Paracas culture (about 600–150 B.C.). Paracas elite wore lavish costumes of mantles, ponchos, skirts, tunics, loincloths, and woven headgear. Even after death, these individuals were covered with many fine weavings. On the dry south coast, careful excavations have uncovered mummified burials still wrapped with brightly colored, embroidered ritual cloths, providing a vivid picture of the symbolic life of these ancient Peruvians.

Although the Paracas textiles have their own distinctive style, they do share certain artistic features with contemporary Chavín cloths. Both portray anthropomorphic and composite zoomorphic figures. Yet on the brightly colored Paracas textiles, these figures have a less somber presence than the supernatural creatures depicted in stone and pottery at Chavín de Huántar.

One of the most frequent images found on the Paracas textiles is a human figure called the Ecstatic Shaman. Arched sharply backward with outstretched arms, head askew, and flailing hair, these figures seem frozen in the midst of rapid movement, perhaps magical flight. The symbolism of the long, untamed hair may have greater significance than simply conveying action, because in the Paracas textiles only these figures and trophy heads are depicted with unbound locks. The Spanish chroniclers tell us that among the later Inca, long hair was considered an important attribute for **shamans** and certain sorcerers.

The Paracas textiles provide a dramatic record of ancient Peruvian weaving skills. Copper and gold ornaments attest to the metallurgical proficiency of other South American peoples during the same period. Small copper tools and ornaments have been recovered in northern Bolivia, where the cold metal was worked by hammering and shaping. In the north, gold was made into earspools, as well as nose, chest, and other head adornments. The latter were crafted by working the metal into thin sheets and then hammering it over a mold, a process referred to as **repoussé.** These gold ornaments, which also frequently were soldered or welded, often bore the composite figures characteristic of the Chavín Horizon.

THE TEXTILES OF PARACAS   375

MOCHE

*Giant pyramids on
Peru's north coast*

The Huaca del Sol at Moche.

The end of the Chavín phenomenon marked the start of an era, 200 B.C.–A.D. 600, primarily characterized by the development of small local polities and their associated distinct regional ceramic traditions. Around the time of Christ, the site of Moche (mo'chay) was established about 6 km (3.5 mi) from the ocean near the modern city of Trujillo in the Moche Valley, on the north coast of Peru. The site is located 600 m (2000 ft) from the Moche River, close to the center of the Moche Valley, and up against Cerro Blanco, a large hill that rises abruptly to a height more than 500 m (1650 ft) above sea level. In its day, Moche was the largest settlement on the north coast of Peru. Unlike most other centers of its time, Moche controlled not only the rest of the Moche Valley but also adjacent coastal valleys for centuries.

The Moche site is dominated by two major pyramids, or **huacas:** the Huaca del Sol and the Huaca de la Luna. The

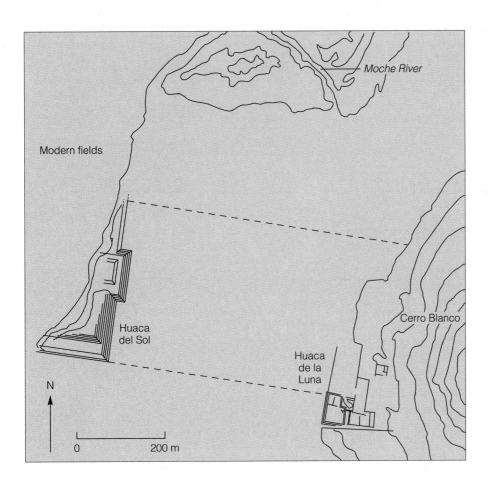

two structures are separated by a 500-m (1650-ft) wide plaza or level area. The Huaca del Sol towers 40 m (130 ft) above the surrounding plain and measures at least 340 × 160 m (1100 × 525 ft, larger than a city block). It was one of the largest, if not the most massive, solid adobe structure ever built in the New World. The pyramid once contained more than 130 million sun-dried bricks. The Huaca de la Luna, which rests on the lower slopes of Cerro Blanco, is a 30-m (100-ft) high complex of platforms, walls, and courtyards. Made of adobe, it was formed by three mounds connected by courts and was constructed in at least three stages.

The two pyramids were used differently. Activities on top of the Huaca del Sol were associated with the accumulation of domestic refuse, while the summit of the Huaca de la Luna was swept clean, and the uppermost structures were decorated with painted murals. The murals were found in 1899 by the archaeologist Max Uhle, who also discov-ered a cemetery area between the two pyramids.

More recently, Michael Moseley and his colleagues have studied the adobe bricks from the two *huacas* and have found more than 100 different symbols impressed on their top surfaces. Because these symbols were applied during production, Moseley reasoned that they may have been makers' marks (stylized signs), used to distinguish the bricks manufactured by different groups. The two *huacas,* which required hundreds of millions of adobe bricks, were constructed segmentally in similar, discrete rectangular units composed of stacked bricks. Moseley found that each adobe segment, or column, generally included bricks marked by a single maker's symbol. While some symbols marked the bricks in numerous construction segments, others appeared less frequently. Thus Moseley suggested that segments of the two pyramids were built by groups of associated laborers, with some work parties involved in the construction more

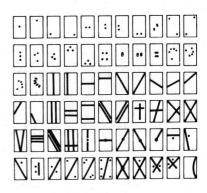

Makers' marks on adobe bricks at Moche.

North coastal Peru, with the location of Moche and other valleys dominated by Moche influence.

Pacific Ocean

Lambayeque R.

Pampa Grande

Chicama R.

Galindo

Trujillo

Moche

Moche R.

Virú R.

Santa R.

Pañamarca

Nepeña R.

ANDES MOUNTAINS

▲ Archaeological site

● Modern town or city

0   150 km

often than others. The use of conscripted laborers to complete discrete organizational tasks, known as the **mit'a system**, was a familiar means of tribute employed by the Inca more than a millennium later.

By A.D. 300–400, Moche influence dominated not only the larger Chicama Valley to the north, but also the adjacent Virú and Santa valleys to the south. In Virú and Santa, Moche pottery appeared suddenly and rapidly displaced the local pottery traditions. This ceramic shift coincided with dramatic changes in settlement pattern, in which the local populations congregated at a few, large settlements. In each valley, a sizable monument was built following the architectural canons used in the two Moche Valley *huacas*. Although these pyramids do not approach the Huaca del Sol in size, each was usually the largest structure of its time in its region, and each was associated with Moche pottery or mural art. Farther south in the Nepeña Valley, Moche pottery appeared somewhat later but is limited to settlements in a small

area around the site of Pañamarca, a large community that may have guarded the southern limits of Moche hegemony. In each of these valleys, Moche influence ceased by A.D. 600, at roughly the same time that the Moche site was abandoned.

Prior to the decline, the Moche people grew cotton, maize, potatoes, peanuts, and peppers by irrigating the coastal desert. Complex canal systems were built to transport water to flat desert lands located kilometers away. The building and maintenance of these water-control systems also may have required labor-recruitment practices similar to those employed in the building of the *huacas*. Fishing and the hunting of sea mammals provided important dietary resources. To date, large public food-storage complexes, similar to those associated with the later Chimú and Inca polities, have not been found at Moche.

Moche society was highly stratified. There were great, and probably inherited, differences in access to wealth and power. Marked disparities have been

noted in the quantity and quality of grave goods found within burials. Graves incorporated into or found near the two Moche huacas tended to be more lavish. Status variation also can be inferred from variability in domestic architecture. Residential structures that were more solidly built also were architecturally more elaborate than other domestic constructions; the former tended to be associated with more highly decorated ceramic forms, such as ornate stirrup-spout vessels, and other objects of value, such as copper implements.

Moche artisans are recognized for their accomplishments in metalworking, making objects of silver and various alloys. They not only used the known techniques of hammering, annealing, embossing, repoussé, and soldering, but began to use turquoise mosiac inlay and simple casting as well. They also developed **lost**

A representation of the Presentation Theme, part of the Moche Sacrifice Ceremony.

wax casting, a technique in which a hollow cast is made by allowing the molten metal to replace a wax lining in the cast. While the bulk of the metal was used for ornaments, copper ingots were smelted for storage. In addition, the Moche smiths made chisels, spearpoints, digging-stick tips, spearthrower hooks, tweezers, and fishhooks.

The most renowned craftspeople were the potters, who, through a wide array of painted ceramic vessel forms and high relief sculptures, have left an unsurpassed portrayal of Moche mythology, ritual, and daily life. Scenes showing deer being hunted with spearthrowers, as well as fishermen at sea in one-man canoes made of bundles of rushes, are common. Other figures often portrayed include warriors, weavers, prisoners, mothers with children, messengers, and rulers carried in litters or sitting on platforms. Battles are frequently depicted, as are scenes in which victorious soldiers accompany naked prisoners with ropes tied around their necks. The pottery also provides further evidence for social stratification. In general, men wore a loincloth and a sleeveless shirt beneath a belted tunic that stopped above the knee. But more important people also wore a large cloth mantle. While all men wore headgear, only a few important individuals had animal skin headdresses decorated with feathers and small pieces of metal.

Moche potters were explicit in their depiction of sexuality, portraying a range of erotic practices. Some of the more graphic depictions are scenes of masturbation and male-female couples engaged in fellatio. Historical data from the time of Spanish contact indicate that the native people on the north coast of Peru practiced sodomy and that some of their ceremonies included orgies.

Traditionally, archaeologists and art historians have implied that the Moche ceramicists depicted all aspects of life. Yet, more recently, Christopher Donnan, of the University of California, Los Angeles, has noted that certain scenes, such as the presentation of a goblet to an important person, tend to recur on Moche pottery. This Presentation Theme, which appears to have been part of a Sacrifice Ceremony, usually includes a series of associated symbolic elements. At the center of the scene is an important individual with rays emanating from his head and shoulders. The rayed figure generally wears a conical helmet topped by a crescent-shaped ornament and holds the tall goblet. The scene usually also features a warrior extracting blood from a naked captive, a composite human-feline who often holds the captive, animated weapons, and a dog near the rayed figure. Elements of this scene appear individually on other Moche vessels. Donnan has proposed that rather than depicting all facets of Moche life, the pottery focuses primarily on a few ritually important themes. This visual record, in conjunction with excavations and settlement pattern studies, provides a more complete picture of the Moche than we have for most other ancient South American peoples.

On the south coast of Peru, the Nazca style developed from the earlier Paracas art around 200 B.C. Most Nazca ceramic art, renowned for brilliantly painted **polychrome** vessels with six or seven colors, comes from looted cemeteries, although a few large Nazca sites have been studied more systematically. Most notable is the site of Cahuachi in the Nazca Valley, a large aggregation of adobe platforms, courts, and associated buildings that covers roughly 1 sq km (0.4 sq mi). Cahuachi, with a large 20-m (65-ft) high stepped pyramid, was the largest center of its day in the Nazca region and may have had a role in the dispersal of the Nazca style to other valleys along the south coast.

Perhaps the most astonishing feature in the Nazca region of southern Peru is spread out over several hundred square kilometers (an area three to four times larger than Manhattan Island) in the desert between the Ingenio and Nazca river valleys. More than 1000 years ago, lines, geometric forms, and various figures were drawn on the desert surface by removing dark rock fragments to expose a light-colored underlying soil. The geometric shapes, mostly triangles and trapezoids, alone cover an amazing 360 ha (900 acres). The majority of the several dozen figures, the most famous of the Nazca lines, are animals, although several are plants and others are human-like. The animals include birds, lizards, and fish, as well as a spider and a monkey. The latter, an inhabitant of the Amazon rain forest and not of the dry coast, is known to have been important in coastal religion and symbolism.

One of the myths about the Nazca lines is that they must be seen from the air to be appreciated. More recent studies indicate that they were meant to be viewed by people on the ground. Most of the lines and drawings are visible from the desert floor, and they can be seen even more clearly from either the low hills or the huge sand dunes that border the dry plain. While it has been suggested that the desert drawings relate to calendrics and astronomy as well as to ritual or ceremonial pathways, the specific intentions of the original makers remain a matter of debate.

An aerial photograph of a monkey at Nazca.

SIPÁN

*Clues to Moche ritual
and politics*

An aerial view of the three pyramids at Sipán. The smallest pyramid, on the left, was the focus of looting and subsequent systematic excavation.

Less than 200 km (124 mi) north of the pyramids of Moche is the fertile Lambayeque Valley. Abundant water resources and rich, level farmland have combined to make this area highly suitable for intensive agriculture. At the center of the valley lies the small village of Sipán (see-pahn'), an agricultural community of approximately 1500 people, distinguished by the presence of ancient pyramids and cemeteries. The impressive Sipán pyramids are visible for miles, rising above the intensively farmed fields that today grow mostly sugarcane.

For decades, some of the farmers of Sipán have supplemented their agricultural income with sporadic looting from the rich archaeological resources in the region. The looters dig deep holes with picks and shovels and often find ceramic vessels or stone and shell beads, which they sell to the antiquities dealers who periodically pass through the region. Yet occasionally they have exposed tombs containing objects of gold or silver, for which the looters receive much larger sums. Such occasional rich finds, and the periodically weak economy in the Lambayeque area, have helped keep this destructive tradition of looting alive. Over generations, some Sipán inhabitants have become adept at learning where to dig to recover the most valuable items, and at avoiding the local police and government officials responsible for protecting archaeological resources.

In November 1986, the local looters, believing they had exhausted nearby cemeteries, focused their attention on the smallest of three Sipán pyramids. Working at night to avoid detection, they dug deep pits into the pyramid's core of solid mud bricks. For months, little was found. But on the night of February 16, 1987, they tunneled into one of the richest burial chambers ever looted, the royal tomb of a Moche ruler. Conflicting accounts make it difficult to know exactly what was removed, but several cloth sacks of priceless artifacts were undoubtedly carted away. Almost immediately, disputes arose over the distribution of the treasure, and one looter, displeased with his share, informed the police. The police went to Sipán, where they arrested some of the other participants and confiscated part of the plunder in their homes. They also notified Walter Alva, Director of the Bruning Museum in the adjacent town of Lambayeque, who had worked for years with the police in an effort to halt the looting.

Alva recognized the richness and scholarly significance of the finds, as well as the need to locate the tomb. In Sipán, word spread quickly about the discovered wealth, and many local residents flocked to the pyramids with window screens, kitchen utensils, and shovels to see what they could recover. Even after the police reached the scene, it took several hours to clear the pyramid of wealth seekers. From that point to the conclusion of the scientific excavations, the exposed pyramid had to be guarded 24 hours a day.

The damage to the funerary chamber was severe, from both the original grave robbers and those who later streamed to the site and ruthlessly hacked at the walls. Alva decided that an archaeological project should start immediately to investigate the pyramid before this important site was entirely destroyed. Although

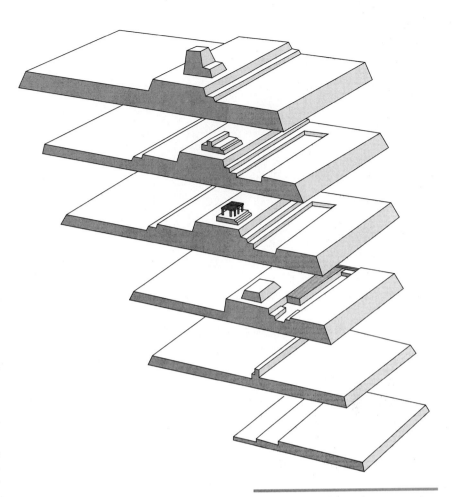

The six building episodes of the small pyramid at Sipán.

some of the looted finds were recovered that first night and a few items were confiscated later by the police, most of the plundered objects were never found. Instead, they were surreptitiously smuggled to Lima. From there, many items eventually were illegally transported to the art markets and private collections of Europe, the United States, and Japan.

Walter Alva, Christopher Donnan, and their colleagues immediately set to work on the Sipán pyramids. They mapped the complex, thereby determining the relationship between the smallest structure (now pitted) and the other, larger pyramids. Because the small mound was in greatest danger of further destruction, they concentrated their efforts there. Detailed architectural analysis of the areas exposed by the looter's trenches led to the discovery that the pyramid was built in six stages. In its earliest phase, thought to have been constructed during the first century A.D., the

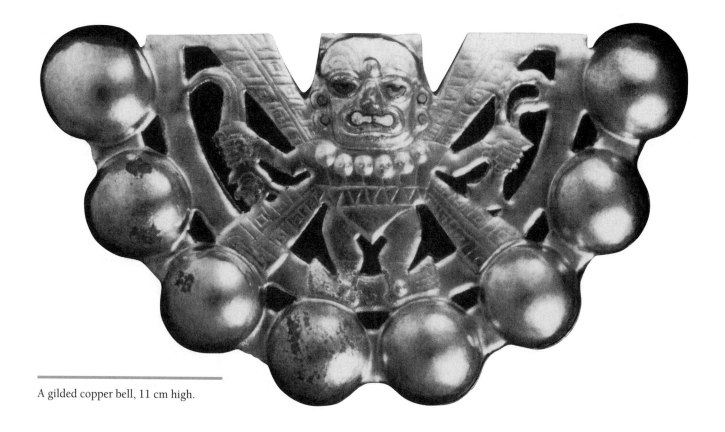

A gilded copper bell, 11 cm high.

pyramid appears only to have been a low rectangular platform with two steps extending along its entire north side. Each subsequent building enlarged the pyramid, encapsulating the previous structure, with the final construction phase completed around A.D. 300.

The richness of the looted finds, as well as elaborate gold, silver, and ceramic artifacts recovered during the cleaning operation, prepared Alva and Donnan for the possibility that an important burial might be recovered. Prior to Sipán, the Moche burials with the most elaborate pieces generally had been looted rather than excavated scientifically. Yet the excavators could never have imagined that they would recover perhaps the richest burial ever found in the Western Hemisphere. Nor could they have known that their findings would help answer a key riddle about the ancient Moche. Were the repetitive scenes recognized in Moche art, such as the Sacrifice Ceremony (see p. 380), really enacted by the Moche people or purely mythic in nature?

Over months of painstaking excavation, the Sipán excavations uncovered three fabulous tombs. In each case, the central figure was elaborately costumed in exquisitely crafted gold and silver ornaments, as well as worked shell, gemstone, and metal finery of all kinds. In the two largest, most elaborate, and latest tombs, the central figures had key costume elements that enabled the excavators to identify them as specific participants in the Sacrifice Ceremony. For example, the central rayed figure, referred to as the Warrior Priest, in the Presentation Theme often was depicted with paired backflaps, a crescent-shaped headdress piece, large circular ear decorations, a crescent nose ornament, and a pair of bells hanging from his belt. This individual is usually shown in military settings, accompanied by a dog, and often with a lamp-shaped scepter. All of these elements were excavated together in Tomb 1 at Sipán. Tomb 2 yielded an individual buried with many of the decorative and symbolic elements that have been linked to a second principal figure in the Sacrifice Ceremony. The earliest of the three excavated tombs was neither as rich nor as closely associated with the de-

A large gold headdress, 62.7 cm wide.

pictions of the Sacrifice Ceremony as the later two. Yet the central figure was entombed with some elements of the Warrior Priest attire. It is possible that the Sacrifice Ceremony was less elaborate and stylized in earlier Moche times; artistic depictions of this event all postdate A.D. 300.

Amputated hands and feet were uncovered at Sipán. These sacrificial offerings would seem to indicate not only that key participants in the Sacrifice Ceremony were buried in the pyramid, but also that the event itself was probably practiced on or near the pyramid.

The Sipán excavations provide a clearer understanding of Moche social and economic organization. Moche society was marked by greater differentials in wealth than previously believed. The elaborate costumes buried with these nobles would have demanded many highly skilled artisans to replenish the great objects of wealth that were buried. This burial custom helps contextualize the extraordinary artistic and technological achievements long associated with Moche craftworkers.

The royal tombs also have yielded significant clues about Moche art and religion. We now recognize that at least some of the art documents actual events enacted by real people. Although the treasures of the Sipán tombs seem priceless, of greater value is the exciting new cultural information they have provided, enabling us to develop a clearer picture of the Moche—one of the most fascinating civilizations of the ancient world.

TIWANAKU

*Bolivia's high-altitude
ancient city*

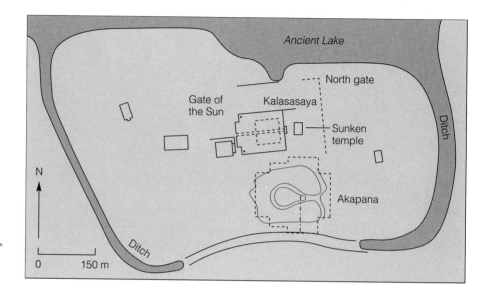

The plan of the civic-ceremonial core of Tiwanaku.

When the Spanish chroniclers asked the Inca rulers about their origins, they were told that the genesis of the first Inca took place in the part of the realm called Collasuyu. This Inca origin myth may have developed from the belief in the sacred nature of Collasuyu's Lake Titicaca, the largest lake in South America. When the great king Pachakuti (A.D. 1438–1470) began the Inca imperial conquests, it is no coincidence that he moved first against polities on the shores of Lake Titicaca.

The first sedentary settlements south of Lake Titicaca, in what is today Bolivia, were established during the second millennium B.C. The inhabitants of these early communities on the wind-swept high-altitude steppe, or **altiplano**, had a mixed agrarian economy in this zone that most North Americans would consider to be too elevated for agriculture. In the cold altiplano, the early villagers subsisted on a range of domesticated species adapted to the torrential rains of the wet season (November–May) as well as an extended dry season (April–October). The most important food re-

sources were hardy tuberous plants like the potato, cold-adapted grains like quinoa, and such domesticated camelids as alpaca and llama.

One of the early villages on the southern shores of Lake Titicaca was Chiripa. At the center of this site was a large, artificial mound first constructed around 1300–1200 B.C. Between 900 and 100 B.C., the mound was expanded, and stone retaining walls were built along three sides. At that time, a series of subterranean houses was arranged around the mound. Later a sunken court (measuring roughly 23 m, or 75 ft, per side) was built at the apex of the mound. The Chiripa court, a prototype for later ceremonial precincts at the site of Tiwanaku, was embellished with carved plaques and limestone columns.

During the last centuries of the first millennium B.C., a small settlement was founded 20 km (12 mi) south of Lake Titicaca, on the site that was to become the great city of Tiwanaku (tee-wah-nok'u). Situated 3850 m (12,600 ft) above sea level in a small valley in the Bolivian altiplano, at more than twice the

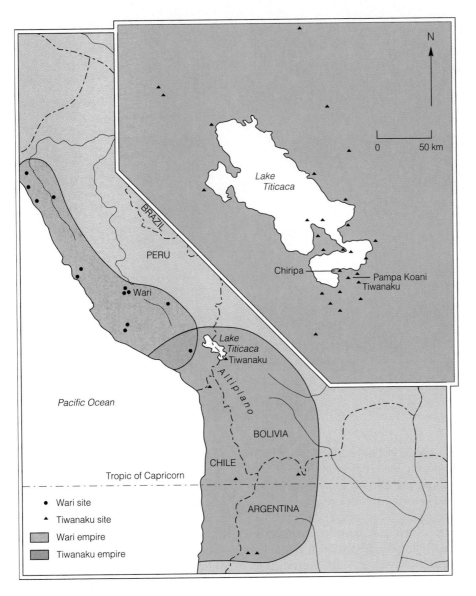

altitude of Denver, Colorado, Tiwanaku was one of the highest urban centers ever established. Monumental architectural construction began during the first centuries A.D., when the site rose to importance in the southern basin of Lake Titicaca. Tiwanaku grew to its greatest geographic size (more than 4 sq km, or 1.5 sq mi) and demographic extent (an estimated 25,000–40,000 people) around A.D. 400. For the next 600–800 years, the city dominated the entire Lake Titicaca region, and ceremonial art styles associated with the capital spread over a far wider area.

The civic-ceremonial core of Tiwanaku was a 20-ha (50-acre) area at the center of the site. This precinct, laid out according to a grid oriented in the four cardinal directions, included a series of truly impressive architectural features. Akapana, an enormous stone-faced, stepped platform mound, 200 m (655 ft) on a side and 15 m (50 ft) high, was the most massive construction. It included huge blocks of stone, some of which weighed as much as 10,000 kg (11 tons) and had to be brought over land and water to Tiwanaku from quarries more than 100 km (62 mi) away. A second platform, Pumapunku, measured more than 5 m (16 ft) high, with walls 150 m (500 ft) long. Tiwanaku's civic-ceremonial core also included a complex of buildings, with a stone drainage system, that may have been a palace.

The Gateway of the Sun at Tiwanaku.

The most famous stone sculpture at Tiwanaku, the Gateway of the Sun, was incorporated into a large rectangular precinct known as the Kalasasaya. The Gateway of the Sun, carved from a single huge stone block, portrays a central figure holding two scepters that end in the heads of condors. This individual is flanked by rows of winged attendants who each carry a condor scepter. The central character recalls a figure with two staffs, frequently shown in Chavín iconography. Inside the Kalasasaya are rectangular sunken courts. These architectural features, which may have been temple precincts, have a precedent at earlier Chiripa.

At Tiwanaku, the local altiplano economy of camelid pastoralism and the cultivation of hardy grains and tubers was supplemented by the reclamation for agriculture of waterlogged lands adjacent to Lake Titicaca. In addition, Tiwanaku maintained long-distance trade connections, establishing economic colonies in both the Pacific Coast zone to the west and the more tropical forested zones to the east. These earlier networks may have laid a foundation for the Inca to link the diverse and distant reaches of the Andean realm. Warm-region crops, such as maize and coca (a native Andean shrub whose dried leaves are chewed as stimulants), were obtained, as well as birds and medicinal herbs from the east and obsidian and coastal products, like shell and dried fish, from the west. Trade connections were maintained by large llama caravans, which traveled throughout the Bolivian altiplano and to southern Peru and the Chilean coast.

Alan Kolata, of the University of Chicago, has studied agrarian reclamation on the Pampa Koani, an area subject to frequent natural flooding on the southern border of Lake Titicaca. During the first millennium A.D., the waterlogged land was reclaimed through the construction of raised fields near the lake, by excavating the heavy Pampa soils on either side of the field surface and mounding the dirt in the center to form an earthen platform elevated above the seasonally high waters. Kolata found that some raised platforms were constructed more elaborately to enhance plant growth. In one field at the lakeshore, the platform consisted of a cobble-

The Kalasasaya at Tiwanaku.

stone base, covered by a thick clay stratum, superceded by three gravel layers and a rich layer of topsoil. In this ingenious structure, the clay, held in place by the cobblestones, prevented the brackish lake water from penetrating into the field from below, while fresh rainwater could percolate down to the roots of the crops from above.

During the latter half of the first millennium A.D., while Tiwanaku was the principal center in the southern Andes, the Peruvian highland site of Wari dominated the more northerly highland and coastal regions. Andean archaeologists suggest that while Tiwanaku developed economic ties with its hinterland, Wari's control over the surrounding area was more militaristic. Wari's regional domination also was shorter, as that site lost its influence and was largely abandoned prior to the tenth century A.D. While the artistic styles associated with Tiwanaku and Wari were similar, both of them featuring jaguars and raptors (birds of prey), the specific relationship between the two centers remains unknown.

Soon after A.D. 1000, Tiwanaku's domination over the basin of Lake Titicaca began to wane. A number of smaller competing states emerged, each maintaining its own local sphere of influence until the middle of the fifteenth century A.D., when the Titicaca basin was unified under Inca domination. The decline of Tiwanaku coincided with the abandonment of the raised fields of the Pampa Koani. The vast landscape of once-productive fields reverted to pasturage, a function they still serve today. Even the Inca did not reclaim the seasonally waterlogged Pampa lands that had once helped feed the population of Tiwanaku, focusing instead on the rocky mountain slopes above the plain. There, the Inca expanded the region's agricultural productivity by constructing terraces that transformed steep hillsides into arable farmland.

Although the specific causes of Tiwanaku's collapse have not been determined, we do know that several of the important organizational features associated with the later Inca empire can be traced to this earlier altiplano center. The widespread Tiwanaku iconographic style seems to presage the broad dissemination of Inca state art. Likewise, Tiwanaku's establishment of small economic colonies in diverse environmental settings augurs an Inca practice. Perhaps the Inca kings recognized the powerful influence of Tiwanaku on the later prehispanic Andean world when they traced their ancestry to the basin of Lake Titicaca. In so doing, the Inca rulers also were invoking the mystique of Tiwanaku's past grandeur to bolster their own efforts to reestablish a far-reaching Andean domain.

A pottery vessel decorated with Tiwanaku/Wari stylistic elements.

CHAN CHAN

Desert city of the Chimú

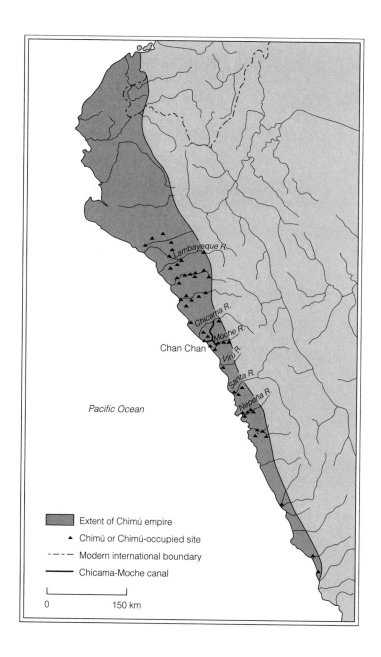

The Chimú area.

On the north coast of Peru, the seventh-century collapse of Moche coincided with a shift in political power. In the Moche Valley, occupation concentrated in the large settlement of Galindo. Yet unlike the Moche site with its huge adobe *huacas*, the nondomestic construction at Galindo was small. At the same time, a much larger settlement, Pampa Grande, with more elaborate architecture, was es-tablished in the Lambayeque Valley to the north. Both Pampa Grande and Galindo were positioned in easily defend-able locations from which they could control local irrigation systems. Thus, although the north coast was not con-quered by Wari invaders from the south, that expansionist polity may have caused sufficient unrest to effect major shifts in population and power.

By approximately A.D. 800–900, a small settlement was founded at the mouth of the Moche Valley at Chan Chan. Although the exact extent of this early occupation has not been determined, it is clear the site grew rapidly in size and importance. By the middle of the fifteenth century, Chan Chan had become a sprawling coastal city, covering more than 20 sq km (8 sq mi). Chan Chan was also the capital of the Chimú state, which stretched 1000 km (620 mi) from southernmost Ecuador to central Peru.

At its height in the mid-fifteenth century A.D., the civic-ceremonial core of Chan Chan covered roughly 6 sq km (2.3 sq mi, roughly twice the size of New York's Central Park). This central area was dominated by 10 rectilinear compounds, or *ciudadelas* (literally, "little cities"), each surrounded by high adobe walls. The nucleus of Chan Chan also included a large platform-court complex, as well as flat-topped mounds and numerous smaller monuments and structures, yet the most striking and massive features were the *ciudadelas*, many of which measured 200–600 m (650–1950 ft) on a side.

The *ciudadelas*, oriented roughly north-south, each had a single entrance through the north wall that opened onto a corridor leading to a broad court. A ramp sloped up to a long bench along the south wall of the court. Human corpses, probably buried when the compounds were constructed, were uncovered during excavations of these ramps. Each compound also included a multitude of storerooms, smaller courts, and living quarters. Usually the last structure built in each *ciudadela* was a burial platform, which presumably held the bodies of the family that occupied each of these mazelike compounds. Later records name 10 Chimú kings, corresponding to the 10 palatial compounds at Chan Chan. Geoffrey Conrad, of Indiana University, believes that each *ciudadela* was a particular king's residence and the administrative center for the Chimú kingdom. Following the death of the ruler, the compound became the mausoleum for the king, maintained by his living kinsmen. Conrad argues that the maintenance of a dead Chimú ruler's personal property by his heirs, who did not succeed him in office, was derived from a broader pan-Andean custom of ancestor worship. Upon succession, each new ruler built his own *ciudadela* to serve as headquarters and royal treasury.

Most of the inhabitants of Chan Chan resided outside these massive compounds in small structures composed of six to eight small rooms. During excavations in these quarters, few farming or fishing implements were found. Instead, the evidence for craft manufacture was abundant, including lapidary and woodworking tools, spinning and weaving implements, and the equipment for metalworking.

As at earlier Moche, most of the monumental construction at Chan Chan was built by a labor force from outside

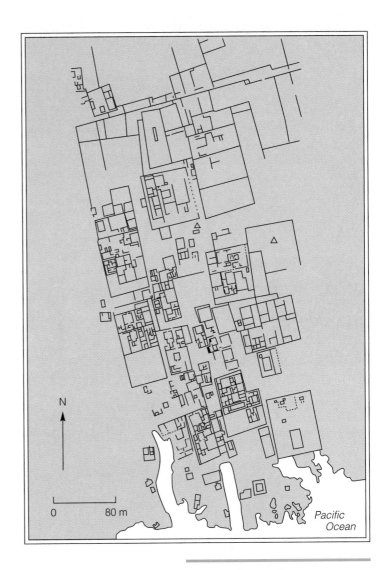

The plan of Chan Chan.

An aerial view of Chan Chan.

the center. Michael Moseley estimates that the population at Chan Chan remained relatively small, perhaps 25,000 people. In the city's hinterland, massive labor investments were made in agricultural intensification. Sophisticated hydraulic systems brought water to the land surrounding Chan Chan. The Chimú even constructed an intervalley canal designed to carry water to the Moche Valley from the Chicama River, 65 km (40 mi) away.

The development of the large irrigation networks around Chan Chan would seem to relate to the Andean practice of labor tribute (the *mit'a* system), as well as to the Chimú pattern of succession. According to one hypothesis, the Chimú, like the Inca, practiced a policy of **split inheritance,** by which the successor to the throne received the inherited office

of the supreme leader, but the land, the palace, and the personal wealth of the dead ruler were left to a corporate group of other junior kinsmen. As a consequence, each new ruler had to raise his own revenues to erect his residential compound and finance his reign. His principal resource was a large labor force that could be employed in monumental construction, agricultural intensification, road building, and militaristic ventures.

Between 1462 and 1470, the Chimú were in competition with the increasingly powerful Inca. By the end of the decade, this conflict ended with the incorporation of the Chimú kingdom into the rapidly growing Inca empire. In this manner, the Inca were able to link their lands and road systems with those previously controlled by the Chimú. Curiously, Chimú artifacts were found more

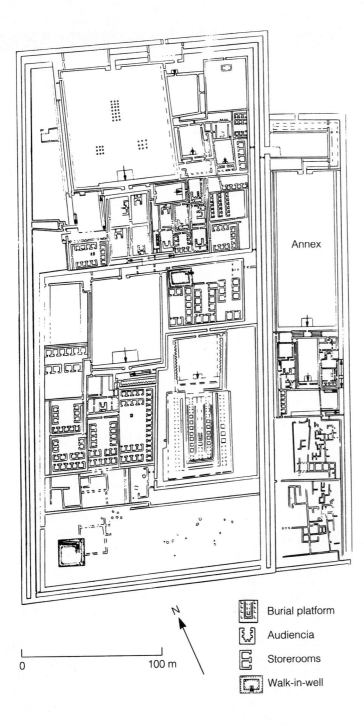

N

0   100 m

Annex

▨ Burial platform

⊔ Audiencia

E Storerooms

▣ Walk-in-well

The plan of one of the *ciudadelas* at Chan Chan. The U-shaped structures, *audiencias,* may have been used by nobles holding audience with lower-status people. Each structure holds only one seated person, and each has its own court.

widely distributed after the Inca conquest than before, perhaps as a result of the emergence of new patterns of trade and taxation, or possibly because of the great admiration the Inca had for Chimú craftspeople. For example, Chimú metalworkers were brought to the capital of Cuzco to work for the Inca state.

Today the quiet desolation of the dry coastal environment is broken only by the nearly continuous howl of onshore winds. No one lives at Chan Chan, but the site is covered by a series of trails and paths that skirt the undulating tops of collapsed adobe ruins that were once the palaces of the Chimú kings. At dawn from a distance, the diffused, weak daylight makes it difficult even to distinguish the massive earthen walls of this once important city from the sky at the horizon.

CUZCO AND MACHU PICCHU

Key centers of the Inca

As with the Aztecs of Mesoamerica, much of what we know about the Inca comes to us not from archaeology but through written documents, filtered through the eyes of European chroniclers, whose goals and experiences differed greatly from those of the Inca themselves. In 1532, a small band of Spaniards led by Francisco Pizarro came into contact with populations in the northern coastal valleys of Peru that were part of a giant centralized political domain called Tawantinsuyu. The capital of this great polity was Cuzco (kuse'co), a city in the southern highlands. The highest-ranked leader was called Inca, son of the deity Inti (the Sun God) and descendant of a long line of heroic dynasties. At that time the empire was in the midst of a severe crisis, provoked by a bitter rivalry between two brothers, Huascar and Atauhualpa. Although Atauhualpa eventually won the power struggle, his costly victory may have lost the empire, as control of the Inca domain was soon in the hands of the Spanish.

According to legend, the rapid rise of the Inca began with hostilities between the inhabitants of Cuzco and the Chanca, a neighboring people. Fresh from military victories over several adjacent polities, the Chanca laid siege to Cuzco, forcing many of the inhabitants, including the reigning Inca, to flee to the surrounding hills. At Cuzco, a son of the Inca ruler, named Cusi Inca Yupanqui, was left to spearhead the final defense of the city. While waiting for the last Chanca onslaught, Cusi Inca Yupanqui had a vision in which he was told by a supernatural being that he would eventually rise to power and conquer many nations. Inspired by the apparition and buoyed by the support of new allies, Cuzco's defenders rallied to defeat the Chanca and drive them far from the Inca homeland. Cusi Inca Yupanqui was crowned Inca and renamed Pachakuti, "he who remakes the world." From that date, generally placed around A.D. 1440, Pachakuti is said to have initiated the dramatic series of conquests that culminated less than a century later in a huge empire that stretched over 4200 km (2600 mi) from north to south.

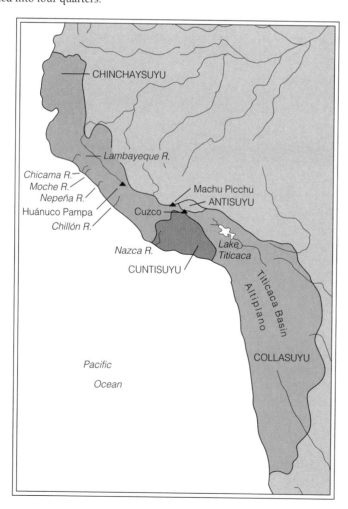

The Inca empire (Tawantinsuyu), which was divided into four quarters.

Inca imperial propaganda proclaimed that the Andean world was in a state of savagery prior to the rise of the Inca. This claim was obviously ethnocentric and fallacious. Clearly, the royal families at Cuzco inherited administrative strategies and systems of legitimization from the rulers of earlier states, centered at Chan Chan and Tiwanaku. Archaeology has shown that at the outset of the second millennium A.D., following the fall of Tiwanaku, the southern highlands around Lake Titicaca did undergo an episode of decentralization in which many small polities fragmented a landscape that had previously been unified by the earlier altiplano center. Supporting the legendary accounts, archaeological analyses indicate that by A.D. 1450, these autonomous competing polities of the Titicaca basin began to come under Inca hegemony. Centered at Cuzco, the Inca rapidly established major ceremonial centers on islands in Lake Titicaca not only to solidify their control of this important geographic resource, but also to legitimize their ancestral link to earlier Tiwanaku.

Cuzco was established by Manco Capac, the first Inca ruler, in a mountain valley nearly 3500 m (11,500 ft) above sea level. Because the site is relatively close to the equator, its climate is reasonably mild in spite of the high elevation. Cuzco remained a small community until it was rebuilt by the victorious Pachakuti. The Inca canalized and straightened several small rivers that cut through the settlement. Cuzco's most elaborate buildings, many of which were constructed entirely of finely hewn stone, were erected in the area between these rivers. An imposing fortress with massive masonry walls was built on a steep hill above this central area, which was not fortified (see Color Plate 20). Drawing on Inca sources, John Rowe, of the University of California, Berkeley, has suggested that Cuzco was intentionally laid out in the shape of a puma, with the fortress representing the animal's head and the intersection of the rivers serving as its tail. The area between the puma's front and back legs was paved with pebbles and served as a central ceremonial square.

The magnificent Temple of the Sun, the most important Inca structure in

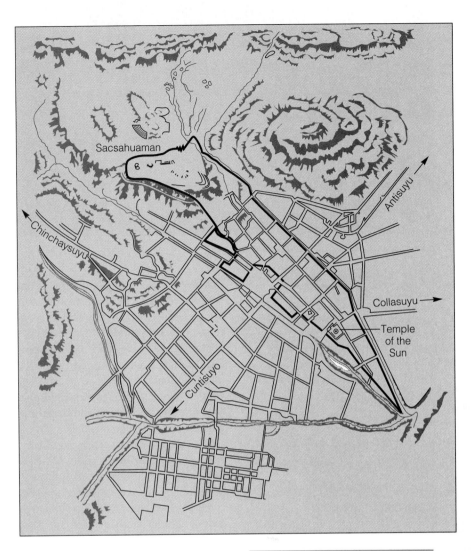

The plan of colonial Cuzco, which was built on Inca remains. The fortress and walls of the Inca city are outlined as a stylized puma.

Cuzco, was built by Pachakuti at the site's center. The building's exterior walls, more than 50 m (160 ft) per side, were decorated with a thick gold **frieze.** Entrances to the structure were covered with heavy gold plates, and the interior walls also were coated with gold. Early Spanish accounts describe a central patio or garden that included both natural and gold-crafted vegetation, including maize plants in which the ears, stalks, and leaves were all made of metal. The temple's principal sanctuary was dedicated to Inti. Inside the room were idols of gold and silver, as well as mummies of former Inca rulers and their wives.

Cuzco also contained other smaller temples, in addition to public buildings and elite residences. Generally, these structures were built of cut stone, finished with such precision that the joints

Fitted-stone architecture at Cuzco.

matched perfectly and mortar was not required. These architectural monuments, which required both great skill and significant labor power, were erected by commoners as part of the *mit'a* system. Pachakuti also erected a special public building that served as a convent for Chosen Women, brought to the capital to weave the finest cloth and to participate in specific religious rituals.

As the nucleus of an empire, Cuzco was not a typical Inca city. Its principal function was administration, and many of its inhabitants were involved in civic-ceremonial activities: priests, nobles, military officers, architects, and servants. Most of the supporting commoner population resided in smaller communities in the surrounding valley. In these settlements, the structures were built of field-stone and adobe rather than cut-stone blocks. A network of state storehouses and religious shrines also marked the well-planned terrain in the immediate vicinity of Cuzco.

The market in Cuzco was small and outside the center of the city. The peripheral nature of commercial activities at Cuzco reflects the administrative-elite character of the capital. However, it also indicates the nature of Inca economy, in which the state had a central role in the collection and redistribution of goods. Craftsworkers and other specialists contributed labor to the imperial government, which thus took control of a wide range of craft items. Compared to the contemporary Aztec polity, private trade and marketing occurred at very low levels in the empire of the Inca.

The Spanish were greatly impressed by Cuzco, its stone architecture, and its treasure of precious metals. Before the arrival of the Europeans in 1532, the accumulation of wealth was fostered by an Inca regulation that forbade anyone from removing gold, silver, or fine cloth from the city, once it was inside. In 1535, Cuzco was systematically burned and largely destroyed by the Inca themselves, when they besieged a Spanish garrison. But because the conquering Spaniards reconstructed the city promptly, often using Inca builders, much of the prehispanic plan has endured. Solid Inca walls still provide the stone foundation for many later buildings. Even the remnants of the once-spectacular Temple of the Sun now stand as the base for the Church of Santo Domingo. Like modern Mexico City, lying above the ruins of ancient Aztec Tenochtitlán, Cuzco is undoubtedly one of the longest continuously occupied cities in the New World.

Today, the most famous archaeological site in Peru and perhaps all of South America is another Inca site, Machu Picchu (ma'chew-pee'chew) (see Color Plate 21). This site is dramatically situated on the eastern frontier of the Inca empire, and the ruins lie on a saddle between two mountain peaks, which tower over the site and overlook a large bend in the Urubamba River. Machu Picchu is a graphic reminder of the architectural grandeur of the Inca. Yet in spite of its international popularity as a tourist attraction, archaeologists know relatively little about this magnificent ruin. Burials at the site included both males and females, suggesting that, despite its remote location, Machu Picchu was not simply a military garrison or fortress. Nevertheless, access to the site was limited by gates and removable rope bridges. The ceremonial core of Machu Picchu could be entered only through a stone gateway, making access to this part of the site especially difficult.

According to Spanish legal documents from the time of conquest, Machu Picchu was the property of the descendants of the Inca ruler Pachakuti. Machu Picchu was one of several royal estates built by Pachakuti, as commemorative memorials to his various military/political

The *intihuatana,* a large stone pillar, recovered at Machu Picchu.

exploits, and it was passed to his kin at his death. Elaborate dwellings at the site housed the king and his court when they were in residence, usually during the dry season. A smaller permanent population, responsible for maintaining the estate, may have resided at the site during the rest of the year. The site's large number of sacred features, as well as its location, reflects Pachakuti's concern with religion. The topography of the area—an impressive canyon surrounded by large rocks, conical peaks, and snowy vistas—combines many features that were important to Inca religion and cosmology.

At the site, an intact *intihuatana,* a large stone pillar thought to have had a ceremonial function, was found. Usually when the conquering Spanish found such features at other Inca sites, they destroyed them because of their suspected association with the native religion. Some researchers have proposed that the *intihuatana* at Machu Picchu was used by Inca priests as a sundial to read the length of the shadows cast by the sun. However, researchers specializing in **archaeoastronomy** have found that the pillar has no obvious astronomical function. Nevertheless, other features at Machu Picchu did have astronomical functions. A cave just below the site is thought to have been an observatory for the December solstice, and from the Torreón, a large masonry tower built on a rock promontory with a clear view to the east, the Inca could record the path of the rising sun during the June solstice.

Although Machu Picchu was inhabited by the Inca late in the prehispanic era, it may not have been visited by the Spanish *conquistadores.* In fact, unlike Cuzco, Machu Picchu was largely unknown to the Euro-American world until it was publicized following an expedition by Hiram Bingham in 1911. Today, amid the clouds and the snow-capped mountain peaks, Machu Picchu remains a magnificent remnant of a once great and powerful civilization that ruled the prehispanic Andean world.

INCA HIGHWAYS

Lifelife of the Inca empire

The movement of goods and information between the Pacific Coast, the Andean highlands, and the Amazonian *montaña* has been an important aspect of the South American world since at least the first millennium B.C. John Murra, of Cornell University, has shown that many Andean ethnic groups established colonies and devised other strategies to gain access to the products from these diverse ecological niches. As in Mesoamerica, much of this long-distance traffic was accomplished by foot. Yet in prehispanic South America, light loads (up to 45 kg, or 100 lb) also were carried by the domesticated llama, slightly easing the cost of long-distance transport.

Archaeologists do not know when the first Andean roads were built. Some scholars have suggested that they date to the time of Chavín de Huántar. By the time Tiwanaku and Wari dominated the Andean landscape, roads were in use. Well-built roads cross right through major Wari centers. Later the Inca linked existing roads into their own extensive

The Inca road system.

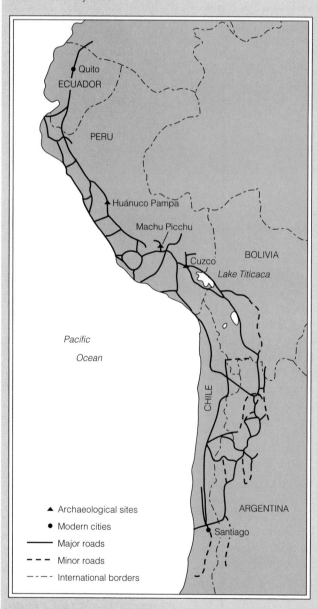

A woven Inca bridge over the Apurimac River in Peru, spanning a gap of about 45 m. This engraving was published by E. George Squier, one of the last travelers to see the bridge, in 1877.

system, creating South America's largest contiguous archaeological remain.

Not surprisingly, Cuzco was the hub of the Inca road system. The principal road ran through the highlands from the capital to Quito (in Ecuador) and into present-day Colombia. A second mountain segment ran south through Bolivia to Santiago (Chile) and northwest Argentina. A long coastal road connected with the highland network at more than a dozen points. The total extent of this road system spanned more than 40,000 km (25,000 mi).

Wheeled transport did not exist, and the Inca roads generally were narrow, ranging from 1 to 16 m (3 to 52 ft) wide. For the most part, the mountain roadways were more winding and narrower than those along the coast, to accommodate the terrain. In some places, the road was little more than a well-beaten path. Deserts and swamps were avoided when possible, although the Inca had means for coping with all of these situations. Across the desert, roads were lined with walls of posts, adobes, or stones to block windblown sands. In wet areas, stone pavements were laid over the road, and drainage canals were built.

The Inca are renowned for the several types of bridges they constructed over deep chasms and waterways. Rope suspension bridges, derived from the ancient Andean weaving tradition, greatly impressed the early Spanish chroniclers. Some of these bridges, where cables were hung from supporting masonry towers, continued in use into the twentieth century. Other Inca bridges were constructed with superstructures of wood, stone, or even floating reeds. In Inca times, most natives of the Andean highlands could not swim. Therefore, when a bridge could not be built or was being repaired, the Inca generally used ferries of balsa wood or reed.

The Inca road system was the lifeline of the Inca state and could not be traveled without an imperial directive. Most often the roads were used to move government messengers, Inca armies, royal

A 10-m-wide Inca road.

litters, or state trade caravans. Sometimes conquered populations were forcibly moved along the road system.

To service road traffic, the Inca built a network of roughly 1000–2000 **tampus,** roadside lodgings and storage places (primarily for food, fodder, firewood, and other commodities). The *tampus,* which tended to be roughly a day's walk apart, also served as seats of local government. Archaeological studies have found evidence of mining, spinning, pottery manufacture, coca exploitation, and ceremonial activities associated with specific *tampu* sites. On the eastern Andean slopes of Bolivia, certain fortified sites may have served *tampu* as well as military functions.

Francisco Pizarro's conquest expedition traveled through Tawantinsuyu along Inca roads and robbed the *tampus* and stole the stored food. Ironically, the great road system, which enabled the Inca to control their widespread empire, may also have contributed to their downfall.

Communications and their maintenance have been a major concern of Andean peoples from Inca times and probably earlier. In Andean conditions, roads, trails, and bridges were probably as essential to the political cohesion of the Inca state and to the redistribution of goods within it, as they are today to political integration or economic development.

    D. E. Thompson and J. V. Murra (1966)

HUÁNUCO PAMPA

*A provincial outpost
of the Inca*

An official (on the right) uses a *quipu* to relate accounting information to the Inca emperor (on the left).

Following his conquest of the Lake Titicaca basin, the Inca Pachakuti began what was to be almost a century of expansion. When possible, Inca ambassadors tried to negotiate a peaceful submission, a strategy that proved successful among smaller polities too weak to defend themselves. Some leaders may have been more willing to join than fight because of the Inca policy that allowed local rulers to retain power as long as they gave their primary allegiance to the Inca. When military action was necessary, the Inca had a large, effective fighting force supplied in part through their road network.

Tawantinsuyu, the Inca empire, was divided into four quarters that, according to Spanish chroniclers, were subdivided for administrative purposes into smaller population units. The latter subdivisions were based on multiples of 10; the **waranqa** of 1000 taxpayers was the unit most frequently used. The decimal system of administrative divisions was probably coordinated with the *quipu,* an Andean recording device that uses knotted strings in a positional decimal system. As far as we know, neither the Inca nor any of the other prehispanic South American peoples devised a formal system of writing.

To minimize provincial rebellion, the Inca used a system of colonization called the **mitmaq,** whereby populations were shifted from one part of the empire to another to break up dissident groups or to improve the exploitation of certain resources. Yet the Inca's effect on the Andean political landscape was less dramatic than it might seem. A common

misconception in popular accounts is that the Inca ruled a monolithic, uniform state. In reality, the empire was an amalgam of many units, which differed in ethnicity, political structure, size, and often language. Inca imperial administration was variable, depending on the economic and political significance of the conquered domain. The Inca tended to make substantial governmental changes only when a region's pre-Inca organization was fragmentary or when resistance to Inca rule persisted.

Spanish chronicles from the sixteenth century emphasize the military and administrative strategies used by the Inca to control their empire. Yet the Inca also established and maintained the authority of the state through a series of civic-ceremonial rituals, as well as through the economic activities on which these ritual events were centered.

An archaeological perspective on Inca provincial rule has been illustrated most clearly at the site of Huánuco Pampa (wan'u-ko-pam'pa), a late prehispanic administrative center located in central Peru. In this highland region, Craig Morris, of the American Museum of Natural History, and Donald Thompson, of the University of Wisconsin, Madison, studied the civic-ceremonial center, as well as the surrounding communities. The Inca rapidly built Huánuco Pampa during the middle of the second half of the fifteenth century A.D. The site was placed on an inhospitable high plain at 3800 m (12,500 ft), an area previously uninhabited and relatively isolated from other settlements. Significantly, Huánuco Pampa lies directly on

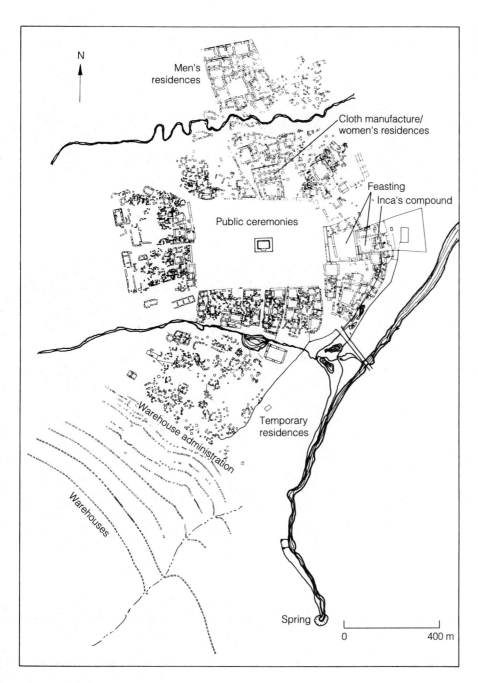

The plan of Huánuco Pampa.

the main Inca road between Cuzco and Quito.

The ruins of the settlement cover roughly 2 sq km (0.8 sq mi). By the time of the Spanish invasion in 1532, Huánuco Pampa included more than 4000 stone buildings. Much of this construction is remarkably different from that found at outlying communities. Both the architectural and the ceramic remains at Huánuco Pampa mimic the imperial Inca tradition found at Cuzco, while smaller

towns and villages retained customary local practices.

The Inca stone masonry was finest at the core of the site. An enormous central plaza (550 × 350 m, or 1800 × 1100 ft, larger than four city blocks) included a giant stone platform and was flanked by several smaller plazas and large stone compounds. The stonework in the platform and central compounds was a good imitation of the Inca style, even though it lacked the precise joining

A giant stone platform at Huánuco
Pampa.

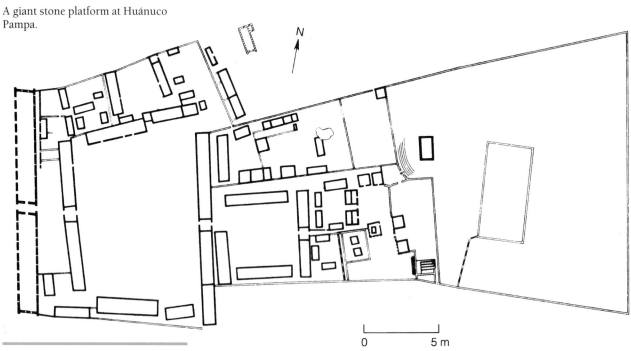

A set of architectural compounds connected by gateways at Huánuco Pampa.

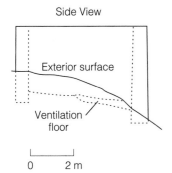

Side View

Exterior surface

Ventilation floor

0   2 m

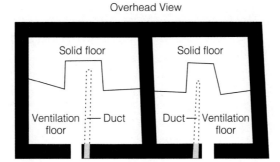

Overhead View

Solid floor | Solid floor

Ventilation floor — Duct | Duct — Ventilation floor

The plan of a two-room rectangular storehouse at Huánuco Pampa.

of intricately shaped stone blocks seen at Cuzco itself.

The extensive storage facilities associated with Huánuco Pampa are indicative of the site's reliance on its supporting hinterland, as well as the great power of the Inca administration. Although Huánuco Pampa's immediate agricultural hinterland could have supplied small quantities of potatoes, it could not have produced sufficient amounts to feed the site's 10,000–15,000 inhabitants. Maize found in storage facilities must have been imported from fields at lower elevations. Food supplies and the labor to construct the center must have been drawn from a wide hinterland.

Huánuco Pampa was not a manufacturing center and lacked a major market. Much of its populace was an administrative elite, along with their retainers and record keepers. However, in Huánuco Pampa's central state compounds, Morris and Thompson found unusual concentrations of giant storage vessels associated with the production of maize beer, or *chicha,* and spindle whorls and other artifacts linked to the manufacture of textiles. Since *chicha* is not easy to store or to transport, it probably was distributed at Huánuco Pampa during feasts and state rituals. The unusual abundance of large food-preparation vessels and serving platters in the ruins of the central compounds at Huánuco Pampa further suggests the importance of such activities. State-sponsored feasts could have been held in the huge open plaza at the core of the preplanned site, next to the food-preparation and serving areas.

Traditionally, the sharing of food and drink was a central feature of prehispanic Andean social relationships. At Huánuco Pampa, customary modes of sharing food and drink probably were used by the Inca state to establish loyalties and encourage the help of the local population in military, political, and economic activities. The state control and centralization of cloth production also may have played a part. As Murra has noted, textiles had an unusual sociopolitical significance in the prehispanic Andes. Cloth was exchanged at most of life's major turning points, such as marriage, as well as during major political events, like conquest and incorporation. The more textiles the Inca state had, the more effectively it could raise and control armies and workers, and the more successfully it could consolidate conquered domains.

Through the control and manipulation of textiles and administration-sponsored feasting and hospitality, the state was able to cement symbolic ties between the Inca and the conquered people. The extensive roadways, military strength, and innovative bureaucratic technology clearly were critical to the growth and maintenance of the Inca empire. Perhaps critical, too, were the rituals that defined participation in the Inca state as involving more than working state lands, helping to build platforms, or fighting in a remote war. Ideological factors also appear to have had a key role in shaping the Inca state.

SUMMARY

THE ORGANIZATION
OF STATE SOCIETY

*Similarities and differences
in two prehispanic worlds*

This chapter's introduction outlined some of the key similarities and differences between the early civilizations of Mesoamerica and the Andean region of South America. The market, an important institution in prehispanic Mesoamerica, was not nearly as important in the ancient South American world. While the Cortés-led conquerors of the Aztecs were amazed by the size and the splendor of the central Mexican market, the sixteenth-century Spaniards in Peru were impressed not by markets, but by the large number of giant storage areas controlled by the Inca state. The Spanish soldier Pedro Cieza de León, writing soon after the fall of the Inca, noted that

> in the more than 1200 leagues of coast they ruled they have their representatives and governors, and many lodgings and great storehouses filled with all necessary supplies. This was to provide for their soldiers, for in one of these storehouses there were lances, and in another, darts, and in others, sandals, and in others, the different arms they employed. Likewise, certain buildings were filled with fine clothing, and others, with coarser garments, and others with food and every kind of victuals. When the lord was lodged in his dwellings and his soldiers garrisoned there, nothing from the most important to the most trifling, but could be provided. (1959, pp. 68–69)

The impressive storage facilities, described in the historical accounts, correspond closely to the large storage features associated with such Inca sites as Huánuco Pampa. Written and archaeological evidence suggest that state-imposed tribute and labor drafts were key to the organization of the Inca, as well as to earlier Andean states.

The development of large-scale storage technologies and massive road systems in Andean South America made possible the later meteoric expansion of the Inca empire, which drew together a remarkable diversity of societies under a single imperial rule. This immense empire, the largest assembled in the prehispanic New World, culminated a long sequence of indigenous strategies through which Andean peoples interconnected the vast environmental and resource mosaic of their world. The naturally fragmented and diverse Andean landscape may have fostered a perpetual search for more productive combinations of goods and resources and for more workable relations with neighboring peoples. In comparison, the largest ancient Mesoamerican political systems were considerably smaller in scale. The cycles of political consolidation and fragmentation ebbed and flowed in both of these global regions.

Despite the obvious differences between the ancient urban civilizations that arose in Mesoamerica and South America, the later prehispanic societies that developed in both regions shared a number of important organizational features. We know that even before the beginning of the modern era, the populations of both areas were characterized by differences in wealth and power, which generally became more apparent later in the prehispanic era. These distinctions were manifest in the clothes and ornaments people wore, the food they ate, the variety of goods they had, and the houses in which they lived.

For example, in Mesoamerica, Aztec lords, most of whom inherited their social status, dressed in cotton, ate venison, and lived in elaborate residences with retainers and servants. Alternatively, the commoners wore clothes made of coarser maguey fibers, ate relatively little animal protein, and lived in small adobe and stone houses. Inca lords ate, dressed, and resided very differently from Andean commoners. Thus, in both regions, these peoples, with powerful government institutions and large population centers, also were characterized by a marked degree of social stratification.

Nevertheless, we know that personal attributes could be important even in highly stratified societies, such as the Inca, where great warriors or capable administrators could achieve noble status. With the Inca, this social mobility was necessary because they expanded their empire so rapidly that there was a nearly constant need to fill administrative posts. Despite social mobility, however, the most powerful ruling positions could in principle be filled only by members of noble lineages. Inca emperors were believed to have ruled by divine right, claiming descent from the sun. Their power was absolute, checked only by the fear of revolt and past custom. Bloodlines were so important in later Inca times that the first wife of the Inca emperor was his full sister. Yet each emperor also had secondary wives, some of whom were the daughters of neighboring rulers.

Archaeological research provides the best avenue for understanding how the state and inherited social differences first emerged in human societies. Marked sociopolitical differences were not institutionalized in the earliest human societies, and they seem uncharacteristic of human populations with extensive hunting-and-gathering economies. Yet as we have seen in the Andes, inherited inequalities, social stratification, and the state developed long before European contact. Postconquest documentary records of the Spanish can never fully inform us about the ways in which social, political, and economic distinctions first emerged in the Andean world. Even in Mesoamerica, where written records have survived the ravages of time, the beginnings of social and political inequality predate the advent of writing. Many clues may exist at sites like El Paraíso and Chavín de Huántar, which were not the capitals of urban states yet show indications of emergent inequities in power and wealth.

While ultimately the solutions to these puzzles lie in the archaeological record, they will not be achieved quickly or easily. Questions about social inequality and the rise of states, as well as convincing explanations for the different historical pathways that we see for Mesoamerica and South America, are the kind of big, messy research issues that require mountains of carefully collected information, as well as brilliant, yet measured, inferences and ideas. Even then, each question probably has more than one answer or at least complex answers that interdigitate a multiplicity of factors. We can only hope to continue to make the kind of rapid progress in understanding our past that we have seen during the last few decades.

SUGGESTED READINGS

Bruhns, K. O. 1994. *Ancient South America*. Cambridge: Cambridge University Press. *A recent synthesis of archaeological research on ancient South America.*

Burger, R. L. 1992. *Chavín and the origins of Andean civilization*. London: Thames & Hudson. *An illustrated discussion of Chavín de Huántar and earlier Andean sites.*

Kolata, A. L. 1993. *The Tiwanaku: Portrait of an Andean civilization*. Cambridge: Blackwell. *A current synthesis of Tiwanaku and its predecessors.*

Moseley, M. E. 1992. *The Incas and their ancestors: The archaeology of Peru*. London: Thames & Hudson. *A readable overview of Andean prehistory.*

Roosevelt, A. C. 1989. Lost civilizations of the lower Amazon. *Natural History* 98:74–82. *A brief overview of lowland prehispanic South America.*

10

OLD WORLD STATES AND EMPIRES

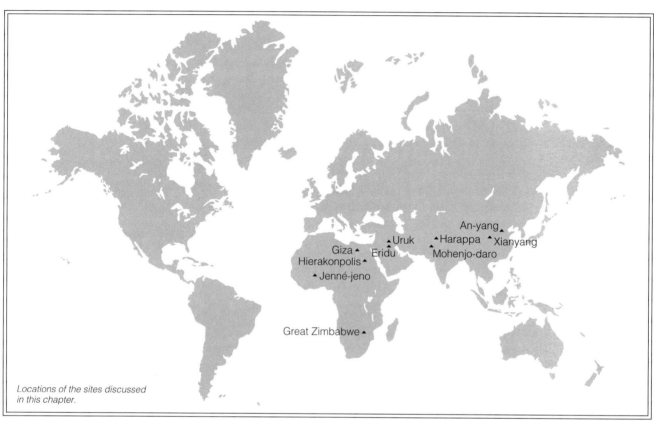

Locations of the sites discussed
in this chapter.

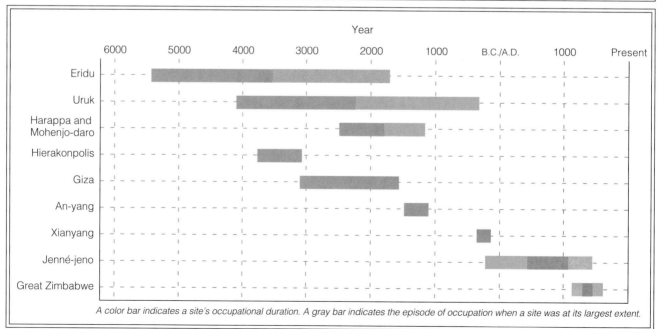

A color bar indicates a site's occupational duration. A gray bar indicates the episode of occupation when a site was at its largest extent.

THE OLD WORLD AFTER THE TRANSITION TO AGRICULTURE

The rise of early states and urban centers

The study of man and civilization is not only a matter of scientific interest, but at once passes into the practical business of life. We have in it the means of understanding our own lives and our place in the world, vaguely and imperfectly it is true, but at any rate more clearly than any former generation. The knowledge of man's course of life, from the remote past to the present, will not only help us to forecast the future, but may guide us in our duty of leaving the world better than we found it. (Tylor, 1960, p. 275)

In many ways, E. B. Tylor's words are as meaningful today as they were when first published in 1871. With more than a century of archaeology behind us, we can describe the trajectories of long-term change for a number of world regions, as well as compare and contrast the sequences from these areas. Although a thorough understanding of these differences and similarities remains ahead of us, today we know much more and therefore can ask research questions that are more specific than was possible in Tylor's day.

In Chapter 6, we examined the transition from hunting and gathering to agriculture and the adoption of more sedentary lifeways in a number of world regions. In Chapters 8 and 9, we began with early sedentary communities in Mesoamerica and South America and examined the various paths of change that led to the rise of the complex polities centered at Tenochtitlán (Aztec) and Cuzco (Inca). In this chapter, we review the transitions from early farming villages to more hierarchical polities in five regions of the Old World: Mesopotamia, South Asia (the Indian subcontinent), Egypt, North China, and Africa. We examine the beginnings of agriculture and the emergence and development of early states in Europe in Chapter 11.

Although the apparent causes of the changes we describe often varied greatly, long-term shifts resulted in the rise of polities and institutions that were hierarchically organized. Such institutions emerged in conjunction with larger, denser populations, where consensual methods of decision making no longer work effectively. At the same time, hierarchical institutions, characterized by differential power and authority, tend to become self-serving as well as system-serving. They work to perpetuate and enhance the extant structure (and its inequalities) so that those who are already advantaged remain the privileged class. Increasing inequality in wealth and power is a hallmark of so-called civilized societies. Such stratification also may be related to the problem of succession that characterizes all hierarchical institutions. By specially marking and treating the offspring of the privileged from birth, society can expose them to the knowledge, personal connections, and traditions necessary for assuming power. At the same time, such marking can limit the number of rightful heirs, thereby minimizing (if not eliminating) the disruptive consequences of succession disputes. Of course, wealth differentials and stratification are associated with the unequal control of power, land, and resources.

As we see in this chapter, the rise of hierarchical polities is generally linked with economic transitions in exchange and production. Particularly in the Old World, where beasts of burden and wheeled vehicles could distribute goods relatively inexpensively, we see the development of increasingly large-scale and specialized craft industries. Although such industries frequently were controlled by independent entrepreneurs, over time they offer central political institutions greater opportunities for limiting access and concentrating wealth. As societies increase in size and organizational complexity, the mechanisms of exchange also shift from face-to-face contacts to tribute and marketing.

Although these general trends are evident for the regions discussed in this chapter, the specific sequences of transition and the rates of change were not uniform. The world's first states evolved in Mesopotamia, where the temple institution became a key focus. We begin our discussion with Eridu, the site with perhaps the earliest Mesopotamian temple, established by the end of the sixth millennium B.C. The Mesopotamian temple functioned differently than the Mesoamerican temple. The former had a key economic role, not seen in the Mesoamerican institution, in that it received goods through tribute and then redistributed a portion during feasts and other activities.

We next examine the early Mesopotamian urban center of Uruk, situated amid a network of ancient canals not far from the Euphrates River. Scholars agree that large-scale canal irrigation was a key feature of early Mesopotamian civilization, and the remnants of the ancient waterways are still evident on the desiccated landscape. However, the specific causal relationship between water management and state development in Southwest Asia, also known as the Near East, remains a matter for debate. While some argue that the allocation of water and the maintenance of the canals necessitated some kind of central authority, others have suggested that the monumental water-control systems were built only after the rise of powerful states. Whichever scenario is eventually supported, the later Near Eastern empires capitalized on the great grain-producing potential of large-scale canal irrigation systems.

Slightly later, during the third millennium B.C., major centers arose along the Indus River and its tributaries in what are today Pakistan and India. Here we focus on the best-known sites of the Indus civilization, Harappa and Mohenjo-daro. Although these South Asian sites have not yielded rich tombs, like those in Mesopotamia, they are known for their highly developed craft industries. Indus centers generally were not as large as those in Mesopotamia, but they appear to have been more systematically planned, with centralized drainage networks for individual houses.

To a degree, the rise of civilization in Egypt was inspired by political and economic ties with the Near East. Yet the course of development was different. Large-scale political centralization was much more in evidence in Egypt than in Mesopotamia. Power was more focused on the principal ruler (viewed as a divine king) in Egypt. The monumental pyramid tombs of Egypt represent an expression of wealth and grandeur unsurpassed in the ancient Near East. For Egypt, we begin with the center of Hierakonpolis, a major settlement along the Nile whose occupation largely predates the unification of northern and southern Egypt. We next discuss the later funerary complex at Giza, located close to the ancient capital at Memphis. Both were important places in Dynastic Egypt. At Giza, several centuries after unification, powerful pharaohs constructed some of the world's largest pyramids.

By early in the second millennium B.C., states developed indigenously in North China. An-yang, the last capital of the Shang dynasty, was excavated first in the late 1920s and remains one of the best-known early Chinese cities. Although early Chinese centers were somewhat less urban than those in early Mesopotamia, they became some of the largest in the world by A.D. 1. During the last centuries B.C., in the reign of the Qin dynasty, a magnificent tomb was built near the capital of Xianyang. The mausoleum included a huge army of life-size **terracotta** (brown-orange earthenware) foot soldiers and cavalrymen, and illustrates the extreme stratification in ancient China.

Finally, we discuss sub-Saharan state development in western Africa at the tell site of Jenné-jeno and in southern Africa at Great Zimbabwe. The early urban center of Jenné-jeno was an important node in long-distance trade between the Sahara and gold-producing areas to the south during the first millennium A.D. Although not the earliest state in southern Africa, Great Zimbabwe is a spectacular site with large stone structures erected early in the second millennium A.D.

The head and torso of a life-size terra-cotta figure from the gallery.

In the chapter's Summary, we return to some of the key models and ideas that have been advanced to account for early state development. In a world that often seems to be dominated by powerful presidents, despots, kings, legislatures, bureaucracies, and tax collectors, one wonders how such hierarchical systems arose in the first place and why individual households lost their autonomy. To answer such questions about the beginnings of inequality and the rise of the first hierarchical decision-making institutions, we must turn to archaeology. In most parts of the world, the processes that culminated in unequal access to power and wealth began centuries before the advent of written records. As a consequence, written histories alone cannot answer these evolutionary questions. Archaeology must continue to focus on the dramatic changes that occurred between the advent of agriculture and the rise of urbanism in many areas of the world. Unraveling the processes and causal connections surrounding these episodes may help us explain the course of recent human history.

ERIDU

*An early ceremonial center
in Mesopotamia*

For nearly 10,000 years, the people of Southwest Asia have lived in farming communities. Their settlements, consisting of small, closely packed mud or clay rectangular structures, are ideally suited to the climate and the available resources. But mud-brick dwellings deteriorate rapidly. They must be rebuilt every 50–75 years, after a few generations of use. Over millennia, mud-brick abodes have been rebuilt repeatedly on top of earlier structures. Gradually, large mounds of accumulated mud and clay, known as tells, form across an entire community. Thousands of tells rise above the landscape of the Near East, some as high as 50 m (165 ft) above the surrounding terrain. These mounds contain debris from thousands of years of habitation. Ancient irrigation canals also cover the landscape of Southwest Asia. For the last 7000 years, irrigation has been practiced in this part of the world, and remnants of canals remain a visible reminder of the region's rich archaeological past.

The soils of the alluvial plain are deposited by the annual floods of the Tigris and Euphrates Rivers. The rivers also provide the water that makes irrigation (and hence agriculture) possible in this region, where rainfall is inadequate for farming. Today, Mesopotamian farmers using irrigation can cultivate a variety of crops, including wheat, barley, dates, lentils, olives, oranges, and onions. Along the swamps formed by the rivers, several kinds of usable plants, such as flax for textiles and rushes for basketry, can be collected. Although scrub forests along the rivers do not support much game,

fish are abundant in the rivers. However, the riverine lowlands of the Mesopotamian alluvium do not contain much in the way of raw materials.

No early agricultural villages, such as those established in the coastal Levant and in the foothills of the Taurus and Zagros mountains (see Chapter 6), have been recorded on the flat plain between the Tigris and Euphrates Rivers in southern Iraq, the area known as Mesopotamia (Greek for "land between two rivers"). The alluvial floodplains and deltas here are hot and dry, composed primarily of inhospitable sand, swamp, and dry mudflats. Yet it was in Mesopotamia that the world's first civilization developed.

By 6000 B.C., the first scattered farming villages were settled on the northern fringe of the Tigris and Euphrates floodplain, an area where seasonal rainfall can sustain agriculture. These communities were generally composed of several houses, entered through the roof, containing two or three rooms each. Ovens and chimneys were common features. By 5500 B.C., a new style of painted pottery, called Halafian, spread throughout a wide area of northern Mesopotamia, replacing the monochrome wares that had been made previously. The remarkable similarity of Halafian pottery over a wide area suggests that small villages were linked into far-reaching networks.

Shortly after the appearance of Halafian ceramics in the north, the focus of Mesopotamian settlement shifted to the southern alluvial plain of the Tigris and Euphrates Rivers, an area known as Sumer. No sedentary villages prior to the sixth millennium B.C. have yet been recorded in this area. This is not surprising, because the area lacks plants and animals that later were domesticated, and even usable stone. In most years, the region receives insufficient precipitation for dry farming. Yet with an economy based on fish, irrigation agriculture, and domestic cattle, Sumer became the demographic and political core of Southwest Asia for most of the next 4000 years. The 'Ubaid (oo-baid') period (5300–3600 B.C.), which begins this sequence, was marked by an increasing reliance on canal irrigation and the establishment of the temple (see "Temples," p. 413).

The first villages in southern Mesopotamia were small, mostly 1–2 ha (2.5–5 acres). Yet, relatively rapidly, a few of the settlements, such as Eridu (air'ih-dew), grew in size and importance. Eridu, the earliest known settlement on the southern Mesopotamian alluvium, was established around 5400 B.C. Ancient Sumerian accounts of creation (written in 3000 B.C.) name Eridu as one of the first communities to emerge from the primeval sea.

Although most of the structures at Eridu were houses, the initial occupational levels feature a significant nonresidential structure. The architectural plan of this public building bears sufficient similarity to later Sumerian temples (depicted in written texts) to suggest that it may have served as an early temple. The building, constructed of mud-bricks, measured 3.5 × 4.5 m (11.5 × 15 ft), with a possible altar facing the entrance and a pedestal in the center of the room. Signs of burning on the pedestal indicate that it may have been used for offerings. This possible temple suggests that the organizational capacity for the construction of minor public architecture was present; however, its small size reflects a much lower level of social complexity than in later times.

Yet the temple institution may have had antecedents that preceded the movement of populations into Mesopotamia's southern alluvium. An earlier T-shaped structure at Tell as-Sawwan, on the border between the northern plain and the southern alluvium, may have been a public building with functions similar to

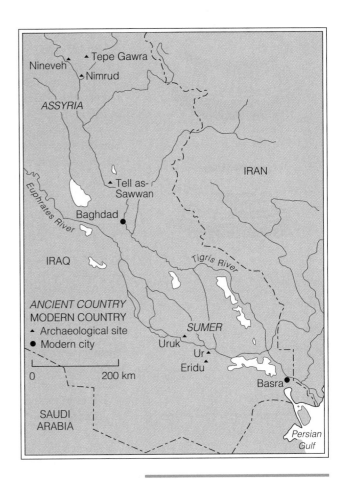

Mesopotamia, with sites mentioned in text.

those of the later temple. In addition, a circular domed structure at Tepe Gawra, on the fringes of the northern plain, was found below a sequence of superimposed temples. At other northern Mesopotamian sites, similar circular structures, often joined to a rectangular entryway and thereby making a keyhole shape, have been found. These structures, or *tholoi*, were distinct from the traditional rectangular dwellings and seem to have had a nonresidential purpose, perhaps related to ritual and storage.

Because the temple institution was a focal point of early civilizations in Southwest Asia, questions about its origin and antecedents are important for Near Eastern prehistory. Yet there also are more general implications. If the temple only emerged in Sumer, its development may be linked to the increasing and necessary reliance on canal irrigation. Social theorists have long argued that the management of irrigation systems requires cooperation among farming populations to

Two examples of painted 'Ubaid pottery.

An artist's reconstruction of the Uruk period temple at Eridu.

allocate water and maintain canals—a particular problem in Sumer, where the rivers carry and deposit great quantities of silt. Alternatively, if antecedents of the temple were established prior to the occupation of the southern Mesopotamian alluvium, perhaps the movement into Sumer became possible only once a central redistributive institution, like the temple, was in place. Without such an integrative institution, the agricultural hazards of flooding, drought, and dust storms could not have been overcome. In this scenario, irrigation management may have been responsible for the expansion and elaboration of the temple institution, but not its initiation. Likewise, another consequence of irrigation is that it tends to enhance disparities in agricultural productivity and hence land value. In Sumer, emerging inequalities in agrarian production may have fostered increasing economic stratification. Much more archaeological research is needed to address these issues adequately.

By 4500 B.C., the southern Mesopotamian alluvium was dotted with full-fledged towns and public buildings. Based on irrigation farming, the economy produced enough food to support a growing population, yielding a surplus that supported craft producers and decision makers. Eridu may have covered 10 ha (25 acres) by this time and had a population as large as several thousand people. The temple at Eridu was rebuilt numerous times and expanded so that it contained multiple altars and offering places. The most elaborate residential dwellings were situated immediately around the temple at the center of the community; craftsworkers and peasants lived at ever-increasing distances from the core of the settlement.

The development of the temple institution and the spread of canal irrigation were key features of the 'Ubaid period in southern Mesopotamia. This period was identified by a widespread monochrome pottery decorated with geometric designs. 'Ubaid times also were characterized by population growth and increases in craftwork. 'Ubaid pottery was made in a wider range of forms than the earlier Halafian ware. Yet it tended to be somewhat less decorated, and the different ceramic varieties were generally more uniformly distributed over space. Most of the 'Ubaid ceramics appear to have been made on a slow-turning potter's wheel, in use for the first time. Because of the absence of suitable sources of stone, hard-fired clay was used to make sickles, mullers (implements used to grind paints, powders, etc.), hammers, and axes.

The complex processes that led to the growth of later civilization in Mesopotamia clearly had begun during the 'Ubaid period. Yet indicators of pronounced social differentiation appeared only at the very end of the period. There are few exotic luxury items at 'Ubaid sites. And despite many excavated 'Ubaid burials, no highly elaborate funerary contexts have been unearthed. Not until the subsequent Uruk period (3600–3100 B.C.) did monumental urban centers arise in accordance with clear indicators of social stratification. Eridu remained an important place for more than 1000 years following the end of the 'Ubaid period. Yet early in the fourth millennium B.C., other centers, such as Uruk (also known as Warka), rapidly surpassed it in size, monumentality, and political significance. Although for much of its early history the centers and polities of Mesopotamia shared a common cultural tradition, rarely was this region dominated politically by a single ruler or core state.

Temples were established in southern Mesopotamia no later than the 'Ubaid period (5300–3600 B.C.), and by the end of the 'Ubaid, the Sumerian pattern of towns with temples was well entrenched. In later Mesopotamian cities, the temple was always the largest and most impressive building, and it had both economic and religious functions. The temple institution became the focal point for the powerful religion and statecraft that integrated and maintained the complex polities that arose in ancient Mesopotamia.

At Eridu, a series of around 20 superimposed temples, spanning 3500 years, was excavated. Built atop earlier ruins, the later temples were raised above the land. The remains of earlier shrines are preserved within the foundations of later buildings. Each structure was separated from the others by deposits of debris, including small animal and fish bones, that may have been offerings.

Although not all temples are associated with great stepped towers known as **ziggurats,** many are. How significant the ziggurats were is evident in the names by which they are known—House of the Mountain, for example. In Mesopotamia, the word *mountain* has great religious significance, as the place where the power of all natural life is concentrated. In a terracotta relief found in a temple from the second millennium B.C., the body of the deity issues from a mountain.

In Mesopotamia, religious order centering on the temple assumed much of the burden for structuring society. Third-millennium texts tell us that the laws of the gods were unchanging and people were governed by the gods' decisions. However, the rapid rise in the importance of the temple cannot be explained fully by religion. The growth of temples and the early cities that developed around them was closely related to the economy. Generally associated with storage facilities, the temple became a redistributive center for agricultural produce and craft goods. It also provided help after floods, dust storms, and scorching winds when agricultural crops failed.

Temple administrators organized the cooperative projects necessary to construct and maintain irrigation channels and probably decided who received how much water. The construction of the irrigation canals created unequal land values and inequities in land holdings. The temple elite became the managers of large sectors of the economy. They owned land, employed people directly, and were extensively involved in farming and manufacturing activities. Because they controlled large quantities of food, they could support full-time craft specialists, including stonemasons, copperworkers, and weavers. The temple also directed the long-distance trade that provided raw materials to the craft specialists. Status goods were received in return, reinforcing the position of the temple elite. Although other private and royal estates also were important, it was the temple that became the central economic force in early Mesopotamian cities.

The building of ziggurats required huge amounts of labor and materials. The fact that so much energy was diverted to nonutilitarian tasks attests to the power of the temple elite. The construction of monumental architecture served to reinforce social and political hierarchies. The temples may have been objects of civic pride, proclaiming the well-being of the communities that built them and the majesty of the gods to whom they were dedicated, while at the same time, through rituals and religious sanctions, validating the power and authority of the ruling elite.

TEMPLES

The role of the temple institution in Mesopotamia

The long sequence of temples excavated at Eridu. Roman numerals indicate the reverse sequence of construction.

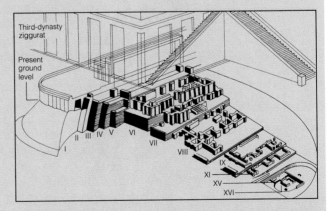

Third-dynasty ziggurat

Present ground level

II III IV V VI

I

VII

VIII

IX

XI

XV

XVI

URUK

The world's first city

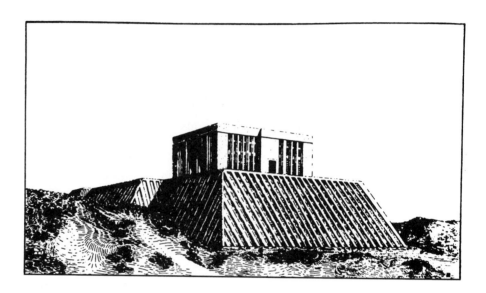

An artist's reconstruction of the Anu Ziggurat at Uruk.

Many of the processes underlying the growth of urban civilization in Sumer began during the 'Ubaid period. Yet it was during the succeeding Uruk (3600–3100 B.C.) and Early Dynastic (3100–2370 B.C.) periods that urban settlements and the earliest states were first established. Based on the great surplus potential of intensive irrigation agriculture, the power of cities and their rulers increased. In Mesopotamia, the site of Uruk (oo-rook′), with its giant stepped pyramid, the Anu Ziggurat, was the largest and most impressive. During the fourth millennium B.C., Mesopotamia also entered the era of history, with the use of a system of writing on clay tablets.

Located on the banks of the Euphrates River less than 160 km (100 mi) north of Eridu, Uruk was settled prior to 4000 B.C. during the 'Ubaid period and became a major city of more than 10,000 people, covering 100 ha (250 acres) by 3100 B.C. Residential architecture at Uruk was made of whitewashed mud brick.

Houses were rectangular in shape and were built along narrow, winding streets.

Most outlying sites were small, only 1–3 ha (2.5–7.5 acres) in size (smaller than a city block), although several settlements of intermediate size were established. Rapid population growth during the Uruk period was probably due to in-migration and perhaps the settling down of nomadic peoples, in addition to natural increases resulting from changes in fertility and mortality rates.

The earliest monumental architecture at Uruk, the Anu Ziggurat, is composed of a series of building levels, the earliest going back to 'Ubaid times. This stepped pyramid, named for the primary god (Anu) in the Sumerian pantheon, attained its maximum size at the end of the Uruk period. At this time, the White Temple was built on top of the Anu Ziggurat, 12 m (40 ft) above the ground. The temple, which measured 17.5 × 22.3 m (57.5 × 73 ft), was made of whitewashed mud brick and decorated

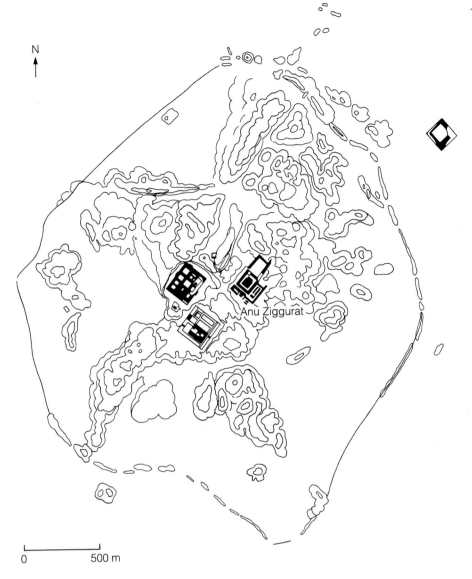

Anu Ziggurat

0   500 m

with elaborate recesses, columns, and buttresses. Inside, the pattern followed the tripartite temple plan described for Eridu centuries earlier, which consisted of a long central room with a row of smaller rooms on each side.

The Anu Ziggurat and the White Temple mark a transition that was occurring in Mesopotamian society. The earlier Eridu temples were small compared to Uruk temples and probably were administered by civic-ceremonial functionaries who had only limited influence over the populace. However, the economic and political power of the temple expanded as the size of its buildings in-creased. The Anu complex, estimated to have taken 7500 man-years to build, represents the control of a large, organized labor force. As has been argued for Medieval Europe: "What constituted the real basis of wealth . . . was not owner-ship of land but power over men, however wretched their condition" (Duby, 1974, p. 13).

As temples became more elaborate, the structures, as well as the individuals associated with them, were separated from the general populace. Platforms and ziggurats elevated the temples above the rest of the community. In the Early Dy-nastic period, temples and the associated

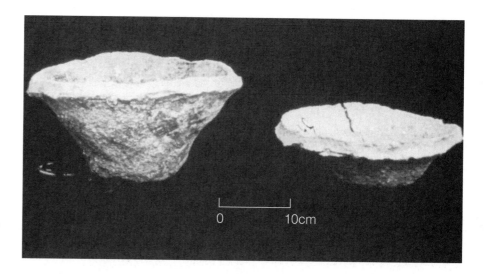

Undecorated, crudely made beveled-rim bowls.

priestly residences were often enclosed by high walls that further divided and protected this increasingly wealthy precinct from the lower socioeconomic strata below.

By the middle of the fourth millennium B.C., economic specialization in a wide variety of arts and crafts was evident, including stone cutting, metallurgy, and pottery production. Earlier Halafian and 'Ubaid potters had crafted beautifully painted vessels, but during Uruk times, these wares were largely replaced by unpainted pottery (a trend that may have begun earlier in the 'Ubaid period). An important Uruk development was the widespread use of the potter's wheel, which allowed for the more rapid production of fired clay containers. Using the wheel and molds, potters began to produce mostly undecorated utilitarian vessels in great volume, including crudely made beveled-rim bowls that may have been used for rations. In earlier Halafian and 'Ubaid times, highly decorated pottery vessels may have served as wealth or status items that also marked or defined certain social, territorial, or kin groups. By the Uruk period, ceramic items appear not to have played these roles, as they were even plainer and more uniformly distributed over space. Perhaps textiles and metal items largely replaced pottery as wealth items and markers of social identity.

As craft specialization and the demand for raw materials increased, trade flourished along major waterways, especially the slow-moving Euphrates. Ships sailed up the rivers from the Persian Gulf, carrying food and raw materials, including shell, carnelian, silver, gold, lapis lazuli, onyx, alabaster, ivory, textiles, timber, and skins. Copper, which first appeared on the plateau to the north as early as the fifth or sixth millennium B.C., was imported into lower Mesopotamia around 3500 B.C. Metal implements soon took on an important role in agriculture and warfare. Coppersmiths were present in most Mesopotamian cities by 3000 B.C. The wheel was introduced during the fourth millennium B.C., and wheeled vehicles, drawn by horses, asses, and oxen, became vital in trade and warfare.

Another important development during the fourth millennium B.C. was the invention of the plow, which resulted in increased agricultural yield. In large part, Uruk's power depended on the city's ability to extract agricultural surplus from the hinterlands. In the southern Mesopotamian alluvium, agricultural surplus was vital, as the region lacks mineral and stone resources. The major crops were wheat, barley, flax, and dates; cattle raising and fishing also were important.

The world's earliest known written documents, clay tablets dating to 3400 B.C., come from Uruk. The principal function of this earliest Mesopotamian writing appears to have been economic, as the clay tablets record lists of commodi-

ties and business transactions. Over 1500 symbols have been identified in these early texts. Signs for carpenter, smith, chariot, copper (in the form of an ingot), plow, and harp have been recognized. Lists of commodities include dairy products, cattle, wheat, barley, bread, beer, clothing, and flocks of sheep. The elements of the early Uruk writing system have been shown to be the forerunners of later Sumerian cuneiform (see "Early Writing Systems," p. 419).

By the beginning of the Early Dynastic period (about 3000 B.C.), Near Eastern civilization was well established. Written records enable us to trace the dynastic succession of specific kings. Metal tools, which were far more efficient than earlier tools, became much more common. Smiths began to alloy copper with tin to produce bronze, which is much harder than copper. The development of bronze weapons was directly linked to the increasing role of warfare as a means of attaining political ends. Armies were equipped with wheeled chariots and wagons. Rulers became more despotic, concentrating wealth and controlling subjects by military strength, religious sanction, and taxation.

During the Early Dynastic, Sumer was divided into 10–15 contemporaneous city-states, which were largely politically autonomous. Uruk grew to 400 ha (1000 acres) and may have contained as many as 50,000 people. This demographic growth was indicative of the great nucleation (in cities) that characterized Early Dynastic Mesopotamia. As the wealth and power of these closely packed cities increased, so did the competition between them. Great defensive walls were constructed around the major urban centers, including Uruk. This period also was characterized by dynastic rule, as individual monarchs and their courts gained increasing independence from long-powerful temple institutions.

After its peak around 2700 B.C., Uruk's supremacy was challenged by other early cities, and its political importance eventually declined. Yet no single city-state dominated the Mesopotamian landscape for long during the Early Dynastic. Ur, a smaller center just 120 km (75 mi) away, became Uruk's economic and military rival. Ur was inhabited as early as the Uruk period, but the settlement rose to great prominence only during the subsequent millennium.

Early Dynastic Ur is renowned for the Royal Cemetery, which was excavated in the late 1920s by British archaeologist Sir Leonard Woolley. More than 2500 burials were unearthed, providing graphic evidence for superb craftsmanship, opulent wealth, and developed social stratification. Fewer than 20 graves actually contained royal individuals, who were placed in private chambers made of stone blocks and mud bricks. The contents of these graves indicated great concentrations of wealth and the trappings of earthly power.

Perhaps the best-known vault is thought to contain the body of Queen Shub-ad. She was lying on her back upon a bed, accompanied by female attendants. Two wagons drawn by oxen and attended by male servants had been backed down the entry ramp, where 59 bodies, mostly female, were on the ground near the tomb chambers. All retainers were lavishly bedecked with crafted ornaments made of gold, silver, carnelian, lapis lazuli, and turquoise. Woolley believed that all the people and animals buried with the queen entered the vault alive. After the queen and her possessions were placed in the pit, the animals were dispatched by their keepers, who then consumed poison that was ready for them in the shafts. No violence or confrontation is evident in the arrangement of the corpses. Although royal interments are few at Ur, numerous graves contain modest quantities of goods, and an even larger number include little or no material wealth. Great disparities in individuals' treatment at death are evident at Ur, suggesting that social stratification was marked.

By the end of the Early Dynastic period, bureaucratic organization, social stratification, trade, crafts, and writing were all highly developed (see Color Plate 22). Yet, if anything, the pace of military conflict and political upheaval was intensified. For Sumer, the history of the third and second millennia B.C. (and beyond) is extremely complicated; political realignments, military conquests, and dynastic replacements occurred frequently. Although increasingly large territorial units and empires were formed periodically, these large polities often were short-lived. In other instances, expansive polities came into contact and conflict with each other, leading to the collapse of at least one of them. The political fluidity that has characterized this part of the world in recent decades may have roots in the distant past.

Early civilizations employed different systems of communication, information storage, and accounting. In the Andes, the *quipu* was used by Inca bureaucrats to keep accounts; no system of writing was developed (see "Huánuco Pampa," Chapter 9, p. 400). Some of the first writing in China was on animal bones and turtle shells. Scapulas (shoulder blades) and other bones were heated until cracks formed. The patterning of the cracks in relation to the written characters was used ritually by diviners to foretell the future, a practice referred to as **scapulimancy** (see "An-yang," p. 442). In the Indus Valley, evidence for early indigenous script is found primarily on soapstone seals that apparently were used to mark ownership. In Egypt, many early texts recorded dynastic and kinship themes. In prehispanic Mesoamerica, writing was frequently used to record dynastic records (births, marriages, accessions, and deaths), to announce military victories, and to document political events. Calendrical inscriptions often were used by the Maya and other Mesoamerican peoples to track historical themes. In Mesopotamia, the principal function of the world's first writing system was similar to that described for the Indus Valley; however, the particular conventions of the Mesopotamian writing system and the actual script and symbols employed were markedly different.

In 1929, a team of German archaeologists discovered written inscriptions on clay tablets at the site of Uruk. These earliest Mesopotamian texts, dating to the late fourth millennium B.C., revealed an already developed writing system that included as many as 1500 different symbols and fairly consistent conventions for the presentation of information. By 3000 B.C., this writing system was in use across southern Mesopotamia. The written symbols were primarily ideographs (abstract signs), although a few of the signs were pictographs that more or less portrayed the represented objects.

In the mid-1960s, French excavations at Susa, on the Susiana Plain east of

A clay envelope, or bulla, approximately 7 cm in diameter.

Uruk, discovered hollow clay spheres or envelopes, called **bullae**, that enclosed modeled clay tokens or geometric forms. Dating to the end of the fourth millennium B.C., these bullae are impressed on the outside, thus providing evidence for writing that is approximately as old as the Uruk tablets. They resemble the hollow clay tablets containing clay tokens that were used for accounting as late as 1500 B.C. in parts of Southwest Asia.

In 1969, Denise Schmandt-Besserat, of the University of Texas, Austin, initiated a study of the earliest uses of clay in the Near East. Traveling to museums around the world, she recorded collections of early pottery, bricks, and figurines. Yet in addition to those expected objects, she noted that most of the collections (made from Turkey to Pakistan) also included hand-modeled clay tokens dating to as early as the ninth millennium B.C. Schmandt-Besserat recognized the similarity between these tokens, which generally had been cataloged as toys, gaming pieces, or ritual objects, and the tokens associated with the later bullae and hollow tablets. She also noticed more than 30 formal correspondences between three-dimensional geometric tokens and the two-dimensional ideographic

(continued)

symbols that were inscribed on the early
tablets.

Based on these correspondences,
Schmandt-Besserat reasoned that Neolithic clay tokens, like the later bulla-
enclosed counterparts, may have been
used to record economic transactions.
The earliest token shapes that could be
associated with later written characters
referred to quantities of various agricultural products. Other common token
forms were linked formally with the two-
dimensional symbols for numbers and
key commodities, like cloth, bread, ani-

mals, and oil. Not surprisingly, the variety
of tokens increased through time, generally becoming more elaborate. Overall,
more than 200 different kinds of tokens
have been identified at sites dating to
9000–1500 B.C. If Schmandt-Besserat's
hypotheses are correct, the first communication revolution—the advent of the
clay tokens—was associated with the
transition to village sedentism, farming,
and an increased volume of economic
transactions and long-distance trade.

Relatively little change in this recording system is evident prior to the

emergence of urbanism and the state during the fourth millennium B.C. Sometime after 3500 B.C., a sizable proportion of the tokens were perforated, as if for stringing. Schmandt-Besserat reasoned that tokens may have been strung together to signify that the objects they represented were part of a single transaction. By the end of the fourth millennium B.C., tokens also began to be placed in bullae. Sealing the tokens within a single bulla could have served to segregate a specific transaction. Seals of the individuals involved were placed on the outside of the bulla, perhaps validating the event. A bulla may have been used like a bill of sale would be used today. The honesty of the deliverer could be checked by matching the goods received with the tokens enclosed in the accompanying bulla. But there was one major drawback to this innovation: Checking the tokens required that a bulla be broken; but to preserve the record, the bulla had to remain intact. The solution was to press the tokens on the exterior of the clay envelope before enclosing the tokens and firing the bulla. In this way, the contents of the load could be checked by the receiver while the validating inscriptions remained intact. In some instances, a finger or a stylus was used to impress the image of the token on the bulla surface. By this time, a system of cylinder seals also was devised. The seals could be impressed on clay, leaving a mark or design that could be associated with a specific person.

By the outset of the third millennium B.C., hollow bullae with tokens inside were generally replaced by clay tablets. Anyone could check the outside of a bulla without destroying the record. An inscribed bulla or tablet was much easier to make and store than clay tokens. Such economizing measures would have become more important as the development of tribute-collecting institutions (the temple) and urban centers fostered an intensified volume of economic transactions. Thus it is not really surprising that the earliest tablets were convex and made of clay, mirroring the shape and material composition of the spherical bullae. Likewise, it is easier to understand the early reliance on ideographs on the tablets, because the earliest written signs followed the shapes of the geometric tokens. The use of Mesopotamian writing to record economic transactions also seems a logical development from the function of the earlier token system. Mesopotamian writing clearly did not emerge in a vacuum; it evolved from an old and widespread system of communication and accounting.

Mesopotamian writing was simplified and made more efficient over time. To simplify writing, Sumerian scribes reduced the number of symbols and substituted wedge-shaped marks for the signs, giving rise to **cuneiform**, the name given to subsequent Mesopotamian scripts. The opposite occurred in Egypt, where the hieroglyphic symbols were made increasingly difficult to execute. In Egypt, writing served fewer purposes for a relatively small segment of the population.

The most significant contribution of writing was expediting the flow of information in increasingly large and stratified societies. It facilitated administrative activities and enabled the further growth and centralization of Mesopotamian cities. Writing also may have crystallized and preserved Mesopotamian cultural and bureaucratic traditions so that they outlived the hegemony of single rulers or dominant city-states.

Yet an alphabetical system was not invented in Mesopotamia, and in 1900 B.C., Sumerian written language still contained 600–700 unique elements, with an organizational structure somewhat analogous to traditional Chinese. The first truly alphabetical written languages developed toward the end of the second millennium B.C. By 1000 B.C., the Greeks adapted the Syrian alphabet to their own language and reduced the number of written signs to 25. The Greek alphabet then became the foundation for all contemporary European language systems.

HARAPPA AND MOHENJO-DARO

Urbanism and the rise of civilization in the Indus Valley

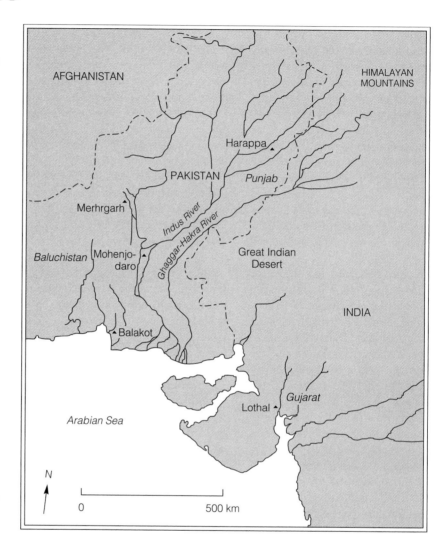

The Indus area, with sites mentioned in the text.

The broad fertile floodplains of the Indus and Ghaggar-Hakra Rivers (the latter is now dry) and their tributaries, in what is now Pakistan, were the principal focus of the Indus Valley civilization, 2600–1900 B.C. Covering about 680,000 sq km (260,000 sq mi, roughly the size of Texas), this area is bordered by the Baluchistan Hills to the west, the Arabian Sea to the south, the Great Indian Desert to the east, and the majestic Himalayan Mountains to the north.

The earliest known sites in the riverine heartland of the Indus civilization date to the late fifth and early fourth millennia B.C., postdating earlier occupations like Mehrgarh, 200 km (125 mi) to the west. These settlements, referred to as Early Harappan, were scattered across the plains in major agricultural areas or along important trade routes. Many of them exhibit artifacts and organizational features directly antecedent to the later sites, suggesting that the Indus Valley civilization had a long, local path of development. The Indus development does not appear to have been a simple consequence of stimuli from the ancient civilizations of Mesopotamia, a view held by previous generations of scholars.

The early Indus Valley settlements consisted of small, contiguous, rectangular mud-brick houses, some of which contained multiple rooms. The size of settlements varied, and a few included monumental construction. Some sites had massive mud-brick walls and neighborhoods laid out with north-south and east-west streets. Plow-based agriculture was practiced. Cattle, sheep, and goats were kept, but hunting and fishing also remained important subsistence activities.

Craft technologies associated with later Indus civilization developed to a high degree at these pre-Indus settlements. Rings, bangles, beads, pins, axes, and celts were manufactured from copper and bronze. Fine stones were ground and polished into beads. Using kilns and the potter's wheel, craftspeople produced a variety of vessel forms, some of which were elaborate, such as serving dishes on stands. Much of the pottery was finely painted. Other important crafted items included terracotta figurines. By the late fourth millennium B.C., potter's marks were present, and seals were inscribed with various geometric symbols.

Indus Valley civilization, also called the Harappan tradition, was first identified by Sir John Marshall in 1921 at the site of Harappa (ha-rap'ah) in the Punjab highlands in the upper Indus Valley. Although few systematic settlement pattern studies have been undertaken, more than 1000 Harappan sites have been reported. Few villages have been excavated, but most appear to be 1–5 ha (2.5–12.5 acres) in size and are located near rivers or streams. There are at least four large urban centers, the best known of which are Harappa and Mohenjo-daro (mo-henge'o-dah'ro), roughly 500 km (310 mi) to the south in the lower Indus plain. The two sites, both of which have been the focus of major archaeological field studies, are surprisingly similar. Both towns are large, covering approximately 150–250 ha (370–620 acres), and contained populations of roughly 40,000–80,000 people. Both Mohenjo-daro and Harappa were built with massive mud-brick walls and platforms that raised the towns above the surround-

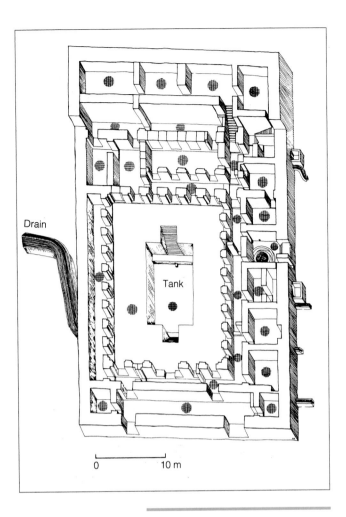

The plan of the Great Bath at Mohenjo-daro.

ing floodplains (see Color Plate 23). Mohenjo-daro was rebuilt at least nine times.

Harappa and Mohenjo-daro consisted of several mounded sectors. Massive foundations of eroded mud-brick walls and traces of large brick gateways have been noted around the edges of these mounds. Both Harappa and Mohenjo-daro have a high rectangular mound on the west and other large mounds to the north, south, and east. Some of the most important public buildings associated with the Harappan tradition are located on the western or tallest mound at Mohenjo-daro. The major structures included a possible "granary," a "great bath," and a great hall ("college") almost 730 sq m (8100 sq ft) in size. Some scholars have argued that the granary (1000 sq m, or 11,000 sq ft, equivalent to an Olympic-size swimming pool) was erected over brick supports

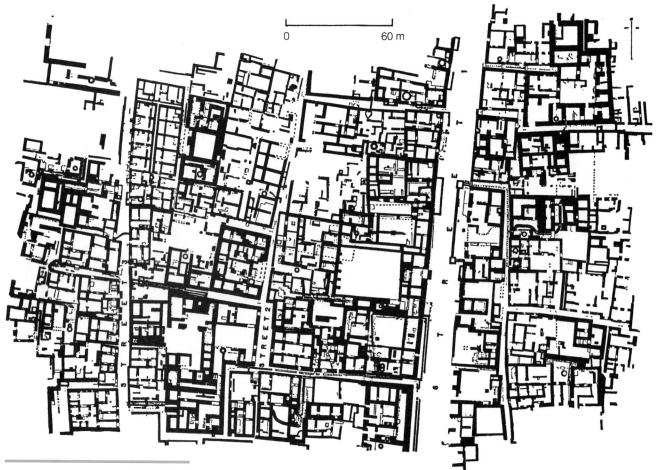

The plan of streets and houses at Mohenjo-daro.

so that air could circulate under the stored grain. Others suggest that it was simply a public building with multiple rooms. The Great Bath—12 × 7 m (39 × 23 ft) and 3 m (10 ft) deep, which may have been used for ceremonial ritual bathing—included eight small private bathrooms or changing cubicles. The bath itself was fed by a well, and its brickwork was sealed with waterproof bitumen or tar. The building was probably the first large water tank in the world.

Mohenjo-daro's other sectors were divided into blocks by streets, the broadest of which were about 10 m (33 ft) wide. Hundreds of houses lined the streets and alleys, some of which were paved with stone. Some of these structures had two stories and were made of baked mud bricks (at smaller settlements, houses generally were built of sun-dried mud bricks). At Mohenjo-daro, more spacious dwellings, per-

haps for high-status individuals and merchants, were laid out around central courtyards. These residences had private bathing areas and toilets connected to a central drainage system built partially underground.

A striking feature of Harappan society is the extent of standardization, including a system of weights and measures. Precisely shaped pieces of chert were used as counterweights in balances. Construction bricks had standard dimensions. Ceramic forms and ornamentation were remarkably similar at sites throughout the Indus system, although there was some regional variation and change over time.

A considerable degree of occupational specialization characterized Indus society, and one's profession was probably an important factor in social differentiation. At the major urban centers, there were designated living and working

A collection of stone cubical weights from Harappa.

quarters for beadmakers, coppersmiths, and weavers. Certain smaller sites were devoted almost entirely to a specific industry, craft, or trade, including beadmaking, shellworking, ceramic production, and coppersmithing. Metallurgy was well developed, and copper and bronze were used for a variety of tools and weapons. The availability of copper, lead, and silver within or close to Indus territory contributed to a greater use of metal tools than was evident in Mesopotamia.

There were significant differences between the Indus Valley and Mesopotamian civilizations. Although the Indus civilization covered a larger geographic area—650,000 sq km (260,000 sq mi), it had a smaller number of major centers. Mesopotamia was composed of many city-states. The similarities between Harappa and Mohenjo-daro suggest that Indus centers were closely linked economically and culturally. The Indus civilization may have had a more equitable distribution of wealth than was the case in other early Old World societies. Exotic stones or metal were not restricted to large sites or clearly elite contexts; considerable quantities of wealth have been recovered at even modest settlements. Indus material culture was simple compared to that of Mesopotamia; little representational or lavish art was constructed on a massive scale. Instead, one finds figurines, small sculptures, carvings on bone and ivory, decorated pottery, and intaglio figures on seals. Indus art is often in miniature.

The Indus elite engaged in fewer lavish public displays; they built no rich tombs, elaborate palaces, or fancy temples. But some mud-brick-lined tombs yielded more grave offerings (pottery, bronze mirrors, and a few beads) than the average burial. Nothing approaching the royal graves at Ur or the Egyptian tombs has yet been found in the Indus region. In fact, whatever rulers and elite the Harappans had remain anonymous. Individual conquests and accomplishments are not enumerated, and few portraits have been found. A steatite (soapstone) figure from Mohenjo-daro depicting a bearded man in an embroidered robe is a rare exception.

Indus settlements were closer to natural resources than Sumerian sites were. The large Harappan centers were connected with outlying rural communities and resource areas through complex trade networks. Both maritime and overland routes were used. Wheeled carts were drawn along regular caravan routes, and deep-sea vessels traveled the Persian Gulf and the Gulf of Oman. Long-distance exchanges moved seals, carnelian beads, and other miscellaneous items from the Indus region to the Persian Gulf, northern and southern Mesopotamia, Iran, and Afghanistan. Imports included lapis lazuli from Afghanistan, conch shells from Gujarat (western India), turquoise from northeastern Iran, carved chlorite (a kind of green stone) bowls from the Iranian Plateau, and

A steatite figure of a ruler from Mohenjo-daro.

serpentine (another green stone) from central Asia. Few Mesopotamian items have been found in the Indus area. A possible explanation is that Mesopotamia exported mostly perishables or specific raw materials, such as barley, fruits, oil, and textiles.

A system of writing that was very different from the early Mesopotamian script developed in the Indus Valley. Over 4000 seals with Indus script have been found. Most inscriptions are short; no known inscription is longer than 21 signs, and the average text is only five or six signs. The lack of long texts has added to the difficulty of interpreting the Indus script. Over 400 different symbols have been identified, yet none has been definitively deciphered. Inscriptions, including both writing and pictures, are found on small copper tablets and potsherds, but most are found on square

seals of soapstone, a material that is easy to carve. Most seals had holes that allowed them to be strung and worn around the neck. The script seems to identify the owner of the seal or the official status of the bearer.

Many animals are depicted on the seals, including elephants, unicorns, water buffalo, rhinoceros, tigers, crocodiles, antelopes, bulls, tigers, and goats. The late Walter Fairservis, Jr., suggested these animals may be totems or symbols representing specific kin groups; some seals depict processions with animal effigies being carried as standards. Each seal may thus identify its owner with a social group, which might help explain why similar scenes are repeated on multiple seals. One common theme is a figure seated in the yogic posture with heels pressed under the groin. Surrounded by various animals, this individual wears a

water buffalo–horned headdress. A second common scene is a pipal tree (a species of fig tree) with various anthropomorphic and human figures. Some archaeologists have suggested that the figure with the headdress may be an early form of a deity that later came to be worshipped as Shiva, Lord of the Beasts, in Hinduism.

The Indus civilization began to decline around 1900 B.C. The major Harappan centers were greatly weakened, and the center of power shifted from the Indus to the Ganges River Valley to the east where, after 600 B.C., large cities were built and state-level organizations formed. Archaeologists now think that the changes in the early part of the second millennium B.C. were not a complete collapse or population replacement but, rather, the beginning of an episode of decentralization. Many elements of the earlier Harappan civilization were retained in these new settlements. The decline of the Indus civilization has been linked to the drying of the ancient Ghaggar-Hakra River and the breakdown of the Indus system of exchange. Traditional views

that proposed an Aryan invasion from the northwest are no longer supported.

The persistence of many aspects and traditions of the Indus civilization into more recent times is startling. Ceremonial bathing, ritual burning, specific body positions (such as the yogic position) on seals, the important symbolic roles of bulls and elephants, decorative arrangements of multiple bangles and necklaces (evident from graves and realistic figurines), and certain distinctive headgear—all are important attributes of ancient Harappan society that remain at the heart of contemporary Hinduism. The standard Harappan unit of weight, equivalent to 0.5 oz (14 g), continued in use at South Asian bazaars and markets into the nineteenth century. Although ancient Harappa and Mohenjo-daro lie in ruins today, the civilization of which they were a part has left an extremely important legacy.

ECONOMIC SPECIALIZATION

Shellworking in the Indus civilization

With population growth, more densely packed communities, and increasing political complexity, household self-sufficiency becomes difficult, if not impossible, to sustain. Gaining access to all the resources that a family requires becomes difficult. As more tasks become specialized, people exchange what they produce for other goods and services through markets and trade networks. In some societies, the control of markets or exchange networks is an important source of power.

Trade and craft production appear to have been key features of Indus Valley society. Complex internal trade networks connected the major urban centers of the Indus civilization with rural agricultural and resource areas. Evidence from Mohenjo-daro suggests that the large Indus cities included craft areas that served as the living and working quarters for specialists. Some crafts, like the working of shell, stone, pottery, and metal, may have developed into hereditary occupations.

Shellworking, an important Indus craft, was undertaken by specialists. The earliest use of shell was limited to simple ornaments that were made by perforating natural shells. Later, during the time of the Indus civilization, shell use increased to include a variety of such decorative, utilitarian, and ritual objects as ornaments (bangles, rings, beads, pendants, and large perforated disks), utensils (ladles), inlay pieces, and other special objects.

According to J. Mark Kenoyer, of the University of Wisconsin, Madison, each of the workshops at Mohenjo-daro specialized in producing different shell items. For example, one area apparently produced mostly inlay pieces. Shell workshops similar to those at Mohenjo-daro were present at Harappa and other urban centers. But at Harappa, there was less variety in shell species and fewer shell artifacts in general, because of its location further inland. At the site of Lothal, on the coast of the Arabian Sea, shell workshops also produced a variety of shell objects.

Another major shell site, at Balakot, on the coast near Karachi, Pakistan, specialized in shell bangles, beads, and smaller objects. The site has workshop areas with stone grinders and hammers, bangles in various stages of manufacture, and unworked shell. One type of shell was cut with a specialized bronze saw. Metal tools were expensive, and at most sites, only craftworkers who were supported or controlled by more affluent individuals had access to metal tools. Most of the bangles were made by an alternative chipping and grinding process that used stone tools. Regardless of the method of manufacture, the resulting bangles at Balakot were almost identical. Even though Indus sites specialized in different types of finished products, a single standardized manufacturing technology and certain decorative conventions often were employed across the region.

Although certain shell items were purely decorative, the function of other Indus shell artifacts remains a mystery. Recent excavations at the cemetery area in Harappa have found many adult women with shell bangles on their left arms. These arm bracelets may have been a symbol of ethnic identity or a signifier of a specific marriage status. Ethnographic data show that shell bangles are still used for various social and ritual functions across the South Asian subcontinent. Through historical accounts, the antiquity of finely crafted shell objects (and their ritual functions) can be traced back to 600 B.C. It seems reasonable to deduce that some of these social and ritual uses may have their ultimate roots in the practices of the Indus civilization.

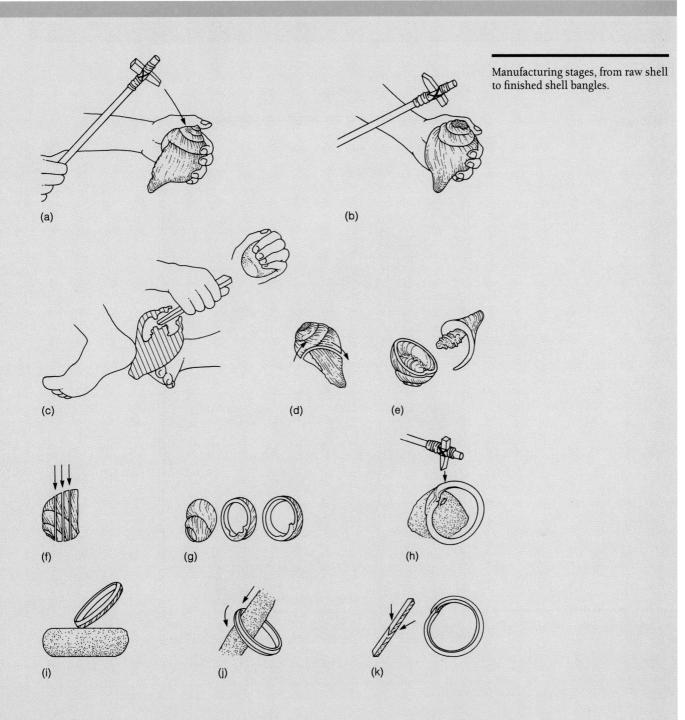

(a)

(b)

(c)

(d)

(e)

(f)

(g)

(h)

(i)

(j)

(k)

HIERAKONPOLIS

The emergence of the Egyptian civilization

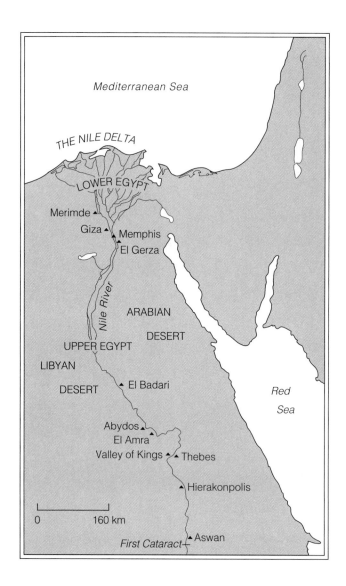

The Nile Valley, with sites mentioned in the text.

In spite of the general popularity of Egyptian archaeology, we know surprisingly little about early Egypt, particularly prior to the rise of early states and the first written documents. What we do know about Egypt suggests that this civilization along the Nile River was different in its long-term history from the ancient civilizations that developed in other parts of the world. For example, Egypt was relatively centralized for almost 2500 years, with only one major episode of political fragmentation, 2200–2000 B.C.

Egyptian civilization centered on the Nile Valley, a long oasis surrounded by desert. The Nile flows to the north and the Mediterranean Sea, more than 6400 km (4000 mi) from its source in the swamps and lakes of equatorial Africa. Its final 1300 km (800 mi) cut through Egypt before fanning out into an enormous delta. In Lower Egypt, an area of rich cultivable floodplains to the north, the river valley is up to 20 km (12.5 mi) wide. The south, known as Upper Egypt, has less alluvial land (only several kilometers wide), forming a narrow strip surrounded by jagged rock escarpments.

Prior to the construction of the Aswan Dam, near the First Cataract (rapids), in the 1960s, annual flooding along the Nile was common, and tons of rich soil were deposited. As a result, the floodplain of the Nile is extremely fertile. Because of sparse rainfall today, irrigation is necessary for farming, but annual temperatures are ideal for the cultivation of a wide range of crops. Staple crops are legumes, barley, onions, cucumber, melons, and figs. Other plants include rushes and reeds used for making baskets, flax for linens, and papyrus for cordage and paper. As in the past, today the area also supports sheep, goats, pigs, cattle, ducks, geese, fish, turtles, crocodiles, hippopotamuses, and other game animals. Although the surrounding deserts provide very little in the way of food, they are rich in building stone and minerals, including copper, gold, and silver.

The floods along the Nile were more predictable and easier to control than those of the Tigris and Euphrates Rivers in Mesopotamia. The Egyptians could very easily modify natural basins on the floor of the Nile Valley to retain floodwater for their crops. Higher levees along the river provided dry locations for settlements.

No definite sedentary villages have been found in the Nile Valley prior to the sixth millennium B.C., when nomadic cattle herders and farmers began to settle in the area. Prior to 6000 B.C., the Nile Valley was occupied by groups of hunter-gatherers who followed an annual round in which they hunted along the margins of the desert for wild cattle, gazelles, and birds during part of the year and took fowl and fish at other times. The presence of grinding stones indicates that wild grains also were an important food item.

Soon after 5000 B.C., food production was established in the Nile Valley. The early farming settlements raised Near Eastern domesticates: wheat, barley, sheep, and goats. Most of what is known about predynastic Egypt comes from the south, where there has been less deposition to bury sites. Yet it is possible that sedentism actually may have occurred earlier in the more fertile north. One floodplain settlement near the Nile Delta, Merimde, dating to as early as 4900 B.C., consisted of a cluster of semi-subterranean, oval houses with roofs of sticks and mud. The inhabitants used stone axes, knives, and flint arrowheads. Grains were stored in ceramic jars, baskets, and pits. Circular clay-lined threshing floors also have been reported.

The earliest occupations in the south (roughly contemporary with those in the north) are called Badarian, after the best-known settlement of El Badari in Upper Egypt. Badarian settlements consisted of clusters of skin tents or small huts. Many of the dead were buried carefully in oval or rectangular pits roofed over with sticks or mats. Utensils and food were commonly placed in the burials. Other grave offerings included rectangular stone palettes (or tablets), ivory spoons, and small ivory or stone vases, all of which have been associated with the preparation and use of green face paint. These items are all common components of the predynastic burial assemblages. The Badarian focus on grave features and the accompanying goods may have been at the root of the later Egyptian emphasis on burial custom.

In the south, materials associated with the Amratian tradition (3800–3500 B.C.) are frequently found directly above Badarian levels. The name Amratian was derived from the site of El Amra near Abydos in Upper Egypt. The Amratian materials seem to reflect direct continuity with the earlier Badarian, yet the latter period is characterized by the appearance of more developed craft industries (particularly pottery, alabaster, and basalt) and a larger number and more widespread distribution of settlements. Copperworking, which may have been initiated in the Badarian, also gained in importance. Amratian metalworkers used copper to make pins, flat axes, awls, and daggers. Scholars do not agree on the origins of Egyptian metallurgy. Many argue that it was introduced from Southwest Asia, whereas others, pointing to earlier metalworking in Upper than Lower Egypt,

The ceremonial macehead of King Scorpion.

(8 × 5 ft) and 1.8 m (6 ft) deep, contained baskets, fine pottery, rope, flint arrowheads, and wooden arrow shafts. Unfortunately, the grave was looted in later times, and the most valuable goods may have been stolen. A second grave contained scraps of **papyrus**, an ancient type of paper made from the papyrus plant, and a disk-shaped macehead made of polished porphyry, a green-and-white stone. Maceheads, which were mounted on wooden staffs called maces, were recognized in Egypt as a sign of authority. The presence of the macehead at Hierakonpolis indicates that the process of political development already may have been well under way. Similar polished, hard-stone maceheads have been found at several other contemporaneous sites, possibly indicating the presence of several small competing political units.

Hierakonpolis also was the center of a very large pottery industry. At least 15 Amratian kilns have been identified, the largest of which covered over 1000 sq m (0.25 acre). Two distinct types of pottery were made: a coarse ware for everyday household or industrial use and a fine, untempered ware for grave offerings. The kilns appear to have been part of one well-organized complex, in that each kiln was used for the firing of a different kind of pottery. The large kilns must have produced far more than was needed locally. The late Michael Hoffman postulated that the people in charge of pottery production acquired considerable economic power.

During the subsequent Gerzean period (3500–3100 B.C.), named after El Gerza, craft activities, including pottery production, metallurgy, and the manufacture of stone bowls from very hard materials such as diorite and basalt, appear to have been carried out at an even larger scale. The use of copper artifacts, which were now cast as well as hammered, increased. Gold also was worked at this time, and some luxury items were wrapped in gold foil. Trade with the Near East intensified in volume. Some of the pottery of this period was painted in Southwest Asian style, in dark red on a buff background. Foreign motifs also were incorporated into the local decorative tradition.

suggest it may have been an indigenous accomplishment.

The best-known Amratian center, Hierakonpolis (high′ra-kon′po-lis), meaning "city of the falcon," had a population of several thousand people. Most inhabitants lived in rectangular, semisubterranean houses of mud brick and thatch. The more important artisans and traders lived in larger houses in separate compounds. Near the site was a large cemetery with part of the burial area reserved for elaborate tombs. Although not as spectacular as later ones in Egypt, these tombs are impressive. The early tombs were constructed by cutting rectangular holes into the terrace of a dry streambed. The size and contents of the tombs varied, perhaps reflecting status and prestige. One grave, measuring 2.4 × 1.5 m

Narmer's carved stone palette.

Gerzean remains have been found in Upper and Lower Egypt, possibly indicating greater integration between the two areas. Yet important differences in ceramic styles and burial customs continued to distinguish Upper and Lower Egypt. On carved palettes and other art, key individuals are depicted wearing distinctive headgear or crowns. These crowns vary from one area of Egypt to another, suggesting that several different polities may have developed along the Nile.

During Gerzean times, social and economic inequalities, evident from tomb size, grave design, and burial inclusions, increased markedly. One macehead found at Hierakonpolis, with a scorpion on it, has been identified as belonging to King Scorpion, the predecessor of Egypt's first pharaoh. Hierakonpolis, whose location shifted slightly closer to the Nile, was one

of the largest known settlements, with 5 ha (12.5 acres) of occupation, including large nonresidential structures such as palaces and temples.

Written records and stone monuments indicate that the incidence of warfare increased at this time, with local kings trying to gain control over adjacent kingdoms. Among the competing kings, it is thought to have been Narmer from Hierakonpolis who finally succeeded in unifying Egypt into one kingdom around 3100 B.C. As Egypt's first pharaoh, Narmer founded a dynasty (3100–2890 B.C.) and a political structure that lasted for nearly 3000 years.

The unification of Upper and Lower Egypt was recorded for posterity on a 64-cm (25-in) carved stone palette discovered by English archaeologists in 1898 at Hierakonpolis. One side of the tablet depicts Narmer, the leader of Upper Egypt,

The Egyptian crowns: the white crown of Upper Egypt (left), the red crown of Lower Egypt (center), and the double crown of unified Egypt (right).

wearing the white crown of Upper Egypt and holding his symbolic mace. The other side shows him wearing the red crown of Lower Egypt. Both sides include scenes of the king in battle.

The Egyptian state was far larger and more complex than any city-state in Mesopotamia. The nature of rule also was much different in Egypt than in Mesopotamia. In Egypt, the royal court centralized power and wealth, and this consolidation is evident in the concentration of resources in the mortuary complexes of the kings. The relative stability of Egyptian rule diminished some of the insecurity that in Mesopotamia led to the construction of great walled complexes around nucleated urban centers. In Egypt, continuity with earlier occupations is apparent in such contexts as stoneworking, death ritual, and the use of the macehead as a symbol of rule.

The unification of Egypt was closely timed with the earliest hieroglyphic writing. Although writing first developed in Mesopotamia, the Egyptians devised their own script, which is very different from Near Eastern writing. Egyptian hieroglyphs consist of both pictographic and phonetic elements, written on papyrus

and carved into public buildings. Egyptian writing was more concerned with rule and kinship than with economic transactions. The deeds and accomplishments of leaders were recorded, and this may have had a role in the consolidation of power in the hands of a limited few.

The widespread adoption of irrigation agriculture also coincided with the unification of Egypt. Ancient Egyptian irrigation practices were very simple, such as modifying natural basins to serve as reservoirs for floodwater. Yet the large surpluses that these techniques permitted clearly were necessary to support the opulent lifestyles and mortuary rituals of the emergent pharaohs.

The earliest tombs in Egypt were small wooden graves in which the dead were buried with utensils and food to sustain them in the afterworld. In late predynastic Egypt (the fourth millennium B.C.), more elaborate tombs were constructed for the burial of elite members of society. These graves contained a variety of goods, including beautiful pottery, baskets, braided leather rope, painted reed arrow shafts, flint arrowheads, pieces of papyrus, and maceheads.

The architectural styles of tomb construction differed in Lower Egypt and Upper Egypt. In the royal **necropolis,** or cemetery, at Hierakonpolis, these differences were utilized symbolically by Narmer or his immediate predecessors. Constructed at the end of the fourth millennium B.C., the cemetery was arranged, according to Michael Hoffman, who excavated at the site, to represent the union of Upper and Lower Egypt, perhaps to legitimize the military conquest of Lower Egypt by the Upper Egyptian rulers.

Tombs in the style of Lower Egypt were constructed at the downstream end of a **wadi,** or dry streambed, which represented the downstream end of the Nile, or Lower Egypt. These tombs were lined with mud bricks, with large, painted wood and reed structures placed over them. Low reed fences surrounded these tombs. The burials occurred in groups of three, four, and five, suggesting that rulers were buried with other family members or members of their court. A fragmented wooden bed was found in one tomb. It was finely carved, with two legs crafted to resemble a bull's legs—a forerunner of the furniture in King Tutankhamen's tomb.

At the opposite end of the necropolis, or upstream with respect to the wadi, was a stone tomb in the architectural style of Upper Egypt. This stone feature is surrounded by apparently similar tombs that have yet to be excavated. Cut into subsoil bedrock, the excavated tomb was a long, narrow trench with an L-shaped hole cut into the middle of the floor. There was no superstructure asso-

ciated with it. Surrounding this stone tomb were animal burials, including the remains of hippopotamuses, elephants, crocodiles, baboons, cattle, goats, sheep, and dogs. Some of the animals were mummified and probably had civic-ceremonial significance. In Dynastic times, the Egyptians used various animals as godlike symbols of the different **nomes,** or geographic provinces, that comprised the Egyptian state. Some of these same animal symbols are portrayed atop standards on Narmer's stone palette. In accordance with the rest of the cemetery, it seems possible that the animal burials also followed a symbolic orientation. For example, the easternmost tomb had six baboons, animals that ancient Egyptians associated with the rising sun.

Hoffman proposed that this desert necropolis presages key attributes of the Egyptian state. These features include the use of the royal death cult and an associated cemetery area as national symbols, the division of the state into the symbolic halves of Upper and Lower Egypt, and the incorporation of conquered polities and peoples through ritual as well as military means. In contrast to the neighboring polities of Southwest Asia, political integration in Dynastic Egypt was tied less directly to specific fortified towns and was linked more closely to elite lineages and cemetery and temple complexes. The roots of that civic-ceremonial organization appear to have extended to Hierakonpolis.

THE CEMETERY AT HIERAKONPOLIS

Steps toward the unification of Egypt

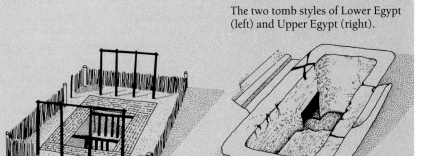

The two tomb styles of Lower Egypt (left) and Upper Egypt (right).

Tomb I
Lined with mud bricks

Tomb II
Cut in stone

GIZA AND DYNASTIC EGYPT

Pyramids and pharaohs

Zoser's step pyramid at Saqqarah.

By 3100 B.C., Upper and Lower Egypt were unified into one state when Narmer, Egypt's first pharaoh, conquered the northern delta. Narmer moved the capital from Hierakonpolis, in Upper Egypt, to Memphis, at the junction of Upper and Lower Egypt, where the Nile Valley spreads out into the broad delta. Memphis remained the political center of Egypt for 1500 years. Although the Nile Valley around Memphis was not a particularly rich agricultural area, the city was strategically positioned for riverine communication between southern and northern Egypt.

The symbol of the pharaoh was the double crown of Upper and Lower Egypt (see p. 434). A series of pharaohs during the first (3100–2890 B.C.) and second (2890–2686 B.C.) dynasties ruled under the double crown, but consolidation of the two disparate regions was not a steady or easy process. The Egyptian kings adopted the strategy of establishing outposts, temples, and shrines throughout their domains, maintaining integration and preventing the monopoly of functions or power in any single place or capital. Intermarriage of the elite from north and south may have been used to solidify the unification.

The Egyptian population was less urban than Near Eastern societies, which generally had larger centers. Apart from a few large sites, most of the Egyptian population continued to live in unwalled, largely self-sufficient villages. This may account for the preoccupation of the Egyptian elite with rural lifeways. Despite this preoccupation, a massive, hereditary bureaucracy developed, devoting official energy to tax collection, harvest yields, and the administration of irrigation. Each nome (province), administered by a local governor, was under overall central control. During the first dynasty, the Egyptian kings also supported an increasing number of craft specialists. Trade links were extended to what is now Sudan (Nubia) and Libya. With the elaboration of the court during the early dynasties, the demand for sub-Saharan products like ivory and ebony intensified, thereby heightening interest in areas to the south.

Between the third dynasty in 2686 B.C. and the Persian conquest in 525 B.C., Egypt was ruled by no fewer than 23 dy-

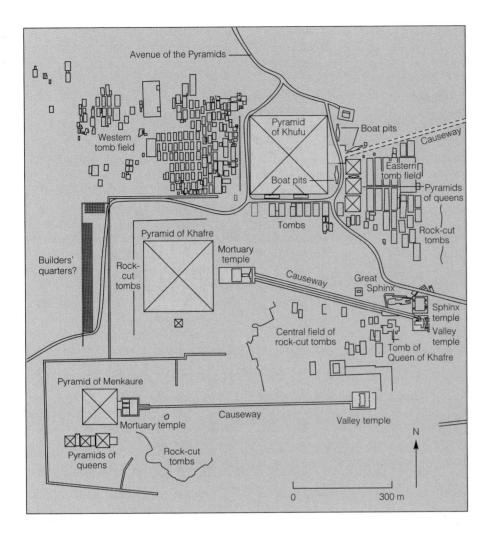

Avenue of the Pyramids

Western
tomb field

Pyramid
of Khufu

Boat pits

Causeway

Boat pits

Eastern
tomb field

Pyramids
of queens

Tombs

Rock-cut
tombs

Pyramid of Khafre

Mortuary
temple

Builders'
quarters?

Rock-
cut
tombs

Causeway

Great
Sphinx

Sphinx
temple

Central field of
rock-cut tombs

Valley
temple

Tomb of
Queen of Khafre

Pyramid of Menkaure

Causeway

Valley temple

Mortuary temple

N

Pyramids of
queens

Rock-cut
tombs

0   300 m

nasties. The third through sixth dynasties comprise what is known as the Old Kingdom (2686–2181 B.C.), a time of despotic pharaohs and grandiose pyramid construction. The largest Egyptian pyramids were constructed by these early dynasties. The first pyramid was a stepped-stone structure constructed by the pharaoh Zoser, as the centerpiece of his funeral complex. The step pyramids were soon followed by the more familiar pyramids with smooth faces. Like all royal tombs until 1000 B.C., the pyramids were constructed in the desert on the west side of the Nile River and were surrounded by the tombs of contemporary officials.

Although few written records have survived from the Old Kingdom, sketchy accounts provide a perspective largely unavailable for earlier periods. Scribes were an important part of the govern-

ment. Special schools trained writers for careers in the palace and the treasury. Contemporary documents on papyrus show that Egyptians were skilled in architecture, surgery, accounting, geometry, and astronomy. But most of the population, as in other early civilizations, consisted of illiterate peasant farmers who maintained the Egyptian agricultural base.

One major site of the Old Kingdom is Giza, located near modern Cairo (see Color Plate 24). Just a short distance from the ancient capital city of Memphis, the Giza Plateau is where King Khufu (known as Cheops in Greek), of the fourth dynasty, built his massive pyramid. Called the Pyramid of Khufu, or the Great Pyramid, this monumental edifice required precise planning and complex engineering, and serves as a clear reflection of state power and labor

The double statue of Menkaure and his sister, Khamerernebti II.

control. The pyramid is 150 m high (500 ft, almost as tall as the Washington Monument), covers 5.3 ha (13.1 acres), and contains a series of internal passages and chambers. Khufu's pyramid was constructed of 2,300,000 stone blocks with an average weight of 2275 kg (2.5 tons). Its construction involved roughly 13,440,000 man-days of labor and incorporated materials from areas as far away as Lebanon, Sinai, Aswan, and Nubia.

Surrounding the Pyramid of Khufu were the much smaller pyramids of three queens and the rectangular tombs of Khufu's closest royal relatives and high officials. Nearby was the king's palace complex and villages for the administrators and workmen. Two other large pyramids were constructed by his successors Khafre (known as Chephren in Greek) and Menkaure (Mycerinus in Greek). Khafre's pyramid is almost as large as Khufu's, but its internal structure is much simpler, with a single tomb chamber at the base of the structure. One of the most famous ancient Egyptian structures, the king-headed lion or Great Sphinx, bears Khafre's features. It was constructed to guard the sacred realm of the dead kings, whose power was believed to have continued to influence the universe in which their successors ruled. While of the same design as the large pyramids, Menkaure's pyramid is much smaller, and its construction marks the end of the era of massive pyramid construction. Those built during the following dynasty were relatively small and poorly constructed.

During the early dynasties, pharaohs were central to the Egyptian state. They were considered divine, sometimes referred to as "the good god." These paramount rulers controlled economic exchange, served at the top of a great bureaucracy, and acted as the heads of state religion. Toward the end of the Old Kingdom, the construction of smaller pyramids paralleled a decline in royal power. Following the pattern that often occurred in ancient states and empires, the Old Kingdom collapsed after five centuries of strong central rule and was followed by a period of decentralization. The provinces became competitive

petty kingdoms that fought with each other, either alone or in small alliances. With the fragmentation of the Egyptian state into these smaller territorial political groups, provincial governors and bureaucrats gained more power. Comparatively large mud-brick tombs were erected in these provinces, displaying the growing power of local authorities.

The beginning of the Middle Kingdom, around 2000 B.C., was marked by the reunification of Upper and Lower Egypt under a dynastic line centered at the city of Thebes in Upper Egypt. The rulers pacified southern Egypt and then overthrew the dynasty in power to the north. The capital was brought back to Memphis, and the fortified towns of the earlier decentralized period disappeared. With increased administrative centralization, a second era of ostentatious pyramid building began. Yet the Middle Kingdom pharaohs were less despotic. Trading contacts were extended, and parts of Nubia, just to the south of Egypt, were conquered. Huge fortresses were erected to solidify control of this frontier along the Nile.

During the first half of the second millennium B.C., central administrative authority again weakened, and a period of short-lived dynasties and regionalization followed. In the sixteenth century B.C., a later Theban dynasty began a third era of unification and centralization, called the New Kingdom. The dynasties of this period are richly documented in historical texts. The kings of the New Kingdom reasserted control from the Nile Delta to Nubia and conquered parts of Lebanon, Palestine, and southern Syria. No earlier Egyptian polity had established such far-ranging external contacts. The highly centralized government of the New Kingdom depended on large external tribute levees for its maintainance and support.

During the New Kingdom, kings were considered quasi-divine, the mediators between humans and the gods. These rulers often married their own sisters to concentrate status and divinity in a dynastic line. The kings lived in elaborate complexes that contained throne rooms and extensive private chambers for the royal family, harems, court officials, and servants. The pharaohs adopted new burial customs; their mummies were buried in rock-cut tombs in the Valley of Kings near Thebes. Among the New Kingdom pharaohs were a number of historically renowned figures: Tuthmosis III, Ahkenaten, Tutankhamen (better known as King Tut), and Ramses II.

During the New Kingdom, an important innovation in irrigation permitted the agricultural development of the broad Nile Delta. The **shaduf,** a labor-saving bucket-and-lever lifting device, enabled one to raise water a few feet from wells or ditches into gardens and fields. This innovation, still in use today, may have contributed to the demographic buildup in the delta during the New Kingdom. The kings of the nineteenth dynasty divided their residence between the traditional centers of power, Thebes and Memphis, and a new royal residence that was established in the eastern delta.

The administrative centralization and stability that characterized the New Kingdom came to an end around 1000 B.C. Hostilities erupted when strong provincial leaders and local army commanders increased their regional power. A period of foreign intervention followed, and for millennia Egypt did not regain its autonomy for anything but a brief interlude. The Nile Valley was ruled in succession by Assyrians, Persians, and then Alexander the Great, king of the Macedonians (northern Greece). The almost 3000-year succession of pharaohs ended when Alexander appointed one of his generals ruler of Egypt.

Several hypotheses have been proposed to explain the highly centralized nature of the early Egyptian state. The constricted distribution and relatively small proportion of usable land (along the Nile) may have fostered the concentration and monopolization of wealth. Commoners and peasants would have had relatively few options when they were heavily taxed or asked to contribute to labor gangs. In an environment such as the fertile Nile Valley, surrounded by desert, it would be very difficult for people to move away and still maintain access to cultivable land.

The critical nature of water control (often requiring centralized maintenance

and adjudication) also may have been a factor; however, according to Karl Butzer, of the University of Texas, Austin, early Egyptian irrigation systems were not highly centralized and were largely under local control. Nevertheless, the disastrous potential of Nile flooding may have encouraged the establishment of a central agency to help alleviate periodic local disasters.

Finally, Egypt had a number of military-political threats on its borders throughout much its history, and this, too, may have encouraged the centralization of power in the hands of a few to coordinate a strong defense. While none of these interpretations is convincing on its own, they do suggest questions and directions for future research.

Using a shaduf to raise water from the Nile to a walled irrigation ditch.

PYRAMIDS

Ancient monuments in the Old and New Worlds

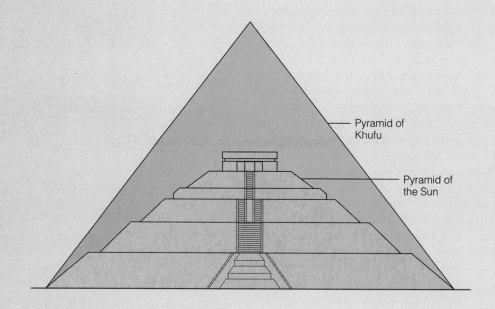

Pyramid of Khufu

Pyramid of the Sun

A comparison of the Pyramid of the Sun at Teotihuacan and the Pyramid of Khufu at Giza, which is approximately 146 m high.

Pyramid-shaped structures were built by ancient civilizations in both the Old World and the New World, representing the wealth and power of those who erected them. Yet the building techniques and the specific uses of these constructions varied greatly from one ancient civilization to another.

The best-known pyramids in the Old World were erected by the ancient Egyptians during the third millennium B.C. The Egyptian pyramids were constructed of cut-stone blocks, with internal passageways and tombs. The first royal pyramid, built around 2680 B.C. at Saqqarah by Zoser, was a six-step pyramid (see p. 436). Over the next century, the pyramid shape was perfected, culminating in the magnificent pyramids at Giza. The construction of these Old Kingdom pyramids required an enormous expenditure of energy and manpower, involving both unskilled labor to quarry and transport the stones and skilled masons who would cut, fit, and smooth the stones. Given the construction techniques known at the time, such large structures had to be in the shape of a pyramid to support their weight.

Constructed as monuments for kings, the Egyptian pyramids have as their origin the tomb architecture of predynastic Egypt. They were built in one episode of construction, without outside stairways, and were not meant to be climbed once they were completed. They served not only as tombs for the pharaohs, but also as their houses for eternity. As such, the pyramids reflect the importance Egyptians placed on life in the afterworld.

Kurt Mendelssohn argues that the construction of monumental tombs for the pharaohs, who could have been interred at much less cost, was not the only goal. It was the erection of the pyramid itself that was important. He suggests that pyramid construction was an administrative strategy used by the pharaohs to institutionalize the state. The thousands of peasants who worked on the pyramids depended on the central government for food during three months of the year. They were fed from food surpluses obtained from villages through taxation. One consequence was that the population became reliant on the state bureaucracy to redistribute food and or-

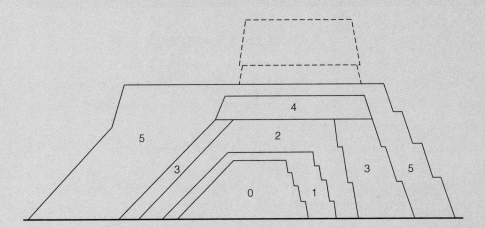

The building episodes of a Late Postclassic pyramid in the Basin of Mexico. The earliest pyramid is represented by 0 and the latest by 5.

ganize labor. Whether this outcome was planned is unclear. Nevertheless, Old Kingdom pyramid construction may have had some of the consequences outlined by Mendelssohn.

Monumental structures in the New World were very different in form from their Egyptian counterparts. For example, in western Mexico, such buildings could be circular as well as square and rectangular. Throughout the New World, most large structures were actually truncated pyramids, with flat tops. Most Mesoamerican pyramids were rubble-filled, with a cut-stone facing. However, some central Mexican pyramids have a core of adobe bricks with a stone facing held together by mortar. Other North American pyramids, such as Monk's Mound at Cahokia, were built almost entirely of earthen fill.

Mesoamerican pyramids were smaller than the earlier Old Kingdom pyramids at Giza. Two of the most massive Mesoamerican pyramids, the Pyramid of the Sun and the Pyramid of the Moon, were constructed at Teotihuacan in central Mexico around 100 B.C. At its base, the Pyramid of the Sun is about the size of the Pyramid of Khufu at Giza but only about half as high. In contrast to the Egyptian pyramids, Mesoamerican structures were often built in a series of con-

struction episodes, in which they were enlarged and often changed drastically in appearance. The largest Mesoamerican pyramid, the Great Pyramid at Cholula (in the state of Puebla), was enlarged many times over hundreds of years.

New World pyramids generally served as foundations for other public buildings, such as temples, shrines, palaces, or elite residences. Stairways provided access to the structures above. The truncated pyramids emulated natural features, such as hills and mountains, raising structures above the ground level. The platforms increased the visibility of the public buildings, while making direct access to them more difficult. Although many New World pyramids include burial features, few were designed or used (as were the Egyptian pyramids) exclusively as the final resting place for a particular ruler or elite figure.

AN-YANG

A late Shang city in China

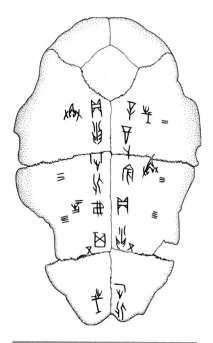

An inscribed oracle bone from the Shang period.

The emergence of Shang civilization initially appeared to have no direct antecedents; it was formerly thought that early Chinese cities and states arose as a result of Mesopotamian contact. But as with Egypt and the Indus Valley, recent archaeological fieldwork has demonstrated that the trajectory from the diversity of the Chinese Neolithic to the rise of early civilizations was more continuous, with outside influences playing a small role. The development of civilization in China was largely indigenous, with its own character and its own writing system. Wheat, barley, and the horse-drawn chariot were significant Western introductions into early China; however, these innovations were not the principal stimuli for the rise of Chinese civilization.

Between 5000 and 3000 B.C., the Huang Ho (Yellow River) region of North China was settled by millet and pig farmers who resided in large villages of up to 100 houses. One such village was Banpo-ts'un (see Chapter 6). The community included large central structures that may have served as clan meeting houses or the residences of certain influential villagers. Marks found on some Yangshao ceramic vessels resemble written Shang characters dating to more than several thousand years later. During the subsequent Longshan period (3000–2205 B.C.), significant changes took place in North Chinese social organization, including marked increases in social ranking. Compared to earlier burials, Longshan mortuary assemblages exhibit more variation; some include jade ornaments and ceremonial weapons. For the first time, many of the Longshan period settlements were walled, and the largest communities were much bigger than ever before.

During Longshan times, scapulimancy, the interpretation of cracking patterns on heated bone, was practiced (see "Early Writing Systems," p. 419). Although no written inscriptions are found on Longshan bones, Chinese written characters have been found on numerous bones at later sites. In later times, such divination rituals involving **oracle bones** were addressed to royal ancestors and were carried out by religious specialists. In addition to scapulimancy, the manifestations of ritual were prevalent in many other ways during the Longshan period. Fantastic or mythical animals were crafted on objects of pottery, wood, and jade. Many of these objects were probably associated with shamanistic rituals that were important during the later Three Dynasties and Shang periods.

The era following Longshan in North China is known as the San dai, or Three Dynasties: Xia, Shang, and Zhou. The Xia (Sha) dynasty (2205–1766 B.C.) is the first hereditary dynasty in recorded Chinese history. Although later historical texts suggest that there were 17 rulers in 471 years, the period is still somewhat of a mystery archaeologically. K. C. Chang, of Harvard University, has suggested that the Erlitou culture, with a spatial and temporal distribution that fits the historical accounts of the Xia dynasty, is the archaeological manifestation of that dynasty.

The Xia dynasty was transitional between the late Neolithic and the Shang

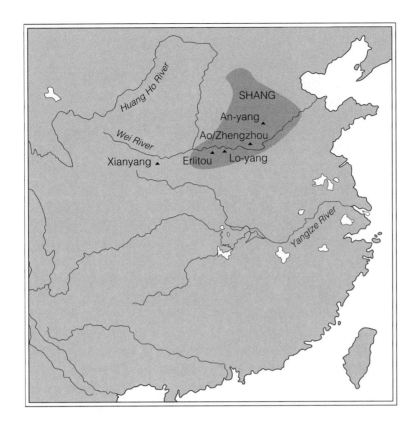

Shang China, indicated by the shaded area.

dynasty. Scapulimancy continued to be practiced. Although there are no known inscriptions on oracle bones, signs and symbols have been found on pottery vessels. Bronzeworking, which was in evidence by the end of Longshan, became an increasingly important craft. According to a first-millennium B.C. text, the two principal affairs of the Chinese state were ritual and warfare. Most of the bronze was used to make ritual food and drink vessels, musical instruments, and weapons. Other valuable objects were fashioned from jade, turquoise, and lacquer. A few basic bronze implements were made, but most utilitarian tools, including knives, sickles, and hoes, were made in stone, shell, wood, antler, or bone. Wheel-thrown ceramic ware, first manufactured during the late Neolithic, increased in abundance, although handmade pottery also continued to be used.

Two palatial house foundations of stamped earth, found in later strata at the site of Erlitou, also indicate a possible break with Longshan. Both palace foundations are much larger than the other houses at the site. The largest foundation, 108 × 100 m (350 × 330 ft), was associated with ritual burials (including one individual with bound hands).

The decline of the Xia dynasty coincided roughly with the rise of the Shang dynasty (1766–1122 B.C.). The Shang period is known from archaeological excavations at its last capital, An-yang, information from other ancient sites, and written records. The Chinese state had developed by Shang times. The major Shang centers were Ao (an early capital located underneath the modern industrial city of Zhengzhou), Lo-yang, and An-yang. Each had a clearly defined ceremonial core, inhabited by a royal household, and a series of nonresidential buildings (meeting halls and ancestral temples). The ceremonial core was surrounded by a service area and the pit-house residences of the commoners.

Today Ao is partially hidden by buildings, but at its height it may have covered 3.4 sq km (1.3 sq mi). The central precinct was enclosed by a huge earthen wall 9 m (30 ft) high and 36 m (118 ft) wide at the base. The quantity and quality of artifacts indicate the presence of

The central precinct of Ao.

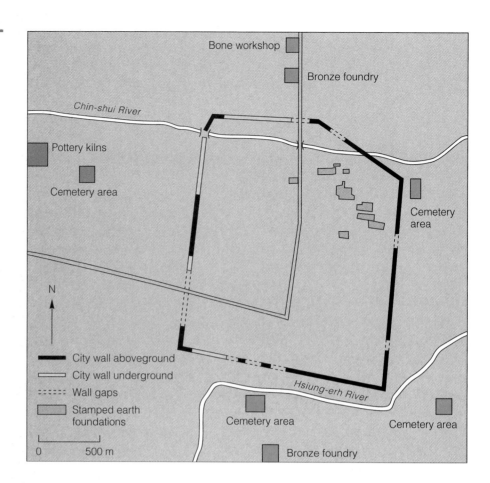

An artist's reconstruction of a Shang palace at Ao.

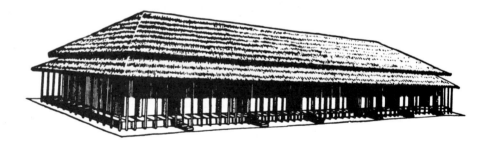

hundreds of skilled craftworkers. One area contained more than a dozen high-temperature pottery kilns, each associated with dense concentrations of oven-fired and broken pottery. In another area, human and animal bones were worked into fishhooks, awls, axes, and hairpins. Bronzeworking was one of the most highly developed crafts. Bronze was fashioned into ornaments as well as tools. In one workshop, molds were used to mass-produce bronze arrow points. As yet, the Shang materials contemporaneous with Ao have yielded no definitive

indications of writing, chariots, or royal mausoleums, all features solidly linked with An-yang and its late Shang materials. However, the construction technology and the basic layout of the palace structure at Zhengzhou were nearly identical to that at subsequent An-yang.

Toward the end of the Shang dynasty, the capital was moved north to An-yang (ahn'yong'). As with the earlier capital, An-yang was a large ceremonial and administrative center with monumental architecture surrounded by craft areas, including bronze foundries, stone

and bone workshops, and pottery kilns. Circling the center were residential hamlets (small concentrations of wooden houses with thatched roofs), a royal cemetery area at Hsi-pei-kang, and more workshops.

An-yang consisted of three groups of buildings with a total of 53 rectangular structures built on top of stamped-earth platforms. The largest structure was 60 m (195 ft) long and is presumed to be a royal palace. Between two of the building groups is a square, earthen foundation thought to have been a ceremonial altar. As a whole, this building complex appears to have been well planned, although it almost certainly was implemented in several construction stages.

Late Shang society was highly stratified into upper and lower classes. The extent of social distinctions, present as early as the Longshan period, was ex-

aggerated by the establishment of An-yang. The king, his family, and officials were at the top. Kings were considered divine, with power flowing from the king to the nobility to the court, and finally to the commoners. Only those of high status possessed the spectacular Shang bronzes, used the Chinese script, and controlled the archives. The king and his court received grain and other forms of tribute, which they used to support a lavish style in life as well as in death. In the 11 large royal tombs at Hsi-pei-kang, Shang kings were buried with sacrificed retainers, horse-drawn chariots, and large quantities of luxury items, including bronze vessels, shell and bone ornaments, jade, and pottery. For each of these graves, moving the earth alone would have required thousands of working days. The royal tombs were surrounded by 1200 smaller and simpler

A bronze vessel from the Shang or
early Zhou period.

graves, most of which lack any grave
goods.

The lower class consisted of farmers
and craftworkers. Some of the more skill-
ful and highly specialized ones (bronzesmiths, lacquerwarers, and wood carvers) may have had some of the privileges
of the upper class; yet overall, the farmers and craftsmen used stone and bone
implements, coarse gray pottery, and
lived in semisubterranean pithouses. The
commoners labored for public works
and military campaigns. At the bottom
of the lower class were the war captives,
who were kept as slaves or served as
sacrificial victims for rituals and temple
dedications.

Shang civilization is famous for its
bronzework. Food and drinking vessels
are the most common bronze items, but
some weapons, chariot and cavalry fit-
tings, and musical instruments also were
made of bronze. Small objects, such as

spearpoints, were made by pouring a
molten mix of copper and tin into molds.
Large ceremonial vessels were made by
a more complex process involving clay
prototypes. During the first half of the
twentieth century, Western scholars familiar with the An-yang bronzes presumed that the metalworking technology
was introduced from Europe or Southwest Asia. Yet the absence of such Western techniques as annealing, hammering,
and lost wax casting, and the presence of
complex mold-casting technologies, indicate an indigenous origin for Shang
bronzeworking. The roots of late Shang
metallurgy may lie in the sophisticated
pottery kilns that were used as early as
the late Neolithic.

At An-yang, scapulimancy became
more complex and sophisticated. In addition to the shoulder blades of cattle
and water buffalo, diviners used the car-
apaces of turtles. Once an answer was

446 CHAPTER 10 OLD WORLD STATES AND EMPIRES

obtained, by consulting ancestral spirits and interpreting the cracks on the oracle bones, both the question and the answer were sometimes recorded on the surface of the bone. A symbol similar to the later written character for "book" is found on one bone, indicating the presence of scribes. The earliest Chinese writing may have been expressed on silk, bamboo, or wooden tablets. These surfaces commonly were used for written inscriptions in the last half of the first millennium B.C.; however, no texts on these highly perishable materials yet have been found for Shang. By late Shang times, Chinese written language had developed to the point where over 3000 phonetic, ideographic, and pictographic symbols were in use. Based on more than 150,000 inscribed turtle shells, in addition to inscriptions made in bronze, pottery, and stone, it is clear that early Chinese writing was related closely to the political, military, and ritual activities of the upper class and had little to do with mercantile matters.

The borders of the Shang state are unknown; however, late Shang rulers had at least some control over a fairly large area in northern China. The extent of their influence varied according to distance from the capital. Shang rulers traveled widely across their domain, and the extent of their influence was related in part to their actual physical presence. The rulers were assisted by a complex hierarchy of local nobles, who had considerable autonomy in their own territories. These local lords were responsible for collecting taxes and supplying men for public projects and military campaigns. On occasion, armies numbering 30,000 soldiers were assembled to wage war against "barbarians" at the edge of the Shang domain. Military success depended on the horse-drawn chariot. War was waged more for people than for land. In these campaigns, thousands of prisoners were taken, most of whom were sacrificed or used as slaves.

Despite major changes in political organization, written communication, and social stratification, the basic subsistence technology of the late Shang period changed little from earlier times. Millet remained the principal food crop in North China, supplemented by rice and wheat. Stone hoes, harvesting knives, and wooden digging sticks remained the primary cultivation implements. In some areas, two crops a year were grown, suggesting irrigation, yet large-scale water control was not implemented until the last centuries B.C.

Changes in labor practices may have constituted the most dramatic shift in the Shang economy. Larger numbers of people were employed in farming, thereby increasing production per unit of land as well as the amount of cultivated terrain. The reliance on human energy may help account for the kind of military campaigns that were waged, as well as the rapid demographic increases that occurred in China during this period. The importance of agricultural labor may have encouraged rural families to grow, since children could work in the fields at an early age. One consequence would have been large-scale population growth.

The Shang dynasty was overthrown by people living on its western periphery in the vicinity of Xianyang on the Wei River. It is unclear whether the defeat resulted from the internal rebellion of a distant Shang province or by the rebellion of an outside group of people forced by nomadic pressures to settle in or near the Shang state (as suggested by one 3000-year-old text). Whatever the case, the new dynasty did not create an entirely new civilization; it incorporated the existing network of towns and officials. It was on the foundation of the Shang dynasty that the subsequent Zhou dynasty established China's first empire.

Western scholars tend to see civilization as a level of human attainment that lifts humans to a higher plane than that of "mere" animals and plants, and as an artificial environment that insulates us from unadulterated and hostile nature. But in ancient Chinese civilizations humans and nature were regarded as one; the Chinese were civilized precisely because they were able, or at least desirous, to be close to and harmonize with nature as a matter of conscious and deliberate choice.

K. C. Chang (1994)

THE ROOTS OF CHINESE CUISINE

Ancient culinary ritual and traditions

Archaeologists often study containers of fired clay, stone, and metal to infer information about chronology or past technologies. However, the main function of these vessels was the preparation and serving of food and drink. The pottery and bronze vessels of the Shang and Zhou (pronounced "jo") dynasties provide one perspective on ancient Chinese culinary traditions. This archaeological perspective is supplemented vividly by historical texts and inscriptions from these times. For example, *The Three Lis,* or *Three Books of Rites,* solemn texts from the Han period (206 B.C.–A.D. 220) that record ritual and courtly behavior from ancient China, provide detailed descriptions of food preparation and feasts, including the types and amounts of food and wine served for certain occasions. Oracle bone and bronze vessel inscriptions from the Shang period include written characters that refer to certain foods, rituals, and cooking techniques and whose shapes suggest ancient practices.

It is not surprising that many groups of people are strongly concerned with food. However, according to K. C. Chang, the Chinese are more concerned with food and eating than any other people. He points out that in contemporary China, a familiar greeting is: "Have you eaten?" Chang believes that this preoccupation has a long history, as do many Chinese culinary traditions. According to one account, when a duke asked Confucius (551–479 B.C.) about military strategy, the sage replied, "I have indeed heard about matters pertaining to meat stands and meat platters, but I have not learned military matters" (quoted in Chang, 1973, p. 496). In ancient China, knowledge and skill in the preparation of food and drink were important personal characteristics; King T'ang, the founder of the Shang dynasty, chose a cook as his prime minister. According to several Zhou texts, a cooking vessel, called the *ting* cauldron, was the primary symbol of the state. Along with differences in dress and adornment, part of the definition of a "barbarian" or a non-Chinese was a person who did not prepare and consume food in the customary manner. Included in the *Three Books of Rites* is a personnel roster of the king's palace; almost 60% of the 4000 people responsible for the king's private residential quarters were involved with food and wine, with specialists assigned to menu preparation, service, meat, fish, game, shellfish, wine, fruits and vegetables, pickling, and salt.

The dualism between *yin* and *yang,* central to much of contemporary Chinese culture, is also present in the categorization of food. A basic dichotomy exists between food and drink. Food is further divided into grain food and "dishes" that are combinations of meat and vegetables. These distinctions, and their associated rules, are integral to the Chinese way of eating today and seem not to have changed much since Zhou times. In the past as well as today, the basic or essential meal consists of grain and water. The basic word *shih,* for food (as opposed to drink), also, in a narrower sense, refers to grain. Meat and vegetable dishes are considered secondary in importance and are to be eaten in moderation.

The historical texts indicate that eating together was a major source of enjoyment in ancient China. Yet it also was a serious social affair, with strict rules to be observed, including correct table manners and an etiquette regarding the appropriate foods to be served at specific occasions. In Shang and Zhou times, people from the upper ranks ate individually, kneeling on mats. The number of dishes served to an individual was primarily determined by one's rank and age. Utensils and serving platters were placed beside the individual in specific arrangements, certain foods on the right and others on the left. In addition, rules specified the arrangement of certain foods on the serving vessels and how they were presented at the table. Children were trained early to eat with their right hand. In late Zhou times, crunching bones with one's teeth, eating too quickly, slurping down soup, and picking one's teeth were all specified as inappropriate etiquette.

In one contemporary Chinese cookbook, 20 methods for heating food are mentioned. Many of these procedures, including boiling, steaming, and roasting, also were important in Zhou texts. Yet the ancient accounts do not mention stir-frying, which is prevalent today. Nevertheless, in the past as well as the present, it is the preparation before cooking that is essential to Chinese cuisine. The word for cooking in the Zhou texts literally means "to cut and cook." Great significance is placed on the art of mixing flavors and ingredients into distinctive soups and stews before they are heated.

Social class was a major factor in dietary variation. Peasants relied on a basic grain diet, using the platters and vessels associated with such foods. According to the textual record, the meat dishes were intended for rituals or upper-class feasts. Meat was usually dried, cooked, or pickled. A few recipes for elaborate dishes of the Shang and Zhou times are known; these are for the so-called Eight Delicacies, which were prepared specifically for the elderly. They included the Rich Fry (pickled meat over rice), the Similar Fry (pickled meat over millet), the Bake (baked stuffed pig or ram), the Pounded (pounded meat fillets softened by pickle and vinegar), the Steeped (newly killed beef steeped in wine), the Grill (dried meat seasoned with cinnamon, ginger, and salt), the Soup Balls (fried cakes of meat and rice), and the Liver and Fat (roasted dog liver cooked in fat).

In ancient Chinese cooking, each variety of food and drink was associated with different ceramic and bronze vessels. There were vessels for boiling and simmering and others for steaming. For serving and eating, ladles and chopsticks were used, although hands were used as often as chopsticks. There were special cups for water and wine. In the era of the Shang dynasty, bronze vessels were used only to serve grains and drinks made from grain, but never to serve meat. The most important vessels for meat dishes were made from wood, basketry, and pottery.

Most excavated Zhou period burial assemblages contain ceramic vessels. The majority of the graves do not include just one or two containers, but a whole range of different vessel forms. Chang reasons that most of these individuals were interred with a set of containers for cooking and serving grain, serving meat, and for drinking. Chang's deduction would have been difficult, if not impossible, to derive without the careful juxtaposition of texts with archaeology. Together, these complementary records are serving to uncover the deep traditions of Chinese cuisine.

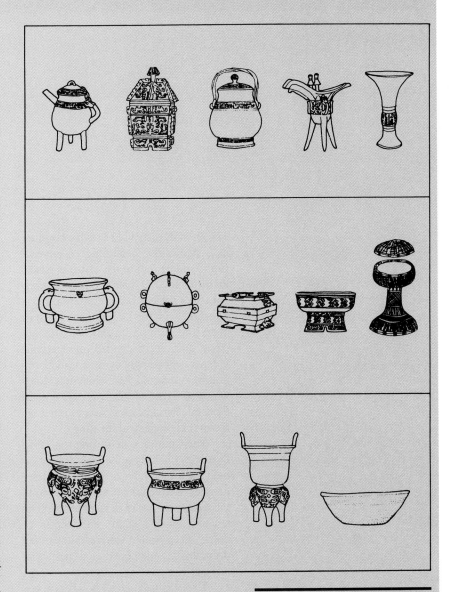

Examples of Shang and Zhou food and drinking vessels: drinking vessels (top), serving vessels (center), cooking vessels (bottom).

XIANYANG

*Terracotta soldiers
and the Qin dynasty*

The Zhou dynasty (1122 to third century B.C.) marks the beginning of imperial China and its traditions, which persisted for the next 2000 years and into the present. Zhou society was highly stratified at its center, with the king and a royal court at the top. Away from this core, the adjacent areas were divided into partially independent provinces, and administration was enacted by semifeudal lords who had great control over their local domains. Periodic civil wars erupted between these lords and the king.

The Chinese state during the Three Dynasties (including the early Zhou) was built on a hierarchical network of large lineages in which the distance away from the main male line of descent determined relative political status and access to power. Each walled town was inhabited primarily by members of a particular lineage.

The latter half of the Zhou period was characterized by great political change and upheaval, with warring states and shifting capitals. It also was a time when Chinese urbanism spread over a much wider area than ever before. Great cities were built, many of which were larger and more nucleated than the earlier Shang cities. The largest Zhou settlement, G'a-to, had 270,000 people. All the large cities were walled. By 600 B.C., iron casting was practiced and iron agricultural tools were in use. Large irrigation works were constructed, and wet-rice irrigation became increasingly important. Changes in agricultural technology enabled rapid increases in population density. Late Zhou

socioeconomic structure placed great emphasis on the taxation of peasants in lieu of labor drafts. Kinship bonds began to diminish, and territorial units and bureaucracies gained importance. Late Zhou was the time of Confucius, who preached order, deference, and family ties, perhaps in response to rapid social transition and transformation. Although large-scale political integration remained relatively weak and fragmentary, a single system of measurement was adopted across most of China. There was increased interregional trade and commercial activity, as well as greater cultural unity.

By the third century B.C., the descendants of the western Zhou kings ruled an increasingly small area outside their original homeland. As the Zhou polity weakened, other states rose in influence. The expansion of the Qin polity and its short-lived dynasty (221–207 B.C.) eclipsed the Zhou, along with five other contemporary states.

Shih Huang Ti inherited the throne of the Qin (pronounced "chin") kingdom at age 13 in 246 B.C. During the first 25 years of his reign, he frequently engaged in battle, eventually conquering six other major kingdoms. For this reason, six was considered the lucky number of the Qin. Through military prowess, Shih Huang Ti unified China into a single imperial kingdom in 221 B.C. and declared himself China's first emperor. The empire was ruled from the capital city of Xianyang (she-on'yong), to which he forced over 100,000 royal and wealthy families from throughout the empire to move.

A terracotta soldier guarding the tomb of Shih Huant Ti.

The Great Wall.

Shih Huang Ti had luxurious palaces built in Xianyang that were replicas of royal residences in the conquered states. By moving local lords to Xianyang, he forcibly detached the feudal aristocracy from the land and its people, weakening their power. This move also served to centralize the Qin empire by concentrating economic and political power in a single capital.

According to historical records, Shih Huang Ti was an ambitious and ruthless emperor. He built the Great Wall along China's northern periphery by joining walls that had been constructed by earlier feudal states. Although the traditional view is that the wall was intended to protect the newly formed empire from the nomadic herders of Asia to the north, other scholars have suggested that its main function was to prevent heavily taxed peasants from escaping taxes and conscription. The 2400-km (1500-mi) wall, built by 700,000 conscripts and

wide enough for six horses abreast, remains the longest fortification anywhere. Many men perished while working on the wall, inspiring some to call it "the longest cemetery in the world." Shih Huang Ti also established China's first standing army, a body that may have contained more than a million people.

To weaken regional autonomy, Shih Huang Ti destroyed the feudal structure that had existed for centuries. Because he saw Confucian philosophy as a threat to his authority, all the books of this school were burned, and Confucian scholars who refused to accept his reforms were buried alive.

The centralizing tendencies of Shih Huang Ti included increasing codification of a Chinese legal system and the standardization of Chinese character writing so that the written language could be understood throughout the empire. Weights and measures, coins, and the gauges of chariot wheels were increas-

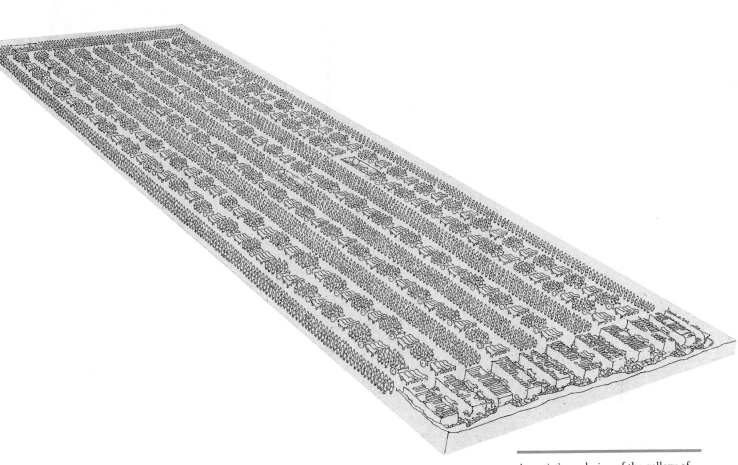

An artist's rendering of the gallery of terracotta soldiers and horses guarding the east gate of the emperor's tomb at Mount Li.

ingly regulated and made more homogeneous. Paper was invented during the Qin dynasty. In the grave of one Qin official, more than 1200 bamboo slips were found, bound into a series of books and containing an explicit legal code specifying particular crimes and their punishments. In addition to intensified road building, a canal system was constructed by Shih Huang Ti to enhance communication and transportation. The canal system was one of the greatest inland water communication systems in the ancient world, and several canals are still functioning today.

As soon as Shih Huang Ti became emperor, he began building his tomb. According to history, 700,000 laborers from all parts of the country worked for 36 years on the project, a virtual subterranean palace for the emperor to live in for eternity. According to early Chinese records, the architects of the tomb conceived of it as a universe in miniature. All

the country's major waterways were reproduced in mercury within the tomb, and they fed into a tiny ocean. Heavenly constellations were painted on the ceiling. The emperor's outer coffin was made of molten copper, and fine vessels, precious stones, and other rarities were buried with him.

The burial tomb, called Mount Li, was at one time 46 m (150 ft) tall. Built in the center of a spirit city, an area enclosed by an inner wall, it contained sacred stone tablets and prayer temples. Beyond this area was an outer city enclosed by a high rectangular stone wall 7 m (23 ft) thick at the base. The total complex covered 200 ha (500 acres). Today, most of the walls and temples have been removed.

About 1370 m (4500 ft) east of Mount Li, excavations have revealed one of the most astonishing ancient spectacles. Guarding the east side of the emperor's tomb is a brick-floored, 1.2-ha

The gallery of terracotta soldiers at Xian.

(3-acre) gallery of terracotta soldiers and horses. Collapsed pillars indicate that a roof once covered the underground battlefield. In the royal tombs of the previous Shang dynasty, kings and high-ranking officials were interred with living warriors, women, servants, and horses. This practice, which had ceased centuries prior to the Qin dynasty, evidently was revived in symbolic fashion by Shih Huang Ti.

Although only part of the gallery has been excavated, some 8000 terracotta figures have been exposed, along with wooden chariots. The terracotta warriors are slightly larger than life-size; they are arranged in battle formations, dressed in uniforms of various rank, and carry real weapons—swords, spears, and crossbows. Traces of pigment indicate that the uniforms were brightly colored. Of the excavated figures, none look exactly alike; their facial expressions vary, suggesting that they were realistic portraits of each individual in the emperor's honor guard. Even the horses were very finely

crafted, appearing alert and tense as they would be in battle.

The army and horses are supplemented by a rich artifact assemblage, including gold, jade, and bronze objects, linen, silk, bamboo and bone artifacts, pottery utensils, and iron agricultural tools. Elemental analysis on the swords has revealed that they were made from an alloy of copper, tin, and 13 other elements. The designers of the tomb's security system, a series of mechanized crossbows, were sealed inside the tomb to die so that none of the tomb's secrets could be divulged.

Shih Huang Ti always lived and worked in guarded secrecy, because several assassination attempts were made on his life. Only a few trusted ministers ever knew where he was. He died on a journey to the eastern provinces, and his death was kept a secret from all except his youngest son. His prime minister and his chief eunuch (a castrated male) apparently plotted to keep the death secret for their own ambitious reasons. They wanted the emperor's youngest son to succeed to the throne, instead of an elder son, as Shih Huang Ti had decreed. The councillors thought they could more easily influence and manipulate the younger son. The elder son, who had been exiled to the northwestern frontier to help build the Great Wall, was sent a fake order to commit suicide, which he did, paving the way for the younger son to become the new emperor. Nevertheless, Shih Huang Ti's efforts to expand his domain to both the north and the south sapped his treasury, so Qin preeminence was short-lived.

While the Qin dynasty was brief, China's first episode of unification was not. Qin rule was followed by the Han dynasty, which lasted for 400 years (206 B.C.–A.D. 220). The Han unification was in part made possible by technological innovations developed in Zhou times: iron tools, wet-rice irrigation, the ox-drawn plow, improved roads, and the crossbow. Under Han rule, China continued as a unified empire, but with greater political stability. The economy was prosperous, and a standardized coinage circulated throughout China.

During the Han dynasty, China became even more densely settled. The world's first census in the years A.D. 1 and 2 lists the population of the empire as 57,700,000, with cities of up to 250,000 people. One late Han city may have contained as many as half a million people. The decisions made by the Han monarchs were implemented through 1500 administrative provinces, each of which was centered at a walled town. No other political system of its era—not even the Roman Empire— was as massive in size or bureaucratic complexity.

JENNÉ-JENO

*An ancient urban center in
West Africa*

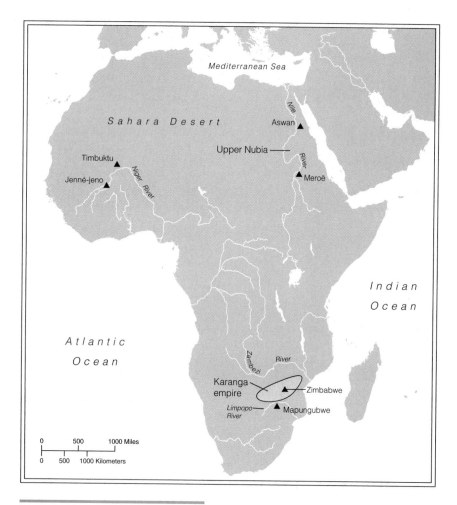

Africa, with places and names mentioned in the text.

penetrations into Upper Nubia, the Nubian kingdom of Kush (in what is now the Sudan) arose. The Kushites were ethnically and linguistically different from the Egyptians, and they had their own tomb style. Egypt later came briefly under Kushite control, and the intermingling of these two East African cultures intensified.

During the fourth century B.C., following an episode of Egyptian control, a major center on this portion of the southern Nile was established at Meroë. For almost a millennium (until the fourth century A.D.), the Meroitic kingdom maintained trade connections with both the Mediterranean world and the southern Sahara. Yet, after its collapse, the fertile grasslands around Meroë became the homeland for more rural lifeways. To the west, state-level societies did not develop on the southern fringes of the Sahara Desert until the first millennium A.D.

The Sahara Desert has undergone several cycles of hyperaridity (extreme drought) that have affected human settlement in the region. Prior to 10,000 B.C., the desert was very dry and uninhabited. Several millennia later, after conditions improved, the Sahara consisted of a mosaic of shallow lakes and marshes linked by permanent streams where communities of hunter-fisher-collectors settled. The technology of these early groups included microliths, bone harpoons, comb-impressed pottery, and grinding stones used to process wild grains. Livestock were added to the subsistence base in the fifth millennium B.C. Sheep and goats were introduced first, most likely from the Near East via Egypt or from North Africa. However, it is unclear whether domestic cattle also were introduced

The ancient Egyptian state, with its close ties to the Mediterranean world, had few direct contacts with regions far to the south and west. Only the area down to the Nile's first rapids (near the present Aswan Dam) was ruled consistently by the pharaohs, although slaves, ebony, and ivory were brought from farther south through trade. Early in the last millennium B.C., following New Kingdom

from the Near East or were domesticated indigenously from a wild local species.

The central and southern Sahara continued to be occupied by **pastoralists** until about 2500 B.C. when a second pronounced dry period began, which continues to the present. Desiccation of the environment led to the southward movement of the Saharan peoples into sub-Saharan Africa. These herder-collectors brought their cattle with them, while the people remaining in the Sahara became more nomadic. The presence of the tsetse fly in the Sahel (the region at the southern edge of the Sahara Desert) and the Sudanic savanna prior to 2500 B.C. had limited the expansion of pastoralists into the region. With the onset of drier conditions, the tsetse fly migrated farther south.

By 1000 B.C., pastoralists of the western Sahel adopted or domesticated cereals. Early West African staples include sorghum and several genera of millet. Yet the subsistence economy remained variable as wild foods continued to be important, and lifeways based on hunting, gathering, and fishing remained dominant in some areas.

Iron metallurgy was introduced into West Africa during the first millennium B.C. In much of Africa (except Egypt), iron was the first metal to be used. This pattern contrasts with the development of metalworking in most of the Old World, where ironworking followed copper and bronze. One explanation is that ironworking was introduced from the north, most likely by iron-using Phoenicians who established trading colonies in North Africa. Yet there is limited evidence for copper smelting in the West African Sahara almost a millennium earlier that may have led to the independent discovery of iron metallurgy in West Africa. Whatever its source, the great efficiency of iron tools spurred the rapid spread of this technology throughout Africa upon its introduction.

The earliest identifiable iron-using society in West Africa is the Nok culture of central Nigeria, known for its distinctive sculpted terracotta heads. Iron-smelting furnaces from the region date to the last half of the first millennium B.C.

Jenné-jeno, located in the floodplain of the Niger River.

One of the few other areas in West Africa that had iron at that time is southwestern Mali, where iron slag and artifacts have been recovered from the earliest occupation levels at the classic tell site of Jenné-jeno. Situated 3 km (1.8 mi) southeast of the present city of Jenné, the site consists of a mound of successive settlements 800 m (2600 ft) long and 6–8 m (20–26 ft) high.

Jenné-jeno is located in the Inland Niger Delta in southwestern Mali along the middle course of the Niger River, an area lined with hundreds of ancient tells.

A funerary urn uncovered in the cemetery at Jenné-jeno.

Jenné-jeno's strategic location along a navigable river in a floodplain lacking raw materials encouraged exchange. The villagers traded their agricultural, fish, and animal products for iron ore and grindstones from at least 50 km (30 mi) away. The development of these regional trade networks within the Inland Niger Delta and immediately adjacent areas was an important factor in Jenné's early expansion.

The practice of camel domestication, which first occurred in Arabia, spread to the Sahara by early in the first millennium A.D. Camel transport had an important effect on the economy by providing a means of regular long-distance trading across the desert. With the development of long-distance trade, villages such as Jenné-jeno developed into important market centers. Jenné-jeno expanded its trading network to include copper and salt from the Sahara to the north, and gold from the savanna and forest country to the south.

Jenné-jeno became increasingly urban after the mid-fourth century. The most frequent mode of interment in the crowded cemeteries of the site was urn burial. The deceased were placed in the bottom of jars measuring 60–90 cm (24–35 in) high and 45–50 cm (18–20 in) in diameter and were buried with few accompanying grave goods. This burial custom was practiced in the Inland Niger Delta into the late nineteenth century.

The city reached its height after A.D. 800, when it expanded to 33 ha (80 acres) and a city wall 3.6 m (11.8 ft) wide was constructed around the mound's 2 km (1.2 mi) circumference. Brick architecture replaced the coursed solid mud technology that was in use earlier. Closely spaced house foundations of mud bricks are still visible on the surface; mud bricks used in constructing the city wall also are visible today along parts of the mound's periphery. Furnace parts, forge debris, and crucibles suggest blacksmiths and coppersmiths worked the iron ore and copper that Jenné-jeno obtained through trade.

When Arabs penetrated western Africa at the end of the first millennium A.D., Jenné-jeno and other early West Af-

This vast inland area of swamps and standing water is remarkably fertile, and the rivers have a great abundance of fish. The alluvial plain, however, is devoid of stone, copper, and iron ore.

The initial settlement at Jenné, dating to around 200 B.C., was confined to a few hectares in the central part of the site. The early inhabitants were mixed agriculturalists who constructed circular houses of straw coated with mud. The earliest direct evidence for domesticated African rice (*Oryza glaberrima*) in West Africa, dating to the first century A.D., was recovered at Jenné-jeno by the site's excavators, Susan and Roderick McIntosh, of Rice University. Fish, reedbuck (African antelope), and domestic cattle (*Bos taurus*) also figured heavily in the inhabitants' diet. Craft skills are evident in the earliest materials recovered at the site, which include iron and slag and significant quantities of well-manufactured ceramics decorated with twine impressions.

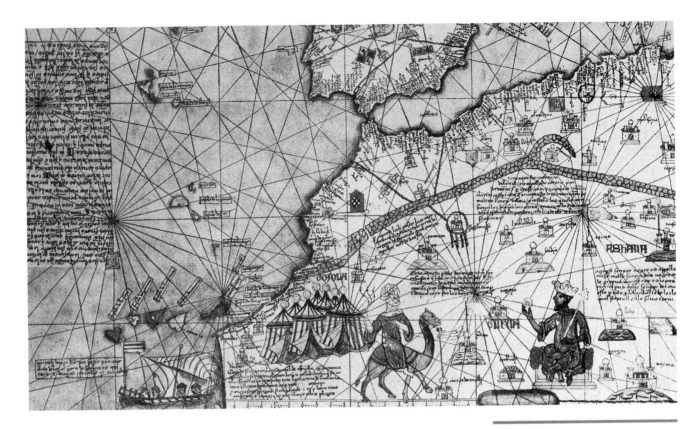

Map of West Africa drawn in A.D. 1375 showing traders on camelback.

rican towns were functioning as fully developed urban centers that were at the apex of regional settlement hierarchies. The rulers of Jenné-jeno presided over a large area of the floodplain extending 60 km (100 mi) downstream.

Jenné-jeno began to decline after A.D. 1150 and was abandoned by 1400, as were most of the rural settlements in its hinterland. The reasons for the abandonment are unknown; however, defensive concerns and the spread of Islam after the arrival of the Arab traders are likely factors. The modern city of Jenné (Jenné-jeno means "ancient Jenné") was established nearby during the twelfth or thirteenth century when Jenné-jeno already was in decline. The new location in an area surrounded by water was easily defended, since it was accessible only by water most of the year. Given the long history of community displacement (both voluntary and coerced) associated with the spread of Islam throughout West Africa, the population base of the new center may have largely come from Jenné-jeno. The new Jenné not only con-tinued to be an important commercial center, but also became a center of Islamic learning.

The Inland Niger Delta has remained an important thoroughfare for exchange throughout much of the second millennium A.D. Another important commercial center on the Niger River was Timbuktu, 500 km (300 mi) north of Jenné, at the edge of the Sahara. From at least the fourteenth century, the two towns served as major ports of trade in western Africa. North African pottery and blocks of Saharan salt arrived by camel caravan at Timbuktu where they were shifted to canoes for transport up the Niger River to Jenné. At Jenné, they were traded for the rich agricultural produce of Jenné's hinterland and for gold mined from areas farther south. Historical texts refer to both cities and this "golden trade of the moors." Today, modern Jenné is famous for its stunning mud architecture and distinctive mosque that reflects both indigenous and North African influences.

GREAT ZIMBABWE

An important trading center in southcentral Africa

Relatively egalitarian political formations were more resilient in southern Africa than they were in West Africa. Farming and domesticated animals did not spread into southern Africa until the third century A.D., coincident with the appearance of ironworking and the spread of Bantu-speaking peoples. These herder-cultivators worked metal and made pottery. Prior to their arrival during the Early Iron Age, southern Africa was occupied by hunter-gatherers whose only tools were stone.

Peasant farmers first settled in southcentral Africa, in what is now Zimbabwe (zim-bob'way), during the fourth century A.D. Northeast of the Kalahari Desert, Zimbabwe is high plateau country (elevation 1200–1500 m, 4000–5000 ft) bounded by rivers. The gently rolling plains are cool and well-watered, covered with savannah woodlands that are free of the disease-carrying tsetse fly, the scourge of equatorial Africa. Mineral deposits are abundant. Iron ores, widespread throughout much of southern and eastern Africa, are present, as are copper and gold.

The querns and grindstones found in these early farming villages indicate that grain was grown. Sheep and goats were kept, but hunting continued to provide an important source of meat. People lived in permanent villages, some as large as several hectares, located on open ground with little apparent concern for defense. Their huts were constructed of a wooden framework covered with mud. The presence of slag fragments suggests that ironworking was a common skill.

Such small iron artifacts as arrowheads, razors, beads, and rings are found in every village. Copper items were rarer; usually no more than a few beads or small strips have been recovered in any one excavation. Handmade ceramics were produced, of which there were several distinct regional variants. Contact with the east coast of Africa is indicated by the presence of glass trade beads and occasional marine shells.

Soon after their introduction, cattle became important both culturally and economically. As in many African societies today, the size of one's cattle herd was probably a sign of status and a basic means of converting grain surpluses into more permanent kinds of wealth. The advent of cattle herding did not eliminate hunting. Grain crops—particularly sorghum, finger millet, cowpeas, and ground beans—also were cultivated. Bananas were introduced from Indonesia by trans-Indian traders around the ninth century A.D.

During the later prehistory of Africa (in the last thousand years), complex states emerged in the central and southern regions. Groups such as the Karanga were led by powerful chiefs, priests, and traders. They had contacts with societies outside the continent, and at the advent of written history, several of them were still actively involved with foreign merchants.

Two of the largest early states in southern Africa were centered on Mapungubwe and Great Zimbabwe. Mapungubwe, the earlier of the two, is located on top of a large sandstone outcrop that rises abruptly from the arid valley of the Limpopo River about 320 km

(200 mi) south of Great Zimbabwe. The earliest farmers in the region built a number of villages close to the river after A.D. 800. Their economy was based on cattle, sheep, and goats, and they obtained such goods as cowrie shells and glass beads through Indian Ocean trade. Excavations at one of these early village sites (Bambandyanalo), only a few kilometers from Mapungubwe, revealed a large cattle enclosure, crude breakers and bag-shaped pots, grindstones, and a few iron tools. The first buildings were constructed on Mapungubwe Hill early in the twelfth century A.D. Excavations at the site have revealed a succession of houses and richly adorned burials accompanied by gold beads and bangles. Mapungubwe quickly became one of the largest towns in the region, controlling a hinterland of lesser settlements up to 60 km (37 mi) away. Its inhabitants specialized in various crafts, including working ivory into bracelets, making bone points, and weaving. However, the real base of Mapungubwe's power came from its intermediary role in coastal trade and the wealth of gold and animal products from its hinterland.

When Mapungubwe was at its peak in the mid-thirteenth century A.D., Great Zimbabwe was a smaller district center. Mapungubwe later went into decline just as Great Zimbabwe was reaching its greatest size and influence. The eventual abandonment of Mapungubwe may in part have been due to Great Zimbabwe's seizure of the gold trade and exchange routes to the coast.

Great Zimbabwe, the largest and most famous site of the Karanga, is located in the central region of Zimbabwe, on a tributary that eventually drains into the Indian Ocean. The area is composed of granite hills, some of which are enormous, bare, rounded domes. Because of their size, these granite features affect rainfall patterns so that the prevailing southeasterly winds drop more rain here than in neighboring areas. To the north, the site is bounded by a narrow ridge of granite that forms a 91-m (300-ft) cliff, strewn with enormous boulders. Just south of the Great Zimbabwe ruins, the land descends into drier, more open

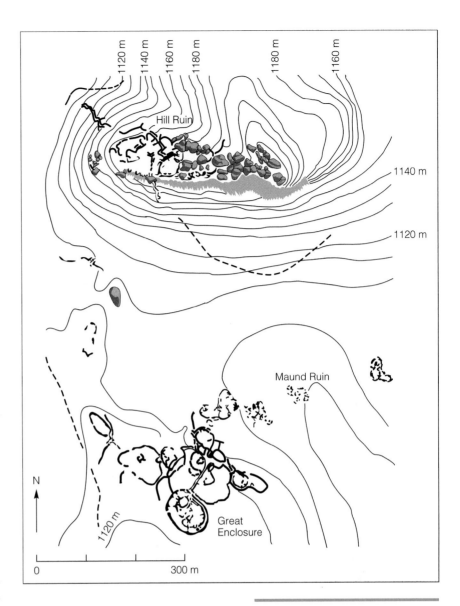

The plan of Great Zimbabwe.

grasslands suitable for cattle. Slabs that break off the granite domes provide abundant building material.

The Karanga began to build stone structures, including field walls, terraces, and stone enclosures, sometime after A.D. 1000. The first stone structures at Great Zimbabwe, built after A.D. 1250, were placed on top of the high cliff, possibly for defense. Simple stone walls enclosed platforms that held pole-and-mud houses. The walls do not follow an obvious plan. The only openings are narrow doorways, topped with simple stone lintels. The quality of the walls varies, from uncoursed sections of irregularly shaped rocks to coursed walls of granite blocks that were carefully matched.

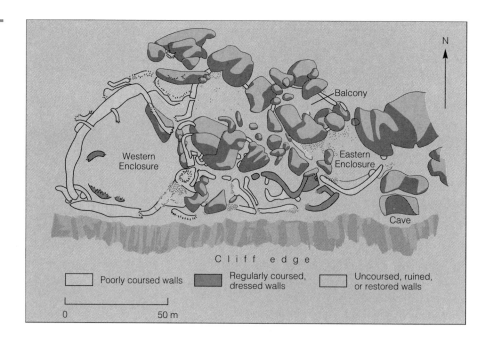

The Hill Ruin at Great Zimbabwe.

The buildings at the site consist of two groups, one on the steep, rocky cliff and the other on the adjacent valley floor. On the cliff, called the Hill Ruin, well-coursed walls were linked to natural boulders, forming a series of easily defended enclosures. The largest and most substantial structure on the hill, called the Western Enclosure, consisted of two curved walls, over 9 m (30 ft) high, circling an area greater than 45 m (150 ft) in diameter. On the other end of the cliff-top was a smaller structure, the Eastern Enclosure, bounded by boulders on the north and a stone wall on the south. Inside this structure were groups of circular stone platforms that held many monoliths. The presence of figurines, including seven carved soapstone birds, suggests that this enclosure was the ceremonial center of the site. The carved birds, about 36 cm (14 in) high, were placed on top of 1-m (3-ft) stone columns. Nothing like these stone carvings has been found elsewhere.

In the valley below, larger, free-standing walled enclosures were built surrounding circular pole-and-mud houses. This pattern is especially clear at the Maund Ruin on the edge of the site, where 29 separate stone walls were built. The walls abut 10 circular dwelling huts, forming 9 separate courtyards, each en-

tered through doorways in the stone walls. These enclosures form single, functional units. Both in the valley and on the hill, large middens of domestic debris have accumulated outside most of the enclosures.

One enclosure on the opposite end of the valley from the Hill Ruin, the Great Enclosure, was especially large and complex, with a perimeter wall over 10 m (33 ft) high and 5 m (16 ft) thick (see Color Plate 25). The outer wall was over 240 m (800 ft) long, forming an irregular ellipse with a diameter of 89 m (292 ft). The top of the wall is decorated with a band of two lines in a chevron pattern. There are several entrances into the enclosure on the north and west sides of the wall. Containing more stonework than all the rest of the ruins at Great Zimbabwe combined, this wall is the largest prehistoric structure in sub-Saharan Africa. Several other smaller walled enclosures are situated within this outer wall, containing dwellings that housed the ruler and his family. The most striking construction inside the Great Enclosure is a solid circular stone tower rising 10 m (33 ft) from its base, which is 6 m (20 ft) in diameter. Called the Conical Tower, this structure was surrounded by platforms and large monoliths. The function of these monoliths, also associated with the Hill Ruin,

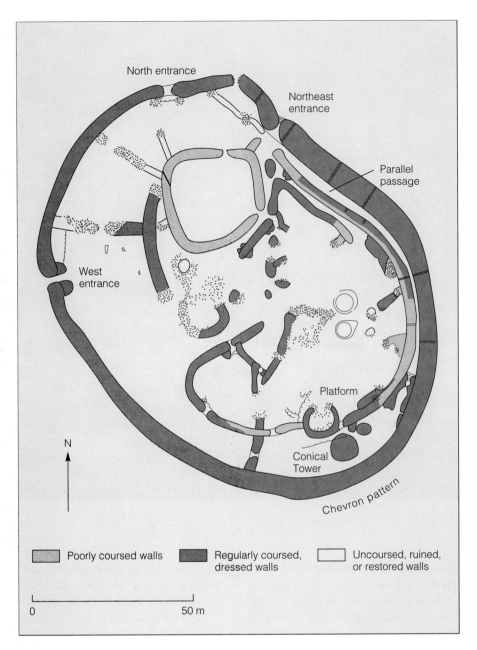

North entrance

Northeast entrance

Parallel passage

West entrance

Platform

Conical Tower

Chevron pattern

N

Poorly coursed walls

Regularly coursed, dressed walls

Uncoursed, ruined, or restored walls

0   50 m

remains somewhat of a mystery. Their distribution was not random; they were placed in areas having a sacred character.

The stone enclosures at the core of Great Zimbabwe—covering 40 ha (100 acres)—are the largest and most elaborate of the more than 150 similar stone structures constructed across the high granite region of the Zimbabwe plateau. Many of these sites were small, having between one and five small enclosures surrounded by freestanding walls. The pottery at all of these sites was similar to that at Great Zimbabwe.

The architectural florescence at Great Zimbabwe was linked to the development of a powerful, strong political authority. The construction of the extensive stone walls clearly required an organized labor effort. Centralized control of expanded trade links with Indian Ocean polities may have been a significant factor, and Great Zimbabwe became an important commercial center, both locally and regionally. Specialized craftworkers made simple forged iron tools, such as hoes, axes, and arrowheads. They alloyed copper with tin and

The Great Enclosure and other ruins at Great Zimbabwe.

made coiled wire bracelets and pins, needles, and razors, and used imported gold to make bracelets, anklets, and beads. These metals were worked at a small scale in certain enclosures set aside for specific tasks. The presence of large numbers of spindle whorls, made from both potsherds and soapstone, indicate that cotton textiles were woven at Great Zimbabwe.

The prosperity of Great Zimbabwe was based largely on its monopolization of coastal and long-distance trade, which it had earlier wrested from Mapungubwe. Exchange with Africa's east coast, which was visited by Arab and Indian merchants, provided a large number of exotic objects, including Persian and Chinese pottery, Near Eastern glass, and cowrie shells from the beaches of the Indian Ocean. These items were prestige

goods, essential to demonstrating rank. Porcelain, glass, and trinkets were found in one hoard at Great Zimbabwe in association with iron gongs, hoes, and seashells. The latter items are still recognized in the region today as symbols of chiefly authority. The traders at Great Zimbabwe also received products from the surrounding area, through either patronage or tribute. Copper was imported from the northern edge of the plateau in the form of standardized ingots. With the initiation of goldworking, the gold trade on the plateau became important by the late twelfth or early thirteenth century A.D.

Zimbabwe reached its period of greatest influence between A.D. 1350 and 1450, when the settlement, with a population estimated between 12,000 and 20,000, extended over 700 ha (1700

The outer wall of the Great Enclosure, capped by the chevron pattern.

acres) and controlled an area of approximately 100,000 sq km (38,600 sq mi) between the Zambezi and Limpopo Rivers. The balance of power then shifted to a more northerly center on the Zambezi River. The increasing importance of copper from the north may have been a factor in redirecting trade. Later, trade and communication routes, focused on the Zambezi, may have bypassed Great Zimbabwe. The Portuguese penetrated the area in the sixteenth century and established a fort on the east coast. Their attempt to control the gold exchange of south-central Africa further disrupted trade, and the Karanga empire disintegrated by the end of the century. Today, Karanga ruins stand tall in the plateau country of Zimbabwe. The word *zimbabwe* means "stone houses" or "venerated houses," and the Karanga used it to identify the houses of chiefs. It is these ruins that now give their name to a contemporary nation.

SUMMARY

THEORIES OF STATE
DEVELOPMENT

*Changing views on the rise of complex
polities and urban societies*

Decades ago, the late V. Gordon Childe described the essence of what we mean by
civilization in a list of ten characteristics (even if he did not succeed in providing a
scientifically precise or universally acceptable definition). Charles Redman, of Arizona
State University, subsequently organized Childe's indices into a list of primary and
secondary characteristics. The primary characteristics are economic, organizational,
and demographic in nature and suggest fundamental changes in societal structure.
They include (1) cities—dense, nucleated demographic concentrations; (2) full-time
labor specialization; (3) state organization, based on territorial residence rather than
kin connections; (4) class stratification—the presence of a privileged ruling stratum;
and (5) the concentration of surplus. According to Redman, Childe's secondary
characteristics serve to document the existence of the primary criteria. They are
(1) monumental public works; (2) long-distance exchange; (3) writing; (4) arithmetic,
geometry, and astronomy; and (5) highly developed, standardized artwork.

Childe's criteria, particularly the secondary ones, are certainly not without problems. For example, the Inca, who established the largest pre-Columbian New World
empire, did not have a standardized system of writing. Conversely, many societies that
are not consensually recognized as civilizations built monumental edifices, engaged in
long-distance exchange, crafted wonderful (and reasonably standardized) artwork, and
were very aware of astronomical cycles. Even the primary criteria are subject to discussion, as kinship is known to have played a very strong organizational role in both
Native American and early Chinese civilizations. Although it is next to impossible
using archaeological data to distinguish full-time from part-time craft specialization,
occupational specialization (of an unknown degree of intensity) is often found at
archaeologically known sites that are not traditionally conceptualized as civilizations.
Nevertheless, Childe's criteria not only provide a valuable starting point for discussion,
but most of them can be examined archaeologically. To the researcher, they provide a
more useful starting point than, for example, the frequently cited definition of the state
as an institution that monopolizes force, a characteristic that cannot be subjected to
straightforward archaeological investigation.

Given the difficulties in defining the state and civilization, as well as the evident
variety in human societies and sequences of societal change, it is not surprising that
no single, satisfactory explanation has been developed to account for these transformations. In anthropology, current interpretive perspectives can be subdivided into
integrative and coercive models. Integrative approaches emphasize coordination and
regulation as roles of emergent institutions. The alternative coercive theories stress the
role of the developing state in the resolution of intrasocietal conflicts that emerge from
disparities in wealth. These alternative frameworks have their philosophical roots at
least as early as the fifth century B.C., when the Greek writer Thucydides described the
Peloponnesian War and its combatants. Thucydides compared different organizational
frameworks, contrasting the democratic and the oligarchic. The former, typified by
Athens under the ruler Pericles, was characterized by government through coopera-

tion, with the populace described as benefitting from state policies and services. Sparta, which typified the latter, more coercive governing structure, was ruled by the propertied class that controlled decision making in order to maintain their disproportionate wealth.

Most states integrate as well as coerce, although their degree of reliance on different governing strategies certainly can vary. For archaeologists, as well as other social and historical scientists, the decipherment of different organizational strategies is a promising domain for research. Yet in modeling the evolution of early states, researchers should recognize that government strategies can undergo change. For example, institutions may initially develop to serve integrative or regulative roles. Once established, they may become more coercive, in the face of new challenges or to maintain whatever benefits their decision makers may have accrued. Therefore, the functions of a governing institution may not provide a complete picture of why that institution arose in the first place.

The preceding discussion contrasts the explanatory merits of integrative versus coercive frameworks. A second analytical pathway compares the relative utility of different "prime-movers," key factors that are proposed to account for many, if not all, cases of state development. The late Karl Wittfogel proposed water control (irrigation) as the key variable in the rise of the "hydraulic state." Wittfogel saw water as having unique properties, essential for agriculture in the dry lands where many of the world's early states developed, yet manipulable by people in ways that other environmental resources are not. Nevertheless, although large-scale canal irrigation systems were eventually used in the domains of many early states (such as in Mesopotamia), the temporal sequence of state formation and the construction of these grand irrigation networks is not clear. In other areas, like Mexico's Valley of Oaxaca, it appears that most pre-Colombian water-control devices could have been managed by a few households at most. Recent ethnographic research also indicates that large-scale irrigation networks do not necessarily require centralized administration.

A second prime-mover, demographic pressure, places the primary cause of political change on imbalances between a human population and its available food supply. Influenced by the work of the agricultural economist Esther Boserup, proponents of this view have turned the work of Thomas Malthus on its head. In the late eighteenth century, Malthus argued that the advent of agriculture led to the production of food surpluses, thereby making human population growth possible and increasing the availability of leisure time. Yet anthropological work, spearheaded by Robert Carneiro, of the Museum of Natural History in New York, Marshall Sahlins, of the University of Chicago, and Richard Lee, of the University of Toronto, has questioned the long-held dogma surrounding surplus and leisure time. As Kent Flannery synthesized:

> The cold ethnographic fact is that the people with the most leisure time are the hunters and gatherers, who also have the lowest productivity; even primitive farmers don't produce a surplus unless they are forced to, and thus the challenge is getting people to work more, or more people to work. With better technology, people simply work less; what produces surplus is the coercive power of real authority, or the demands of elaborate ritual. (1972a, pp. 405–406)

Recently, anthropologists have questioned the arguments of Lee and Sahlins concerning leisure time. They note that most hunter-gatherer populations suffered seasonal or periodic food shortages or frequently lacked certain key resources, like fat or protein. Yet the fact remains that, except when encouraged, few hunter-gatherers or village people produced a great deal more than their families required.

Primarily concerned with the contemporary Third World (where runaway demographic growth is not unusual), Boserup argues that technological changes and increased productivity also could be spurred by excessive population. Archaeological adherents of Boserup's position view ancient population growth as an independent variable and the principal cause of social and economic transformations. As we saw in many of the site discussions in this chapter and in Chapters 8 and 9, demographic

If population pressure was a problem in the Nile Valley, a circumscribed situation par excellence, the Pharaoh should have been delighted to see the last of Moses and his cogeners [followers]. That he was not, and indeed expended considerable effort to retain the Jews within his territories, suggests that population pressure was not perceived as a threat to social stability.

A. T. Rambo (1991)

growth often coincided with episodes of great social change, and in many regions it was an important variable. Yet correlation does not equal causality. What is not clear in most cases is the nature of the interconnections—whether population growth was the cause or the consequence of political and economic transitions.

In rural, preindustrial contexts where child labor can be economically valuable, increases in tribute and the labor demands on households (often associated with political development) can spur cycles of demographic growth, as families opt to have more children. In other words, political and economic strategies can greatly influence demographic change. In many of the cases we have examined, the nucleation of population around an emerging center also may have been spurred by in-migration, as people were attracted by or coerced to settle near an increasingly powerful institution.

Furthermore, population growth does not necessarily imply population pressure, the latter being a notoriously difficult concept to measure. Archaeological and historical findings from many areas indicate that long-term population change is not regular, uniform, or ever-increasing, making it theoretically problematic to assume continuous and autonomous growth. Finally, in several cases, archaeological findings have shown that regional populations were markedly below any reasonable estimate of available agrarian production at the time of early state development.

Exchange also has been advanced as a prime-mover, although, like warfare, it is practically a human universal and therefore too broadly defined to account for the development of the state. Thus the occurrence of exchange is not as evolutionarily significant as are the nature and mode of the transactions, whether they are monopolized or controlled and by whom, the volume of the transactions involved, and the kinds of items moved (and their local importance). Until these considerations are empirically considered and refined theoretically, exchange cannot be convincingly employed as a prime-mover in state development.

Another general model for state development was proposed by Carneiro. Stimulated by his ethnographic work among tribal groups in the Amazon Basin of South America, Carneiro has suggested that warfare and bounded conditions may account for the origin of states. Carneiro recognized that warfare, almost universal in human society, cannot alone account for the rise of the state. Warfare was present (even endemic) in many places, yet the state never formed in those areas. In Carneiro's scenario, a population first must have increased in size beyond the limits of its local resources. **Circumscription** by either environmental (mountains, oceans, rivers) or social boundaries (neighboring groups) would then require warfare and conquest to obtain more food. Although warfare does appear to have been an important factor in some cases, such as the rise of Monte Albán in the Valley of Oaxaca, Mexico (see Chapter 8, p. 322), Carneiro's formulation, which tends to make warfare and population pressure into dual prime-movers, has not met with unanimous support. For example, it is hard to envision how circumscription played a major role on the extensive, flat North China Plain, where the early Chinese state appears to have arisen. Even in Oaxaca, the connection between the concentration of political power and militarism began during a period when the regional population was small.

Today, most archaeologists have adopted multivariate approaches, recognizing that the process of state development was probably triggered by a suite of factors (including some of the prime-movers), rather than a single causal stimulus in each instance, and that even the same set of factors may not have been involved in each case. Our examination of Old World state formation illustrates that factors such as population growth, new technologies, changing exchange and interaction (including warfare) patterns, and shifts in the organization of labor and specialization were often intertwined with episodes of managerial restructuring, yet we have sorted out neither the specific interlinkages between these factors nor their relative importance in each case.

The contingent or historical nature of social change provides a further challenge. In each region, earlier changes always constrain and underpin subsequent shifts. Consequently, the nature of the states in each of these regions varied somewhat because of

The regularities set forth by Steward, and the models constructed by Wittfogel, Carneiro, and others, have guided a great deal of fruitful research leading to knowledge about the material forces important in the rise of complex chiefdoms and states. What constructs, however, will guide us in the future?

H. T. Wright (1986)

I have sometimes compared models to ships. What interests me, once the ship is built, is to launch it, to see if it floats, then to make it sail wherever I please, up and down the currents of time. The moment of shipwreck is always the most meaningful.

F. Braudel (1970)

the nature and organization of the specific polities that preceded them. If we concede that the rise of new forms of government are often accompanied by other significant (and interdependent) shifts at both higher and lower scales (e.g., households, boundary relations), then the analytical tasks in front of us seem all the more challenging.

Nevertheless, there has been tremendous progress in the study of the state during the last several decades. Recent archaeological surveys, large-scale excavations, the study of ancient households, and ethnohistoric breakthroughs, which have helped us to unravel some of the ideological changes that made new managerial formations possible, have enriched the empirical foundation necessary for examining this key societal transformation. In the Near East, South Asia, Egypt, North China, and sub-Saharan Africa, recent findings enable us to refine and improve our models as we expand our knowledge of the history of each of these regions. If these contributions continue apace (especially in the face of our dwindling, threatened archaeological record), and if a series of crucial definitional and theoretical challenges are met, the opportunity for taking giant steps forward in our understanding lies immediately ahead.

Men make their own history, but they do not make it just as they please; they do not make it under circumstances chosen by themselves, but under circumstances directly encountered, given and transmitted from the past.

K. Marx (1863)

SUGGESTED READINGS

Baines, J., and J. Málek. 1980. *Atlas of ancient Egypt.* New York: Facts on File. *A well-illustrated overview of ancient Egyptian civilization.*

Burenhult, G., ed. 1994. *Old World civilizations: The rise of cities and states.* New York: HarperCollins. *An amply illustrated compilation of essays focused on ancient Old World civilizations.*

Feinman, G. M., and J. Marcus, eds. 1998. *Archaic states.* Santa Fe, NM: School of American Research Press. *A stimulating collection of essays that highlights the diversity of ancient states.*

Garlake, P. S. 1973. *Great Zimbabwe.* London: Thames & Hudson. *A descriptive discussion of a key site in Africa.*

Kenoyer, J. M. 1998. *Ancient cities of the Indus Valley civilization.* Oxford: Oxford University Press. *A timely overview by an areal specialist.*

Murowchick, R. E., ed. 1994. *Cradles of civilization: China.* Norman: University of Oklahoma Press. *A well-illustrated collection of articles examining the early civilizations of China.*

Redman, C. L. 1978. *The rise of civilization: From early farmers to urban society in the ancient Near East.* San Francisco: W. H. Freeman. *A classic review of the ancient Near East.*

Wright, H. T. 1986. The evolution of civilizations. In *American archaeology, past and future,* ed. D. J. Meltzer, D. D. Fowler, and J. A. Sabloff. Washington, DC: Smithsonian Institution Press. *A comparative synthesis of long-term change in several world regions.*

Yoffee, N., and G. L. Cowgill, eds. 1988. *The collapse of ancient states and civilizations.* Tucson: University of Arizona Press. *A comparative collection of scholarly papers on collapse by experts from several disciplines.*

11

PREHISTORIC EUROPE

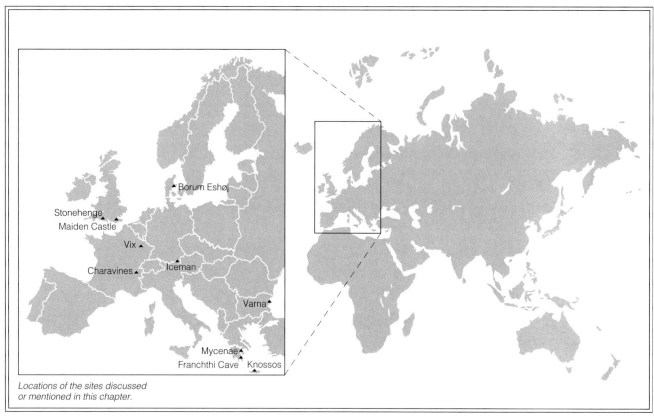

Locations of the sites discussed
or mentioned in this chapter.

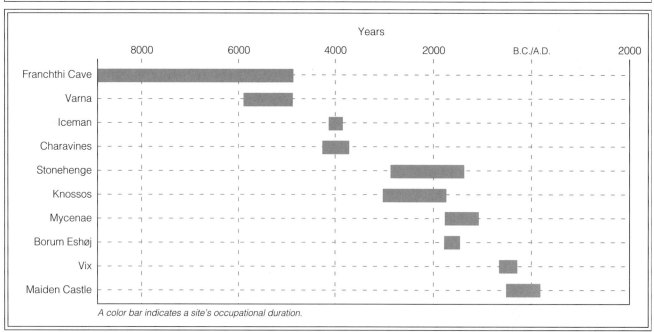

A color bar indicates a site's occupational duration.

FROM THE FIRST FARMERS TO THE ROMAN EMPIRE

A story in change

From the appearance of the first farmers to the historic events of the Roman conquest, the archaeology of the last 8000 years in Europe is a story of the spread of agriculture, technological innovation, and the development of economically and politically powerful groups. This period is of interest to us today because many of the basic tenets of western civilization come from prehistoric Europe. Languages, customs, traditions, forms of government, and many of our fundamental solutions to the uncertainties of the world emerged in Europe during this period. The period also interests us because, in the span of a few thousand years, we can trace the development of human societies from small, simple bands of hunter-gatherers to large, complex states with thousands of citizens.

Many major innovations—domesticated plants and animals, pottery, metallurgy, writing, and others—came to Europe from the Near East, appearing initially in the southeast and moving gradually to the north and west. Incipient farming communities appeared in the Aegean area and Greece, with domesticated plants and animals, architecture, and ceramics brought or borrowed from the Near East (Southwest Asia). Agriculture in southeastern Europe initially appeared shortly before 7000 B.C. and arrived in northwestern Europe around 4000 B.C.

Excavations at the site of Franchthi Cave in Greece document the introduction of agriculture to southeastern Europe at the end of the eighth millennium B.C. During the next millennium, farming and pottery followed two main pathways from Greece into Europe: by land into the center of the continent, and by sea along the north coast of the Mediterranean. The package of pottery, mud-brick houses, and domestic plants and animals was spread by 6500 B.C. via the Danube and other rivers to the Balkan Peninsula of southeastern Europe (Bulgaria, the present countries of the former Yugoslavia, Romania, and Hungary). In the other direction, distinctive Cardial pottery, decorated with the scalloped edge of a shell from the marine shellfish *Cardium*, wheat, and the bones of domesticated sheep appeared in caves and rockshelters along the Mediterranean shore after 6000 B.C. The coastal location and sporadic distribution of these sites suggest a spread of agricultural products arriving by sea.

The fifth millennium, 6000–5000 B.C., witnessed the flowering of Neolithic cultures in southeastern Europe—the appearance of large settlements, elaborate religious systems, copper mining, and extensive trade networks. Major sites, such as Starcevo outside of Belgrade in Serbia and Karanovo in Bulgaria, are known from large tells throughout the area. These sites contain numerous houses, elaborate pottery, and copper artifacts. Probably the oldest metal production in the world, copper was mined from rich deposits in Serbia and elsewhere; finished axes and copper jewelry were traded throughout Europe. The cemetery at Varna documents the extraordinary wealth in copper and especially gold that accumulated in southeastern Europe during this period.

During the sixth millennium B.C., agriculture continued to spread from the original two arms of expansion. The coastal branch moved inland from the Mediterranean

471

A schematic view of the spread of agriculture from the Near East into Europe.

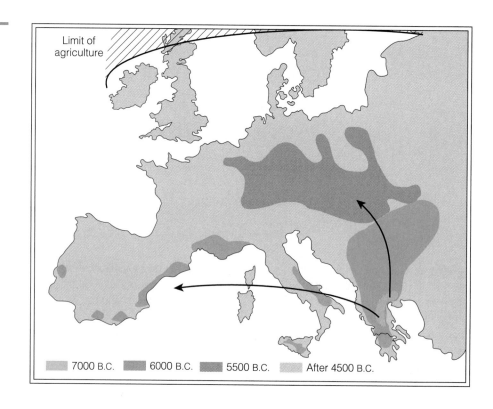

Limit of agriculture

7000 B.C.   6000 B.C.   5500 B.C.   After 4500 B.C.

A megalithic tomb in Denmark. The tomb itself lies under the capstone.

shore into Spain, France, and Italy. By 4000 B.C., farming communities were distributed across most of southern Europe. The Iceman came from one of these communities in northern Italy before he died at the top of the Alps. A number of very well preserved settlements, often described as lake dwellings, are known from Switzerland, France, and elsewhere during this period. The village of Charavines in southeastern France provides an extraordinary glimpse into the Neolithic because of the remarkable preservation of wood and other organic deposits at the site.

The other arm of agricultural expansion in Europe reached into central and eastern Europe during this same period. The first Neolithic communities in central Europe are known as **Bandkeramik,** or Linear Pottery. The Bandkeramik had its origin around 5500 B.C. in villages along the middle Danube and its tributaries in eastern Hungary. From this core area, farmers migrated east, north, and west, to the loess-covered valleys of central Europe to Belgium, southern Poland, and Ukraine. Within a period of a few hundred years around 5500 B.C., small farming villages appeared throughout this area. Although early farming adaptations spread westward very quickly from the Near East into southeastern Europe and the Mediterranean Basin, the first crops and domesticated animals did not appear in central Europe before 5500 B.C. What is impressive is the very rapid expansion of the Bandkeramik. The uniformity of the architecture, artifacts, burials, and settlement plan that characterizes these settlements is remarkable.

The end of the fifth millennium B.C. witnessed the spread of agriculture to northwestern Europe: the Netherlands, northern Germany, northern Poland, southern Scandinavia, and the British Isles. Neolithic farming societies in western Europe began to erect megalithic constructions—large, stone tombs and monuments such as Stonehenge. Across Europe, Neolithic groups began to develop local traditions as independent societies. In spite of such widespread traditions and increasing trade, conflict and warfare are documented in the increasingly defensive nature of settlement location.

The third millennium B.C. saw several major innovations from the farmers of Europe, including the introduction of bronze, new weapons, the wheel, draft animals and the plow and ox cart, the horse and chariot, and extensive maritime contacts.

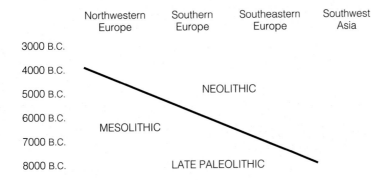

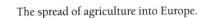

	Northwestern Europe	Southern Europe	Southeastern Europe	Southwest Asia	The spread of agriculture into Europe.

3000 B.C.

4000 B.C.

5000 B.C. NEOLITHIC

6000 B.C.

MESOLITHIC

7000 B.C.

8000 B.C. LATE PALEOLITHIC

Secondary animal products, such as milk and wool, become important for food and raw materials. Bronze first appeared in the form of weapons and jewelry and was largely in the possession of the elite. Bronze swords and spears must have provided a distinct military advantage. Trade and conflict appear to have escalated during this period as well.

The second millennium B.C. was important in the Aegean area. First on Crete, and later in Greece, Bronze Age lords directed powerful polities. The palaces of Knossos and Mycenae provide evidence of the vitality of these early states. The palace economy involved writing systems, craft specialization, taxation, and extensive trade networks. This commerce attracted goods and materials from most of temperate Europe to the Aegean. The second millennium B.C. was also the time of the Bronze Age north of the Alps. Large polities arose in those areas where raw materials and trade routes coincided. The elaborate tombs of elite individuals under large earthen mounds in southern England, the Czech Republic, Spain, and southern Scandinavia are evidence of local wealth and high status in these areas. The Danish site of Borum Eshøj provides examples of such tombs and the monuments of these societies.

The first millennium, from 1000 B.C. to the birth of Christ, is known as the Iron Age because of the introduction of this new metal. The classical civilizations of Greece and Rome arose in the Mediterranean region during this time. These literate polities are the subject of classical archaeology. North of the Alps, prehistory continued somewhat longer. In temperate Western Europe, Celtic and Germanic tribes with distinctive traditions and art styles were present during the Iron Age. The fortresses of these warrior societies, known by their Roman name **oppida**, centers of trade and warfare, dotted the landscape of western Europe. The princess burial at Vix in France documents the wealth and interaction of those Celtic elite; her tomb is located at the foot of Mont Lassois, one of the largest fortified towns of Celtic Europe. Iron Age sacrifices and executions preserved in the bogs of the north provide a startling glimpse of some of the inhabitants of that area.

The discipline and strength of the legions finally overwhelmed the Celts, or Gauls, as Julius Caesar and his successors carried the legacy of Rome to western Europe. The Iron Age fortress of Maiden Castle in southern England was razed in A.D. 43. Only those areas north and east of the Rhine River remained free of Roman rule and continued a tribal way of life for a short while longer. Eventually the spread of Christianity brought a new religion, and the literate priesthood recorded history, closing the prehistoric part of Europe's past.

FRANCHTHI CAVE

The arrival of the Neolithic in Europe

Franchthi Cave, on the coast of the Aegean in southern Greece.

A view down the "chimney" of Franchthi Cave at the excavations beneath.

Franchthi (fraunk'tee) Cave in southern Greece provides early evidence for the introduction of agriculture to the European continent. Today the cave is situated at the coast; in the early Holocene, however, the Aegean Sea was some distance from the cave, and a fairly level plain stood where its waters are now. Investigations at the cave led by Thomas Jacobsen, of Indiana University, revealed layers of trash and other debris that contained a detailed picture of human residence over the last 20,000 years. The early Mesolithic inhabitants of Franchthi exploited a wide range of terrestrial and marine resources at the end of the Pleistocene. Evidence for the hunting of red deer and other large game animals, the collecting of marine mollusks and land snails, and the use of several types of wild plants, including leafy greens, pistachio nuts, almonds, and various grasses, is found in the Upper Paleolithic deposits. The variety and seasonal availability of the foods at the site suggest that the cave may have been occupied year-round by 10,000 years ago.

Period	Sea Level	Proportion of Wild Animal Bones				Fish	Plants	Years B.P.
Late Mesolithic	−25 m	Deer			Pig	Large and common	Wild barley, vetch, and lentils	8500
Middle Mesolithic		Deer			Pig	Small and rare	Wild barley, vetch, and lentils	10,500
Early Mesolithic		Deer	Horse	Goat	Pig	Small and rare	Wild barley, vetch, and lentils	
Hiatus								
Late Paleolithic	−50 m	Deer	Horse	Cattle	Goat	—	Wild barley, vetch, and lentils	12,500
Upper Paleolithic	−90 m	Deer	Horse			—	—	22,000

The major layers at Franchthi Cave.

The Mesolithic levels at the site indicate an increasing reliance on the sea. The remains of tuna and the presence of obsidian document the seafaring abilities of the residents around 10,000 years ago. Bones from large tuna comprise about 50% of the animal remains in these cave layers. Measuring up to 2.5 m (8 ft) long and weighing up to 200 kg (450 lb), tuna live only in the deeper waters of the Aegean. The obsidian in some of the artifacts at Franchthi comes from the island of Melos, some 150 km (100 mi) away.

After 7000 B.C., domesticated plants and animals were present at Franchthi. Sheep and goats were abundant in the cave levels from this period, as well as domesticated wheats and barley. Red deer and tuna were less common among the animal remains. Plant species consumed earlier declined, including wild oats, pistachios, and barley. Some stone blades have **sickle polish** along their edges, a substance that remains when blades are used to cut the stems of plants such as grasses and reeds. The presence of sickle polish indicates that the inhabitants of the cave were harvesting plants in substantial quantities. Coriander seeds were also found among the plant remains. Coriander grows as a weed in cultivated or disturbed areas; its presence suggests that crops may have been cultivated. Finally, the lentils preserved from this level at Franchthi are large, the same size as the later domesticated variety.

The occupation area increased in size at this time. A terrace in front of the cave was now used for the houses of a small farming community with a population of perhaps 75 people. Contacts with other areas increased. New exotic materials such as marble appeared in the cave deposits for the first time. However, the introduction of domestic plants and animals, as well as pottery, did not disrupt all aspects of Franchthi Cave; there was some continuity in the previous way of life.

The domesticated plants and animals appeared rather suddenly at Franchthi and must have come from the Near East. There are several possible scenarios for this introduction of agriculture. One involves the influx of people bringing domesticates to Greece and the Aegean islands. Another possibility is the adoption of exotic domesticates and pottery by the indigenous peoples of southeastern Europe. It seems unlikely that the inhabitants of the cave would have changed completely with the arrival of the Neolithic. Perhaps the domesticated plants and animals were introduced by seafarers from Turkey or the Near East, looking for exotic materials to trade or exchange. Whatever the initial mechanism of introduction, these innovations initiated a series of changes that would eventually be felt throughout Europe. Within 3000 years of their first appearance in Greece, farming societies replaced hunter-gatherers across most of the European continent.

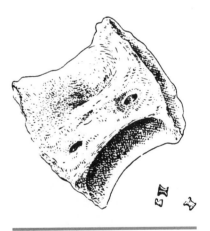

Evidence for deep-sea fishing at Franchthi Cave: bones from species such as tuna (top), which are much larger than those from earlier periods (bottom).

VARNA

Golden burials on the Black Sea coast of Bulgaria

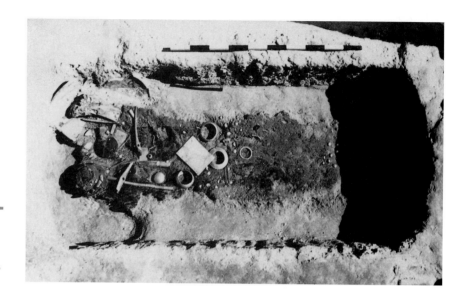

Grave 4 at Varna. This grave was a cenotaph, a grave without a skeleton, but it had an extraordinary amount of artifacts, including pottery, stone axes, and 320 pieces of gold.

Workers digging near the town of Varna on the coast of the Black Sea in 1972 uncovered several graves containing unusual metal objects. Thinking the metal was copper, they called in local archaeologists, who excavated the cemetery from 1973 to 1982. The discoveries at Varna have dramatically altered our impressions of early farmers in southeastern Europe because of the rare and valuable materials that accompanied the burials.

The cemetery contained at least 190 graves in an area of 6500 sq m (1.6 acres). The graves are simple rectangular pits with rounded corners, dug into the earth to varying depths, up to 3 m (almost 10 ft). Red ochre was spread over most of the burials. The "copper" the workers discovered was in fact gold, and more than 6 kg (about 14 lb) were found during the excavation of the cemetery. A wide range of other materials were found in the graves as well, including flint, obsidian, bone, clay, ochre, shell, graphite, marble, and copper. Impressions of decayed textiles could be seen on the walls of the graves and were preserved in some of the copper artifacts. Radiocarbon methods date the site to approximately 6500 B.C., contemporary with the Vinča culture in Yugoslavia.

The dead were buried with their head toward the Black Sea. Most of the burials were males, lying extended on their back. A few women were buried in a flexed position on their right side. There were no graves with children; the youngest individual in the cemetery was about 14 years old. The graves contained relatively few furnishings. Most male burials included a copper axe or pottery and flint tools; female graves held only a few ceramic pots. Almost 20% of the graves did not contain a body—a pattern seen elsewhere in the Neolithic of southeastern Europe. Most of these empty graves, or **cenotaphs**, contained only a few offerings, usually gold rings and copper axes.

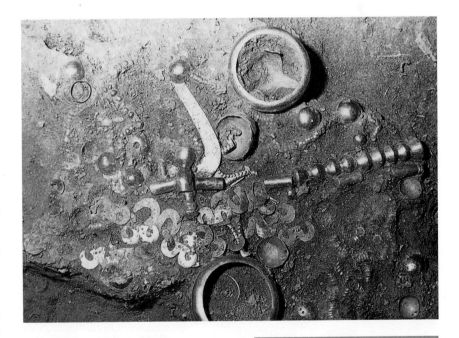

The earliest example of the use of gold for painting decorations on pottery at Varna.

Several of the graves were quite distinctive. Three empty graves contained life-size clay masks of human faces. Certain facial features, such as the teeth and decorations on the ear, chin, or forehead, were made from gold plaques. In addition, thousands of gold pins and beads of *Spondylus* and *Dentalium* shell, copper needles, marble drinking cups, figurines, and graphite-and-gold-painted pottery were found in these three "mask" graves. The graphite and gold ceramics are exceptional examples of the technological sophistication of the potters of this period. Graphite is applied as a powder to the burnished clay surface of the pottery and must be fired at a temperature of at least 1000°C (1800°F) to fix the graphite. Gold powder may have been applied to pottery in a similar fashion, but the exact technique is unknown.

Three other empty graves, numbered 1, 4, and 36 during the excavations, contained even more wealth. The offerings and grave goods were arranged in these tombs as though a body were present. Grave 1 contained 1225 gold objects weighing 2093 g (4.5 lb), in 15 groups. (At the price of gold today, the value would be roughly $1,000,000.) These items included two gold tubes and parts of the shaft of axes. Golden masks

Some of the contents of Grave 36 at Varna.

were found in several of the graves. Grave 36 included a solid gold axe and shaft, two gold bull effigies, 30 miniature golden horns, and various gold adornments and jewelry, a marble dish, four pottery vessels, and miscellaneous bone and flint tools.

Grave 4 contained 320 gold pieces weighing 1500 g (3.3 lb). The list of items in the grave is remarkable:

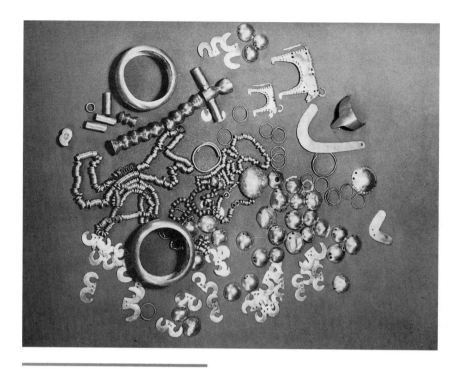

Some of the gold artifacts from Grave 36 at Varna, including an axe and shaft, two bull effigies, 30 miniature horns, and pieces of jewelry.

Some of the *Dentalium* shells, carnelian and other stone beads, and gold disks in Grave 1 at Varna.

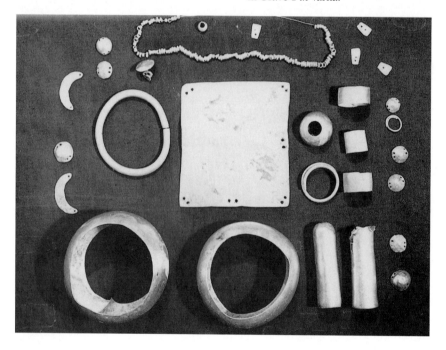

A stone axe of beautiful workmanship with a tubular gold shaft was placed as if at the right shoulder of the missing skeleton. Other grave goods included: a copper pick-axe of the same shape as found in the . . . copper [mines]; a shaft-hole axe; a flat axe; a chisel and awls [one with a preserved bone handle]; a dark green stone axe; an enormous flint blade [over 40 cm long]; oblong and rectangular breastplates of gold, having two small perforations in each corner; a circular convex gold disc 7 cm across, lying at the shoulder next to the golden shaft of the axe; one very large globular gold bead placed at the head; round gold earrings; a necklace of annular gold beads; three massive armrings of gold in the center of the grave; 41 circular convex discs of gold with perforations on the side, probably garment ornaments; and a mass of beads of *Spondylus* and *Dentalium* shell and of semi-precious orange, red, and black stone. At the head were a large gold-painted dish and vase and three other pots with lids. (Gimbutas, 1977, p. 48)

The graves at Varna provide spectacular evidence for **status differentiation** in the Neolithic of southeastern Europe. The different categories of people in this society were distinguished by the wealth that accompanied the burials. The rich graves may have been those of religious or political leaders or merchants. Certainly, the location of this important cemetery points to a role in trade and exchange. Varna is located at the shore of a former inlet from the Black Sea, perhaps a natural harbor, and near the mouth of the Danube River. Trade routes for gold, copper, obsidian, marble, shell, pottery, and many other items must have run through or very near this area. Such a strategic location may well have led to the rise of an elite at Varna and the accumulation of extraordinary amounts of wealth. The fact that the wealth of the living was buried with the dead is both a remarkable testimony to the complexity of Neolithic society in the Balkan peninsula and a boon for archaeology.

*A frozen mummy
from the Neolithic*

One of the most remarkable finds in the last century was made in 1991 in the high Alps, near the border between Austria and Italy. Hikers noticed a human body, half-frozen, face-down, in the snow and ice along the trail (Color Plate 26). The hikers contacted the authorities, who assumed it was the recent remains of an unfortunate mountaineer, as a number of people die in the Alps each year. The remains were somewhat carelessly removed from the ice and taken to a morgue. After inspection of the body and particularly the items found with the corpse, it became clear that this was not the result of a skiing accident—it was the frozen mummy of a man from the Stone Age.

The body was taken to the University of Innsbruck for study, and a wide range of scientists have been involved in the research. More than 150 specialists are examining all aspects of Ötzi the Iceman, as he has come to be known. The Iceman is the highest archaeological find in Europe, at 3200 m (10,500 ft). Sometime fairly soon after his death, snow buried his body; there are no traces of scavenging by birds or other animals. He is mummified, dried by the sun, wind, and ice of the mountaintops. Over time, a small glacier on the mountaintop expanded to cover the depression in which the Iceman lay. Amazingly, this thick, heavy layer of ice did not crush the body, but sealed it into the small depression for 6000 years, as if in a huge freezer. The glacier retreated during the warm summer of 1991 and exposed the corpse.

The extent of preservation of the body is remarkable, and most of the internal organs, as well as the eyeballs, are intact. Although the body was hairless from the effects of freezing and thawing, hair was found around the body. Tattoos were clearly visible on his back and right leg. X-rays revealed several broken ribs

(continued)

The body of the Iceman and his tools.

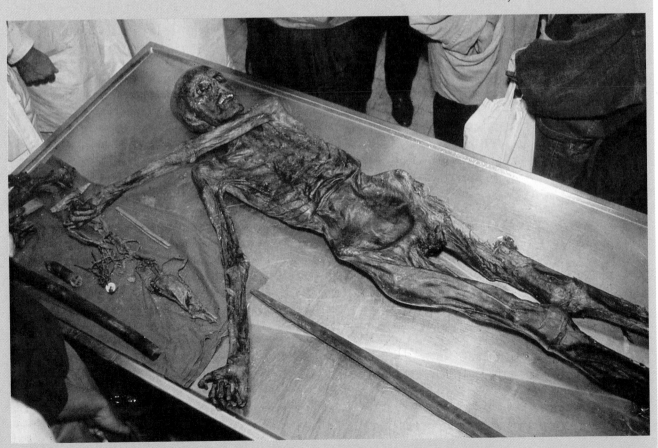

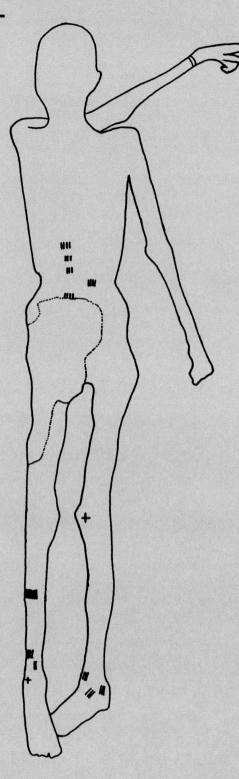

The location of tattoos on the body of the Iceman.

and indicate that the Iceman suffered from arthritis in his neck, lower back, and right hip. An absence of stomach contents and the presence of material in the large intestine indicate that he had not eaten for 8 hours. His last meal included unleavened bread, some greens, and meat. The Iceman was approximately 50 years old at the time of his death. Pollen analysis indicates the time of death between March and June. Radiocarbon dates from the body and the equipment the Iceman carried indicate an age of around 4300 B.C., clearly in the Neolithic period.

The Iceman was carrying a substantial amount of gear with him, consisting of seven articles of clothing and twenty items of equipment. The items were a bow and quiver of arrows, bow strings, bone points, a needle, a hafted copper axe, a wooden rucksack frame, two birch-bark containers, a hafted knife of flint and its sheath, several flint tools (including a scraper, an awl, a flake, and a tool for pressure flaking flint), a net (perhaps for catching birds), a piece of ibex horn, a marble pendant, and birch fungus (possibly used as medicine). Most of the arrows were unfinished; he carried several items that were incomplete or in need of repair. No food was found among his possessions. His clothing included a large belt with pouch, holding up a leather loincloth and skin leggings, a coat of deerskin, a cape of woven grass, a conical leather cap with fur on the inside and a chin strap, and shoes of calfskin filled with grass.

One of the more interesting finds is the copper axe; it is almost pure. This new metal documents the widespread use of copper during the latter half of the Neolithic period. Copper was being mined and smelted in several areas of eastern Europe by this time and traded as far as Scandinavia. There was also an unexpectedly high level of copper in the Iceman's hair.

The difficult questions about the Iceman include where he came from and how he died. He probably came from valleys to the south in Italy, less than a day's walk away. He carried a small ember of charcoal, for starting fires, that came from the wood of trees that grow south of the Alps. Pollen found in his intestines came from the hornbeam tree, which grew only to the south of the Alps. The grain of wheat attached to his clothing and his last meal suggest connections with farming villages. His lungs are black with the hearth smoke that filled early Neolithic houses.

Of the several theories about how the Iceman died in the high Alps, the two most likely involve either an accident or some kind of escape. He may well have been a shepherd in the mountains, caught by an early fall blizzard. The evidence suggests that he lay down in the depression where he was found, went to sleep, and froze to death. The cloak of grasses he wore is not atypical for shepherds in the Alps up to recent times. The lack of supplies, the broken ribs, and the obviously unprepared and damaged belongings indicate that he must have fled to this mountain refuge following some dispute or personal disaster. Analysis of a fingernail revealed interrupted periods of growth, suggesting that the Iceman underwent several periods of stress in the months before his death. Thus, the arthritic Iceman, under stress, and with several broken ribs, must have been in a weakened state before his death.

The Iceman is one of those rare finds in archaeology that attract enormous public attention because of the unusual conditions of preservation. The mysteries of the Iceman—how the body was preserved for so long, and how and why he died— add to the aura of intrigue surrounding the discovery. Equally important, however, is how much we are learning from the Iceman about the artifacts, clothing, and equipment of the Neolithic—and, perhaps, especially how those people were not very different from ourselves.

The Iceman has now been returned to the cold. His body today is displayed through a window in a freezer in a $1.9 million exhibit in a museum in northern Italy.

The Iceman's outerwear, made of grass and leather.

CHARAVINES

A Neolithic lakeside village

Preserved wooden posts on the lake floor at Charavines. The posts were exposed during low lake levels in 1906.

The past is also found under water. Underwater archaeological explorations have been going on for some time. Although survey and excavation conditions are more difficult, the exceptional preservation of organic materials often makes the effort worthwhile. Perhaps the most famous finds have been of Greek and Roman ships in the Mediterranean, but earlier Bronze Age shipwrecks are also well known. In fact, there have been underwater finds from every period of Euro-

pean prehistory. The Upper Paleolithic cave of Cosquer off the southern coast of France is one example. Numerous Mesolithic sites have been found off the coasts of Denmark and Sweden in the Baltic Sea. Several submerged Neolithic settlements have been discovered and excavated in Switzerland and France. Originally described as lake dwellings, these settlements were thought to have stood over the water on raised pilings. It is clear today, however, that the lake levels are

Underwater excavations at Charavines. Divers conducted the excavations using standard archaeological techniques.

higher now than in the Neolithic, and these villages, once along the shoreline, are now under water.

One of the best examples of such a Neolithic lakeshore settlement comes from the site of Charavines (shar'a-vans), located between Lyon and Grenoble in southeastern France. The site was originally observed in 1906 when the tops of hundreds of large wooden posts were seen under the water, approximately 100 m (330 ft) off the shore of Lake Paladru. Charavines was excavated by a team from the Institute for Alpine Prehistory at the University of Grenoble, headed by Amié Boquet. These excavations, under 2–4 m (7–13 ft) of water, lasted from 1972 through 1986 and produced a remarkable array of food remains and items of wood, bone, fiber, and other materials, preserved in the oxygen-deficient mud of the lake bottom. The finds from this site prompted Boquet to humorously suggest changing the other name for the Neolithic from the Stone Age to the "wood age." Hundreds of specialists have worked for years analyzing the various materials recovered in the excavations.

The excavations at Charavines revealed that there had been two major phases of occupation at this lakeshore. Each one lasted 20–25 years, separated

Artist's interpretation of the divers at work.

by about 3 years of abandonment more than 5000 years ago. This detailed information is based on dendrochronological analysis of the wooden beams used in house construction. Most of the beams have traces of bark remaining, so the date the trees were felled can be determined from the tree rings. Fir trees were felled during winter for timber to build the first

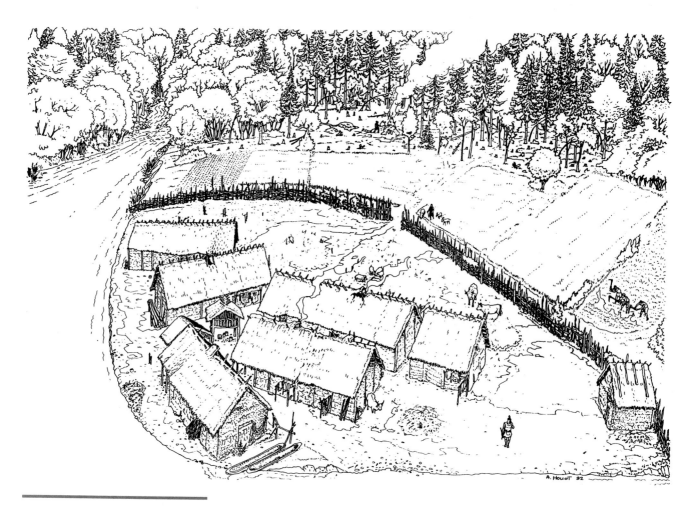

Artist's interpretation of the Neolithic village at Charavines around 3600 B.C. The age has been determined by dendrochronology.

two houses at Charavines; 9 years later, new posts were cut and used to rebuild the houses, and 8 years later they were rebuilt again.

The number of structures per settlement phase ranged from three to eight. The excavators were able to map the precise location of the houses, and their contents were preserved in the mud floors. Houses were large, 10–12 m (40–50 ft) long and 3–4 m (10–14 ft) wide. Low platforms of clay were built on the floors for the hearths. Different activity areas and trash dumps were apparent from the distribution of artifacts and other materials at the site.

The food remains are remarkable; millions of fruit pits, nutshells, and seeds have been collected. The excellent preservation provides an unusual opportunity to reconstruct the complete diet of a prehistoric people. The diet of the inhabitants of Charavines was varied and nutritious. The occupants practiced farming, collecting, hunting, and fishing to

obtain the foods they needed. A sizable portion of the diet came from wild sources.

The animal bones at Charavines provide evidence of meat in the diet. The bones from the later phase of settlement represent at least 504 animals from numerous species (Table 11.1). Although there are several domesticated animals, they represent fewer than 10% percent of the animals in the diet by weight. Wild animals provided the bulk of the meat portion of the diet.

The plant foods included a variety of dried or charred grains, seeds, nuts, berries, and fruits. More than 80 different species of plants were found in the deposits at Charavines, including 17 species of weeds. Cultivated plants included three kinds of wheat, barley, flax, and poppy. Several spices, including oregano and thyme, were present. Fruits, nuts, and berries included wild apples, strawberries, plums, grapes, sloe berries, acorns, walnuts, hazelnuts, pine nuts, and beech seeds. Other wild plants included carrots,

Table 11.1   The Distribution of Animals During the Later Occupation at Charavines, Based on 504 Individuals

	Percentage of Individuals	Percentage of Meat Used*	Wild or Domestic
Red deer	60.5%	61.0%	W
Wild boar	22.7	29.3	W
Goat	6.0	1.7	D
Sheep	5.0	1.7	D
Roe deer	4.5	1.3	W
Cattle	1.3	5.0	D

*Estimated meat obtained, assuming all animals were eaten.

Dried apples for storage. They were preserved among the materials from Charavines.

grapes, a material for tinder for fires, and wild roses.

Food-preparation techniques are clear from the preserved remains. Whole dried apples are preserved in the deposits at the site, along with baked breads and other materials. Cooking utensils such as wooden spoons and whisks, and baking stones for making bread, were also found. Both gardens and fields were used for growing plants. Small gardens next to the houses were used for herbs, spices, medicinal plants, and some vegetables. Agricultural fields were used for cereal crops of wheat and barley. Cultivating tools such as antler hoes were found in large numbers at the site.

A great deal of information on the technology of the inhabitants is preserved in the submerged layers at Charavines. The abundant wooden objects include bows and arrows; handles for axes, knives, and other tools; canoes and paddles; and planks for construction. Textiles and tools for cloth making are preserved as well, including spindle whorls for spinning yarn from wool and flax fiber, wooden combs used as weaving tools, and bone needles for sewing. Numerous pieces of rope and string were also found. Beads and pendants of shell, shist, calcite, and greenstone were also recovered.

Other items at Charavines document long-distance trade during the Neolithic. Some of the flint used for daggers comes from a source known as Grand Pressigny in northern France. An amber bead must have originally come from the shores of the Baltic, hundreds of kilometers to the north. Stone for a polished axe was brought from Switzerland or southwestern Germany. Clearly there were connections for trade and exchange across large areas of Europe, even during the Neolithic.

Prehistoric sites with preservation such as that at Charavines are rare, and for that reason all the more important. Certainly, the information gained in the recovery of this underwater treasure was well worth the time, effort, and money expended.

Two hafted flint knives.

THE MEGALITHS OF WESTERN EUROPE

Trademark tombs of the first farmers

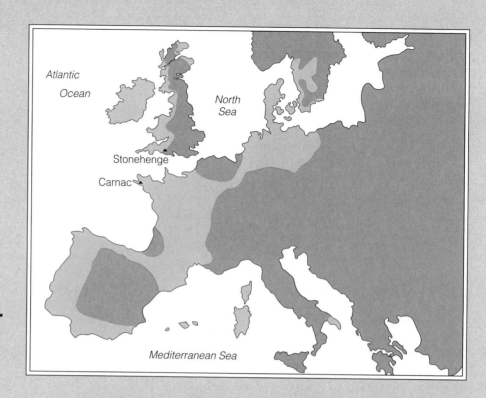

The distribution of megalithic tombs (shaded areas) in western Europe and the location of Stonehenge, England, and Carnac, France.

Agriculture spread to western and northern Europe at the beginning of the fourth millennium B.C. Almost immediately, farming societies began to erect structures made of massive stone slabs and boulders. These **megaliths,** as they are called, usually involved a burial area in or on the ground, surrounded by a chamber made of huge stones laid on top of one another without mortar. The entire stone tomb was then buried beneath a mound of earth to create an artificial cave. Often a covered passage at the edge of the mound provided an entrance for later use of the tomb.

Tens of thousands of these structures are found along the coast of the Atlantic Ocean and the North Sea, in Spain, Portugal, France, Belgium, the Netherlands, Ireland, Britain, Germany, Denmark, and Sweden. The megaliths are distributed in a curious, patchy pattern that defies current explanation. Different traditions of pottery and house construction were associated with these monuments; apparently different groups of people built the same kinds of tombs.

The absence of metal objects in these structures makes it clear that they predate the Bronze Age in western Europe. Radiocarbon dates indicate an age between 4000 and 2000 B.C., during the Neolithic. Most of the megalithic structures were built early in this period. Varying greatly in size and in the number of stones used for construction, they were all built to withstand the test of time—to last for many, many generations.

The megaliths fall into three major groups: menhirs, henges, and dolmens. **Menhirs** are large standing stones, erected either singly or collectively in linear arrangements. Standing stones, either intentionally shaped or selected as long narrow blocks to be set upright in the ground, occur in various heights, usually in the range of 1–5 m (3–15 ft). The largest known menhir comes from the town of Locmariaquer on the peninsula of Brittany in northwestern France. It

The largest series of aligned menhirs in Europe at Carnac. There are approximately 3000 standing stones at the site.

now lies on the ground, broken into five huge pieces. Originally this menhir was 23 m (75 ft) long, the height of a six-story building, and weighed at least 350 tons.

Perhaps the most impressive of the stone lines is found at Carnac, also in Brittany, where approximately 3000 large stones have been arranged in 13 parallel lines, stretching almost 6 km (4 mi) across the landscape. The stones are smaller at the eastern end of this arrangement, around 1 m (3 ft) high, and reach up to 4 m (13 ft) at the western end. The purpose of these linear arrangements is unclear, but they may have been intended to measure the cycles of the moon and predict eclipses. What is striking is that a smaller arrangement of wooden poles could easily have been used in place of such massive stone sentinels.

Henge monuments, or circles, are defined by an enclosure, usually a circular ditch and bank system, up to 500 m (1600 ft) in diameter. Not all henges contain stones; some appear to have been large timber structures. Stone circles, found primarily in the British Isles, are a special form of alignment with a definite astronomical significance. While the best known of these is at Stonehenge (see p. 490), hundreds of other stone circles dot the landscape of northern England and Scotland.

A **dolmen** is a megalithic tomb or chamber with a roof. Large stones and piles of earth were used to create these chambers. In spite of the enormous amount of labor required to obtain the stones and move them to the site of the tomb, the entire structure was often buried under a mound of earth. Megalithic dolmens range from small, single chamber structures to enormous hills of rock and soil that may hide a number of rooms and crawlways. Passage and gallery graves are two types of these larger tombs. A **passage grave** is entered via a long, low, narrow passage that opens into a wider room, generally near the center of the

(continued)

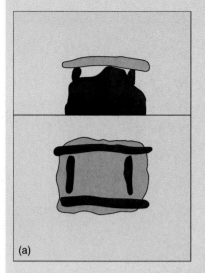

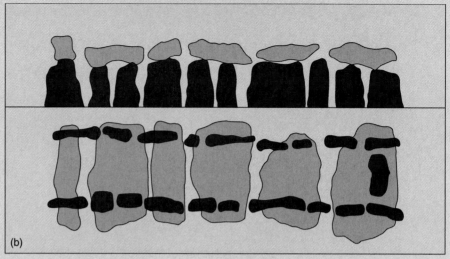

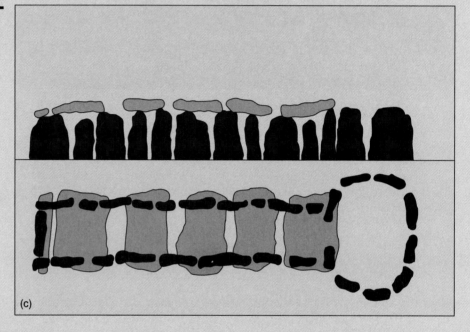

The three major types of megalithic tombs in western Europe: (a) dolmen, (b) gallery grave, and (c) passage grave.

structure. A **gallery grave,** or long tomb, lacks an entrance passage, and the burial room or rooms form the entire internal structure.

The earliest examples of megalithic tombs come from Brittany, dating to around 4000 B.C., at the time of the transition to agriculture in this area. The first large tombs in Scandinavia at about the same time were earthen long **barrows,** or mounds, with a single log tomb inside, apparently imitating the plan of a Neolithic house. These earthen structures,

intended for the burial of a single individual, could be transformed into larger, stone chambers for the collective burial of several individuals. Some of the tombs had a movable stone door that could be opened to permit the interment of new bodies. Remains of the previous occupants were pushed to the sides to make room. These tombs may have been intended for all the members of a related group of farmsteads or hamlets; the tomb symbolized the collective and cooperative nature of the group.

These tombs served an important purpose for the living, as well. Such "cults of the dead" likely involved both ancestor worship and property rights. Elaborate burial ritual and monument construction integrated the cult. Ancestor veneration may have supported claims to agricultural fields for local communities of farmers. The construction of a permanent burial monument provides dramatic evidence of one's tenure in place and the inheritance of rights to the land.

Part of the ritual associated with a cult of the dead apparently dictated that burials be placed in large stone tombs after lengthy ceremonies and activities elsewhere. Only the bones of the deceased were placed in the tombs; the flesh had decomposed or had been removed prior to entombment. The tombs do not appear to have been major repositories for wealth or elaborate furnishings for the dead. Grave goods are rare; usually only a few pots, stone tools, and bones are found. There is, however, evidence that pottery vessels with food and drink were regularly placed at the entrance of the tombs in ceremonial offerings for the deceased.

Megalithic structures provide dramatic and enduring evidence of the impact of agriculture on the inhabitants of western Europe. Construction of monumental architecture is one clue to the increasing complexity of societies in this area. Shortly after farming was adopted, a pronounced trend toward regionalization appeared. In spite of the evidence of a widespread cult such as megalithic burials, various regional styles in material culture arose in conjunction with the fortification of settlements and increasing evidence for warfare. It appears that more distinct and delineated societies were identifying themselves across the continent, and this pattern continued into the succeeding Bronze Age and Iron Age.

A model of the relationship between type of tomb, grave goods, and population density in Neolithic Denmark. Megalithic tombs occur in areas with higher population clustering; more grave goods occur in areas with fewer people.

STONEHENGE

A temple to the sun on England's Salisbury Plain

The most impressive prehistoric monument in the British Isles, and perhaps all of Europe, is Stonehenge on the Salisbury Plain in southern England. Stonehenge holds an enormous fascination, as much for the mysterious aura that surrounds it as for the impressive feat of construction. Some of the stones have been taken away over the centuries; many have fallen and lie half-buried in the earth. Other stark, brooding, gray stones still stand, arranged in the circles and arches that outline this "observatory"

and ceremonial center of late Neolithic and Bronze Age Britain.

The construction and elaboration of Stonehenge took place over a period of 1500 years, from approximately 3000 to 1500 B.C. On the one hand, Stonehenge was rebuilt almost continuously during this period, changing in purpose and function. At the same time, the previous constructions remained visible to subsequent generations and were respected as part of the continuity of the monument from beginning to end. This area of the

An aerial view of Stonehenge, with the Aubrey holes in the background.

What is Stonehenge: it is the roofless
*   past;*
Man's ruinous myth; his uninterred
*   adoring*
Of the unknown in sunrise cold and red;
His quest of stars that arch his doomed
*   exploring.*

And what is Time but shadows that were
*   cast*
By these storm-sculptured stones while
*   centuries fled?*
The stones remain; their stillness can
*   outlast*
The skies of history hurrying overhead.
                              Siegfried Sasson (1961)

490

The megalithic monument that is Stonehenge, on the Salisbury Plain in southern England.

Salisbury Plain must have held a fascination for its prehistoric inhabitants as well. In addition to the focus on Stonehenge, the landscape around the site is filled with tombs and monuments to the dead.

The earliest stage of the monument was built between 3000 and 2900 B.C. It consisted of a circular bank and ditch, almost 100 m (330 ft) in diameter, cut into the chalk of the subsoil. The bank on the inside of the circle would have stood almost 2 m (6 ft) high, piled up with material dug from the ditch. It is probable that a wooden palisade was erected along the bank in the fashion of other causewayed enclosures known in England at this time. A broad entrance

to the circle lay on the northeast side with two smaller ones to the south. Inside this circle and bank were dug the 56 "Aubrey" holes, named after their seventeenth-century discoverer, regularly spaced around the perimeter. These holes were filled shortly after their original excavation, and their purpose is unknown.

During a second stage of construction, until 2500 B.C., the monument was extensively remodeled. The major addition was the construction of a circle of upright timbers or posts in the center of the monument. Similar structures, known as wood henges, have been found in other parts of the Salisbury Plain from this period. The entrances were elaborated and one of the southern entrances

Stonehenge A

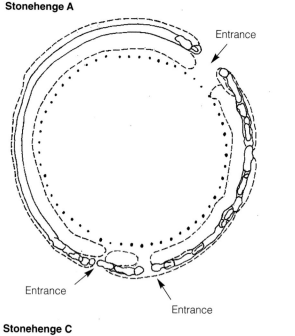

Entrance

Entrance

Entrance

Stonehenge B

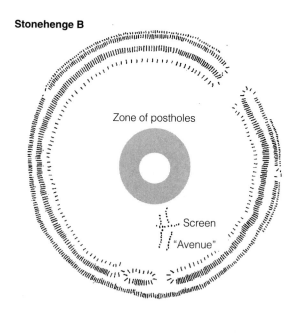

Zone of postholes

Screen

"Avenue"

Stonehenge C

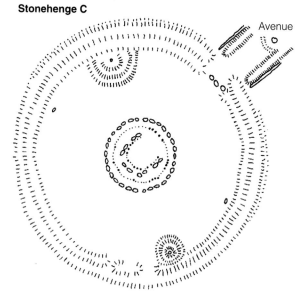

Avenue

Stonehenge D

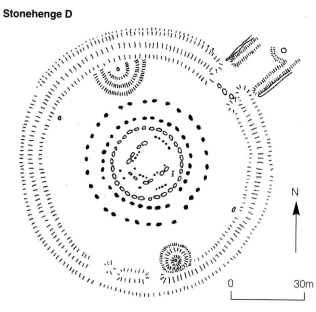

N

0   30m

Four major stages in the construction of Stonehenge: (a) causewayed enclosure with an internal palisade, ca. 3000–2900 B.C.; (b) a timber construction with avenue and screen and central zone of postholes, 2900–2500 B.C.; (c) the major stone structure, 2500–1600 B.C.; and (d) final phase with two rings of pits surrounding the central stones, 1600–1500 B.C.

was closed. A short "avenue" of wooden posts was added toward the southern entrance, and a substantial timber screen was built across it to block the view to the center. Cremation burials were placed in a few of the depressions and also in the bank and ditch areas around the perimeter of the monument.

The third stage of construction involved a series of major additions between 2500 and 1600 B.C. The timber circle at the center of the monument was replaced with stone in a series of episodes. A circle of carefully shaped pillars and lintels of Sarsen sandstone was

erected in the center. Huge columns of this sandstone were quarried as far away as 30 km (20 mi), shaped into pillars, and dragged to the site. Five **trilithons** (two upright pillars with a crosspiece on top) of Sarsen stone were erected in a horseshoe-shaped arrangement open toward the northeastern entrance. One of these trilithons is distinctly taller than the other four, standing 8 m (25 ft) high. The lintel on this trilithon is 5 m (16 ft) long and over 1 m (3 ft) thick. The larger Sarsen pillars weigh as much as 50 tons (equivalent to a loaded train car) and were likely moved on oak rollers. A system of scaffolding was probably used to raise the stones into position. The individuals involved in the various construction phases of Stonehenge must have numbered in the hundreds or thousands.

Two parallel, crescent-shaped rows of standing bluestones were erected in the center of the circle, along with several upright stones. This blue-tinted volcanic dolerite came from a source some 250 km (150 mi) distant in the Prescelly Mountains of southern Wales. Certainly, part of their journey was by water, but the movement of such large stones was a major accomplishment in itself. More standing stones were added near the entrance and inside the periphery of the ditch. Slightly later, a new circle of standing bluestones was placed inside the horseshoe of trilithons. In the final stage of construction, a ring of bluestone pillars was raised inside the Sarsen circle, but outside the horseshoe. In addition, two rings of large holes were dug around the outer circle. These may have held standing stones that are now missing.

An "avenue" some 500 m (1600 ft) long and 15 m (50 ft) wide, flanked on either side by an earthen ditch and bank, was constructed running to the northeast from the circle of Stonehenge, leading to the River Avon. This avenue runs through one of the densest concentrations of prehistoric burial monuments in England. The Heel Stone was brought to the site at this time and erected in the avenue about 10 m (33 ft) from the northeastern edge of the circle. This irregular boulder rises almost 5 m (16 ft) above ground level and weighs at least 35 tons (equivalent to an 18-wheel truck).

Stonehenge functioned in part as an observatory to record the summer solstice. On the 21st or 22nd of June each year, the dawn sun rises directly over the Heel Stone. When the weather is clear, the new sunlight passes across the Heel Stone and through the double standing stones at the entrance, bisects the two horseshoes of standing stones, and reaches the altar stone in the very center of the circle. Today the sun just misses the exact top of the Heel Stone as a result of small changes in the earth's axis since construction. This shift was used by the Royal Astronomer, Sir Norman Lockyer,

Construction technique at Stonehenge. Wooden scaffolding was probably used to raise the lintel stone into place.

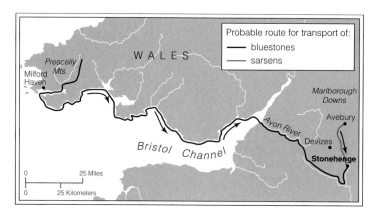

Probable routes of transport for bluestones from the Prescelly Mountains in Wales and Sarsen stone from near Avebury to Stonehenge.

in 1905 to estimate the age of the monument as 1900 B.C., an accurate prediction made many years before other methods of absolute dating were available.

Some have argued that Stonehenge was an astronomical computer, used to record various lunar and stellar alignments. One of the more popular theories is that the circle of stone and holes could have been used to predict lunar eclipses. There is no strong evidence, however, for any alignments other than the summer solstice.

The last stage of Stonehenge reflects its declining use in the period between 1600 and 1500 B.C. Two concentric rings of pits were added around the stone circles in the middle of the monument. Their function is unknown. In addition, several carvings were added to the trilithons, including a depiction of a bronze dagger.

Stonehenge has been a problem for British archaeology in recent years. Although a mecca for tourists to England, just behind the Tower of London in popularity, the wear and tear wrought by visitors has led to more careful regulation of the monument grounds. Years of postwar tourism had dire consequences—inquisitive fingers had worn down the engravings on the stones, and the weight borne by millions of feet had worn the ground down to the chalk bedrock. At the summer solstice in late June, huge festivals celebrated the summer as present-day Druids welcomed the sunrise. Today, most of the monument is not directly accessible; walkways direct the visitor past the mute sentinels of the past. While such means of protection distance the

visitor from the stones, they do serve to help ensure that Stonehenge and its heritage will remain for the future as a monument to and from the ancient Britons.

Locations of important Minoan and Mycenaean sites in the Aegean region.

The wine dark waters of the Aegean Sea bathe the shores of Turkey to the east and Greece to the north and west. The long, mountainous island of Crete marks the southern border of this part of the sea, which is splattered with small rocky and volcanic islands. These islands, actually the summits of a submerged mountain range, generally have thin, poor soil and a dry climate.

These rugged, barren conditions may have held a hidden benefit for the early inhabitants. The absence of large areas of fertile farmland meant that crops other than cereals had to be cultivated. Wheat could be grown in more sheltered areas with deeper soils, but grapes, olive trees, and sheep flourished on the rocky slopes of the islands. Olives are remarkably nutritious and provide oil that can be burned, rubbed on, cooked, or eaten. Grapes are not only a delicious fruit, but their fermented juice makes wine. Oil, wine, and wool became important exports for the economies of these small

islands. The inhabitants must have also relied on the sea for fish and other foods; sailing and a knowledge of the sea would have been essential.

Seafaring and trade permitted the movement of goods and foods between islands, and between the islands and the mainland. The strategic location of Crete and the Aegean islands along the main avenues of sea trade enabled the inhabitants to become the middlemen in moving goods between the civilizations of Egypt and the Near East and the settlements of Europe.

The demand for wine, olive oil, pottery, textiles, and other goods enhanced the economic well-being of the people of the Aegean islands. A pattern was apparently established rather early in which raw materials were taken to the islands and made into finished products. Craftworkers used the potter's wheel to make fine ceramic vessels. Others carved stone, bone, and ivory seals for economic transactions, produced wooden tools, sculpted

(continued)

figurines and bowls of marble, obsidian, and other colorful stones, or created jewelry and other luxury items. After 3000 B.C., the craftworkers of the Aegean also began to make objects of metal: bronze, silver, and gold. Smiths produced bronze tools and weapons by the thousands for both local use and export. This metal was the signature material of the Bronze Age, and its production was one of the primary reasons for the growth of economic and political power in the Aegean region.

The discovery and use of metals in the Old World was a relatively slow process. A few small pieces of copper, in the form of jewelry, appeared in the Near East by 7000 B.C. at early Neolithic sites. This was native copper, simply hammered from its original shape into a new form. The melting and casting of copper began in southeastern Europe and the Near East shortly before 4000 B.C. Copper mines were opened in Yugoslavia, and various copper artifacts, primarily axes and jewelry, found their way throughout much of Europe. Gold objects also began to appear during the fourth millennium B.C.

Bronze was discovered, probably by accident, shortly before 3000 B.C. Bronze is a mixture of copper and tin or arsenic. Copper ores sometimes naturally contain arsenic. In all likelihood, early smiths discovered that those ores that included arsenic produced a slightly harder material which was easier to cast. Further experimentation must have led to the discovery of tin as another alloy, and bronze metallurgy had begun. Bronze has several advantages over copper. It can be recycled repeatedly, whereas copper loses its tensile strength in recasting. Bronze holds an edge much better than copper, and most of the early bronze objects were weapons: swords, daggers, spearheads, and arrowheads.

The advent of metallurgy, first of copper and then of bronze, silver, and gold, greatly increased trade and the movement of goods throughout the Aegean region and the rest of Europe. Much

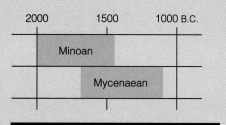

A chronology of the Minoans and the Mycenaeans.

of Europe was involved in the movement of materials and goods into the economic magnet of the eastern Mediterranean.

The Aegean Bronze Age dates to about 3000–1000 B.C., ending with the beginning of the Iron Age and the rise of the classical Greek civilization of Plato and Homer. There were two major centers of development and power in the Aegean: one on Crete and one on mainland Greece. The civilization that emerged on the island of Crete was known as the Minoan and reached its peak between 2000 and 1450 B.C. During this period, the Minoans dominated the Aegean through sea power and the control of trade in the eastern Mediterranean. The seats of power on Crete were in palaces and villas, residences of the local rulers who directed this early state. Defensive fortifications were not needed by the islanders, because they were protected by their ships.

Three different writing systems were used on Crete, including an early hieroglyphic system, replaced around 1700 B.C. by a system known as Linear A, which is still undeciphered. A second writing system, Linear B, has been decoded and is related to the archaic Greek language. Linear B was developed on mainland Greece and later introduced to Crete by the Mycenaeans.

The Mycenaeans on mainland Greece controlled most of the Aegean between 1600 and 1100 B.C. and took over Crete after 1450 B.C. The Mycenaean civilization was dominated by a series of hilltop

(a)

(b)

(c)

(d)

Pictographic scripts, used in early writing in the Aegean area. These tablets are from Crete and show both Linear A and Linear B systems: (a) Linear A, with a four-wheeled wagon; (b) Linear B, with sword, chariot, and horse; (c) Linear B, describing the issue of a set of armor; and (d) Linear B, counting gold cups and bull's head drinking vessels.

fortresses, or **citadels**, interconnected by roads. These citadels were ruled by powerful warrior-kings, whose graves are among the richest ever uncovered in Europe. Episodic alliances among the citadels led to greater political, economic, and military power, and the Mycenaeans became the major force in the Aegean after 1500 B.C. The collapse of Mycenaean power and the abandonment of the heavily fortified citadels after 1100 B.C. is one of the most intriguing mysteries of Aegean archaeology.

The Bronze Age in the Aegean marks a watershed in the prehistory of Europe. In the Mediterranean Basin, early civilizations rose in the Aegean, on mainland Greece, and later on the peninsula of Italy. These societies were literate and ruled by kings; they inhabited large towns, kept armies and navies, collected taxes, and established laws. These states controlled trade over large areas and extracted a variety of raw materials and other products from the rest of Europe.

North of the Alps, there was much less political integration; societies operated at a tribal or chiefdom level, on a smaller scale. This pattern continued essentially until the Roman conquest of France and much of Britain, shortly before the birth of Christ. The Romans introduced writing systems and true statecraft into northwestern Europe for the first time. Prehistory ended much earlier south of the Alps, where the literate civilizations of Greece, in the first half of the first millennium B.C., and of Rome, in the second half, dominated the Mediterranean Basin.

KNOSSOS

*The mythical halls
of the Minotaur
on the island of Crete*

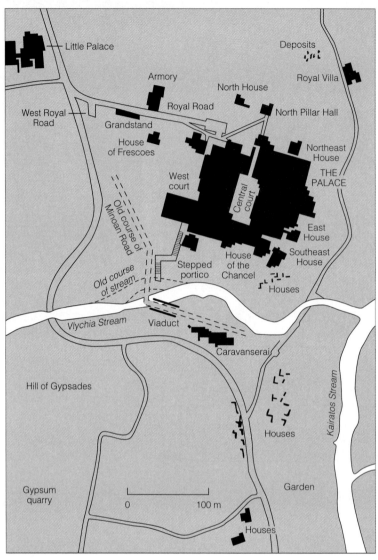

The plan of Knossos around 1900 B.C., including the palace, several adjacent mansions, smaller houses, and other buildings, along with a system of paved roads. The original settlement at this location was a Neolithic village at the junction of the two streams.

Sir Arthur Evans, the keeper of the Asmolean Museum in Oxford, England, traveled to Crete in 1894 and discovered an extensive group of ruins, buried under a low mound of soil and collapsed walls, at a place known as Knossos (kuh'nos-sus). Beginning in 1900, Evans spent the remaining 35 years of his life excavating at Knossos. He restored many of the areas he had excavated, rebuilding the walls and repainting the plaster in the vivid colors that had been preserved in the ruins. Today, the palace that he uncovered is a monument to his labor and his vision of the restoration.

The first Bronze Age palace at Knossos was erected around 3000 B.C. on top

of 7 m (22 ft) of Neolithic deposits that had accumulated for several thousand years. A series of palaces were built on top of one another, each larger and more elaborate, as the settlement and administrative structure grew. Knossos covers almost 25,000 sq m (6 acres, an area the size of a large basketball arena), in a complex of buildings and construction that included the palace itself, several surrounding large mansions, and many smaller houses, connected by roads.

The palaces were the centers of the Minoan state, laid out and built according to plan, with a large, rectangular central court surrounded by myriad rooms, numerous corridors, a maze of courtyards, grand staircases, private apartments, administrative chambers, enormous storerooms, baths, and even a sophisticated plumbing system. The complex of rooms and buildings housed many of the administrative, economic, and religious functions of the government. Many important craft workshops were also located in the palace or housed in adjacent buildings. Functional space was carefully designed and separated according to residential, administrative, storage, religious, and manufacturing uses. The palace was a multistory building with extensive storerooms. Long, narrow rooms held enormous storage jars, or *pithoi,* along the walls for oils, wine, and other liquids, and stone-lined pits in the floor were filled with wheat and other cereals. It is clear from this arrangement that the palace complex controlled the economic activities of the state.

Frescoes and murals decorated the walls of the palace, depicting various aspects of Minoan life. Shrines are scattered throughout the palace as well, documenting the integration of church and state in the early Aegean civilizations. Much attention has been focused on the open-bodice costumes of the goddesses and the acrobatic bullfighters who are often depicted. Religious ceremonies appear to have combined several elements, including the bull, a sacred axe, and snakes.

The extensive network of trade that was directed from Knossos and other Minoan centers is evidenced by the variety of raw materials found in the palace: copper from Cyprus and Turkey; ivory, amethyst, carnelian, and gold from Egypt; lapis lazuli from Afghanistan; amber from Scandinavia. These commodities, and the Cretan ships that carried them, were the foundation of the wealth and power of the Minoan state. The Egyptians feared the "great green sea," yet the sturdy Minoan ships, with their deep keels and high prows, weathered the storms of the Mediterranean and controlled the sea lanes.

The palace of Knossos was destroyed at least twice during its history. The first destruction, in 1700 B.C., was marked by extensive wall collapse and evidence of a major fire. Many of the

A portion of the reconstructed palace at Knossos, Crete, showing a street and the facade of a building.

other palaces and villas on Crete show evidence of similar destruction at the same time; it seems clear that a major earthquake must have occurred. Most of the palaces were rebuilt following this episode of destruction. The second period of destruction at Knossos dates to approximately 1450 B.C. and marks the end of the Minoan civilization. The palace was reoccupied following this episode, but the pottery and other artifacts indicate that Mycenaeans from the mainland were in control. Other palaces on Crete also were destroyed at this time, but not simultaneously, as in 1750 B.C. The reason for this last episode of destruction and the collapse of the Minoans is less clear but probably involves the growing power of the Mycenaeans.

Basement storerooms at Knossos. These palace basements were warehouses with storage pits in the floor for grains and huge storage jars, or *pithoi,* for liquids along the walls.

MYCENAE

*Fortress of the warrior-kings
of Bronze Age Greece*

An aerial photograph of the citadel of
Mycenae in Greece. The grave circles
are in the foreground.

*Not even those who lived long ago before
us and were sons of our lords, the gods,
themselves half-divine, came to an old
age and the end of their days without
hardship and danger, nor did they live
forever.*

Simonides, in Vermeule (1972)

The Bronze Age in Europe, and its accompanying weaponry, ushered in a period of conflict and warfare in which the
skills, attitude, and power of the military
seemed to take precedence over other
aspects of society. A new warrior class
emerged during this period; weapons
and armor were the primary burial
goods, and martial and hunting scenes
dominated decorative art. A military
presence is strongly visible in the Bronze
Age citadels of southern Greece, the
"halls of the heroes." These are the people, so vividly described in *The Iliad* of
Homer, who sailed to Troy on the west
coast of Turkey, and eventually sacked
the city around 1250 B.C. This is the civilization of Agamemnon and Ulysses.
These early Greeks gradually wrested
power away from Crete and the Minoans
and came to dominate the Aegean between 1600 and 1100 B.C., a time known
as the Mycenaean period in prehistoric
archaeology.

The citadels, of which the site of Mycenae (my-seen'ee) is the best known,
were fortified palace towns, located on
high, defendable points on the landscape. The early rulers of the citadel of
Mycenae were buried in **shaft graves,**
pits 6–8 m (20–25 ft) deep, cut into
the soft rock of their hilltop settlement.
Groups of shaft graves were enclosed in
a circle of standing limestone slabs. Two
such grave circles have been excavated at
Mycenae, and several tombs were found
in each shaft. The walls of the tombs
were lined with brick or stone, and the
entire structure was covered with a timber roof. At a later date the shaft was reopened and another tomb added. A total
of 19 individuals were buried in the six
shaft graves of grave circle A at Mycenae,
two to five people in each shaft. There
were nine men, eight women, and two
children.

The grave goods from Mycenae are
among the most spectacular finds from

the Bronze Age. The graves included precious metals and stone in the form of weapons, vessels, masks, and other objects. One early grave in these tombs contained more than 5 kg (11 pounds) of gold. There are gold and bronze masks and drinking cups, necklaces, earrings, a crystal bowl carved in the shape of a goose, and swords and daggers with gold and lapis inlays. Ninety swords were found in the graves of three individuals. Amber from northern Europe, ivory from Africa, silver from Crete, glass from Egypt, and great amounts of gold were entombed along with these early rulers. In addition, the corpses were apparently covered with hundreds of leaves, flowers, butterflys, and stars cut from thin sheets of gold.

Heinrich Schliemann, excavator of the graves, described opening one of the shafts in a letter to a friend in 1876:

> There are in all five tombs, in the smallest of which I found yesterday the bones of a man and a woman covered by at least five kilograms of jewels of pure gold, with the most wonderful archaic, impressed ornaments; even the smallest leaf is covered with them. To make only a superficial description of the treasure would require more than a week. Today I emptied the tomb and still gathered more than $^{6}/_{10}$ kilogram of beautifully ornamented gold leafs; also many earrings and ornaments representing an alter with two birds. . . . There were also found two scepters with wonderfully chiselled crystal handles and many large bronze vessels and many gold vessels. (Quoted in Vermeule, 1972, p. 86)

Schliemann was convinced that he had found the gold death mask and body of Agamemnon, who was murdered by his wife's lover when he returned from the conquest of Troy (see Color Plate 27). Although that individual was probably not Agamemnon, and the mask may well have been a forgery brought in by Schliemann, the contents of the graves of Mycenae

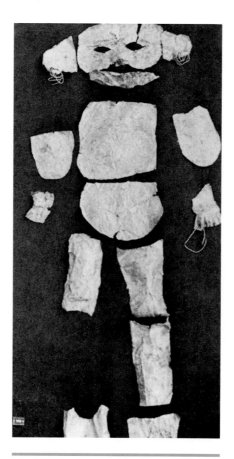

A gold suit placed over a buried child at Mycenae. Gold masks were placed on the faces of several of the individuals buried here and at other Mycenaean sites.

clearly document the wealth of this civilization and its rulers.

By 1400 B.C., a new kind of grave, the vaulted, beehive-shaped *tholos* **tomb**, was constructed for the major rulers. Several of these architectural wonders still stand today. The Treasury of Atreus at Mycenae is the finest example of a *tholos* tomb. The roof of the vault stands more than 13 m (40 ft) above the floor and is 15 m (50 ft) in diameter. The dramatic doorway to the tomb is 5 m (16 ft) high, and the lintel across the door weighs more than 100 tons. Unfortunately, the contents of the tomb were stolen long ago.

Many large and small settlements from this time period were scattered across southern Greece. A sophisticated system of graveled roads for chariots and carts, with stone bridges and culverts, connected the towns and villages. Mycenaean towns were heavily fortified with walls known as **Cyclopean stone walls** because of their massive size. Major citadels from this period are known from Mycenae itself, Tiryns, Pylos, and Thebes. At the citadel of Tiryns, the great walls are 15 m (50 ft) thick with internal passages.

At Mycenae, the hilltop was leveled and terraced to accommodate the walls of the fortress as well as the inhabitants of the palace and town. A long, narrow road, flanked by high stone walls, leads up to the Lion Gate, the entrance to the citadel, so named because of the enormous stone sculpture of two lions that crowns the gate. The monumental stone walls of Mycenae encircle an area 1100 m (3500 ft) in diameter (the equivalent of two city blocks), enclosing the palace of the king as well as a number of residences and other structures. The Mycenaean palaces combined many of the administrative, military, and manufacturing functions of the kingdom within the residence of the ruler. Workshops for crafts, guardrooms, storerooms, and kitchens were attached to the rear of the palace. There was a small postern gate at the back of the citadel. During a siege, fresh water was available from a cistern, located at the bottom of a rock-cut tunnel and staircase deep inside the hill of Mycenae.

The surrounding villages supplied plant foods and meat, men and materials, to the lord of the citadel. This information comes from preserved clay tablets with Linear B script. In some instances, these soft clay tablets were burned in fires that swept the citadels and hardened the clay, thereby preserving the script. The subjects of the texts are primarily economic, dealing with inventories, shipments, and quotas of items to be paid to the palace in tribute. At the palace of Pylos, where a major hoard of tablets was preserved, a list of different occupations in the kingdom was recorded: bakers, bronzesmiths, carpenters, heralds, masons, messengers, potters, shepherds, and "unguent boilers." Many other skills are also evidenced

The entrance to a *tholos* tomb, in which the later kings of Mycenae were buried. This example at Mycenae is called the Treasury of Atreus and dates to 1400 B.C.

in the artifacts and architecture of the citadel, such as delicate ivory carving, fresco painting, metal inlaying, and weapons manufacturing.

The reason for the collapse of Mycenaean civilization remains a mystery. Unrelated to drought or outside conquest, perhaps it was simply the result of a culmination of centuries of conflict and competition. After 1100 B.C., Athens began to assert its importance in Greece as the center of a new industry of ironmaking, and the citadels of the Mycenaeans fell into ruin. The beginning of the Iron Age civilization in classical Greece, 600–300 B.C., gave rise to the golden age of Athens, the exploits of Pericles, the wisdom of Socrates and Plato, the inventions of Archimedes, the writings of Homer, and the foundations of much of Western civilization.

THE BRONZE AGE NORTH OF THE ALPS

Innovation and growing populations

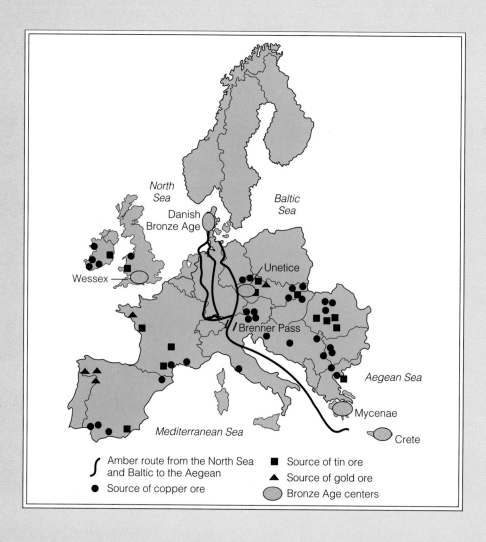

The major sources of gold, copper, tin, and amber in Europe and some of the trade routes to the Mediterranean. Three of the major centers of the Bronze Age north of the Alps were in southern England, Denmark, and the Czech Republic.

Map labels: North Sea, Baltic Sea, Danish Bronze Age, Unetice, Wessex, Brenner Pass, Aegean Sea, Mycenae, Mediterranean Sea, Crete

Legend:
- Amber route from the North Sea and Baltic to the Aegean
- Source of copper ore
- Source of tin ore
- Source of gold ore
- Bronze Age centers

One of the more pronounced trends in the European Neolithic was regionalization, the development of distinctly local traditions. Initial farming cultures expanded over broad regions. Settlements were generally located in open and unprotected spaces, and pottery styles were similar across very large areas. Very quickly, however, population growth and the development of permanent field systems resulted in competition and conflict between groups. By 3000 B.C., the continent was occupied by well-entrenched farming populations making stone tools and pottery—cultivating, trading, and fighting.

Later Neolithic settlements were often located in defensive positions and heavily fortified. Pottery styles became more limited in their distribution. At the same time, trade and exchange expanded in scope. A variety of materials and finished goods were moved long distances across Europe. Obtaining raw materials, manufacturing trade items, and transporting finished goods became an important part of Neolithic economic systems. Flint, for example, was mined in Denmark, Belgium, England, and elsewhere and polished into fine axes for trade.

Metals appeared later in the northern part of Europe than in the Aegean area. Copper first appeared north of the Alps around 4000 B.C., coming primarily from southeastern Europe. Bronze objects began to appear in graves and cemeteries of farming settlements in this region after 2000 B.C. By this time, Bronze Age cultures in the eastern Mediterranean had developed into powerful political entities through a combination of alliance, sea power, craft production, and the control of trade.

The eastern Mediterranean acted like a magnet for the valued raw materials of the rest of Europe. Copper, tin, and gold from sources in Ireland and England moved across the English Channel, down the Seine and Rhone rivers in France, to the Mediterranean for shipment to the Aegean. Copper ores and ingots from the Carpathian Mountains in eastern Europe were brought overland through the Brenner Pass in the Alps to Greece. Amber from the Baltic and North Sea coasts of Denmark and Poland was also imported to the Aegean. Other exports, such as furs and slaves, may have also been shipped to the Aegean in exchange for finished bronze weapons, pottery vessels, and bronze and gold jewelry.

New objects and ideas filtered back into Europe along these corridors of trade. The third millennium B.C. in northern and western Europe witnessed a number of major innovations, including bronze and gold, the plow, oxen as draft animals, the wheel, the ox cart, the horse and chariot, and new weapons. Secondary animal products such as milk and wool became more important and fostered new industries.

Wealthy and powerful hierarchical societies arose at the centers of these important trade routes in the early Bronze Age after 2500 B.C. The Wessex culture in England elaborated the construction of Stonehenge and erected hundreds of burial mounds, or barrows, across southern England. The Unetice culture in the Czech Republic, known from several "princely" burials, dominated central Europe. The Bronze Age in Denmark and southern Sweden was spectacular in terms of the quantity of fine metal objects that were buried in many funerary mounds and caches. In fact, much of what is known about the Bronze Age comes from large barrows or caches of metal objects hidden in the ground; relatively few houses or settlements have been discovered or excavated. Such information provides a limited, but spectacular, view of only a small, wealthy segment of Bronze Age society.

A wooden plow from the Bronze Age of southern Scandinavia.

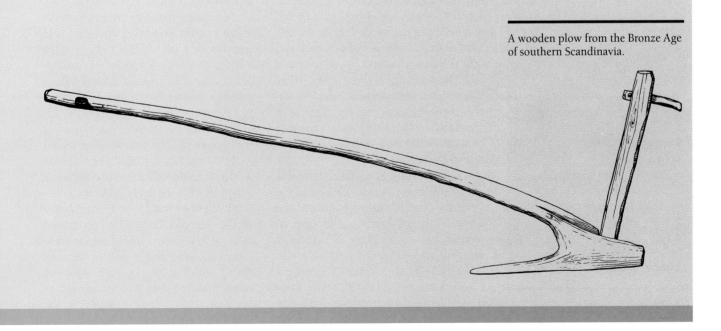

BORUM ESHØJ

A Bronze Age grave in Denmark

The log coffin of the 20-year-old male at Borum Eshøj.

Two Bronze Age barrows (burial mounds) along the coast of Denmark.

Bronze Age barrows dot the landscape of southern Scandinavia. These high circular mounds were often placed dramatically on the horizon to emphasize the importance of the buried individuals. In a few instances, the contents of barrows have been preserved to the present, providing a glimpse of the elite of Bronze Age society in northwestern Europe. Dressed in their finest clothing and jewelry, deceased individuals were placed in a coffin, a huge log of oak, split in half and hollowed out inside. This coffin was then covered under a pile of stones and buried under a mound of cut sods and soil. The coverings of these tombs sometimes sealed the contents from the air, and the log coffins quickly filled with groundwater. These conditions preserved both the coffins and the contents to a remarkable extent.

Borum Eshøj (bore'um-es'hoy) was one of the largest Bronze Age barrows in Denmark, located slightly north of the present city of Aarhus. The original mound was almost 9 m (30 ft) high (equivalent to a three-story building) and 40 m (130 ft) in diameter. The barrow was first opened in 1875 by the landowner who was removing the rich soil of the mound to add to his fields. Three oak coffins were found in the mound, containing an elderly man, a woman, and a younger man. The central log coffin was 3 m (10 ft) long and contained the body of a 50-to-60-year-old man, lying on a cowhide. He wore a wool cap over hair that was once blond, now stained black by tannic acid. His chin, also stained dark, was clean-shaven, and his teeth were in good condition. He was dressed in a wool skirt with a rope belt. The body of the younger man, age 20, was found in another coffin. Wearing a wool shirt held together by a leather belt and a wooden button, he was buried with a bronze dagger in a wooden sword scabbard, a bone comb, a round bark container, and a wooden pin to fasten his cloak.

The elderly woman was extremely well preserved. She was 50–60 years old and 1.57 m (5 ft, 2 in) tall. The first item found when the coffin was opened was a cowhide with the hairs still intact. Beneath the hide was a woolen rug on top of the woman's body. She was buried wearing a skirt and tunic of brown wool, a tasseled belt, and a hairnet of wool thread with her long hair still inside. A comb made of horn was found next to her hair. Various bronze objects in the coffin included a pin, a dagger with a

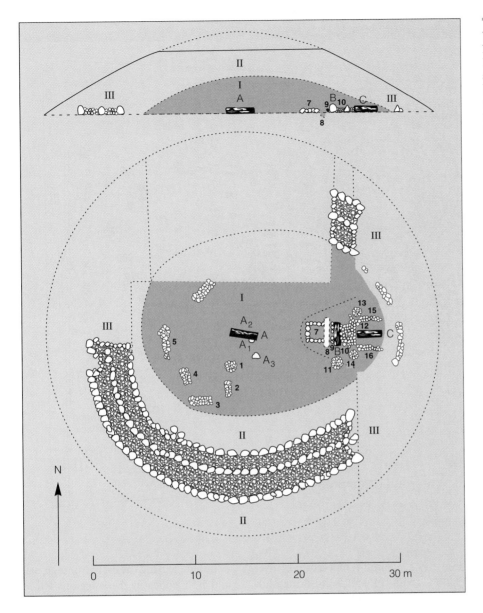

horn handle, a belt disk, and rings for the fingers, arms, and neck.

Bronze Age barrows were built for the wealthier members of society and placed near where the living had died. The distribution of thousands of such barrows in Denmark provides some information on the use of the landscape and the organization of early Bronze Age society. Most barrows in Denmark are located in areas of productive farmland, evidence of the important relationship between wealth and the control of agricultural resources.

The amount of metal, bronze, and gold in these burials provides some indication of the wealth of the deceased individuals as well. All bronze and gold in southern Scandinavia had to be imported because the ores are not indigenous. Gold was more valuable; only 1 g (0.04 oz) of gold is found for every 1000 g (2.2 lb) of bronze. There are pronounced differences in buried wealth between the sexes and between individuals. Male graves are more frequent than female graves, and they contain more wealth. Some individuals were buried with a great deal of bronze and gold and some without any, suggesting that social differentiation was pronounced in this area. An elite segment of the population must have controlled most of the resources as well as the trade.

A woman's woolen tunic and belted skirt from one of the log coffins.

VIX

A princess burial from the late Hallstatt Iron Age

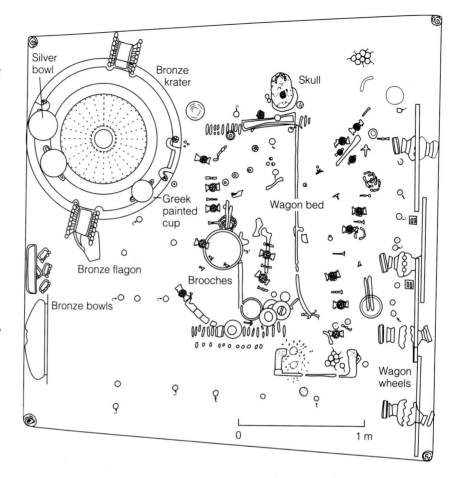

The ground plan of the princess burial at Vix. The wagon bed in the center was used as a burial platform, and the wheels of the wagon were placed along the wall to the right. An enormous bronze krater (storage vessel) was placed in the upper-left corner of the tomb, along with a number of other vessels.

Iron has a melting temperature of over 3000°C (5400°F), and sophisticated furnaces and smelting techniques are required for reducing the ore. Ironmaking was discovered in Turkey shortly before 2000 B.C. The technology was probably a well-guarded secret for some time, to gain military advantage—iron can cut bronze. The new metal was used initially to make stronger, more durable weapons and later for making more practical tools and equipment. Iron came to Europe around the beginning of the first millennium B.C., slightly earlier in the eastern Mediterranean, slightly later in the northwestern part of the continent.

The Iron Age in western Europe, the time of the Celtic tribes, can be divided into two phases: Hallstatt and La Tène. Hallstatt, the earlier period, approximately 800–500 B.C., was centered in Austria, southern Germany, and the Czech Republic. During the early Iron Age, salt and iron mines in these regions led to economic boom times. The La Tène period followed Hallstatt. The major concentrations of sites from this period are found in eastern France, Switzerland, southern Germany, and the Czech Republic. The Celtic Iron Age came to an end in most of western Europe shortly before the birth of Christ with the Roman conquest, led by Julius Caesar, during 58–51 B.C. Most of England was conquered by the emperor Claudius slightly later. Remnants of the Celtic traditions continued in Ireland for centuries, however, largely untouched by the Roman Empire. Germanic tribes in central and northern Europe also remained in the Iron Age on the fringes of the Roman Empire for another 1000 years, essentially until the arrival of Christianity.

A distinctive Celtic art style was practiced throughout western Europe during this time. Both Hallstatt and La Tène are defined primarily by styles of artistic depiction and decoration and by types of pottery. Designs from the La Tène period are both flamboyant and hypnotic. Complex patterns of concentric circles, spirals and meanders, and a variety of bird and animal figures appear on metal and ceramic objects (see Color Plate 28). Disembodied heads with almond-shaped eyes and fierce moustaches, long fanciful horse heads, and willowy statues of women characterize the tradition. Weapons, tools, jewelry, and everyday equipment were ornamented with this distinctive art.

This art style, along with certain religious practices and beliefs, was shared by several distinct societies in western Europe. These groups were headed by strong leaders and organized along similar lines. Some areas had elected magistrates. Julius Caesar, who encountered these groups in battle and in negotiations, wrote of their social structure, describing three major groups below the king: an aristocratic class of warriors and priests, the common people, and slaves—a stratified society.

The tombs of the elite of Celtic society are among the best-known finds from this period. The grave at Vix (pronounced "vicks") was excavated in 1953 by René Joffroy at the foot of an Iron Age hillfort known as Mont Lassois in northern France. A princess had been buried there beneath an earthen mound, along the headwaters of the Seine River, around 500 B.C. A large square chamber was dug into the ground and lined with wooden planks. The body of a 35-year-old woman was placed on the bed of a ceremonial cart or hearse in the center of the grave. The wheels of the cart were removed and stacked against the sides of the tomb. Her body was covered with a leather blanket, and a bronze-headed staff was placed across her body. She was buried with a heavy gold collar of foreign manufacture and wore Baltic amber beads, locally made bronze brooches, and other pins and jewelry.

The tomb was filled with a wealth of exotic, funerary offerings. A huge bronze

krater, or vessel for mixing and storing wine, more than 1.5 m (5 ft) high, weighing 208 kg (450 lb), with a volume of more than 1000 liters (280 gal), was set in one corner of the grave. It was crafted in a Greek bronze workshop, probably located in southern Italy. The krater was designed to be dismantled for transport, and the assembly instructions were labeled with Greek letters. The design around its rim depicts Greek warriors and horse-drawn chariots. A number of bronze, silver, and gold bowls were placed alongside the krater, including a bronze flagon from Italy and two painted pottery cups from Greece.

The origins of the materials found in the princess burial at Vix indicate the extensive trade taking place in Europe at that time and emphasize the importance of the major rivers as transportation routes. The Rhône, the largest river in Europe that joins the Mediterranean, provided a major corridor from the south into temperate Europe. The modern city

The enormous bronze krater found in the tomb at Vix. The vessel is 1.5 m high and weighs more than 200 kg.

The imported gold collar found with the princess burial at Vix, 23 cm in diameter.

Part of the decoration of a Gundestrup caldron from Denmark, a classic example of Celtic art.

of Marseilles, at the mouth of the Rhône River in southern France, was originally a Greek colony called Massilia, founded in 600 B.C. Wine from the Aegean was sent to Massilia for shipment into western Europe. Various goods and materials from the interior of the continent were exported through this colony to the eastern Mediterranean. Fragments of a garment of Chinese silk, found in a Hallstatt tomb in Germany, are one example of the extent of trade at this time. The quantity of materials flowing through Marseilles must have been remarkable.

The fortress of Mont Lassois, directly above the grave at Vix, was one of the major political and commercial centers of late Hallstatt Europe. Mont Las-sois dominates the upper Seine Valley at the spot where the river becomes navigable and flows west to the Atlantic. The Rhône and its tributaries lie just to the east. Thus, Mont Lassois is at a strategic point in the main route of commerce between the western Mediterranean and the Atlantic coast of western France, the English Channel, and the British Isles. Iron ore and forests for wood to make charcoal for reducing the ore were also available in the area. The richness of the offerings in the tomb of the princess at Vix, some 500 km (300 mi) north of Marseilles, suggests that the Greeks were giving gifts to the elite of Celtic society in order to obtain favorable trading status and secure commerce.

Crauballe Man, found in a Danish bog in 1952. His throat had been cut, and he was placed naked in the waters of the Grauballe bog around 20 B.C.

Archaeologists rarely find flesh on the bones of the past. Much of what we know about our ancestors and their lifeways comes from the detective work of piecing together information from fragments of pots and tools, discarded bones and buried skeletons—the broken, forgotten, and hidden remnants of what human society once created. Unusual situations, especially in the case of human bodies preserved from the past, immediately capture our attention. These discoveries emphasize the fragile nature of the human condition and generate much interest in the past.

Among the most remarkable series of preserved prehistoric bodies are the "bog people" from northern Europe. Hundreds of individuals have been found in the peat bogs of northern Germany and southern Scandinavia, dating to the centuries around the birth of Christ. These bogs have marvelous preservative powers. The accumulation of peat and organic detritus that fills these swamps and mires contains tannic acid from the needles of coniferous trees. Tannic acid, used for tanning hides, is one essential factor in the preservation of the skin of the bog bodies. The second factor is the waterlogged condition of the bogs, which creates an environment where bacteria cannot break down soft tissues.

The bog bodies are not the result of accidental drowning or disappearance. They are a curious consequence of the beliefs and practices of early Iron Age society. These people viewed the bogs as sacred places where sacrifices were made to the gods. Long braids of human hair were cut off and thrown in the bogs as one type of offering. Weapons and jewelry of bronze, iron, and gold were also placed in the mire to appease the gods. Individuals were also intentionally sacrificed to the sacred bogs. Lindlow Man, found in an English bog in 1984, was bludgeoned with an axe and strangled, and finally his throat was cut.

One of the best-known examples is Tollund Man, exhumed from the bogs of Denmark by P. V. Glob, of the Danish National Museum (see Color Plate 29). Tollund Man was placed in the murky waters of a peat bog in central Denmark almost 2000 years ago. As Glob describes, the body was very well preserved; even his eyelashes and beard were readily visible. Tollund Man had been strangled; a thin leather garrotte was still tightly wound around his neck. He was naked except for a small leather cap and a belt around his waist. Tollund Man was well groomed when he died and his hands were soft and uncalloused, not used for hard labor. His last meal was a gruel of many different kinds of seeds and grains. He died in the spring, and his execution may have been related to the rituals of Iron Age society that required sacrifice and offerings for the resurrection of the year and the bounty of the earth.

In the peat cut, nearly seven feet down, lay a human figure in a crouched position, still half buried. A foot and a shoulder protruded, perfectly preserved but dark brown in color like the surrounding peat, which had dyed the skin. Carefully we removed more peat, and a bowed head came into view. As dusk fell, we saw in the fading light a man take shape before us. He was curled up, with legs drawn under him and arms bent, resting on his side as if asleep. His eyes were peacefully shut . . . his brows were furrowed and his mouth showed a slightly irritated quirk, as if he were not overpleased by this unexpected disturbance of his rest.

P. V. Glob (1970a)

MAIDEN CASTLE

The end of the Celtic Iron Age

Maiden Castle in Dorset, England, showing the fortifications of multiple walls and ditches. Excavations in progress can be seen on the top of the hill.

The largest settlements from the Iron Age in Europe are defended hilltops, found throughout southern Germany, France, and Britain. Mont Lassois above the Vix burial is one example, and there are many others across central and western Europe. These fortresses and their inhabitants were formidable. The Romans frequently remarked on the strength of the Gaelic walls that surrounded these hilltops. Roman writers reported on the ferocity of the Celtic warriors, describing the bold *gaesatae,* spearmen who went naked into battle. Roman statuary commemorated the valor of the Celts as fair-

haired warriors with drooping moustaches. In a famous sculpture, a defiant, yet defeated, Celt puts himself to the sword rather than surrender to the Romans. That the Romans should so admire the character of their boisterous and aggressive enemy is itself a remarkable statement about the Celts.

Hundreds of Iron Age hillforts are found in Britain and Ireland in various sizes, from less than an acre to many hectares. These hillforts served as both population centers and retreats during the Iron Age, distinguished by the fortifications that surround them. Maiden Castle

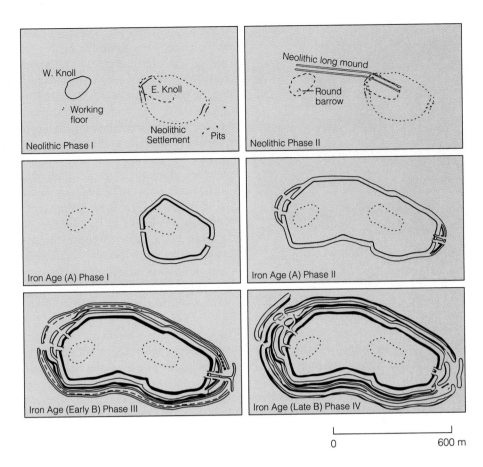

is one of the largest hillforts in Britain; in its final form, it enclosed an area of almost 18 ha (45 acres). Situated atop a high, saddleback hill in the downs of Dorset, near the southern coast of England, Maiden Castle dominated the Iron Age Dorset landscape.

Sir Mortimer Wheeler excavated parts of the site from 1934 through 1937, and more recent excavations were undertaken during the 1980s. Wheeler was a major figure in British archaeology, highly respected for both the quality of his work and his concern with the education of archaeologists. After his college studies, Wheeler served as an officer in World War I, the commander of a battery in the Royal Artillery. Returning at the end of the war to head the archaeology section of the National Museum of Wales, in 1925 he became director of the London Museum. His excavations at Maiden Castle were intended both to reveal the past history of the site and to train new students in archaeology.

Wheeler's forte was the **stratigraphic section**, the excavation of trenches and squares across manmade features to reveal the sequence and methods of construction. This vertical wall, or profile, of excavated trenches and squares provides information essential to understanding the history of a site. Recording these sections in photographs and drawings creates a permanent record of the sequence of events for the archaeologist to interpret. Wheeler's precise excavations and recording methods have revealed much about the prehistory of Maiden Castle, from the Neolithic to the Roman conquest of Britain.

The hilltop was first used around 3700 B.C. as a Neolithic camp; an enormous barrow was erected here during the same period, overlooking the adjacent valley. This extraordinary Neolithic long barrow ran for over 550 m (1800 ft) across the hilltop, marked by two parallel ditches, each 5 m (16 ft) wide, 15 m (50 ft) apart. Maiden Castle was the center of an elaborate landscape of henge monuments, timber settings, and causewayed camps, comparable to other major Neolithic centers in the British Isles.

A Roman catapult arrowhead lodged in the back of one of the defenders of Maiden Castle.

During the Iron Age around 500 B.C., fortifications were first constructed around a growing market center on the hilltop. The first fort at Maiden Castle was univallate, having one wall, and enclosed some 6 ha (15 acres). Large hillforts such as Maiden Castle appear to have had administrative, religious, economic, and residential functions in a proto-urban context, an early form of the walled town. There are several distinct areas within Maiden Castle. An Iron Age shrine or temple was uncovered on the most prominent part of the hilltop. This structure was later replaced by a Roman temple, documenting the continuity of religious significance and focus.

The hilltop served as a residence as well as a fortified storehouse for the agricultural surplus from the rich farmlands. Residential structures dot the hilltop; evidence of dense occupation suggests that as many as 2000–4000 people lived there. Large pits were dug into the chalk, as much as 3 m (10 ft) deep for storage, water reservoirs, and other purposes. Excavations also revealed the parallel ruts of wagon wheels crossing the defended interior; the standard wheel-to-wheel distance in the later Iron Age was 1.46 m (4.8 ft). More recent excavations have uncovered numerous structures and an enormous quantity of refuse in the form of pottery, bronze and iron artifacts, and animal bones. Most of the animal bones were from sheep, and several had signs of malnutrition.

By 50 B.C., shortly before the first Roman invasion of Britain, the fortifi-

tions were enormously expanded, and the enclosed area inside the hillfort tripled in size. The final set of fortifications consisted of a set of three enormous concentric banks and two ditches enclosing almost 18 ha (45 acres). A fourth bank was built at the south end for additional protection. The term **multivallate** is used to describe large hillforts with complex defenses of multiple ditches and ramparts. Some of the walls at Maiden Castle stand as high as 20 m (65 ft) today. These walls had a 4-m (13-ft) high foundation of stone and a massive wooden palisade on top. A narrow, serpentine, and dangerous path guards the entrance at the eastern end of the hilltop. At the entrance were wooden gates 4 m (13 ft) wide. Some 22,000 slingstones were found in caches near the walls of Maiden Castle, representing one of the important defensive weapons in use during that period.

In spite of its massive defenses against attack, Maiden Castle fell to the Roman legions and their siege artillery in A.D. 43. Wheeler's depiction of the final hours of the defenders of Maiden Castle is a masterpiece of archaeological interpretation and prose:

> Before the close fighting began, the regiment of catapults or *ballistæ*, which habitually accompanied a legion on campaign, put down a barrage across the gateway, causing casualties at the outset. Following the barrage, the Roman infantry advanced up the slope, cutting its way from rampart to rampart, tower to tower. In the innermost bay of the entrance, a number of huts had been recently built; these were now set alight, and under the rising clouds of smoke the gates were stormed. But resistance had been obstinate and the attack was pushed home with every savagery. The scene became that of a massacre in which the wounded were not spared. Finally, the gates were demolished and the stone walls which flank them reduced to the lowly and ruinous condition in which we found them, nineteen centuries later. (Wheeler, 1943, p. 47)

A Roman catapult arrowhead, found in the back of the skeleton of one of the defenders of Maiden Castle, poignantly marks the end of the Celtic Iron Age in western Europe and its replacement by the Romans.

SUMMARY

LESSONS FROM PREHISTORIC EUROPE

The growth of European civilization

The story of European prehistory is one of spectacular growth and change. Because of a long history of archaeological research and the richness of prehistoric remains, we know more about the past of Europe than anywhere else. The prehistory of Europe is, in fact, a model of the evolution of society, from small bands of hunter-gatherers in the late Pleistocene and early Holocene, through the first hierarchical societies of the early Neolithic and the states of the Bronze Age and Iron Age.

The introduction of agriculture resulted in major changes in European society and economy over the six millennia before Christ. The initial spread of farming was slow, taking place over a period of roughly 3000 years. The first farming communities in Europe are known from Greece and the Aegean area and date to around 6500 B.C. By 3000 B.C., farming had penetrated to the coasts of western Europe and reached its climatic limits in northern Scandinavia and Britain. By that time, virtually all the cultivable areas of Europe were inhabited by farming populations, and hunter-gatherers continued only in the most northerly, marginal areas. In the third millennium B.C., these initial Neolithic societies became more regionalized, following distinctive trends toward increasing warfare, wealth, and trade.

The transition to farming appears to have followed a common pattern in much of Europe, as domesticated plants and animals were slowly incorporated into a subsistence pattern based largely on wild foods. In northern Europe, at least, the shift from a reliance on wild foods to a predominance of domesticates took several thousand years. The spread of agriculture was accompanied by significant changes in social relations.

New religious beliefs must have been spreading at this time as well. One manifestation is the appearance of megalithic tombs along the Atlantic coastline of Europe, whose construction represented enormous efforts. The monuments themselves would have been dramatic statements of the authority of the individuals buried within them. This inequality was also represented by the appearance of rare objects such as copper and gold. Apart from the elite control of highly valued materials, economies were probably based on barter and reciprocal exchange. This trend toward hierarchical organization in the Neolithic accelerated with the introduction of bronze, around 3000 B.C.

The third and second millennia B.C. witnessed the appearance of early states and empires in Mesopotamia, the Nile Valley, and the Aegean. Before the literate civilizations of classical Greece and Rome, the Aegean area witnessed the emergence of state-level societies on Crete and the Greek mainland. The Minoan palaces and Mycenaean citadels were urban centers of these civilizations and the focal points of industry, commerce, religion, military power, and central accumulation.

During the third millennium B.C. in Europe, several major changes in technology and transportation occurred, including the manufacture of bronze weapons and jewelry, the widespread adoption of the plow and the wheel, and the use of draft animals such as oxen and horses to pull carts and chariots. Weapons and martial motifs dominated the symbols of status in European society during this time. Local warfare and

The evolution of European society.

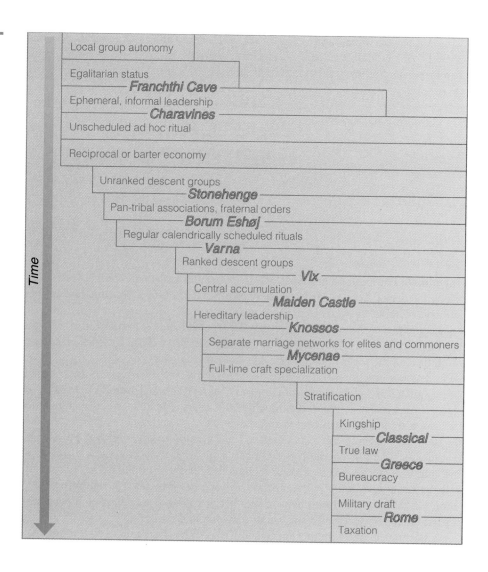

Time

Local group autonomy

Egalitarian status
Franchthi Cave

Ephemeral, informal leadership
Charavines

Unscheduled ad hoc ritual

Reciprocal or barter economy

Unranked descent groups
Stonehenge

Pan-tribal associations, fraternal orders
Borum Eshøj

Regular calendrically scheduled rituals
Varna

Ranked descent groups
Vix

Central accumulation
Maiden Castle

Hereditary leadership
Knossos

Separate marriage networks for elites and commoners
Mycenae

Full-time craft specialization

Stratification

Kingship
Classical

True law
Greece

Bureaucracy

Military draft
Rome

Taxation

conflict contrasted strongly with the long-distance patterns of trade, commerce, and cooperation. Textiles of wool and linen, metal dress pins, and amber and gold necklaces characterized the clothing of the elite. A bronze razor (for shaving) was a means to alter one's appearance as a mark of status and power.

Certainly by this time, rituals were scheduled according to regular times of the year. The solar "computer" of Stonehenge and the myriad stone and wood circles of northwestern Europe clearly functioned in this manner. North of the Alps, political and social organization seems to have involved alliances of ephemeral chiefs who cooperated in the exchange of exotic materials and warfare. The economy and social relations were intertwined. As wealth accumulated and increased during the Bronze Age, there was a marked trend toward fortification. The most notable features of the Bronze Age landscape, aside from exceptional monuments such as Stonehenge, are large barrows, the tombs of the elite. There was a dramatic, intentional contrast between the elevated graves of the nobility and the flat cemeteries of the commoners.

The introduction of iron after 1000 B.C. brought new tools and weapons to Europe. Iron produced harder and sharper implements and was in great demand. In contrast to copper and tin, whose sources were limited to only a few areas in Europe, iron ores in a variety of different forms were found in many places across the continent. Veins of iron ore were exploited in Iberia, Britain, the Alps, the Carpathian Mountains, and elsewhere. Bog iron was exploited in northern Europe, and carbonate sources in other areas enabled local groups to obtain the raw materials necessary for producing this important material.

At the same time, the collapse of the dominant civilizations of the Aegean area around 1000 B.C. changed the flow of raw materials and finished products across Europe. However, new centers in the Mediterranean, first in the classic civilization of Greece and later in the Roman Empire, brought history to Europe as these powerful empires emerged. Again, we can observe important and dramatic differences between the "classic" areas of the Mediterranean and the northern parts of "barbarian" Europe.

Several events marked the beginning of the La Tène period of the Iron Age, between 500 B.C. and the birth of Christ. The collapse of trade with the Mediterranean, rapid population increase, and conflict led to expansion and a series of migrations to the south and east of the Celtic heartland. The Celts, or Gauls, moved into northern Italy and the Po River Valley, and farther east into Romania and eventually Anatolia in Asia Minor. Around 390 B.C., the Gauls sacked Rome. With the decline of long-distance trade, local craftsmanship improved, and a spectacular, powerful style of art and decoration predominated among the Celts. These crafts, along with many other aspects of society, were concentrated in towns in the Celtic part of Europe. These towns most often occupied the oppida, the heavily walled and fortified centers of political and economic power. Maiden Castle is just one of many examples of these Celtic towns that fell to the Romans as the empire expanded.

A very different sequence of events characterized the Mediterranean. By 800 B.C., the effects of growing population and urbanization led to the emergence of Greek city-states as major powers. Conquest and continuing population expansion led to Greek colonization of several areas to the east and west of the homeland. Colonies appeared in Sicily, southern Italy, southern France, and Spain, as the eastern Mediterranean could not contain the growing numbers of Greeks, Etruscans, and Carthaginians. Local demand for Greek goods was high in these areas. At a site in Spain, for example, 1400 Greek pottery vessels were found in a single, small excavation. At another site in Spain, a single grave contained gold jewelry that included a seal from Syria and an earring from Egypt. The Greeks, and later the Romans, had encoded systems of law, military drafts, and elaborate bureaucracies, characteristics of high-level state societies. As the Greece of Homer and Socrates declined in power, Rome began to build its empire. The Macedonians under Phillip, and later Alexander the Great (356–323 B.C.), had turned to the east, setting out against Asia.

Trade and colonization during the earlier half of the Iron Age, the first millennium B.C., changed to warfare after 400 B.C., as the dynamics of power shifted to the Italian peninsula. By 290 B.C. the Romans had spread into most of Italy, and by 140 B.C. they had eliminated their major rivals at Corinth in Greece and Carthage in North Africa. Rome controlled the Mediterranean and turned toward the interior of Europe. Roman trade and colonization at first focused on Spain as an important source of raw materials. Soon, however, trade routes and the wealth of northern Europe captured the attention of the Romans. Julius Caesar led the legions against the Gauls who occupied France, the British Isles, and parts of central and eastern Europe. From 59 to 51 B.C., Caesar pushed the boundaries of the Roman Empire across France to the Rhine River, largely destroying Celtic society in the process. In one instance, following the conquest of the town of Cenabrum, the Romans killed all but 300 of the 40,000 men, women, and children taking refuge in the fortress. A few years later, the empire extended across the Channel into much of England. By the birth of Christ, Rome controlled virtually all of southern Europe. A few pockets of Celts remained in Ireland and Scotland and on the islands.

North of the Rhine, however, the Germanic tribes resisted and eventually outlasted the Roman Empire. The Germanic Iron Age followed the Roman period and extended from the birth of Christ through most of the first millennium A.D. In this area of Germany, Scandinavia, and eastern Europe, warrior societies continued and flourished. These societies were small, yet highly productive, agricultural communities. Society was largely egalitarian, and authority was vested in individuals of demonstrated strength and wit. Through time, these communities grew larger and more powerful, gradually forming alliances to create larger polities. While the Roman conquest effectively ended prehistory in southern Europe and Britain, the spread of Christianity marked the beginning of the historic period in most of Europe north of the Alps. The spread of Christianity was followed by the Dark Ages, the Renaissance, and eventually the industrial era, bringing us to the present.

SUGGESTED READINGS

Bradley, R. 1998. *The significance of monuments.* London: Routledge. *A refreshing review and innovative perspective on the burial monuments of western Europe.*

Chadwick, J. 1976. *The Mycenaean world.* Cambridge: Cambridge University Press. *A classic treatise on the Mycenaeans, with particular emphasis on the written language.*

Chippendale, C. 1983. *Stonehenge complete.* Ithaca, NY: Cornell University Press. *A well-illustrated compendium on the evolution of Stonehenge and our understanding of it.*

Coles, J. M., and A. F. Harding. 1979. *The Bronze Age in Europe.* London: Methuen. *Details about the Bronze Age civilizations of Europe, with an emphasis on areas north of the Alps.*

Cunliffe, B., ed. 1994. *The Oxford illustrated prehistory of Europe.* Oxford: Oxford University Press. *The most up-to-date synthesis of European prehistory, written by various experts in the field.*

Powell, T. G. E. 1980. *The Celts.* London: Thames & Hudson. *An updated classic on the Celtic peoples of Europe and their art.*

Whittle, A. 1996. *Europe in the Neolithic: The creation of new worlds.* Cambridge: Cambridge University Press. *A synthesis of the evidence on the Neolithic of Europe.*

IN CONCLUSION

The past as present and future

Perhaps the best way to conclude this book is to ask the question, What have we learned? We know that archaeology includes stunning museum pieces, travel, and exotic places. Archaeology is puzzles, mysteries, and detective work. Archaeology is intriguing methods for getting answers about the past and a stimulating career in which any number of interests can be explored by looking at the variety of times, places, and ways in which people lived in the past. Archaeology is digging holes and recovering architecture and artifacts. Archaeology is good, dirty fun.

But we also learn larger lessons from the past. The Spanish American philosopher Santayana wrote that those who cannot remember the past are condemned to repeat it. Certainly, there are lessons about the long span of our prehistory on earth and about the evolution of our species and our behavior. In terms of the vastness of geological or archaeological time, the role of humans on the planet is minuscule indeed. Yet the impact of our species is immeasurable. Although relative newcomers to earth's history, we have an obligation and a responsibility toward all that is around us. Humans have tremendous destructive power as well as creative abilities. Through looting, careless development, and the wanton destruction of archaeological resources, we even have the potential to eliminate our abilities to reconstruct and understand our own past.

There is no present or future—only the past, happening over and over again—now.

Eugene O'Neill

Society has so much to learn from its ancestors—their successes and failures—and contemporary archaeology is developing the tools and techniques to examine this ancient record carefully and with the degree of objectivity that science requires.

A corollary to the immensity of prehistoric time is the tempo of change. The rate of change in our societies and in ourselves is ever-increasing. If we consider the passage of time as a straight line, the major milestones in the evolution of life occur more and more frequently as we approach the present. The complexity and rate of change in human prehistory are clearly accelerating. We took our first steps some 5–4 m.y.a., made our first tools 3–2 m.y.a., first buried our dead perhaps 100,000 years ago, painted on the walls of caves about 25,000 years ago, domesticated plants and animals 10,000 years ago, built cities and began to write on clay around 5000 years ago, and began to harness fossil fuels and machinery less than 500 years ago.

The pace of life, science, and living has become so rapid that today almost everything around us changes in the short period between birth and death. It becomes more and more difficult to understand or cope with changes in the society that fostered us. We must deal with what philosopher and visionary Alvin Toffler has called future shock:

> By now the accelerative thrust triggered by man has become the key to the entire evolutionary process on our planet. The rate and direction of the evolution of other species, their very survival, depends on decisions made by man. Yet there is nothing inherent in the evolutionary process to guarantee man's own survival.
>
> Throughout the past, as successive stages of social evolution unfolded, man's awareness followed rather than preceded the event. Today unconscious adaptation is no longer

adequate. Faced with the power to alter the gene, to create new species, to populate the planets, or depopulate the earth, man must now assume conscious control of evolution itself. Avoiding future shock as he rides the waves of change, he must master evolution, shaping tomorrow to human need. Instead of rising in revolt against it, he must, from this historic moment on, anticipate and design the future. (1970, p. 438)

Perhaps the final lesson of archaeology is a lingering sense of hope about the future. Our strongest feelings from what we as archaeologists have learned remain a basic optimism for our species. In every way we are artifacts, manufactured over a very long period of time, created by the experiences of our ancestors. We have been on the planet for several million years. In that time, we have evolved from a chimpanzeelike ape to the man on the moon. We have expanded geographically and survived under a wide range of difficult conditions. There is an unusual quality about the human species—the enormous potential in the human intellect, with its remarkable inventiveness for coping with change. A large brain and creativity managed to get us through a very long and difficult journey in the past. For that very reason, the future should be just as exciting.

In my beginning is my end.

T. S. Eliot

One of Europe's earliest stone sculptures from Stone Age Yugoslavia.

APPENDIX

COMMON MEASUREMENT CONVERSIONS AND EQUIVALENTS

LENGTH or HEIGHT

1 centimeter (cm) = 0.394 inch (in)
1 inch = 2.54 centimeters
1 meter (m) = 3.281 feet (ft)
1 foot = 0.305 meter
1 meter = 1.0936 yards (yd)
1 yard = 0.9144 meter
1 kilometer (km) = 0.6214 mile (mi)
1 mile = 1.6094 kilometers

APPROXIMATE EQUIVALENTS	Feet	Meters
Average person	5.5	1.7
Height of basketball basket	10	3.0
High-diving platform	32.8	10
Bowling alley	60	18
Ten-story building	100	30
Arc de Triomphe	164	50
High ski jump	196.8	60
Football field	300	91
Washington Monument	555	169
Golf course	20,000	6098

AREA

1 square centimeter (sq cm) = 0.155 square inch (sq in)
1 square inch = 6.452 square centimeters
1 square meter (sq m) = 10.764 square feet (sq ft)
1 square foot = 0.0929 square meter
1 square meter = 1.196 square yards (sq yd)
1 square yard = 0.8361 square meter
1 square kilometer (sq km) = 0.386 square mile (sq mi)
1 square mile = 2.59 square kilometers
1 hectare (ha) = 10,000 square meters
1 hectare = 2.47 acres
1 acre = 0.405 hectare

APPROXIMATE EQUIVALENTS	Length	Width	Square Feet	Square Meters	Acres	Hectares
Average bedroom	12 ft	10 ft	120	11	0.0027	0.0011
Soccer goal	24 ft	8 ft	192	18	0.0045	0.0018
Doubles tennis court	36 ft	78 ft	2808	261	0.0645	0.0261
Basketball court	84 ft	45.75 ft	3843	357	0.0882	0.0357
Average house lot	80 ft	80 ft	6400	595	0.1469	0.0595
Baseball infield	90 ft	90 ft	8100	753	0.1859	0.0753
Olympic pool	50 m	21 m	11,298	1050	0.2594	0.1050
Football field	300 ft	60 ft	18,000	1673	0.4132	0.1673
Hockey rink	200 ft	100 ft	20,000	1859	0.4591	0.1859
Soccer field	100 m	80 m	86,080	8000	1.9760	0.8000
Union Square, New York City	650 ft	650 ft	422,500	39,250	9.6948	3.9250
Average city block	700 ft	700 ft	490,000	45,539	11.2481	4.5539

	Miles	Miles	Square Miles	Acres	Hectares
Churchill Downs (horse racetrack)	1.25	oval	0.018522	11.849	4.797
Indianapolis racetrack	2.5	oval	0.4112	263.057	106.501
Central Park, New York City	2.5	0.5	1.25	799.663	323.750
Manhattan Island	12.5	2.5	22	14,074.060	5698.000

VOLUME

1 cubic centimeter (cc) = 0.061 cubic inch (cu in)
1 cubic inch = 16.39 cubic centimeters
1 cubic meter (cu m) = 35.314 cubic feet (cu ft)
1 cubic foot = 0.0283 cubic meter
1 cubic meter = 1.308 cubic yards (cu yd)

APPROXIMATE EQUIVALENTS	Cubic Meters
Refrigerator	2
Home bathroom	10
UPS delivery truck	25
School bus	50
Large room	100
Medium-size house	1000
Small church	10,000
Modern oil tanker	100,000

DENSITY

25 people/sq km	=	0.2 person/soccer field	=	65 people/sq mi
500 people/sq km	=	4 people/soccer field	=	1300 people/sq mi
5000 people/sq km	=	40 people/soccer field	=	13,000 people/sq mi

absolute dating A method of assigning archaeological dates in calendar years so that an age in actual number of years is known or can be estimated. *See also* relative dating.

accelerator mass spectrometry (AMS) A method of radiocarbon dating using an accelerator to count the individual isotopes of the carbon sample; advantages include small sample size, speed of counting, and accuracy.

Acheulean A major archaeological culture of the Lower Paleolithic, named after the site of St. Acheul in France. A hallmark of the Acheulean is the handaxe.

achieved status Social status and prestige attributed to an individual according to achievements or skills rather than inherited social position. *See also* ascribed status.

acropolis (plural **acropoli**) (Greek) A raised complex of palaces and courtyards, especially in Mesoamerica and Greece.

Adena A burial mound complex that developed in the Ohio River Valley toward the end of the last millennium B.C.

adobe A mud mixture used to make sundried bricks for buildings in arid areas.

adze A heavy, chisel-like tool.

alloying A technique of combining or mixing two or more metals to make an entirely new metal; for example, mixing copper and tin creates bronze.

alpaca A domesticated South American herbivore with long, soft wool.

altiplano (Spanish) The high-altitude plain between the eastern and western ridges of the Andes in Peru.

Anasazi One of three major cultural traditions of the American Southwest during late prehistoric times. The Anasazi were centered in the northern Southwest, on the high plateau of the Four Corners region.

ancient DNA Genetic material preserved in archaeological remains of bones and plants that can be studied for information about past genetic relationships.

annealing The process of heating and gradually cooling metal (or other materials) to reduce brittleness and enhance toughness.

anthropomorphic Having human form or attributes.

archaeoastronomy The study of ancient alignments and other aspects of the archaeological record and their relationship to ancient astronomical knowledge and events.

archaeology The study of the human past, combining the themes of time and change.

archaeozoology The study of animal remains from archaeological sites.

Archaic The term used for the early Holocene in the New World, from approximately 6000 B.C. until 1500–1000 B.C.

artifact Any object or item created or modified by human action.

ascribed status Social status and prestige attributed to an individual at birth, regardless of ability or accomplishments. *See also* achieved status.

assemblage The set of artifacts and other remains found on an archaeological site or within a specific level of a site.

association The relationship between items in an archaeological site. Items in association are found close together and/or in the same layer or deposit. Often used for dating purposes, as items found in association are assumed to be of the same age.

Atlantean column A carved human figure serving as a decorative or supporting column, such as at the Mesoamerican site of Tula.

atlatl A spearthrower, or wooden shaft, used to propel a spear or dart; first appeared in the Upper Paleolithic, also used in the precontact New World.

australopithecine The generic term for the various species of the genus *Australopithecus,* including *A. ramidus, A. afarensis,* and *A. africanus.*

bajo (Spanish) A broad, flat, clay-lined depression in the Maya lowlands that fills with water during the rainy season.

ball court An I-shaped or oval prehispanic structure, found throughout Mesoamerica and the southwestern United States, that was the site of ritual ballgames.

Bandkeramik An archaeological culture of the early Neolithic in central Europe, referring to the style of pottery: linear bands of incised designs on hemispherical bowls.

barrow An earthen mound covering a burial, found in prehistoric Europe and Asia.

bas-relief A type of sculptural relief in which the figures project slightly from the background.

bifacial A term describing a flaked stone tool in which both faces or sides are retouched to make a thinner tool. *See also* unifacial.

bipedalism The human method of locomotion, walking on two legs; one of the first human characteristics to distinguish the early hominids, as opposed to quadrupedalism, walking on four legs.

blade A special kind of elongated flake with two parallel sides and a length at least twice the width of the piece. The regular manufacture of blades characterized the Upper Paleolithic, with an efficient way of producing mass quantities of cutting edge.

bow-drill A device for perforating beads or other small objects, in which a bow is used to rotate the shaft of the bit.

breccia The accumulated materials from cave deposits that harden into a conglomerate rock, including sediments, rocks, and animal bones.

brow ridge That part of the skull above the eye orbits. This ridge of bone was particularly pronounced in the early hominids, when cranial capacity was less and the forehead absent or sloping. Brow ridges are largely absent in *Homo sapiens sapiens.*

bulla (plural **bullae**) (Latin) A hollow clay sphere or envelope used to enclose clay tokens in ancient Mesopotamia.

burin A stone tool with right-angle edges used for planing and engraving.

cacao A bean of the cacao tree, native to Mesoamerica; used to make chocolate. Cacao beans also were used as money by the Aztecs.

cache A collection of artifacts, often buried or associated with constructed features, that has been deliberately stored for future use.

calibrated dates Dates resulting from the process of calibration, the correction of radiocarbon years to calendar years, by means of a curve or formula derived from the comparison of radiocarbon dates and tree rings from the bristlecone pine. Calibration extends approximately 6000 years into the past.

camelid   A ruminant mammal—such as camel, llama, and extinct related forms—having long legs and two toes.

cannibalism   The practice of eating human flesh.

carnelian   A red or reddish variety of chalcedony (a translucent variety of quartz) used in jewelry.

cayman   A tropical South American alligator.

cenotaph   A grave that does not contain a skeleton.

cenote   The Maya word for a sinkhole, a natural well in the Yucatán that provides water for drinking and bathing.

Cenozoic   The most recent geological era, spanning the last 65 million years and characterized by the rise of birds, mammals, and flowering plants; sometimes called the Age of Mammals.

chac mool (Maya)   A life-size stone figure in a reclining position, with flexed legs and head raised and turned to one side. *Chac mools* served as altars and were often placed in temple doorways to receive offerings.

charnel house   A house in which the bodies of the dead are placed.

chert   A dull-colored, subtranslucent rock resembling flint that was often used for making flaked stone tools.

chicha   A South American beer made from maize.

Chichimec   A term loosely applied to the peoples who lived beyond the northern limits of Mesoamerica; nomadic people, considered to be uncivilized barbarians.

chinampa (Spanish)   An agricultural field created by swamp drainage or landfill operations along the edges of lakes. This intensive form of agriculture was especially prevalent in the Basin of Mexico but also was used elsewhere in the central highlands of Mexico.

circumscription   The process or act of being enclosed by either environmental boundaries, such as mountains, oceans, and rivers, or social boundaries, such as neighboring groups of people.

citadel   A hilltop fortress, the characteristic settlement of the ruling elite of Mycenaean civilization, 1700–1100 B.C.

Clactonian   A term used for assemblages from the Lower Paleolithic, lacking handaxes and characterized by large flakes with heavy retouching and notches.

cleaver   A companion tool of the Acheulean handaxe. Cleavers have a broad leading edge, whereas handaxes come to a point.

Clovis   An archaeological culture during the Paleoindian period in North America, defined by a distinctive type of fluted point; named for the original find spot near Clovis, New Mexico.

codex (plural **codices**) (Latin)   A hand-painted book on bark paper or animal skins folded like a screen. In Mesoamerica, codices, which record historical, religious, and tribute information, were made both before and after the Spanish conquest.

comal (Spanish)   A flat, ceramic griddle used for cooking tortillas.

conquistador (Spanish)   A conqueror; referring to the Spanish explorers who conquered Mexico in the early 1500s and also ventured into the southern United States.

coprolite   Fossilized feces.

cord-marking   A decorative technique in Jomon Japan and elsewhere, in which cord or string is wrapped around a paddle and pressed against an unfired clay vessel, leaving the twisted mark of the cord.

core   The stone from which other pieces or flakes are removed. Core tools are shaped by the removal of flakes.

cosmology   The worldview of a group or society, encompassing their understanding of the universe, their origins and existence, and nature.

cultigen   A cultivated plant.

cultivation   The human manipulation or fostering of a plant species (often wild) to enhance or ensure production, involving such techniques as clearing fields, preparing soil, weeding, protecting plants from animals, and providing water to produce a crop.

cultural resource management   The survey and/or excavation of archaeological and historical remains threatened by construction and development.

culture   A uniquely human means of non-biological adaptation; a repertoire of learned behaviors for coping with the physical and social environment.

cuneiform   A writing system of ancient Mesopotamia involving a series of wedge-shaped marks to convey a message or text.

cutmark   A trace left on bone by a stone or metal tool used in butchering a carcass; one of the primary forms of evidence for meat-eating by early hominids.

Cyclopean stone walls   The huge stone walls of Mycenaean tombs and fortresses; from Cyclops, the mythical giant.

danzante (Spanish)   Dancer; a life-size carving of a captive or prisoner of war depicted in bas-relief on stone slabs at San José Mogote or Monte Albán, Oaxaca.

débitage (French)   A term referring to all the pieces of shatter and flakes produced and not used when stone tools are made; also called waste material.

dendrochronology   The study of the annual growth rings of trees as a dating technique to build chronologies.

dolmen   A generic term for a megalithic tomb or chamber with a roof. *See also* gallery grave; passage grave.

domestication   The taming of wild plants and animals by humans. Plants are farmed and become dependent on humans for propagation; animals are herded and often become dependent on their human caretakers for food.

dryopithecine   The generic term for the Miocene fossil ancestor of both the living apes and modern humans, found in Africa, Asia, and Europe.

ecofact   Any of the remains of plants, animals, sediments, or other unmodified materials that result from human activity.

economy   The management and organization of the affairs of a group, community, or establishment to ensure their survival and productivity.

edge hypothesis   A revised version of the population pressure hypothesis about the origins of agriculture, suggesting that the need for more food was initially felt at the margins of the natural habitat of the ancestors of domesticated plants and animals.

effigy   A representation or image of a person or animal.

egalitarian   A term that refers to societies lacking clearly defined status differences between individuals, except for those due to sex, age, or skill. *See also* hierarchical.

E group   An arrangement of buildings designed to mark the position of the rising sun during important solar events, such as equinoxes and solstices in Mesoamerica.

El Niño (Spanish)   A warm-water counter-current that periodically appears off the Peruvian coast, usually soon after Christmas, and alters the normal patterns of water temperature, flow, and salinity. These changes diminish the availability of nutrients to marine life, causing large schools of fish and flocks of seabirds to either migrate or die.

emblem glyph A set of Maya hieroglyphs; generally, each emblem glyph is specific to a given Classic Maya city. Although most Maya epigraphers agree that emblem glyphs have a geographic referent, they do not agree on whether such glyphs stand for a place or for the royal family that ruled the place.

endocast A copy or cast of the inside of a skull, reflecting the general shape and arrangement of the brain and its various parts.

epigraphy The study of inscriptions.

epiphysis (plural **epiphyses**) The end of a long bone in humans and other mammals, which hardens and attaches to the shaft of the bone with age.

epoch A subdivision of geological time, millions of years long, representing units of eras.

equinox A time when the sun crosses the plane of the equator, making night and day the same length all over earth, occurring about March 21 and September 22.

era A major division of geological time, tens or hundreds of millions of years long, usually distinguished by significant changes in the plant and animal kingdoms. Also used to denote later archaeological periods, such as the prehistoric era.

estrus The cycle of female sexual receptivity in many species of animals. The female is sexually receptive only a few days a month or year, rather than continually. Estrus is absent in the human female.

ethnocentrism Evaluating other groups or societies by standards that are relevant to the observer's culture.

ethnography The study of human cultures through firsthand observation.

ethnohistory The study of ancient (often non-Western) cultures using evidence from documentary sources and oral traditions, and often supplemented with archaeological data. Traditionally, ethnohistorians have been concerned with the early history of the New World, the time of European contact, and later settlement and colonization by Europeans.

evolution The process of change over time due to shifting conditions of the physical and cultural environment, involving mechanisms of mutation and natural selection. Human biology and culture evolved during the Pliocene, Pleistocene, and Holocene.

excavation The exposure and recording of buried materials from the past.

facade The face, or front, of a building.

feature An immovable structure or layer, pit, or post in the ground having archaeological significance.

fieldwork The search for archaeological sites in the landscape through surveys and excavations.

flake A type of stone artifact produced by removing a piece from a core through chipping. Flakes are made into a variety of different kinds of tools or used for their sharp edges (without further retouching).

flint A fine-grained, crystalline stone that fractures in a regular pattern, producing sharp-edged flakes; highly prized and extensively used for making flaked stone tools.

flintknapping The process of making chipped stone artifacts; the striking of stone with a hard or soft hammer.

floodwater farming A method of farming that recovers floodwater and diverts it to selected fields to supplement the water supply.

flotation A technique for the recovery of plant remains from archaeological sites. Sediments or pit contents are poured into water or heavy liquid; the lighter, carbonized plant remains float to the top for recovery, while the heavier sediments and other materials fall to the bottom.

fluted point The characteristic artifact of the Paleoindian period in North America. Several varieties of fluted points were used for hunting large game. The flute refers to a large channel flake removed from both sides of the base of the point to facilitate hafting.

Folsom An archaeological culture during the Paleoindian period in North America, defined by a distinctive type of fluted point and found primarily in the Great Plains.

fossil The mineralized bone of an extinct animal. Most bones associated with humans in the Pliocene, Pleistocene, and Holocene are too young to have been mineralized, but the term *fossil skull* or *fossil bone* is often used generically in these cases as well.

frieze A decorative band or feature, commonly ornamented with sculpture, usually near the top of a wall.

galena A common, heavy mineral that is the principal ore of lead.

gallery grave A megalithic tomb lacking an entrance passage; the burial room or rooms form the entire internal structure; found in Neolithic western Europe. *See also* dolmen; passage grave.

glacial A cold episode of the Pleistocene, in contrast to a warmer interglacial period; also called an ice age. The classic European sequence of the Günz, Mindel, Riss, and Würm glacials has recently been revised, with the recognition of a large number of cold/warm oscillations in the Pleistocene. *See also* interglacial.

glume The tough seed cover of many cereal kernels. In the process of the domestication of wheat, the tough glume becomes more brittle, making threshing easier.

glyph (Greek) A carving; a drawn symbol in a writing system that may stand for a syllable, a sound, an idea, a word, or a combination of these. *See also* emblem glyph.

gorget A circular ornament, flat or convex on one side and concave on the other, usually worn over the chest.

grave goods The items that are placed in graves to accompany the deceased.

guano Bird excrement.

half-life A measure of the rate of decay in radioactive materials; half the radioactive material will disappear within the period of one half-life.

hammerstone A stone used to knock flakes from cores; part of the toolkit of a flintknapper.

handaxe The characteristic artifact of the Lower Paleolithic: a large, teardrop-shaped stone tool bifacially flaked to a point at one end and a broader base at the other, for general-purpose use that continued into the Middle Paleolithic. The Acheulean handaxe is the signature tool of *Homo erectus* and early *Homo sapiens*.

hard hammer technique A percussion technique for making stone tools by striking one stone, or core, with another stone, or hammer. *See also* soft hammer technique.

hematite A common heavy mineral that is the principal ore of iron.

hemp A tall annual plant whose tough fibers are used to make coarse fabrics and ropes.

henge A monument defined by the presence of an enclosure, usually made by a circular ditch and bank system, up to 500 m in diameter. Henges were erected during the Neolithic and early Bronze Age in western Europe.

hierarchical A term referring to societies that have a graded order of ranks, statuses, or decision makers. *See also* egalitarian.

hieroglyph Originally, the pictographic script of ancient Egypt; any depictive, art-related system of writing, such as that of Mesoamerica. Also may refer to an individual symbol.

Hohokam One of three major cultural traditions of the American Southwest during late prehistoric times. The Hohokam were centered in the deserts of southern Arizona.

Holocene The most recent geological epoch, which began 10,000 years ago with the close of the Pleistocene and continues today. Some describe this epoch only as a warmer episode between glacial periods. Also called Postglacial, Present Interglacial, and Recent.

hominid The term used to describe only the human members of the primates, both fossil and modern forms.

hominoid A descriptive term for any human or ape, past or present, characterized by teeth shape, the absence of a tail, and swinging arms.

Hominoidea The taxonomic group (family) that includes the human and ape members of the primates, both fossil and modern forms.

Hopewell Interaction Sphere A complex trade network involving goods and information that connected distinct local populations in the midwestern United States from approximately 200 B.C.– A.D. 400.

horizon A widely distributed set of cultural traits and artifact assemblages whose distribution and chronology suggest they spread rapidly. A horizon is often composed of artifacts associated with a shared symbolic system.

huaca (Quechua) An Andean word for pyramid.

hunter-gatherer A hunter of large wild animals and gatherer of wild plants, seafood, and small animals, as opposed to farmers and food producers. Hunting and gathering characterized the human subsistence pattern prior to the domestication of plants and animals and the spread of agriculture. Also called foragers.

hyoid bone A delicate bone in the neck that anchors the tongue muscles in the throat.

iconography The study of artistic representations or icons that usually have religious or ceremonial significance.

ideograph A written symbol that represents an abstract idea rather than the sound of a word or the pictorial symbol of an object (pictograph).

ideology A conceptual framework by which people structure their ideas about the order of the universe, their place in that universe, and their relationships among themselves and with other objects and forms of life around them.

incensario (Spanish) An incense burner made of pottery and sometimes stone, used in Mesoamerican religious and political ceremonies.

inflorescence The flowering part of a plant.

interglacial A warm period of the Pleistocene, in contrast to a colder period called a glacial.

isotope One of several different atomic states of an element; for example, carbon occurs as ^{12}C, ^{13}C, and ^{14}C, also known as carbon-14 or radiocarbon.

isotopic technique A technique for absolute dating that relies on known rates of decay in radioactive isotopes, especially carbon, potassium, and uranium.

jasper A high-quality flint, often highly colored, often used as a raw material for the manufacture of stone tools, beads, and other ornaments.

jet A compact, black coal that can be highly polished; used to make beads, jewelry, and other decorative objects.

Jomon The archaeological culture of late Pleistocene and early Holocene Japan; primarily associated with groups of hunter-gatherers, but recent evidence suggests that these groups were practicing some rice cultivation.

kiln A furnace or oven for baking or drying objects, especially for firing pottery.

kiva A semisubterranean ceremonial room found at sites throughout the American Southwest.

krater A large metal vessel for mixing and storing wine, traded over a large part of Europe during the Iron Age.

lactational amenorrhea The suppression of ovulation and menstruation during breast-feeding.

laguna (Spanish) Lagoon; a manmade depression in Mesoamerica that may have begun as a borrow pit for the construction of an earthen mound. *Lagunas* were often lined with waterproof bentonite blocks and may have been used for ritual bathing.

lapis lazuli A semiprecious stone of deep blue color, used and traded widely in antiquity in the form of beads, pendants, and inlay.

lateralization The division of the human brain into two halves. One side controls language; the other regulates perception and motor skills.

Levallois A technique for manufacturing large, thin flakes or points from a carefully prepared core, first used during the Lower Paleolithic and remaining common during the Middle Paleolithic. The method wasted flint and was generally not used in areas of scarce raw materials.

Levant A mountainous region paralleling the eastern shore of the Mediterranean, including parts of the countries of Turkey, Syria, Lebanon, and Israel.

lintel A horizontal beam of wood or stone that supports the wall above a doorway or window.

lithic Pertaining to stone, or rock; paleolithic means old stone, neolithic means new stone, microlithic means small stone, and megalithic means giant stone.

living floor The actual surface of occupation at a prehistoric site, sometimes preserved under unusual conditions of deposition.

llama A woolly South American ruminant camelid, used as a beast of burden.

locomotion A method of movement, such as bipedalism.

loess Wind-blown silt deposited in deep layers in certain parts of the Northern Hemisphere.

lomas (Spanish) Vegetation that is supported by fog in otherwise arid environments.

Long Count The Classic Maya system of dating that records the total number of days elapsed from an initial date in the distant past (3114 B.C.). The system is based on multiples of 20, beginning with the *kin* (1 day), *uinal* (20 *kins* or 20 days), *tun* (18 *uinals* or 360 days), *katun* (20 *tuns* or 7200 days), and *baktun* (20 *katuns* or 144,000 days).

longhouse A wooden structure that is considerably longer than it is wide; served as a communal dwelling, especially among native North Americans in the Northeast and on the Northwest Coast.

lost wax casting A technique for casting metal in which a sand or clay casing is formed around a wax sculpture; molten metal is poured into the casing, melting the wax. The cooling metal takes on the shape of the "lost" wax sculpture preserved on the casing.

maguey Any of several species of arid-environment plants with fleshy leaves that conserve moisture, the fiber and needles of which were used to make rope and clothing in Mesoamerica.

mano The hand-held part of a stone-milling assembly for grinding maize or other foods.

manuport A natural stone carried into an archaeological site and used without significant modification as a seat, anvil, pillow, and the like; recognized as exotic to the specific location where found.

marketing An exchange system that frequently involves currencies and generally extends beyond close kinsmen and a small group of trading partners. Market participants try to minimize their costs and maximize their returns to make a profit.

megalith (Greek) A large stone monument.

menhir A large, standing stone, erected either singly or collectively in a linear arrangement.

Mesoamerica The region consisting of central and southern Mexico, Guatemala, Belize, El Salvador, and the western parts of Honduras and Nicaragua that was the focus of complex, hierarchical states at the time of Spanish contact. The people of this area shared a basic set of cultural conventions. Also called Middle America.

Mesolithic The period of time of hunter-gatherers in Europe, North Africa, and parts of Asia between the end of the Pleistocene and the introduction of farming; the Middle Stone Age. *See also* Neolithic; Paleolithic.

Mesozoic The geological era spanning approximately 225–65 m.y.a., often called the Age of Dinosaurs.

mesquite A tree or shrub of the southwestern United States and Mexico whose beanlike pods are rich in sugar.

metallurgy The art of separating metals from their ores.

metate The stone basin, often trough-shaped, or lower part of a stone-milling assembly for grinding maize or other foods.

microband A small family group of hunter-gatherers.

midden An accumulated pile of trash and waste materials near a dwelling or in other areas of an archaeological site. *See also* shell midden.

Milankovitch forcing A term describing the phenomenon considered to be the prime reason for glacial fluctuations and climatic change. Changing factors are the distance between earth and the sun and the tilt of earth's axis, which play major roles in the amount of sunlight reaching earth, atmospheric tempera-ture, and the expansion and retreat of continental glaciation. The cyclical nature of variation in these factors was recognized by Yugoslavian mathematician Milutin Milankovitch.

millennium (plural **millennia**) A period of 1000 years. The millennia before Christ run in reverse; the first millennium is 0–1000 B.C., the second is 1000–2000 B.C., and so on.

Mississippian The collective name applied to the societies that inhabited portions of the eastern United States from approximately A.D. 700–1600. Mississippian peoples practiced an agricultural way of life, constructed earthen platform mounds, and shared certain basic cultural conventions.

mit'a system A means of tribute in prehispanic Andean South America that involved the use of conscripted laborers to complete discrete organizational tasks.

mitmaq A system of colonization used by the Inca to minimize provincial rebellion by moving people around to break up dissident groups.

mitochondrial DNA Genetic material in the mitochondria of human cells that mutates at a relatively constant rate. Because mitochondrial DNA is inherited only from the mother, it provides an unaltered link to past generations.

Mogollon One of three major cultural traditions of the American Southwest during late prehistoric times. The Mogollon were centered in the mountainous areas of southeastern Arizona and southwestern New Mexico.

montaña (Spanish) Mountain, specifically referring to the wet, tropical slopes of the Amazonian Andes.

mortar A bowl-shaped grinding tool, used with a wood or stone pestle for grinding various materials.

Mousterian A term describing the stone tool assemblages of the Neanderthals during the Middle Paleolithic, named after the site of Le Moustier in France. *See also* Acheulean.

multivallate A term describing complex defenses of multiple ditches and ramparts at large Iron Age hillforts.

mural art One of the two major categories of Paleolithic art, along with portable art. Mural art consists of painting, engraving, and sculpting on the walls of the caves, shelters, and cliffs of southwestern Europe; one of the hallmarks of the Upper Paleolithic.

natural habitat hypothesis A theory about the origins of agriculture associated with Robert Braidwood, suggesting that the earliest domesticates appeared in the area their wild ancestors inhabited.

necropolis (Greek) Cemetery.

Neolithic The period of time of early farmers with domesticated plants and animals, polished stone tools, permanent villages, and often pottery; the New Stone Age. *See also* Mesolithic; Paleolithic.

net-sinker A small weight attached to fishing nets.

nome A geographic province incorporated within the ancient Egyptian state.

oasis hypothesis A theory about the origins of agriculture associated with V. Gordon Childe and others, suggesting that domestication began as a symbiotic relationship between humans, plants, and animals at oases during the desiccation of the Near East at the end of the Pleistocene.

obsidian Translucent, gray to black or green, glasslike rock from molten sand; produces extremely sharp edges when fractured and was highly valued for making stone tools.

occipital bun A distinctive shelf or protrusion at the lower base of the skull; a feature usually associated with Neanderthals.

Oldowan A term used to describe the earliest kinds of stone tools from the end of the Pliocene and the early Pleistocene, discovered at Olduvai Gorge. Oldowan assemblages contain various types of unifacial and bifacial pebble tools and flakes.

Olmec The Aztec name for the late prehispanic inhabitants of the Gulf Coast region of Mexico. This term has been extended by archaeologists to describe the sites, monuments, and art found in the same region during the Formative period. Aspects of this art style and related motifs have a wider distribution across Mesoamerica during the Early and Middle Formative periods (1150–700 B.C.). This broader distribution is called the Olmec Horizon.

oppidum (plural **oppida**) (Latin) A massive fortification in western Europe, often on a hilltop or bluff, built for defensive purposes during the Iron Age; described in some detail and often conquered by the Romans.

optical emission spectroscopy A technique used in the analysis of the elemental composition of artifacts. Material is heated to a high temperature, causing its electrons to release light of a particular wavelength, depending on the elements present. Because of different characteristic wavelengths for different elements, it is possible to determine what elements are present in the tested material.

oracle bone   An animal bone with cracks (due to heating) or other markings, used to foretell the future.

oxygen isotope ratio   The ratio of different isotopes of oxygen in ocean water, varying with the temperature of the water; measured in seashells and used as an indicator of temperature change over time.

paleoanthropology   The branch of anthropology that combines archaeology and physical anthropology to study the biological and behavioral remains of the early hominids.

paleoethnobotany   The study of plant remains from archaeological sites.

Paleoindian   The period of large-game hunters in North America at the end of the Pleistocene. Paleoindian remains are characterized by the presence of fluted points and frequently the bones of extinct animals.

Paleolithic   The first period of human prehistory, extending from the time of the first tools, more than 2.5 m.y.a., until the end of the Pleistocene, 10,000 years ago; characterized by the use of flaked stone tools, it is also known as the Old Stone Age.

Paleozoic   The geological era spanning 600–225 m.y.a., that witnessed the appearance of the first vertebrate species— fish, amphibians, and reptiles—and the spread of plants to the land.

palisade   A fence of posts or stakes erected around a settlement for defensive purposes.

palynology   The study of pollen for the reconstruction of past climate and environment. Also called pollen analysis.

papyrus   An ancient type of paper made from the papyrus plant, used by the ancient Egyptians for writing.

Paranthropus   Genus of early hominids, contemporary with *Australopithecus,* that includes *boisei* and *robustus* as species.

passage grave   A megalithic tomb entered via a long, low, narrow passage that opens into a wider room, generally near the center of the structure. *See also* dolmen; gallery grave.

pastoralist   An animal herder; pastoralism is a subsistence strategy generally associated with a mobile lifeway.

patrilocal   Describing a residence pattern in which married couples live with or near the husband's family.

pectoral   An ornament worn across the chest, especially for defensive purposes.

percussion flaking   A technique for producing stone artifacts by striking or knapping crystalline stone with a hard or soft hammer. *See also* pressure flaking.

petroglyph   A drawing that has been carved into rock.

petty state   A small, socially stratified political unit prevalent in Mesoamerica at the time of the Spanish conquest. Similar political formations have been found in other regions as well.

phonetic   Pertaining to the sounds of speech.

photomicrograph   A photograph of a microscopic object, taken through a microscope.

pictograph   A written or painted symbol that more or less portrays the represented object. *See also* ideograph.

pithos (plural *pithoi*) (Greek)   A large clay storage jar.

pithouse   A prehistoric semisubterranean dwelling in which the lower parts of the walls are the earthen sides of a shallow pit; the top part of the walls often consisted of a framework of poles intertwined with small twigs, covered with mud.

Pleistocene   The geological epoch from 2 m.y.a. to 10,000 B.P., characterized by oscillations in climate between warm and cold, the expansion of continental ice sheets, significant changes in sea level, and much of the evolution of the human species.

Pliocene   The geological epoch spanning 5.5–2 m.y.a., which witnessed the appearance of the first hominids.

Plio/Pleistocene   A combination term used to describe the time between the appearance of the earliest hominids during the Pliocene and the beginning of the Pleistocene.

pochteca   A privileged, hereditary guild of long-distance Aztec traders.

pollen diagram   A chart showing the proportions of different species of pollen in a stratigraphic sequence.

polychrome   Multicolored; describing pottery that has been decorated with three or more colors.

polygynous   Having more than one mate.

population pressure hypothesis   A theory about the origins of agriculture espoused by Lewis Binford in terms of an equilibrium between people and food, a balance that could be upset by either a decline in available food or an increase in the number of people; because cli-

matic and environmental changes appeared to be minimal in the Near East, population increase upset the balance, forcing people to turn to agriculture as a way to produce more food.

portable art   One of the two major categories of Paleolithic art, along with mural art. Portable art includes all decorated materials that can be moved or carried; found throughout Europe and much of the Old World.

Postglacial   *See* Holocene.

posthole   *See* post mold.

post mold   The circular remains, often just a dark stain in the soil, of a wooden post that formed part of the frame of prehistoric structures. Also called a posthole.

potassium-argon dating   *See* radiopotassium dating.

potlatch   A large feast among Northwest Coast Native Americans that included the display and dispersal of accumulated wealth to the assembled guests.

potsherd   A fragment of a clay vessel or object.

Precambrian   The first major era of geological time, extending from the formation of the earth to approximately 600 m.y.a.

prehistory   In general, the human past; specifically, the time before the appearance of written records.

Present Interglacial   *See* Holocene.

pressure flaking   A technique for producing stone artifacts by removing flakes from a stone core by pressing with a pointed implement. *See also* percussion flaking.

primate   The order of animals that includes lemurs, tarsiers, monkeys, apes, and humans, characterized by grasping hands, flexible limbs, and a highly developed sense of vision.

provenience   The established position of an artifact; in the context of a specific site, the horizontal and vertical locations of an object in relation to an established coordinate system. When the position of a specific object is known to archaeologists, it is considered well provenienced.

pueblo   A stone-masonry complex of adjoining rooms found in the American Southwest.

puna (Spanish)   High grassland plateaus in the Peruvian Andes.

quern   A stone grinding surface for preparing grains and other plant foods and for grinding other materials.

quetzal   A bird native to the humid mountain forests of Mesoamerica, prized for its brilliant feathers.

quipu The Inca word for a numerical device consisting of a horizontal cord from which a series of smaller strings hung. The Inca used the *quipu* to record numbers by tying knots at various intervals along the strings.

rachis The stem that holds seeds to the stalk in wheat and other plants; changes from brittle to tough when wheat is domesticated.

radiocarbon dating An absolute dating technique based on the principle of decay of the radioactive isotope of carbon, ^{14}Carbon; used to date archaeological materials within the last 40,000 years.

radiopotassium dating An absolute dating technique based on the principle of decay of the radioactive isotope of potassium, ^{40}K; used to date materials ranging in age from 500,000 years ago to the age of the oldest rocks in the universe. Also called potassium-argon dating.

Recent *See* Holocene.

reciprocity The exchange of goods between known participants, involving simple barter and face-to-face exchanges.

red ochre An iron mineral that occurs in nature, used by prehistoric peoples in powdered form as a pigment for tanning animal skins; often found in burials from the late Paleolithic and Mesolithic.

redistribution The accumulation and dispersal of goods through a centralized agency, individual, or institution.

reducing atmosphere The oxygen-deficient atmosphere that is achieved in kilns for baking pottery or smelting ores.

reduction In archaeology, a manufacturing process involving the removal (as opposed to the addition) of materials from a core that becomes the finished product; includes techniques like flintknapping and wood carving.

refitting A technique for reassembling the scattered pieces of stone, pottery, or bone at an archaeological site to study patterns of manufacture and disposal.

relative dating A technique used to *estimate* the antiquity of archaeological materials, generally based on association with materials of known age or simply to say that one item is younger or older than another. *See also* absolute dating.

repoussé (French) The process of forming a raised design on a thin sheet of metal by placing it over a mold and hammering it in place.

retouching The shaping or sharpening of stone artifacts through percussion or pressure flaking; a technique of flintknapping.

rhizome An edible, rootlike subterranean plant stem.

sacbe The Maya word for a raised causeway constructed of stone blocks and paved with gravel and plaster.

sarcophagus A stone coffin, usually decorated with sculpture and/or inscriptions.

scapulimancy The ancient practice of seeking knowledge by reading cracks on bones. Symbols were written on an animal's scapula (shoulder blade); the bone was heated until a series of cracks formed; then diviners interpreted the pattern of cracking to foretell the future.

scheduling The process of arranging the extraction of resources based on their availability and the demands of competing subsistence activities.

seasonality The changing availability of resources according to the different seasons of the year.

sedentism The transition from a mobile way of life to living in more permanent contexts, such as villages.

setaria A wild grass with edible seeds.

sexual dimorphism A difference in size between the male and female members of a species; for example, male gorillas are significantly larger than females.

sexual division of labor The cooperative relationship between the sexes in hunter-gatherer groups.

shaduf An Egyptian bucket-and-lever lifting device that enables one to raise water a few feet from a well or ditch into fields and gardens.

shaft grave A vertical tunnel cut into rock in which the tombs of Mycenaean elite were placed.

shaman An anthropological term for a spiritualist, curer, or seer.

shattering A natural mechanism of seed dispersal.

shell midden A mound of shells accumulated from human collection, consumption, and disposal; a dump of shells from oysters, clams, mussels, or other species found along coasts and rivers, usually dating to the Holocene.

shicra The Inca word for meshed bags containing rocks, used as fill in the reconstruction of ancient Andean structures.

sickle A tool for cutting the stalks of cereals, especially wheat. Prehistoric sickles were usually stone blades set in a wood or antler handle.

sickle polish A clear polish that forms along the edges of flakes and blades that are used to cut reeds, grass, wheat, and other long-stemmed plants.

site The accumulation of artifacts and/or ecofacts, representing a place where people lived or carried out certain activities.

slash and burn A type of farming in which the ground is cleared by cutting and burning the vegetation on the spot. The burned vegetation serves as a natural fertilizer. The field is farmed until yields decrease; then it is allowed to lie fallow. Also called swidden farming.

slate A fine-grained rock, with a dull, dark bluish-gray color, that tends to split along parallel cleavage planes, often producing thin plates or sheets.

social hypothesis A theory about the origins of agriculture, suggesting that domestication was the solution to a social problem, allowing certain individuals to accumulate food surplus and to transform those foods into more valued items, such as rare stones or metals, and even social alliances.

social organization The roles and relationships among people in a society.

soft hammer technique A flintknapping technique that involves the use of a hammer of bone, antler, or wood, rather than stone. *See also* hard hammer technique.

solifluction A phenomenon in which freezing and thawing of the ground results in slippage of the surface.

solstice The time of year when the sun is at its greatest distance from the equator, occurring about June 21 and December 22.

sondage (French) A test excavation or test pit made at an archaeological site to determine the content and/or distribution of prehistoric materials.

Southern Cult A network of interaction, exchange, and shared information present over much of the southeastern (and parts of the midwestern) United States from around A.D. 1200 until the early 1500s. Also called Southeastern Ceremonial Complex.

spindle whorl A cam or balance wheel on a shaft or spindle for spinning yarn or thread from wool, cotton, or other material; usually made of clay.

split inheritance An Andean practice by which the successor to the throne inherited only the office of the dead ruler, while his junior kinsmen received the lands, palace, and personal wealth of the dead ruler.

state A form of government with an internally specialized and hierarchically organized decision-making apparatus. A state generally has three or more administrative levels. Societies that have state institutions are referred to as state societies or state-level societies.

status differentiation Inequality in human society in which certain individuals or groups have access to more resources, power, and roles than others. Differentiation occurs through ranking of descent groups or the creation of classes of people. *See also* egalitarian; hierarchical.

steatite Soapstone, a variety of talc with a soapy or greasy feel, often used to make containers or carved ornaments.

stela (plural **stelae**) (Latin) An erect stone monument that is often carved.

stone boiling The process of heating stones in a fire and then adding them to containers to boil water or cook other foods.

stratigraphic section The excavation of trenches and squares across manmade features to expose a cross section of the deposits and reveal the sequence and methods of construction.

stucco A type of plaster, often made of lime, used for decoration.

survey A systematic search of the landscape for artifacts and sites on the ground through aerial photography, field walking, soil analysis, and geophysical prospecting.

talud-tablero (Spanish) An architectural style characteristic of Teotihuacan during the Classic period, in which recessed rectangular panels (the *tablero*) are separated by sloping aprons (the *talud*).

tampu A roadside lodging and storage place along the Inca road system; *tampus* were located roughly one day's walk apart.

technology The combination of knowledge and manufacturing techniques that enable people to convert raw materials into finished products.

tell A mound composed of mud bricks and refuse, accumulated as a result of human activity. The mound of Jericho built up at a rate of roughly 26 cm (10 in) per 100 years, almost a foot a century.

temper A nonplastic material (such as sand, shell, or fiber) that is added to clay to improve its workability and to reduce breakage during drying and firing.

temporal marker A morphological type, such as a design motif on pottery or a particular type of stone tool, that has been shown to have a discrete and definable temporal range.

teosinte (Aztec *teocentli*) A tall annual grass, native to Mexico and Central America, that is the closest relative of maize.

terracotta A hard, brown-orange earthenware clay of fine quality, often used for architectural decorations, figurines, etc.

tholos tomb A large, beehive-shaped tomb, constructed using the corbel arch technique, characteristic of the Mycenaean civilization of Greece.

tlachtli The Aztec word for their ritual ballgame.

totem pole A pole or post that has been carved and painted with totems or figures, such as animals, that serve as the emblems of clans or families. Native Americans of the Pacific Northwest often erected these poles in front of their houses.

transhumance A pattern of seasonal movement usually associated with pastoralists who take their herds to the mountains in summer and the valleys in winter; more generally, a regular pattern of seasonal movement by human groups.

trilithon A massive stone lintel occurring in prehistoric structures, such as Stonehenge and the *tholos* tombs in Greece.

tuber A fleshy, usually oblong or rounded outgrowth (such as the potato) of a subterranean stem or root of a plant.

tumpline A strap that is passed over the forehead or the chest to facilitate the transportation of a heavy load carried on the back.

tzompantli The Aztec word for skull rack. The Aztec often placed the skulls of sacrificial victims on a wooden pole or frame; in some cases, large blocks of stone were sculpted to look like skull racks.

unifacial A term describing a flaked stone tool in which only one face or side is retouched to make a sharp edge. *See also* bifacial.

wadi (Arabic) A dry streambed.

waranqa A subdivision of the Inca empire that was used for administrative purposes, consisting of 1000 taxpayers.

wattle and daub A building technique that uses a framework of poles, interspersed with smaller poles and twigs; the wooden frame is plastered with mud or a mud mixture.

were-jaguar A representation of a deity that is half jaguar and half human, a common symbol in Preclassic Mesoamerica.

wet-site excavation The technique of excavating waterlogged sites by pumping water through garden hoses to spray the dirt away and expose archaeological features and artifacts.

wheel-thrown pottery Pottery that is made using the potter's wheel.

woodhenge A circular feature demarcated by large upright timbers, probably used by prehistoric groups as astronomical observatories.

ziggurat A large pyramid in Mesopotamia consisting of many stepped levels.

zoomorphic Having animal form or attributes.

REFERENCES

Aaris-Sørensen, K., and E. Brinch Petersen. 1986. The Prejlerup aurochs—an archaeozoological discovery from Boreal, Denmark. *Striae* 24:111–117.

Adams, D. 1980. *The hitchhiker's guide to the galaxy.* New York: Harmony.

Adams, R. E. W. 1991. *Prehistoric Mesoamerica,* rev. ed. Norman: University of Oklahoma Press.

Adams, R. E. W., W. E. Brown, and T. P. Culbert. 1981. Radar mapping, archeology and ancient Maya land use. *Science* 213:1457–1463.

Adams, R. Mc. 1981. *Heartland of cities.* Chicago: University of Chicago Press.

Aiello, L. C. 1993. The fossil evidence for modern human origins in Africa: A revised view. *American Anthropologist* 95: 73–96.

Aikens, C. M., and T. Higuchi. 1982. *The prehistory of Japan.* New York: Academic Press.

Aikens, R. J. C. 1956. *Stonehenge.* Baltimore: Pelican.

Aitken, M. J. 1985. *Thermoluminescence dating.* New York: Academic Press.

Akazawa, T. 1980. Fishing adaptation of prehistoric hunter-gatherers at the Nittano site, Japan. *Journal of Archaeological Science* 7:325–344.

Allchin, B., and R. Allchin. 1982. *The rise of civilization in India and Pakistan.* Cambridge: Cambridge University Press.

Alva, W., and C. B. Donnan. 1993. *Royal tombs of Sipán.* Los Angeles: Fowler Museum of Cultural History, University of California.

Ames, K. M. 1981. The evolution of social ranking on the Northwest Coast of North America. *American Antiquity* 46: 789–805.

Ammerman, A. J., and L. L. Cavalli-Sforza. 1984. *The Neolithic transition and the genetics of populations in Europe.* Princeton: Princeton University Press.

Anawalt, P. R. 1982. Understanding Aztec human sacrifice. *Archaeology* 35(3): 38–45.

Anderson, A. 1987. Recent developments in Japanese prehistory: A review. *American Antiquity* 61:270–281.

Appenzeller, T. 1994. Clashing Maya superpowers emerge from a new analysis. *Science* 226:733–734.

Arens, W. 1979. *The man-eating myth: Anthropology and anthropophagy.* New York: Oxford University Press.

Arnold, B., and D. B. Gibson, eds. 1998. *Celtic chiefdom, Celtic state.* Cambridge: Cambridge University Press.

Aveni, A. F. 1986. The Nazca lines: Patterns in the desert. *Archaeology* 39(4):32–39.

Bahn, P. G., and C. Renfrew. 1996. *The Cambridge illustrated history of archaeology.* Cambridge: Cambridge University Press.

Baines, J., and J. Málek. 1980. *Atlas of ancient Egypt.* New York: Facts on File.

Banning, E. B., and B. F. Byrd. 1987. Houses and changing residential units: Domestic architecture at PPNB 'Ain Ghazal, Jordan. *Proceedings of the Prehistoric Society* 53:8–65.

Barber, R. L. N. 1988. *The Cyclades in the Bronze Age.* Iowa City: University of Iowa Press.

Bareis, C. J., and J. W. Porter, eds. 1984. *American Bottom archaeology.* Urbana: University of Illinois Press.

Barker, G. 1985. *Prehistoric farming in Europe.* Cambridge: Cambridge University Press.

Bar-Yosef, O. 1986. The walls of Jericho: An alternative explanation. *Current Anthropology* 27:157–162.

Bar-Yosef, O. 1998. The Natufian culture in the Levant: Threshold to the origins of agriculture. *Evolutionary Anthropology* 6: 159–177.

Bar-Yosef, O., and A. Belfer Cohen. 1992. Foraging to farming in the Mediterranean Levant. In *Transitions to agriculture in prehistory,* ed. A. B. Gebauer and T. D. Price. Madison, WI: Prehistory Press.

Bayard, D. 1971. *Non Nok Tha: The 1968 excavation procedure, stratigraphy, and a summary of evidence.* University of Otago: Studies in Prehistoric Anthropology, Vol. 4. Dunedin, NZ.

Bayard, D. 1980. East Asia in the Bronze Age. In *The Cambridge encyclopedia of archaeology,* ed. A. Sherratt. New York: Crown.

Beadle, G. 1980. The ancestry of corn. *Scientific American* 242:112–119.

Becker, M. J. 1979. Priests, peasants, and ceremonial centers: The intellectual history of a model. In *Maya archaeology and ethnohistory,* ed. N. Hammond and G. R. Willey. Austin: University of Texas Press.

Bellwood, P. 1978. *Man's conquest of the Pacific.* Oxford: Oxford University Press.

Bellwood, P. 1990. Foraging towards farming: A decisive transition or a millennial blur? *Review of Archaeology* 11:14–24.

Bender, B. 1978. Gatherer-hunter to farmer: A social perspective. *World Archaeology* 10:204–222.

Bennett, W. C. 1934. Excavations at Tiahuanaco. *Anthropological Papers of the American Museum of Natural History* 34(3):359–494.

Bennett, W. C. 1947. The archaeology of the central Andes. In *Handbook of South American Indians: Vol. 2, The Andean civilizations,* ed. J. Steward. Washington, DC: Smithsonian Institution, Bureau of American Ethnology, Bulletin 143.

Benson, E. P., ed. 1968. *Dumbarton Oaks conference on the Olmec.* Washington, DC: Dumbarton Oaks.

Benson, E. P., ed. 1971. *Dumbarton Oaks conference on Chavín.* Washington, DC: Dumbarton Oaks.

Benson, E. P., ed. 1981. *The Olmec and their neighbors: Essays in memory of Matthew W. Stirling.* Washington, DC: Dumbarton Oaks.

Berdan, F. 1982. *The Aztecs of central Mexico: An imperial society.* New York: Holt, Rinehart & Winston.

Berger, R., R. Chohfi, A. V. Zegarra, W. Yepez, and O. F. Carrasco. 1988. Radiocarbon dating Machu Picchu, Peru. *Antiquity* 62:707–710.

Berlo, J. C., ed. 1992. *Art, ideology, and the city of Teotihuacan.* Washington, DC: Dumbarton Oaks.

Bermudéz de Castro, J. M. A. 1998. Hominids at Atapuerca: The first human occupation in Europe. In *The first Europeans: Recent discoveries and current debate,* ed. E. Carbonell, J. Bermudéz de Castro, J. L. Arsuaga, and X. P. Rodriguez, pp. 45–66. Burgos, Spain: Aldecoa.

Bernal, I. 1965. Archaeological synthesis of Oaxaca. In *Handbook of Middle American Indians, Vol. 3: Archaeology of southern Mesoamerica,* ed. G. R. Willey. Austin: University of Texas Press.

Bernal, I. 1980. *A history of Mexican archaeology: The vanished civilizations of Middle America.* London: Thames & Hudson.

Bicchieri, M. G. 1972. *Hunters and gatherers today.* New York: Holt, Rinehart & Winston.

Bickerton, D. 1991. *Language and species.* Chicago: University of Chicago Press.

Binford, L. R. 1968. Post-Pleistocene adaptations. In *New perspectives in archaeology,* ed. S. R. Binford and L. R. Binford. Chicago: Aldine.

Binford, L. R. 1983. *In pursuit of the past.* New York: Thames & Hudson.

Binford, L. R., and S. R. Binford. 1966. A preliminary analysis of functional variability in the Mousterian of Levallois facies. In *Recent studies in paleoanthropology,* ed. J. D. Clark and F. C. Howell. *American Anthropologist,* special issue 68 (2,2):238–295.

Binford, L. R., and C. K. Ho. 1985. Taphonomy at a distance: Zhoukoudien, the cave home of Beijing man. *Current Anthropology* 26:413–442.

Bingham, H. 1915. The story of Machu Picchu: The Peruvian expeditions of the National Geographic Society and Yale University. *National Geographic* 27(2):172–216.

Bingham, H. 1948. *Lost city of the Incas.* New York: Duell, Sloan & Pearce.

Black, D. 1931. On an adolescent skull of *Sinanthropus pekinensis* in comparison with an adult skull of the same species and with other hominid skulls, recent and fossil. *Palaeontologica Sinica,* Series D, Vol. 7, Fasicule 2.

Blanton, R. E. 1978. *Monte Albán: Settlement patterns at the ancient Zapotec capital.* New York: Academic Press.

Blanton, R. E. 1983. The ecological perspective in highland Mesoamerican archaeology. In *Archaeological hammers and theories,* ed. J. A. Moore and A. S. Keene. New York: Academic Press.

Blanton, R. E., S. A. Kowalewski, G. M. Feinman, and L. M. Finsten. 1993. *Ancient Mesoamerica: A comparison of change in three regions.* 2d ed. Cambridge: Cambridge University Press.

Blumenschine, R. J. 1987. Characteristics of the early hominid scavenging niche. *Current Anthropology* 28:383–407.

Bogucki, P. 1988. *Forest farmers and stockherders.* Cambridge: Cambridge University Press.

Bordaz, J. 1971. *Tools of the Old and New Stone Age.* New York: American Museum of Natural History.

Bordes, F. 1968. *The Old Stone Age.* New York: McGraw-Hill.

Bordes, F. 1972. *A tale of two caves.* New York: Harper & Row.

Bordes, F., and D. de Sonneville-Bordes. 1970. The significance of variability in Paleolithic assemblages. *World Archaeology* 2:61–73.

Boserup, E. 1965. *The conditions of agricultural growth: The economics of agrarian change under population pressure.* Chicago: Aldine.

Boule, M. 1911–1913. L'homme fossile de La Chapelle-aux-Saintes. *Annales de Paléontologie,* VI–VIII.

Bowen, D. Q. 1978. *Quaternary geology.* Oxford: Pergamon Press.

Bradley, R. 1984. *The social foundations of prehistoric Britain.* Harlow, Great Britain: Longman.

Braidwood, R. J. 1960. The agricultural revolution. *Scientific American* 203(3): 130–148.

Brain, C. K. 1981. *The hunters or the hunted? An introduction to African cave taphonomy.* Chicago: University of Chicago Press.

Braudel, F. 1970. History and the social sciences: The long term. *Social Science Information* 9:145–174.

Brewer, D. J., and E. Teeter. 1999. *Egypt and the Egyptians.* Cambridge: Cambridge University Press.

Brose, D., J. Brown, and D. Penney. 1985. *Ancient art of the American Woodland Indians.* New York: Harry N. Abrams.

Browman, D. L. 1981. New light on Andean Tiwanaku. *American Scientist* 69(4): 408–419.

Bruhns, K. O. 1994. *Ancient South America.* Cambridge: Cambridge University Press.

Brunhouse, R. L. 1973. *In search of the Maya.* New York: Ballantine Books.

Bryan, A. L. 1978. *Early man in America from a circum-Pacific perspective.* Edmonton: Archaeological Researches International.

Bryan, A. L. 1986. *New evidence for the Pleistocene peopling of the Americas.* Orono, ME: Center for the study of Early Man.

Burenhult, G., ed. 1994. *Old World civilizations: The rise of cities and states.* New York and San Francisco: HarperCollins.

Burger, R. L. 1984. *The prehistoric occupation of Chavín de Huantar, Peru.* Berkeley: University of California Press.

Burger, R. L. 1985. Concluding remarks: Early Peruvian civilization and its relation to the Chavín horizon. In *Early ceremonial architecture in the Andes,* ed. C. B. Donnan. Washington, DC: Dumbarton Oaks.

Burger, R. L. 1989. An overview of Peruvian archaeology (1976–1986). *Annual Review of Anthropology* 18:37–69.

Burger, R. L. 1992. *Chavin and the origins of Andean civilization.* London: Thames & Hudson.

Burl, A. 1976. *Stone circles of the British Isles.* New Haven: Yale University Press.

Butzer, K. W. 1980. Civilizations: Organisms or systems? *American Scientist* 68: 148–160.

Butzer, K. 1982. *Archaeology as human ecology.* Cambridge: Cambridge University Press.

Calnek, E. E. 1976. The internal structure of Tenochtitlan. In *The Valley of Mexico: Studies in pre-Hispanic ecology and society,* ed. E. R. Wolf. Albuquerque: University of New Mexico Press.

Cann, R. L., M. Stoneking, and A. C. Wilson. 1987. Mitochondrial DNA and human evolution. *Nature* 325:31–36.

Carneiro, R. L. 1970. A theory of the origin of the state. *Science* 169:733–738.

Caso, A., and I. Bernal. 1965. Ceramics of Oaxaca. In *Handbook of Middle American Indians, Vol. 3: Archaeology of southern Mesoamerica,* ed. G. R. Willey. Austin: University of Texas Press.

Chakrabarti, D. 1980. Early agriculture and the development of towns in India. In *The Cambridge encyclopedia of archaeology,* ed. A. Sherratt. New York: Crown.

Chang, K. C. 1973. Food and food vessels in ancient China. *Transactions of the New York Academy of Sciences* 35(6): 495–520.

Chang, K. C. 1977a. Chinese archaeology since 1949. *Journal of Asian Studies* 36(4):623–646.

Chang, K. C. 1977b. The continuing quest for China's origins, I: Early farmers in China. *Antiquity* 30(2):116–123.

Chang, K. C. 1977c. The continuing quest for China's origins, II: The Shang civilization. *Antiquity* 30(3):187–193.

Chang, K. C. 1981. In search of China's beginnings: New light on an old civilization. *American Scientist* 69:148–160.

Chang, K. C. 1986. *The archaeology of ancient China.* New Haven: Yale University Press.

Chang, K. C. 1989. Ancient China and its anthropological significance. In *Archaeological thought in America,* ed. C. C. Lamberg-Karlovsky. Cambridge: Cambridge University Press.

Chang, K. C. 1994. Ritual and power. In *Cradles of civilization: China,* ed. R. E. Murowchick. Norman: University of Oklahoma Press.

Changeux, J.-P., and J. Chavillon, eds. 1995. *Origins of the human brain.* Oxford: Oxford University Press.

Chesterton, G. K. 1933. *All I survey: A book of essays.* London: Methuen.

Childe, V. G. 1950. The urban revolution. *The Town Planning Review* 21:3–17.

Childe, V. G. 1951. *Man makes himself.* New York: New American Library.

Childe, V. G. 1956. *A short introduction to archaeology: Man and society.* London: F. Muller.

Churchill, S. E. 1998. Cold adaptation, heterochrony, and Neandertals. *Evolutionary Anthropology* 7:46–61.

Cieza de León, P. 1959. *The Incas,* trans. H. de Onis, ed. V. von Hagen. Norman: University of Oklahoma Press.

Clark, J. D. 1970a. *Kalambo Falls.* Cambridge: Cambridge University Press.

Clark, J. D. 1970b. *The prehistory of Africa.* London: Thames & Hudson.

Clark, J. D., and S. A. Brandt, eds. 1984. *From hunters to farmers.* Berkeley: University of California Press.

Clark, J. D., and J. W. K. Harris. 1985. Fire and its roles in early hominid lifeways. *African Archaeological Review* 3:3–28.

Clark, J. E. 1986. From mountains to molehills: A critical review of Teotihuacan's obsidian industry. In *Research in Economic Anthropology, Supplement 2,* ed. B. L. Isaac. Greenwich, CT: JAI Press.

Clutton-Brock, J. 1999. *A natural history of domesticated animals.* Cambridge: Cambridge University Press.

Coe, M. D. 1977. *Mexico.* 2d ed. New York: Praeger.

Coe, M. D. 1984. *The Maya.* 3d ed. London: Thames & Hudson.

Coe, M. D., and R. A. Diehl. 1980. *In the land of the Olmec: The archaeology of San Lorenzo Tenochtitlan.* Austin: University of Texas Press.

Coe, M., D. Snow, and E. Benson. 1986. *Atlas of ancient America.* New York: Facts on File.

Coe, W. R. 1965. Tikal: Ten years of study of a Maya ruin in the lowlands of Guatemala. *Expedition* 8:5–56.

Coe, W. R. 1967. *Tikal: A handbook of the ancient Maya ruins.* Philadelphia: University Museum.

Coe, W. R., and W. A. Haviland. 1982. Introduction to the archaeology of Tikal, Guatemala. *University Museum Monograph 46.* Philadelphia: University of Pennsylvania.

Coggins, C. 1979. A new order and the role of the calendar: Some characteristics of the Middle Classic period at Tikal. In *Maya archaeology and ethnohistory,* ed. N. Hammond. Austin: University of Texas Press.

Cohen, M. N. 1977. Population pressure and the origins of agriculture: An archaeological example from the coast of Peru. In *The origins of agriculture,* ed. C. Reed. The Hague: Mouton.

Cole, S. 1975. *Leakey's luck: The life of Louis Seymour Bazett Leakey, 1903–1972.* New York: Harcourt Brace Jovanovich.

Coles, J. M. 1982. The Bronze Age in northwestern Europe. *Advances in World Archaeology* 1:265–321.

Coles, J. M., and E. S. Higgs. 1969. *The archaeology of early man.* London: Faber & Faber.

Conkey, M. W. 1980. The identification of prehistoric hunter-gatherer aggregation sites: The case of Altamira. *Current Anthropology* 21:609–630.

Conkey, M. W. 1981. A century of Paleolithic cave art. *Archaeology* 34:20–28.

Conrad, G. W. 1981. Cultural materialism, split inheritance, and the expansion of ancient Peruvian empires. *American Antiquity* 46:3–26.

Coope, G. R. 1975. Climatic fluctuations in northwest Europe since the Last Interglacial, indicated by fossil assemblages of Coleoptera. In *Ice Ages: Ancient and modern,* ed. A. E. Wright and F. Moseley. Liverpool: Seel House Press.

Cordell, L. S. 1979. Prehistory: Eastern Anasazi. In *Handbook of North American Indians, Vol. 9: Southwest,* ed. A. Ortiz. Washington, DC: Smithsonian Institution Press.

Cordell, L. S. 1997. *Archaeology of the Southwest.* 2d ed. San Diego: Academic Press.

Costantini, L. 1984. The beginning of agriculture in the Kachi Plain: The evidence of Mehrgarh. In *South Asian archaeology 1981,* ed. B. Allchin. New York: Cambridge University Press.

Cowan, C. W., and P. J. Watson. 1992. *Origins of agriculture in world perspective.* Washington, DC: Smithsonian Institution Press.

Cowgill, G. L. 1975. Population pressure as a non-explanation. In *Population studies in archaeology and biological anthropology,* ed. A. C. Swedlund. *American Antiquity, Memoir* 30:127–131.

Cowgill, G. L. 1997. State and society at Teotihuacan, Mexico. *Annual Review of Anthropology* 26:129–161.

Crawford, G. W., and H. Takamiya. 1990. The origins and implications of late prehistoric plant husbandry in northern Japan. *Antiquity* 64:889–911.

Crook, J. H. 1972. Sexual selection, dimorphism, and social organization in the primates. In *Sexual selection and the descent of man, 1871–1971,* ed. B. Campbell. Chicago: Aldine.

Crown, P. L., and W. J. Judge, eds. 1991. *Chaco and Hohokam: Prehistoric regional systems in the American Southwest.* Santa Fe, NM: School of American Research.

Culbert, T. P. 1988. Political history and the Maya glyphs. *Antiquity* 62(234): 135–152.

Culbert, T. P., and D. S. Rice, eds. 1990. *Precolumbian population history in the Maya lowlands.* Albuquerque: University of New Mexico Press.

Cunliffe, B. 1994. *The Oxford illustrated prehistory of Europe.* Oxford: Oxford University Press.

Dahlin, B. H. 1984. The colossus in Guatemala: The Preclassic Maya city of El Mirador. *Archaeology* 37(5):18–25.

Dales, G. F. 1986. Some fresh approaches to old problems in Harappan archaeology. In *Studies in the archaeology of India and Pakistan,* ed. J. Jacobson. New Delhi: Oxford and IBH Publishing.

D'Altroy, T. N. 1992. *Provincial power in the Inka empire.* Washington, DC: Smithsonian Institution Press.

D'Altroy, T. N., and T. K. Earle. 1985. Staple finance, wealth finance, and storage in the Inka political economy. *Current Anthropology* 26(2):187–206.

Dart, R. A. 1953. The predatory transition from ape to man. *International Anthropological Linguistics Review* 1:201–219.

Darwin, C. 1981. *The descent of man, and selection in relation to sex.* With an introduction by John Bonner and Robert M. May. Princeton, NJ: Princeton University Press. Originally published in 1871.

Davidson, B. 1970. *The lost cities of Africa.* Rev. ed. Boston: Little, Brown.

Day, M. 1977. *Guide to fossil man.* London: Cassell.

Deacon, H. 1989. Late Pleistocene paleoecology and archaeology in the southern Cape, South Africa. In *The human revolution,* eds. P. A. Mellars and C. B. Stringer. Princeton: Princeton University Press.

Deacon, H. J., and J. Deacon. 1999. *Human beginnings in South Africa: Uncovering the secrets of the Stone Age.* Cape Town: David Philip.

Dearborn, D. S. P., and K. J. Schreiber. 1986. Here comes the sun: The Cuzco-

Machu Picchu connection. *Archaeoastronomy* 9(1–4):15–37.

Dearborn, D. S. P., K. Schreiber, and R. E. White. 1987. Intimachay: A December solstice observatory at Machu Picchu, Peru. *American Antiquity* 52(2):346–352.

de Borhegyi, S. F. 1980. The pre-Columbian ballgames: A pan-Mesoamerican tradition. *Contributions in Anthropology and History: 1*. Milwaukee: Milwaukee Public Museum.

Decker-Walters, D., T. Walters, C. W. Cowan, and B. D. Smith. 1993. Isozymic characterization of wild populations of *Cucurbita pepo*. *Journal of Ethnobiology* 13:55–72.

de Lumley, H. 1969. A Paleolithic camp at Nice. *Scientific American* 220(5):42–50.

de Mortillet, G. 1872. Classification des ages de la pierre. *Comptes rendues congress International d'Anthropologie et d'Archéologie prehistorique, VI session*. Brussels.

Dennell, R. C. 1983. *European economic prehistory: A new approach*. New York: Academic Press.

Deuel, L. 1977. *Memoirs of Heinrich Schliemann*. New York: Harper & Row.

Diamond, J. 1997. *Guns, germs, and steel: The fates of human societies*. New York: Norton.

Díaz del Castillo, B. 1956. *The discovery and conquest of Mexico*. New York: Farrar, Straus & Giroux.

Diehl, R. A. 1976. Pre-Hispanic relationships between the Basin of Mexico and north and west Mexico. In *The Valley of Mexico*, ed. E. R. Wolf. Albuquerque: University of New Mexico Press.

Diehl, R. A. 1981. Tula. In *Supplement to the handbook of Middle American Indians*, ed. J. A. Sabloff. Austin: University of Texas Press.

Diehl, R. A. 1983. *Tula: The Toltec capital of ancient Mexico*. London: Thames & Hudson.

Diehl, R. A., and J. C. Berlo, ed. 1989. *Mesoamerica after the decline of Teotihuacan, A.D. 700–900*. Washington, DC: Dumbarton Oaks.

Dikov, N. N. 1994. The Paleolithic of Kamchatka and Chukotka and the problem of the peopling of America. In *Anthropology of the North Pacific Rim*, ed. W. W. Fitzhugh and V. Chausronnet. Washington, DC: Smithsonian Institution Press.

Dillehay, T. 1984. A late Ice-Age settlement in southern Chile. *Scientific American* 254(4):100–109.

Dillehay, T. 1987. By the banks of the Chinchihuapi. *Natural History* 4:8–12.

Dillehay, T. 1997. *Monte Verde, a late Pleistocene settlement in Chile*. Washington, DC: Smithsonian Institution Press.

Dixon, J. E., J. R. Cann, and C. Renfrew. 1968. Obsidian and the origins of trade. *Scientific American* 211(3):44–53.

Doebley, J. 1990. Molecular evidence and the evolution of maize. *Economic Botany* 44(3 Supplement):6–27.

Donnan, C. B. 1976. *Moche art and iconography*. Los Angeles: UCLA Latin American Center Publications.

Donnan, C. B., ed. 1985. *Early ceremonial architecture in the Andes*. Washington, DC: Dumbarton Oaks.

Dorweiler, J., A. Stec, J. Kermicle, and J. Doebley. 1993. Teosinte glume architecture 1: A genetic locus controlling a key step in maize evolution. *Science* 262:233–235.

Drucker, P. 1955. *Indians of the Northwest Coast*. New York: McGraw-Hill.

Drucker, P., R. Heizer, and R. Squier. 1959. Excavations at La Venta, Tabasco. *Bureau of American Ethnology, Bulletin 170*. Washington, DC: Smithsonian Institution.

Dubois, E. 1894. *Pithecanthropus erectus, eine Menschenahnliche Ubergangsform aus Java*. Cologne: Batavia.

Duby, G. 1974. *The early growth of the European economy: Warriors and peasants from the seventh to the twelfth century*. Ithaca, NY: Cornell University Press.

Dye, D. 1989. Death march of Hernando de Soto. *Archaeology* 42(3):27–31.

Elvin, M. 1973. *The pattern of the Chinese past*. Stanford, CA: Stanford University Press.

Engel, F. A. 1976. *An ancient world preserved*. New York: Crown.

Fagan, B. M. 1995a. *Ancient North America*. 2d ed. London: Thames & Hudson.

Fagan, B. M. 1995b. *People of the earth: An introduction to world prehistory*. 8th ed. New York: HarperCollins.

Fairservis, W. A. 1983. The script of the Indus Valley civilization. *Scientific American* 248(3):58–66.

Fairservis, W. A. 1986. A review of the archaeological evidence in connection with the identity of the language of the Harappan script. In *Studies in the archaeology of India and Pakistan*, ed. J. Jacobson. New Delhi: Oxford and IBH Publishing.

Falk, D. 1984. The petrified brain. *Natural History* 93(9):36–39.

Farnsworth, P., J. E. Brady, M. J. deNiro, and R. S. MacNeish. 1985. A re-evaluation of the isotopic and archaeological reconstructions of diet in the Tehuacán Valley. *American Antiquity* 50:102–116.

Fash, W. L. 1991. *Scribes, warriors, and kings: The city of Copán and the ancient Maya*. London: Thames & Hudson.

Feder, K. L. 1996. *Frauds, myths, and mysteries: Science and pseudoscience in archaeology*. 2d ed. Mountain View, CA: Mayfield.

Feder, K. L., and M. A. Park. 1997. *Human antiquity*. 3d ed. Mountain View, CA: Mayfield.

Fedigan, L. M. 1986. The changing role of women in models of human evolution. *Annual Review of Anthropology* 15:25–66.

Feinman, G. M., S. A. Kowalewski, L. Finsten, R. E. Blanton, and L. Nicholas. 1985. Long-term demographic change: A perspective from the Valley of Oaxaca. *Journal of Field Archaeology* 12:333–362.

Feinman, G. M., and J. Marcus, eds. 1998. *Archaic states*. Santa Fe, NM: School for American Research Press.

Feldman, R. A. 1983. From maritime chiefdom to agricultural state in Formative coastal Peru. In *Civilization in the ancient Americas: Essays in honor of Gordon R. Willey*, ed. R. M. Leventhal and A. L. Kolata. Albuquerque: University of New Mexico Press.

Fiedel, S. J. 1992. *Prehistory of the Americas*. Cambridge: Cambridge University Press.

Finlayson, W. D. 1985. The 1975 and 1978 rescue excavations at the Draper site: Introduction and settlement patterns. *National Museum of Man Mercury Series*, Paper #130. Ottawa: Archaeological Survey of Canada.

Finney, F. A., and J. B. Stoltman. 1991. The Fred Edwards site: A case of Stirling phase culture contact in southwestern Wisconsin. In *New perspectives on Cahokia*, ed. J. B. Stoltman. Madison, WI: Prehistory Press.

Fish, S. K., and S. A. Kowalewski, eds. 1990. *The archaeology of regions: A case for full-coverage survey*. Washington, DC: Smithsonian Institution Press.

Fisher, H. E. 1982. *The sex contract. The evolution of human behavior*. New York: Quill.

Fitting, J. E. 1978. Regional cultural development, 300 B.C. to A.D. 1000. In *Handbook of North American Indians, Vol. 15: Northeast,* ed. W. C. Sturtevant and B. G.

Trigger. Washington, DC: Smithsonian Institution Press.

Flannery, K. V. 1968a. Archaeological systems theory and early Mesoamerica. In *Anthropological archeology in the Americas,* ed. B. J. Meggers. Washington, DC: Anthropological Society of Washington.

Flannery, K. V. 1968b. The Olmec and the Valley of Oaxaca: A model for interregional interaction in Formative times. In *Dumbarton Oaks conference on the Olmec,* ed. E. Benson. Washington, DC: Dumbarton Oaks.

Flannery, K. V. 1972a. The cultural evolution of civilizations. *Annual Review of Ecology and Systematics* 3:399–426.

Flannery, K. V. 1972b. The origins of the village as a settlement type in Mesoamerica and the Near East: A comparative study. In *Man, settlement, and urbanism,* ed. P. J. Ucko, R. Tringham, and G. W. Dimbleby. London: Duckworth.

Flannery, K. V. 1973. The origins of agriculture. *Annual Review of Anthropology* 2: 271–310.

Flannery, K. V., ed. 1976. *The early Mesoamerican village.* New York: Academic Press.

Flannery, K. V., ed. 1986. *Guilá Naquitz: Archaic foraging and early agriculture in Oaxaca, Mexico.* New York: Academic Press.

Flannery, K. V., and J. Marcus. 1976. Evolution of the public building in Formative Oaxaca. In *Cultural change and continuity: Essays in honor of James Bennett Griffin,* ed. C. Cleland. New York: Academic Press.

Flannery, K. V., and J. Marcus. 1983. The growth of site hierarchies in the Valley of Oaxaca: Part 1. In *The cloud people: Divergent evolution of the Zapotec and Mixtec civilizations,* ed. K. V. Flannery and J. Marcus. New York: Academic Press.

Flinders Petrie, W. M. 1904. *Methods and aims of archaeology.* London: Macmillan.

Flint, R. F. 1971. *Glacial and quaternary geology.* New York: Wiley.

Foley, R. 1987. Hominid species and stone-tool assemblages: How are they related? *Antiquity* 61:380–392.

Ford, J. A., and C. H. Webb. 1956. Poverty Point: A Late Archaic site in Louisiana. *Anthropological Papers,* vol. 46, part 1. New York: American Museum of Natural History.

Ford, R. I., ed. 1984. *The origins of plant husbandry in North America.* Ann Arbor: University of Michigan Museum of Anthropology.

Foster, M. S., and P. C. Weigand, eds. 1985. *The archaeology of west and northwest Mesoamerica.* Boulder, CO: Westview Press.

Fowler, M. L. 1974. *Cahokia: Ancient capital of the Midwest.* Reading, MA: Addison-Wesley.

Fowler, M. L. 1975. A pre-Columbian urban center on the Mississippi. *Scientific American* 232:92–101.

Fowler, M. L. 1991. Mound 72 and Early Mississippian at Cahokia. In *New perspectives on Cahokia,* ed. J. B. Stoltman. Madison, WI: Prehistory Press.

Fowler, M. L., and R. L. Hall. 1978. Late prehistory of the Illinois area. In *Handbook of North American Indians, Vol. 15: Northeast,* ed. W. C. Sturtevant and B. G. Trigger. Washington, DC: Smithsonian Institution Press.

Frankfurt, H. 1956. *The birth of civilization in the Near East.* Garden City, NY: Doubleday.

Frayer, D. W., M. H. Wolpoff, A. G. Thorne, F. H. Smith, and G. G. Pope. 1993. Theories of modern human origins: The paleontological test. *American Anthropologist* 95:14–50.

Funk, R. E. 1978. Post-Pleistocene adaptations. In *Handbook of North American Indians, Vol. 15: Northeast,* ed. W. C. Sturtevant and B. G. Trigger. Washington, DC: Smithsonian Institution Press.

Fyfe, C. 1994. The development of African states: 3000 B.C.–A.D. 1500. In *Old World civilizations: The rise of cities and states,* ed. G. Burenhult. San Francisco: HarperCollins.

Galinat, W. C. 1971. The origin of maize. *Annual Review of Genetics* 5:447–478.

Gamble, C. 1986. *The Paleolithic settlement of Europe.* Cambridge: Cambridge University Press.

Gamble, C. 1999. *The Paleolithic societies of Europe.* Cambridge: Cambridge University Press.

Garlake, P. S. 1973. *Great Zimbabwe.* London: Thames & Hudson.

Garlake, P. S. 1980. Early states in Africa. In *The Cambridge encyclopedia of archaeology,* ed. A. Sherratt. New York: Crown.

Garrod, D. A. E., and D. M. A. Bate. 1937. *The Stone Age of Mount Carmel.* Oxford: Clarendon Press.

Geertz, C. 1963. The transition to humanity. *Anthropological Series* 3:1–9. Washington, DC: Voice of America, United States Information Service.

Gibson, J. L. 1974. Poverty Point: The first North American chiefdom. *Archaeology* 27:97–105.

Gibson, J. L. 1987. The Poverty Point earthworks reconsidered. *Mississippi Archaeology* 22:15–31.

Gimbutas, M. 1977. Varna, a sensationally rich cemetery of the Karanova culture about 4500 B.C. *Expedition* 19:39–47.

Gingerich, P. D. 1985. Nonlinear molecular clocks and ape-human divergence times. In *Hominid evolution: Past, present, and future,* ed. P. V. Tobias. New York: A. R. Liss.

Gleeson, P., and M. Fisken. 1977. *Ozette archaeological project, interim final report, phase X.* Pullman: Washington Archaeological Research Center, Washington State University.

Gleeson, P., and G. Grosso. 1976. Ozette site. In *The excavation of water-saturated archaeological sites (wet sites) on the Northwest Coast of North America,* ed. D. R. Croes. Ottawa: Archaeological Survey of Canada.

Glob, P. V. 1970a. *The bog people.* Ithaca, NY: Cornell University Press.

Glob, P. V. 1970b. *The mound people.* Ithaca, NY: Cornell University Press.

Glover, I. C. 1977. The Hoabinhian: Hunter-gatherers or early agriculturalists in Southeast Asia? In *Hunters, gatherers, and first farmers beyond Europe,* ed. J. V. S. Megaw. Leicester: Leicester University Press.

Glover, I. C. 1980. Agricultural origins in East Asia. In *The Cambridge encyclopedia of archaeology,* ed. A. Sherratt. New York: Crown.

Goebel, T., A. P. Derevianko, and V. T. Petrin. 1993. Dating the Middle-to-Upper Paleolithic transition at Kara-Bom. *Current Anthropology* 34:452–458.

Goodall, J. 1986. *The chimpanzees of Gombe Reserve.* Cambridge: Harvard University Press.

Gorman, C. H. 1970. Excavations at Spirit Cave, North Thailand: Some interim interpretations. *Asian Perspectives* 13: 79–107.

Gorman, C. H. 1971. The Hoabinhian and after: Subsistence patterns in Southeast Asia during the Late Pleistocene and Early Recent periods. *World Archaeology* 2(3):300–320.

Gorman, C. H. 1977. A priori models and Thai prehistory: A reconsideration of the beginnings of agriculture in southeastern Asia. In *The origins of agriculture,* ed. C. A. Reed. The Hague: Mouton.

Goudie, A. 1983. *Environmental change.* Oxford: Clarendon Press.

Gould, S. J. 1984. A short way to corn. *Natural History* 93(3):12–20.

Gowlett, J. A. J. 1984a. *Ascent to civilization: The archaeology of early man.* New York: Knopf.

Gowlett, J. A. J. 1984b. Mental abilities of early man. In *Community ecology and human adaptation in the Pleistocene,* ed. R. A. Foley. London: Academic Press.

Gowlett, J. A. J. 1987. The archaeology of accelerator radiocarbon dating. *Journal of World Prehistory* 1:127–170.

Graham, I. 1967. *Archaeological explorations in El Petén, Guatemala.* Middle American Research Institute, Publication 33. New Orleans: Tulane University.

Grayson, D. K. 1987. Death by natural causes. *Natural History* 5:8–12.

Grayson, D. K. 1991. Late Pleistocene mammalian extinctions in North America: Taxonomy, chronology, and explanations. *Journal of World Prehistory* 5:193–232.

Grayson, D. K. 1993. *The desert's past: A natural history of the Great Basin.* Washington, DC: Smithsonian Institution Press.

Green, M. W. 1981. The construction and implementation of the cuneiform writing system. *Visible Language* 15(4):345–372.

Griffin, J. B. 1967. Eastern North American archaeology: A summary. *Science* 156:175–190.

Griffin, J. B. 1980. Agricultural groups in North America. In *The Cambridge encyclopedia of archaeology,* ed. A. Sherratt. New York: Crown.

Griffin, J. B. 1983. The Midlands. In *Ancient North Americans,* ed. J. Jennings. San Francisco: Freeman.

Grove, D. C. 1981. The Formative period and the evolution of complex culture. In *Supplement to the handbook of Middle American Indians, Vol. 1,* ed. J. A. Sabloff. Austin: University of Texas Press.

Grove, D. C. 1984. *Chalcatzingo: Excavations on the Olmec frontier.* London: Thames & Hudson.

Gumerman, G. J., ed. 1991. *Exploring the Hohokam: Prehistoric desert peoples of the American Southwest.* Dragoon, AZ: Amerind Foundation. (and Albuquerque: University of New Mexico Press.)

Gumerman, G. J., and E. W. Haury. 1979. Prehistory: Hohokam. In *Handbook of North American Indians, Vol. 9: Southwest,* ed. A. Ortiz. Washington, DC: Smithsonian Institution Press.

Haas, J. S. 1982. *The evolution of the prehistoric state.* New York: Columbia University Press.

Haas, J., S. Pozorski, and T. Pozorski, eds. 1987. *The origins and development of the Andean state.* Cambridge: Cambridge University Press.

Haddingham, E. 1979. *Secrets of the Ice Age.* London: Walker & Co.

Hall, M. 1996. Mapungubwe and Toutswemogala. In *The Oxford companion to archaeology,* ed. B. M. Fagan. New York: Oxford University Press.

Hall, R. L. 1977. An anthropocentric perspective for eastern United States prehistory. *American Antiquity* 42(4):499–518.

Halloway, R. L. 1983. Cerebral brain endocast pattern of *Australopithecus afarensis. Nature* 303:420–422.

Hammond, N. 1982. *Ancient Maya civilization.* New Brunswick, NJ: Rutgers University Press.

Hammond, N. 1987. The discovery of Tikal. *Archaeology* 40(3):30–37.

Hantman, J. L. 1990. Between Powhatan and Quirank: Reconstructing Monacan culture and history in the context of Jamestown. *American Anthropologist* 92:676–690.

Harlan, J. R. 1967. A wild wheat harvest in Turkey. *Archaeology* 20(3):197–201.

Harlan, J. R. 1995. *The living fields: Our agricultural heritage.* Oxford: Oxford University Press.

Harlan, J. R., J. M. J. de Wet, and A. B. L. Stemler, eds. 1976. *Origins of African plant domestication.* The Hague: Mouton.

Harlan, J. R., and D. Zohary. 1966. Distribution of wild wheats and barley. *Science* 153:1074–1080.

Harner, M. 1977. The enigma of Aztec sacrifice. *Natural History* 86:47–52.

Harris, D. R., and G. C. Hillman, eds. 1989. *Foraging and farming: The evolution of plant exploitation.* London: Unwin Hyman.

Harrison, R. J. 1980. *The Beaker Folk.* London: Thames & Hudson.

Hassan, F. A. 1981. *Demographic archaeology.* Cambridge: Academic Press.

Hassan, F. A. 1997. Global population and human evolution. *Human evolution* 12:3.

Hastings, C. M., and M. E. Moseley. 1975. The adobes of Huaca del Sol and Huaca de la Luna. *American Antiquity* 40:196–203.

Hastorf, C. A., and V. S. Popper. 1989. *Current paleoethnobotany.* Chicago: University of Chicago Press.

Haury, E. W. 1976. *The Hohokam: Desert farmers and craftsmen.* Tucson: University of Arizona Press.

Hayden, B. 1990. Nimrods, piscators, pluckers and planters: The emergence of food production. *Journal of Anthropological Archaeology* 9:31–69.

Hedges, R. E. M. 1981. Radiocarbon dating with an accelerator. *Archaeometry* 23:3–18.

Henderson, J. S. 1981. *The world of the ancient Maya.* Ithaca: Cornell University Press.

Henry, D. 1989. *From foraging to agriculture: The Levant at the end of the Ice Age.* Philadelphia: University of Pennsylvania Press.

Hesse, B. 1982. Slaughter patterns and domestication: The beginnings of pastoralism in western Iran. *Man* 17:403–417.

Higham, C. F. W. 1977. Economic change in prehistoric Thailand. In *The origins of agriculture,* ed. C. A. Reed. The Hague: Mouton.

Higham, C. F. W. 1984. Prehistoric rice cultivation in Southeast Asia. *Scientific American* 250(4):138–146.

Higham, C. F. W., and A. Kijngam. 1982. Prehistoric man and his environment: Evidence from the Ban Chiang faunal remains. *Expedition* 24(4):17–24.

Hill, B., and R. Hill. 1974. *Indian petroglyphs of the Pacific Northwest.* Saanichton, Canada: Hancock House.

Hill, J. N. 1970. *Broken K Pueblo: Prehistoric social organization in the American Southwest.* Tucson: University of Arizona Press.

Hillman, G. C., and M. S. Davies. 1990. Measured domestication rates in wild wheats and barley under primitive cultivation, and their archaeological implications. *Journal of World Prehistory* 4:157–222.

Hoffman, M. A. 1976. The city of the hawk. *Expedition* 18:32–41.

Hoffman, M. A. 1983. Where nations began. *Science* 83 October:42–51.

Hole, F., K. V. Flannery, and J. A. Neely. 1969. *Prehistory and human ecology of the Deh Luran Plain.* Ann Arbor: University of Michigan Press.

Holloway, R. L. 1975. *The role of human social behavior in the evolution of the brain.* New York: American Museum of Natural History.

Hood, S. 1973. *The Minoans.* London: Thames & Hudson.

Hsu, C. 1965. *Ancient China in transition.* Stanford, CA: Stanford University Press.

Huckell, B. B. 1996. The Archaic prehistory of the North American Southwest. *Journal of World Prehistory* 10:305–373.

Hyslop, J. 1984. *The Inka road system.* New York: Academic Press.

Ikawa-Smith, F. 1980. Current issues in Japanese archaeology. *American Scientist* 68:134–145.

Iltis, H. H. 1983. From teosinte to maize: The catastrophic sexual transmutation. *Science* 222:886–894.

Isaac, G. 1977. *Olorgesailie: Archaeological studies of a Middle Pleistocene lake basin in Kenya.* Chicago: University of Chicago Press.

Isaac, G. 1984. The archaeology of human origins: Studies of the Lower Pleistocene in East Africa, 1971–1981. *Advances in World Archaeology* 3:1–87.

Isaac, G., and R. Leakey. 1979. *Human ancestors. Readings from Scientific American.* San Francisco: Freeman.

Isbell, W. H. 1978. The prehistoric ground drawings of Peru. *Scientific American* 238:140–153.

Jackson, H. E. 1989. Poverty Point adaptive systems in the lower Mississippi Valley: Subsistence remains from the J. W. Copes site. *North American Archaeologist* 10:173–203.

Jacobsen, T. 1976. Seventeen thousand years of Greek prehistory. *Scientific American* 234(6):76–87.

Jacobson, J. 1979. Recent developments in South Asian prehistory and protohistory. *Annual Review of Anthropology* 8: 467–502.

Jacobson, J. 1986. The Harappan civilization: An early state. In *Studies in the archaeology of India and Pakistan,* ed. J. Jacobson. New Delhi: Oxford and IBH Publishing.

Jarrige, J.-F., and R. H. Meadow. 1980. The antecedents of civilization in the Indus Valley. *Scientific American* 243(2):122–133.

Jawad, A. J. 1974. The Eridu material and its implications. *Sumer* 30:11–46.

Jefferson, T. 1797. *Notes of the state of Virginia.* London: J. Stockdale.

Jeffries, R. W., and M. Lynch. 1985. Dimensions of Middle Archaic cultural adaptation at the Black Earth site, Saline County, Illinois. In *Archaic hunters and gatherers in the American Midwest,* ed. J. L. Phillips and J. A. Brown. New York: Academic Press.

Jelinek, A. J. 1982. The Tabun Cave and Paleolithic man in the Levant. *Science* 216:1369–1375.

Jelinek, A. J. 1988. Technology, typology, and culture in the Middle Paleolithic. In *Upper Pleistocene prehistory,* ed. H. Dibble and A. Montet-White. Philadelphia: University of Pennsylvania Press.

Jennings, J. D., ed. 1983. *Ancient South Americans.* San Francisco: Freeman.

Jiménez Moreno, W. 1941. Tula y los toltecas según las fuentes históricas. *Revista Mexicana de Estudios Antropológicos* 5: 79–83.

Joffroy, R. 1962. *Le Trésor de Vix. Historie et porteé d'une grande decouverte.* Paris: Fayard.

Johanson, D. C. 1976. Ethiopia yields first "family" of early man. *National Geographic* 150(6):790–811.

Johanson, D. C., and M. A. Eddy. 1981. *Lucy: The beginnings of humankind.* New York: Simon & Schuster.

Jolly, C. 1970. The seed eaters: A new model of hominid differentiation based on a baboon analogy. *Man* 5:5–26.

Jones, C. 1977. Inauguration dates of three Late Classic rulers of Tikal, Guatemala. *American Antiquity* 42:28–60.

Jones, C., and L. Satterthwaite. 1982. *The monuments and inscriptions of Tikal: The carved monuments.* Tikal Report 33A. University Museum Monograph 44. Philadelphia: University of Pennsylvania.

Jones, M. K., R. G. Allaby, T. A. Brown, F. Hole, M. Heun, B. Borghi, and F. Salamini. 1998. Wheat domestication. *Science* 279:202–204.

Jurmain, R., H. Nelson, and W. A. Turnbaugh. 1987. *Understanding physical anthropology and archaeology.* 3d ed. St. Paul, MN: West Publishing Co.

Keatinge, R. W., ed. 1988. *Peruvian prehistory.* Cambridge: Cambridge University Press.

Keeley, L. H. 1981. *Experimental determination of stone tool uses: A microwear analysis.* Chicago: University of Chicago Press.

Keeley, L. H., and N. Toth. 1981. Microwear polishes on early stone tools from Koobi Fora, Kenya. *Nature* 293(8):464–465.

Keightley, D. N., ed. 1983. *The origins of Chinese civilization.* Berkeley: University of California Press.

Kenoyer, J. M. 1984. Shell working industries of the Indus civilization: A summary. *Paleorient* 10(1):49–63.

Kenoyer, J. M. 1985. Shell working at Moenjo-daro, Pakistan. In *South Asian archaeology 1983,* ed. J. Schotsmans and M. Taddei. Naples: Instituto Universitario Orientale.

Kenoyer, J. M. 1991. The Indus Valley tradition of Pakistan and western India. *Journal of World Prehistory* 5:331–385.

Kenoyer, J. M. 1998. *Ancient cities of the Indus Valley civilization.* Oxford: Oxford University Press.

Kense, F. J., and J. A. Okoro. 1993. Changing perspectives on traditional iron production in West Africa. In *The Archaeology of Africa: Food, metals and towns,* ed. T. Shaw, P. Sinclair, B. Andah, and A. Okpoko. London: Routledge.

Kenyon, K. 1954. Ancient Jericho. *Scientific American* 190(4):76–82.

Kenyon, K. 1960. *Excavations at Jericho. I.* Jerusalem: British School of Archaeology.

Kirchhoff, P. 1952. Mesoamerica: Its geographic limits, ethnic composition, and cultural characteristics. In *Heritage of conquest,* ed. S. Tax. New York: Free Press.

Kirk, R., and R. D. Daugherty. 1978. *Exploring Washington archaeology.* Seattle: University of Washington Press.

Klein, R. G. 1995. Anatomy, behavior, and modern human origins. *Journal of World Prehistory* 9:167–198.

Klein, R. G. 1999. *The human career.* 2d ed. Chicago: University of Chicago Press.

Klein, R. G., and K. Cruz-Uribe. 1984. *The analysis of animal bones from archaeological sites.* Chicago: University of Chicago Press.

Klein, R. G., and K. Cruz-Uribe. 1987. Large mammal and tortoise bones from Eland's Bay Cave Province, South Africa. In *Papers in the prehistory of the Western Cape, South Africa,* ed. J. Parkington and M. Hall. British Archaeological Reports, Series 332.

Klima, B. 1962. The first ground plan of an Upper Paleolithic loess settlement in middle Europe and its meaning. In *Courses toward urban life,* ed. R. J. Braidwood and G. R. Willey. Chicago: Aldine.

Klima, B. 1963. *Dolni Vestonice.* Prague: Nakladatelstvi Ceskoslovenske Akademie Ved.

Knight, V. J., Jr. 1990. Social organization and the evolution of hierarchy in southeastern chiefdoms. *Journal of Anthropological Research* 46:1–23.

Kolata, A. L. 1983. The South Andes. In *Ancient South Americans,* ed. J. D. Jennings. San Francisco: Freeman.

Kolata, A. L. 1986. The agricultural foundations of the Tiwanaku state. *American Antiquity* 51(4):748–762.

Kolata, A. L. 1987. Tiwanaku and its hinterland. *Archaeology* 40(1):36–41.

Kolata, A. L. 1993. *The Tiwanaku.* Cambridge, MA: Blackwell.

Kramer, S. N. 1988. The temple in Sumerian literature. In *Temple in society,* ed. M. V. Fox. Winona Lake, IN: Eisenbrauns.

Krings, M., A. Stone, R. W. Schmitz, H. Krainitzki, M. Stoneking, and S. Pääbo. 1997. Neanderthal DNA sequences and the origin of modern humans. *Cell* 90: 19–30.

Kristiansen, K. 1998. *Europe before history. The European world system in the 2nd millennium B.C.* Cambridge: Cambridge University Press.

Kurtén, B. 1968. *Pleistocene mammals of Europe.* Chicago: Aldine.

Kurtén, B., and E. Anderson. 1980. *Pleistocene mammals of North America.* New York: Columbia University Press.

Laitman, J. T. 1984. The anatomy of human speech. *Natural History* 93(9): 20–27.

Lamberg-Karlovsky, C. C., and J. A. Sabloff. 1979. *Ancient civilizations: The Near East and Mesoamerica.* Prospect Heights, IL: Waveland Press.

Lanning, E. P. 1967. *Peru before the Incas.* Englewood Cliffs, NJ: Prentice-Hall.

Larsson, L. 1988. *The Skateholm Project. I. Man and environment.* Lund, Sweden: Almqvist & Wiksell International.

Leacock, E. B. 1971. *North American Indians in historical perspective.* New York: Random House.

Leakey, M. D. 1971. *Olduvai Gorge.* Cambridge: Cambridge University Press.

Leakey, M. D. 1978. Pliocene footprints at Laetoli, Tanzania. *Antiquity* 52:133.

Leakey, M. D., and J. M. Harris, eds. 1987. *Laetoli: A Pliocene site in northern Tanzania.* Oxford: Clarendon Press.

Leakey, M. D., and R. E. Leakey, eds. 1978. *Koobi Fora research project.* Oxford: Clarendon Press.

Leakey, R. 1981. *The making of mankind.* London: M. Joseph.

Leakey, R., and R. Lewin. 1977. *Origins reconsidered.* New York: Dutton.

Lechevallier, M., and G. Quivron. 1985. Results of the recent excavations at the Neolithic site of Mehrgarh, Pakistan. In *South Asian archaeology 1983,* ed. J. Schotmans and M. Taddei. Naples: Instituto Universitario Orientale.

Lee, R. B., and R. Daly, eds. 1999. *Cambridge encyclopedia of hunters and gatherers.* Cambridge: Cambridge University Press.

Lee, R. B., and I. DeVore. 1968. *Man the hunter.* Chicago: Aldine.

Legge, A. J., and P. A. Rowley-Conwy. 1988. *Star Carr revisited.* London: University of London.

LeGros Clark, W. E., and B. G. Campbell. 1978. *The fossil evidence for human evolution.* Chicago: University of Chicago Press.

Lekson, S. H., T. C. Windes, J. R. Stein, and W. J. Judge. 1988. The Chaco Canyon community. *Scientific American* 259(1):72–81.

León-Portilla, M. 1987. Ethnohistorical record for the Huey Teocalli. In *The Aztec Templo Mayor,* ed. E. H. Boone. Washington, DC: Dumbarton Oaks.

Leroi-Gourhan, A. 1957. *Prehistoric man.* New York: Philosophical Library.

Leroi-Gourhan, A. 1968. The archaeology of Lascaux Cave. *Scientific American* 219(4):104–111.

Leroi-Gourhan, A. 1984. *The dawn of European art: An introduction to Paleolithic cave paintings.* Cambridge: Cambridge University Press.

Leroi-Gourhan, A., and M. Brezillon. 1972. Fouilles de Pincevent: Essai d'analyse ethnographique d'un habitat Magdalenien (sec. 36). VII supplément a *Gallia Prehistoria.* Paris: Editions du Centre National de la Recherche Scientifique.

Levtzion, N. 1976. The early states of the western Sudan to 1500. In *History of West Africa,* vol. 1, 2d ed., ed. J. F. A. Ajayi and M. Crowder. New York: Columbia University Press.

Lewin, R. 1984. *Human evolution: An illustrated introduction.* San Francisco: Freeman.

Lewin, R. 1988. *In the age of mankind.* Washington, DC: Smithsonian Institution Press.

Lipe, W. 1983. The Southwest. In *Ancient North Americans,* ed. J. Jennings. San Francisco: Freeman.

Lister, R. H., and F. C. Lister. 1981. *Chaco Canyon, archaeology and archaeologists.* Albuquerque: University of New Mexico Press.

Lloyd, S., and F. Safar. 1943. Tell Uqair: Excavations by the Iraq government directorate of antiquities in 1940 and 1941. *Journal of Near Eastern Studies* 2:131–189.

Loewe, M., and E. L. Schaughnessy. 1999. *The Cambridge history of ancient China.* Cambridge: Cambridge University Press.

Long, A., B. F. Benz, D. J. Donahue, A. J. T. Jull, and L. J. Toolin. 1989. First direct AMS dates on early maize from Tehuacán, Mexico. *Radiocarbon* 31(3):1035–1040.

Lovejoy, C. O. 1981. The origin of man. *Science* 211:341–350.

Lumbreras, L. 1974. *The peoples and cultures of ancient Peru,* trans. B. J. Meggers. Washington, DC: Smithsonian Institution Press.

Lynch, T. F. 1980. *Guitarrero Cave: Early man in the Andes.* London: Academic Press.

Lynch, T. F., R. Gillespie, J. A. J. Gowlett, and R. E. M. Hedges. 1985. Chronology of Guitarrero Cave, Peru. *Science* 229: 864–867.

MacNeish, R. S. 1978. *The science of archaeology?* North Scituate, MA: Duxbury Press.

MacNeish, R. S. 1981. Tehuacán's accomplishments. In *Supplement to the handbook of Middle American Indians, Vol. 1,* ed. J. A. Sabloff. Austin: University of Texas Press.

MacNeish, R. S., F. A. Peterson, and K. V. Flannery. 1970. *Prehistory of the Tehuacán Valley, Vol. 3: Ceramics,* ed. R. S. MacNeish. Austin: University of Texas Press.

Malek, J., ed. 1993. *Cradles of civilization: Egypt.* Norman: University of Oklahoma Press.

Maloney, B. K., C. F. W. Higham, and R. Bannanurag. 1989. Early rice cultivation in Southeast Asia: Archaeological and palynological evidence from the Bang Pakong Valley, Thailand. *Antiquity* 63:363–370.

Manzanilla, L., L. Barba, R. Chávez, A. Tejero, G. Cifuentes, and N. Peralta. 1994. Caves and geophysics: An approximation of the underworld of Teotihuacan, Mexico. *Archaeometry* 36(1):141–157.

Marcus, J. 1976a. *Emblem and state in the Classic Maya lowlands: An epigraphic approach to territorial organization.* Washington, DC: Dumbarton Oaks.

Marcus, J. 1976b. The origins of Mesoamerican writing. *Annual Review of Anthropology* 5:35–67.

Marcus, J. 1980. Zapotec writing. *Scientific American* 242(2):50–64.

Marcus, J. 1983a. The conquest slabs of Building J, Monte Albán. In *The cloud people: Divergent evolution of the Mixtec and Zapotec civilizations,* ed. K. V. Flannery and J. Marcus. New York: Academic Press.

Marcus, J. 1983b. Lowland Maya archaeology at the crossroads. *American Antiquity* 48:454–488.

Marcus, J. 1987. Prehistoric fishermen in the kingdom of Huarco. *American Scientist* 75(4):393–401.

Marcus, J. 1992a. *Mesoamerican writing systems: Propaganda, myth, and history in* four ancient civilizations. Princeton: Princeton University Press.

Marcus, J. 1992b. Political fluctuations in Mesoamerica. *National Geographic Research and Exploration* 8(4):392–411.

Marcus, J., ed. 1990. *Debating Oaxaca archaeology.* Ann Arbor: University of Michigan, Museum of Anthropology, Anthropological Papers, No. 84.

Marcus, J., and K. V. Flannery. 1996. *Zapotec civilization: How urban society evolved in Mexico's Oaxaca Valley.* London: Thames & Hudson.

Marshack, A. 1972a. *The roots of civilization.* New York: McGraw-Hill.

Marshack, A. 1972b. Upper Paleolithic symbol and notation. *Science* 178: 817–828.

Martin, P. S., and F. Plog. 1973. *The archaeology of Arizona: A study of the Southwest region.* New York: Natural History Press.

Martin, P. W., and H. E. Wright, Jr. 1967. *Pleistocene extinctions: The search for a cause.* New Haven: Yale University Press.

Martin, S., and N. Grube. 1995. Maya superstates. *Archaeology* 48:41–46.

Marx, K. 1963. *The eighteenth Brumaire of Louis Bonaparte.* New York: International Publishers.

Masuda, S., I. Shimada, and C. Morris. 1985. *Andean ecology and civilization: An interdisciplinary perspective on Andean ecological complementarity.* Tokyo: University of Tokyo Press.

Matheny, R. T. 1986. Investigations at El Mirador, Petén, Guatemala. *National Geographic Research* 2(3):332–353.

Matheny, R. T., ed. 1980. El Mirador, Petén, Guatemala: An interim report. *New World Archaeological Foundation, Papers* 45.

Mathien, F. J., and R. H. McGuire, eds. 1986. *Ripples in the Chichimec Sea: New considerations of Southwestern-Mesoamerican interactions.* Carbondale: Southern Illinois University Press.

Matos Moctezuma, E. 1984. The great temple of Tenochtitlan. *Scientific American* 251(2):80–89.

Mayr, E. 1970. *Population, species, and evolution.* Cambridge, MA: Harvard University Press.

McDonald, K. 1996. Early Iron-Age settlement of sub-Saharan Africa. In *The Oxford companion to archaeology,* ed. B. M. Fagan. New York: Oxford University Press.

McHenry, H. M. 1982. The pattern of human evolution: Studies on bipedalism, mastication, and encephalization. *Annual Review of Anthropology* 11:151–173.

McIntosh, S. K., ed. 1995. *Excavations at Jenné-jeno, Hambarketolo, and Kaniana (Inland Niger Delta, Mali), the 1981 seasons.* Berkeley: University of California Press.

McIntosh, S. K., ed. 1999. *Beyond chiefdoms: Pathways to complexity in Africa.* Cambridge: Cambridge University Press.

McIntosh, S. K., and R. J. McIntosh. 1980. Jenné-jeno: An ancient African city. *Archaeology* 33:8–14.

McIntosh, S. K., and R. J. McIntosh. 1981. West African prehistory. *American Scientist* 69:602–612.

McIntosh, S. K., and R. J. McIntosh. 1983. Current directions in West African prehistory. *Annual Review of Anthropology* 12:215–258.

McIntosh, S. K., and R. J. McIntosh. 1984. The early city in West Africa: Towards an understanding. *The African Archaeological Review* 2:73–98.

McIntosh, S. K., and R. J. McIntosh. 1993. Cities without citadels: Understanding urban origins along the middle Niger. In *The Archaeology of Africa: Food, metals and towns,* ed. T. Shaw, P. Sinclair, B. Andah, and A. Okpoko. London: Routledge.

Mead, J. I., and D. J. Meltzer. 1985. *Environments and extinctions: Man in late glacial North America.* Orono, ME: Center for the Study of Early Man.

Meadow, R. H. 1984. Animal domestication in the Middle East: A view from the eastern margin. In *Animals and archaeology 3,* ed. J. Clutton-Brock and C. Grigson. Oxford: British Archaeological Reports S202.

Meggers, B. J., and C. Evans. 1957. *Archaeological investigations at the mouth of the Amazon.* Washington, DC: Smithsonian Institution, Bureau of American Ethnology, Bulletin 167.

Mellaart, J. 1964. Excavations at Catal Hüyük, 1963: Third preliminary report. *Anatolian Studies* 14:39–119.

Mellaart, J. 1967. *Catal Hüyük: A Neolithic town in Anatolia.* London: Thames & Hudson.

Mellaart, J. 1975. *The Neolithic of the Near East.* New York: Scribner.

Mellars, P., and C. Stringer. 1989. *The human revolution: Behavioural and biological perspectives on the origins of modern humans.* Edinburgh: Edinburgh University Press.

Mendelssohn, K. 1974. *The riddle of the pyramids.* New York: Praeger.

Milisauskas, S. 1978. *European prehistory.* New York: Academic Press.

Millon, R. 1967. Teotihuacan. *Scientific American* 216:38–48.

Millon, R. 1973. *Urbanization at Teotihuacan, Mexico, Vol. 1: The Teotihuacan map.* Austin: University of Texas Press.

Millon, R. 1976. Social relations in ancient Teotihuacan. In *The Valley of Mexico,* ed. E. R. Wolf. Albuquerque: University of New Mexico Press.

Millon, R. 1981. Teotihuacan: City, state, and civilization. In *Supplement to the handbook of Middle American Indians, Vol. 1: Archaeology,* ed. J. A. Sabloff. Austin: University of Texas Press.

Montague, A. 1964. *The concept of race.* New York: Free Press.

Moore, A. M. T. 1985. The development of Neolithic societies in the Near East. *Advances in World Archaeology* 4:1–70.

Moore, A. M. T., G. C. Hillman, and A. J. Legge. 2000. *Village on the Euphrates: The excavation of Abu Hureyra.* Oxford: Oxford University Press.

Moore, C. B. 1905. Certain aboriginal remains of the Black Warrior River. *Journal of the Academy of Natural Sciences of Philadelphia* 13:125–244.

Moorehead, W. K. 1922. *The Hopewell mound group of Ohio.* Chicago: Field Museum of Natural History, Publication 211, Anthropological Series 6(5). (Reprinted in 1968.)

Morley, S. G. (ed. R. J. Sharer). 1994. *The ancient Maya.* 5th ed. Stanford: Stanford University Press.

Morley, S. G., and G. W. Brainerd. 1956. *The ancient Maya.* 3d ed. Stanford: Stanford University Press.

Morris, C., and D. E. Thompson. 1985. *Huánuco Pampa: An Inca city and its hinterland.* London: Thames & Hudson.

Morris, C., and A. von Hagen. 1993. *The Inka empire and its Andean origins.* New York: Abbeville Press.

Moseley, M. E. 1975a. Chan Chan: Andean alternative of the preindustrial city? *Science* 187:219–225.

Moseley, M. E. 1975b. *The maritime foundations of Andean civilization.* Menlo Park, CA: Benjamin/Cummings.

Moseley, M. E. 1975c. Prehistoric principles of labor organization in the Moche Valley, Peru. *American Antiquity* 40:191–196.

Moseley, M. E. 1983. Central Andean civilization. In *Ancient South Americans,* ed. J. D. Jennings. San Francisco: Freeman.

Moseley, M. E., and K. C. Day, eds. 1982. *Chan Chan: Andean desert city.* Albuquerque: University of New Mexico Press.

Movius, H. L. 1948. The Lower Paleolithic culture of southern and eastern Asia. *Transactions of the American Philosophical Society* 38:329–351.

Muller, J. 1983. The Southeast. In *Ancient North Americans,* ed. J. Jennings. San Francisco: Freeman.

Mulvaney, D. J. 1975. *The prehistory of Australia.* 2d ed. Baltimore: Pelican.

Mulvaney, J., and J. Kamminga. 1999. *The prehistory of Australia.* Washington, DC: Smithsonian Institution Press.

Muro, M. 1998. New finds explode old views of the American Southwest. *Science* 279:653–654.

Murowchick, R. E., ed. 1994. *Cradles of civilization: China.* Norman: University of Oklahoma Press.

Murra, J. V. 1962. Cloth and its function in the Inca state. *American Anthropologist* 64:710–728.

Murra, J. V. 1972. El "control vertical" de un máximo de pisos ecológicos en la economia de las sociedades andinas. In *Visita de la provincia de Leon de Huanuco (1562), Vol. 2,* ed. J. V. Murra. Huanuco, Peru: Universidad Nacional Hermilio Valdizan.

Ndoro, W. 1996. Great Zimbabwe. In *The Oxford companion to archaeology,* ed. B. M. Fagan. New York: Oxford University Press.

Neitzel, J. 1989. The Chacoan regional system: Interpreting the evidence for social complexity. In *The sociopolitical structure of prehistoric southwestern societies,* ed. S. Upham, K. G. Lightfoot, and R. A. Jewett. Boulder, CO: Westview Press.

Nicholas, L. M., and G. M. Feinman. 1989. A regional perspective on Hohokam irrigation in the lower Salt River Valley, Arizona. In *The sociopolitical structure of prehistoric southwestern societies,* ed. S. Upham, K. G. Lightfoot, and R. A. Jewett. Boulder, CO: Westview Press.

Nissen, H. J. 1986. The archaic texts from Uruk. *World Archaeology* 17(3):317–334.

Nissen, H. J. 1988. *The early history of the ancient Near East, 9000–2000 B.C.* Chicago: University of Chicago Press.

Normile, D. 1997. Yangtze seen as earliest rice site. *Science* 275:309.

Oakley, K. P. 1955. Fire as a Paleolithic tool and weapon. *Proceedings of the Prehistoric Society* 21:36–48.

Oates, J. 1980. The emergence of cities in the Near East. In *The Cambridge encyclo-*

pedia of archaeology, ed. A. Sherratt. New York: Crown.

O'Connor, D. 1980. Egypt and the Levant in the Bronze Age. In *The Cambridge encyclopedia of archaeology,* ed. A. Sherratt. New York: Crown.

Oliver, R., and B. M. Fagan. 1975. *Africa in the Iron Age: c. 500 B.C. to A.D. 1400.* Cambridge: Cambridge University Press.

Ortiz de Montellano, B. 1978. Aztec cannibalism: An ecological necessity? *Science* 200:611–617.

Otto, M. P. 1979. Hopewell antecedents in the Adena heartland. In *Hopewell archaeology: The Chillicothe conference,* eds. D. S. Brose and N. Greber. Kent, OH: Kent State University Press.

Parkington, J. E. 1972. Seasonal mobility in the Late Stone Age. *African Studies* 31:223–243.

Parkington, J. E. 1981. Stone tools and resources: A case study from South Africa. *World Archaeology* 13:16–30.

Parkington, J. E. 1984. Changing views of the Later Stone Age of South Africa. *Advances in World Archaeology* 3:89–142.

Parpola, A. 1986. The Indus script: A challenging puzzle. *World Archaeology* 17(3):399–419.

Parsons, J. R. 1972. Archaeological settlement patterns. *Annual Review of Anthropology* 1:127–150.

Pauketat, T. R. 1998. Refiguring the archaeology of greater Cahokia. *Journal of Archaeological Research* 6:45–89.

Paul, A., and S. A. Turpin. 1986. The ecstatic shaman theme of Paracas textiles. *Archaeology* 39(5):20–27.

Pearsall, D. 1989. *Paleoethnobotany.* Orlando, FL: Academic Press.

Pearsall, D. 1992. The origins of plant cultivation in South America. In *Origins of agriculture in world perspective,* ed. C. W. Cowan and P. J. Watson. Washington, DC: Smithsonian Institution Press.

Pearson, R., and A. Underhill. 1987. The Chinese Neolithic: Recent trends in research. *American Anthropologist* 89(4):807–822.

Peebles, C. S., and C. A. Black. 1987. Moundville from 1000–1500 A.D. as seen from 1840 to 1985 A.D. In *Chiefdoms in the Americas,* ed. R. D. Drennan and C. A. Uribe. Lanham, MD: University Press of America.

Peebles, C. S., and S. Kus. 1977. Some archaeological correlates of ranked society. *American Antiquity* 42:421–448.

Perony, D. 1930. Le Moustier. *Revue Anthropologique* 14.

Perrot, J. 1966. Le Gisement Natoufien de Mallaha (Eynan), Israel. *L'Anthropologie* 47:437–484.

Peterson, I. 1988. Tokens of plenty. *Science News* 134:408–410.

Pfeiffer, J. E. 1982. *The creative explosion: An enquiry into the origins of art and religion.* New York: Harper & Row.

Pfeiffer, J. E. 1985. *The emergence of humankind.* New York: Harper & Row.

Phillipson, D. 1977. *The later prehistory of eastern and southern Africa.* London: Heinemann.

Phillipson, D. 1980. Iron Age Africa and the expansion of the Bantu. In *The Cambridge encyclopedia of archaeology,* ed. A. Sherratt. New York: Crown.

Phillipson, D. 1985. *African archaeology.* Cambridge: Cambridge University Press.

Phillipson, D. W. 1996. Prehistory of Africa. In *The Oxford companion to archaeology,* ed. B. M. Fagan. New York: Oxford University Press.

Pilbeam, D. 1985. Distinguished lecture: Hominoid evolution and hominoid origins. *American Anthropologist* 88:295–312.

Pollock, S. 1999. *Ancient Mesopotamia: The Eden that never was.* Cambridge: Cambridge University Press.

Possehl, G. L. 1990. Revolution in the urban revolution: The emergence of Indus urbanization. *Annual Review of Anthropology* 19:261–282.

Possehl, G. L. 1997. The transformation of the Indus civilization. *Journal of Archaeological Research* 11:425–472.

Price, T. D. 1987. The Mesolithic of western Europe. *Journal of World Prehistory* 1:225–305.

Price, T. D., ed. 1989. *The chemistry of prehistoric bone.* Cambridge: Cambridge University Press.

Price, T. D., and E. Brinch Petersen. 1987. A Mesolithic community in Denmark. *Scientific American* 255(3):111–121.

Price, T. D., and A. B. Gebauer, eds. 1995. *Last hunters—first farmers: New perspectives on the prehistoric transition to agriculture.* Santa Fe, NM: School for American Research.

Pringle, H. 1997. Oldest mound complex found at Louisiana site. *Science* 277:1761–1762.

Prufer, O. 1964. The Hopewell cult. *Scientific American* 211(6):90–102.

Puleston, D. E. 1973. Ancient Maya settlement patterns and environment at Tikal, Guatemala: Implications for subsistence models. Ph.D. dissertation, University of Pennsylvania, Philadelphia.

Puleston, D. E. 1977. The art and technology of hydraulic agriculture in the Maya lowlands. In *Social processes and Maya prehistory,* ed. N. Hammond. New York: Academic Press.

Puleston, D. E. 1978. Terracing, raised fields, and tree cropping in the Maya lowlands: A new perspective on the geography of power. In *Prehispanic Maya agriculture,* ed. P. D. Harrison and B. L. Turner, II. Albuquerque: University of New Mexico Press.

Quilter, J. 1985. Architecture and chronology at El Paraíso, Peru. *Journal of Field Archaeology* 12:279–297.

Quilter, J. 1991. Late preceramic Peru. *Journal of World Prehistory* 5(4):387–438.

Quilter, J., B. Ojeda, D. M. Pearsall, D. H. Sandweiss, J. G. Jones, and E. S. Wing. 1991. Subsistence economy of El Paraíso, an early Peruvian site. *Science* 251:277–283.

Quilter, J., and T. Stocker. 1983. Subsistence economies and the origins of agriculture. *American Anthropologist* 85(3): 545–562.

Rambo, A. T. 1991. The study of cultural evolution. In *Profiles in cultural evolution: Papers from a conference in honor of Elman R. Service,* ed. A. T. Rambo and K. Gillogly. Ann Arbor: University of Michigan, Anthropological Papers, Museum of Anthropology, No. 85.

Randsborg, K. 1975. Social dimensions of early Neolithic Denmark. *Proceedings of the Prehistoric Society* 41:105–118.

Raymond, J. S. 1981. The maritime foundations of Andean civilization: A reconsideration of the evidence. *American Antiquity* 46(4):806–821.

Redman, C. 1978. *The rise of civilization: From early farmers to urban society in the ancient Near East.* San Francisco: Freeman.

Redmond, E. M. 1983. *A fuego y sangre: Early Zapotec imperialism in the Cuicatlán Cañada, Oaxaca.* Ann Arbor: University of Michigan, Museum of Anthropology, Memoirs 16.

Reed, C. A., ed. 1977. *The origins of agriculture.* The Hague: Mouton.

Renfrew, C. 1974. *Before civilization.* New York: Knopf.

Renfrew, J. 1973. *Palaeoethnobotany.* New York: Columbia University Press.

Rice, G. 1987. La Ciudad: A perspective on Hohokam community systems. In *The Hohokam village: Site structure and organization,* ed. D. E. Doyel. Glenwood Springs, CO: Southwestern and Rocky Mountain Division of the American Association for the Advancement of Science.

Rindos, D. 1984. *The origins of agriculture: An evolutionary perspective.* New York: Academic Press.

Robson, J. R. K., R. I. Ford, K. V. Flannery, and J. E. Konlande. 1976. The nutritional significance of maize and teosinte. *Ecology of Food and Nutrition* 4: 243–249.

Roe, D. 1981. *The Lower and Middle Paleolithic periods in Britain.* London: Routledge & Kegan Paul.

Rolland, N., and H. L. Dibble. 1990. A new synthesis of Middle Paleolithic variability. *American Antiquity* 55:480–499.

Rollefson, G. O. 1985. The 1983 season at the Early Neolithic site of 'Ain Ghazal. *National Geographic Research* Winter: 44–62.

Ronen, A., ed. 1982. *The transition from Lower to Middle Paleolithic and the origin of modern man.* Oxford: British Archaeological Reports.

Roosevelt, A. 1989. Lost civilizations of the lower Amazon. *Natural History,* February, 74–82.

Roosevelt, A. C., R. A. Housley, M. Imazio da Silveira, S. Maranca, and R. Johnson. 1991. Eighth millennium pottery from a prehistoric shell midden in the Brazilian Amazon. *Science* 254:1621–1624.

Rosenberg, M., R. Nesbitt, R. W. Redding, and B. L. Peasnall. 1998. Hallan Çemi, pig husbandry and post-Pleistocene adaptations along the Taurus-Zagros archaeology (Turkey). *Paléorient* 24: 25–41.

Rosenberg, M., and R. W. Redding. 1996. Hallan Cemi, feasting, and the beginnings of animal domestication in highland southwestern Asia. *Paléorient.*

Rosman, A., and P. G. Rubel. 1971. *Feasting with mine enemy: Rank and exchange among Northwest Coast societies.* New York: Columbia University Press.

Rowe, J. H. 1947. Inca culture at the time of Spanish conquest. In *Handbook of South American Indians: Vol. 2, The Andean civilizations,* ed. J. H. Steward. Washington, DC: Smithsonian Institution, Bureau of American Ethnology, Bulletin 143.

Rowe, J. H. 1967. What kind of settlement was Inca Cuzco? *Nawpa Pacha* 5:59–76.

Rowe, J. H. 1987. Machu Pijchu: A la luz de los documentos del siglo XVI. *Kuntur* 4:12–20.

Ruddiman, W. F., and J. E. Kutzbach. 1991. Plateau uplift and climatic change. *Scientific American* 264(3):66–75.

Ruz Lhuillier, A. 1973. *El Templo de las Inscripciones: Palenque.* Mexico, D.F.: Instituto Nacional de Antropología e Historia.

Sabloff, J. A. 1990. *The new archaeology and the ancient Maya.* New York: Freeman.

Sahagún, F. B. 1950–1982. *Florentine codex: General history of the things of New Spain,* trans. A. J. O. Anderson and C. E. Dibble (11 vols.). Santa Fe, NM: School for American Research, and Provo: University of Utah.

Sahlins, M. D. 1968. Notes on the original affluent society. In *Man the hunter,* ed. R. B. Lee and I. DeVore. Chicago: Aldine.

Sahlins, M. D. 1972. *Stone Age economics.* Chicago: Aldine.

Sanders, W. T., J. R. Parsons, and R. S. Santley. 1979. *The Basin of Mexico: Ecological processes in the evolution of a civilization.* New York: Academic Press.

Sanders, W. T., and B. Price. 1968. *Mesoamerica: The evolution of a civilization.* New York: Random House.

Sarich, V. 1983. Retrospective on hominid macromolecular systematics. In *New interpretations of ape and human ancestry,* ed. R. L. Ciochon and R. S. Corrucini. New York: Plenum Press.

Sauer, C. O. 1952. *Agricultural origins and dispersals.* New York: American Geographical Society.

Saunders, J. W., and T. Allen. 1994. Hedgepeth mounds, an Archaic mound complex in north-central Louisiana. *American Antiquity* 59:471–489.

Saunders, J. W., R. D. Mandel, R. T. Saucier, E. T. Allen, C. T. Hallmark, J. K. Johnson, E. H. Jackson, C. M. Allen, G. L. Stringer, D. S. Frink, J. K. Feathers, S. Williams, K. J. Gremillion, M. F. Vidrine, and R. Jones. 1997. A mound complex in Louisiana at 5400–5000 years before the present. *Science* 277: 1796–1799.

Scarborough, V. L., and D. R. Wilcox, eds. 1991. *The Mesoamerican ballgame.* Tucson: University of Arizona Press.

Schele, L., and M. E. Miller. 1986. *The blood of kings: Dynasty and ritual in Maya art.* Fort Worth, TX: Kimball Art Museum.

Schmandt-Besserat, D. 1978. The earliest precursor of writing. *Scientific American* 238(6):50–59.

Schmandt-Besserat, D. 1980. The envelopes that bear the first writing. *Technology and Culture* 21(3):357–385.

Schmandt-Besserat, D. 1990. Accounting in the prehistoric Middle East. *Archeomaterials* 4(1):15–23.

Schwartz, J. H. 1995. *Skeleton keys.* Oxford: Oxford University Press.

Service, E. R. 1975. *Origins of the state and civilization: The process of cultural evolution.* New York: Norton.

Shackleton, N. J., and N. D. Opdyke. 1973. Oxygen isotope and paleomagnetic stratigraphy of equatorial Pacific core V28-238: Oxygen isotope temperatures and ice volume on a 10^5 and 10^6 year scale. *Quarternary Research* 3: 39–55.

Sharer, R. J., and D. C. Grove, eds. 1989. *Regional perspectives on the Olmec.* Cambridge: Cambridge University Press.

Sherratt, A., ed. 1980. *The Cambridge encyclopedia of archaeology.* New York: Crown.

Shipman, P. 1983. Early hominid lifestyle: Hunting and gathering or foraging and scavenging? In *Animals and archaeology: Hunters and their prey,* ed. J. Clutton-Brock and C. Grigson. Oxford: British Archaeological Reports.

Shutler, R., Jr. 1983. *Early man in the New World.* Beverly Hills, CA: Sage Publications.

Siemens, A. H., and D. E. Puleston. 1972. Ridged fields and associated features in southern Campeche: New perspectives on the lowland Maya. *American Antiquity* 37:228–239.

Simons, E. 1972. *Primate evolution.* New York: Macmillan.

Simpson, G. G. 1967. *The meaning of evolution.* Rev. ed. New Haven: Yale University Press.

Singer, R., and J. Wymer. 1982. *The Middle Stone Age at Klasies River Mouth in South Africa.* Chicago: University of Chicago Press.

Skelton, R. R., H. M. McHenry, and G. M. Drawhorn, 1986. Phylogenetic analysis of early hominids. *Current Anthropology* 27:21–43.

Smith, B. D. 1986. The archaeology of the southeastern United States: From Dalton to de Soto, 10,500–500 B.P. *Advances in World Archaeology* 5:1–92.

Smith, B. D. 1989. Origins of agriculture in eastern North America. *Science* 246: 1566–1571.

Smith, B. D. 1992. *Rivers of change: Essays on early agriculture in eastern North America.* Washington, DC, and London: Smithsonian Institution Press.

Smith, B. D. 1995. *The emergence of agriculture.* San Francisco: Freeman.

Smith, B. D. 1997. Reconsidering the Ocampo caves and the era of incipient cultivation in Mesoamerica. *Latin American Antiquity* 8:342–383.

Smith, C. E. 1980. Plant remains from Guitarrero Cave. In *Guitarrero Cave,* ed. T. F. Lynch. New York: Academic Press.

Smith, F. H., and F. Spencer, eds. 1984. *The origins of modern humans.* New York: A. R. Liss.

Soffer, O. 1985. *The Upper Paleolithic of the central Russian plains.* New York: Academic Press.

Solecki, R. 1971. *Shanidar: The first flower people.* New York: Knopf.

Solheim, W. G., II. 1972a. An earlier agricultural revolution. *Scientific American* 226:34–41.

Solheim, W. G., II. 1972b. Early man in Southeast Asia. *Expedition* 14(3):25–31.

Spence, M. W. 1974. Residential practices and the distribution of skeletal traits in Teotihuacan, Mexico. *Man* 9:262–273.

Spence, M. W. 1981. Obsidian production and the state in Teotihuacan. *American Antiquity* 46(4):769–787.

Spencer, C. S. 1982. *The Cuicatlán Cañada and Monte Albán: A study of primary state formation.* New York: Academic Press.

Spindler, K. 1994. *The man in the ice.* London: Weidenfeld & Nicholson.

Spooner, B., ed. 1972. *Population growth: Anthropological implications.* Cambridge: MIT Press.

Stanford, C. 1998. The social behavior of chimpanzees and bonobos. *Current Anthropology* 39:399–420.

Stein, G. J. 1998. Heterogeneity, power, and political economy: Some current research issues in the archaeology of Old World complex societies. *Journal of Archaeological Research* 6:1–44.

Stein, G., and M. S. Rothman. 1994. *Chiefdoms and early states in the Near East.* Madison, WI: Prehistory Press.

Stephens, J. L. 1841. *Incidents of travel in Central America, Chiapas, and Yucatán.* 2 vols. New York: Harper & Row. (Reprinted by Dover, 1962.)

Stephens, J. L. 1843. *Incidents of travel in Yucatán.* 2 vols. New York: Harper & Row. (Reprinted by Dover, 1963.)

Steponaitis, V. 1983. *Ceramics, chronology, and community patterns: An archaeological study at Moundville.* New York: Academic Press.

Steponaitis, V. 1986. Prehistoric archaeology in the southeastern United States, 1970–1985. *Annual Review of Anthropology* 15:363–404.

Steponaitis, V. 1991. Contrasting patterns of Mississippian development. In *Chiefdoms: Power, economy, and ideology,* ed. T. Earle. Cambridge: Cambridge University Press.

Stirling, M. W. 1943. *Stone monuments of southern Mexico.* Washington, DC: Smithsonian Institution, Bureau of American Ethnology, Bulletin 138.

Stoltman, J. B., ed. 1991. *New perspectives on Cahokia: Views from the periphery.* Madison, WI: Prehistory Press.

Stringer, C. B. 1985. Middle Pleistocene hominid variability and the origin of Late Pleistocene humans. In *Ancestors: The hard evidence,* ed. E. Delson. New York: A. R. Liss.

Stringer, C. B. 1988. *The Neanderthals.* London: Thames & Hudson.

Stringer, C. B. 1990. The emergence of modern humans. *Scientific American* 259(12):98–103.

Sudgen, D. E., and B. S. John. 1976. *Glaciers and landscape.* London: E. Arnold.

Susman, R. L., and J. T. Stern. 1982. Functional morphology of *Homo habilis. Science* 217:931–934.

Swaminathan, M. S. 1984. Rice. *Scientific American* 250(1):80–93.

Tanner, N. 1981. *On becoming human.* London: Cambridge University Press.

Tattersall, I. 1995. *The fossil trail: How we know what we think we know about human evolution.* Oxford: Oxford University Press.

Tattersall, I., C. Delson, and J. V. Couvering, eds. 1988. *Encyclopedia of human evolution and prehistory.* New York: Garland.

Tauber, H. 1981. ^{13}C evidence for dietary habits of prehistoric man in Denmark. *Nature* 292:332–333.

Taylor, R. E. 1988. *Radiocarbon dating.* New York: Academic Press.

Taylour, W. 1989. *The Mycenaeans.* London: Thames & Hudson.

Te-k'un, C. 1959. *Archaeology in China, Vol. I: Prehistoric China.* Cambridge: W. Heffer & Sons.

Te-k'un, C. 1960. *Archaeology in China, Vol. 2: Shang burials.* Cambridge: W. Heffer & Sons.

Te-k'un, C. 1966. *Archaeology in China: New light on prehistoric China.* Cambridge: W. Heffer & Sons.

Tello, J. C. 1943. Discovery of the Chavín culture in Peru. *American Antiquity* 9: 135–160.

Templeton, A. R. 1993. The 'Eve' hypothesis: A genetic critique and reanalysis. *American Anthropologist* 95:51–72.

Thomas, D. H. 1979. *Archaeology*. New York: Holt, Rinehart, & Winston.

Thomas, D. H. 1983. *The archaeology of Monitor Valley 2: Gatecliff Shelter*. New York: American Museum of Natural History.

Thomas, D. H. 1989. *Archaeology*. New York: Holt, Rinehart & Winston.

Thompson, D. E., and J. V. Murra. 1966. The Inca bridges in the Huánuco region. *American Antiquity* 31:632–639.

Thorne, A. G., and M. H. Wolpoff. 1992. The multiregional evolution of humans. *Scientific American* 266(4):76–83.

Tobias, P. 1971. *The brain in hominid evolution*. New York: Columbia University Press.

Todd, I. A. 1976. *Çatal Hüyük in perspective*. Menlo Park, CA: Cummings.

Toffler, A. 1970. *Future shock*. London: Pan Books.

Topic, T. L. 1982. The Early Intermediate period and its legacy. In *Chan Chan*, ed. M. E. Moseley and K. C. Day. Albuquerque: University of New Mexico Press.

Topping, A. 1978. The first emperor's army, China's incredible find. *National Geographic* 153(4):440–459.

Toth, N. 1987. The first technology. *Scientific American* 256(2):112–121.

Townsend, R. F., ed. 1992. *The ancient Americas: Art from sacred landscapes*. Chicago: Art Institute of Chicago.

Trask, L. 1998. The origins of speech. *Cambridge Archaeological Journal* 8:69–94.

Trigger, B. G. 1978. Early Iroquoian contacts with Europeans. In *Handbook of North American Indians, Vol. 15: Northeast,* ed. W. C. Sturtevant and B. G. Trigger. Washington, DC: Smithsonian Institution Press.

Trigger, B. G. 1980a. Archaeology and the image of the American Indian. *American Antiquity* 45:662–675.

Trigger, B. G. 1980b. *Gordon Childe: Revolutions in archaeology*. New York: Columbia University Press.

Trigger, B. G., B. J. Kemp, D. O. O'Connor, and A. B. Lloyd. 1985. *Ancient Egypt: A social history*. Cambridge: Cambridge University Press.

Tringham, R. 1971. *Hunters, fishers, and farmers of Eastern Europe 6000–3000 B.C.* London: Hutchinson University Library.

Trinkaus, E., ed. 1990. *The emergence of modern humans*. Cambridge: Cambridge University Press.

Trinkaus, E., and W. W. Howells. 1979. The Neanderthals. *Scientific American* 241:94–105.

Tuck, J. A. 1978a. Northern Iroquoian prehistory. In *Handbook of North American Indians, Vol. 15: Northeast,* ed. W. C. Sturtevant and B. G. Trigger. Washington, DC: Smithsonian Institution Press.

Tuck, J. A. 1978b. Regional cultural development, 3000 to 300 B.C. In *Handbook of North American Indians, Vol. 15: Northeast,* ed. W. C. Sturtevant and B. G. Trigger. Washington, DC: Smithsonian Institution Press.

Turner, B. L., II, and P. D. Harrison, eds. 1983. *Pulltrouser Swamp: Ancient Maya habitat, agriculture, and settlement in northern Belize*. Austin: University of Texas Press.

Tylor, E. B. 1960. *Anthropology*. Ann Arbor. University of Michigan Press. (Originally published in 1881.)

Ubelaker, D. H. 1978. *Human skeletal remains*. Washington, DC: Taraxacum Press.

Ucko, P. J., and A. Rosenfeld. 1967. *Paleolithic cave art*. London: Weidenfeld & Nicholson.

Underhill, A. 1997. Current issues in Chinese Neolithic archaeology. *Journal of World Prehistory* 11:103–160.

U.S. Congress, Office of Technology Assessment. 1986. *Technologies for prehistoric and historic preservation*. OTA-E-319. Washington, DC: U.S. Government Printing Office.

Vaillant, G. C. 1966. *Aztecs of Mexico*. Harmondsworth, England: Pelican.

Vermeule, E. 1972. *Greece in the Bronze Age*. Chicago: University of Chicago Press.

Villa, P. 1982. Conjoinable pieces and site formation processes. *American Antiquity* 47:276–290.

Wainwright, G. 1989. *The henge monuments*. London: Thames & Hudson.

Walker, A. 1981. Diet and teeth: Dietary hypotheses and human evolution. *Philosophical Transactions of the Royal Society of London* B292:57–64.

Wallace, A. R. 1869. *Malay archipelago*. New York: Harper and Brothers.

Warren, P. 1975. *The Aegean civilizations*. Oxford: Elsevier Phaidon.

Warrick, G. A. 1983. Reconstructing Iroquoian village organization. *National Museum of Man Mercury Series,* Paper #124. Ottawa: Archaeological Survey of Canada.

Warrick, G. A. 1988. Estimating Ontario Iroquoian village duration. *Man in the Northeast* 36:21–60.

Watson, W. 1960. *Archaeology in China*. London: Max Parrish.

Weaver, M. P. 1981. *The Aztecs, Maya, and their predecessors: Archaeology of Mesoamerica*. New York: Academic Press.

Webb, C. H. 1982. *The Poverty Point culture*. 2d ed. Baton Rouge: Louisiana State University School of Geoscience.

Wenke, R. J. 1990. *Patterns in prehistory*. 3d ed. Oxford: Oxford University Press.

Wheeler, R. E. M. 1943. *Maiden Castle, Dorset*. London: Society of Antiquaries 12.

Wheeler, R. E. M. 1968. *The Indus civilization*. Cambridge: Cambridge University Press.

Wheeler, T. S., and R. Maddin. 1976. The techniques of the early Thai metalsmith. *Expedition* 18(4):38–47.

White, J. C. 1982. *Discovery of a lost Bronze Age: Ban Chiang*. Philadelphia: University of Pennsylvania Press.

White, L. A. 1959. *The evolution of culture*. New York: McGraw-Hill.

Wilcox, D. R., T. R. McGuire, and C. Sternberg. 1981. *Snaketown revisited*. Arizona State Museum Archaeological Series 155. Tucson: University of Arizona.

Willey, G. R. 1953. *Prehistoric settlement in the Virú Valley, Peru*. Washington, DC: Smithsonian Institution Press.

Willey, G. R. 1966. *An introduction to American archaeology, Vol. 1: North and Middle America*. Englewood Cliffs, NJ: Prentice-Hall.

Willey, G. R. 1971. *An introduction to American archaeology, Vol. 2: South America*. Englewood Cliffs, NJ: Prentice-Hall.

Willey, G. R. 1974. The Classic Maya hiatus: A rehearsal for the collapse? In *Mesoamerican archaeology: New approaches,* ed. N. Hammond. London: Duckworth.

Wills, W. H. 1988. Early agriculture and sedentism in the American Southwest: Evidence and interpretations. *Journal of World Prehistory* 2(4):445–488.

Wilmsen, E. N. 1974. *Lindenmeier: A Pleistocene hunting society*. New York: Harper & Row.

Wilmsen, E. N. 1978. *Lindenmeier, 1934–74*. Washington, DC: Smithsonian Institution Press.

Wilson, A. C., and R. L. Cann. 1992. The recent African genesis of humans. *Scientific American* 266(4)68–73.

Wilson, D. J. 1981. Of maize and men: A critique of the maritime hypothesis of state origins on the coast of Peru. *American Anthropologist* 83(1):93–120.

Wing, E. S. 1980. Faunal remains. In *Guitarrero Cave: Early man in the Andes,* ed. T. S. Lynch. New York: Academic Press.

Wittfogel, K. 1957. *Oriental despotism*. New Haven: Yale University Press.

Wood, J. W., D. Lai, P. L. Johnson, K. L. Campbell, and I. M. Masler. 1985. Lactation and birth spacing in highland

New Guinea. *Journal of Biosocial Science, Supplement* 9:159–173.

Woodman, P. C. 1981. A Mesolithic camp in Ireland. *Scientific American* 245(2): 120–132.

Woolley, C. L. 1954. *Excavations at Ur.* London: Benn.

Wright, G. A. 1969. *Obsidian analyses and prehistoric Near Eastern trade: 7500–3500 B.C.* Ann Arbor: University of Michigan Museum of Anthropology.

Wright, H. E. 1971. Late Quaternary vegetational history of North America. In *The Late Cenozoic ice ages,* ed. K. K. Turekian. New Haven: Yale University Press.

Wright, H. T. 1986. The evolution of civilizations. In *American archaeology, past and future,* ed. D. J. Meltzer, D. D. Fowler, and J. A. Sabloff. Washington, DC: Smithsonian Institution Press.

Wright, H. T., and G. A. Johnson. 1975. Population, exchange and early state formation in southwestern Iran. *American Anthropologist* 77:267–289.

Wymer, J. 1968. *Lower Paleolithic archaeology in Britain.* London: John Baker.

Yen, D. E. 1977. Hoabinhian horticulture: The evidence and the questions from northwest Thailand. In *Sunda and Sahul: Prehistoric studies in Southeast Asia, Melanesia, and Australia,* ed. J. Allen, J. Golson, and R. Jones. London: Academic Press.

Yen, D. E. 1982. Ban Chiang pottery and rice. *Expedition* 24(4):51–64.

Yerkes, R. W. 1988. The Woodland and Mississippian traditions in the prehistory of midwestern North America. *Journal of World Prehistory* 2(3)307–358.

Yoffee, N., and G. L. Cowgill, eds. 1988. *The collapse of ancient states and civilizations.* Tuscon: University of Arizona Press.

Zohary, D., and M. Hopf. 1993. *Domestication of plants in the Old World: The origin and spread of cultivated plants in West Asia, Europe, and the Nile Valley.* Oxford: Clarendon Press.

zur Nedden, D., K. Wicke, R. Knapp, H. Seidler, H. Wilfing, G. Weber, K. Spindler, W. A. Murphy, G. Hauser, and W. Platzer. 1994. New findings on the Tyrolean "Ice Man": Archaeological and CT-body analyses suggest personal disaster before death. *Journal of Archaeological Science* 21:809–818.

Zvelebil, M., and P. M. Dolukhanov. 1991. The transition to farming in eastern and northern Europe. *Journal of World Prehistory* 5(3):233–278.

CREDITS

Contents p. vii, Robert F. Sisson, © National Geographic Society; p. viiiL, Courtesy J. Edward Kidder, Jr.; p. viiiR, © Board of Trustees, Southern Illinois University; pp. ixL, ixR, xL, Courtesy Linda M. Nicholas; p. xR, © Forhistorisk Museum, Moesgård. **Introduction** p. 1, Courtesy Department of Library Services. American Museum of Natural History. Neg. #108781; p. 4, Courtesy Michael Kienitz. **Chapter 1** p. 2, © Courtesy T. Douglas Price and Anne Birgitte Gebauer; p. 3, © Courtesy T. Douglas Price and Anne Birgitte Gebauer; p. 4, Courtesy of Dr. Douglas Crice, Georadar, Inc.; p. 5, 8, 9, Courtesy Michael Kienitz; p. 7T, © Courtesy T. Douglas Price and Anne Birgitte Gebauer; p. 7B, © Courtesy T. Douglas Price and Anne Birgitte Gebauer, Courtesy of Michael Kienitz; p. 10T, Courtesy of Dr. James Stoltman; p. 10B, Courtesy of Michael Kienitz; p. 11T, Courtesy of Michael Kienitz; p. 11B, 12, © T. Douglas Price; p. 13, © Statens Historiska Museum. Photo: Soren Hallgren; p. 14, © Board of Trustees, Southern Illinois University; p. 17, From *Rock Art of Spanish Levant*, Antonio Beltran. Reprinted with permission of Cambridge University Press. p. 20, Reproduced with permission, from *The Annual Review of Ecology and Systematics*, Volume 3., © 1972 by Annual Reviews Inc.; p. 21, © T. Douglas Price. **Chapter 2** p. 28, Courtesy Department of Library Services. American Museum of Natural History, Neg #108781; p. 32, © Institute of Human Origins; p. 34, Redrawn from original drawings by Bobbie Brown in *Lucy: The Beginnings of Humankind*, by Donald C. Johanson and Maitland Edey, 1981, Simon and Schuster; p. 33, 35 © John Reader/Science Photo Library/ Photo Researchers, Inc.; p. 36, © Kevin O'Farrell Concepts; p. 41, Courtesy Bob Campbell; p. 40,42, 45T © John Reader/Science Photo / Photo Researchers, Inc.; p. 45B, Courtesy Transvaal Museum, D.C. Panagos; p. 46T, From *Human Evolution*, Second Edition by Joseph Birdsell. Copyright © 1975, 1981 by Harper and Row Publishers, Inc. Reprinted by permission of HarperCollins Publishers; p. 46B, From C.K. Brain, 1981. *Who Were the Hunters or the Hunted?* Chicago: The University of Chicago Press. Reprinted with permission of the publisher; p. 47, Courtesy Richard Potts; p. 48, © Baron Hugo Van Lawick / National Geographic Image Collection; p. 51, *Olduvai Gorge*, Volume 3, by Mary Leakey, 1971, Cambridge University Press. Reprinted with permission of the publisher; p. 52, 54 © John Reader / Science Photo Library/Photo Researchers, Inc.; p. 53, Robert F. Sisson, © National Geographic Society; p. 55, 56, © T. Douglas Price and Anne Birgitte Gebhauer; p. 59L, From *"The First Technology,"* by Nicholas Toth. p. 59R, Courtesy F.E. Grine, SUNY, Stony Brook. Photo by Chester Tarka; p. 62, © Warren & Genny Garst/ Tom Stack and Associates. **Chapter 3** p. 65, McKern and McKern, *Living Prehistory*, Copyright © 1974, Benjamin-Cummings Publishing Company; p. 68, © Douglas T. Price; p. 69, From A. Leroi-Gourhan. 1957. Prehistoric Man. New York: Philosphical Library. Reprinted with permission of the author; p. 70, Courtesy Department of Library Services. American Museum of Natural History. Neg # 298897; p. 72, © John Reader / Science Photo Library/ Photo Researchers, Inc.; p. 74, From Miller, et. al., "Paleoceanography," 2: 1-19, 1987, © American Geophysical Union; p. 77, Courtesy Department of Library Services. American Museum of Natural History. Neg# 124667; p. 78, From Professor Huang Weiwen. Institute of Paleontology & Paleoanthropology, Beijing; p. 79, Courtesy Department of Library Services. American Museum of Natural History. Neg # 335651; p. 82T, © Staatliches Museum für Naturkunde, Stuttgart; p. 82B, From the Laboratiore de Préhistoire,

Musée de l'Homme, Paris. Courtesy Henry de Lumly; p. 83, Courtesy of F. Clark Howell; p. 84, Courtesy of Henry de Lumly, Musee National d'Histoire Naturelle, Paris; p. 85, © T. Douglas Price; p. 86, From "A Paleolithic Camp in Nice," by Henry de Lumly; p. 87, Peabody Museum of Natural History, Yale University. Painted by Rudolph F. Zallinger; p. 89T, Aaris-Sorensen and Brinch Petersen, STRIAE, 24: 111-117, photo by Geert Brovad; p. 89B, Source material courtesy Richard Klein; p. 90, 90L, 90T, 91B, From J. Desmond Clark, 1970; p. 91T, © Laurence Bartram; p. 92, Used with permission from Francois Bordes. 1968. *The Old Stone Age*. Courtesy of McGraw-Hill Book Company; p. 93, © British Museum; p. 94, © The Natural History Museum, London; p. 95, © T. Douglas Price. **Chapter 4** p. 98T, Reconstruction of Homo sapiens neanderthalensis by Jay H. Matternes, © Copyright 1981; p. 98R, After Feder and Park, 1997; p. 100, From *Human Antiquity*, 2/e, by Kenneth L. Feder and Michael Alan Park, © 1993. Mayfield Publishing Company, p. 208; p. 101, © John Reader/ Science Photo Library/Photo Researchers, Inc.; p. 102, Courtesy Hillary Deacon; p. 104, From Singer and Wymer, *The Middle Stone Age at Klasies River Mouth in South Africa*, Reprinted by permission of The University of Chicago Press; p. 103, Source material courtesy Richard Klein; p. 106, "Mosaic," Vol. 10, No. 2, Mar/Apr. 1979; p. 108, © Musee de l'Homme; p. 110, Used with permission from Francois Bordes. 1968. *The Old Stone Age*. Courtesy McGraw-Hill Book Company; p. 111T, Reprinted by permission from p.439 of *Understanding Physical Anthropology and Archaeology*, 3/e by Robert Jurmain, Harry Nelson and William Turnbaugh, © 1987 by West Publishing; p. 111B, © The Natural History Museum, London; p. 112, Redrawn from Clark Spenser Larsen and Robert M. Hatter, *Human Origins: The Fossil Record*, 2/e. p. 175. © 1985 Waveland Press, Inc. Prospects Heights, IL. Second Edition published in 1991. Used by permission of the publisher. p. 113, 115, © Ralph S. Solecki. p. 118T, Redrawn from Clark Spenser Larsen and Robert M. Hatter, *Human Origins: The Fossil Record*, 2/e. p. 175. © 1985 Waveland Press, Inc. Prospect Heights, IL. Second Edition published in 1991. Used by permission of the publisher; p. 118B, © T. Douglas Price; p. 119, Courtesy F. Leveque/Ministere de la Culture, de la Communication, Des Grands Travaux et du Bicentenaire; p. 120, From *Oxford Illustrated Prehistory of Europe* by Barry Cunliffe. © 1994. Reprinted by permission of Oxford University Press; p. 121, Courtesy Peter Vemming Hansen; p. 122, © The National Museum of Denmark, Copenhagen; p. 123, G. LaPlace. 1974. La Typologie Analytique et Structurale , Paris. Editions du Centre National de la Recherche Scientifique, Paris; p. 124, Collection of the Institute fur Ur-and Fruhgeschichte, University of Tubingen, Germany; p. 125, Courtesy of Archeologicky Ustav, Brno, Czechoslovakia; p. 126T, From B. Kilma. 1963. Dolni Vestonice. Prague: Czechoslavakia Academy of Science; p. 126B, Courtesy Department of Library Services. American Museum of Natural History. Neg #69368fr.15; p. 127T, 127B, From B. Kilma. 1963. Dolni Vestonice. Prague: Czechoslavakia Academy of Science; p. 127M, From H. Muller-Karpe. 1966. Handbuch vor Vorgeschichte. Munich: C.H. Beck; p. 127, From B. Kilma. 1963. Dolni Vestonice. Prague: Czechoslavakia Academy of Science; p. 128, Courtesy Department of Library Services. American Museum of Natural History. Neg #15204; p. 130T, 131B, E. Haddingham. 1979. *Secrets of The Ice Age*. New York: Walker and Co.; p. 130B, Illustration by Zdenek Burian. Reproduced with permission of Jiří Hochman; p. 131, F. Haddingham, 1979. *Secrets of the Ice Age*. New

York: Walker and Co.; p. 132, From A. Leroi-Gourhan 1982. *The Dawn of European Art: An Introduction to Paleolithic Cave Painting*. New York: Cambridge University Press; p. 135T, From A. Leroi-Gourhan 1982. *The Dawn of European Art: An Introduction to Paleolithic Cave Painting*. New York: Cambridge University Press; p. 135B, Drawing by Ann Hatfield from *Plato Prehistorian*, by Mary Settegast, Rotenberg Press 1986; p. 133, Photo by Jean Vertut, Issy-Les Moulineaux, France; p. 134, Courtesy Department of Library Services. American Museum of Natural History. Neg # 39686. Photo by Kirschner; p. 135T, Drawing by Ann Hatfield from Plato Prehistorian, by Mary Settegast, Rotenberg Press 1986; p. 136, © Professor Leroi-Gourhan. From *The Old Stone Age*, p. 236. Weidenfeld & Nicholson Ltd; p. 137B, Editons du Centre National de la Recherche Scientifique, Paris; p. 137T, After Leroi-Gourhan and Brezillion, 1966. Reprinted with permission of the publisher. Editons du Centre National de la Recherche Scientifique, Paris; p. 138, Courtesy Alexander Marshack; p. 139T, Courtesy Department of Library Services. American Museum of Natural History. Neg # 2A17536; p. 139B, Courtesy Alexander Marshack; p. 141, ©Thomas Hoepker/ Magnum Photos; p. 143, From "How to Cope with Calibration," by R. Pearson. 1987. Antiquity, 61: 98-103; p. 145, From "Elephant Hunting in North America," by C. Vance Haynes, Jr. © 1966. Scientific American, p. 104; p. 146, Courtesy R.M. Gramly/G.L.A.R; p. 148, 150, Courtesy Tom Dillehay; p. 152T, Photo by Vance T. Holiday; p. 152B, D.H. Thomas 1978. *Archaeology* p. 64 New York: Holt, Rinehart, and Winston; p. 154, From The National Anthropological Archives, Smithsonian Institution; p. 153T, From The National Anthropological Archives, Smithsonian Institution; p. 153B, Courtesy of the Royal Ontario Museum, Toronto, Canada; p. 155, Courtesy George Frison; p. 155L, J. Mead and D, Meltzer. 1985. *Environments and Extinctions : Man in Late Glacial North America*. Corvalis, OR. Center for the Study of the First Americans.

Chapter 5   p. 161, © The National Museum of Denmark, Copenhagen; p. 164, Courtesy Dr. Peter C. Woodman/ University College Cork, Ireland; p. 165T, Courtesy Dr. Peter C. Woodman/ University College Cork, Ireland; p. 165B, From "A Mesolithic Camp in Ireland," by Peter C. Woodman, © 1981 Scientific American; p . 166, From J.G.D. Clark, 1954. *Star Carr*. New York: Cambridge University Press; p. 167, After Coope, 1975; p. 168, © T. Douglas Price; p. 169, Courtesy Lars Larsson, Institute of Archaeology, Sweden; p. 170, © T. Douglas Price; p. 171, Courtesy Danish National Museum; p. 172, From "American Scientist," Journal of Sigma Xi, The Scientific Research Society; p. 174, © T. Douglas Price; p. 176, Source material courtesy Richard G. Klein; p. 177, Courtesy John Parkington/ University of Capetown; p. 178, The Jomon-Seasonal Hunting-Gathering Cycle. Drawing adapted from the original of Tatsuo Kobayashi. By Gordon Miller. In "Image and Life 50,000 years of Japanese Pre-History." Museum note No. 5 by permission of the Museum of Anthropology, The University of British Columbia, Vancouver, B.C, Canada; p. 179T, © T. Douglas Price; pp. 179B, 180T, © J. Edward Kidder; p. 180B, From C.M. Aikens and T. Higuchi 1982, *Prehistory of Japan*, Orlando Press, FL. Academic Press; p. 182T, 182B, 183, 185, © Board of Trustees, Southern Illinois University; p. 184, © Board of Trustees, Southern Illinois University, drawing by Thomas Gatlin; p. 189, Michael A. Hampshire, National Geographic Society; p. 190, Gary Friedman © National Geographic Society; p. 191L, Gary Friedman © National Geographic Society; p. 191R, 192T, 192B Courtesy David Hurst Thomas. American Museum of Natural History; p. 193T, © Laurence Bartram; p. 193B, Courtesy T. Douglas Price & Anne Birgitte Gebauer.   **Chapter 6**   p. 199, From *Archaeology: Theories, Methods and Practice*, by Colin Renfrew and Paul Bahn, 2nd Edition, 1996. Published by Thames and Hudson, Inc. New York.; p. 200, © T. Douglas Price; p. 203, From *Transitions in Agriculture in Prehistory*,

Edited by Anne Birgitte Gebauer and T. Douglas Price; p. 204, Courtesy James L. Phillips; p. 205T, After Jean Perrot, Centre de Recherche Francais de Jerusalem; p. 205B, From *The Rise of Civilization : From Early Farmers to Urban Society in the Ancient Near East,* by Charles Redman, © 1978 by W.H. Freeman and Company. Reprinted by permission; p. 208T, © Dr. Bryan Byrd, University of Wisconsin and Dr. E.B. Banning, University of Toronto, drawn by Jonathan Mabry; p. 208B, © Andrew M. T. Moore; p. 210, © Andrew M.T. Moore; p. 212, Courtesy Charles M. Niquette/Cultural Resource Analysts, Inc.; p. 213, Courtesy Institute of Archaeology, University College, London; p. 214, Courtesy James L. Phillips; p. 215, Courtesy University of London, Dept. of Archaeology; p. 216, © T. Douglas Price; p. 217, Drawings by Ann Hatfield from *Plato Prehistorian* by Mary Settegast, published by the Rotenberg Press, 1986. Permission to reprint courtesy of the Rotenberg Press; p. 219, From "Gazelle Drives in the Ancient Near East," by Anthony J. Legge and Peter A. Rowley-Conway. © 1967 by Scientific American, Inc. All rights reserved; p. 220, © T. Douglas Price; p. 221, Drawings by Eliza McFadden from Plato Prehistorian by Mary Settegast, published by the Rotenberg Press, 1986. Permission to reprint courtesy of the Rotenberg Press; p. 221, Drawings by Eliza McFadden from Plato Prehistorian by Mary Settegast, published by the Rotenberg Press, 1986. Permission to reprint courtesy of the Rotenberg Press; p. 222, © T. Douglas Price; p. 223, © T. Douglas Price; p. 224T, © Mission Archeologique de l'Indus, photo by Catherine Jarrige; p. 224B, M. Lechevallier and G. Quivron, 1985, "Results of the Recent Excavations at the Neolithic Site Mehrgarh, Pakistan," South Asian Archaeology 1983. J. Schotmans and M. Taddei, eds. Instituto Universitario Orientale, Departimento Di Studi Asiatici, series minor 23, Naples; p. 225, Data from J-F Jarriage and R. H. Meadow. 1980. "The Antecedents of Civilization in the Indus Valley." Scientific American 243:(2); p. 226, Courtesy Susan Kepecs; p. 228, From T. Cheng, 1966. Archaeology in China: New Light on Prehistoric China. Cambridge: W. Heffer and Sons. Reprinted with permission of the author; p. 233, Courtesy William G. Solheim II. University of Hawaii at Manoa; p. 234, From *Ben Chiang: Discovery of a Lost Bronze Age,* by Joyce White, the University Museum, University of Pennsylvania, 1982. Reprinted with permission; p. 235T, Metalworking and photomicrography by Sim Adler, Charles Latham Brown, Clive Scorey, and Phillip Clapp of The Physics and Metallury Group, Ledgemont Research Library; p. 235B, Metalworking and photomicrography by Sim Adler, Charles Latham Brown, Clive Scorey, and Phillip Clapp of The Physics and Metallury Group, Ledgemont Research Library; p. 237, Courtesy Kent V. Flannery; p. 238, Courtesy Kent V. Flannery; p. 239, Redrawn from H. Iltis. 1987. *Grass Systematics and Evolution*, T.R. Soderstrom, K.W. Hilu, C.S. Campbell, and M.E. Barkworth, eds.; p. 240, © Robert S. Peabody Museum of Archaeology. Phillips Academy, Andover, MA. All rights reserved; p. 241, Redrawn from G. Beadle. 1980. "The Ancestry of Corn," Scientific American 242:113; p. 243, Robert S. Peabody Museum of Archaeology. Phillips Academy, Andover, MA. All rights reserved; p. 244, Adapted from "The Origins of New World Civilization," by Richard MacNeish. ©1964 by Scientific American, Inc. All rights reserved; p. 247, 248T, 248B, 249, © Thomas F. Lynch; p. 251, Courtesy Bruce Smith.   **Chapter 7**   p. 261B, Jesse Jennings, *Prehistory of North America*, Second Edition, McGraw-Hill © 1968 and 1974; p. 262, From *The Poverty Point Culture, 2/e*, by Clarence H. Webb, p. 51 © 1982 Geoscience and Man, Vol. 17; p. 263, © The Field Museum, Neg. #94855; p. 264, © Ohio Historical Society; p. 265, © The Field Museum, Neg. #A91198; p. 266, © The Field Museum of Chicago, Neg. #A110016; p. 268T, Courtesy Peabody Museum, Harvard University. Photograph by Hillel Burger. Photo #N27081; p. 268B, American Indian Pipe, anonymous loan to the Brooklyn Museum;

C. Morris and D. Thompson. 1985. *Huanuco Pampa: An Inca City and its Hinterland*, London: Thames and Hudson. Reproduced with permission of the authors; p. 402, From C. Morris and D. Thompson. 1985. Huanuco Pampa: An Inca City and its Hinterland, London: Thames and Hudson. Reproduced with permission of the authors. **Chapter 10** p. 409, © Audrey R. Topping; p. 412, From *Art of the Near East*, by Seton Lloyd, © 1961 Thames and Hudson, p. 259, Praeger Publishers, an imprint of Greenwood Publishing Group, Inc. Reprinted with permission; p. 413, © State Antiquities and Heritage Organization, Baghdad; p. 414, A. Noldecke. 1936. Uruk Vorbericht 7, Figure 5; p. 415, A. Nöldecke, A. von Haller, H. Kenzen, and E. Heinrich, 1937. Abhandlungen der Preussischen Akademie der Wissenschaften, Figure I. Berlin: Verlag der Akademie der Wissenschaften; p. 416, Courtesy Gregory Johnson, Hunter College, CUNY; p. 417, 419, Courtesy Denise Schmandt-Besserat. With permission of Deutsches Archaoloisches Institut, Orient, Abteilung; p. 420, Courtesy Denise Schmandt-Besserat. University of Texas, Austin; p. 422, Permission to redraw courtesy of M.K. Kenoyer; p. 423, From Civilizations Anciennes du Pakistan. 1989. Bruxelles: Musees Royaux d'Art et d'Histoire; p. 424, From M. Wheeler. 1968. *The Indus Civilization*. New York: Cambridge University Press. Reprinted with permission of the publisher; p. 425, 427, Courtesy George Dales and the Harappa Project, University of California at Berkeley; p. 426, Photo by J.M. Kenoyer, courtesy of the Department of Archaeology and Museums, Government of Pakistan; p. 429, Permission to redraw from original illustration by M.K. Kenoyer; p. 432, Ashmolean Museum, Oxford; p. 433, © Giraudon/Art Resource, NY; p. 434, K. Mendelssohn. 1974. *The Riddle of the Pyramids*. New York: Praeger Publications. © Thames and Hudson 1974. Reprinted with permission of Henry Holt and Company; p. 435, From Michael Hoffman, "Where Nations Began." Science 83. October 1983. pp. 42-51. © by the AAAS; p. 437, Lovell Johns/ Andromeda Oxford, Ltd; p. 436, © Alain Choisnet/ The Image Bank; p. 438, Acct. no. 11.1738, pair statue of Mycerinus, and his queen, from Giza, dynasty IV, 2599-1571 B.C., slateschist, H (composite statue) : 54-1/2 in. Harvard-MFA Expedition. Courtesy Museum of Fine Arts, Boston. Reproduced with permission. © 2000 Museum of Fine Arts, Boston; p. 440, 441, K. Mendelssohn. 1974. *The Riddle of the Pyramids*. New York: Praeger Publications. © Thames and Hudson 1974. Reprinted with permission of Henry Holt and Company; p. 444T, From K.C. Chang. 1986. Studies of *Shang Archaeology*. New Haven: Yale University Press; p. 444B, From Wenwu, 1984; p. 445, Courtesy of the Institute History and Philology, Academy Sinica, Taiwan; p. 446, Courtesy the Metropolitan Museum of Art, Gift of Mrs. John Marriott, Mrs. John Barry Ryan, Gilbert W. Kahn, Roger Wolfe Kahn, 1949. #49. 136.5; p. 449, From K.C. Chang, "Food and Vessels in Ancient China," Transactions of the New York Academy of Sciences 35 (6) 1973. Reprinted with permission of the annals of the New York Academy of Sciences; p. 451, © Audrey R. Topping; p. 453, Yang Hsien-Min, © National Geographic Society; p. 452, 454, Courtesy Linda M. Nicholas; p. 457, 458, © R.J. McIntosh; p. 459, © The Granger Collection, New York; p. 461, 462, P. Garlake. 1973. Great Zimbabwe. London: Thames and Hudson; p. 464, © 1989 Robert Holmes; p. 465, © Walter Meayers Edwards/ National Geographic Image Collection. **Chapter 11** p. 472, © T. Douglas Price; p. 474T, 474B, Courtesy Thomas Jacobsen, Indiana University; p. 475, From "17,000 Years of Greek Prehistory, " by Thomas W. Jacobsen, Illustration by Alan D. Islen. Copyright © June 1976 by Scientific American, Inc. All rights reserved; p. 476, 477, 478, Courtesy Dr. Ivan Ivanov; p. 479, © Gerha Hinterleitner/Liaison Agency, Inc.; p. 480, Courtesy the Forschungsinstitut fur Alpine Vorzeit; p. 481, Courtesy the Forschungsinstitut fur Alpine Vorzeit; p. 482, Courtesy Musee Dauphinois; p. 483T, Courtesy A. Bocquet/ Centre de Documentation de la Prehistoire Alpine; p. 483B, Courtesy Dr. Ullrich Ruoff; p. 484, Courtesy A. Houot/ Centre de Documentation de la Prehistoire Alpine; p. 485T, 485B, A. Bocquet/ Centre de Documentation de la Prehistoire Alpine; p. 487, From Ancient Europe from the Beginnings of Agriculture to Classical Antiquity, by Stuart Piggott. Reprinted with permission from Edinburgh University Press; p. 489, Reproduced with the permission of The Prehistoric Society; p. 490, © British Crown Copyright/ M.O.D. Reproduced with the permission of the Controller of Her Britannic Majesty's Stationary Office; p. 491, Courtesy Department of Library Services. American Museum of Natural History. Neg#269817; p. 492, 493, After C. Chippendale. 1983. *Stonehenge Complete*. London: Routledge; p. 499T, Courtesy John Bennet; p. 499, Courtesy John Bennet; p. 500, From Emily Townshend Vermeule. 1972. *Greece in The Bronze Age,* Chicago: The University of Chicago Press. Reprinted with permission of the publisher; p. 501, Courtesy Jack Davis; p. 502, Photo by J. McCredie, National Museum, Athens; p. 503, Courtesy Jack Davis; p. 505, From J. Jensen. 1979. Bronzealderen, Volume 1. Copenhagen: Sesam. Reprinted with permission of the publisher; p. 506B, Four bronze age barrows along the coast of Denmark. From Danish Prehistoric Monuments, by P.V. Glob, 1971, page 27, figure 4. Reprinted with permission of Glydendal, Copenhagen; p. 506T, Published by permission of the Danish National Museum; p. 507, From P.V. Glob. 1970. The Mound People. Ithaca, NY: Cornell University Press. Originally published by Glydendal, Copenhagen; p. 508, From T. Champion, C. Gamble, S. Shennan, and A. Whittle. 1984. Prehistoric Europe. London: Academic Press. Reprinted with permission of the publisher; p. 509, Cliche Musee Archeologique de Chatillon sur Seine; p. 510, © The National Museum of Denmark, Copenhagen; p. 511, © Forhistorisk Museum, Moesgard; p. 512, Ashmolean Museum, Oxford; p. 513, 514, Courtesy the Society of Antiqaries of London; p. 518, Courtesy Linda M. Nicholas Color Insert Color Insert Plates 1, 2, 3, © John Reader/Science Source Photo Library/Photo Researchers, Inc.; Plate 4, Photo by Jean Vertut, Issey-les-Molineaux, France; Plate 5, © The National Museum of Denmark, Copenhagen; Plate 6, Photo by Peter Dorell and Stuart Laidlaw, Courtesy University of London, Institute of Archaeology; Plate 7, Courtesy of the authorsPlate 8, © David Cavagnaro/Peter Arnold, Inc.; Plate 9, Courtesy Thomas F. Lynch; Plates 10, 11, 12, 13, 14, 15, Courtesy Linda M. Nicolas; Plate 16, © Kenneth Garrett 1982. All rights reserved.; Plates 17, 18 © British Museum; Plate 19, Courtesy Dumbarton Oaks Research Library and Collections, Washington, DC; Plate 20, Courtesy Jennifer Blitz; Plate 21, © Robert Frerck/Woodfin Camp and Associates; Plate 22, © British Museum; Plate 23, © Dilip Mehta/Woodfin Camp and Associates; Plate 24, Photri, Inc.; Plate 25, © Robert Holmes; Plate 26, Courtesy the Forschungsinstitut für Alpine Vorzeit; Plate 27, National Archaeological Museum, Athens, Hellenic Republic; Plate 28, © British Museum; Plate 29, © Ira Block 1986

References to illustrations and tables are in *italics*.